The New Economics

Keynes' Influence on Theory
and Public Policy

EDITED WITH INTRODUCTIONS BY

SEYMOUR E. HARRIS

PROFESSOR OF ECONOMICS, HARVARD UNIVERSITY

NEW YORK: ALFRED A. KNOPF: 1947

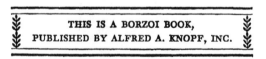

THIS IS A BORZOI BOOK,
PUBLISHED BY ALFRED A. KNOPF, INC.

JOHN MAYNARD KEYNES, 1883—1946

This volume is dedicated by its editor to those economists who, following the leadership of Lord Keynes, are endeavoring to make of economics a useful tool for the diagnosis and treatment of economic disease.

Preface

THE READER will learn what this book is about by reading the brief opening chapter. In sum, the book includes thirty-one chapters of new material (inclusive of ten chapters by the editor which summarize, integrate, and fill in some gaps, and a bibliography), and sixteen chapters of old material, inclusive of three speeches in the House of Lords by Keynes, the plan for a Clearing Union, and his 1937 *Quarterly Journal* article.

I acknowledge the aid I have had from my Secretary, Miss Lillian Buller, from Mrs. Anna Thorpe, for typing large parts of the manuscript, and especially from my research assistant, Mrs. Margarita Willfort, for editorial help, for checking references, and for numerous other aids. In providing some financial help, the Graduate School of Public Administration has also contributed in an important way to the consummation of this task.

SEYMOUR E. HARRIS

Four Winds Farm
West Acton, Massachusetts

Acknowledgments

THE FOLLOWING essays in this volume have been reprinted with the permission of the authors, publishers, and holders of copyright mentioned below, to whom especial thanks are due:

American Economic Association, Evanston, Illinois: "John Maynard Keynes, 1883–1946," by J. A. Schumpeter, in *American Economic Review*, September 1946

Controller of His Britannic Majesty's Stationery Office: three speeches in the House of Lords (May 18, 1943; May 23, 1944; December 10, 1945) from the Official Report (Clerk of the Parliaments) "Proposals for an International Clearing Union" (British Information Services)

The Econometrica Society: "Mr. Keynes and Traditional Theory," by R. F. Harrod, in *Econometrica*, January 1937

"Lord Keynes and the General Theory," by P. A. Samuelson, in *Econometrica*, July 1946

International Labour Organization: "Mr. Keynes' 'General Theory of Employment, Interest and Money.'" by A. P. Lerner, in *International Labour Review*, October 1936

London School of Economics: "A Simplified Model of Mr. Keynes' System," by J. E. Meade, in *Review of Economic Studies*, February 1937

Macmillan and Company, Ltd.: "Alternative Formulations of the Theory of Interest," by A. P. Lerner, in *Economic Journal*, June 1938

"The International Currency Proposals," by J. Robinson, in *Economic Journal*, June–September 1943

The President and Fellows of Harvard College, Cambridge, Massachusetts: "The General Theory of Employment," by J. M. Keynes, in *Quarterly Journal of Economics*, February 1937

"Saving Equals Investment," by A. P. Lerner, *ibid.*, February 1938

"Saving and Investment: Definitions, Assumptions, Objectives," *ibid.*, August 1939

"Interest Theory—Supply and Demand for Loans or Supply and Demand for Cash," by A. P. Lerner, in *Review of Economic Statistics*, May 1944

Science and Society, Inc., Chicago, Illinois: "John Maynard Keynes," by P. M. Sweezy, in *Science and Society*, Fall 1946 (London)

Times: Obituary, April 26, 1946

In addition, permission has been granted by the publishers (Macmillan and Company, Ltd.; Harcourt Brace & Co.) to use quotations from the following works of Lord Keynes: *General Theory of Employment, Interest and Money; Essays in Persuasion; Means to Prosperity; Treatise on Money; Economic Consequences of the Peace; Tract on Monetary Reform;* from Taussig *International Trade;* and from two works by J. Robinson.

Contributors

ARTHUR I. BLOOMFIELD, *Chief, Reports and Analysis Division, Federal Reserve Bank of New York*

GERHARD COLM, *Council of Economic Advisers, Executive Office of the President*

DOUGLAS B. COPLAND, *Economist for various Australian Governments, and now Minister to China*

RICHARD M. GOODWIN, *Assistant Professor of Economics, Harvard University*

GOTTFRIED HABERLER, *Professor of Economics, Harvard University*

ALVIN H. HANSEN, *Lucius N. Littauer Professor of Political Economy, Harvard University*

SEYMOUR E. HARRIS, *Professor of Economics, Harvard University*

R. F. HARROD, *Managing Editor, The Economic Journal, and Student of Christ Church, Oxford University*

ALBERT G. HART, *Professor of Economics, Columbia University*

BENJAMIN HIGGINS, *Professor of Economics, McGill University*

RANDALL HINSHAW, *Assistant Professor of Economics, Amherst College*

JOHN MAYNARD KEYNES

WASSILY LEONTIEF, *Professor of Economics, Harvard University*

ABBA P. LERNER, *Professor of Economics, New School for Social Research*

JOHN LINTNER, *Assistant Professor of Finance, Harvard University School of Business Administration*

J. E. MEADE, *Director of Economics Section, Cabinet Secretariat, His Majesty's Government*

LLOYD A. METZLER, *Associate Professor of Economics, University of Chicago*

Contributors

RAGNAR NURKSE, *Professor of Economics, Columbia University*

JOAN ROBINSON, *University Lecturer in the Faculty of Economics and Politics, Cambridge University*

PAUL A. SAMUELSON, *Professor of Economics, Massachusetts Institute of Technology*

JOSEPH A. SCHUMPETER, *George F. Baker Professor of Economics, Harvard University*

ARTHUR SMITHIES, *Bureau of the Budget*

ALAN SWEEZY, *Professor of Economics, Williams College*

PAUL M. SWEEZY, *Formerly Assistant Professor of Economics, Harvard University*

J. TINBERGEN, *Professor of Statistics, Rotterdam School of Economics, and with the Central Government Planning Office, The Hague*

JAMES TOBIN, *Junior Fellow, Harvard University*

Abbreviations

AER	*American Economic Review*
EC	*Econometrica*
EJ	*Economic Journal*
ECN	*Economica*
FRB	*Federal Reserve Bulletin*
ILR	*International Labour Review*
JPE	*Journal of Political Economy*
JRSS	*Journal of the Royal Statistical Society*
LA	*Living Age*
LBMR	*Lloyd's Bank Monthly Review*
MGCRE	*Manchester Guardian Commercial, Reconstruction in Europe*
N&A	*The Nation and Athenaeum*
NBER	National Bureau of Economic Research
NICB	National Industrial Conference Board
NR	*The New Republic*
NST&N	*The New Statesman and Nation*
NYT	*The New York Times*
PQ	*Political Quarterly*
QJE	*Quarterly Journal of Economics*
RES	*Review of Economic Statistics*
TL	*The Times* (London)
TNEC	Temporary National Economic Committee
YR	*Yale Review*

Contents

PART FOUR

Special Aspects

PART FIVE

International Economic Relations

Contents

PART SIX

Economic Fluctuations and Trends and Fiscal Policy

PART SEVEN

X Money and Prices

X PART EIGHT

Effective Demand and Wages

PART NINE

Some Earlier Discussions

PART TEN

Bibliography of Keynes' Writings

OBITUARY: The Times (*London*), *April 22, 1946*

Lord Keynes

A GREAT ECONOMIST

LORD KEYNES, the great economist, died at Tilton, Firle, Sussex, yesterday from a heart attack.

By his death the country has lost a very great Englishman. He was a man of genius, who as a political economist had a world-wide influence on the thinking both of specialists and of the general public, but who was also master of a variety of other subjects which he pursued through life. He was a man of action as well as of thought, who intervened on occasion with critical effect in the great affairs of state, and carried on efficiently a number of practical business activities which would have filled the life of an ordinary man. And he was not merely a prodigy of intellect; he had civic virtues—courage, steadfastness, and a humane outlook; he had private virtues—he was a good son, a devoted member of his college, a loyal and affectionate friend, and a lavish and unwearying helper of young men of promise.

The Right Hon. John Maynard Keynes, C.B., Baron Keynes, of Tilton, Sussex, in the Peerage of the United Kingdom, was born on June 5, 1883. His father, John Neville Keynes, was a distinguished writer on political economy and logic and was for many years Registrary of Cambridge University. His mother was Mayor of Cambridge as lately as 1932. They both survive him. He was brought up in the most intellectual society of Cambridge. He was in college at Eton, which he dearly loved, and he was proud at being nominated by the masters to be their representative governor later in life. He won a scholarship to King's College in mathematics and classics, writing his essay on Héloïse and Abélard. He was President of the Cambridge Union, won the Members' English Essay Prize for an essay on the political opinions of Burke, and was twelfth wrangler in the mathematical tripos. Although he did not take another tripos, he studied deeply in philosophy and economics and was influenced by such men as Sidgwick, Whitehead, W. E. Johnson, G. E. Moore, and, of course, Alfred Marshall.

In 1906 he passed second into the Civil Service, getting his worst mark in economics—"the examiners presumably knew less than I did"—and chose the India Office, partly out of regard for John Morley and partly because, in those days of a smooth working gold standard, the Indian currency was the livest monetary issue and had been the subject of Royal Commissions and classic controversies. During his two years there he was working on his fellowship dissertation on Probability, which gained him a prize fellowship at King's. This did not oblige him to resign from the Civil Service, but Marshall was anxious to get him to Cambridge, and, as token, paid him £100 a year out of his private pocket to supplement the exiguous fellowship dividend—those were before the days of his bursarship of the college. Anyhow, his real heart lay in Cambridge. He lectured on money. He was a member of the Royal Commission on Indian Currency and Finance (1913–14). He served in the Treasury 1915–19, went with the first Lord Reading's mission to the United States, and was principal representative of the Treasury at the Paris Peace Conference and deputy for the Chancellor of the Exchequer on the Supreme Economic Council. After his resignation he returned to teaching and to his bursar's duties at King's, but he always spent part of his time in London. He was a member of the Macmillan Committee on Finance and Industry, and parts of its classic report bear the stamp of his mind.

In 1940 he was made a member of the Chancellor of the Exchequer's Consultative Council and played an important part in Treasury business. He was made a director of the Bank of England. In 1942 he was created Lord Keynes, of Tilton, and made some valuable contributions to debate in the Upper House. He was made High Steward of Cambridge (Borough) in 1943. His continued interest in the arts was marked by his trusteeship of the National Gallery and chairmanship of the Council for the Encouragement of Music and the Arts. In 1925 he married Lydia Lopokova, renowned star of the Russian Imperial Ballet—"the best thing Maynard ever did," according to the aged Mrs. Alfred Marshall. She made a delightful home for him, and in the years after his serious heart attack in 1937 was a tireless nurse and vigilant guardian against the pressures of the outside world.

Lord Keynes's genius was expressed in his important contributions to the fundamentals of economic science; in his power of winning public interest in the practical application of economics on critical occasions; in his English prose style—his description of the protagonists at the Versailles Conference, first fully published in his *Essays in Biography* (1933), is likely long to remain a classic—and, perhaps one should add, in the brilliant wit, the wisdom, and the range of his private conversation, which would have made him a valued member of any intellectual salon or coterie in the great ages of polished discussion.

In practical affairs his activities in addition to his important public services were legion. As bursar of King's he administered the college finances with unflagging attention to detail. By segregating a fund which could be invested outside trustee securities he greatly enlarged the resources of the college, and, unlike most college bursars, he was continually urging the college to spend more money on current needs. From 1912 he was editor of the *Economic Journal*, which grew and flourished under his guidance, and from 1921 to 1938 he was chairman of the National Mutual Life Assurance Society. He ran an investment company. He organized the Camargo Ballet. He built and opened the Arts Theatre at Cambridge, and, having himself supervised and financed it during its period of teething troubles, he handed it over, when it was established as a paying concern, as a gift to *ex-officio* trustees drawn from the university and city. He became chairman of C.E.M.A. in 1942 and of the Arts Council in 1945. He was chairman of the *Nation*, and later, when the merger took place, of the *New Statesman;* but he had too scrupulous a regard for editorial freedom for that paper to be in any sense a reflection of his own opinions. He also did duty as a teacher of undergraduates at King's College and played an important and inspiring part in the development of the Economics faculty at Cambridge. The better students saw him at his most brilliant in his Political Economy Club. He was interested in university business and his evidence before the Royal Commission (1919–22) was an important influence in causing it to recommend that the financial powers of the university should give it greater influence over the colleges.

To find an economist of comparable influence one would have

to go back to Adam Smith. His early interest was primarily in
money and foreign exchange, and there is an austere school of
thought which regards his *Indian Currency and Finance* (1912)
as his best book. After the 1914–18 war his interest in the relation
between monetary deflation and trade depression led him on to
reconsider the traditional theory about the broad economic forces
which govern the total level of employment and activity in a
society. He concluded that, to make a free system work at optimum capacity—and so provide "full employment"—it would be
necessary to have deliberate central control of the rate of interest
and also, in certain cases, to stimulate capital development. These
conclusions rest on a very subtle and intricate analysis of the
working of the whole system, which is still being debated wherever economics is seriously studied.

Popularly he was supposed to have the vice of inconsistency.
Serious students of his work are not inclined to endorse this estimate. His views changed in the sense that they developed. He
would perceive that some particular theory had a wider application. He was always feeling his way to the larger synthesis. The
new generalization grew out of the old. But he regarded words as
private property which he would define and redefine. Unlike most
professional theorists, he was very quick to adapt the application
of theory to changes in the circumstances. Speed of thought was
his characteristic in all things. In general conversation he loved
to disturb complacency, and when, as so often, there were two
sides to a question he would emphasize the one more disturbing
to his present company.

His *Treatise on Probability* is a notable work of philosophy. Although using mathematical symbols freely, it does not seek to add
to the mathematical theory of probability, but rather to explore
the philosophical foundations on which that theory rests. Written
clearly and without pedantry, it displays a vast erudition in the
history of the subject which was reinforced by and reinforced his
activities as a bibliophile.

Keynes had on certain occasions an appreciable influence on
the course of history. His resignation from the British delegation
to the Paris Peace Conference and his publication a few months
later of *The Economic Consequences of the Peace* had immediate
and lasting effects on world opinion about the peace treaty. The
propriety of his action became a matter of controversy. Opinions
still differ on the merits of the treaty, but about the point with

which he was particularly concerned, Reparations, there is now general agreement with his view that the settlement—or lack of settlement—was ill-conceived and likely to do injury to the fabric of the world economy. His subsequent polemic against the gold standard did not prevent a return to it in 1925, but largely added to the ill repute of that system in wide circles since. It was mainly through his personal influence some years later that the Liberal Party adopted as their platform in the election of 1929 the proposal to conquer unemployment by a policy of public works and monetary expansion.

He had a footing in the British Treasury in two wars. The idea of deferred credits was contained in the pamphlet entitled *How to Pay for the War*, which he published in 1940. From 1943 Lord Keynes played a principal part in the discussions and negotiations with the United States to effect a transition from war to peace conditions of trade and finance which avoided the errors of the last peace, and to establish international organization which would avoid both the disastrous fluctuations and the restrictions which characterized the inter-war period. He was the leader of the British experts in the preparatory discussions of 1943 and gave his name to the first British contribution—"the Keynes Plan" —to the proposals for establishing an international monetary authority. In July, 1944, he led the British delegation at the Monetary Conference of the United and Associated Nations at Bretton Woods, where an agreed plan was worked out. He was the dominant figure in the British delegation which for three months, from September to December, 1945, hammered out the terms of the American Loan Agreement, which he defended brilliantly in the House of Lords. He was appointed in February Governor of the International Monetary Fund and the International Bank for Reconstruction and Development, and in these capacities had just paid a further visit to the United States, whence he returned only two weeks ago. These continuous exertions to advance the cause of liberality and freedom in commercial and financial policies as a means to expand world trade and employment imposed an exceptionally heavy and prolonged strain which, in view of his severe illness just before the war, Lord Keynes was physically ill-fitted to bear.

His life-long activities as a book-collector were not interrupted even by war. His great haul of unpublished Newton manuscripts on alchemy calls for mention. He identified an anonymous pamphlet entitled *An Abstract of a Treatise of Human Nature*, acquired by his brother, Mr. Geoffrey Keynes, as being the authentic work of David Hume himself. He had it reprinted in 1938, and it will no doubt hereafter be eagerly studied by generations of philosophers. During the second war his hobby was to buy and then, unlike many bibliophiles, to read rare Elizabethan works. His interest in and encouragement of the arts meant much to him. From undergraduate days he had great friendships with writers and painters and, while his activities brought him in touch with many distinguished people of the academic world and public life, he was probably happiest with artistic people. At one period he was at the centre of the literary circle which used to be known as "Bloomsbury"—Lytton Strachey, Virginia Woolf, and their intimate friends. More than fame and worldly honours, he valued the good esteem of this very cultivated and fastidious society.

His published works included *Indian Currency and Finance* (1913), *The Economic Consequences of the Peace* (1919), *A Treatise on Probability* (1921), *A Revision of the Treaty* (1922), *A Tract on Monetary Reform* (1923), *A Short View of Russia* (1925), *The Economic Consequences of Mr. Churchill* (1925), *The End of Laissez Faire* (1926), *A Treatise on Money* (two volumes) (1930), *Essays in Persuasion* (1931), *Essays in Biography* (1933), *The General Theory of Employment, Interest, and Money* (1936), and *How to Pay for the War* (1940).

And finally there was the man himself—radiant, brilliant, effervescent, gay, full of impish jokes. His entry into the room invariably raised the spirits of the company. He always seemed cheerful; his interests and projects were so many and his knowledge so deep that he gave the feeling that the world could not get seriously out of joint in the end while he was busy in it. He did not suffer fools gladly; he often put eminent persons to shame by making a devastating retort which left no loophole for face-saving. He could be rude. He did not expect others to bear malice and bore none himself in the little or great affairs of life. He had many rebuffs but did not recriminate. When his projects were rejected, often by mere obstructionists, he went straight ahead and produced some more projects. He was a shrewd judge of men and often plumbed the depths in his psychology. He was a humane man genuinely devoted to the cause of the common good.

PART ONE

Introduction: The Issues

SEYMOUR E. HARRIS

CHAPTER I

About This Book

THE OCCASION

LORD KEYNES was born in 1883 and died in 1946. This volume was conceived as a tribute to the man and the economist. But it is more than that. We intend to appraise Keynes' contributions to economics: to add up the gains and to explore the weaknesses.

A volume on Keynesian economics, written mainly by Keynes' followers, naturally would be largely panegyric. But there is criticism also—both by the followers and by the minority of writers in this volume who might not be classed as Keynesian. These critics, however, unlike many of the detractors of Keynes, have read and absorbed the *General Theory*. Even the most enthusiastic imbibers at the Keynesian fountain will find impurities and indigestible and incongruous substances—examine the essays by Messrs. Colm, Smithies, and Samuelson in this volume, for example.

The larger part of this book is an interpretation by Keynesians of Keynes' economics and Keynesian economics. This is as it should be: I am not a supporter of Marxist economics; but when I want to learn about Marxist economics, I find it much more helpful to consult Marxists than anti-Marxists. Those who want unfriendly interpretations and destructive criticisms should consult the growing anti-Keynesian literature. The miracle of Keynes is that, despite the vested interests of scholars in the older theory, despite the preponderant influence of press, radio, finance, and subsidized research against Keynes, his influence both in scientific circles and in the arena of public policy has been extraordinary, and much beyond what could have been expected by Keynes or others in 1936.

That Keynes made large and lasting contributions to economics, all the contributors to this volume would undoubtedly agree. However, that he said the last word would most likely be denied by them. Even the most avid followers of Keynes are scarcely prepared to state that all economic problems have been solved by him, and that no further work remains to be done. One hundred years ago, J. S. Mill rashly announced the solution of the problem of the theory of value, that further work was unnecessary. Mill proved to be a poor prophet. Jevons, Marshall, Walras, Pigou, Hicks, Chamberlin, *et al.*, contributed significant improvements and not mere embellishments to the theory of value. During World War I, a professor of economics at Harvard, impressed by the founding of the Federal Reserve System, warned his students that further work in money would be sterile. Keynesians are not guilty of such temerity. Economics is an evolutionary science and, therefore, is protean. Even foundation stones, like the contributions of Bentham, Ricardo, and others, require supplementation, amplification, and, frequently, revision.

Keynes' great contribution (cf. Mr. Copland in this volume) was to adapt economics to the changing institutional structure of modern society. Economics had failed to keep pace with the developments of science, of government, of changes in the marketplace, of organization by groups, and in general with institutional developments. Up to 1936, when the *General Theory* was first published, accepted economics in general belonged much more to the vanished age of competition, of capital deficiencies, of full employment or transitional unemployment, and the like, than to the twentieth-century economy which tolerated and, to some extent encouraged, monopolies, rigidities, excessive savings, deficiency of demand, and unemployment. To make up for the growing lag, Keynes sailed boldly and vigorously into uncharted waters. Navigators in the classical waters were necessarily upset by the resulting ripples or, better, waves. Many of them, and particularly the older ones, suspecting the intruder of piracy, steered their boats as best they could out of his way. Younger navigators, impressed by the greater skill shown by Keynes in the new waters, were tempted to follow him; and since their investments in the older economics were not large, they were less cautious than their teachers. Advance by easy steps, as suggested by the Marshall motto, *Natura non facit saltum*, had not proved enough. Keynes, therefore, set sail in new waters.

Keynes' activity as an economist extended over a period of thirty-five years; and in the last fifteen years he was the outstanding figure in the world of economists. In the wide scope of his interests, in his eloquence and persuasiveness, in the virtually complete command over economic forums, both of subjects to be discussed and manner of discussing them, in the impression he made upon our quasi-capitalist system, in the influence upon economists and men of action of his day—in these jointly, and probably in each separately, Keynes has not had an equal. Like Adam Smith, he could write with charm and persuasiveness (though with more brilliance) for the enlightenment of men of action; like Ricardo, he could write for economists and inspire them to meditation and debate; and somewhat like Marx, Keynes could awaken in his disciples an almost religious fervor for his economics, which could be effectively harnessed for the dissemination of the new economics.

Keynes indeed had the Revelation. His disciples are now dividing into groups, each taking sustenance from the Keynesian larder. The struggle for the Apostolic Succession is on. At one extreme there is apostle Beveridge, who would both socialize demand and support a controlled economy. At the other extreme is Polanyi, who finds Keynesianism consistent with complete laissez faire, and interprets the gains in the Soviet Economics as originating essentially from pumping money into the system. In between are other groups who adhere much more conventionally to the teachings of Keynes: i.e., laissez faire is outmoded; the excrescences of capitalism must be removed; government control of money, interest, savings, and investment is recommended; but individual liberties to choose occupations, to select goods for consumption, to make profits, should not be impaired.

At this point, it may be well to insist that Keynes was essentially a defender of capitalism. Only the stupidity of those whom he supports can account for any other interpretation. Keynes indeed offers government a larger degree of control over the economic process and a larger degree of operation than the old-fashioned classical economist; but his motive is to save capitalism, not destroy it. Those who are not prepared to accept this interpretation should read Part IV of the *Essays In Persuasion*. Keynes wanted government to assume responsibility for demand, because otherwise the system would not survive. It was possible to have both *more* government activity and *more* private activity—if unemployment could only be excluded. And above all, Keynes would not remove the foundations of capitalism: free choice, the driving force of the quest for profits, the allocation of resources in response to the price incentive. His last book, *How to Pay for the War*, confirms his life-long faith in these ingredients of capitalism.

It is appropriate to end this introductory section with a few final words on Keynes' position in economics. As this book is about to go to press, a visit to Harvard by Professor Bertil Ohlin, an eminent economist and head of the Swedish Liberal Party, offers a jumping off point for these remarks. On this occasion, Professor Ohlin presented a stimulating paper on over-employment, in the afternoon, and participated in an informal discussion from 6:30 to 10:30 P.M. At the evening meeting, Professors Hansen, Samuelson, and the writer, all staunch Keynesians, discussed the contributions of Keynes with Dean Williams, Professors Ohlin, Haberler, Chamberlin, and Black, the last five critical in varying degrees.

Several aspects of the evening meeting struck me. Here was an informal meeting where, as so often happens, the discussion inevitably gravitated to Keynes. This was not by any means planned, but it is, however, a very significant fact. Then again, I was impressed by the manner in which supporters and critics alike used the Keynesian terminology and analysis. How few economists there are who have not been infected by the Keynesian "poison"!

All the participants, supporters and critics both, in varying degrees and varying states of enthusiasm indulged in the popular pastime of criticizing parts of the Keynesian system: Keynes' confused discussion of the relation of savings and investment; his over-emphasis of the importance of the rate of interest and his faulty analysis of its determinants; his over-simplified and unrealistic theory of wages; the sterility of his consumption function; his unawareness and his ungenerous appraisal of much of the work of his predecessors; the lack of originality in his work—these were among the points under discussion.

On the trek home after the stimulating meeting I ran over the points made and tried to draw some conclusions concerning Keynes' place in economics. I had agreed with many of the criticisms directed against Keynes. Yet my final appraisal remained, that Keynes was undoubtedly the great figure in economics of the twentieth century and may well prove to be the giant of modern economics. I was reminded of Ingersoll's *Top Secret*. According to Ingersoll, General Eisenhower had made every possible error: in dealing with the British; in failing to achieve cooperation; in failing to mobilize resources properly; in planning his strategy and tactics. He had in this sense lost every battle, only to win the war. And I am reminded of Republican appraisal of the late President Roosevelt. From a perusal of their pronouncements, one would not know that the Roosevelt administration had achieved important reforms, had raised incomes from 40 to 80 to 160 billion dollars, and finally had contributed importantly to the victory.

Keynes, indeed, also had lost many battles and made many errors. He also, however, had won the war. Out of the straws of his predecessors, with some additions of his own, he had built a structure which no economist or economic practitioner can afford not to inspect and use.

Others undoubtedly had similar ideas, though the system is essentially new. What matters is not who had an idea first. Historians of economic thought will deal with that problem, though the search for the origin of ideas is not a very productive occupation. Historians have found precursors of A. Smith, Ricardo, and Marx; and I am sure the historians, aided and abetted by the Keynes baiters, will be equally successful in finding that the essentials of Keynesian economics were in classical or Scandinavian economics. That does not matter, however. What matters is who put the "new" economics across. Here there cannot be two views. The persistence of the critics, the attention given to Keynes' writings, the mobilization of virtually all economic criticism on the pastime of examining Keynes' writings, are ample evidence of an underlying (in some cases sub-conscious) agreement that what Keynes had to offer was of transcendent importance.

READER'S GUIDE

(a) The Scope

The object of this book is to present, within the limits of a single volume, an analysis of the economics of John Maynard Keynes. It includes not only an analysis of Keynes' writings, but also, in the light of the spate of appraisals and criticisms of Keynesian economics, an evaluation of the present status of Keynesian economics. No book in economics within a *hundred years* of publication has received as much attention and criticism, both pre-natal and post-natal, as Keynes' *General Theory* over a period of less than *twelve years*. In this volume also, it receives the major attention; but we also deal with Keynes' important earlier contributions, which were the seeds from which the *General Theory* grew, as well as his work after 1936.

(b) The Contents

The volume contains contributions by twenty-six leading economists—the majority members of the American Keynesian school. The volume includes, in addition to some of Keynes' papers, contributions by several distinguished foreign followers (and important names in the development of Keynesian economics): Messrs. Copland, Harrod, and Meade, and Mrs. Robinson; an outstanding Continental economist, Professor Tinbergen; and at least six economists who, though undoubtedly influenced by Keynes, are clearly not members of his school: Professors Haberler, Hart, Leontief, Schumpeter, P. Sweezy, and Tinbergen. There are a few others who are not easily classified. I have also included in this volume Keynes' three famous speeches before the House of Lords, the *Proposals for an International Clearing Union* (largely his work), a speech on the International Bank, the excellent obituary in *The Times* (London), and several important interpretations of Keynes. In all, old material accounts for about one-third of the book.

(c) The Audience

This is perhaps the first volume of Keynesian economics prepared since Lord Keynes' death. Keynesiana may well ultimately account for more printed words than Marx. This early volume, we hope, will occupy an important place in that literature. We hope especially that over the years it will appeal to able college and graduate students and economists generally. We also anticipate that many informed citizens, and particularly those concerned with public policy, will become better acquainted with Keynes' views on public policy and his influence on policy, and that many errors concerning the implications of Keynesian economics will be corrected.

(d) Reader's Guide

Readers will find the introductions, accounting for some 40,000 words, helpful in getting their bearings. The introductions also fill in some of the gaps necessarily left in a cooperative enterprise. Non-technical readers might wish to skip the able essays by

Messrs. Goodwin, Hart, Leontief, Tinbergen, and Tobin, and all of Part Nine. They are more advanced and technical than the remainder of the book.

THE BOOK IN GREATER DETAIL

My general introduction (Part One) is a catch-all, dealing as it does with the outlines of the volume, Keynes' influence on public policy (in general, on New Dealism, on blueprints for the future), the appraisal of Keynes in 1936–37, the present status of Keynesian economics, its relation to classical economics, and finally Keynes' economics in the literature.

Part Two contains three evaluations of Keynes' economics: one by Mr. Harrod, a British disciple; one by Professor Schumpeter, a brilliant critic to the right; and one by Dr. Paul Sweezy, one of the most able critics of the left.

In Part Three, the Keynesian bible, *The General Theory*, is subjected to microscopic examination. Three of the world's leading Keynesians—Messrs. Hansen, Lerner, and Samuelson—contributed essays. Dr. Lerner's essay, the first in this part, is an early examination of the *General Theory* in language which makes it much more comprehensible than the original. The appraisals by Professors Hansen and Samuelson have the advantage of being written eleven years later and thus have perspective. Professor Haberler, an enlightened critic of Keynes, also contributed an essay to this part, which many will consider an antidote to the essays by Keynes himself and his enthusiastic supporters. Finally, I have included an essay by Keynes written in 1937, which gives an indication of what, after two years of consideration and one year of criticism, Keynes conceived his position and main contributions to be.[1]

Professor Hansen in the United States and Mr. Copland in Australia in recent years have probably played a greater part in influencing public policy than any other economist in their respective countries. It is, therefore, appropriate that these two

---

[1] Three other recent appraisals should not go unnoticed. The first (A. Neisser, "Keynes As An Economist," *Social Research,* June, 1946, pp. 225–236) summarizes briefly and admirably Keynes' major contributions. The second (D. Dillard, "The Pragmatic Bases of Keynes' Political Economy," *The Journal of Economic History,* Nov., 1946) is a thorough review of Keynes' writings and in particular his impact on policy. Finally, Mr. Robinson's article in the forthcoming issue of the British *Economic Journal* is likely to be the most important of all.

economists, greatly in sympathy with Keynes' viewpoint, should give their views on Keynes and public policy. Part Four also includes some comments on Keynes' important contributions to econometrics by one of the world's leading econometricians, Professor Tinbergen. Finally, Professor Leontief, an able critic of Keynes, suggests why and to what extent Keynes has misinterpreted classical economics; and he incidentally deals with Keynes' views on wages and unemployment—a problem discussed more fully in Part Eight.

I shall say little about Parts Five (International Economic Relations), Six (Economic Fluctuations and Trends and Fiscal Policy), and Eight (Effective Demand and Wages). Each of these parts has an introduction in which the subject matter is discussed and various aspects of the relevant material are treated. The part on international economic relations is especially long, and quite appropriately, since Keynes had an intense interest in this field. There are few problems in this area that did not receive Keynes' attention and which are not discussed here. Part Six also treats an important aspect of Keynesian economics, for it deals with economic fluctuations, trends, unemployment, and what should be done about unemployment. Part Seven, by the way, deals only with Keynes' views on money and prices—it was not possible to include the interesting essay by Professor Lintner in any of the other parts. Part Eight, in addition to the introduction, presents the skeleton of Keynes' theory, with particular emphasis on unemployment and wage rates.

In Part Nine, we have reprinted some of the earlier contributions to Keynesiana. In particular, the essays by Messrs. Harrod and Meade present the *General Theory* in a systematic manner, as Keynes himself had failed to do. (I wish that there had been space to include Dr. Lange's excellent essay along somewhat similar lines.) [2] I have also included four brief essays by Dr. Lerner, which are able defenses of Keynes on two of the most controversial issues, savings and investment, and the rate of interest.[3] This selection is not by any means adequate. Lack of

[2] O. Lange, "The Rate of Interest and the Optimum Propensity to Consume," (ECN, 1938).

[3] The inclusion of these is justified by the inadequate consideration given in this volume to Keynes' position on the equality of savings and investment and the rate of interest. For criticisms of the Keynes-Lerner position, the reader should consult especially the able contributions of Professors D. H. Robertson and B. Ohlin (EJ, 1937) and Professor F. Lutz (QJE, 1938).

space and unavailability of some items account for the choices made.

Finally, we present a complete (?) bibliography of Keynes' writings. This is the first of its kind. There must be omissions and errors—please inform the editor of them.

S. E. H.

CHAPTER II

Keynes' Influence on Public Policy

KEYNES' CONTRIBUTIONS TO PUBLIC POLICY

IN AN INTRIGUING appraisal of Keynes, Professor Schumpeter explains the appeal of Keynesian economics as follows: "The *General Theory* seems to reduce it once more to simplicity, and to enable the economist once more to give simple advice that everybody could understand. But exactly as in the case of Ricardian economics, there was enough to attract, to inspire even, the sophisticated." [1]

Professor Haberler also writes: ". . . But we can safely assume that the concrete content and the policy recommendations which Keynes and others deduced from his system had even more to do with its persuasiveness (even for his theoretically-minded followers) than its theoretical beauty and simplicity." [2]

Keynes' influence, both in theory and practice, has of course been outstanding. It is indeed doubtful whether any other economist ever had so large an influence on policy, and particularly in so short a time. [3] The policy issues are clear and, therefore, I start with them. [4]

Keynes contributed importantly to the solution of the following problems: reparations, exchange rates, international equilibrium, appropriate rates of interest, central banking policy, inflation, deflation and wastage of economic resources, and employment. These problems are, of course, interrelated; they are not, and

[1] Below, p. 100.
[2] Below, p. 162. Cf. also H. Neisser, *op. cit.*, p. 233. Prof. Neisser emphasizes Keynes' success in reducing the thousands of equations in neo-classical economics to a few manageable and simple relations.
[3] Cf. the stimulating essay by Prof. Hansen on "Keynes on Economic Policy."
[4] The reader should consult my Introductions to Parts Five, Six, and Eight, where most of the issues are discussed more fully and references given.

perhaps never will be, solved satisfactorily; nevertheless, by re-moving underbrush, building foundations, and illuminating the signposts, Keynes prepared the road to full employment and stability. It was not, however, easy to induce the journalists, the radio commentators, and the men of action to travel over these safe roads.

In the acrimonious discussions of reparations, Keynes indeed gave birth to the modern transfer problem. Can there be any doubt that Keynes, more than anyone else, was responsible for the clarification of this problem, and with the resulting decisions to have little to do with the explosive transfer problem after
· World War II (e.g., Lend-Lease, reparations policies)? Keynes was indeed the architect of modern programs of international monetary policies, inclusive of flexible but not free exchange rates (and therefore the proud destroyer of the gold standard), for the provision of international reserves, the concentration of gold for the settlement of international balances, and, as a corol-lary of these, the independence of each country to pursue full employment policies unfettered by rigid exchanges or un-co-operative economic policies abroad. Who, more than Keynes, is responsible for the growing freedom from the tyranny of gold, for the increased disposition to determine monetary supplies and rates of interest according to the requirements of the domestic economy, for using money as the handmaid of industry instead of sacrificing resources in order to maintain fixed exchanges?

Keynes concentrated most of his fire on the target of full em-ployment. Since the period during which he wrote was largely a period of depression for Great Britain and to some extent for the world, Keynes' economics has frequently been dubbed "depres-sion economics" (see Schumpeter, below). I do not share this view, and I shall return to it.[5] Here we are concerned with Keynes' anti-depression policies.

In the twenties, his attack on depression revolved around money and the rate of interest, his concern with international economics originating in the effects of the balance of payments upon monetary supplies and the rate of interest. Even in 1930, he could characterize the year as the death struggle over whether current high rates of interest or the low rates of pre-war days were to prevail.[6] In the middle twenties, he presented important

[5] See page 22.
[6] *Treatise,* Vol. II, pp. 196–197; see also Chapter 37.

evidence to the Colwyn Committee on the need of low rates, on the propriety of a large floating debt (a market for public debt at low rates of interest), and on the unwisdom of repaying debt.[7] (Had he not again, Cassandra-like, anticipated the nature of the market for government securities, for the next generation at any rate?) As late as December 31, 1933, in his famous open letter to President Roosevelt, he stressed the need of lower rates and inquired with prophetic vision why the rate on long-term U. S. debt could not be reduced to 2½ per cent? (It yielded about 4 per cent at the time.) In the *General Theory*, Keynes continued to be concerned over the rate of interest. Many would say that he was still too much concerned with it.

Yet between 1930 and 1936 a fundamental change had occurred. In fact, as early as 1929 (*Can Lloyd George Do It?*) Keynes had seen clearly that monetary policy alone could not do the job. His letter to the President was emphatic that loan-expenditure was the way out (though he mentioned the possibility of improved prospects for business, reduced rates of interest, and increased consumption), and that the recession of the latter part of 1933 had been primarily due to the failure to put through a program of loan expenditure. The *General Theory*, with its emphasis on marginal efficiency of capital (both its instability and declining trend), on the institutional difficulties of getting the rate of interest down sufficiently, and on the difficulties of raising the propensity to consume, necessarily led him to put much emphasis on government loan expenditure. Near the end of his book, Keynes admitted that the manipulation of the rate of interest would not provide the optimum rate of investment and, though an appropriate tax program and interest policy would exercise a guiding influence on consumption, that they would not be enough. Only a comprehensive socialization of investment would secure an approximation to full employment conditions.[8] Keynes was also explicit in a later elaboration of his views—cf. his well known essay (1937) for the *Eugenics Review*.[8a] In it he anticipated that consumption would not rise by more than 1 per cent per year. Therefore, strong institutional measures were required in order to combat stagnation. It should be clear now why I can-

[7] Committee on National Debt and Taxation, *Report* (*Colwyn Report*), *Minutes of Evidence*, 1927, pp. 277–283, 536–537.

[8] *General Theory*, p. 378; see also pp. 163–164, 219–220, 307–309.

[8a] "Some Economic Consequences of a Declining Population," *Eugenics Review*, April, 1937.

not accept my distinguished colleague Professor Haberler's statement that from the "point of view of the *General Theory what is needed to prevent mass unemployment is monetary policy and, at the most, a mild form of fiscal policy.*" [9]

Certainly, the economic historian interpreting the middle years of the 20th century will characterize the period as the struggle for, and over, full employment. He may well refer to the period as the Keynesian period in the same manner as we now refer to the Mercantilist, the Physiocratic, and the Classical periods. He will point to Keynes' emphasis on the level of employment against the classical concern with the allocation of economic resources; he will stress Keynes' skill in marshalling available weapons and techniques and inventing of new ones for attaining the *objective;* and he will comment on the persuasive manner in which the message was passed on to disciples and policy-makers. He may well praise Keynes as the supporter of capitalism, who would remove the tumors and preserve the essentials of capitalism—free choice by consumers, free allocation of economic resources, the quest for profits. It would be worth while to live to the year 2000 to see whether this analysis of current economic history will stand the tests of perspective and the passage of time. I believe it will if democracy survives. Perhaps a twenty-first century Clapham will read this passage and honor it by a footnote and an answer.

KEYNES AND NEW DEALISM

In this country, the view is widely held that Keynes contributed greatly to the evolution of New Deal economic policies; and the mere mention of his name will bring forth the most vituperative remarks by conservative American businessmen. Indeed, American economic policies in the thirties conformed to the Keynesian pattern much more than did the British. Both countries, indeed, relied on exchange instability. The United States, however, renounced exchange stability for but a year. In fact, within a month of Keynes' advice to the President to maintain the *status quo* and to be prepared to adjust exchanges in response to changes in underlying conditions, the United States had returned once more essentially to gold. Here at least Great Britain's behavior was more Keynesian than America's: in 1935, in a paper in *Lloyd's Bank Monthly Review*, Keynes stressed the need for continued

[9] See below, pp. 177–8. (Italics mine.)

flexibility of exchanges; and up to the outbreak of the war Great Britain reserved the right to manipulate her exchanges.

In the acceptance of deficit financing and loan expenditures, the United States authorities put into practice the theories of Keynes. Whereas the British nullified the gains of exchange depreciation to some extent by imposing measures of economy, the United States embraced deficit financing. In the years 1931–1938, for example, the public debt of *all governments* in this country rose by $24.8 billion, and federal net capital investments accounted for $11.6 billion.[10]

In other respects, also, the American economy seemed to have become a testing laboratory for Keynes' ideas. The National Recovery Administration (NRA), the Agricultural Adjustment Administration (AAA), various relief programs, the Social Security Act were interpreted in part as programs which would transfer purchasing power from non-spenders to spenders. As General Johnson, the querulous head of the NRA, said, since the millionaire cannot buy forty dollars' worth of ham and eggs daily, the way out of a depression is to enable each American to buy fifty cents' worth of ham and eggs. A rise in the average propensity to consume was also to some extent the objective of "punitive" tax legislation of 1935.[11] Again, in accordance with sound Keynesian theories, the government, through the Thomas Amendments and the revaluation of gold, prepared the way for monetary expansion and declining rates of interest. From 1932 to 1940, the monetary gold stock had risen by $17.8 billion, the deposits of all banks by $23.4 billion, the gross *federal* debt by $24.2 billion, and yet the rate of interest on long-term federal issues had dropped from over 4.5 per cent in 1932 to 2.5 per cent in 1940.[12]

Yet Keynes did not fully approve of early New Dealism. He was not pleased with the gyrations of the dollar; nor with the attempts to raise prices by restrictions of output or by increasing wages and farm incomes; nor with the failure (1) to raise prices through monetary policies, and (2) to expand demand through

[10] Hearings, TNEC, 1940, *Investigation of Concentration of Economic Power*, pp. 4090–4092, 4149; and S. E. Harris, *Economics of Social Security* (McGraw-Hill, 1941), pp. 34–43.

[11] B. Rauch, *The History of the New Deal* (Creative Age Press, 1944), pp. 175–178.

[12] S. E. Harris, *The Economics of American Defense* (1941), p. 30; and NBER, *Basic Yields of Corporate Bonds, 1900–1942* (1942), p. 15.

loan expenditure. All of this was made evident in his letter to *The New York Times* of December 31, 1933.[13] Even while he was criticizing, however, the Administration, disturbed by the setback in the latter part of 1933, began to accelerate its spending program. The Brookings Institution could report that at about this time the view had crystallized that high government expenditures were the primary requisite of economic recovery.[14] In 1934, Keynes visited the White House. According to the report of Mrs. Perkins (*The Roosevelt I Knew*, 1946), the President reported that Keynes had visited him, and apparently the President was not pleased with Keynes' "rigmarole" of figures. Keynes, on his part, expressed surprise that the President was not more literate in economic matters.

American economic policy was indeed full of inconsistencies and paradoxes. The Administration supported concomitantly a program to assure monetary expansion (revaluation of the dollar, the gold clause, and the Thomas Amendments), and the Banking Act of 1933, which in many respects was deflationary. While favoring a program to expand loan expenditure, the Administration in 1933 took severe measures to balance the budget: in fact the $3 billion public works measure was tied to the NRA Act on the theory that, with prosperity retrieved by the NRA, the country could afford the public works. Instead of loan expenditure bringing advances, the gains were to make possible the loan expenditure! In the platforms of both 1932 and 1936, the Democrats stressed their intention to balance the budget. Close advisers to President Roosevelt are well aware that he had never really accepted unorthodox theories of public finance: he would not, however, balance the budget at the expense of human lives. Dr. Smithies is undoubtedly right when he argues that the planned use of deficits to bring recovery, rather than their use incidental to other objectives, did not come until 1938, when the President recommended the use of fiscal policy to achieve recovery.[15] In his budget measure of January, 1940, the President came close to accepting the Keynesian thesis: the experience of 1938–39 should remove any doubt as to the effectiveness of fiscal policy related to economic need; with government intervention, the decline of in-

[13] See also LT, Jan. 3, 1938.
[14] The Brookings Institution, *The Recovery Program of the United States* (1936), pp. 449–450.
[15] A. Smithies, "The American Economy in the Thirties," *Proceedings of the American Economic Association* (1946), p. 16.

come from 1937 to 1938 had been kept down to $8 billion—compare the drop of $42 billion from 1929 to 1932; and whereas in 1937–1938 productive activity had turned upwards in 9 months, in the earlier episode the country had experienced four years of liquidation and depression.[16]

In short, it is not easy to find indubitable evidence of Keynes' direct influence on New Dealism. Dr. Colm is right in emphasizing in this volume the difficulty of tracing Keynes' influence on American fiscal policy. A survey of economic policies, particularly in the early years of the New Deal, reveals so much confusion, so many inconsistencies, and so many serious errors, that Keynes would undoubtedly not want to take too much credit for what was done. That the President, or his early advisers (e.g., Moley, Berle, Baruch, Morgenthau, Tugwell), had been indoctrinated with Keynesian economics (the 1930 variety of course) is most doubtful. Their policies were indeed largely of the shotgun variety.

Yet the general pattern, especially as New Dealism evolved, checked well with Keynes' strategy and tactics. More money, lower rates of interest, loan expenditure, measures to raise the propensity to consume, some freedom from dictation from abroad —all of these were the ingredients out of which the New Deal cocktail was made.[17] The severely restrictive measures, the excesses of economic nationalism, the over-emphasis on raising money incomes as the means to rising output—all of these were ultimately largely repudiated. And though the President never quite understood Keynes, many of his later advisers (a significant proportion of whom learned their Keynes at Harvard) became supporters of the new economics. Keynes' theories and programs undoubtedly had a substantial effect, even if it is difficult to trace. By 1933, the supporters of the new policies and even the man in the street, though unaware of the sources, were using arguments that Keynes had made commonplace. It was another case of getting Hamlet without reading it. Critics of Keynes and New Deal policies might point out that one might well succumb to

[16] TNEC, Monograph 20, *Taxation, Recovery, and Defense* (1940), pp. 53, 56.

[17] It is scarcely necessary to remind the reader of the catastrophic results anticipated. Even the Brookings Institution in 1936 anticipated that, as soon as confidence in the ability to balance the budget was lost, the government would no longer be able to borrow; and the great German inflation was held up as an example of what might be expected. *Op. cit.*, pp. 473–78, 484–89.

radioactivity though the investigators might not be able to trace the exact manner in which the substance had reached the victim.[18]

BLUEPRINTS FOR THE FUTURE

What about Keynes' influence beyond the United States—for example, as evidenced in recent programs for the future?

In this volume, Professor Lintner observes that, in tying his theory to the ballast of national income, Keynes put at the disposal of the economist and practitioner the vast storehouse of income and related statistics. And Professor Hansen and Dr. Copland elaborate on the significance of Keynes' economics for recent advances in public policy. Here my objective is merely to indicate the broad relations of Keynes' economics and the sketches by economic architects of the post-war economy.

In recent years the world has been flooded with a spate of analyses of national income and its constituent elements: consumption, investment, government spending, the export balance, etc. All these owe much to Keynes' *Treatise*, and especially to the *General Theory*. As examples of this type of analysis we can cite the famous annual volume of the British Government on income, expenditures, etc.,[19] the National Resources Planning Board, the important *Markets After the War*, innumerable models—e.g., by the National Planning Assoc., Mosak, Smithies, the Bureau of the Budget, Wallace, Bowles. These attempts to account for income, or income changes, originate in Keynes' analysis. Even the attempt to forecast on the basis of past relationships of these variables is an outgrowth of the *General Theory*. Undoubtedly these models have often been crude and misleading; but they continue to improve. At first it was deemed necessary, on the basis of a simple past relationship, to estimate the net effect upon national income of variations in the independent variables—e.g., export balance, public investment. Now it is generally agreed that we

[18] In addition to the sources already quoted, the reader might consult: S. E. Harris, "Economic Legislation of the United States, 1933," ɪ.ᴊ., 1933, pp. 619–651; Seven Harvard Economists, *The Economics of the Recovery Program* (McGraw-Hill, 1934, 5th Printing); S. E. Harris, *Exchange Depreciation* (Harvard University Press, 1936), Chap. 7. The reader will find further references in these items.

[19] E.g., *An Analysis of the Sources of War Finance and Estimates of the National Income and Expenditure in the Years 1938 to 1943* (Cmd. 4520, 1944).

must allow for the effects of changing distribution of income, accumulation of liquid assets, cyclical variations in relationships, lags in the adjustment of spending to income, population changes, relative price changes, etc., etc. The danger now is that the models may become so complicated as to become useless.[20]

Official White Papers on employment and the post-war economy owe much to Keynes.[21] Authors of these reports also break up income on the Keynesian model; they seek full employment, or full use of resources, or high levels of employment; they emphasize the need of maintaining purchasing power adequate to take the goods produced off the market; in varying degrees of enthusiasm, they urge programs of public investment, consumer subsidies, the use of the tax power to raise consumption, reduction of the rate of interest to stimulate investment, adaptation of public spending to oscillations in private spending. In short, the essentials of Keynes' economics have become the property of the government planner, now to be trumpeted to the masses through blue books, the press, and the radio.

It would be a mistake, however, to assume that Keynes has been victorious on every issue, or to the same degree in all countries though indeed the Keynesian devil, unemployment or stagnation, if not openly admitted, can be seen between the lines. If we were to compare the various reports, we should find the strongest statement of the Keynesian position in the Australian White Paper with emphasis on the objective of full employment, and on the need of offsetting fluctuations in the most volatile item, the foreign balance. The British White Paper stressed the need for taking action at the first onset of a depression, which,

[20] See, especially, the discussion between Hart and Mosak in AER, March and September, 1946; National Planning Association, *National Budgets for Full Employment* (April, 1945); and numerous articles in RES, particularly in 1946. I have discussed these issues in my *Inflation and the American Economy* (McGraw-Hill, 1945) and *National Debt and the New Economics* (in press).

[21] Cf., especially, the following: (1) H. M. Stationery Office, *Employment Policy* (1944); (2) U. S. Council of Economic Advisers, *First Annual Report to the President* (Dec., 1946); (3) *The Economic Report of the President Transmitted to the Congress*, January 8, 1947; (4) *Canadian White Paper on Employment and Income*, reprinted in FRB, June, 1945, pp. 536–549; (5) *Full Employment in Australia*, May 30, 1945, reprinted in *Senate Hearings on Full Employment Act of 1945*, pp. 86–104; (6) Union of South Africa, Social and Economic Planning Council, Report No. 7, *Taxation and Fiscal Policy*, Sept., 1945. Cf. also A. Hansen, *Economic Policy and Full Employment*, Part III (McGraw-Hill, 1947).

without early intervention, might grow like cancerous cells, rather than on the need for permanent government intervention. The government would limit dangerous swings in expenditures and public investment. For Canadian authorities, it was also imperative to stabilize income levels, and not to rely too much on public investment. Both Canada and Australia urged programs of full employment abroad as necessary ingredients of the proposed programs. Perhaps the American "Brown" papers were least Keynesian. A caricature of what might be called Keynesian policy is presented for criticism on pages 12–14 of the *First Report of the Council of Economic Advisers*. The place of public investment is, on the whole, a very limited one. Interest rates are not even mentioned. This document should, however, be judged in the light of the political atmosphere of 1947, in which deficits, public controls, salvation by government are politically unpalatable. Even in the American report, however, the council stresses the need for consumer subsidies, for adequate incomes to assure sales of the annual output, the need of government aid to combat depression. The nation's economic budget is, moreover, presented with ultra-Keynesian embroidery.[22]

Virtually all these reports stress the need of controlling inflation; the urgency of rising productivity; the imperative necessity of attaining higher degrees of mobility and discouraging featherbedding. No thoughtful reader of Keynes will deny his great concern over rising prices with expanding output. Many thoughtful readers will, however, interpret Keynes' economics as too exclusively concerned with general measures for maintaining demand, and not adequately interested in structural maladjustments, price rigidities, monopolies, and the other items mentioned above. One senses such an interpretation of Keynesian economics in the Report of the Economic Council. But any careful reader will discover many instances in which Keynes discusses wage and price rigidities, problems of rationalization, etc. (See my Introductions to Parts Five and Six.) Impressed by the difficulties of correcting structural maladjustments and of dealing with institutional obstacles to flexibility, Keynes was primarily concerned with general measures. Certainly history is on his side and not on that of the Council of Economic Advisers. Price flexibility downwards,

---

[22] See especially *Report of the United Nations Conference on Trade and Employment* (Oct., 1946), pp. 4–6, where the reader will find the fruits of Keynes' teachings in an economic blueprint for the world.

to a historically-minded economist, seems rather visionary.[23] Inter-war experience suggests the greater effectiveness of general meas-ures for controlling depression than rationalization, cost-cutting, population movements, *et hoc genus omne.*[24] I certainly would not agree with Polanyi when he contends that monetary expan-sion is all that there is to Keynesian economics or that the Soviet expansion can be explained in terms of monetary manipulation. I would admit that Keynes and perhaps his followers have been too disposed to neglect problems of allocation of economic re-sources, increased productivity, and the like. In extenuation, I would add that these problems had received sufficient attention elsewhere; theirs was the task to disinter the neglected general measures which largely had been buried with Malthus more than a century ago.

IS KEYNES A DEPRESSION ECONOMIST?

As has been noted, Keynes has been described as a "depres-sion" economist. A more appropriate description would be to characterize him as an anti-cyclical, or better as an anti-deflation and anti-inflation economist.[25] Those who associate Keynes' eco-nomics merely with curative suggestions for a depressed econ-omy, may have forgotten his important contributions in the years 1919–1924, significant passages in the *General Theory,* and his last book, *How to Pay for the War.*

In 1919, Keynes vigorously criticized those European states-men who were debauching the currency, who were attacking the "profiteers," that is to say, the capitalists, "the active and construc-tive element in the whole capitalist society"; and, in his view, these statesmen were responsible for the disordered state of debtor-creditor relations, the ultimate foundation of capi-talism."[26]

By 1923, Great Britain and other countries had experienced a severe dose of deflation. Keynes now reflected on the favorable effects of the long-run tendency of money to depreciate: it was a "weighty counterpoise against the cumulative results of com-pound interest and the inheritance of fortunes . . . . a loosening

[23] Cf. Prof. Hansen, "Keynes on Economic Policy."

[24] See my *National Debt and the New Economics.*

[25] Cf. Dr. Goodwin's essay below, which shows how well the Keynesian system deals with an inflationary situation.

[26] *Essays in Persuasion,* pp. 77–79.

influence against the rigid distribution of old-won wealth and the separation of ownership from activity." [27]

Yet even at this time Keynes was not prepared to acquiesce in large doses of inflation, though businessmen and, probably, labor might gain in periods of inflation. In his view, the most striking consequence of inflation was the injustice to "those who in good faith have committed their savings to titles to money rather than to things." Emphasizing the loss of confidence, the impairment of savings, the *need of new savings* to support a growing body of labor, Keynes highly disapproved of the inflationary practices current on the Continent.[28]

As early as 1939, Keynes proposed heroic measures as a means of precluding wartime inflation. He showed that, as soon as the underlying conditions required the change, he could turn off the expansion spigot, which served him so well in his *General Theory*, and turn on the contraction spigot. Following a series of three articles in *The Times* in 1939 and one in the *Economic Journal*, Keynes issued his pamphlet on *How to Pay for the War* (1940).

At this early date, Keynes gave birth to the concept of the inflationary gap and proposed measures to deal with it. Taxes and voluntary savings would not be adequate; comprehensive rationing and price control were inefficient methods of achieving sterilization of cash and, with their exclusion of consumers' choice, were both distasteful and costly; the inflation technique, which might be used and would provide the necessary resources, was undesirable for obvious reasons.[29] Although he would not spurn limited recourse to rationing and price control and to subsidies, and though he would also rely on increases in voluntary savings and taxation, his novel proposal, a bold and vigorous attack on inflation, was a program of forced savings or deferred pay. It was not anticipated by his critics, who were inclined to associate Keynesianism with monetary expansion and inflationary policies.[30]

---

[27] *Ibid.*, p. 87.

[28] *A Tract on Monetary Reform*, Chap. I, especially pp. 29–32.

[29] Keynes' masterly demonstration of the government's capacity to obtain required revenues under the inflationary process, and his discussion of the relation of income to the ensuing price rises, should not go unnoticed. *How to Pay for the War*, pp. 61–62.

[30] Keynes' failure to win favor for the forced savings program did not prove to be costly. Actually the contributions of controls, subsidies, savings,

Keynesians are frequently accused of glibly proposing a full employment economy without taking adequate account of its inflationary potentials. Our recent experience with a full—better—an over-employed economy is ample evidence that the full employment economy is allergic to inflation. In a full employment economy, wage rates are likely to rise more than efficiency; and each group (e.g., farm groups operating through government), strategically placed, can exact higher rates of pay by threatening to shut down the economy. (These are, of course, not the only sources of inflation.) In such periods (*e.g.*, the United States in 1946), the production of capital goods may be too large relative to the flow of consumers' goods—with inflationary pressures on consumption markets. Furthermore, accumulated liquid assets, which tend to expand in years of high employment, are a constant threat to price stability.

Keynes was far from blind to the inflationary dangers of full employment economics. His plan for a Clearing Union was proposed in part as a means of preventing the evils which follow "from countries failing to maintain stability of domestic efficiency—costs and moving out of step with one another in their national wage-policies without having at their disposal any means of orderly adjustment." [31]

At this time (1943), Keynes wrote:

> Some people argue that a capitalist country is doomed to failure because it will be found impossible in conditions of full employment to prevent a progressive increase of wages. According

and taxes, proved to be much greater than Keynes had anticipated; despite the unexpected increase in the scale of war, inflation was well contained; and British consumption was reduced by 20 per cent in contrast to Keynes' objective of 10 per cent. Public revenues actually rose from £977 million in 1939 to £3268 million in 1945—Keynes proposed increased taxes of £500 million and deferment of earnings of £600 million; actually, private savings rose to £1500 million. Keynes had *assumed* total savings of £700–800 million, and despite a rise of war expenditures from £754 million in 1939 to £3986 million in 1945, the cost of living rose by only 30 per cent—though there is some justice to the charge that the index number was kept down more than the cost of living. The differences between Keynes' projected figures and the actual ones stem from a small rise of prices as well as bolder control and fiscal policies than could have been anticipated. *How to Pay for the War,* especially pp. vi, 6–11, 36–37, 53, 61–67; *Royal Economic Society Memo. No. 106* (June, 1946), pp. 13–16; FRB, July, 1946, p. 741.

[31] Lord Keynes, "The Objective of International Price Stability," EJ, 1943, p. 186.

to this view, severe slumps and recurrent periods of unemployment have been hitherto the only effective means of holding efficiency wages within a reasonably stable range. Whether this is so remains to be seen. The more conscious we are of this problem, the likelier shall we be to surmount it.[32]

While on this subject, we should underline the brilliant discussion in Chapter 21 of the *General Theory*. At this early date, Keynes showed clearly that inflation was a threat long before full employment was reached.[33]

> Thus, in addition to the final critical point of full employment at which money-wages have to rise, in response to an increasing effective demand in terms of money, fully in proportion to the rise in the prices of wage-goods, we have a succession of earlier semi-critical points at which an increasing effective demand tends to raise money-wages though not fully in proportion to the rise in the price of wage-goods; and similarly in the case of decreasing effective demand.[34]

Instead of constant prices with an expansion of money so long as unemployment prevails, prices rise gradually as employment increases. There are various reasons for this—Keynes lists five important reasons: the disproportion between the rise of money and effective demand, non-homogeneity and non-substitutability of resources, early rise in wage rates and the other factors entering into marginal cost.[35]

In conclusion, Keynes has had an unprecedented influence on public policy, an influence which may be explained in part by his disposition to adapt his theoretical models to the problems and institutions of the day. His models clarify both inflationary and deflationary episodes, and prosperous and depressed economies. The British and American economies of the last generation, the blueprints for the future—all of these owe much to Keynes, and the debt is real even when the exact locus of the influence is not easily traced.

S. E. H.

[32] *Ibid.*, p. 187.
[33] Especially pp. 292–304.
[34] *Ibid.*, p. 301.
[35] See the full discussion in Professor Lintner's essay below.

CHAPTER III

The Appraisal of the *General Theory*, 1936–37

THIS CHAPTER is largely of historical interest; and those not conversant with the elements of the *General Theory* might find it difficult.

A BRIEF CATALOGUE OF KEYNES' CONTRIBUTIONS

In parts of these introductory chapters and later in this book, the reader will find the contributions of Keynes listed and analyzed. The additions made by Keynes, as we shall see, will vary according to the critic and with the passage of time. Here, in order to give the reader his bearings, I shall attempt little more than a brief and superficial presentation.

Almost all will agree that Keynes' propensity to consume was an outstanding contribution (cf. Hansen). Professor Metzler shows that Keynes' theory of cycles rests largely on this element in the system in that the failure to spend increments of income on consumption ultimately brings an upper turning point, that is a decline in business activity, and the failure of consumption to decline as much as output accounts for a lower turning point, that is, a rise in activity.[1] It is not, therefore, in Metzler's view, now necessary to explain the turning points by reference to limiting factors such as inadequate supplies of money. Again, the independence of wage rates, on the one hand, and employment and output, on the other, rests in part, in the Keynesian system, on the marginal propensity to consume (cf. Smithies and Tobin). Again, the total effect of a rise in investment upon income depends on the multiplier, which now is the reciprocal of the marginal pro-

---

[1] Cf. J. R. Hicks, "Mr. Keynes' Theory of Employment," EJ, 1936, who interprets Keynes' cycle theory in terms of changing marginal efficiency of capital.

pensity to consume.[2] Keynes' theory of consumption plays a large part also in the evaluation of the declining trend in the marginal efficiency of capital: as the need for capital declines, little help can be expected from a rising propensity to consume; for this function (i.e., the relation of consumption to income) is held to be relatively stable and to depend upon a psychological law.[3] Say's Law is also related to Keynes' consumption function. Indeed, the goods produced may not be taken off the market because consumption does not respond adequately or quickly enough to rising output. What is especially important is that, with a stable consumption function, the determinant of income becomes investment.

In his essay in this volume, Professor Haberler, in commenting on Dr. P. Sweezy's essay, contends that Say's Law had in effect been repudiated by classical economists long before Keynes wrote. Undoubtedly Keynes exaggerated the degree to which classicists had swallowed Say's Law, though Keynes himself admitted that it was not held in extreme favor by modern economists. Moreover, the neo-classicist was, of course, aware of unemployment, of business cycles, and the like; and he must, therefore, have known that all the goods produced are not sold, or that supplies do not necessarily create their own demand. Yet this is not a complete refutation of Keynes' position. The point is that they did not make (1) failure to buy all the goods produced, (2) the related propensity to consume, and (3) underemployment equilibrium part of their *general* economics. In this sense, Say's Law remained part of their general economics.

Keynes' propensity to consume has already played a large part in twentieth-century economics. As has been so often true, the Master throws out a few seeds; and the economists, both friendly and critical, have rushed to plant them. In many instances, they have grown into seedlings and full-sized trees. Keynes himself did not insist that the *percentage* of consumption declines with rising income; he merely contended that some part of the additional income would be saved. Others have examined the actual

---

[2] See Haberler and Goodwin below, and also G. Haberler, "Mr. Keynes' Theory of the 'Multiplier': A Methodological Criticism," in *Readings in Business Cycle Theory* (The Blakiston Co., 1944), pp. 193–202.

[3] Cf. my discussion in the Introduction to Part Six, especially on Keynes' article in the *Eugenics Review*, 1937. Keynes was not too clear, as he was not in the *Treatise*, on the degree of dependence of investment on consumption.

relation of consumption to income: as affected by population changes, size of family, cyclical variations, amount of unemployment, etc., etc.

Another important contribution made by Keynes was in the use of expectations. Hicks, in his review of Keynes in the *Economic Journal* in 1936, put the greatest emphasis on this aspect of the *General Theory;* and Keynes himself, in a full-dress reply to critics and an elaboration and reiteration of his views (his article republished below), emphasized the importance of expectations.[4] In this volume, Professor Hart discusses critically Keynes' contribution in this field, which brought forth such important advances by others. In 1946 Hart can indeed underline weaknesses in Keynes' theory of expectations, some of them substantial. In 1936, however, Keynes' integration of expectations with his theory of money and marginal efficiency marked a notable advance—even over Wicksell, whose natural rate of interest had indeed failed to make use of a theory of expectations. To be sure, there had been important advances in the treatment of expectations in Scandinavian and even British economics. In Keynes' view, decisions to invest depend on long-run prospects which cannot be accurately forecast. Examination of the past would indicate how little businessmen could cope with such uncertainties as war, the price of copper, etc. They might, indeed, take refuge in the average appraisal of uncertainties or in average behavior; but the estimation of future prospects based on an average of ignorance could be little more than the economics of crystal gazing. Emphasizing the uncertainties of the distant future, Keynes largely explains the instability of the marginal efficiency of capital and the large swings in investment which are so devastating in their effect on the economy. Uncertainties and unstable marginal efficiency of capital are also a bridge to Keynes' theory of money; for liquidity preference (i.e., the preference for cash over income-yielding assets) is explained by unstable marginal efficiencies of capital. If one were certain that an asset yielding, say, 3 per cent would not depreciate, his disposition to hold money other than to meet minimum requirements to carry through transactions could not be justified on rational grounds.

In this brief survey, I shall mention only one other fundamental contribution, namely, the emphasis on under-employment equilibrium. Severe criticism may be leveled against Keynes' equilib-

---

[4] Below, p. 184.

rium at less than full employment.[5] Yet it was one of Keynes' most significant gifts to economics. Whereas classical economics either had assumed full employment, or had assumed that, under conditions of less than full employment, adjustments in wages, etc., would bring full employment, Keynes made clear the need of studying economies operating at less than full employment, and the difficulties, short of government intervention, of removing the obstacles in the path of full employment. Workers were unwilling to accept reductions in money wages, and the unemployed, anxious to work at real wage rates below current rates, were unable to effect a reduction. (The explanation of the last difficulty lay largely in the relation of wages and marginal costs and prices.) A reduction in wages, moreover, could not improve the status of industry, for demand would decline *pari passu* with the decline of wages; favorable effects on investment, either as a result of the increased availability of money associated with falling wages or through active monetary expansion, would be excluded by the high elasticity of demand for cash in relation to falling rates of interest (as interest rates tend to fall, the public absorbs the additional cash created), and the small response of investment to any practical decline in the rate of interest.

THE EARLY CRITICS

From the first reviews of the *General Theory*, one would not have suspected that Keynes had written a book which might rival *The Wealth of Nations* or *Das Kapital* in the attention which it would receive. Not a single enthusiastic review has come to my attention; and there were many very critical ones. Let us discuss the latter first.

Perhaps the most critical was a review by Pigou.[6] After castigating Keynes for presenting his ideas in a "matrix of sarcastic comment upon other people," he went on: "Einstein actually did for Physics what Mr. Keynes believes himself to have done for Economics. He developed a far-reaching generalization, under which Newton's results can be subsumed as a special case."[7]

Perhaps in a somewhat repentant mood, Pigou also wrote: "I may even have missed, as has happened before now to critics of

---

[5] Cf., especially, Professors Haberler and Leontief below.
[6] A. C. Pigou, "Mr. J. M. Keynes' *General Theory of Employment, Interest and Money*," ECN, May, 1936, pp. 115–132.
[7] *Ibid.*, p. 115.

new works, some vital and pathbreaking contribution to thought." [8]

"We have watched an artist firing arrows at the moon. Whatever we thought of his marksmanship, we can all admire his virtuosity." [9]

In this review, Pigou touched upon almost every topic in the *General Theory* which later attracted the attention of critics. In lumping all classicists together, Pigou held, Keynes was able to attribute mistakes of one to all (p. 116). Pigou denied that he (Pigou) had failed, in discussing the elasticity of real demand for labor, to consider the *position* of the schedule, or that he had failed to take account of the effect of monetary happenings upon the real supply schedule of labor (pp. 117–118). As many others have pointed out, Keynes' treatment of liquidity preference was not consistent; liquidity preference related money to the rate of interest; but at another point, the demand for money was accounted for by the *real* value people choose to hold in money, and this was related to income (pp. 120–121). When the marginal rate of efficiency of capital rises, moreover, the demand for illiquid assets rises; and therefore, with any probable monetary policy, the rate of interest would rise (p. 124). Here, of course, Pigou was attacking where Keynes was vulnerable—his attempt to associate the interest rate mainly with the demand for money to satisfy liquidity preference. Pigou was prepared to accept Keynes' theory of the multiplier; but, in his view, Keynes had failed to account for the limitations imposed by the requirements of additional money and rising rates of interest (p. 124).

On the savings-investment issue, Pigou was not so pessimistic as Keynes. Once savings grow at a steady rate, investments will also grow correspondingly. Just as people extract teeth with the intentions of substituting artificial teeth, so savers refrain from consumption in order to invest. Savings are made in order to be invested (pp. 126–127). On the wage issues, Pigou did not interpret Keynes' position as a complete break with the classicists; for through various repercussions a reduction of money wages might bring a rise of employment. Keynes, in Pigou's view, had failed to see the relation of the reduction in wage rates and banking policy. It was the latter that made the problem determinate. Even with full employment established, labor would choose between

[8] *Ibid.*, p. 122.
[9] *Ibid.*, p. 132.

higher real wages with less employment and lower real wages with more employment (pp. 127–129, 131).

Later Pigou recanted. In a debate with Kaldor, he yielded much to the Keynesian position on the relation of employment and wage rates.[10] In the introduction to his *Lapses from Full Employment,* he denied the point that now he "was attacking the problem of unemployment by manipulating wages rather than by manipulating demand." And at the end of a discussion of the Keynesian *vs.* the classical position, Pigou admitted that there are subtleties of theory which the classicists did not envisage, though, for practical purposes, he believed their conclusions were correct. Note, however, that full employment will follow only if friction and immobility are ruled out and thorough going competition among wage earners is assured; and even then full employment is assured only on the assumption that opportunities for real investment are sufficient.[11]

Professor Knight was equally bitter in 1937. In discussing Keynes' interpretation of "the postulates of classical economics," he wrote: ". . . throughout the book, his references under this phrase are, in general, the sort of caricatures which are typically set up as straw men for purposes of attack in controversial writing."[12]

"This section (Chapter 24 of the *General Theory,* with the 'inferences' to be drawn from it) is of special interest to the present writer as one inclined to take economics as a 'serious subject' rather than an intellectual puzzle for the diversion or even the improvement of the mind" (p. 117).

". . . We must simply 'forget' the revolution in economic theory and read the book as a contribution to the theory of business oscillations" (p. 121).

Professor Knight found very little in the book with which he could agree. Unemployment, in Keynes' system, is explained by

[10] A. C. Pigou, "Money Wages in Relation to Unemployment," *EJ,* March, 1938, pp. 134–138. In this note, Professor Pigou agreed that a cut in money wages would increase employment only if it would bring about a reduction in the rate of interest; but he added that a reduction in money wages would almost certainly bring about a reduction in the rate of interest.

[11] A. C. Pigou, *Lapses from Full Employment* (1944), p. 25.

[12] F. H. Knight, "Unemployment and Mr. Keynes' Revolution in Economic Theory," *Canadian Journal of Economics and Political Science,* 1937, p. 101.

the manner of fixing prices, by the assumption of monopoly labor conditions, by the manner of operation of the price mechanism (pp. 102–3). Keynes sets up an economic system on assumptions which imply that the variables are fixed or determined other than by the mutual adjustment of supply and demand: he brings in the *deus ex machina*, e.g., public authority, psychology (p. 105 *n.*).

According to Knight, expectations, though important, were badly integrated; the failure of individual savings to be invested was merely Keynes' manner of restating the old theory of accumulation of hoards(p. 108); the independence of savings and the rate of interest are old stuff (p. 108); the monetary assumptions upon which the multiplier theory is based are inadequate (p. 110); the theory of interest is the part of the whole construction that it is most difficult to take seriously (p. 112); apparently in Keynes' system money that is saved is different from money lent (p. 112); the speculative demand needs emphasis but has application much more generally than Keynes allows (p. 113); socialization of investment is "more like the language of the soap box reformer than an economist writing a tome for economists" (p. 119).

Professor Schumpeter also on the whole was critical.[13] If one is to judge by the position given the review in the number of the *Statistical Journal*, the editors did not consider the *General Theory* an important book.

> It is, however, vital to renounce communion with any attempt to revive the Ricardian practice of offering, in the garb of general scientific truth, advice which—whether good or bad—carries meaning only with references to the practical exigencies of the unique historical situation of a given time and country (p. 792).

> Ricardian as the book is in spirit and content, so it is in workmanship. There is the same technique of skirting problems by artificial definitions which, tied up with highly specialized assumptions, produce paradoxical-looking tautologies, and of constructing special cases which in the author's own mind and in his exposition are invested with a treacherous generality (p. 792).

More specifically, Schumpeter was critical of Keynes for applying Marshall's supply and demand curves to aggregate supply

[13] *Journal of the American Statistical Association*, December, 1936, pp. 791–795.

and demand, whereas, in Marshall's view, these schedules should be applied only to unimportant commodities; for relating variants in output uniquely with employment and thus assuming an invariant production function—with this elimination of new capital, stagnation follows indeed; for bringing in expectations as an independent variable and ultimate determinant of economic action; and for bringing in as a *deus ex machina* the psychological law of marginal propensity to consume.

Schumpeter's excellent but critical appraisal presented in this volume is certainly more favorable to Keynes than his 1936 review. It is a fair generalization to say that the reviewers of 1936 —both favorable and unfavorable—are ten years later much more impressed by the book than they were in 1936. The curve representing the grading of the book for 1936 has bodily been shifted upwards to a higher position in 1946.

In this connection, I should also comment on the very able reviews by Professors Robertson and Viner in the November, 1936, *Quarterly Journal of Economics*. Professor Robertson's views are so well known that I shall comment but briefly. In particular, he was critical—as have been Hansen, Samuelson, Goodwin, Lutz, and many others—of Keynes' terminology which made savings equal to investment. (The problem is ably discussed by Robertson in the *Economic Journal* rather than in the article under discussion.) [14] There is indeed much to be said for Robertson's contention that definitions which yield inequality of savings and investment are very useful as guides for policy. Many will agree, however, that the debate was rather sterile and that even Robertson's "Day" approach has many pitfalls and obscurities. Keynes, on the other hand, has not consistently allowed savings to be equal to investment at every moment of time. In fact, at one point he discusses the adjustments of income which will make savings equal to investment.

Robertson concentrated much of his ammunition upon Keynes' attempt to explain the rate of interest as the rate which equates supply and demand for money. Here he was indeed successful in showing that Keynes in fact failed to exclude the effect upon the rate of interest of the shape and height of the productivity curve for capital. Robertson shows that, with expanding output,

[14] Cf. also Lerner, Part Nine of this volume, and the important debate between Keynes and Professor Ohlin in EJ, June, September, December, 1937.

the increased demand for money for investments will ultimately raise the rate of interest.[15] This is undoubtedly one of the most unsatisfactory aspects of Keynes' theory; and Robertson has had support from Pigou, Viner, Haberler, Knight, and many others.

Professor Viner's able review, though critical, was in many respects a favorable one. "The indebtedness of economists to Mr. Keynes has been greatly increased by this latest addition to the series of brilliant, original, and provocative books, whose contribution to our enlightenment will prove, I am sure, to have been greater in the long than in the short run." [16]

Viner dealt especially with three problems: wages and unemployment, liquidity preference, and the propensity to consume. On the first, he commented on the apparent difficulty of increasing employment through a reduction of money wages. First, wages are rigid downwards; second, a rise of employment will be stopped by the upward movement of short period marginal costs. (To this assumption concerning the shape of the Keynesian supply curve, Viner rightly raises objections.) Third, Viner does not find Keynes' association of declining demand with falling wage rates an insuperable obstacle to reducing unemployment: the entrepreneur will gain through the time lag between the drop in wages and in prices. (This argument is not convincing.)

Viner's most important contribution is in his discussion of liquidity preference. Here Viner showed, at an early stage in the discussion, many of the weaknesses of Keynes' analysis: the failure to consider (1) the possibility of increasing money supplies as liquidity preference rose, (2) the nexus of various assets (e.g., if purchases of long-term assets were discouraged, others would be purchased, with favorable effects on the former), and (3) that many buy assets for redemption price, not on the basis of rate of interest. Viner's discussion of these problems is one of the best. Hicks also dealt with them, as have Lerner, Haberler, Hardy, Lintner, and others.

Finally, in his discussion of the propensity to consume, Viner anticipated to some extent the later developments of this con-

---

[15] D. H. Robertson, "Some Notes on Mr. Keynes' *General Theory of Employment*," QJE, November, 1936, especially pp. 175–191. Cf. also Lerner's two essays on interest rates, below.

[16] J. Viner, "Mr. Keynes on the Causes of Unemployment," QJE, November, 1936, p. 146.

cept. For example, he underlined the significance of wealth as a factor tending to influence the propensity to consume.[17]

EARLY APPRAISALS BY LATER KEYNESIANS

So far we have presented the appraisal by those who on the whole might not be classed as followers of Keynes. But one will also find an under-estimation of the importance of the book in 1936–37, even among strong supporters of Keynesian economics. Let us consider the examination of the *General Theory* by three of the leading Keynesians—Hansen, Hicks, and Harrod—who of course are not only followers of Keynes but have made important advances on their own.

Professor Hansen, for example, wrote as follows:

> The book under review is not a landmark in the sense that it lays a foundation for a "new economics." It warns us once again, in a provocative manner, of the danger of reasoning based on assumptions which no longer fit the facts of economic life. . . . The book is more a symptom of economic trends than a foundation stone upon which a science can be built.[18]

Professor Hansen noted that the ultimate causal factors, the three fundamental psychological propensities, were outside of the price system. Keynes' break with the classicists, Hansen observed, was complete on the rate of interest and the relation of savings and investment. On the latter issue, Hansen sided with

[17] Among the early critics who made some effective criticism, Professor Leontief also should be mentioned (QJE, November, 1936). C. O. Hardy (AER, September, 1936, pp. 490–493) saw in the book a greatly increased emphasis upon the liquidity preference as a disturbing element in the equilibrium of the market. Among reviewers in foreign languages, we should mention W. Lautenbach ("Zur Zinstheorie von John Maynard Keynes," *Weltwirtschaftliches Archiv*, 1937, pp. 493–525), who was especially critical of Keynes' theory of interest; and G. Krämer ("J. M. Keynes über Kapitalersparung und -anlegung," *Schmollers Jahrbuch*, June, 1937, pp. 59–72), who approves of Keynes' strictures on laissez faire and sees a need of governmental intervention to stimulate investment. In his view, Keynes' proposals relate more to Anglo-Saxon countries than to Germany. Finally, E. Mantoux ("La théorie générale de M. Keynes," *Revue d'Economie Politique*, 1937, pp. 1559–1590) was especially critical of Keynes' objective of low interest rates, his unfairness to his predecessors, his identity of savings and investment, the overemphasis of full employment as against the national dividend, the attempt to make the multiplier a causal factor; and he stressed the inevitability of socialism should Keynes' proposals be accepted.

[18] A. H. Hansen, "Mr. Keynes on Underemployment Equilibrium," JPE, October, 1936, pp. 667–686 (esp. p. 686).

Robertson, who, it seemed to him, made much more clear than Keynes the disequilibrating factors. At that time, Hansen had apparently not yet embraced the maturity theory, for he thought that stable underemployment equilibrium was not possible without price and wage rigidity and monopolistic control of supplies. And he much preferred technical gains and new discoveries as the means of perpetuating our economic system to Keynes' routes; and he did not seem to approve public measures to convert savings into investments.[19] With further consideration, as we all know, Hansen's views on economic maturity and public investment changed.[20]

In one of the most interesting reviews of the book, Professor Hicks wrote as follows:

> The technique of this work is on the whole conservative: more conservative than in the *Treatise*. It is the technique of Marshall, but it is applied to problems never tackled by Marshall and his contemporaries. . . . That testing has now been done, and the Ricardian conclusions found badly wanting.[21]

In a later study, Hicks wrote: *"The General Theory of Employment* is a useful book; but it is neither the beginning nor the end of dynamic economics."[22]

After reading all or almost all of the reviews of Lord Keynes' *General Theory,* I conclude that, as viewed from the vantage point of 1947, Hicks' evaluation was about as acute as any. According to him, the book presents a theory of output in general; of shifting equilibrium vis-à-vis the static or stationary theories of general equilibrium such as those of Ricardo, Böhm-Bawerk and Pareto; a theory of money, bringing it out of isolation and integrating it with the theory of general equilibrium. Since the ordinary economics cannot explain the norm, it cannot explain *deviations* from the norm. Once anticipations are added, equilibrium analysis can be used not only to deal with remote stationary condition, but with the real world of disequilibrium. "From the standpoint of pure theory, the use of the method of expectations

[19] *Op. cit.,* pp. 680–683.

[20] Cf. his essays below, as well as his notable *Fiscal Policy and Business Cycles* (1941), and *Economic Policy and Full Employment* (1946).

[21] J. R. Hicks, EJ, June, 1936, p. 253.

[22] J. R. Hicks, "Mr. Keynes and the Classics: A Suggested Interpretation," EC, April, 1937, p. 159.

is perhaps the most revolutionary thing about this book. . . ." The book, in Hicks' view, reintroduces determinateness into a process of change. Keynes deals with short and long period expectations, and presents a monetary theory of interest. Hicks observes, however, that the more important transactions are, the less important are the advances of Keynes' theory of interest over the classical theory. In ordinary theory, the rate of interest is determined by the demand and supply for loans; and the equation for demand and supply of money becomes otiose. In the Keynesian system, the rate of interest is determined by the supply and demand for money: the equation for loans then becomes otiose. Hicks also saw the important part played by secular stagnation in the *General Theory*, and in general approved Keynes' solution. We either accept the policy of stimulating investment or repressing saving, or our once "benevolent science becomes a paean to destruction, whose terrors are earthquakes, war, and conflagration. . . ." [23]

Finally, Harrod wrote:

> I may say at once that in my opinion Mr. Keynes' conclusions need not be deemed to make a vast difference to the general theory, but that they do make a vast difference to a number of short-cut conclusions of leading importance. [24]

The achievement of Keynes has been, according to Harrod, to consider certain features of traditional theory which were unsatisfactory, because the problems involved tended to be slurred over, and to reconstruct that theory in a way which resolves the problem. "In my judgment, Mr. Keynes has not affected a revolution in fundamental economic theory but a readjustment and a shift in emphasis . . . And in the sphere of departmental economics and short cuts, which are of greatest concern for the ordinary working economist, Mr. Keynes' views constitute a genuine revolution in many fields." At another point, Mr. Harrod had assured economists, whose main interest was in general theory and who had laid their foundations well, that they might

[23] This paragraph follows closely Hicks' article in the EJ (pp. 238–253). In the EC article, Hicks attempted to reconcile the economics of the classicists and Keynes, and in particular to show under what relationship of demand for money and changing rates of interest Keynes and (or) the classicists were right.

[24] R. Harrod, "Mr. Keynes and the Traditional Theory," EC, February, 1937, p. 75. See below, p. 592.

look down "with a smile of indifference on the fulminations of Mr. Keynes." [25]

I shall not comment fully on Mr. Harrod's essay, for it is republished in this volume. In his view, the most important single point in Keynes' analysis was that it is illegitimate to assume "that the level of income in the community is independent of the amount of investment decided upon." [26]

In the Keynesian system, the schedule of the marginal productivity of capital, the propensity to consume, the liquidity preference function (with money given), will determine the investment level of income and the rate of interest. Whereas in the traditional theory the level of activity is an unknown and prices are determined by the money equation, and the level of activity is determined by money supply factors and marginal productivity schedules; in the Keynesian system, the level of activity is determined by equations governing the savings-interest complex. Money is determinate, and the price level is determined otherwise than by the money equation. [27]

S. E. H.

[25] *Ibid.*, pp. 75, 85. See below, pp. 592–3, 604.

[26] *Ibid.*, p. 76. See below, p. 594.

[27] Perhaps a word should be said concerning two other discussions of the *General Theory.* D. G. Champernowne ("Unemployment, Basic and Monetary: The Classical Analysis and the Keynesian," *Review of Economic Studies*, June, 1936, pp. 201–216) attempted to reconcile Keynes' and the classical theory of wages and unemployment. Champernowne suggested that, if labor is discontented with its real wages, it will induce disequilibrium unemployment and raise wages; and if unemployed labor tries to reduce real wages, the monetary authority will ultimately stop the decline in prices and enable workers to cut real wages (p. 201). The real supply curve of labor is, in his view, a useful concept for estimating the trend of unemployment and real wages (p. 216).

W. B. Reddaway ("*The General Theory of Employment, Interest, and Money,*" *Economic Record*, June, 1936, pp. 28–36) dealt especially with the dynamic elements and at this early time presented the mathematical skeleton of the Keynesian system.

CHAPTER IV

Three Problems in the *General Theory*

IN THIS CHAPTER, I deal with three important criticisms levelled against the *General Theory*: (1) the theory is not general; (2) it is not dynamic; (3) the equilibrium at under-employment levels is not established.[1]

THE THEORY IS NOT GENERAL

Keynes has indeed been blessed with critics. No book on economics in the last one hundred years, or even before, has received the attention bestowed upon the *General Theory*. Friendly critics attempted to systematize it, remove the underbrush, cut out the dead wood, in general to clarify the arguments and to build upon it. Unfriendly critics by the hundreds, on the other hand, wrote books or articles in which they tried to show that classical economics was not Keynes' "classical" economics; that Keynes' assumptions were not justified; that, building on unrealistic assumptions, his economics was unreal and sterile; that his practical proposals for policy would destroy capitalism. Scarcely an economist is to be found who has not at least quoted Keynes in support of his position or taken a pot shot at the *General Theory*.

It would be impossible to list all the criticisms directed against the *General Theory*. Some economists contend that Keynes, confronted with a leak in the classical house, instead of filling the hole, tried to raze the whole structure: it is another case of burning the house in order to roast the pig (cf. Leontief's essay below). Others contend that Keynes has not gone far enough. Instead of trying to patch up classical economics, they would have him remove the underpinnings and build afresh. Lord

---

[1] The reader should consult the very able volume by M. F. Timlin, *Keynesian Economics* (The University of Toronto Press, 1942).

Beveridge would not go so far, but the reader should compare Dr. Paul Sweezy's essay in this volume.

In a review of the *General Theory* published in the *Journal of the American Statistical Association* (December, 1936), Professor Schumpeter expressed well a criticism which has since been made several times, namely, that in writing his *General Theory*, Keynes always had in mind public policy, and particularly British problems. In Schumpeter's view, Keynes was doing economics a disservice in presenting as universal truths, in the Ricardian tradition, economics which consciously or subconsciously were the product of British problems of the day. The only result of this kind of economics was bound to be further cleavages and differences among economists, originating in the attempt to blend economics and politics.

Undoubtedly, there is substance in Professor Schumpeter's thesis. Those who seek universal truths, applicable in all places and at all times, had better not waste their time on the *General Theory*. By general theory, Keynes meant merely theory that dealt with full employment as but a special case. Impressed by institutional changes and considerations, Keynes was impelled to rewrite economics. But one man's meat is another's poison. What repelled Professor Schumpeter has a certain attraction for me. Universal truths are of little use in my box of tools. Does what Keynes has tried to do differ fundamentally from the attempt of Professor Chamberlin, a strong defender of classical economics, to take account of institutional factors in revising and rewriting the classical theory of value and distribution?

Nor am I able to agree with Professor Schumpeter that Keynes' medicine is curative only for Great Britain. I find it even more helpful in the American economy, with its institutional rigidities, strong group interests, a political system that caters to special interests excessively, and with the difficulty, short of strong government interference, of nullifying or offsetting the dynamic forces that make for unemployment. Keynesian economics applies to hybrid economic societies—partly capitalist and partly socialist—and, so long as these societies prevail, Keynes' economics will serve as very useful guideposts for policy. In a changing institutional set-up, Keynesian economics will have to be adapted and modified: on the same grounds that the *General Theory* replaces Mill's *Political Economy* or Marshall's *Principles of Economics*, a newer general theory will ultimately replace

Keynes' *General Theory*. The last may well live as a rule book to be used by the economic practitioners of the next twenty-five to one hundred years. Unlike the Chinese, we do not deal with timeless societies. A system that will serve for this period and, if appropriately modified, perhaps for centuries, is indeed a contribution beyond any of recent generations.

DYNAMIC ELEMENTS

Another criticism of the *General Theory* is that it is not dynamic. In his Preface, Keynes wrote concerning the *Treatise*, that "it seemed to be the outstanding fault of the theoretical parts of that work (namely, Books III and IV) that I failed to deal thoroughly with the effects of *changes* in the level of output. My so-called 'fundamental equations' were an instantaneous picture taken on the assumption of a given output. . . . But the dynamic development, as distinct from the instantaneous picture, was left incomplete and extremely confused. This book, on the other hand, has evolved into what is primarily a study of forces which determine changes in the scale of output and employment as a whole. . . ." [2]

Professor Schumpeter, for example, in his 1936 article, was critical because, in assuming a unique relation between output and employment, Keynes was in fact assuming an invariant production function and ruling out all the changes involved in the capitalist process. Even the use of expectations received unfavorable comment: it was not linked by Keynes to cyclical situations that gave rise to them and hence becomes an independent variable and the ultimate determinant of economic action. By 1946, Schumpeter, in his appraisal of Keynes' work, recanted to some extent and was prepared to find some dynamic elements in Keynes, particularly in the discussion of expectations. He commented, however, on Keynes' reluctance to use the process or period analysis. "The exact skeleton of Keynes' system belongs, to use the term proposed by Ragnar Frisch, to macrostatics, not to macrodynamics." [3]

Harrod, in a paper in *Econometrica* republished in this volume, was also critical of Keynes' failure to present a truly dynamic element. The only criticism of Mr. Keynes which he was prepared to offer was that Keynes' system was still static. Reference

[2] *General Theory*, pp. vi–vii.
[3] AER, Sept., 1946, p. 511. See below, pp. 92–3.

to anticipations was not in Harrod's view enough to make a theory dynamic. Anticipations and other circumstances still help to explain a static equilibrium. In a dynamic theory, one of the determinants will be the rate of growth of supplies of commodities and factors. "The distinguishing feature of the dynamic theory will not be that it takes anticipations into account, for these may affect the static equilibrium also, but that it will embody new terms in its fundamental equations, rate of growth, acceleration, deceleration, etc." [4]

In contrast to the views of Messrs. Schumpeter, Harrod, and Leontief, Hicks underlined Keynes' contribution to a dynamic theory—Hicks' emphasis on expectations as a central contribution of the *General Theory* naturally led to this interpretation. "It is a theory of shifting equilibrium vis-à-vis the static or stationary theories of general equilibrium, such as those of Ricardo, Böhm-Bawerk, or Pareto."

> The changing, progressing, fluctuating economy has to be studied on its own and cannot usefully be referred to the norm of a static state.[5]
>
> Once the missing element—anticipations—is added, equilibrium analysis can be used, not only in the remote stationary conditions to which many economists have found themselves driven back, but even in the real world, even in the real world in "disequilibrium."
>
> The point of the method is that it reintroduces determinateness into a process of change.[6]

UNDEREMPLOYMENT EQUILIBRIUM

In the *General Theory*, Keynes explained the manner in which underemployment equilibrium was reached, and stressed its

[4] R. F. Harrod, "Mr. Keynes and Traditional Theory," EC, Jan., 1937, p. 86 (see below, p. 605). Cf. also Professor Leontief's paper, in which he notes that Keynes has recourse to the exclusively dynamic liquidity preference theory. (Changes in liquidity preference react not to the absolute magnitudes of the relevant variables but only to rates of changes of these variables.) The treatment is not, however, truly dynamic in Leontief's view; and Leontief is critical of Keynes for applying the stickiness assumption in dynamic analysis.

[5] J. R. Hicks, "Mr. Keynes' Theory of Employment," EJ, June, 1936, pp. 238–239.

[6] *Ibid.*, pp. 240–241. Cf. Metzler's essay below. Both Hicks and Metzler emphasize that the *General Theory* does not try to deal with deviations from the norm, since economics has not explained the norm.

importance. The classical case of full employment was only a special case. In Haberler's view (see below, p. 166–7) the under-employment equilibrium is generally considered the most substantial contribution by Keynes. Indeed it has served to concentrate attention on less-than-full employment economics. It has also been the target of innumerable criticisms.

In contrast to the classical theory, which emphasized the relation of declining wage rates and rising employment, and the presence of unemployment with sticky wages, Keynes emphasized the concern of workers with money wages, and the unwillingness of the unemployed to accept a reduction of money wages, and especially their inability to depress real wage rates by cutting their supply price in money terms. Some of the links in the argument will become apparent as we go on.[7]

Keynes undoubtedly exaggerated the extent to which workers watch their money as against their real wage rates.[8] In 1936, Champernowne attempted to reconcile Keynes' wage theory and the classical theory. For the short run, say a year, Keynes' theory, according to Champernowne, had substance. But not for the longer run. "If labor is so disorganized by unemployment that the competition of the unemployed continually lowers money wages, a situation must eventually arise in which the monetary authority takes action to check any resultant fall in prices, and so makes effective the attempt of the unemployed to accept a lower real wage."[9] Champernowne concluded that, so long as there was a "real" tendency for labor to insist on a certain standard of life, and for labor's bargaining power to increase as unemployment declines, and provided that the monetary authority does not allow workers to be misled too long by rises or declines in the cost of living, the real supply curve of labor may be more significant than the money wage in determining the trend of unemployment and real wages.[10]

Critics of Keynes' under-employment equilibrium were inclined especially to concentrate on his liquidity preference. Keynes did not, of course, assume that a reduction of wages did

[7] The reader should compare essays by Messrs. Smithies and Tobin in Part Eight.

[8] Cf. Professor Pigou's review in ECN, 1936, and also Leontief, below.

[9] D. G. Champernowne, "Unemployment, Basic and Monetary: the Classical Analysis and the Keynesian," *Review of Economic Studies*, June, 1936, especially pp. 201–204.

[10] *Ibid.*, p. 226.

not necessarily influence output—rather his argument was that any effect had to be through the changes in the rate of interest, marginal propensity to consume, and the marginal efficiency of capital. Pigou, Champernowne, Haberler, and Leontief, all consider the relation of Keynes' liquidity preference to the under-employment equilibrium.[11] The latter two are not satisfied that a reduction of wages via its effects upon the supply of money and the rate of interest—with reduced wages, more money becomes available—would not bring about the required expansion of output. Pigou's discussion in 1936 seemed to miss the point that, in Keynes' view, a rise in output might follow a reduction in wages via the monetary effects, for he criticizes Keynes for failing to show the relevance of banking policy.[12] Keynes' conclusions rest on the assumption that the liquidity preference schedule is highly elastic—increased supplies of money are absorbed rather than spent, with the result that they do not contribute towards reduced interest rates; and investments are insensitive to declines in the rate of interest. Writing in response to critics in 1937, Keynes admitted that, if the knowledge of the future were calculable and not subject to sudden change, the liquidity curve might be stable and very inelastic. In that case, a small amount of additional money, or money spilled from the industrial circulation as a result of reduced wages, might bring about a large reduction in the rate of interest.[18]

A good many other issues are raised by Keynes' discussion of underemployment equilibrium and wages. In Part Eight, Dr. Smithies and Mr. Tobin show that the skeleton theory is not adequate to explain the relation of money wages and output; that if assumptions are relaxed and consideration paid for example to international repercussions, the budgetary situation, monopolistic conditions, and the like, then changes in money wage rates may well greatly influence output.

In an interesting article in the 1939 *Economic Journal,* Keynes had in fact made considerable concessions. First, on the basis of works by Messrs. Kalecki, Dunlop, and Tarshis, he allowed that his assumption of inverse relationship between changes in the volume of output and real wages might well not be justified.

[11] Champernowne, p. 216; and below.

[12] A. C. Pigou, *op. cit.*; Pigou was, however, clear on this point in his recent *"Lapses from Full Employment."*

[18] J. M. Keynes, "The General Theory of Employment," QJE, Feb. 1937, pp. 218–29. (Below, pp. 181–93.)

In one sense, this discovery might strengthen Keynes' earlier position. For now expanding output would be accompanied by a rise in real wages; and, therefore, another obstacle would be placed in the way of workers who sought to escape unemployment through a reduction in wages. (We should not, however, leave out of account the resulting windfall to the employers and the incentive to add workers.) As a matter of fact, the concessions were made grudgingly. Keynes was careful to show that short of high levels of employment, marginal prime costs did not rise substantially; that the Dunlop-Tarshis thesis applied to weekly, not to the more relevant hourly, wages; that recent experience had demonstrated a relationship similar to the one suggested by him in the *General Theory*. And he was careful to gloat over his implied victory over Pigou, for he could now contend that an expansionist program would not be at the expense of labor—through a cut in real wages, as Pigou had claimed. At least he could put this opposite the black mark against his theory.[14]

More important, he now emphasized the point that he was interested in the relation of changes in real wage rates in response to movements in output. Changes in real wage rates and output in response to *revisions of the wage contract* were another matter. Recent critics of Keynes, we should note, frequently pass over this important article. Keynes was prepared to admit, as he had in the *General Theory*, that changes in wage rates might have some effects; but they were difficult to estimate.[15] *Moreover, he now pointed out that there were five important factors which fluctuate with output; and these obviously might upset the simple relation of money wages and real wages presented in the* General Theory. Here indeed substance was put into the shell; and of course the result is to some extent a repudiation of the money-wage, real-wage, output-and-employment relations in the *General Theory*. For example, it was necessary to consider stickiness and imperfection of competition, the relation of prices of goods bought outside the system (e.g., housing and imports) to money wages; the relation of marginal *wage* costs and marginal prime costs.[16]

S. E. H.

[14] "Relative Movements of Real Wages and Output," EJ, March, 1939, pp. 34–45.

[15] *Ibid.*, p. 35.

[16] *Ibid.*, p. 50.

CHAPTER V

Ten Years After : What Remains
of the *General Theory* ?

IT IS NOW almost twelve years since the *General Theory* went to press. It is time to tally the results. Many will say that it is too soon; and in a sense it is, for Keynes' standing in the year 2000 will undoubtedly not be that of 1947. Much will depend upon political and institutional developments. If communism comes, Keynes will be as dead as Ricardo is in the U.S.S.R. (Like Ricardo, however, Keynes may have great influence on a future Marx.)

In a period of ten to twelve years, despite the interruptions caused by war, the *General Theory* has probably received more attention than did Ricardo over a period of more than one hundred years, or Marshall over the last fifty years. In its pre-natal state, the *General Theory* apparently received a thorough going over by a brilliant group of economists at Cambridge; and, undoubtedly, the book owes much to many of these critics, Mrs. Robinson and Mr. Kahn among others. Since 1936, literally thousands of economists all over the world have read the *General Theory;* and large numbers examined it with painstaking care and, in fact, subjected almost every paragraph to microscopic study. The *General Theory* has given birth to hundreds, if not thousands of articles, inspired the writing of many books in support or against; and in fact there are few books in general economics written since 1936 that have not been influenced consciously or subconsciously by Keynes.

UNDER-EMPLOYMENT EQUILIBRIUM

With the passage of time, Keynes' demonstration that the economy is in equilibrium with less-than-full employment is increasingly considered his major contribution. In fact, under-employment equilibrium is the theme of the *General Theory*—Say's Law, marginal propensity to consume, marginal efficiency of capital, and the liquidity function, are the raw materials out of which Keynes processed the final product, under-employment equilibrium. Critics indeed have dealt severely with each link in the chain; and they have shown, for example, that on other assumptions (e.g., non-rigidity of wages—Haberler; inelastic liquidity function—Hicks, Haberler, Leontief) the position of under-employment may not be one of stable equilibrium. I shall return to these dissensions.

Here it is only necessary to point out that the under-employment equilibrium, despite the barrage of criticisms to which it has been subjected and the weakening of the props supporting it, is a major contribution. Economists will no longer be content to discuss the relevant problems on the assumption of full employment, or on the assumption that forces prevail which drive the economy towards full employment. No longer will they relegate the discussion of unemployment to treatises on the trade cycle, nor be content with concentrating their attention on long-period equilibrium and the optimum allocation of economic resources. The present interest in full employment economics, in non-wastage of resources, and in short-run economics, owes much to Keynes; probably more to him than to anyone else.

In an 858-page volume on general economics, Marshall, for example, scarcely touched the problem of unemployment. The index contains one reference to unemployment (pp. 710–711). Here Marshall briefly comments on the relation of availability of income and the unwillingness to spend it. (Incidentally the passage may be interpreted as a criticism of Mill for having uncritically accepted Say's Law.) Marshall, however, dismisses the difficulty by assuring us that the unwillingness to put the purchasing power to use originates in a lack of confidence. In another passage (pp. 687–688), in discussing the inconstancy of employment, Marshall emphasizes the point that its magnitude is greatly exaggerated. These are the only passages I could find that relate to unemployment.

WAGES AND EMPLOYMENT

Until Keynes' *General Theory* appeared, few economists were prepared to challenge the view that downward flexibility of wages would solve the unemployment problem. Keynes' earlier writings had indeed challenged the accepted views on wage-cutting. But in 1933, Professor Pigou's *Theory of Unemployment* was devoted especially to proving that a reduction of real wages would have a significantly favorable effect on employment. Once and for all, Keynes has established the fact that the economics of the individual firm which concentrates attention on wages as a cost, is inadequate for dealing with the economy as a whole. No economist now could possibly analyze the relation of wage rates and employment or output without considering the effects on demand as well as on costs. This is indeed a great achievement.

This contribution remains, even if it is admitted that Keynes' theory in this area is inadequate to cope with public policy. The main thesis is that employment and output are independent of changes in money wage rates. In view of Keynes' insistence during the inter-war period that unwise international economic policies had left Great Britain saddled with excessive wage rates and with unfavorable effects on employment, Keynes' position in the *General Theory* might well occasion surprise. The explanation is, of course, that in the *General Theory* he was dealing with a closed system—and therefore certainly in relation to Great Britain (but less so the United States!) with an unreal system. It is also unexpected that he should exclude from consideration the effects of fiscal operations of the government. For the response of government contributions to spending in the midst of an inflationary process will influence output.[1] Of course, in the real world, Keynes was aware of the repercussions of external forces upon wage rates, employment, and output, and of fiscal policy. His failure to deal with them in his theoretical skeleton, in the light of his earlier work, should not be interpreted as an unawareness of their importance.

Before turning to another subject, I should mention some criticisms of Keynes' theory of wages and output. It will be recalled that he had developed his theory of the relation of wages and output on the assumption of a rising short period supply curve—marginal prime costs increase with the expansion of output. A reduction of wages would then not raise employment because the gains would be offset by rising costs. Professor Viner, and later Professors Dunlop and Tarshis, denied the validity of

[1] See Dr. Smithies, below.

this assumption. Apparently real wages rise with rising output. In replying to these critics in his 1939 *Economic Journal* article, Keynes was prepared to admit that the supply curve might be horizontal over a considerable range.

It will serve no purpose to chronicle all the attacks on the theory of wages in relation to employment. For example, Keynes considerably exaggerated the "money illusion," that is, the excessive attention paid to money wages by workers. (Pigou, Leontief, Champernowne, Knight, Tobin, etc.) This distorted view of the attitude of labor explained, in Keynes' system, labor's refusal to accept a cut in money wages and its acquiescence to a cut in real wages. Once Keynes' assumptions of perfect competition, unchanged techniques, infinite elasticity of demand for money in relation to the rate of interest, a closed system, allowance for economies of large scale output, etc. are relaxed or changed, the independence of changes in money wage rates and output or employment can no longer be sustained. Perhaps in this sense Professor Haberler is right when he says that Keynes' theory does not offer an adequate guide for policy. In the real world, as we all know, changes in wage rates do influence output; and they do so because the economy is not a closed one; changes influence expectations, the rate of interest, and the marginal propensity to consume, and so on.

In fact, all of this is not really inconsistent with Keynes. In the early part of the *General Theory*, his presentation is rather rigid and not open to any realistic interpretation. In Chapter 19, however, and his later comments (the 1939 article quoted), he admitted that changes in wage rates might influence employment; but the influence would be via the propensity to consume, the marginal efficiency of capital, and the rate of interest; and the net effect is not easy to calculate.[2]

His outstanding contribution, then, was to show the relation of wage rates to effective demand; to disprove the old-fashioned theory, which associated falling wage rates and rising employment; and to show the importance of rigid wage rates on the decline as a bulwark against continued declines in spending, prices, and output.[3]

[2] Messrs. Leontief, Smithies, and Tobin, deal fully with Keynes' pure theory of wages, below.

[3] On the last point, see especially Professor Hansen's second essay below.

THE RATE OF INTEREST AND MARGINAL EFFICIENCY OF CAPITAL

The rate of interest is a cornerstone in the Keynesian system. In the pre-*General Theory* period, Keynes was very optimistic concerning the effectiveness of monetary expansion operating through the rate of interest in pulling a country out of the quagmire of deflation. In the *General Theory*, he stressed the relation of the rate of interest and marginal efficiency of capital as a determinant of the amount of investment and hence of employment. He was, however, much less optimistic than in the *Treatise* that, in the light of the low and uncertain marginal efficiency of capital and institutional difficulties, public policy could depress interest rates adequately to achieve required levels of investment; and he, therefore, would depend largely on influencing the propensity to consume and public investment.

What then were his contributions in this area? First, there is the increased attention given to the rate of interest. Many will say that here Keynes has gone too far, though in saying so they often admit the significance of the rate for debt management and the importance of the availability of credit—points brought out so well by Keynes. Yet here is a causal factor that is of importance, and that can be manipulated. If Keynes has overemphasized, he also has helped correct an under-emphasis. Second, there is the liquidity-preference theory of the rate of interest. No one can afford now to neglect the importance of holding money as an alternative to holding assets, nor the changing appraisal of alternatives under varying rates of interest. Many old-fashioned economists will say that in established theories this was all treated under hoarding. I simply do not agree. The economist is aware, as he never was before, that an increased preference for liquidity will raise interest rates; and that attempts to depress rates by monetary expansion may well be frustrated when the elasticity of demand for money in relation to the rate of interest is infinite or very high.

Third, it is clear to all now that the marginal efficiency of capital may be lower than had generally been assumed and that uncertainty plays a very significant part. An estimate of what an investment will earn five, ten, or twenty years hence is based largely on guesswork, on animal spirits, on adapting estimates to the average estimate, which in turn is based on uninformed guesses. This uncertainty clearly must be a deterrent to investment. Keynes' views on expectations (cf. Hart's essay below) and marginal efficiency of capital (cf. A. Sweezy's essay below) raise some doubts concerning the capacity of private enterprise to provide adequate demand.

The theme is not, however, that Keynes' theory of interest or expectations or marginal efficiency of capital is invulnerable. Attacks have been numerous and, in many respects, effective. Robertson, Pigou, Hicks, and others have all shown that Keynes was not exactly successful in excluding the demand for capital as a determinant of the rate of interest; and in fact Keynes himself vacillated between the old presentation and his novel concentration on liquidity preference. For oversimplifying the alternatives, i.e., cash or gilt edge securities, Keynes' liquidity theory became an easy target for those (e.g., Viner, Hicks, Lerner, Lintner) who perceived that in the real world the alternatives were much more numerous. Keynes' under-employment equilibrium further rests on the assumption of infinite elasticity of demand for money in relation to the rate of interest, and also (derived from his views on marginal efficiency of capital) inelastic demand for investment funds in response to reductions in the rate of interest. Other assumptions are of course possible (cf. Haberler and Leontief below), though the crucial issue is which assumptions are more appropriate in the real world. The writer's predilections here are towards Keynes'.

PROPENSITY TO CONSUME AND THE MULTIPLIER

The consumption function, or the propensity to consume, is one of the cornerstones of the Keynesian structure; and, despite the constant attention given it and the related concept of the multiplier, it has stood up well under scrutiny.[4] With the passage of time, the consumption function has come to occupy a more important place than was admitted by critics in 1936.

Economists and economic practitioners now more than ever stress the relation of (1) consumption and total demand and (2) demand and output. That they do so stems in no small part from Keynes' emphasis on the consumption function and the multiplier. Keynes was impressed by the failure of income recipients in a

[4] Cf. Professors Hansen and Samuelson, below. D. Dillard (*op. cit.*, pp. 125–26) shows that Keynes was troubled by the fear of under-consumption as early as 1919.

rich society to spend increments of income: part would be saved. He was also impressed by the fact that an injection of purchasing power (via public investment) would yield smaller and smaller successive increments of income—largely explained by leakages of various kinds, and in particular by the failure to spend all of the new increments of income. In fact, one of Keynes' important contributions (as Professor Goodwin observes below) was to generalize the multiplier concept to apply not only to the relation of public investment and the ensuing rise of income, but as one giving the relation of any injection to the gains of income.

The consumption function helps to explain why all goods produced are not sold (as suggested by Say's Law); the declining marginal efficiency of capital; [5] the theory of secular stagnation (Sweezy); the independence of changes in wage rates and employment (Tobin); the theory of the trade cycle (Metzler).

In the discussion of the multiplier, many economists have gone on fishing expeditions; but though they had many bites, they did not catch any large fish. Indeed, they *have* added much to Keynes' relatively simple and unverified presentation. Keynes had presented the elements of the theory in *Can Lloyd George Do It?* In an important article in 1931, Kahn further elaborated the theory of the multiplier; and in 1933 (*The Means to Prosperity*), Keynes presented the essentials of the problem for the informed layman. Chapters 8–10 of the *General Theory* in some respects are an improvement over Kahn's presentation; for now the relationship is one of investment and income rather than investment and the gains of consumption.

In the *General Theory*, Keynes writes: "I have found, however, in discussion that this obvious fact often gives rise to some confusion between the logical theory of the multiplier, which holds good continuously, without time-lag, at all moments of time, and the consequences of an expansion in the capital-goods industries which take gradual effect, subject to time-lag and only after an interval." [6]

This assumption that in logic the multiplier "holds good con-

---

[5] In the *General Theory*, the marginal efficiency of capital *seems* to be independent of consumption; but in the *Treatise*, Keynes had devoted much space to the relation of prices of consumption and investment goods, vacillating between independence and dependence.
[6] See pp. 122–123.

tinuously" has been subjected to much criticism (Robertson, Lerner, Goodwin). The failure to deal specifically with the acceleration principle, the relation of a rise of consumption and the ensuing gain of investment—perhaps justified in a low-employment recovery—also aroused much criticism. This was an oversight by Keynes that was, however, quickly dealt with by his leading supporters—Harrod, Hansen, and Samuelson.

Even more important are the empirical studies of the multiplier and the consumption function: studies of leakages by Bretherton *et al.*, C. Clark, J. M. Clark, Villard, etc.; development of the theory of the export multiplier by Machlup; further attention to rising taxes as a leakage, discussion of monetary aspects (Pigou, Neisser). In the stimulus given to the study of the consumption function, Keynes made one of his greatest contributions: To mention but a few of these studies—that of the National Resources Committee (*Consumer Expenditures in the United States*),[7] the contributions of Bean, Woytinsky, Miss Brady, Bassie, Friend, Bennion, Staehle, Mrs. Gilboy, and others, in the *Review of Economic Statistics*, the war-time studies (C. Madge, *War-Time Patterns of Saving and Spending*, 1943, and recent studies of the Bureau of Labor Statistics, Department of Commerce, etc.). At last we are beginning to know something about the relation of consumption to income; and we are beginning to take account of population changes, accumulation of liquid assets, changing cyclical conditions, distribution of income, etc., etc.[8] Many of the empirical studies, indeed, rest on misinterpretation of Keynes' consumption function; but they nevertheless help to clarify consumption behavior.

In concluding this discussion of the consumption function, I should emphasize what must be obvious by now, namely, that, in assuming a stable consumption function, Keynes in fact stressed the decisive importance of investment as the determinant of income—as had Wicksell, Spiethoff, and Hansen. His novel concentration on the consumption function attracted attention once more to the importance of investment, and encouraged scores of in-

[7] This, however, could not be considered an outgrowth of the *General Theory*.

[8] The views of A. F. Burns on the consumption function are not so different from those of Keynesians as he seems to think. (A. F. Burns, *Economic Research and the Keynesian Thinking of Our Times*, in the Twenty-Sixth Annual Report of the NBER, pp. 9–10.)

vestigators to study the relation of consumption and income and to draw conclusions about the stability or instability of the function. At the present writing there is a large accumulation of evidence which supports Keynes' psychological law of a stable consumption function.

S. E. H.

CHAPTER VI

In Relation to Classical Economics :
Evolution or Revolution ?[1]

It is a matter of judgment whether the *General Theory* is simply classical economics, further developed or embroidered, or whether Keynesian economics represents a genuine break. It is not easy to give a satisfactory answer. A new lilac shrub springs up from the roots of the old shrubbery; and if one gets under the dirt, one will find the new shoot sprouting up from the roots of the old. In the same manner, Keynesian economics may seem like and may largely be a new plant; and yet its debts to the older economics are quite clear.

Where are the departures from classical economics?

One: On to the classical theory of long-term equilibrium and Marshall's principle of substitution Keynes has grafted an analysis of the short run and particularly of the level of employment. Short-run economics, whether it covers one year or ninety (as Keynes suggests at one point), will certainly play a much larger part in economics as a result of his influence. Concern with the level of employment marks also an interest in distribution which the classicists, with their excessive concern over the optimum allocation of economic resources, were inclined to neglect. Here we have at least a coup if not a revolution.

Two: Keynes' all-out attack on thriftiness and his espousal of spending is, in Schumpeter's view, the revolutionary element in Keynesian economics. Keynes was not the first to extol the virtues of spending, and indeed he disinterred Mandeville's *Fable of the Bees* and Malthus' views in favor of spending. Over-saving and under-consumption theories of the business cycle also have been popular; and Robertson's brilliant *Banking Policy and the Price Level* (1926) had made clear to all the conflict of interest in de-

[1] See Introduction to Part Eight.

pression periods between individuals who save excessively, and those of society: savings fail to be achieved. It remained for Keynes, both in his *Treatise* and in the *General Theory,* to launch a vigorous attack on thriftiness and to integrate excess savings with his theory of under-employment equilibrium and stagnation. He put the message across so effectively that few thinking men living in a Western democracy, unhurt by war, will be unmindful of the conflict between the individual's quest for security via savings and society's interest in his spending. And those who are inclined to forget will be reminded by public policy.[2]

Three: In reviewing Keynes' *General Theory,* in *Economica,* Professor Pigou adumbrated that the complete break with classical economics would have been achieved if Keynes had denied the relationship of falling wage rates and rising employment. Actually, according to Pigou, Keynes had left a loop-hole. Yet in view of Pigou's recantation in his debate with Professor Kaldor and also in *Lapses from Full Employment,*[8] Keynes' views on wages and employment might be termed revolutionary. In this book Pigou still adhered to the view that, *in ordinary circumstances,* a reduction in money wages would raise employment. His concession was that, under certain monetary conditions, the rate of interest would not fall following a cut in wages, and, therefore, the reduction of wage rates would not contribute towards increased employment, and that the effect had to be via the rate of interest. The vital issue here is merely that, after the *General Theory,* the economic theorist and economic practitioner are much less certain of the favorable effects of wage cutting than they were before 1936, or, for that matter, before Keynes began his campaign against wage cutting in the twenties and had as yet presented his views in the formal dress of a general theory.

Four: It is not necessary to elaborate here on Keynes' under-employment state of equilibrium; for it is discussed elsewhere. All will not agree that the under-employment equilibrium is stable; for much depends on assumptions concerning rigidity of wages, monetary policy, the relation of money and rate of interest, and the latter and investment. But all will agree that under-employment equilibrium will receive much more attention in economics than ever before.

Five: Keynes definitely has tied the theory of money to general

[2] Cf. Chap. V of A. C. Pigou, *Lapses from Full Employment.*
[8] See pp. 10–17.

theory. No longer are we likely to get treatises dealing with the theory of value and distribution with little or no attention paid to money; or treatises on money unrelated to the theory of output and distribution. Money is, moreover, in Keynes' system the bridge from the present to the future. Expectations explain why the public holds money rather than non-monetary assets; and expectations are the dynamic element in Keynes' theory, making significant advances over the static theories of Mill, Marshall, Jevons, Pareto.

Six: Keynes' theory, in the Cambridge tradition, starts from income, and includes the first systematic explanation of income formation. It remained for Keynes to integrate the theory of money, employment, and interest, with income theory. In this manner he puts at the disposal of general theory the vast storehouse of statistics of income, consumption, savings, and investment, with the result that much material becomes available for verification, and the theory becomes much more realistic.[4]

Seven: Keynes' economics is perhaps institutional in that it takes account of institutional factors explaining high rates of interest, inadequate supplies of money, over-saving, cumulative errors, uncertainties, rigidities, etc., etc. Useful general theory, in his view, must take account of these institutional factors, and, in doing so, it will suggest solutions to the contemporary economic problems. In this sense, undoubtedly, Professor Schumpeter is correct in suggesting that the appeal of Keynesian economics lies in its simplicity and effectiveness in yielding answers to the economic problems of the day, the solution of which is demanded by the public that supports economists. As the institutional factors change, the underlying theory will be revised. The contrast between Keynes' theory in the realm of public policy and, say, Marshall or Walras may be put crudely as the difference between a key which in its dimensions is, insofar as the theory is correct, an average of all keys, but which may well fit no doors, and a key which is made expressly to fit a particular door, or a few doors. Perhaps this explains why Keynes has had the answer to so many problems: fiscal policy, the rate of interest and monetary policy, exchange rates, tax policy, the propensity to consume, *et hoc genus omne*. In 1960 or 1970, it may be necessary to file off the edges of Keynes' key to fit the door of the American economy in 1960 or the British economy of 1970.

[4] See Professor Lintner's essay below.

In short, as a result of the Keynesian attack, neo-classical economics will never be the same. In many ways, Keynes was unfair to his predecessors; but as a result of his work, the classicists will have to check their assumptions, pay much more attention to institutional and short-run problems, better integrate the theory of money and income and output, make their theory more useful in the area of public policy, be more concerned with general demand, thrift, and expectations, and be less certain on the relation of wage cutting and employment. If the "new" economics is not a complete break with the economics of the nineteenth century, the economics after 1936 shall at the very least be marked by a jagged line.[5]

S. E. H.

[5] Despite the urgings of my publishers not to add, and particularly to page proof, I cannot refrain from inserting a few comments which stem from Mr. Robinson's brilliant biography of Keynes. (The relevant number of the *Economic Journal* just reached me.) Here one will find the story of Keynes' life, or rather many lives—his successes as a student, teacher, editor, writer, statesman, financier and entrepreneur. Close to Keynes in many capacities over a generation, Mr. Robinson tells his story with charm, reveals many aspects of Keynes' life which are unknown to most of us, and does it all with a remarkable degree of detachment.

Among Robinson's conclusions on Keynes' economics, the following stand out: (1) Keynes was not primarily a tool-maker: he fashioned a tool only to use it for a particular task. (2) His concern with employment dates back to the middle twenties; and each objective (e.g., equilibrium in the balance of payments) was related to the primary one of employment. (3) According to Robinson, the important contributions of Keynes were the emphasis on the relation of savings and investment, the monetary theory of the rate of interest, and the demonstration that the rate of interest does not necessarily afford an automatic link between savings and investment at full employment. (4) Keynes' debt to Prof. D. H. Robertson and to Wicksell were great indeed, and particularly on the relation of savings and investment, and the monetary aspects of the rate of interest. (5) Among Keynes' most significant contributions were his success in relating the academic economics to the economics of government, and in integrating the analytical and statistical approaches to economics.

CHAPTER VII

Keynes and the Literature

DESPITE HIS activities as teacher, insurance executive, editor, college bursar, government servant, and theatrical manager, Keynes proved to be a prolific writer. This volume contains a bibliography of Keynes' writings, classified by form (books, reviews, articles) and by subject matter. The bibliography is as complete as we could make it, though I am sure that many items have escaped us. (The Editor would appreciate any suggestions on this score.) This bibliography includes ten books, and five pamphlets; seventeen reviews of official reports and thirty-two other reviews; and approximately three hundred articles. Many of the articles were indeed reprinted, and notably in the *Essays in Persuasion* and *Essays in Biography.* We have included in this bibliography a large number of anonymous articles written while Keynes was editor of the *Nation and Athenaeum.* The extent to which credit should go to H. D. Henderson or others, rather than to Keynes, is not clear. What is especially striking is the range of subject matters: politics, biography, population, statistics, probability, dramatics, industry, literature, war economics, labor, economic institutions, and especially money and international trade. The catholicity of Keynes' interests and his ability to breathe an air of freshness in fields where discussion had become dull and sterile were indeed among his greatest accomplishments.

In the process of preparing this volume, I put together in mimeographed form a bibliography of writings about Keynes or writings influenced by Keynes; and more recently I ferreted out many additional items. At the last moment, I decided not to publish this bibliography, for two reasons. First, many economists who have been influenced by Keynes are not aware of that influence, or, if they are, they do not like to be reminded of it. Second, to write a complete bibliography of books and articles influenced by Keynes is almost like writing a bibliography of economic writings—a rather uncongenial task.

I shall, however, briefly summarize the results of my bibliographical stillbirth. First, there are books which deal primarily with Keynesian economics, or have been greatly influenced by Keynes. Among those who have written one or more books, since 1936, the following would fit this description: Beveridge, Boulding, Bretherton *et al.*, C. Clark, D. B. Copland, Hansen, Harris,[1] Harrod, Hicks, Kalecki, Lerner, Madge, Meade, E. V. Morgan, Six Oxford Economists (*Economics of Full Employment*), Polanyi, Reddaway, J. Robinson, Samuelson, Shackle, Timlin, Villard, and D. Wright.

Second, one should also list those who, though rather critical of Keynes, nevertheless have been influenced both in the subject matter covered and in the manner of handling it. Perhaps the following authors of books should be included, though I realize that those listed might not agree, and the list is not all-inclusive: Angell, Ayres, J. M. Clark, Haberler, Hart, Hawtrey, Hayek, Machlup, Marget, Moulton *et al.*, Nurkse, Pigou, Robertson, Schumpeter, P. Sweezy, Tinbergen, and J. H. Williams. It is difficult, indeed, to think of an outstanding economist who would not fall into one of the two categories. I do not list, moreover, the large and growing anti-Keynesian literature which has appeared in this country in recent years, and which in no small part is the product of subsidized research, with the partial object of ridding American economics of the Keynesian "poison" which has percolated even to top policy makers. I shall mention merely Moulton, *The New Philosophy of the Public Debt* (Brookings), Terborgh, *The Bogey of Economic Maturity* (Machinery and Allied Products Institute), and Swanson and Schmidt, *Economic Stagnation or Progress?* (U. S. Chamber of Commerce). There are other research organizations which also have shown considerable enthusiasm in subsidizing research in order to disprove the Keynesian theories.

Our bibliography contained also some three hundred articles from leading scientific periodicals over the last ten years—articles commenting on Keynes' writings, and particularly the *General*

---

[1] I confess responsibility for eleven volumes (1936 and later) which were greatly influenced by Keynes.

Theory, or largely inspired by Keynes' work. But there is no space to elaborate this theme further. Keynes indeed has largely determined the subjects to be discussed and the manner of discussing them in the contemporary economic periodicals.

S. E. H.

PART TWO

Keynes, the Economist:
Three Views

CHAPTER VIII

Keynes, the Economist (1)

By R. F. HARROD

THE SON of a distinguished Cambridge economist (still living), John Maynard Keynes was nurtured in the atmosphere of high Cambridge intellectuality. In economics the authority of Alfred Marshall was supreme. In the *Principles of Economics*, which appeared when Keynes was seven, Marshall had embodied the gathered lore of the subject; all that was acceptable in the great writers of the past was preserved with loving piety; warring schools were reconciled; above all he had welded the materials into a single system and stamped it with the characteristic impress of his master mind. The work had architectonic quality and seemed to have finality.

Jevonian and other revolutions having been put in their proper perspective, Marshall gave his pupils the sense that it would be vain and injurious to attempt any radical reconstruction in the fundamentals of the subject. His program of work for them was to study the workings of the economic system in all their rich and varied detail, with the aid of principle; it was a program for the development of applied economics. Although Keynes had gifts qualifying him to be a pioneer in fundamentals, he had many other gifts well qualifying him to be an applied economist. Marshall's program was therefore quite acceptable and attractive. Much of Keynes' best work was done before he showed any signs of breaking away from that program.

In his masterly obituary notice of Marshall,[1] he defined the relation of the *Principles* to the progress of the subject in terms that might well have been acceptable to Marshall. While his tribute to Marshall's many-sided gifts is ample and sincere, it is

---

[1] EJ, September, 1924. Reprinted in *Memorials of Alfred Marshall*, ed. A. C. Pigou, 1925, and in *Essays in Biography* by J. M. Keynes, 1933.

possible to read into his appraisal of the *Principles* a certain attenuating tendency. "Marshall," he wrote, "arrived very early at the point of view that the bare bones of economic theory are not worth much in themselves and do not carry one far in the direction of useful, practical conclusions."[2]

From a broad methodological point of view there is something anomalous in a body of principles being both constructive and final. We have, of course, examples in the relative finality of Euclid and Newton. But economics . . . It must be remembered that Keynes was also a logician, author of the notable *Treatise on Probability.* He was a pupil or associate of such deep philosophers as W. E. Johnson, A. N. Whitehead, G. E. Moore, and Bertrand Russell. This would guarantee intellectual emancipation. Pupils of Marshall with a more circumscribed methodological horizon might easily fall into the error of attaching undue authority to a settled corpus of economic doctrine. Surely one must suppose that the "principles" were either less constructive or less final than appeared at first sight. Keynes' appreciation tends to minimize their constructive character. I remember, some time after this notice had appeared but long before he had thoughts of himself making a radical reconstruction, his saying to me about the *Principles,* with his quick mischievous twinkle, "haven't you yet discovered that that book is void of content?"

Applied economics being the prescribed fare, what should he select? Currency, and, in particular, the Indian currency, was the answer. The British gold standard did not at that time offer much scope for original work. The Indian currency was a live issue, and Marshall himself had done some of his best work on this subject, embodied in his monumental evidence before a succession of Royal Commissions. Keynes derived some practical knowledge from his short spell in the India Office. The result was his book on *Indian Currency and Finance* (1913), a work of quite incredible maturity and authority for a young man of 29, and his contributions to the Report of the Royal Commission (1914). Chapter two of the book remains a classic, and there are many other passages scattered through its pages that retain a live interest.

Some points may be worth noting. His classification of the various kinds of gold and gold exchange standards gives a practical illustration of both the Marshallian maxims, "*natura non facit*

[2] *Op. cit.* p. 342.

saltum" and "the one in the many." Then there is his great penetrating power, a desirable but rare attribute in applied economists, which exposed the essential and actual working of the
systems. The formal garb had to be torn asunder. The book is
impregnated with a correct appreciation of the best monetary
theory of the time; but there is also a strong sense of institutional
development and the changing modes of operation of the fundamental laws. And there is the notion that collective wisdom can
help in the perfecting of institutions, to make them better vehicles
of the fundamental forces. He was far from those who thought of
the gold standard as a rigid formula. It was a complex arrangement which could be progressively developed to relieve the lot
of humanity. He has to rout the conservatives, as on later occasions, with incisive argument and satire. In his enthusiasm for the
gold exchange standard, he throws out the hint that it may be
nearer to the future ideal than the British gold standard system
(p. 36). In this he could draw support from Ricardo, a more
respectable authority, really, than Lord Overstone. He stresses
the point—a familiar type of argument, later, with him in other
connections—that what the British took to be the orthodox model
of a gold standard was really something quite exceptional. It was
made possible by the peculiarly dominant position of London in
the international short-loan market. It is worth noticing that at
this time he fully supported Marshall in urging, against the advocates of silver monometalism for India, that the advantages of
exchange depreciation were trivial and short-lived. In one passage
(p. 101) he hints that the time may not be far distant when we
shall be ready to put something better in place of the gold (or
gold exchange) standard itself.

Marshall wrote in glowing terms about Keynes' Annex to the
report of the Royal Commission. He was "entranced by it as a
prodigy of constructive work. Verily we old men will have to
hang ourselves. . . ." [3] A later tribute from Marshall on Keynes'
Tract on Monetary Reform (1923) may be worth quoting. "I am
soon to go away; but, if I have opportunity, I shall ask new-comers
to the celestial regions whether you have succeeded in finding a
remedy for currency maladies." [4] Is it fanciful to detect in this
pleasant expression of congratulation a governessy—and pro-

[3] *Memorials of Alfred Marshall*, p. 479.
[4] *Op. cit.* p. 33.

phetic—note? You are a currency expert; you are doing very well; but remember your place; you are a specialist in a certain branch of applied economics! Did he scent danger?

However, his pride in his pupil was great and genuine. Edgeworth, too, generous but critical, cosmopolitan in his economic studies, and not in the least likely to be carried away by the fashion of a school, had an unbounded admiration for Keynes. On two occasions I remember his throwing his arms to high heaven and wagging his beard in a transport of eulogy.

The Economic Consequences of the Peace (1919) is a great work, ever fresh. Keynes' mastery of prose, his power of characterization, of debate and persuasion, his easy handling of quantitative problems, glow. The trend of his thought undoubtedly was that Germany must continue to play an important part in the economic progress of Europe. Her elimination would impose an unbearable strain on the world economy. (The idea that a state of affairs which all have taken for granted—in this case the international economic equilibrium—was something special and precarious recurs.) Thus the tendency was towards a kinder treatment of Germany; whether that would have been wise at that time is still a matter of controversy. But his explicit point, on which most stress is laid, that the quantitative reparations proposals were ill thought out, impractical, and absurd, has not been seriously challenged.[5]

The currency expert shows his hand in the book. It is interesting to notice that the allegedly inflationist Keynes gives perhaps the most powerful indictment of inflation that has ever been penned (pp. 220–35).

His mind was much occupied by the question of inflation in those days. In October, 1922, he was summoned to advise the German Government on how to end it; he returned shocked by the apathy and defeatism that he found in Berlin. But he was also exercised by the problem of deflation; and he began a series of warnings in the press and in his *Tract on Monetary Reform* of the

---

[5] A book has recently appeared by M. Étienne Mantoux, unhappily killed in action, entitled *The Carthaginian Peace—or the Economic Consequences of Mr. Keynes*. While he has much of interest to say on the broad issue of a more lenient peace and appears to make some rather effective points against Keynes on matters of detail, the careful reader will observe that the treatment of the central Keynes thesis—the absurdity and impracticality of the actual proposals—is confined to pp. 117–32. The argument of these pages is singularly thin and unconvincing.

foolishness and injuriousness of attempting to raise the value of the currency.

By this avenue he was led to embark upon his prolonged speculations on the workings of deflation, on the depression phase of the trade cycle, then more generally on depression and unemployment. He was bound to break loose from the confines of the "currency expert." His so-called *Treatise on Money* in two volumes (1930) had already got beyond the purely monetary aspect; he was there discussing the questions of investment and saving, familiar subjects for the trade cycle theorist. Was it the shade of Marshall that dictated the title of this treatise? Then, finally, he broke loose altogether and laid his profane hand on fundamental principles in *The General Theory of Employment, Interest, and Money* (1936). By this time there is no doubt that he conceived that he had a contribution to make to the groundwork of economics second only in importance to that of Adam Smith.

Will the claim be justified? How, in particular, is his contribution related to the broad generalization implicit in economic tradition from Adam Smith to Edgeworth that property and freedom provide a framework within which enterprising man will achieve for himself his greatest economic good?

It is rash indeed to attempt to sum up his contribution in a sentence. No one had a greater sense than he of the complexity of economic adjustments and of the numerous reservations that had to be made to a generalization. In his case these reservations always sprang from a strong sense of their importance, and not in the least, as in some writers, merely to safeguard himself from criticism—for on the latter point he was notoriously and signally indifferent. The theory of interest is, I think, the central point in his scheme. He departs from old orthodoxy in holding that the failure of the system to move to a position of full activity is not primarily due to friction, rigidity, immobility or to phenomena essentially connected with the trade cycle. If a certain level of interest is established, which is inconsistent with full activity, no flexibility or mobility in the other parts of the system will get the system to move to full activity. But this wrong rate of interest, as we may call it, is not itself a rigidity or inflexibility. It is natural, durable, and, in a certain sense, in the free system inevitable. That is why he lays what may seem an undue emphasis on the doctrine that interest is essentially the reward not for saving but for parting with liquidity. Given the complex of forces affecting liquidity preference, such and such is the rate of interest that will naturally and necessarily and, so long as underlying forces remain unchanged, permanently obtain. Yet that rate of interest may be inconsistent with the full activity of the system.

Sitting back in our chairs and thinking of the whole development since Adam Smith, what are we to make of this point? In itself it seems to lack the generality one would expect that a point having such fundamentally disturbing corollaries would require. It seems to be a special point, a minor flaw in a free system. None the less his argument hangs together. It has a cogency, a simplicity, a lack of the need of supporting assumptions, that are extraordinarily impressive. It sweeps many cobwebs away. It renders volume upon volume that have been written on cyclical depression outmoded. In this kind of work, so much depends on the selection of the right concepts and the right assumptions. Otherwise the argument tends to leave a mounting total of alternative possibilities unconsidered. This power of selection is the kind of scientific genius required by our subject. I believe that Keynes had it. But this is not the place to attempt a verdict on his *General Theory*.

In the field of policy Keynes had a keen sense of the realities of the situation. He was practical and a man of the world. He was a tremendous fighter, prepared to take on great odds, but he was not inclined to be a crusader for a merely Utopian aim. I will only mention one point of weakness, which is relevant to' his influence on very broad questions. He did not under-estimate the difficulty of persuading men of action to take a sensible line—the Paris Peace Conference was not his only experience of that! But he may have over-estimated his own influence over the thinking minority. I remember his coming into my room, in 1930, and saying, "I intend to advocate a revenue tariff." l knew what he had in mind. It would have been altogether vain then to renew the campaign against the British gold standard as established in 1925; there was no sign of a move toward an international getting-together; the clouds of depression were fast piling up; he had an accurate foresight that acute depression would cause domestic disturbances in many countries and war; he felt it important that the British external balance should be above suspicion, so that we at least might pursue an active recovery policy. None the less, I said, "For Heaven's sake don't do that." He hastened to reassure me. "It is quite all right. We can reverse the process, when this

phase is past." Few men in history can have had so great an influence as Keynes in moving the minds of men on social and economic questions. But I do not recollect anyone who, having initiated a movement of educated public opinion in one direction on a
great topic, was subsequently able to "reverse the process."

When Britain left the gold standard in 1931, the case for the
tariff disappeared and he said no more of it. It was some years,
however, before circumstances seemed propitious for a renewed
effort on behalf of economic internationalism. The movement to
autarchy was everywhere gaining strength. Mr. Cordell Hull's
initiative was a lone move, and Keynes certainly did not regard a
reduction of trade barriers as a sufficient basis for a workable
economic internationalism. When the war came with its crushing
burdens it seemed more than ever likely that Britain would have
to be prepared to protect her own economic position by all methods available. When he began his draft of the "Clearing Union,"
he may still have felt it was rather a forlorn hope. But as the
tokens of American co-operativeness began to come in, he became
quite convinced that this was the occasion for a renewed effort on
behalf of internationalism. He was always an internationalist at
heart.

And so after a dozen years the time had come to "reverse
the process." Alas, he found that it was not so easy. He found
"how much modernist stuff, gone wrong and turned sour and silly,
is circulating in our system, also incongruously mixed, it seems,
with age-old poisons." [6] Has he succeeded in "reversing the
process" in Britain? Time will show. He certainly gave his sword
to those who would carry on the fight on behalf of internationalism.

The question may be asked how he should be classed if we
make a dichotomy into "centralist planners" and advocates of a
free economy. Presumably he cannot be classified by this method.
He certainly believed that a great increase of central management
was necessary. On the other hand he wished to confine it to
achieving those results which could not be secured as a result of
uncoordinated individual effort. He advocated the broad qualitative controls involved in currency policy, budget policy, foreign
exchange adjustment, etc. Latterly he often referred to the "hor-
rible world" which seemed likely to result if the more detailed
planners had their way. There is a fine balanced statement on pp.

[6] EJ, June, 1946, p. 186.

377–81 of the *General Theory* most worthy of study. The case for individualism is excellently stated.

To me the moral of his work seems clear. If we accept the broad diagnosis of the *General Theory*—if we do not accept it, his main work has presumably no moral!—then, knowing what impedes the free system from working to the best advantage, we can remove the impediment. His lifelong effort to understand what is wrong with the machine implies an interest in the machine, implies that he wanted us to continue to use the machine, implies, in fact, that he was at bottom an individualist. For a totalitarian, all that life work would have been of merely academic interest. But in contemporary economics Keynes had little interest in what was only academically interesting.

Whatever the final verdict on the *General Theory*, Keynes' greatness as an economist will not be questioned. His mental capacities had a far wider range than those usually found in professional economists. He was a logician, a great prose writer, a deep psychologist, a bibliophile, an esteemed connoisseur of painting; he had practical gifts of persuasion, political finesse, businesslike efficiency; he had personal gifts which made him have profound influence on those who came into direct contact with him. Economics, still young, only in part a fully specialist subject as yet, has gained from its contact with such a comprehensive intellect. I remember his once describing Ricardo as "the most distinguished mind that had found Economics worthy of it." We must surely judge Keynes' mind to be more distinguished than Ricardo's.

CHAPTER IX

Keynes, the Economist (2)

By JOSEPH A. SCHUMPETER

1.

In his sparkling essay on the Great Villiers Connection,[1] Keynes revealed a sense of the importance of hereditary ability—of the great truth, to use Karl Pearson's phrase, that ability runs in stocks—that fits but ill into the picture many people seem to harbor of his intellectual world. The obvious inference about his sociology is strengthened by the fact that in his biographical sketches he was apt to stress ancestral backgrounds with unusual care. He would therefore understand my regret at my inability, owing to lack of time, to probe into the past of the Keynes Connection. Let us hope that someone else will do this and content ourselves with an admiring glance at the parents. He was born on the fifth of June, 1883, the eldest son of Florence Ada Keynes, daughter of the Reverend John Brown, D.D., and of John Neville Keynes, Registrar of the University of Cambridge—a mother of quite exceptional ability and charm, one-time mayor of Cambridge, and a father who is known to all of us as an eminent logician and author of, among other things, one of the best methodologies of economics ever written.[2]

[1] The essay, a review of W. I. J. Gun, *Studies in Hereditary Ability*, was published in N&A, March 27, 1926, and has been reprinted in the volume *Essays in Biography* (1933). This volume sheds more light on Keynes the man and Keynes the scholar than does any other publication of his. I shall accordingly refer to it more than once.

[2] *Scope and Method of Political Economy* (1891). The well-earned success of this admirable book is attested by the fact that a reprint of its fourth edition (1917) was called for as late as 1930: in fact, so well has it kept its own amidst the surf and breakers of half a century's controversies about its problems that even now students of methodology can hardly do better than choose it for guide.

Let us note the academic-clerical background of the subject of
this memoir. The implications of this background—both the
eminently English quality of it and the gentry element in it—become still clearer when we add two names: Eton and King's
College, Cambridge. Most of us are teachers, and teachers are
prone to exaggerate the formative influence of education. But nobody will equate it to zero. Moreover, there is nothing to show
that John Maynard's reaction to either place was anything but
positive. He seems to have enjoyed a thoroughly successful scho-
lastic career.[3] In 1905 he was elected President of the Cambridge
Union. In the same year he emerged as twelfth Wrangler.

Theorists will notice the latter distinction, which cannot be
attained without some aptitude for mathematics plus hard work
—work hard enough to make it easy for a man who has gone
through that discipline to acquire any more advanced technique
he may wish to master. They will recognize the mathematical
quality of mind that underlies the purely scientific part of Keynes'
work, perhaps also the traces in it of a half-forgotten training.
And some of them may wonder why he kept aloof from the current of mathematical economics which gathered decisive momentum at just about the time when he first entered the field. Nor
is this all. Though never definitely hostile to mathematical economics—he even accepted the presidency of the Econometric
Society—he never threw the weight of his authority into its scale.
The advice that emanated from him was almost invariably negative. Occasionally his conversation revealed something akin to
dislike.

Explanation is not far to seek. The higher ranges of mathematical economics are in the nature of what is in all fields referred to
as "pure science." Results have little bearing—as yet, in any case
—upon practical questions. And questions of policy all but mo-
nopolized Keynes' brilliant abilities. He was much too cultivated
and much too intelligent to despise logical niceties. To some extent he enjoyed them; to a still greater extent he bore with them;
but beyond a boundary which it did not take him long to reach,
he lost patience with them. *L'art pour l'art* was no part of his
scientific creed. Wherever else he may have been progressive, he
was not a progressive in analytic method. We shall see that this

---

[3] Eton always meant much to him. Few of the honors of which he was the
recipient later on pleased him so much as did his election, by the masters,
as their representative on Eton's governing board.

also holds in other respects that are unconnected with the use of higher mathematics. If the purpose seemed to justify it, he had no objection to using arguments that were as crude as those of Sir Thomas Mun.

2.

An Englishman who entered adult life from Eton and Cambridge, who was passionately interested in the policy of his nation, who had conquered the presidential chair of the Cambridge union in the symbolic year 1905 that marked the passing of an epoch and the dawn of another [4]—why did such an Englishman not embark upon a political career? Why did he go to the India Office instead? Many pro's and con's enter into a decision of this kind, money among others, but there is one point about it which it is essential to grasp. Nobody could ever have talked to Keynes for an hour without discovering that he was the most unpolitical of men. The political game as a game interested him no more than did racing—or, for that matter, pure theory *per se*. With quite unusual gifts for debate and with a keen perception of tactical values, he yet seems to have been impervious to the lure —nowhere anything like so strong as it is in England—of the charmed circle of political office. Party meant little or nothing to him. He was ready to co-operate with anyone who offered support for a recommendation of his and to forget any past passage of arms. But he was not ready to co-operate with anyone on any other terms, let alone to accept anyone's leadership. His loyalties were loyalties to measures, not loyalties to individuals or groups. And still less than a respector of persons was he a respector of creeds or ideologies or flags.

Was he not, therefore, cut out for the rôle of an ideal civil servant, by nature made to become one of those great permanent Undersecretaries of State whose discreet influence counts for so much in the shaping of England's recent history? Anything but that. He had no taste for politics, but he had less than no taste for patient routine work and for breaking in, by gentle arts, that refractory wild beast, the politician. And these two negative propensities, the aversion to the political arena and the aversion to red tape, propelled him toward the rôle for which he was indeed by nature made, for which he quickly found the form that suited

[4] The Campbell-Bannerman victory was won and a parliamentary Labor Party emerged in January, 1906.

him to perfection, and from which he never departed throughout his life. Whatever we may think of the psychological laws which he was to formulate, we cannot but feel that, from an early age, he thoroughly understood his own. This is, in fact, one of the major keys to the secret of his success—and also to the secret of his happiness: for unless I am much mistaken his life was an eminently happy one.

Thus, after two years at the India Office (1906–08), he went back to his university, accepting a fellowship at King's (1909), and quickly established himself in the circle of his Cambridge fellow economists and beyond. He taught straight Marshallian doctrine with the Fifth Book of the *Principles* as the center, the doctrine that he mastered as few people did and with which he remained identified for twenty years to come. A picture survives in my memory of how he then looked to a casual visitor to Cambridge—the picture of the young teacher of spare frame, ascetic countenance, flashing eyes, intent and tremendously serious, vibrating with what seemed to that visitor suppressed impatience, a formidable controversialist whom nobody could overlook, everybody respected, and some liked.[5] His rising reputation is attested by the fact that as early as 1911 he was appointed editor of the *Economic Journal* in succession to its first editor, Edgeworth. This key position in the world of economics he filled without interruption and with unflagging zeal until the spring of 1945.[6] Considering the length of his tenure of this office and all the other interests and avocations in the midst of which he filled it, his editorial performance is truly remarkable, in fact, almost unbelievable. It was not only that he shaped the general policy of the *Journal* and of the Royal Economic Society, of which he was secretary. He did much more than this. Many articles grew out of his suggestions; all of them received, from the ideas and facts presented down to punctuation, the most minute critical attention.[7] We all know the results, and everyone of us has—no doubt —his own opinion about them. But I feel confident of speaking

[5] My own acquaintance with Keynes, productive of a totally different impression, dates only from 1927.

[6] Edgeworth served once more, as joint editor, 1918–1925. He was succeeded by D. H. Macgregor, who served, 1925–1934, to be in turn succeeded by Mr. E. A. G. Robinson (who had been appointed assistant editor in 1933).

[7] Once he patiently explained to a foreign contributor that, while it is permissible to abbreviate *exempli gratia* into *e.g.*, it is not permissible to abbreviate *for instance* into *f. i.*—and would the author sanction the alteration?

for all of us when I say that, taken as a whole, Keynes the editor has had no equal since Du Pont de Nemours managed the *Ephémérides.*

The work at the India Office was not more than an apprenticeship that would have left few traces in a less fertile mind. It is highly revealing not only of the vigor but also of the type of Keynes' talent that it bore fruit in his case: his first book—and first success—was on *Indian Currency and Finance.*[8] It appeared in 1913, when he was also appointed member of the Royal Commission on Indian Finance and Currency (1913–14). I think it fair to call this book the best English work on the gold exchange standard. Much more interest attaches, however, to another question that is but distantly related to the merits of this performance taken by itself; can we discern in it anything that points toward the *General Theory?* In the Preface to the latter, Keynes himself claimed not more than that his teaching of 1936 seemed to him "a natural evolution of a line of thought which he had been pursuing for several years." On this I shall offer some comments later on. But now I will make bold to assert that, though the book of 1913 contains none of those characteristic propositions of the book of 1936 that have been felt to be so "revolutionary," the general attitude taken toward monetary phenomena and monetary policy by the Keynes of 1913 clearly foreshadowed that of the Keynes of the *Treatise* (1930).

Monetary management was then no novelty, of course—which is precisely why it should not have been heralded as a novelty in the twenties and thirties—and preoccupation with Indian problems was particularly likely to induce awareness of its nature, necessity, and possibilities. But Keynes' vivid appreciation of its bearing, not only upon prices and exports and imports, but also on production and employment, was nevertheless something new, something that, if it did not uniquely determine, yet conditioned, his own line of advance. Moreover, we must remember how closely his *theoretical* development in post-war times was related to the particular situations in which he offered practical advice and which neither he nor anyone else foresaw in 1913: add the theoretical implications of the English experience in the twenties to the theory of *Indian Currency and Finance,* and you

---

[8] In 1910–11 he gave lectures on Indian Finance at the London School of Economics. See F. A. Hayek, "The London School of Economics, 1895–1945," ECN, Feb., 1946, p. 17.

will get the substance of the Keynesian ideas of 1930. This statement is conservative. I could go further—a little—were I not
afraid of falling into an error that is very common among bi-
ographers.

3.

In 1915, the potential public servant in the academic gown
turned into an actual one: he entered the Treasury. English finance during the First World War was eminently "sound" and
spelled a moral performance of the first order. But it was not
conspicuous for originality, and it is possible that the brilliant
young official then acquired his dislike of the Treasury Mind and
the Treasury View that became so marked later on. His services
were, however, appreciated, for he was chosen to serve as Principal Representative of the Treasury at the Peace Conference—
which might have been a key position if such a thing could have
existed within the orbit of Lloyd George—and also as Deputy
for the Chancellor of the Exchequer on the Supreme Economic
Council. More important than this, speaking from the biographer's
standpoint, is his abrupt resignation in June 1919, which was so
characteristic of the man and of the kind of public servant he
was. Other men had much the same misgivings about the peace,
but *of course* they could not possibly speak out. Keynes was made
of different stuff. He resigned and told the world why. And he
leapt into international fame.

The *Economic Consequences of the Peace* (1919) met with a
reception that makes the word *success* sound commonplace and
insipid. Those who cannot understand how luck and merit inter-
twine will no doubt say that Keynes simply wrote what was on
every sensible man's lips; that he was very favorably placed for
making his protest resound all over the world; that it was this
protest as such and not his particular argument that won him
every ear and many thousands of hearts; and that, at the moment
the book appeared, the tide was already running on which it was
to ride. There is truth in all this. Of course, there was an unique
opportunity. But if we choose, on the strength of this, to deny the
greatness of the feat, we had better delete this phrase altogether
from the pages of history. For there are no great feats without pre-
existing great opportunities.

Primarily the feat was one of moral courage. But the book is a
masterpiece—packed with practical wisdom that never lacks

depth; pitilessly logical yet never cold; genuinely humane but nowhere sentimental; meeting all facts without vain regrets but also without hopelessness: it is sound advice added to sound analysis. And it is a work of art. Form and matter fit each other to perfection. Everything is to the point, and there is nothing in it that is not to the point. No idle adornment disfigures its wise economy of means. The very polish of the exposition—never again was he to write so well—brings out its simplicity. In the passages in which Keynes tries to explain, in terms of the *dramatis personae*, the tragic failure of purpose that produced the peace, he rises to heights that have been trodden by few.[9]

The economics of the book, as well as of *A Revision of the Treaty* (1922) that complements and in some respects amends its argument, is of the simplest and did not call for any refined technique. Nevertheless, there is something about it that calls for our attention. Before embarking on his great venture in persuasion, Keynes drew a sketch of the economic and social background of the political events he was about to survey. With but

[9] See pp. 26–50, on the Council of Four, republished, with an important addendum, the Fragment on Lloyd George, in the *Essays in Biography*. It is painful to report that, at the time, some opponents of Keynes' views, in full retreat before his victorious logic, seem to have resorted to sneers about his presentation of certain facts and his interpretation of motive, neither of which, so they averred, he was in a position to judge. Since this indictment of Keynes' veracity has been repeated recently in a *causerie* published in an American magazine, it is first of all necessary to ask the reader to satisfy himself that not a single result of Keynes' analysis and not a single recommendation of his depends on the correctness or incorrectness of the picture he drew of the motives and attitudes of Clemenceau, Wilson, and Lloyd George. But, secondly, since it is part of the purpose of this memoir to delineate a character, it is further necessary to prove that there is absolutely no foundation for the aspersion that Keynes indulged in a flight of "poetic fantasy" and that he pretended to an intimate knowledge of "arcana" that cannot have been known to him—which, at best, would convict him of petty vanity and, at worst, of more than that. But the proof in question is not difficult to supply. If the reader will refer to that masterly sketch, as I hope he will, he is bound to find that Keynes claimed no intimacy with those three men and personal acquaintance only with Lloyd George. He said nothing about the private meetings of the four (the fourth was Orlando), but merely described scenes at the regular meetings of the Council of Four, which, along with all other leading experts, he must have normally attended in his official capacity. Moreover, his presentation of the personal aspects of the steps on the road that led to the disastrous result is amply supported by independent evidence: his brilliant story is nothing but a reasonable interpretation of a course of events that is common knowledge. Finally, critics had better bear in mind that this interpretation is distinctly generous and perfectly free from traces of any resentment, however justifiable, that Keynes may have felt.

slight alterations of phrasing, this sketch may be summed up like
this: *Laissez faire* capitalism, that "extraordinary episode," had
come to an end in August, 1914. The conditions were rapidly passing in which entrepreneurial leadership was able to secure success
after success, propelled as it had been by rapid growth of popula-
tions and by abundant opportunities to invest that were in-
cessantly recreated by technological improvements and by a
series of conquests of new sources of food and raw materials.
Under these conditions, there had been no difficulty about absorbing the savings of a *bourgeoisie* that kept on baking cakes "in
order not to eat them." But now (1920) those impulses were giving out, the spirit of private enterprise was flagging, investment
opportunities were vanishing, and bourgeois saving habits had,
therefore, lost their social function; their persistence actually
made things worse than they need have been.

Here, then, we have the origin of the *modern* stagnation thesis
—as distinguished from the one which we may, if we choose, find
in Ricardo. And here we also have the embryo of the *General
Theory*. Every comprehensive "theory" of an economic state of
society consists of two complementary but essentially distinct
elements. There is, first, the theorist's view about the basic features of that state of society, about what is and what is not important in order to understand its life at a given time. Let us call
this his vision. And there is, second, the theorist's technique, an
apparatus by which he conceptualizes his vision and which turns
the latter into concrete propositions or "theories." In those pages
of the *Economic Consequences of the Peace* we find nothing
of the theoretical apparatus of the *General Theory*. But we find
the whole of the vision of things social and economic of which
that apparatus is the technical complement. The *General Theory*
is the final result of a long struggle *to make that vision of our age
analytically operative.*

4.

For economists of the "scientific" type, Keynes is, of course,
the Keynes of the *General Theory*. In order to do some justice to
the straight-line development which leads up to it from the
Consequences of the Peace, and of which the main stages are
marked by the *Tract* and by the *Treatise*, I shall have to brush
aside ruthlessly many things that ought not to go unrecorded.
Three foothills of the *Consequences* are, however, mentioned in

the note below,[10] and a few words must be said on *A Treatise on Probability* which he published in 1921. There cannot be, I fear, much question about what Keynes means for the theory of probability, though his interest in it went far back: his fellowship dissertation had been on the subject. The question that is of interest to us is what the theory of probability meant for Keynes. Subjectively, it seems to have been an outlet for the energies of a mind that found no complete satisfaction in the problems of the field to which, as much from a sense of public duty as from taste, he devoted most of his time and strength. He entertained no very high opinion about the purely intellectual possibilities of economics. Whenever he wished to breathe the air of high altitudes, he did not turn to our pure theory. He was something of a philosopher or epistemologist. He was interested in Wittgenstein. He was a great friend of that brilliant thinker who died in the prime of life—Frank Ramsey, to whose memory he erected a charming monument.[11] But no merely receptive attitude could have satis-

[10] These are: his article on population and the ensuing controversy with Sir William Beveridge (EJ, 1923); his pamphlet, *The End of Laissez-Faire* (1926); and his article on the "German Transfer Problem" in the EJ, March, 1929, with subsequent replies to the criticism of Ohlin and Rueff. The first attempts to conjure Malthus' ghost—to defend (at the threshold of the period of unsalable masses of food and raw materials!) the thesis that, since somewhere about 1906, nature had begun to respond less generously to human effort and that overpopulation was the great problem, or one of the great problems, of our time: perhaps the least felicitous of all his efforts and indicative of an element of recklessness in his makeup which those who loved him best cannot entirely deny. All that needs to be said about *The End of Laissez-Faire* is that we must not expect to find in this piece of work what the title suggests. It was not at all what the Webbs wrote in that book of theirs that invites comparison with Keynes'. The article on German reparations reveals another side of his character: it was evidently dictated by the most generous motives and by unerring political wisdom; but it was not good theory, and Ohlin and Rueff found it easy to deal with it. It is difficult to understand how Keynes can have been blind to the weak spots in his argument. But, in the service of a cause he believed in, he would sometimes, in noble haste, overlook defects in the wood from which he made his arrows. Perusal of the collection entitled *Essays in Persuasion* (1931), is perhaps the best method of studying the quality of his reasoning in the not-quite-professional part of his work.

[11] In NST&N, October 3, 1931, republished in the *Essays in Biography*. To this essay, the most warm-hearted thing he ever wrote, is appended an anthology of gleanings from Ramsey's notes. These express Ramsey's views, of course, and not Keynes', but, for an occasion like this, nobody would choose passages that do not strike a sympathetic note. Thus, Ramsey's sayings become indicative of Keynes' philosophy.

fied him. He had to have a flight of his own. It is highly revelatory of the texture of his mind that he chose probability for the purpose—a subject bristling with logical niceties yet not entirely without utilitarian connotation. His indomitable will produced what, seen as I am trying to see it, was no doubt a brilliant performance, whatever specialists, non-Cambridge specialists particularly, might have to say about it.

We are drifting from the work to the man. Let us then use this opportunity for looking at him a little more closely. He had returned to King's and to his pre-war pattern of life. But the pattern was developed and enlarged. He continued to be an active teacher and research worker; he continued to edit the *Journal;* he continued to make the public cares his own. But though he strengthened his ties with King's by accepting the important (and laborious) function of Bursar, the London house at 46 Gordon Square became second headquarters before long. He acquired an interest in, and became chairman of, *The Nation*—which superseded the *Speaker* in 1921, absorbed the *Athenaeum,* and was, in 1931, merged with *The New Statesman* (*The New Statesman and Nation*)—to which he directed a current stream of articles that would have been full-time work for some other men. Also, he became chairman of the National Mutual Life Assurance Society (1921–38), to which he gave much time, and managed an investment company, earning a considerable income from such business pursuits. There was no nonsense about him, in particular no nonsense about business and money making: he frankly appreciated the comforts of a proper establishment; and not less frankly he used to say (in the twenties) that he would never accept a professorial appointment because he could not afford to do so. In addition to all this, he served actively on the Economic Advisory Council and on the Committee on Finance and Industry (Macmillan Committee). In 1925, he married a distinguished artist, Lydia Lopokova, who proved a congenial companion and devoted helpmate—"in sickness and in health"—to the end.

That combination of activities is not unusual. What made it unusual and, indeed, a marvel to behold is the fact that he put as much energy in each of them as if it had been his only one. His appetite and his capacity for efficient work surpass belief, and his power of concentration on the piece of work in hand was truly Gladstonian: whatever he did, he did with a mind freed from everything else. He knew what it is to be tired. But he hardly seems to have known dead hours of cheerlessness and faltering purpose.

Nature is wont to impose two distinct penalties upon those who try to beat out their stock of energy to the thinnest leaf. One of these penalties Keynes undoubtedly paid. The quality of his work suffered from its quantity and not only as to form: much of his secondary work shows the traces of haste, and some of his most important work, the traces of incessant interruptions that injured its growth. Who fails to realize this—to realize that he beholds work that has never been allowed to ripen, has never received the last finishing touch—will never do justice to Keynes' powers.[12] But the other penalty was remitted to him.

In general, there is something inhuman about human machines that fully use every ounce of their fuel. Such men are mostly cold in their personal relations, inaccessible, preoccupied. Their work is their life, no other interests exist for them, or only interests of the most superficial kind. But Keynes was the exact opposite of all this—the pleasantest fellow you can think of; pleasant, kind, and cheerful in the sense in which precisely those people are pleasant, kind, and cheerful who have nothing on their minds and whose one principle it is never to allow any pursuit of theirs to degenerate into work. He was affectionate. He was always ready to enter with friendly zest into the views, interests, and troubles of others. He was generous, and not only with money. He was sociable, enjoyed conversation, and shone in it. And, contrary to a widely spread opinion, he could be *polite*, polite with an old-world *punctilio* that costs time. For instance, he refused to sit down to his lunch, in spite of telegraphic and telephonic expostulation, until his guest, delayed by fog in the Channel, put in an appearance at 4 P.M.

His extracurricular interests were many, and each of them he pursued with joyful alacrity. But this is not all of it. Once more,

---

[12] The most obvious example for this is his most ambitious venture in research, the *Treatise on Money*, which is a shell of several pieces of powerful but unfinished work, very imperfectly put together (see below, p. 87). But the instance that will convey my meaning best is the biographical essay on Marshall (EJ, Sept., 1924). He evidently lavished love and care upon it. As a matter of fact, it is the most brilliant life of a man of science I have ever read. And yet, the reader who turns to it will not only derive much pleasure and profit, but also see what I mean. It starts beautifully, it ends beautifully; but in order to be perfect, it would have needed another fortnight's work.

people are not uncommon who, in spite of absorbing avocations, enjoy some recreative activities in a passive way. The Keynesian touch is that with him recreation was creative. For instance, he loved old books, niceties of bibliographic controversy, details of the characters, lives, and thoughts of men of the past. Many people share this taste, which may have been fostered in him by the classical ingredients in his education. But whenever he indulged it, he took hold like the workman he was, and we owe to his hobby several not unimportant clarifications on points of literary history.[13] He also was a lover and, up to a point, a good judge of pictures, to a modest extent also a collector. He thoroughly enjoyed a good play, and founded and generously financed the Cambridge Arts Theatre, which no one who went to it will forget. And, once upon a time, an acquaintance of his received the following note from him, evidently dashed off in high good humor: "Dear . . . , if you wish to know what at the moment *exclusively* occupies my time, look at the enclosed."[14] The enclosure consisted of a program or prospectus of the "Camargo Ballet."

5.

I return to the highway. As stated above, our first stop is at the *Tract on Monetary Reform* (1923). Since, with Keynes, practical advice was the goal and beaconlight of analysis, I will do what in the case of other economists I should consider an offense to do, viz., invite readers to look first at what it was he advocated. It was, in substance, stabilization of the domestic price level for the purpose of stabilizing the domestic business situation, secondary attention being paid also to the means of mitigating short-run fluctuations of foreign exchange. In order to achieve this he rec-

---

[13] The literature of philosophy and economics attracted him most. In this pursuit Professor Piero Sraffa became to him a much-appreciated ally. The best example I can offer of results is the edition of Hume's abstract of his *Treatise on Human Nature* "reprinted with an Introduction by J. M. Keynes and P. Sraffa" (1938). The Introduction is a curious monument of philological ardor.

[14] The acquaintance, a most disorderly person, does not keep letters. The exact wording of Keynes' note can therefore not be verified. But I am positive that it contained a single brief sentence and that the import of this sentence was as stated. It must have been about ten or fifteen years ago, perhaps more.—In his last years, those artistic activities and tastes led to his being elected trustee of the National Gallery and Chairman of the Council for the Encouragement of Music and the Arts. More work!

ommended that the monetary system created by the necessities of warfare should be carried over into the peace economy, the boldest of the various suggestions offered—with an evident trepidation quite unlike him—being the separation of the note issue from the gold reserve which he wished, however, to retain and of which he was anxious to emphasize the importance.

There are two things in this piece of advice that should be carefully noticed: first, its specifically English quality; second, *ex visu of England's short-run interests and of the kind of Englishman the adviser was,* its sober wisdom and conservativism.[15] It cannot be emphasized too strongly that Keynes' advice was in the first instance always English advice, born of English problems even where addressed to other nations. Barring some of his artistic tastes, he was surprisingly insular, even in philosophy, but nowhere so much as in economics. And he was fervently patriotic—of a patriotism which was indeed quite untinged by vulgarity but was so genuine as to be subconscious and therefore all the more powerful to impart a bias to his thought and to exclude full understanding of foreign (also American) viewpoints, conditions, interests, and especially creeds. Like the old free-traders, he always exalted what was at any moment truth and wisdom for England into truth and wisdom for all times and places.[16] But we can not stop at this. In order to locate the standpoint from which his advice was given, it is further necessary to remember that he was of the high intelligentsia of England, unattached to class or party, a typical pre-war intellectual, who rightly claimed, for good and ill, spiritual kinship with the Locke-Mill connection.

What was it, then, that this patriotic English intellectual beheld? The generalization we have already noticed in the pages of the *Consequences.* But England's case was more specific than that. She had not emerged from the war as she had emerged from the war of the Napoleonic era. She had emerged impoverished; she had lost many of her opportunities for the moment and some of them for good. Not only this, but her social fabric had been weakened and had become rigid. Her taxes and wage rates were incompatible with vigorous development, yet there was nothing that could be done about it. Keynes was not given to

---

[15] It should surprise no one that he was eventually (1942) elected director of the Bank of England.

[16] This also explains what his opponents called his inconsistency.

vain regrets. He was not in the habit of bemoaning what could not be changed. Also he was not the sort of man who would bend the full force of his mind to the individual problems of coal, textiles, steel, shipbuilding (though he did offer some advice of this kind in his current articles). Least of all was he the man to preach regenerative creeds. He was the English intellectual, a little *déraciné* and beholding a most uncomfortable situation. He was childless, and his philosophy of life was essentially a short-run philosophy. So he turned resolutely to the only "parameter of action" that seemed left to him, both as an Englishman and as the kind of Englishman he was—monetary management. Perhaps he thought that it might heal. He knew for certain that it would soothe—and that return to a gold system at pre-war parity was more than *his* England could stand.

If only people could be made to understand this, they would also understand that practical Keynesianism is a seedling which cannot be transplanted into foreign soil: it dies there and becomes poisonous before it dies. But in addition they would understand that, left in English soil, this seedling is a healthy thing and promises both fruit and shade. Let me say once and for all: all this applies to every bit of advice that Keynes ever offered. For the rest, the advocacy of monetary management in the *Tract* was anything but revolutionary. There was, however, a novel emphasis on it as a means of general economic therapeutics. And concern with the saving-investment mechanism is indicated in the first lines of the Preface and throughout the first chapter.[17] Thus, though the immediate task before the author prevented him from going very far into these matters, the book does indicate further advance toward the *General Theory.*

Analytically, Keynes accepted the quantity theory which "is fundamental. Its correspondence with facts is not open to question" (p. 81). All the more important is it for us to realize that this acceptance, resting as it does on the very common confusion between the quantity theory and the equation of exchange, meant much less than it seems to mean, exactly as Keynes' later repudia-

[17] See, e.g., the highly characteristic passages on p. 10, and also the description of the "investment system" on p. 8, which anticipates some of the very inadequacies of the analysis of the *General Theory.* Even then, and indeed from first to last, Keynes displayed a curious reluctance to recognize a very simple and obvious fact and to express it by the no less simple and obvious phrase, that typically industry is financed by banks.

tion of the quantity theory means much less than it seems to mean. What he intended to accept was the equation of exchange —in its Cambridge form—which, whether defined as an identity or as an equilibrium condition, does not imply any of the propositions characteristic of the quantity theory in the strict sense. Accordingly, he felt free to make velocity—or k, its equivalent in the Cambridge equation—a variable of the monetary problem, very properly giving Marshall credit for this "development of the traditional way of considering the matter" (p. 86). This is the liquidity preference in embryonic form. Keynes overlooked that this theory can be traced back to Cantillon—at least—and that it had been developed, though sketchily, by Kemmerer,[18] who said that "large sums of money are continually being hoarded" and that "the proportion of the circulating medium which is hoarded . . . is not constant." We cannot go into the many excellent things in the *Tract*, e.g., the masterly section on the forward market in exchanges (Chap. III, sec. IV) and on Great Britain (Chap. V, sec. I) which it is impossible to admire too highly. We must hurry on to our "second stop" on the road to the *General Theory*, the *Treatise on Money* (1930).

With the exception of the *Treatise on Probability*, Keynes never wrote another work in which the hortatory purpose is less visible than it is in the *Treatise on Money*. It is there all the same, and not confined to the last book (VII), in which, among other things, we find all the essentials of Bretton Woods—what an extraordinary achievement! Primarily, however, those two volumes are no doubt Keynes' most ambitious piece of genuine research, of research so brilliant and yet so solid that it is a thousand pities that the harvest was garnered before it was ripe. If only he had learned something from Marshall's craving for "impossible perfection" instead of lecturing him about it! (*Essays*

[18] E. W. Kemmerer, *Money and Credit Instruments* (1907), p. 20. But on p. 193 of the *Tract*, Keynes commits himself to the untenable statement that "the internal price level is mainly determined by the amount of credit created by the banks," and from this he never departed. To the end, this credit remained for him an independent variable, given to the economic process, though determined, not by gold production as it was of old, but either by the banks or by the "monetary authority" (Central Bank or Government). This, however—considering quantity of money as "given"—is one of the characteristic features of the quantity theory in the strict sense. Hence my statement in the text that he never abandoned the quantity theory as completely as he thought he did.

in Biography, pp. 211–12).[19] Moreover, Professor Myrdal's gentle sneer at "that Anglo-Saxon kind of unnecessary originality" is amply justified.[20] Nevertheless, the book was the outstanding performance in its field and day. All I can do, however, is to collect the most important signposts that point toward the *General Theory*.[21]

There is, first, the conception of the theory of money as the theory of the economic process as a whole that was to be fully developed in the *General Theory*. This conception is, second, embedded in the vision or diagnosis of the contemporaneous state of the economic process that never changed from the *Consequences*. Third, saving and investment decisions are resolutely separated, quite as resolutely as in the *General Theory*, and private thrift is well established in its rôle of villain of the piece. The recognition extended to the work of "Mr. J. A. Hobson and others" (Vol. I, p. 179) is highly significant in this respect. And we learn that a thrift campaign is not the way to bring down the rate of interest (e.g., Vol. II, p. 207). Differences in conceptualization—sometimes only in terminology—obscure but do not eliminate the fundamental identity of the ideas the author strives to convey. Thus, fourth, much of the argument runs in terms of

[19] A semi-apologetic passage in the Preface of the *Treatise* shows that he was not unaware of the fact that he was offering half-baked bread.

[20] Gunnar Myrdal, *Monetary Equilibrium* (English translation, by Bryce and Stolper [1939], of a German version of the Swedish original that appeared in the *Ekonomisk Tidskrift* in 1931), p. 8. Myrdal's protest was not, of course, made on his own behalf but on behalf of Wicksell and the Wicksellian group. But a similar protest would have been in order on behalf of Böhm-Bawerk and his followers, especially of Mises and Hayek. The latter's *Geldtheorie und Konjunkturtheorie* had been published, it is true, only in 1929. But Böhm-Bawerk's work was available in English, and Taussig's *Wages and Capital* dates from 1896. Nevertheless, Keynes wrote the capital theory of Book VI exactly as if they had never lived. But there was no obliquity in this. He simply did not know. Proof of his good faith is the ample credit he gave to all authors he did know, Pigou and Robertson among them.

[21] This, of course, involves injustice to the work as a whole, and in particular to the first two books: the conventional but nonetheless brilliant Introduction (Nature of Money, Book I) and the almost independent treatise on price levels (Value of Money, Book II) which is full of suggestive ideas. It must be remembered—and this is really the most fundamental difference between the *Treatise* and the *General Theory*—that the work professes to be an analysis of the dynamics of price levels, "of the way in which the fluctuations of the price level actually come to pass" (Vol. I, p. 152), though in reality it is much more than this.

the Wicksellian divergence between the "natural" and the "money" rate of interest. To be sure, the latter is not yet *the* rate of interest, and neither the former nor profits are as yet turned into the "marginal efficiency of capital." But the argument clearly suggests both steps. Fifth, the emphasis upon expectations, upon the "bearishness" that is not yet liquidity preference from the speculative motive, and the theory that the fall in money wage rates in depression ("reduction in the rate of efficiency-earnings") will tend to re-establish equilibrium *if and because it will act on interest (bank rate) by reducing the requirements of Industrial Circulation*—all these and many other things (bananas, widows' cruises, Danaïdes' jars) read like imperfect and embarrassed first statements of *General Theory* propositions.

6.

The *Treatise* was not a failure in any ordinary sense of the word. Everybody saw its points and, with whatever qualifications, paid his respects to Keynes' great effort. Even damaging criticism, such as Professor Hansen's criticism of the Fundamental Equations,[22] or Professor von Hayek's criticism of Keynes' basic theoretical structure,[23] were as a rule tempered with well-deserved eulogy. But from Keynes' own standpoint it was a failure, and not only because its reception did not measure up to his standard of success. It had somehow missed fire—it had not really made a mark. And the reason was not far to seek: he had failed to convey the essence of his own personal message. He had written a treatise and, for the sake of systematic completeness, overburdened his text with material about price indices, the *modus operandi* of bank rates, deposit creation, gold, and what not, all of which, whatever its merits, was akin to current doctrine and hence, for his purpose, not sufficiently distinctive. He had entangled himself in the meshes of an apparatus that broke down each time he attempted to make it grind out his own meanings. There would have been no point in trying to improve the work in

[22] Alvin H. Hansen, "A Fundamental Error in Keynes' Treatise on Money," AER, 1930; and Hansen and Tout, "Investment and Saving in Business Cycle Theory," EC, 1933.

[23] F. A. von Hayek, "Reflections on the Pure Theory of Money of Mr. Keynes," I and II, *Economica*, 1931 and 1932. Hayek went so far as to speak of an "enormous advance." Nevertheless, Keynes replied not without irritation. As he himself remarked on another occasion, authors are difficult to please.

detail. There would have been no point in trying to fight criticisms, the justice of many of which he had to admit. There was nothing for it but to abandon the whole thing, hull and cargo, to renounce allegiances and to start afresh. He was quick to learn the lesson.

Resolutely cutting himself off from the derelict, he braced himself for another effort, the greatest of his life. With brilliant energy he took hold of the essentials of his message and bent his mind to the task of forging a conceptual apparatus that would express these and—as nearly as possible—nothing else. He succeeded to his satisfaction. And so soon as he had done so—in December, 1935—he buckled on his new armor, unsheathed his sword and took the field again, boldly claiming that he was going to lead economists out of errors of 150 years' standing and into the promised land of truth.

Those around him were fascinated. While Keynes was remodeling his work, he currently talked about it in his lectures, in conversation, in the "Keynes Club" that used to meet in his rooms at King's. And there was a lively give and take. ". . . I have depended on the constant advice and constructive criticism of Mr. R. F. Kahn. There is a great deal in this book which would not have taken the shape it has except at his suggestion" (*General Theory*, Preface, p. viii). Considering all the implications of Richard Kahn's article on "The Relation of Home Investment to Unemployment," published in the *Economic Journal* as early as June, 1931, we shall certainly not suspect those two sentences of overstatement. Some credit was also given, in the same place, to Mrs. Robinson, Mr. Hawtrey, and Mr. Harrod.[24] There were

---

[24] Mr. Hawtrey's relation to the book can never have been any other than that of an understanding and, up to a point, sympathetic critic. He never was, of course, a Keynesian. From the *Tract* to the *Treatise,* Keynes was a Hawtreyan. Mr. Harrod may have been moving independently toward a goal not far from that of Keynes, though he unselfishly joined the latter's standard after it had been raised. Justice imposes this remark. For that eminent economist is in some danger of losing the place in the history of economics that is his by right, both in respect to Keynesianism and in respect to imperfect competition. Not less do I feel bound to advert to Mrs. Robinson's claims. It is highly revelatory of the attitude of the academic mind to women that she was excluded from the above-mentioned seminar (at least she was not invited on the one occasion when I addressed it). But she was in the midst of things. Proofs of this are her "Parable on Saving and Investment" (*Economica*, February 1933), an article which was a most skillfully fought rear-guard action covering retreat from the *Treatise;* and, still more

others—some of the most promising young Cambridge men among them. And they all talked. Glimpses of the new light began to be caught by individuals all over the Empire and in the United States. Students were thrilled. A wave of anticipatory enthusiasm swept the world of economists. When the book came out at last, Harvard students felt unable to wait until it would be available at the booksellers: they clubbed together in order to speed up the process and arranged for direct shipment of a first parcel of copies.

7.

The social vision first revealed in the *Economic Consequences of the Peace*, the vision of an economic process in which investment opportunity flags and saving habits nevertheless persist, is theoretically implemented in the *General Theory of Employment, Interest, and Money* (Preface, dated December 13, 1935) by means of three schedule concepts: the consumption function, the efficiency-of-capital function, and the liquidity-preference function.[25] These together with the given wage-unit and the equally given quantity of money "determine" income and *ipso facto* employment (if and so far as the latter is uniquely determined by the former), the great dependent variables to be "explained." What a *cordon bleu* to make such a sauce out of such scanty material! [26] Let us see how he did it.

---

significant of her rôle in the evolution of the *General Theory,* her "Theory of Money and the Analysis of Output," published as early as October, 1933, in *Review of Economic Studies.*

[25] Distinctive terminology helps to drive home the points an author wishes to make and to focus his readers' attention. This (though nothing else) justifies the re-naming of Irving Fisher's marginal rate of return over cost—the priority of which Keynes fully recognized—and also the use of the phrase *liquidity preference,* instead of the usual one, *hoarding. Consumption function* is certainly a better shell for Keynes' meaning than the Malthusian phrase, *effective demand,* which he also used, for nothing but confusion can come from using the concepts of Demand and Supply outside of the domain (partial analysis) in which they carry rigorously definable meaning. It is not without interest to note that Keynes called his assumptions about the forms of the consumption and liquidity preference functions *psychological laws.* This was of course, another emphasizing device. But no tenable meaning can be attached to it, not even so much meaning as attaches to the *law of satiable wants.* In this, as in some other respects, Keynes was distinctly old-fashioned.

[26] It is really an injustice to Keynes' achievement to reduce it to the bare bones of its logical structure and then to reason on these bones as if they were all. Nevertheless, great interest attaches to the attempts that have been made

(i) The first condition for simplicity of a model is, of course, simplicity of the vision which it is to implement. And simplicty of vision is in part a matter of genius and in part a matter of willingness to pay the price in terms of the factors that have to be left out of the picture. But if we place ourselves on the standpoint of Keynesian orthodoxy and choose to accept his vision of the economic process of our age as the gift of genius whose glance pierced through the welter of surface phenomena to the simple essentials that lie below, then there can be little objection to his aggregative analysis that produced his results.

Since the aggregates chosen for variables are, with the exception of employment, monetary quantities or expressions, we may also speak of monetary analysis and, since national income is the central variable, of income analysis. Richard Cantillon was the first, I think, to indicate a *full-fledged* schema of aggregative, monetary, and income analysis, the one worked out by François Quesnay in his *Tableau Économique*. Quesnay, then, is the true predecessor of Keynes, and it is interesting to note that his views on saving were identical with those of Keynes: the reader can easily satisfy himself of this by looking up the *Maximes*. It should, however, be added that the aggregative analysis of the *General Theory* does not stand alone in modern literature: it is a member of a family that had been rapidly growing.[27]

(ii) Keynes further simplified his structure by avoiding, as much as possible, all complications that arise in process analysis. The exact skeleton of Keynes' system belongs, to use the terms

----

to cast his system into exact form. I want in particular to mention: W. B. Reddaway's review in the *Economic Record*, 1936; R. F. Harrod, "Mr. Keynes and Traditional Theory," EC, January, 1937 (See below, pp. 591–605); J. E. Meade, "A Simplified Model of Mr. Keynes' System," *Review of Economic Studies*, February, 1937 (See below, pp. 606–18); J. R. Hicks, "Mr. Keynes and the 'Classics'," EC, April, 1937; O. Lange, "The Rate of Interest and the Optimum Propensity to Consume," *Economica*, February, 1938; P. A. Samuelson, "The Stability of Equilibrium," EC, April, 1941 (with dynamical reformulation); and A. Smithies, "Process Analysis and Equilibrium Analysis," EC, January, 1942 (also a study in the dynamics of the Keynesian schema). In the hands of writers less in sympathy with the spirit of Keynesian economics, some of the results presented in these papers might have been turned into serious criticisms. This is still more true of F. Modigliani, "Liquidity Preference and the Theory of Interest and of Money," EC, January, 1944.

[27] The quickest way to learn how far aggregative analysis had progressed before the publication of the *General Theory* is to read Tinbergen's survey article in EC, July, 1935.

proposed by Ragnar Frisch, to macrostatics, not to macrodynamics. In part this limitation must be attributed to those who
formulated his teaching rather than to his teaching itself which
contains several dynamic elements, expectations in particular.
But it is true that he had an aversion to "periods" and that he concentrated attention upon considerations of static equilibrium.
This removed an important barrier to success—a difference equation as yet affects economists as the face of Medusa.

(iii) Furthermore, he confined his *model*—though not always
his argument—to the range of short-run phenomena. While
points (i) and (ii) are commonly emphasized, it does not seem
to be realized sufficiently how very strictly short-run his model
is and how important this fact is for the whole structure and all
the results of the *General Theory.* The pivotal restriction is that
not only production functions and not only methods of production but also the quantity and quality of plant and equipment are
not allowed to change, a restriction which Keynes never tires of
impressing upon the reader at crucial turns of his way (see, e.g.,
p. 114 and p. 295).[28]

This permits many otherwise inadmissible simplifications: for
instance, it permits treating employment as approximately proportional to income (output) so that the one is determined as
soon as the other is. But it limits applicability of this analysis to
a few years at most—perhaps the duration of the "forty months'
cycle"—and, in terms of phenomena, to the factors that *would*
govern the greater or smaller utilization of an industrial apparatus *if* the latter remains unchanged. *All the phenomena incident
to the creation and change in this apparatus, that is to say, the
phenomena that dominate the capitalist processes, are thus excluded from consideration.*

As a picture of reality this model becomes most nearly justifiable in periods of depression when also liquidity preference
comes nearest to being an operative factor in its own right. Professor Hicks was therefore correct in calling Keynes' economics
the economics of depression. But from Keynes' own standpoint,
his model derives additional justification from the secular stagnation thesis. Though it remains true that he tried to implement an
essentially long-run vision by a short-run model, he secured, to

---

[28] Strictly, some change in the quantity of equipment must be admitted,
but it is conceived of as so small, at any given point of time, that its effect
upon the existing industrial structure and its output can be neglected.

some extent, the freedom for doing so by reasoning (almost) exclusively about a stationary process or, at all events, a process that stays at, or oscillates about, levels of which a stationary full-employment equilibrium is the ceiling. With Marx, capitalist evolution issues into breakdown. With J. S. Mill, it issues into a stationary state that works without hitches. With Keynes, it issues into a stationary state that constantly threatens to break down. Though Keynes' "breakdown theory" is quite different from Marx's, it has an important feature in common with the latter: in both theories, the breakdown is motivated by causes inherent to the working of the economic engine, not by the action of factors external to it. This feature naturally qualifies Keynes' theory for the rôle of "rationalizer" of anti-capitalist volition.

(iv) Quite consciously, Keynes refused to go beyond the factors that are the *immediate* determinants of income (and employment). He himself recognized freely that these immediate determinants which may "sometimes" be regarded as "ultimate independent variables . . . would be capable of being subjected to further analysis, and are not, so to speak, our ultimate atomic independent elements" (p. 247). This turn of phrase seems to suggest no more than that economic aggregates derive their meaning from the component "atoms." But there is more to it than this. We can, of course, greatly simplify our picture of the world and arrive at very simple propositions if we are content with arguments of the form: *given A, B, C* . . . , then *D* will depend upon *E*. If *A, B, C* . . . are things external to the field under investigation, there is no more to be said. If, however, they are part of the phenomena to be explained, then the resulting propositions about what determines what may easily be made undeniable and acquire the semblance of novelty without meaning very much. This is what Professor Leontief has called implicit theorizing.[29] But for Keynes, as for Ricardo,[30] arguments of this type were but emphasizing devices: they served to single out and, by so doing, to emphasize a particular relation. Ricardo did not say: "Under present English conditions, as I see them, free trade in foodstuffs and raw materials will, everything considered, tend to raise the rate

---

[29] Cf. his article under that title in QJE, Vol. 51, pp. 337–51.

[30] The intellectual affinity of Keynes with Ricardo merits notice. Their methods of reasoning were closely similar, a fact that has been obscured by Keynes' admiration of Malthus' anti-saving attitude and by his consequent dislike of Ricardo's *teaching*.

of profit." Instead he said: "The rate of profit depends upon the price of wheat."

(v) Forceful emphasis on a small number of points that seemed to Keynes to be both important and inadequately appreciated being the keynote of the *General Theory*, we find other emphasizing devices besides the one just mentioned. Two we have noticed already.[31] Another is what critics are apt to call overstatements—overstatements, moreover, which cannot be reduced to the defensible level, because results depend precisely upon the excess. But it must be remembered not only that, from Keynes' standpoint, these overstatements were little more than means to abstract from non-essentials but also that part of the blame for them lies at our own door: we, as a body, simply will not listen unless a point be hammered in with one-sided energy. Granting, for the sake of argument, that the points in question were actually important enough to merit being hammered in, and remembering that the gems of unqualified overstatement do not occur in the *General Theory* itself but in the writings of some of Keynes' followers, we shall appreciate this method of flavoring what I have described as the sauce.

Three examples must suffice. First, every economist knows—if he did not, he could not help learning it from conversation with businessmen—that any sufficiently general change in money wage rates will influence prices in the same direction. Nevertheless, it was not the practice of economists to take account of this in the theory of wages. Second, every economist *should* have known that the Turgot-Smith-J. S. Mill theory of the saving and investment mechanism was inadequate and that, in particular, saving and investment decisions were linked together too closely. Yet, had Keynes presented a properly qualified statement of their true relation, would he have elicited more from us than a mumble to the effect: "Yes . . . that's so . . . of some importance in certain cyclical situations. . . . What of it?" Third, let any reader look up pages 165 and 166 of the *General Theory* —the first two pages of Chapter 13, on the "General Theory of Interest." What will he find? He will find that the theory, according to which the investment demand for savings and the supply of savings that is governed by time-preference ("which I have called the propensity to consume") is equated by the rate of interest, "breaks down" because "it is impossible to deduce the rate

[31] See above, n. 25.

of interest merely from a knowledge of these two factors." Why is this impossible? Because the decision to save does not *necessarily* imply a decision to invest: we must also take account of the possibility that the latter does not follow or not follow promptly. I will lay any odds that this perfectly reasonable improvement in the tenor of current teaching would not have greatly impressed us had he left the matter at this. It had to be liquidity preference to the fore—and interest *nothing* but the reward for parting with money (which cannot be so on the showing of his own text)— and so on in a well-known sequence in order to make us sit up. And we were made to sit up to some purpose. For many more of us will now listen to the proposition that interest is a purely monetary phenomenon than were ready to listen thirty-five years ago.

But there is one word in the book that cannot be defended on these lines—the word *general*. Those emphasizing devices—even if quite unexceptionable in other respects—cannot do more than individuate very special cases. Keynesians may hold that these special cases are the actual ones of our age. They cannot hold more than that.[32]

(vi) It seems evident that Keynes *wished* to secure his major results without appeal to the element of rigidity, just as he spurned the aid he might have derived from imperfections of competition.[33] There were points, however, at which he was unable to do so, especially the point at which the rate of interest has to become rigid in the downward direction because the elasticity of the liquidity-preference demand for money becomes infinite there. And at other points, rigidities stand in reserve, to be appealed to in case the front-line argument fails to convince. It is, of course, always possible to show that the economic system will cease to work if a sufficient number of its adaptive organs are paralyzed. Keynesians like this fire escape no more than do other theorists. Nevertheless, it is not without importance. The classical example is equilibrium under-employment.[34]

[32] This has first been pointed out by O. Lange, *op. cit.*, who also paid due respect to the only truly general theory ever written—the theory of Léon Walras. He neatly showed that the latter covers Keynes' as a special case.

[33] The latter factor was, however, inserted by Mr. Harrod.

[34] I have sometimes wondered why Keynes attached so much importance to proving that there may—and under his assumptions generally will—be less than full employment in *perfect equilibrium of perfect competition*. For there is such an ample supply of verifiable explanatory factors to account for

(vii) I must, finally, advert to Keynes' brilliance in the forging of individual tools of analysis. Look, for instance, at the skillful use made of Kahn's multiplier or at the felicitous creation of the concept of user cost which is so helpful in defining his concept of income and may well be recorded as a novelty of some importance. What I admire most in these and other conceptual arrangements of his is their *adequacy*: they fit his purpose as a well-tailored coat fits the customer's body. Of course, precisely because of this, they possess but limited usefulness irrespective of Keynes' particular aims. A fruit knife is an excellent instrument for peeling a pear. He who uses it in order to attack a steak has only himself to blame for unsatisfactory results.

8.

The success of the *General Theory* was instantaneous and, as we know, sustained. Unfavorable reviews, of which there were many, only helped. A Keynesian school formed itself, not a school in that loose sense in which some historians of economics speak of a French, German, Italian school, but a genuine one which is a sociological entity, namely, a group that professes allegiance to one master and one doctrine, and has its inner circle, its propagandists, its watchwords, its esoteric and its popular doctrine. Nor is this all. Beyond the pale of orthodox Keynesianism there is a broad fringe of sympathizers, and beyond this again are the many who have absorbed, in one form or another, readily or grudgingly, some of the spirit or some individual items of Keynesian analysis. There are but two analogous cases in the whole history of economics—the Physiocrats and the Marxists.

This is in itself a great achievement that claims admiring recognition from friends and foes alike and, in particular, from every teacher who experiences the enlivening influence in his classes.

the actual unemployment we observe at any time that only the theorist's ambition can induce us to wish for more. The question of the presence of involuntary unemployment in perfect equilibrium of perfect competition, a state that even the straw man whom Keynes called "classical economist" never believed in as a reality, is no doubt of great theoretical interest. But practically, Keynes should have fared equally well with the unemployment that may exist in a permanent state of disequilibrium. As it is, he clearly failed to prove his case. But inflexibility of wages in the downward direction stands ready to lend its aid. The theoretical question itself is the subject of a discussion that suffers from the failure of participants to distinguish between the various theoretical issues involved. But we cannot enter into this.

There cannot be any doubt, unfortunately, that in economics such enthusiasm—and correspondingly strong aversions—never flare up unless the cold steel of analysis derives a temperature not naturally its own from the real or putative political implications of the analyst's message. Let us therefore cast a glance at the ideological bearings of the book. Most orthodox Keynesians are "radicals" in one sense or another. The man who wrote the essay on the Villiers Connection was not a radical in *any* ordinary sense of the word. What is there in his book to please them? In an excellent article in *The American Economic Review*, Professor Wright[35] has gone so far as to say that "a conservative candidate could conduct a political campaign largely on quotations from the *General Theory.*" True, but true only if this candidate knows how to use asides and qualifications. Keynes was no doubt too able an advocate ever to deny the obvious. To some extent, though probably to a small extent only, his success is precisely due to the fact that even in his boldest rushes he never left his flanks quite unguarded—as unwary critics of either his policies or his theories are apt to discover to their cost.[36] Disciples do not look at qualifications. They see one thing only—an indictment of private thrift and the implications this indictment carries with respect to the managed economy and inequality of incomes.

In order to appreciate what this means, it is necessary to recall

[35] D. McC. Wright, "The Future of Keynesian Economics," AER, Vol. XXXV, No. 3 (June, 1945), p. 287. This article, in spite of some differences of opinion, usefully complements my own in many points into which considerations of space forbid me to enter.

[36] This is why there is such ample room for that turn of phrase that occurs so often in the Keynesian literature: "Keynes did not *really* say this" or "Keynes did not *really* deny that." In the *General Theory* most of the explicit qualifications occur in Chapters 18 and 19. But the only possible reference to all the implicit ones is *passim.* The logic of the classical system is not *really* impugned (p. 278). Even Say's law (in the sense defined on p. 26) is not completely thrown out; even the existence of a mechanism that tends to equilibrate saving and investment decisions—and the rôle of interest rates in this mechanism—and even the possibility that a reduction of money wages may stimulate output is not absolutely denied; though, to be sure, only in application to very special cases, the validity of the first and the existence of the other two are occasionally recognized. Critics are therefore in constant danger of being convicted of "gross misrepresentation" exactly as unwary critics of Malthus' first Essay invariably run into a volley of quotations from the second edition—in which, in fact, Malthus went far toward explaining away Malthusianism. But it is impossible to go into all this here. In the article quoted, Professor Wright offers instructive examples.

that, as a result of a long doctrinal development, saving had come to be regarded as the last pillar of the bourgeois argument. In fact, old Adam Smith had already disposed pretty much of every other: if we analyze his argument closely—I am speaking, of course, only of the ideological aspects of his system—it amounts to all-around vituperation directed against "slothful" landlords and grasping merchants or "masters," plus the famous eulogy of parsimony. And this remains the keynote of most non-Marxist economic ideology until Keynes. Marshall and Pigou were in this boat. They, especially the latter, took it for granted that inequality, or the existing degree of inequality, was "undesirable." But they stopped short of attack upon the pillar.

Many of the men who entered the field of teaching or research in the twenties and thirties had renounced allegiance to the bourgeois scheme of life, the bourgeois scheme of values. Many of them sneered at the profit motive and at the element of personal performance in the capitalist process. But so far as they did not embrace straight socialism, they still had to pay respect to saving —under penalty of losing caste in their own eyes and ranging themselves with what Keynes so tellingly called the economist's "underworld." But Keynes broke their fetters: here, at last, was theoretical doctrine that not only obliterated the personal element and was, if not mechanistic itself, at least mechanizable, but also smashed the pillar into dust; a doctrine that may not actually say but can easily be made to say both that "who tries to save destroys real capital" and that, via saying, "the unequal distribution of income is the ultimate cause of unemployment." [37] *This* is what the Keynesian Revolution amounts to. Thus defined, the phrase is not inappropriate. And *this*, and only this, explains and, to some extent, justifies Keynes' change of attitude toward Marshall which is neither understandable nor justifiable upon any scientific ground.

But though this attractive wrapper made Keynes' gift to scientic economics more acceptable to many, it must not divert attention from the gift itself. Before the appearance of the *General Theory*, economics had been growing increasingly complex and

[37] And, after all, a glance at pp. 372–73 and 376 of the *General Theory* will convince anyone that Keynes actually came pretty near to authorizing both statements. One must be as punctiliously conscientious as is Professor Wright in order to say that he did not actually do so.

increasingly incapable of giving straightforward answers to straightforward questions. The *General Theory* seemed to reduce it once more to simplicity, and to enable the economist once more to give simple advice that everybody could understand. But, exactly as in the case of Ricardian economics, there was enough to attract, to inspire even, the sophisticated. The same system that linked up so well with the notions of the untutored mind proved satisfactory to the best brains of the rising generation of theorists. Some of them felt—still feel for all I know—that all other work in "theory" should be scrapped. All of them paid homage to the man who had given them a well-defined model to handle, to criticize, and to improve—to the man whose work symbolizes at least, even though it may not embody, what they wanted to see done.

And even those who had found their bearings before, and on whom the *General Theory* did not impinge in their formative years, experienced the salutary effects of a fresh breeze. As a prominent American economist put it in a letter to me: "It (the *General Theory*) did, and does, have something which supplements what our thinking and methods of analysis would otherwise have been. It does not make us Keynesians, it makes us better economists." Whether we agree or not, this expresses the essential· point about Keynes' achievement extremely well. In particular, it explains why hostile criticism, even if successful in its attack upon individual assumptions or propositions, is yet powerless to inflict fatal injury upon the structure as a whole. As with Marx, it is possible to admire Keynes, even though one may consider his social vision to be wrong and every one of his propositions to be misleading.

I am not going to grade the *General Theory* as if it were a student's examination book. Moreover, I do not believe in grading economists—the men whose names one might think of for comparison are too different, to incommensurable. Whatever happens to the doctrine, the memory of the man will live—outlive both Keynesianism and the reaction to it.

At this I will leave it. Everyone knows the stupendous fight the valiant warrior put up for the work that was to be his last.[38] Everyone knows that during the war he entered the Treasury again

---

[38] His last great work, that is. He wrote many minor pieces almost to his dying day.

(1940), and that his influence grew, along with that of Churchill, until nobody thought of challenging it. Everyone knows of the honor that has been conferred upon the House of Lords and, of course, of the Keynes Plan, Bretton Woods, and the English loan. But these things will have to engage some scholarly biographer who has all the materials at his disposal.

CHAPTER X

Keynes, the Economist (3)

By PAUL M. SWEEZY

LORD KEYNES, who died at the age of 62 on April 21, 1946, was unquestionably the most famous and controversial of contemporary economists. Moreover, like the great figures of the classical school—Adam Smith, David Ricardo, and John Stuart Mill [1]—he was no narrow specialist working in the seclusion of an academic ivory tower. Both as critic and as participant, he played a very important and certainly a unique rôle in the public life of Britain in the period of the two World Wars; as a patron of the arts, he was a power in the cultural life of his country; as head of a great insurance company and as Bursar of King's College, Cambridge, he proved that the economic theorist can be a highly successful businessman; while his non-economic writings range from the standard (literary as opposed to mathematical) *Treatise on Probability* to the incisive *Essays in Biography*. Keynes was, in short, one of the most brilliant and versatile geniuses of our time; and one can be sure that his place in history—not only doctrinal economic history—will be a subject of discussion and controversy for an indefinite period to come. It would be presumptuous at this early date to attempt anything in the way of definitive judgments, and in writing this note I am far from entertaining any such intentions. I think it should be possible nevertheless to set out some of the factors in Keynes' work and in his influence on

[1] Keynes himself used the term "classical economists" to include the subjective value theorists—especially Marshall and his followers in the Cambridge group—of the late nineteenth and twentieth centuries. For reasons which should be clarified by the subsequent discussion, this practice seems to me to be misleading. It is preferable to regard John Stuart Mill as the last of the classical economists and to label the Marshallians the "neo-classical" school.

others which will have to be taken into account in any evaluation of the man, present or future.

In order to understand Keynes, one must first understand where he stood in relation to other economists and schools of economic thought; for, as we shall see, it was what might be called an accident of location which accounts for much of the influence as well as for many of the shortcomings of his work. Modern economics—the economics of industrial capitalism and of the world market—had its origins in the later decades of the seventeenth century. During the next hundred and fifty years England was the home of the most important advances on both the industrial and the theoretical fronts; and by the time of Ricardo (1772–1823), English Political Economy enjoyed a degree of authority and prestige throughout the western world which has never been equalled before or since. In the second half of the nineteenth century, the unity of the classical tradition was broken; what had been a single trunk with only minor off-shoots divided itself into two great branches, each with its own sub-branches, which have on the whole been growing apart ever since. These two branches may be called socialist, or Marxian, and neo-classical respectively. To vary our metaphor, each can and does claim to be the legitimate child of classical Political Economy, but it must be said that for brothers they have had remarkably little to do with one another. This striking fact is due to a variety of reasons: for one thing, the two schools have diverged in their manner of selecting and discarding elements of the classical theory; for another, they have (openly in the case of Marxism, under cover of a pretended scientific neutrality in the case of neo-classicism) become intellectual weapons on opposite sides of a bitter class struggle; and, finally, Marxism—partly no doubt as a result of the historical accident of Marx's own nationality—took root on the continent of Europe but failed for many years to win a significant following in the English-speaking world. Thus the two schools, despite their common origin, became intellectually, politically, and geographically estranged. Such contacts as they had, which were almost entirely outside Britain and the United States, were the contacts of battle and produced intolerance rather than understanding.

When Keynes took up the study of economics about the turn of the century, neo-classicism was in undisputed possession of the field in the English-speaking countries; dissent was regarded as a sign of incompetence. Keynes himself accepted the prevailing doctrines unquestioningly and soon came to be rated as a brilliant but essentially orthodox representative of the neo-classical school. There is no evidence that he was ever seriously influenced by conflicting or incompatible intellectual trends. He borrowed occasionally from foreign authors,[2] and when his own ideas had finally taken shape he was generous in giving credit for having anticipated them to a long line of heretics and dissenters; but these were essentially adventitious elements in Keynes' thought. By training he was a strict neo-classicist, and he never really felt at home except in argument with his neo-classical colleagues. In fact, one would be perfectly justified in saying that Keynes is both the most important and the most illustrious product of the neo-classical school.

This points, I think, to the true nature of Keynes' achievement. His mission was to reform neo-classical economics, to bring it back into contact with the real world from which it had wandered farther and farther since the break with the classical tradition in the nineteenth century; and it was precisely because he was one of them and not an outsider that Keynes could exercise such a profound influence on his colleagues. The very same reasons, however, account for the fact that, as we shall see below, Keynes could never transcend the limitations of the neo-classical approach which conceives of economic life in abstraction from its historical setting and hence is inherently incapable of providing a reliable guide to social action.

Keynes' *magnum opus, The General Theory of Employment, Interest, and Money* (1936) opens with an attack on what he calls orthodox economics—neo-classical economics, in the terminology of this paper—and sustains it almost continuously to the end. The gist of this Keynesian criticism can be summed up simply as a flat rejection of what has come to be known as Say's Law of Markets [3] which, despite all assertions to the contrary by

[2] For example, the concept of a "natural rate of interest," which plays an important part in *A Treatise on Money* (1930), was taken from the Swedish economist Knut Wicksell (1851–1926). Wicksell himself, however, was essentially a neo-classicist.

[3] Say's Law in effect denies that there can ever be a shortage of demand in relation to production. Ricardo expressed it as follows: "No man produces but with a view to consume or sell, and he never sells but with an intention to purchase some other commodity which may be useful to him, or which

orthodox apologists, did run like a red thread through the entire
body of classical and neo-classical theory. It is almost impossible
to exaggerate either the hold which Say's Law exercised on professional economists or its importance as an obstacle to realistic
analysis. The Keynesian attacks, though they appear to be directed against a variety of specific theories, all fall to the ground
if the validity of Say's Law is assumed. Having once rejected
Say's Law, Keynes was obliged to search the neo-classical theoretical structure from top to bottom to separate those propositions
which depend upon it from those which do not. The result of this
search, as it appears in the *General Theory,* is almost incompre-
hensible to any one but an adept in neo-classical economics. As
Keynes himself says in the Preface, "the composition of this book
has been for the author a long struggle of escape, and so must
the reading of it be for most readers if the author's assault upon
them is to be successful"—obviously implying that he expects the
readers to have the same type of training and the same general
background as his own. And then he adds, with refreshing candor,
"the ideas which are here expressed so laboriously are extremely
simple and should be obvious. The difficulty lies, not in the new
ideas, but in escaping from the old ones, which ramify, for those
brought up as most of us have been, into every corner of our
minds."

Keynes undoubtedly exaggerates the simplicity of his own contribution—it is noteworthy that pride in theoretical virtuosity was
utterly foreign to his nature—but I think that almost all teachers
will agree that it is easier to get his essential ideas across to a
beginner than to a student who has already been steeped in the
doctrines of the neo-classical school. Historians fifty years from
now may record that Keynes' greatest achievement was the
liberation of Anglo-American economics from a tyrannical
dogma, and they may even conclude that this was essentially a
work of negation unmatched by comparable positive achieve-
ments. Even, however, if Keynes were to receive credit for nothing else—which is most unlikely—his title to fame would be
secure. He opened up new vistas and new pathways to a whole

---

may contribute to future production. By producing then, he necessarily becomes either the consumer of his own goods, or the purchaser and consumer
of the goods of some other person . . . Productions are always bought by
productions, or by services; money is only the medium by which the exchange
is effected." *Principles of Political Economy,* Gonner ed., pp. 273, 275.

generation of economists; he will justly share the credit for their accomplishments.[4]

I have tried to show that the opportunity to which Keynes responded was essentially a crisis in traditional economics, a crisis which was both accentuated and laid bare by the Great Depression. He was able to demonstrate that his fellow economists, by their unthinking acceptance of Say's Law, were in effect asserting the impossibility of the kind of economic catastrophe through which the world was indubitably passing.[5] From this starting point he was able to go on to a penetrating analysis of the capitalist economy which shows that depression and unemployment are in fact the norms to which that economy tends, and which explodes once and for all the myth of a harmony between private and public interests which was the cornerstone of nineteenth-century liberalism. But Keynes stopped here in his critique of existing society. Our troubles, he believed, are due to a failure of intelligence and not to the breakdown of a social system; "the problem of want and poverty and the economic struggle between classes and nations," he wrote in 1931, "is nothing but a frightful muddle, a transitory and unnecessary muddle."[6]

That Keynes held this view was, of course, no accident. He could reject Say's Law and the conclusions based on it, because he thought they were largely responsible for the muddle; but it never occurred to him to question, still less to try to escape from, the broader philosophical and social tradition in which he was reared. The major unspoken premise of that tradition is that capitalism is the only possible form of civilized society. Hence Keynes, exactly like the economists he criticized, never viewed

[4] Probably only those who (like the present writer) were trained in the academic tradition of economic thinking in the period before 1936 can fully appreciate the sense of liberation and the intellectual stimulus which the *General Theory* immediately produced among younger teachers and students in all the leading British and American Universities.

[5] Apologists for the orthodox view are always ready with quotations to prove that economists were never such fools as this would imply. Keynes' answer, I think, is correct and convincing: "Contemporary thought," he wrote, "is still deeply steeped in the notion that if people do not spend their money in one way they will spend it in another. Post-war economists seldom, indeed, succeed in maintaining this standpoint *consistently*; for their thought to-day is too much permeated with the contrary tendency and with facts of experience too obviously inconsistent with their former view. But they have not drawn sufficiently far-reaching consequences; and have not revised their fundamental theory." *General Theory*, p. 20.

[6] *Essays in Persuasion*, p. vii.

the system as a whole; never studied the economy in its historical setting; never appreciated the interconnectedness of economic phenomena on the one hand and technological, political, and cultural phenomena on the other. Moreover, he was apparently quite ignorant of the fact that there was a serious body of economic thought, as closely related to the classical school as the doctrines on which he himself was brought up, which attempted to do these things. In Keynes' eyes, Marx inhabited a theoretical underworld along with such dubious characters as Silvio Gesell and Major Douglas;[7] and there is no evidence that he ever thought of any of Marx's followers as anything but propagandists and agitators.

This is not the place for a review of Marxian economics.[8] I raise the issue only in order to show that the school of thought to which Keynes belongs is rather isolated and one-sided, that some of his most important discoveries were taken for granted by socialist economists at least a generation before Keynes began to write, and that many of the most vital problems of the capitalist system are completely ignored in the *General Theory*. Marx rejected Say's Law from the outset;[9] already before 1900 his followers were carrying on a spirited debate among themselves not only on the subject of periodic crises but also on the question whether capitalism could be expected to run into a period of permanent or chronic depression.[10] Keynes ignores technological change and technological unemployment, problems which figure as an integral part of the Marxian theoretical structure. Keynes treats unemployment as a symptom of a technical fault in the capitalist mechanism, while Marx regards it as the indispensable means by which capitalists maintain their control over the labor market. Keynes completely ignores the problems of monopoly, its distorting effect on the distribution of income and the utilization of resources, the huge parasitic apparatus of distribution and advertising which it foists upon the economy. A socialist can only blink his eyes in astonishment when he reads that there is "no

[7] *General Theory*, p. 32.

[8] I have tried to provide such a review in *The Theory of Capitalist Development*, 1942.

[9] Marx remarked, in connection with the passage from Ricardo quoted in note [8] above, that "this is the childish babbling of a Say, but unworthy of Ricardo." *Theorien über den Mehrwert*, Vol. II, Pt. 2, p. 277.

[10] See *The Theory of Capitalist Development*, Chap. IX ("The Breakdown Controversy").

reason to suppose that the existing system seriously misemploys the factors of production which are in use. . . . When nine million men are employed out of ten million willing and able to work, there is no evidence that the labor of these nine million men is misdirected." [11] Many other examples of the insularity and comparative narrowness of the Keynesian approach could be cited. But perhaps most striking of all is Keynes's habit of treating the state as a *deus ex machina* to be invoked whenever his human actors, behaving according to the rules of the capitalist game, get themselves into a dilemma from which there is apparently no escape. Naturally, this Olympian interventionist resolves everything in a manner satisfactory to the author and presumably to the audience. The only trouble is—as every Marxist knows—that the state is not a god but one of the actors who has a part to play just like all the other actors.

Nothing that has been said should be taken as belittling the importance of Keynes' work. Moreover, there has been no intention to imply that Marxists "know it all" and have nothing to learn from Keynes and his followers. I have no doubt that Keynes is the greatest British (or American) economist since Ricardo, and I think the work of his school sheds a flood of light on the functioning of the capitalist economy. I think there is a great deal in Marx—especially in the unfinished later volumes of *Das Kapital* and in the *Theorien über den Mehrwert*—which takes on a new meaning and fits into its proper place when read in the light of the Keynesian contributions. Moreover, at least in Britain and the United States, the Keynesians are far better trained and equipped technically (e.g., in the very important sphere of gathering and interpreting statistical data) than Marxist economists; [12] and as matters stand now there is no doubt at all which group can learn more from the other.

But while it is right to recognize the positive contributions of Keynes, it is no less essential to recognize his shortcomings. They

[11] *General Theory*, p. 379. It is only fair to point out that Keynes' neglect of monopoly is not characteristic of present-day academic economics. It remains true, however, that the neo-classical treatment of the subject over-concentrates on the problems of the individual firm and has not done very much to relate monopoly to the functioning of the economy as a whole. In the latter field it would be hard to name a book even today which rivals *Das Finanzkapital* written by the Marxist economist Rudolf Hilferding in the first decade of the present century.

[12] How few there are who really deserve the name!

are for the most part the shortcomings of bourgeois thought in general: the unwillingness to view the economy as an integral part of a social whole; the inability to see the present as history, to understand that the disasters and catastrophes amidst which we live are not simply a "frightful muddle" but are the direct and inevitable product of a social system which has exhausted its creative powers, but whose beneficiaries·are determined to hang on regardless of the cost. Keynes himself, of course, could never have recognized, let alone transcended, the limitations of the society and the class of which he was so thoroughly a part. But the same cannot be said of many of his followers. They did not grow up in the complacent atmosphere of Victorian England. They were born into a world of war, and depression, and fascism. Some no doubt, treading in the footsteps of the master, will seek to preserve their comforting liberal illusions as long as humanly possible. Some, in all probability, will range themselves on the side of the existing order and will sell their skill as economists to the highest bidder. But still others, while retaining what is valid and sound in Keynes, will take their place in the growing ranks of those who realize that patching up the present system is not enough, that only a profound change in the structure of social relations can set the stage for a new advance in the material and cultural conditions of the human race.

This last group, I think, will inevitably be attracted to Marxism as the only genuine and comprehensive science of history and society. Perhaps the clearest indication of this is Joan Robinson's little book, *An Essay on Marxian Economics,* published in England early in the war. Mrs. Robinson, a member of the inner Keynesian circle, is one of perhaps half a dozen top-flight British economic theorists. Marxists will not be able to agree with everything she says, but they will find in her a sympathetic critic, ready and anxious to discuss problems with them in a sober and scientific spirit. Can it be pure accident that one of the most prominent followers of Keynes should be the author of the first honest work on Marxism ever to be written by a non-Marxist British economist?

PART THREE

The General Theory:
Five Views

CHAPTER XI

The *General Theory* (1)

By ABBA P. LERNER

IN AN *important book recently published,*[1] *Keynes has attempted to solve the general problem of variations in the volume of output and employment. As the book is largely an attack on the adequacy of the existing orthodox economic theory as a means for handling the problems of fluctuations in employment, trade cycles, and the like, it is clear that it has an important bearing on many of the questions which are at present in the forefront of the interests of the International Labor Organization. The argument, however, which deals primarily with questions of theory and only in the second place with the application of this theory to practice, is by no means easy to follow, partly from the intrinsic nature of the subject, partly from the highly specialised terminology employed. The Office has therefore thought that many readers of the [International Labour] Review would welcome an account in simpler terms of the main argument of the book. This is the purpose of the following article, whose author is thoroughly familiar with Mr. Keynes' writings. It should be added that the article has been read in manuscript by Keynes himself, who has expressed his approval of it.*

1.

The object of this article is to provide as simple as possible an account of the most important line of argument that runs through J. M. Keynes' book *The General Theory of Employment, Interest, and Money,* so that, except perhaps in some details of presentation, it contains nothing original. I have endeavored, where possible, to follow the traditional use of language more closely than

[1] John Maynard Keynes: *The General Theory of Employment, Interest, and Money* (London, Macmillan, 1936). xii, 403 pp. 5s.

Keynes does, as I have found that this renders the argument both
more intelligible and more acceptable to those who are not familiar with the oral tradition of Cambridge. While necessarily
simplifying the argument considerably in order to be able to
encompass it in an article of appropriate length, I do not think
I have left out anything fundamental. In discovering what are the
points in the argument or its presentation at which students are
liable to jib, I have learned much from innumerable discussions
with economists and students in London, Cambridge, and Geneva, and of these certainly the most helpful was Dr. Gottfried
Haberler, who has been working towards similar results along a
quite different route. I must add that I would certainly not have
been able to attempt this task were it not for the time I spent in
Cambridge in 1934–35 while Leon Fellow of the University of
London.

* * * * *

Keynes wishes sharply to distinguish his own system from what
he calls the "classical" economics. By that he means the orthodox
body of doctrine, first conceived in fairly complete outline by
Ricardo, and developed by almost all economists of repute from
that time on, both in England and elsewhere, which finds its
present culmination in the works of Pigou. Keynes is so keen
on making clear the difference between the classical and his own
scheme that he perhaps over-emphasizes it, willingly taking this
risk in order to be certain of avoiding the other error, which he
considers more dangerous, of permitting a reader to overlook the
revolutionary nature of the change. He has no patience whatever
for the interpreter who would try to read Keynes' views into the
classical writers. This is not at all—as is frequently suggested—
because that would diminish his claims to originality (in fact
I believe he is over-generous in his estimate of how near the
Mercantilists and the Monetary Cranks were to his thesis) but
because he is convinced that such identification is made plausible
only by obscurity. Keynes therefore complains that: "Those who
are sufficiently steeped in the old point of view simply cannot believe that I am asking them to step into a new pair of trousers,
and will insist on regarding it as nothing but an embroidered
version of the old pair that they have been wearing for years." [2]

I have insisted at some length on this because it helps to explain the extraordinary psychological resistance to Keynes' new

[2] ECN, Nov. 1931, p. 390.

argument that is always displayed by classical economists. (I shall use this word throughout in Keynes' sense.)

It is this psychological resistance that so frequently leads people to reject a proposition of Keynes' as a paradox and then to turn uneasily and, almost in the same breath, to scorn it as a platitude. "It's absolutely wrong"—"we all knew that before!"

The last sentence in Keynes' preface reads: "The difficulty lies, not in the new ideas, but in escaping from the old ones, which ramify, for those brought up as most of us have been, into every corner of our minds." I would like to underline that sentence.

✿　✿　✿　✿　✿

Keynes is concerned with the problem of unemployment. The classical view is that, in the absence of State interference or other rigidities, the existence of any unemployment will have the effect of lowering wages.

This follows immediately from the definition of unemployment, for any man who is not in employment but who does not try to get work at a lower wage is no more considered to be unemployed than the man who refuses to work overtime or on Sundays. At the current wage he prefers leisure to employment. He may be idle but he is not unemployed—at any rate he is not involuntarily unemployed. If he really wanted to work, if he were really unemployed, he would offer himself at a lower wage and this would reduce the level of wages. Unemployment is incompatible with equilibrium.

The reduction of wages, the argument goes on, will make industrial activity more profitable so that business men will employ more people. As long as there is any unemployment, wages will fall; and as long as wages fall, profits rise; and as profits rise, employment increases until all the unemployed are absorbed in industry, and we have equilibrium and no more unemployment.

Unemployment can therefore persist only if the State, or the trade unions, or some other institution prevents the unemployed from offering their services at lower wages and so from setting in motion the automatic mechanism which leads to equilibrium and full employment. What is necessary, therefore, is simply to remove the rigidity and allow the unemployment to liquidate itself by reducing wages.

Keynes accepts neither the definition nor the argument. Like the classical economists, he is concerned only with *involuntary* unemployment, but he defines as *involuntarily* unemployed a man who would be willing to work at a lower *real* wage than the current real wage, whether or not he is willing to accept a lower *money* wage. If a man is not willing to accept a lower *real* wage, then he is *voluntarily* unemployed, and Keynes does not worry about him at all. But there are millions of people who on Keynes' definition are unemployed but who fall outside of the classical definition of unemployed, and these provide one of the most pressing of modern social problems. These are willing to work for less than the current real wage—they would be willing to work for the current money wage even if the cost of living were to go up a little—yet they cannot find jobs. What determines the number of people in a society who find themselves in this position? Or, to put the question the other way round, what determines the number of people who do find employment? The object of Keynes' book is to indicate the road leading to the answer to this question.

The classical refusal to consider these men as really involuntarily unemployed resolves itself into a recipe for finding them employment. They have only to agree to accept lower wages and they will find work. Keynes objects to this procedure of economists on two separate grounds. His first objection is on the practical ground of the uselessness of tendering advice that one knows will not be accepted, even if it is sound advice. It is time for economists who wish to give statesmen practical advice to realise that money wages are sticky—that workers will, in fact, refuse to reduce money wages.

But Keynes' main objection consists of a denial of the theory which is put forward as an excuse for the treatment. If money wages are reduced, it does not follow that there will be any increase in employment. A general reduction of wages will reduce marginal costs, and competition between producers will reduce prices of products. Equilibrium will be reached only when prices have fallen as much as wages, and it will not pay to employ more men than in the beginning. The workers, who are able to make agreements with their employers about their *money* wage, cannot adjust their *real* wage. If they could reduce their real wage, more would be employed; but they can only attempt to reduce their real wage by reducing their money wage at the existing price level. This, however, only brings about a proportionate fall in prices so that they are in fact not able to vary their *real* wage. That is why their unemployment is *involuntary* even if they refuse to accept a lower money wage. For that would not have the desired effect of reducing the real wage and increasing employment—it would merely remove a certain stability of prices.

It has hardly been disputed that a cut in money wages, by reducing costs, will have some tendency to reduce prices, but it remains to be shown why prices should fall *proportionately* to the reduction in money wages so that there is *no* fall in the real wage and so *no* increase in employment in the manufacture of consumption goods. (Employment in investment industry depends on other factors considered below. For the time being this is taken as given.)

Whether this will be the case or not cannot be decided at all by looking merely at the effect of the wage cut upon *costs*. It is necessary also to consider the effect of the wage cut upon *demand;* whether directly or whether indirectly through the change in employment that might be initiated by the first impact of the wage cut. Until we bring this into the picture, we have not sufficient data to be able to decide what the result must be.

This has made it possible for one eminent economist to argue that a cut in money wages will increase employment, and for another eminent economist to argue that a cut in money wages will not increase employment. The first is able to show that his thesis is consistent with the cost conditions; for with a larger volume of employment—with more labor applied to the given productive equipment of society—the marginal productivity of labor is less, marginal costs are higher relatively to wages; prices (which, with the same degree of imperfection of competition, must in equilibrium bear the same ratio to marginal costs) are also higher relatively to wages, so that the workers by cutting their money wages have been successful in reducing their *real* wages. The second is also able to show that his conclusions are consistent with the cost conditions; for if there is no increase in employment, marginal costs will fall as much as wages, and prices have to fall in the same proportion as costs, so that there is no change in real wages. Further, each economist is able to accuse the other of assuming his conclusions, and then each can complain of the pot calling the kettle black. So that we have an infinite regress but no answer to our question.

The necessity of bringing in the demand side is seen even more clearly if we suppose for a moment that wages are the only item that enters into marginal costs and that marginal costs are constant. In this case there is no inverse relation between employment and real wages. If wages are cut, marginal costs fall in the same proportion as wages whether there is an increase in employment or not. There will be no fall in real wages, but that tells us nothing about the volume of employment. To get the answer to our question, we have to consider the effects of the wage cut on demand, direct as well as indirect.

The essence of the analysis whereby Keynes obtains the result that there will be no change in employment comes from a consideration of demand conditions. If there is initially an increase in employment—and, since employers very often think that a wage cut is a good thing, this impact effect is very likely—the demand conditions will be such as to bring about losses which tend to induce the entrepreneurs to curtail employment until the previous equilibrium level of employment is restored. Similarly, if the impact effect is to reduce employment, this will bring about profits which induce entrepreneurs to raise employment to the previous level.

The losses that accompany an increase in employment in the manufacture of consumption goods are due to the tendency of people whose income is increased to increase their expenditure by *less* than the increase in the outlay on their production, so that there emerges a net loss. This loss may be mitigated, but not entirely escaped, by the withholding of stocks with the intention of selling them at a more propitious moment; but this procedure, while diminishing losses, has the effect of building up superfluous stocks. The losses and the accumulation of stocks both tend to reduce employment, and these forces must persist and accumulate as long as employment remains above the equilibrium level. The whole of this phenomenon is reversed for the case where the initial effect of the wage cut is to diminish employment.

We must now consider how all this works if items other than wages enter into marginal costs. Where this is the case, these other items are payments for the use of productive resources which, in the short period, are fixed in supply. This is because they accept whatever they can get, their reward falling relatively to wages until all those that are of any use whatever are employed.

If, then, wages are reduced, the attempt to substitute labor for those other productive resources will increase employment and may reduce the earnings of these resources. As long as these earnings have not fallen in the same proportion as wages, costs and prices will not have fallen as much as wages but will have fallen more than the rewards of the other productive resources. Real wages will be lower while the real reward to the other productive factors will be greater. More men will be employed, and the total real income will be greater; since, with more men employed on the given resources, a greater real product is forthcoming. The aggregate real income of the other productive resources is increased, since the quantity employed is unchanged and the real rate of reward is increased. The aggregate real income of labor may be greater or less than in the beginning, according as the increase in employment is greater or less than the reduction in the real wage.

As long as this situation remains, prices have not fallen as much as wages have been reduced; and the workers have been able to reduce their real wages by reducing their money wages and thus to increase employment. Such a position cannot be expected to persist, but contains within itself forces which will still further reduce the rewards of the factors other than labor until costs and prices have fallen proportionately to wages, and real wages and employment are back again at the original level.

In the situation we have just described, total real income is greater than in the initial position, because more men applied to the same equipment produce more goods. There is an increase in the total real costs of the consumption entrepreneurs exactly equal to this increase in real income (since the incomes of the factors of production are the costs of the entrepreneurs). Out of this extra income, some will be saved, so that the total receipts of consumption entrepreneurs increase (in real terms) less than their outgoings. Entrepreneurs make losses which cause them to restrict their (output and) demand for productive resources. This goes on as long as more men are employed than in the initial equilibrium and as long as the real reward of the productive resources other than labor is greater than in the initial position. These two phenomena disappear at the same time, since the tendency to substitute labor for other productive resources, which led to the increase in employment in the first place, disappears just at the point where the real reward to the other productive factors has fallen in the same proportion as prices and wages. A new equilibrium is reached only when employment has gone back to its original level and the reward of the other resources has fallen to its old *real* level. This will only be when their prices have fallen in the same proportion as wages. As long as these have fallen only in a smaller proportion than wages, prices will be higher than before relatively to wages and lower than before relatively to the reward of the other productive resources, and the disequilibrium described will continue.

In a longer period, it will be possible to increase or decrease the supply of productive resources other than labor by varying the application of current factors of production to their manufacture, so that the above argument, which rests on the fixity of supply of productive resources other than labor, would not apply. But there will be no inducement to vary their supply since their price, determined in the longer period by their cost of production, will have varied in just the same proportion as wages. There is therefore no point in departing—except as a temporary mistake —from the initial level of employment.

This does not mean that a reduction of money wages may not have all sorts of indirect influences which ultimately react on the level of employment. There will be effects on the demand for money, on the rate of interest, on intrepreneurs' expectations of future prices (or rather of the relation of these future prices to present costs), on the distribution of wealth and spending—all these and other influences will have an effect on the number of people that entrepreneurs consider it profitable to employ—but these work in divergent directions and some of them only after a considerable interval, so that nothing can be said as to the effect of the sum of these influences on employment as a result of a reduction in wages until a complete set of assumptions have been provided as to the form and strength of these influences. Before we have all this information, we must either assume them to cancel out and say that there is no effect on employment, or else, if we wish to be more realistic, we must say that what happens to employment if money wages are reduced will depend upon other conditions, so that employment might go either up or down. Anything might happen. There is no simple rule such as the classical economists envisage relating the level of employment to the money wage.

2.

If the level of employment is not affected in any simple way by the money wage, what is it that does determine the amount of employment? Before answering this question it is useful to contemplate some very simple equations.

The income of the whole society is earned by the members of the society in producing either consumption goods or other kinds of goods. We call these other goods investment goods. This gives us our first equation. The total income of society (Y) is made up of the income earned in making consumption goods (C) and the income earned in making investment goods (I). $Y = C + I$.

Now C, which stands for income earned in making consumption goods, must also stand for the amount spent on buying consumption goods, since these two are in fact the same thing. (Similarly I stands also for the amount of money spent on investment goods.) The aggregate amount of saving in any period (S) is defined as the excess of aggregate income in the period over the expenditure on consumption goods. This, the almost universal definition of saving, gives us our second equation $S = Y - C$ (definition).

From these two equations it follows that saving must always be equal to investment. $S = I$.

This appears rather peculiar to many people when they first meet it, since there is obviously no mechanism whereby any individual's decision to save causes somebody to invest an exactly equal amount. Mr. Keynes has ineradicably impressed that upon the mind of everyone who has read his *Treatise on Money*. And of course Keynes was right in this. Yet there is no paradox.

It is perfectly possible for any individual to save more without investing more himself. The proposition applies only to *aggregate* saving and investment. Neither is it necessary that aggregate investment should increase whenever any individual decides to increase the amount that he saves. This would be so if an increase in an individual's saving left unchanged the amount saved by all other individuals together, so that it always meant an increase in aggregate saving. But we cannot assume that, because the individual must decrease his expenditure on consumption goods to the extent that he increases his saving. This diminution in C (if others have not changed their expenditure on consumption goods) diminishes Y (by diminishing the income of those who sell consumption goods) and therefore leaves $(Y - C)$, which by definition is S, the same as before. Others have saved as much less as he has saved more, so that aggregate saving is unchanged and equal to the unchanged *I*. If there is no change in *I*, there can be no change in *S*.

Individuals deciding how much to spend out of their incomes seem to be able to decide how much to save, and, if we consider one individual in a large society, this has sense, because the effect on his own income of an individual's expenditure on consumption goods can be neglected. But if we take society altogether and neglect the effect of changes in expenditure on total incomes, we naturally get into trouble, for we are then making the contradictory assumptions (a) that when people save more they spend less on consumption goods and (b) that the people who sell consumption goods do not receive any less. And nobody expects to get sensible results by deduction from contradictory assumptions, not even those who are most scornful of the canons of "bourgeois" logic.

The classical view that an individual, in deciding to save more, increases the aggregate amount of saving (*S*), can be supported by another argument which does not, at first sight, appear to be quite as illogical as that just given. We must leave this however until we have examined the classical theory of the determination of saving and investment and the rate of interest.

A more common-sense objection to the proposition that saving and investment must always and inevitably be equal to each other is to be found in the query whether the identity of these two cannot be upset by *hoarding*. In the case of any individual it is clear that there is no need for his saving to be equal to his investment. When an individual saves more than he invests he is said to *hoard* the difference. Why cannot society do the same? And if society hoards (or dishoards) will that not make saving greater (or less) than investment?

We must note more carefully what is meant by *hoarding*. Our individual who invested only a part of his saving was left with the difference in cash. His store of money has increased and it is in fact this increase in his store of money that *is* his hoarding. Any individual who saves more than he invests in any period increases his holding of money by the difference. Any individual who increases his store of money in any period must have saved more than he invested in the period by just that amount.

The question "Can the society hoard?" means, then, nothing else than "Can the society increase its store of money?" This will depend upon whether or not the monetary authority has increased the amount of money in the society during the period we have been considering.

If the monetary authority does not increase the amount of money, it is impossible for the society to hoard. If any individual hoards, other individuals have to dishoard to the same extent, for it is impossible for anybody to increase his store of money without somebody else diminishing *his* store of money as long as the total store is unchanged. There cannot therefore be any *net* hoarding (or dishoarding) by all the members of the society taken together, so that there cannot for the society be any excess of saving over investment (or of investment over saving). $S = I$.

If the monetary authority does increase the amount of money, then there not merely *can* be net hoarding by the whole society, but there *must* be net hoarding exactly equal to the increase in the society's holdings of money. This does not mean that there is any divergence between saving and investment. There is indeed an excess of saving over investment by the individuals who are left with the extra money that has been put into the society and which must be in somebody's hands. But this is exactly balanced by the expenditure of money by those individuals who borrowed the extra money from the monetary authority (the banks). These borrowers were enabled by the banks to consume or to invest out of borrowed money that was not part of their income. Insofar as they spend the money on consumption, this constituted negative saving which has to be subtracted from the excess saving by the hoarders. The rest of the borrowed money is invested and provides the investment that balances the excess saving and shows again the inevitable equality of saving to investment. We always get back to this really very obvious if not very informative bit of arithmetic. It only appears strange or suspicious because of the habit of looking at the saving from the point of view of the individual who has got his income and is wondering whether to save it or not. He is naturally unable to see the whole social process. Our suspicions should vanish when we realize that all that the proposition says is that the excess of total income over income earned in making consumption goods is equal to the income earned in other ways.

What we have done now is to replace the suspect proposition that $S = I$ by the even more suspect proposition that it is impossible for a society to hoard if the banks do not increase the amount of money. Does this not imply that everything that has been said in economic discussions about the effects of hoarding is sheer nonsense?

This is, of course, not the case. The trouble arises from a confusion of two meanings of *hoarding*. When people consider, say, the deflationary effects of hoarding, they are talking sound and important sense. But if they are to use the word *hoarding* in the sense we have used it, so that it indicates an excess of saving over investment, they should speak of the deflationary effects of "attempts to hoard." These effects are of the utmost importance. They involve a reduction of prices, of profits, of employment, of incomes, of prosperity generally, and of many concomitants of these. But they do not involve an increase in hoarding—in our exact sense of increasing the money held—unless the amount of money is increased. It is only saying the same thing in other words to show that an attempt by people to save more than they invest will diminish consumption and incomes and employment, etc., but will never succeed in making saving greater than investment.

We see then that decisions of income receivers as between spending and saving do not affect the aggregate volume of saving but do determine the size of both income and consumption. The difference between them, which is the amount actually saved, is determined by those who decide the size of I (which is equal to the excess of income over consumption, because it is that part of income which is not earned in making consumption goods).

If we have given the size of I, we can say that Y is determined by the propensity to save. If we suppose that the amount people save depends only on the size of their income, and that it increases with the size of income, we can see that income must be at that level where the amount people wish to save is equal to I.

As long as income is below this level people will wish to save less than is being invested, i.e., they will want to spend on consumption goods more than is being earned in making consumption goods, and since these two are identical this means that they will *wish* to spend on consumption goods more than they *are* spending on consumption goods. This will lead to increased demand and profits in the manufacture of consumption goods, which will lead to an expansion of employment and income until this level is reached. People then wish to save just as much as is being invested, i.e., they spend on consumption goods an amount that is less than their income by exactly the expenditure on

(= the earnings in the manufacture of) investment goods, i.e., they spend on consumption goods just as much as is earned in making consumption goods, i.e., just as much as the cost incurred in making consumption goods. There is neither profit nor loss but equilibrium. If employment and income had risen above the level where people wish to save just as much as is being invested, losses would have emerged to bring incomes and employment down again to the equilibrium level where people wish to save just as much as is being invested. $S = I$. Although there is no mechanism whereby decisions about saving bring about an equal value of investment, which is what makes the equation suspicious, because of the long-standing habit of expecting the influences to work *from* saving *to* investment, *there is* a mechanism whereby decisions to invest bring about an equal amount of saving, which is what makes the equation true. $I = S$.

From the expenditure on consumption at this level of income, we can derive the number of men employed in making consumption goods—for there is a functional relation between this number of men and expenditure on their product. Similarly, from the expenditure on investment goods, we can derive the number of people at work in making the investment goods. This gives us the total number of men employed. This number is determined by the amount of investment and the propensity to save (or its complement: the propensity to consume, which is the relationship between income and consumption). The propensity to consume may also depend upon other things, such as the rate of interest. These can be brought in and they fit quite well into the theory, but it is a reasonable simplification to assume that small changes in the rate of interest will affect different people in opposite directions; and the net effect may here be neglected.

3.

There remains to be considered what determines the rate of investment. It is in the analysis of this that some of the more subtle and more valuable innovations in the theory are made by Keynes. Investment consists in the application of productive resources to the manufacture of capital goods. Capital goods are goods which are valuable on account of services they are expected to yield in the future. The efficiency of a capital good, or the rate of return over cost, as Irving Fisher calls this, is the rate of yield of the capital good, i.e., it is that rate of discounting the expected future yields of the capital good which makes the sum of the discounted yields equal to the cost of making it. For example, if it costs £300 to make a machine which gives off two services, one in one year's time which is then worth £220 and one in two years' time which is then worth £121, the efficiency of this machine is 10 per cent, because, if the values of the services are discounted at the rate of 10 per cent down to the present, the sum of their values is £300.

$$\left(£220 \times \frac{100}{110} = £200, £121 \times \left(\frac{100}{110}\right)^2 = £100, \text{ and } £200 + £100 = £300.\right)$$

The *marginal* efficiency of any particular type of capital good is the ~~efficiency of the~~ marginal item of that type of capital good, in the use where its installation would show the greatest possible efficiency. The marginal efficiency of capital in general is the highest of the marginal efficiencies of all capital goods that still remain to be made.

It should be noted that the marginal efficiency of any capital good is described in the same way (has the same dimensions) as the rate of interest, so that it can be measured against it. It is a percentage of so much per annum. But it must on no account be confused with the rate of interest. The rate of interest is the rate at which money has to be paid for the privilege of borrowing money; or, from the point of view of the lender, it is the rate at which one is remunerated in money for the service of lending money.

There is, however, a certain relationship between the rate of interest and the marginal efficiency of capital. For it will pay entrepreneurs to borrow money in order to increase the rate of construction of capital goods—which is the rate of investment— as long as the rate of interest is less than the marginal efficiency of capital. As the rate of investment increases, the best opportunities for investment are used up, and the marginal efficiency of capital diminishes. This happens in two ways. As the amount of capital increases, the expected values of the services of new capital goods fall as these have to compete with a larger supply of existing capital goods. This will be a very slow process since the rate at which capital is increased—the output in a short period—is small relatively to the existing stock of capital goods.

But the other way in which the marginal efficiency falls is operative in the short period. As the rate of investment increases, the marginal cost of making capital goods increases, and this immediately tends to reduce the marginal efficiency of capital to the rate of interest. For each rate of interest there is a corresponding rate of investment. This relationship is the schedule of the marginal efficiency of capital.

The schedule of the marginal efficiency of capital is sometimes called the demand curve for savings because the entrepreneurs, who undertake the investment and have to obtain the funds to finance it, are conceived to obtain them from the savings of individuals which when summed constitute the "supply" of savings. This is important in so far as it is brought in to explain the amount of investment that takes place, and upon the amount of investment depends—as we have seen—the amount of employment which is the *quaesitum* of the whole book.

It is clear that the amount of investment undertaken by entrepreneurs in any given position, given the marginal efficiency schedule of capital, will be determined by the' rate of interest. The crux of the matter lies then in the theory of the determination of the rate of interest.

According to the classical theory, the rate of interest is given by the supply and demand schedules for savings. The rate of interest is the price of savings and that amount of saving and investment comes about that is indicated by the intersection of these demand and supply schedules. If the supply of savings is greater than the rate of investment, the rate of interest will fall so as to bring them into equilibrium, and vice versa. Savings and investment are brought into equality with each other in an equilibrium by the movement of the rate of interest.

This line of reasoning is not merely wrong—it is meaningless. The equations on page 121 show that savings can never be different from investment whatever the rate of interest, so that it is nonsense to say that the rate of interest brings them to equality with each other. This can be shown in another way. The supply schedule of savings in this scheme is supposed to be independent of the demand curve for saving (which is the marginal efficiency schedule of capital). This means that, given the rate of interest, the amount of saving is independent of the amount of investment and also of the size of people's incomes. In fact, of course, it is ridiculous to assume that this is so, for what happens is that if there is an increase in investment, incomes increase immediately, so that saving is increased by exactly the amount that investment is increased. The supply curve does not keep still. Whatever the point one takes on the demand curve, the supply curve moves to the right or to the left so that it intersects the demand curve at the point taken.

We can now consider the alternative argument, referred to above, which is sometimes put forward in defense of the proposition that any individual, in deciding to save more, thereby increases S, the aggregate amount of saving of the whole society. Instead of assuming that when an individual saves more and spends less on consumption goods the seller of consumption goods continues to receive the same amount as before, so that Y, the aggregate income of society, is unaffected, it is assumed that whenever an individual decides to increase his saving by a certain amount, either he or somebody else always increases investment by the same amount. This increases the incomes of those engaged in the production of investment goods by as much as the income of the producers of consumption goods diminishes, so that Y, the aggregate income, remains the same. C, the expenditure on consumption goods, has diminished, and $(Y - C)$ or S has increased as much as the first individual increases his own saving.

There are two difficulties about this argument. The first is that there is no satisfactory indication of any mechanism in a monetary economy whereby the decision to save necessarily carries with it an instantaneous and equal decision to invest. The second difficulty is that, if there were some mechanism which did make somebody decide to invest exactly as much as anybody saved, the classical explanation of the determination of saving and investment would be upset in a manner similar to the one we have indicated. For this would mean that the investment curve—which constitutes the demand curve for the supply of savings—coincided throughout with the supply curve of savings. At each rate of interest people decide to save a certain amount (supposing for the moment that the supply curve of saving is not shifted about by changes in income due to changes in investment)—and if there is some mechanism whereby an individual's decision to save calls into being an equal amount of investment, then saving again equals investment throughout (though not for the reasons given above). There is only one curve, which is both the supply curve and the demand curve for savings, so that the rate of interest remains unexplained.

This argument sometimes takes the form of assuming MV (the amount of money multiplied by its velocity of circulation) as unchanging. This means that the total amount spent altogether, both on consumption and on investment, is unchanged, so that if £1 less is spent on consumption £1 more must be spent on investment. This assumption is frequently very tacit, and when made explicit it appears in extremely innocent-looking forms like assuming "other things remaining the same" or considering what happens "in the absence of hoarding." This really means that unless something special from outside—"hoarding"— intervenes, we may expect MV to remain constant and that any decision to save will somehow result in somebody investing an equal amount. This criticism of the illegitimate and sometimes unconscious assumption of a constant MV is not Keynes' way of dealing with the argument. He usually refuses to have anything to do with such simple "quantity equations." Dr. Haberler, however, concentrates on this line of attack, which is only a more orthodox (and more complicated) route that leads to the same conclusions as are obtained by Keynes.

There remains unexplained what it is that determines the rate of interest. The explanation of this is given by Keynes, who derives it from the inadequate theories of the Mercantilists by an easy development of a line of thought that had been shut out of economic theory for over a century. This line of thought has only recently been coming back into respectable economics under very heavy disguise in the writings associated with such esoteric concepts as the "natural rate of interest" and "neutral money."

The rate of interest is what people pay for borrowing money. It is what people who have money—cash—obtain for lending it to other people instead of holding it themselves. It is not payment for saving, for one can save without lending the money saved; and in that case one does not get any interest payments. On the other hand, one can lend the money out of what one previously held; and in that case one gets interest payments without saving. The relevant demand is then the demand to *hold* money. The supply is simply the total amount of money that there exists. This demand schedule Keynes called *liquidity preference*, and it is the intersection between the liquidity preference schedule and the supply of money (which is a perpendicular line if the amount of money is fixed) that gives the rate of in-. terest upon which the whole thing depends. The higher the rate of interest the greater the cost—in terms of interest foregone—of holding money and the smaller the amount of money people will want to hold. Conversely, if there is an increase in the amount of money, the rate of interest will fall until people want to hold the larger amount of money. They are induced to want to hold more money by the fall in the rate of interest, for then, to some people, the convenience and feeling of security of holding cash can be satisfied to a greater extent because the cost is less.

Our conclusion is that the amount of employment can be governed by policy directed toward affecting the amount of investment. This may be done either by lowering the rate of interest or by direct investment by the authorities. There may be difficulties for institutional or psychological reasons in reducing the rate of interest to sufficiently low a level to bring about that rate of investment which, with the existing propensity to consume, is necessary in order to bring about full employment. It is because of such difficulties that Keynes thinks that public works are necessary, and may become more and more necessary as the wealth and capital equipment of the community increase. For this means that, on the one hand, people wish to save more out of the larger income corresponding to full employment while, on the other hand, the accumulation of capital lowers the marginal efficiency schedule of capital. Equilibrium with full employment is then possible only at lower interest rates than are practicable unless either (a) investment is increased by State production of capital goods whose efficiency is less than the rate of interest or which for any other reason would not be manufactured by private entrepreneurs, or (b) the propensity to save is diminished—consumption increased—by State expenditure on social services or by redistribution of income from the rich to the poor, or by any other means.

The reader may have noticed a considerable similarity between this last argument and the classical argument that was so vehemently attacked on pp. 127 and 128. Here in fact an equilibrium is indicated by the intersection of demand and supply curves for savings. What the argument amounts to is that, if for institutional reasons the rate of interest cannot be brought down to the level which equates the supply and demand, the demand curve must be moved to the right or the supply curve moved to the left until they meet at a level of the rate of interest that *is* practicable. But what was impossible in the classical explanation of the rate of interest is permissible here because for this argument we were assuming full employment in order to be able to consider what are the necessary conditions for that to exist. There is then a given income so that there is a given supply schedule of savings. The criticism of the classical explanation of the determination of the rate of interest is that its argument—in assuming a given supply curve of saving—is implicitly assuming a given degree of employment, namely, full employment. And it is not useful to consider what determines the amount of employment on the assumption that there is full employment—or even to discuss the determination of the rate of interest under those conditions without considering whether in fact there is any force which will bring about full employment.

Keynes' conclusion that the amount of employment has to be governed by operating on the amount of consumption and investment, via the rate of interest or otherwise, may seem at first sight to be a very small mouse to emerge from the labor of mountains. Everybody has known that cheaper money is good for business, and so is any increase in net investment or expenditure. But except for occasional lapses from scientific purity to momentary commonsense, the pundits of economic science have been declaring that people should practice more thrift. There has been a weakening of this attitude recently—I am not clear to what extent this is due to the cyclical fluctuations in the attitude of economists and how much to the influence of Keynes' ideas and some parallel development by J. R. Hicks and the Swedish writers. But we must not forget that it is not so very long ago that we had Professor Robbins and Keynes on the wireless, respectively advising the world to save more and to spend more. And there is still in Milan a World Institute for the Encouragement of Thrift. It will be a long time before the view that thrift "since it enriches the individual can hardly fail to benefit the community" is seen to be an important example of the common logical error of composition. What Keynes has done is to show that what the ordinary man has often felt in his bones can be justified by a keener analysis than has so far been applied to the problem. He has shown further that it is *only* by working indirectly on these same determinants that any other remedies can ever work. Thus, even in the case when a reduction of money wages increases employment, it does so only in so far as it indirectly reduces the rate of interest. The direct effect is merely to reduce both prices and money incomes, leaving the *real* situation as before. At the lower price level, people find that they need less money to carry on their business, so that, if there is no change in the amount of money, its supply is greater than the demand to hold it, and the attempt of money holders to lend the spare money to others, or to buy other assets for money, raises the value of the other assets and reduces the rate of interest. The reduction of the rate of interest does the trick by making a larger rate of investment profitable. Incomes then increase, in accordance with the propensity to consume, until a level of income and employment is reached which induces people to save at a rate equal to the greater rate of investment. From this it follows that any objections that may be raised against the dangers inherent in lowering the rate of interest in an attempt to increase employment apply just as much or as little to the policy of increasing employment by lowering wages, since that works only via lowering the interest rate. It is not denied that there are any dangers, but such as they are, they are inherent in *any* successful attempt to increase employment. To run away from these is to refuse to be cured because that will make it possible to become sick again.

To seek the alleviation of depression by reducing money wages, rather than by directly reducing the rate of interest or otherwise encouraging investment or consumption, is to abandon the high road for a devious, dark, difficult, and unreliable path, for no better reason than that the dangers that await one at the common destination are more clearly seen when it is approached by the broad highway.

CHAPTER XII

The *General Theory* (2)

By *ALVIN H. HANSEN*

1.

I⊤ WOULD BE a mistake, I think, to make too sharp a dividing line between pre-Keynesian and Keynesian economics. That some line has to be drawn I do not believe will be denied by anyone who will examine the economic literature before and after 1936. But every contributor to any field of knowledge stands on the shoulders of his predecessors. Specialists in any field of knowledge know that no one man ever single-handed invented anything. In a sense there are no "revolutionary" discoveries. Nevertheless, in the progress of man's thinking new plateaus are from time to time cast up not unlike a geological upheaval. And these *are* revolutionary developments even though the constituent elements composing the structure can be found elsewhere and have long been well known.

If a stranger from Mars should undertake to read the literature of economics from, say, 1700 to the present day, he would be struck, I believe, particularly by the new direction and outlook injected by the publication of (a) *Wealth of Nations*, (b) the works of Jevons, the Austrians, and Walras, and (c) Keynes' *General Theory*. Scarcely has any issue of an economic journal or any serious volume since 1936 appeared which has not been influenced by, or primarily concerned with, the concepts and thinking of Keynes.

The record will also verify, I think, that friend and foe alike have experienced a considerable enrichment of their "mental furniture" by reason of the Keynesian contribution. This indeed is nothing new. Alfred Marshall's *Principles of Economics* was profoundly influenced by Jevons and the Austrians, though he was far from sympathetic when this "attack" on the classicals first appeared. There are plenty of parallels today.

While it is not possible now to assess the ultimate place of Keynes in the history of economic thought, it is safe to say that no book in economics has ever made such a stir within the first ten years of its publication as has the *General Theory*. And this interest continues unabated. It is further true, I believe, that economic research has tackled new problems and is better equipped with tools of analysis by reason of the work of Keynes. Moreover, a correct appraisal of Keynes' work cannot be made by confining attention to the contents of the *General Theory*. The Keynesian "revolution" is far from having been completed, and it is, accordingly, not possible this early accurately to appraise the importance of his work in relation to the great peaks of intellectual achievement which have gone before.

Keynes proved to be quite right when he predicted in his Preface to the *General Theory* that many economists would fluctuate between a belief that he was quite wrong and a belief that he was saying nothing new. This conundrum, it appears, still torments some economists; but many more, during the process of criticizing Keynes, have acquired as a by-product the new analytical apparatus. Keynes himself felt he was "treading along unfamiliar paths," and that the composition of the *General Theory* had been a long "struggle of escape from habitual modes of thought and expression." In the literature of the last ten years, one cannot fail to be impressed with the change that has occurred in the "habitual modes of thought and expression" of Keynes' critics, also.

2.

David McCord Wright, in a recent article on the "Future of Keynesian Economics" [1] put his finger quite accurately on the basic change in *outlook* effected by the "Keynesian Revolution." We cannot follow, he says, the main lines of Keynes' argument and say that the capitalist system, left to itself, will automatically bring forth sufficient effective demand. Keynes' ideas "derive much of their unpopularity because they form the most widely known arguments for intervention even though such intervention may be quite capitalist in nature." It is the analysis of the problem of *aggregate demand,* together with the implications of this

[1] AER, June, 1945.

analysis for practical policy, which challenges the old orthodoxy.

In this connection an illuminating passage appears in the Preface to Pigou's recent pamphlet, *Lapses from Full Employment*, as follows:

"Professor Dennis Robertson . . . has warned me that the form of the book may suggest that I am in favour of attacking the problem of unemployment by manipulating wages rather than by manipulating demand. I wish, therefore, to say clearly that this is not so."

This sentence would not likely have been written prior to the *General Theory*.

3.

It has been my conviction for many years [2] that the great contribution of Keynes' *General Theory* was the clear and specific formulation of the consumption function. This is an epoch-making contribution to the tools of economic analysis, analogous to, but even more important than, Marshall's discovery of the demand function.[3] Just as Marshall's predecessors were fumbling around in the dark because they never grasped the concept of a demand *schedule*, so business-cycle and other theorists from Malthus to Wicksell, Spiethoff, and Aftalion, never could quite "reach port" because they did not have at hand this powerful tool. It is illuminating to re-read business-cycle and depression theories in general prior to 1936 and to see how many things settle neatly into place when one applies the consumption function analysis—things that were dark and obscure and confused without it. The consumption function is by far the most powerful instrument which has been added to the economist's kit of tools in our generation. It is perfectly true that embryonic suggestions (as also with the demand function) appear in earlier literature, but the consumption function was never fashioned into a workmanlike instrument until the *General Theory*. This, I repeat, is Keynes' greatest contribution. And in more general terms, the effect of variations in income upon all manner of economic variables has, since Keynes, become an important field for research and analysis. Income analysis at long last occupies a place equally as im-

---

[2] See my *Fiscal Policy and Business Cycles*, Chapter XI.

[3] Not until Marshall did the demand function play a significant rôle in economic analysis. Yet Cournot (and perhaps others) had formulated the principle before.

portant as price analysis. This part of the Keynesian contribution
will remain, regardless of what happens to that which relates to
policy.

Time and again when I thought I had discovered this or that
error in the Keynesian analysis, either on my own or at the suggestion of a critic, I have been surprised to find how often, upon
examination, the point had already been anticipated and covered
in the *General Theory*. I regret that I have not kept a list of these
points, but only recently I came upon another interesting example
which relates to the consumption function. In my *Fiscal Policy
and Business Cycles* I had pointed out (p. 233 *et seq.*) that, on
grounds of general reasoning and such facts as are available
(Kuznets' long-run data) we may assume an upward *secular*
drift in the consumption function. Later, this was elaborated
more fully by Paul Samuelson.[4] This upward secular drift is often
(but erroneously) cited as proof that the consumption function
analysis is not valid. Until recently, I had supposed that Keynes
had overlooked the secular aspect of the problem, and it was
therefore of great interest for me to discover that his particular
formulation does in fact (possibly inadvertently) cover the matter in a fairly satisfactory manner. The consumption function of
two periods, widely separated in time, can be made comparable
by correcting for changes in prices, per capita productivity, and
population increase.[5] This would correct for the secular drift, and,
if the corrected functions were found to be similar, we could say
that the consumption function was stable over time. Now Keynes
achieves a fairly satisfactory result by casting his consumption
function in terms of wage-units. When the consumption-income
schedules of two different periods are cast in terms of wage units,
the effect is to correct for price and productivity changes. Thus
the schedules become quite comparable over time,[6] and we are
accordingly in a position to determine whether or not a shift has
in fact occurred in the consumption function.

Not only is consumption a function of income in the short run,
but also in the long run. The secular upward shift in the con-

---

[4] See Chapter II, in *Postwar Economic Problems* (edited by Seymour E.
Harris, New York, 1943).

[5] This would amount to much the same thing as calculating each schedule
as ratios of a full-employment income in each period. Thus the consumption
function could be said to be stable over time if the schedules so constructed
had the same relation to a full-employment income in each period.

[6] This, at any rate, is true if the schedules are reduced to a per capita basis.

sumption function [6a] could not occur except *as a result of* the prior rise in income. It is sometimes argued that the fact that the historical data reveal an upward secular drift in the consumption function itself proves that consumption is autonomously determined so far as the *long-run* relationship is concerned. But this is, I believe, wrong. The upward shift in the consumption function is a result of the secular rise in income. For example, the statistical evidence points to the conclusion that the *secular* upward shift in the consumption function did not occur from 1929 to 1940. In other words, the consumption schedule, measured in terms of a "full employment" income, had fallen from 1929 to 1940. Thus, at corresponding income levels (measured as ratios of a full employment income in each period), individuals saved a higher per cent in 1940 than in 1929.[7] Had a full employment income been reached, however, in the late thirties, the higher income would have "educated" the public to higher consumption standards so that the per cent saved of the higher income might have been no higher than in 1929. The point is that it is necessary first to *achieve* the higher potential income level which progress makes possible, in order to induce people to live at a higher standard. The rising standard follows from the rising income, not the other way around.

The rôle and significance of the consumption function can be illustrated by a comparison of the *Treatise* with the *General Theory*. In the *Treatise* $\pi o = E + (I - S)$, where πo is the current income, E the normal (full employment) income, and S is the current saving which *would* be made from a normal full-employment income. Thus the current realized income is, according to the *Treatise*, less than the normal or full-employment income by the amount that current investment falls below the potential saving at full employment. But this, of course, is wrong, since it leaves out the multiplier. The missing link is supplied by the consumption function. This in a nut shell reveals one of the great advances of the *General Theory* over the *Treatise*.

In this connection it is interesting to compare Robertson's $Y_1 = Y_0 + (I_1 - S_1)$ with Keynes' $\pi o = E + (I - S)$ in the *Trea-*

[6a] See my *Fiscal Policy and Business Cycles*, p. 233; and Paul Samuelson in Harris' *Post-war Economic Problems*.

[7] See Louis Bean's estimates in RES, Nov., 1946. Bean, however, appears mistakenly to conclude that his data point to the conclusion that the consumption function may be expected to remain low, relative to 1929, even though we achieve a full employment income.

tise. They bear a superficial resemblance. An important difference is that Robertson's is a period analysis which does not pretend to explain the *level* of Y_1 but only its relation to Y_0, while Keynes' (*Treatise*) equation pretends to explain the *level* of π_0. By combining Robertson's formulation with the consumption function analysis (as I have done in Chapter XII in *Fiscal Policy and Business Cycles*), one can solve by the period analysis the problem attacked by Keynes in the *Treatise*. Keynes, however, chose in the *General Theory* to implement the consumption function analysis in terms of a logical or mathematical formulation [8] involving no time-lags. Thus if the consumption function is given, the level of income is uniquely determined (time-lags assumed away) by the volume of investment.

4.

With respect to the determinants of investment—the marginal efficiency of capital and the rate of interest—Keynes' contribution relates chiefly to the latter. The real factors, in a dynamic society, which determine the marginal efficiency of capital are largely taken for granted. The psychological and institutional aspects are indeed at points well treated, but the "real" or "objective" aspects —the dynamics of technical progress—are passed by almost unnoticed. Keynes, however, contributed greatly to the theory of the rate of interest. As a result of his analysis we now place less emphasis than formerly on the rate of interest as a means of increasing the volume of investment. The rate of interest is indeed enormously important in the effective implementation of fiscal policy (debt management, lending and guaranteeing operations in such areas as housing, etc.), but as a means of increasing purely private investment it could *only* be of great importance as a determinant of income and employment if the marginal efficiency schedule were very highly elastic. And even so, once a minimum low rate of interest had been reached (Keynes' liquidity prefer-

[8] It is not correct, as is often done, to identify the Keynesian *logical* formulation with the "ex post" or "statistical" formulation. Nevertheless, Keynes was realistic enough to recognize that time-lags do occur, and so the *actual* marginal propensity to consume may, for a time, until the adjustment is made, fall below the *normal* marginal propensity to consume. Thus the "statistical" formulation and the Keynesian realistic formulation (involving time lags) are alike in that saving and investment are both equal to *current* income minus *current* consumption. See *General Theory*, pp. 122–4.

ence), nothing more could be accomplished by means of monetary policy. In so far as anything can be achieved (and something can within limits be done) by reducing as far as possible the rate of interest, this method obviously, from the long-run standpoint, is non-recurring and quickly runs out. The movement *along* the marginal efficiency curve would be a "once for all" movement were it not for the *upward shift* of the curve, due to growth and technical progress. It is the upward shift of the marginal efficiency schedule that provides the outlet for a *continuing* flow of investment.

The volume of investment during the last century can be accounted for mainly by growth and technical progress. "Growth" has provided vast outlets for investment of the "widening" type; technical progress has provided outlets of the "deepening" type (greater capital intensity per worker). In addition, some "deepening of capital" has been achieved through some secular decline in the rate of interest.[9] This is important in the sense that we have in consequence more nearly approached the condition of "full investment"—a fuller realization of the potentialities of technical progress. But the contribution which the secular fall in the rate of interest has made to *annual* investment over the last century is surely negligible compared with the contribution to annual investment made by population growth and technical progress.

It is not necessary to argue that the marginal efficiency schedule is highly inelastic. The movement *down* the curve cannot be of great importance for *continuing* income and employment creation. What is needed in order to develop a considerable flow of investment is a continuing upward shift of the marginal efficiency schedule such as may be caused by technological improvements, the discovery of new resources, the growth of population, or public policy of a character which opens up new investment outlets. The effect of *lowering* the rate of interest would quickly wear off in the absence of an upward shift in the marginal efficiency schedule. Thus, little can be expected for *continuing* investment from progressively lowering the rate of interest, even though this were feasible. A low rate of interest is desirable, nevertheless, because this permits an approach to "full investment" which would

[9] I am aware that secular upswings and downswings in the rate of interest have occurred; these have been associated particularly with the so-called "long waves." Moreover, the rate of interest reached a low level, roughly comparable to that of the present period, in the eighteen-nineties.

mean higher productivity per worker. But in the absence of dynamic growth and innovation, a constant level of the rate of interest, no matter how low, would ultimately result in zero net investment.

5.

The liquidity preference analysis is important as an explanation of the enormous volume of liquid assets which it is possible for an advanced and rich industrial society to hold without inflationary consequences. And while the growth of liquid assets beyond a certain point may have little effect on the rate of interest, it may nevertheless affect income and employment by raising the consumption function. How important this may or may not be depends upon certain circumstances to which I refer below. Mere *volume* alone is not the controlling factor.

Thus under-employment equilibrium may be reached, given a fairly low consumption function, not merely because of an elastic liquidity preference schedule, but mainly because of limited investment opportunities (technical progress, etc.) combined with a marginal efficiency schedule which is not very highly elastic. Keynes, however, rests his case heavily on the liquidity preference analysis, from which it follows that the economy does not tend toward full employment merely through the automatic adjustment of the rate of interest.

6.

Wage reduction, as a means of increasing employment via the fall in the interest rate (Pigou), is thus, along with other policies designed to lower the interest rate, relatively ineffective.[10] And with respect to the effect of increased liquid assets (whether in terms of an *absolute* increase in the quantity of money or a *relative* increase caused by wage reductions) on the consumption

[10] Professor Haberler's quotation from Keynes (p. 17, *General Theory*), that an "increase in employment can only occur to the accompaniment of a decline in the rate of real wages," fails to include the very important conditions which must be assumed to make this statement true, namely, no change in "organization, equipment and technique"; in other words, no change in productivity. Moreover, Keynes (March, 1939, EJ) explicitly repudiated the notion that employment must increase *by or through* a lowering of real wages and a movement *along* a declining so-called general demand curve for labor. In his view, employment is increased by raising effective demand, thereby causing an upward *shift* in the demand curve for labor. For Professor Haberler's article see Chapter XIV.

function, that all depends upon who it is that holds the liquid assets. If the liquid assets are largely in the possession of the rich, the consumption function can rise very little unless, indeed, the accumulation of such assets in the hands of a concentrated few is pushed far beyond the limits of tolerance in a democratic society.

7.

It is therefore important *how* the liquid assets came into being and who it is that holds them. The method of *relative* increase in liquid assets (via wage reductions) is clearly not a realistic method of increasing the consumption function for the general population. And with respect to the method of *absolute* increase brought about by the action of the monetary authorities, it makes considerable difference whether the monetary expansion merely came about through monetizing assets held by investors and wealthy individuals, or whether the new money was created as part of an expansionist's fiscal program of subsidization of mass consumption—school lunches, housing and household equipment for low-income groups, family allowances, etc.—or for public construction projects which directly increase the income of workers and start a round of expenditures (multiplier effect) throughout the economy. There is no assurance that a mere increase in liquid assets (whether absolute or relative) will raise the consumption function appreciably. That depends. Thus it is that monetary policy may be relatively ineffective unless combined with appropriate fiscal policy.[11] And it is considerations such as

[11] Professor Haberler, in his contribution to the RES symposium, argues that under-employment equilibrium with flexible wages and prices is impossible since wages and prices will under these conditions fall continually. But considerations of this kind have been fully and effectively discussed and answered by Keynes himself in Chapter 19 of the *General Theory*. (The reader who may feel confused in consequence of recent discussions about the rôle of wage rigidity in the Keynesian system should carefully study this chapter. See also my Chapter, "Keynes on Economic Policy," below.) Completely flexible wages and prices would indeed give us a system so unstable as to be unworkable.

But this is not the question. The question is rather whether an orderly reduction of wages and prices which are *relatively* rigid could promote an increase in employment. And it was presumably such a policy which Professor Haberler had in mind when he discussed the *relative* increase of liquid assets (via wage reductions) and the effect of this on the interest rate or on the consumption function. Whether or not this is effective depends, as I have noted above, on circumstances. You cannot cure unemployment *merely* by

these here under discussion that reveal the essential differences
between pure monetary policy and pure fiscal policy.

8.

After ten years of criticism, the Keynesian analytical apparatus
remains as essential equipment if one pretends to work on the
determinants of income and employment. The consumption function has become and will remain the pivotal point of departure
for any attack on the problem of aggregate demand. Moreover,
with respect to policy, little reliance in the future will be placed
on the notion that it matters little what the consumption function
may be, since, whatever its level, a volume of investment adequate
to fill the "gap" will always automatically tend to develop if only
wage and monetary adjustments are made. Special models set up
to show how wage flexibility under certain conditions might so
operate are notoriously unrealistic and unworkable in the practical world and so fail to come to grips with economic reality.
Finally, a mere increase in the quantity of money, apart from the
manner in which it is created and put into circulation, and apart
from its distribution among the members of society, is not capable
per se of raising the consumption function to a level adequate to
insure full employment. On the other hand, Keynesian economics
has itself been the means of showing the important rôle of monetary expansion in conjunction with fiscal policy in the creation of
adequate aggregate demand. Monetary policy is an essential
instrument for an effective full-employment program. The volume
of liquid assets and the rate of interest are indeed important,
though if applied alone relatively ineffective.

These, then, are the essentials of the Keynesian system and
these are the considerations with which we must grapple in appraising its continuing effectiveness for analysis and policy. Under-employment equilibrium is not dependent upon wage rigidity
(properly defined). The fundamental explanation is to be found

---

expanding the money supply (absolutely or relatively) without regard to
how this increase is brought about or who holds the money. The position of
Modigliani, Polanyi, and others is, I think, a modern recrudescence of an excessive preoccupation with the mere *quantity* of money—a preoccupation no
less indefensible than the old. I say this despite the fact that I myself place
great stress upon the importance of adequate (but not excessive) monetary
expansion as a part of fiscal policy.

in (a) the consumption function, (b) investment outlets, and (c) the liquidity preference analysis.[12] There are no automatic processes that will produce under all circumstances adequate aggregate demand. Private consumption and private investment outlays will not automatically produce this result. And no other explanation for this has so far been offered that is as satisfactory as that presented by Keynes.

9.

It is evident that a new outlook was injected into economics, both with respect to theory and policy, by the publication of the *General Theory.* That it was not just "old stuff" is evidenced by the terrific effort it required for economists to readjust their thinking and, indeed, the difficulty they had in understanding what it was all about. Witness, for example, the first reviews (including my own) and the endless controversial articles on concepts which, in retrospect, are rarely a credit to the profession.[18] More and more, even those who professed to see little in Keynes that was new or valid began to reveal that they had experienced a rebirth despite their protestations to the contrary. Add to this the fact that the influence of Keynes permeates all official international gatherings grappling with economic problems and is present wherever internal economic problems are under consideration (witness postwar governmental pronouncements). It is difficult to avoid the conclusion that nothing like it has happened in the whole history of economics. It is too early to say, but it does not

[12] Professor Haberler's criticism of the elasticity of the liquidity preference schedule seems to me to require cautious interpretation. It relates to factors affecting a *shift* in the schedule rather than to *elasticities* along a given schedule. To be sure, a long-run schedule can sometimes be traced out by determinate shifts of short-run schedules; but Haberler's theory seems to be a special one, which denies, among other things, that as the rate of interest gets nearer and nearer to zero, the difficulties of lowering it further begin to increase.

[18] A recent example disclosing a number of elementary misconceptions is the pamphlet by Arthur F. Burns, on *Economic Research and the Keynesian Thinking of Our Times* (NBER, 1946). However, the pamphlet does strikingly reveal (perhaps inadvertently) how economic theory—whether Ricardian or Keynesian—serves the highly useful purpose of pointing up what factual data are relevant to a useful investigation. See my article, "Dr. Burns on Keynesian Economics," RES, Nov., 1947.

now appear an extravagant statement, that Keynes may in the end rival Adam Smith in his influence on the economic thinking and governmental policy of his time and age. Both lived at profound turning points in the evolution of the economic order. Both were products of their times. Yet both were also powerful agents in giving direction to the unfolding process of institutional change.

CHAPTER XIII

The *General Theory* (3)

By PAUL A. SAMUELSON

THE DEATH of Lord Keynes will undoubtedly afford the occasion for numerous attempts to appraise the character of the man and his contribution to economic thought. The personal details of his life and antecedents very properly receive notice elsewhere in this volume.

It is perhaps not too soon to venture upon a brief and tentative appraisal of Keynes' lasting impact upon the development of modern economic analysis. And it is all the more fitting to do so now that his major work has just completed the first decade of its very long life.

THE IMPACT OF THE GENERAL THEORY

I have always considered it a priceless advantage to have been born as an economist prior to 1936 and to have received a thorough grounding in classical economics. It is quite impossible for modern students to realize the full effect of what has been advisably called "The Keynesian Revolution"[1] upon those of us brought up in the orthodox tradition. What beginners today often regard as trite and obvious was to us puzzling, novel, and heretical.

To have been born as an economist before 1936 was a boon— yes. But not to have been born too long before!

> *Bliss was it in that dawn to be alive,*
> *But to be young was very heaven !*

---

[1] I owe much in what follows to discussions with my former student, Dr. Lawrence R. Klein, whose rewarding study shortly to be published by Macmillan Company bears the above title.

The *General Theory* caught most economists under the age of 35 with the unexpected virulence of a disease first attacking and decimating an isolated tribe of south sea islanders. Economists beyond fifty turned out to be quite immune to the ailment. With time, most economists in-between began to run the fever, often without knowing or admitting their condition.

I must confess that my own first reaction to the *General Theory* was not at all like that of Keats on first looking into Chapman's Homer. No silent watcher, I, upon a peak in Darien. My rebellion against its pretensions would have been complete, except for an uneasy realization that I did not at all understand what it was about. And I think I am giving away no secrets when I solemnly aver—upon the basis of vivid personal recollection—that no one else in Cambridge, Massachusetts, really knew what it was about for some twelve to eighteen months after its publication. Indeed, until the appearance of the mathematical models of Meade, Lange, Hicks, and Harrod, there is reason to believe that Keynes himself did not truly understand his own analysis.

Fashion always plays an important role in economic science; new concepts become the *mode* and then are *passé*. A cynic might even be tempted to speculate as to whether academic discussion is itself equilibrating: whether assertion, reply, and rejoinder do not represent an oscillating divergent series, in which—to quote Frank Knight's characterization of sociology—"bad talk drives out good."

In this case, gradually and against heavy resistance, the realization grew that the new analysis of *effective demand* associated with the *General Theory* was not to prove such a passing fad, that here indeed was part of "the wave of the future." This impression was confirmed by the rapidity with which English economists, other than those at Cambridge, took up the new Gospel: e.g., Harrod, Meade, and others, at Oxford; and, still more surprisingly, the young blades at the *London School*, like Kaldor, Lerner, and Hicks, who threw off their Hayekian garments and joined in the swim.

In this country it was pretty much the same story. Obviously, exactly the same words cannot be used to describe the analysis of income determination of, say, Lange, Hart, Harris, Ellis, Hansen, Bissell, Haberler, Slichter, J. M. Clark, or myself. And yet the Keynesian taint is unmistakably there upon every one of us.

Instead of burning out like a fad, today, ten years after its birth, the *General Theory* is still gaining adherents and appears to be in business to stay. Many economists who are most vehement in criticism of the specific Keynesian policies—which must always be carefully distinguished from the scientific analysis associated with his name—will never again be the same after passing through his hands.[2]

It has been wisely said that only in terms of a modern theory of effective demand can one understand and defend the so-called "classical" theory of unemployment. It is perhaps not without additional significance, in appraising the long-run prospects of the Keynesian theories, that no individual, having once embraced the modern analysis, has—as far as I am aware—later returned to the older theories. And in universities, where graduate students are exposed to the old and new income analyses, I am told that it is often only too clear which way the wind blows.

Finally, and perhaps most important from the long-run standpoint, the Keynesian analysis has begun to filter down into the elementary text-books; and, as everybody knows, once an idea gets into these, however bad it may be, it becomes practically immortal.

THE GENERAL THEORY

Thus far, I have been discussing the new doctrines without regard to their content or merits, as if they were a religion and nothing else. True, we find a Gospel, a Scriptures, a Prophet, Disciples, Apostles, Epigoni, and even a Duality; and if there is no Apostolic Succession, there is at least an Apostolic Benediction. But by now the joke has worn thin, and it is in any case irrelevant.

The modern saving-investment theory of income determination did not directly displace the old latent belief in Say's Law of Markets (according to which only "frictions" could give rise to unemployment and over-production). Events of the years following 1929 destroyed the previous economic synthesis. The economists' belief in the orthodox synthesis was not overthrown, but had simply atrophied: it was not as though one's soul had faced a showdown as to the existence of the Deity and that faith was unthroned, or even that one had awakened in the morning to find that belief had flown away in the night; rather it was realized

---

[2] For a striking example of the effect of the Keynesian analysis upon a great classical thinker, compare the fructiferous recent writings of Professor Pigou with his earlier *Theory of Unemployment.*

with a sense of belated recognition that one no longer had faith, that one had been living without faith for a long time, and that what, after all, was the difference?

The nature of the world did not suddenly change on a black October day in 1929 so that a new theory became mandatory. Even in their day, the older theories were incomplete and inadequate: in 1815, in 1844, 1893, and 1920. I venture to believe that the eighteenth and nineteenth centuries take on a new aspect when looked back upon from the modern perspective, that a new dimension has been added to the rereading of the Mercantilists, Thornton, Malthus, Ricardo, Tooke, David Wells, Marshall, and Wicksell.

Of course, the great depression of the thirties was not the first to reveal the untenability of the classical synthesis. The classical philosophy always had its ups and downs along with the great swings of business activity. Each time it had come back. But now for the first time, it was confronted by a competing system—a well-reasoned body of thought containing among other things as many equations as unknowns; in short, like itself, a synthesis; and one which could swallow the classical system as a special case.

A new *system,* that is what requires emphasis. Classical economics could withstand isolated criticism. Theorists can always resist facts; for facts are hard to establish and are always changing anyway, and *ceteris paribus* can be made to absorb a good deal of punishment. Inevitably, at the earliest opportunity, the mind slips back into the old grooves of thought, since analysis is utterly impossible without a frame of reference, a way of thinking about things, or, in short, a theory.[3]

Herein lies the secret of the *General Theory.* It is a badly written book, poorly organized; any layman who, beguiled by the author's previous reputation, bought the book was cheated of his five shillings. It is not well suited for classroom use.[3a] It is arrogant, bad-tempered, polemical, and not overly generous in its

[3] This tendency holds true of everybody, including the businessman and the politician, the only difference being that practical men think in terms of highly simplified (and often contradictory) theories. It even holds true of a literary economist who would tremble at the sight of a mathematical symbol.

[3a] The dual and confused theory of Keynes and his followers concerning the "equality of savings and investment" unfortunately ruled out the possibility of a pedagogically clear exposition of the theory in terms of schedules of savings and investment determining income.

acknowledgments. It abounds in mares' nests or confusions: involuntary unemployment, wage units, the equality of savings and investment, the timing of the multiplier, interactions of marginal efficiency upon the rate of interest, forced savings, own rates of interest, and many others. In it the Keynesian system stands out indistinctly, as if the author were hardly aware of its existence or cognizant of its properties; and certainly he is at his worst when expounding its relations to its predecessors. Flashes of insight and intuition intersperse tedious algebra. An awkward definition suddenly gives way to an unforgettable cadenza. When finally mastered, its analysis is found to be obvious and at the same time new. In short, it is a work of genius.

It is not unlikely that future historians of economic thought will conclude that the very obscurity and polemical character of the *General Theory* ultimately served to maximize its long-run influence. Possibly such an analyst will place it in the first rank of theoretical classics, along with the work of Smith, Cournot, and Walras. Certainly, these four books together encompass most of what is vital in the field of economic theory; and only the first is by any standards easy reading or even accessible to the intelligent layman.

In any case, it bears repeating that the *General Theory* is an obscure book, so that would-be anti-Keynesians must assume their position largely on credit unless they are willing to put in a great deal of work and run the risk of seduction in the process. The *General Theory* seems the random notes over a period of years of a gifted man who in his youth gained the whip hand over his publishers by virtue of the acclaim and fortune resulting from the success of his *Economic Consequences of the Peace.*

Like Joyce's *Finnegan's Wake,* the *General Theory* is much in need of a companion volume providing a "skeleton key" and guide to its contents: warning the young and innocent away from Book I (especially the difficult Chapter 3) and on to Books III, IV, and VI. Certainly in its present state, the book does not get itself read from one year to another even by the sympathetic teacher and scholar.

Too much regret should not be attached to the fact that all hope must now be abandoned of an improved second edition, since it is the first edition which would in any case have assumed the stature of a classic. We may still paste into our copies of the *General Theory* certain subsequent Keynesian additions, most particularly the famous chapter in *How to Pay for the War* which first outlined the modern theory of the inflationary process.

This last item helps to dispose of the fallacious belief that Keynesian economics is good "depression economics" and only that. Actually, the Keynesian system is indispensable to an understanding of conditions of over-effective demand and secular exhilaration; so much so that one anti-Keynesian has argued in print that *only* in times of a great war boom do such concepts as the marginal propensity to consume have validity. Perhaps, therefore, it would be more nearly correct to aver the reverse: that certain economists are Keynesian fellow-travellers only in boom times, falling off the band wagon in depression.

If time permitted, it would be instructive to contrast the analysis of inflation during the Napoleonic and first World War periods with that of the recent War and correlate this with Keynes' influence. Thus, the "inflationary gap" concept, recently so popular, seems to have been first used around the Spring of 1941 in a speech by the British Chancellor of the Exchequer, a speech thought to have been the product of Keynes himself.[4]

No author can complete a survey of Keynesian economics without indulging in that favorite indoor guessing game: wherein lies the essential contribution of the *General Theory* and its distinguishing characteristic from the classical writings? Some consider its novelty to lie in the treatment of the *demand for money*, in its liquidity preference emphasis. Others single out the treatment of *expectations*.

I cannot agree. According to recent trends of thought, the interest rate is less important than Keynes himself believed; therefore, *liquidity preference* (which itself explains part of the lack of importance of the interest rate, but only part) cannot be of such crucial significance. As for expectations, the *General Theory* is brilliant in calling attention to their importance and in suggesting many of the central features of uncertainty and speculation. It paves the way for a theory of expectations, but it hardly provides one.[5]

I myself believe the broad significance of the *General Theory*

[4] In the present writer's opinion this "neo-Austrian" demand analysis of inflation has, if anything, been overdone; there is reason to suspect that the relaxations of price controls during a period of *insufficient* general demand might still be followed by a considerable, self-sustaining rise in prices.

[5] [See Chapter XXXI, below.]

to be in the fact that it provides a relatively realistic, complete system for analyzing the level of effective demand and its fluctuations. More narrowly, I conceive the heart of its contribution to be in that subset of its equations which relate to the propensity to consume and to saving in relation to offsets-to-saving. In addition to linking saving explicitly to income, there is an equally important denial of the implicit "classical" axiom that motivated investment is *indefinitely expansible or contractable*, so that whatever people *try* to save will always be fully invested. It is not important whether we deny this by reason of expectations, interest rate rigidity, investment inelasticity with respect to over-all price changes and the interest rate, capital or investment satiation, secular factors of a technological and political nature, or what have you. But it is vital for business-cycle analysis that we do assume definite amounts of investment which are highly variable over time in response to a myriad of exogenous and endogenous factors, *and which are not automatically equilibrated to full-employment saving levels by any internal efficacious economic process.*

With respect to the level of total purchasing power and employment, Keynes denies that there is an *invisible hand* channeling the self-centered action of each individual to the social optimum. This is the sum and substance of his heresy. Again and again through his writings there is to be found the figure of speech that what is needed are certain "rules of the road" and governmental actions, which will benefit everybody, but which nobody by himself is motivated to establish or follow. Left to themselves during depression, people will try to save and only end up lowering society's level of capital formation and saving; during an inflation, apparent self-interest leads everyone to action which only aggravates the malignant upward spiral.

Such a philosophy is profoundly capitalistic in its nature. Its policies are offered "as the only practicable means of avoiding the destruction of existing economic forms in their entirety and as the condition of the successful functioning of individual initiative." [6]

From a perusal of Keynes' writing, I can find no evidence that words like these resemble the opportunistic lip-service paid in much recent social legislation to individual freedom and private enterprise. The following quotations show how far from a radical was this urbane and cosmopolitan provincial English liberal:

[6] *General Theory*, p. 380.

How can I accept [the communistic] doctrine which sets up as its bible, above and beyond criticism, an obsolete economic textbook which I know to be not only scientifically erroneous but without interest or application for the modern world? How can I adopt a creed which, preferring the mud to the fish, exalts the boorish proletariat above the bourgeois and intelligentsia who, with all their faults, are the quality of life and surely carry the seeds of all human advancement. Even if we need a religion, how can we find it in the turbid rubbish of the Red bookshops? It is hard for an educated, decent, intelligent son of Western Europe to find his ideals here, unless he has first suffered some strange and horrid process of conversion which has changed all his values. . . .

So, now that the deeds are done and there is no going back, I should like to give Russia her chance; to help and not to hinder. For how much rather, even after allowing for everything, if I were a Russian, would I contribute my quota of activity to Soviet Russia than to Tsarist Russia.[7]

Nothing that I can find in Keynes' later writings shows any significant changes in his underlying philosophy. As a result of the great depression, he becomes increasingly impatient with what he regards as the stupidity of businessmen who do not realize how much their views toward reform harm their own true long-run interests. But that is all.

With respect to international co-operation and autonomy of national policies, Keynes did undergo some changes in belief. The depression accentuated his post-World War I pessimism concerning the advisability of England or any other country's leaving itself to the mercy of the international gold standard. But in the last half dozen years, he began to pin his hopes on intelligent, concerted, multilateral co-operation, with, however, the important proviso that each nation should rarely be forced to adjust her economy by *deflationary* means.

PORTRAIT OF THE SCIENTIST

There is no danger that historians of thought will fail to devote attention to all the matters already discussed. Science, like capital, grows by accretion, and each scientist's offering at the altar blooms forever. The personal characteristics of the scientist can only be captured while memories are still fresh; and only then, in all honesty, are they of maximum interest and relevance.

[7] J. M. Keynes, *Essays in Persuasion* (1932), pp. 300 and 311.

In my opinion, nothing in Keynes' previous life or work really quite prepares us for the *General Theory.* In many ways his career may serve as a model and prescription for a youth who aspires to be an economist. First, he was born into an able academic family which breathed in an atmosphere of economics; his father was a distinguished scholar, but not so brilliant as to overshadow and stunt his son's growth.

He early became interested in the philosophical basis of probability theory, thus establishing his reputation early in the technical fields of mathematics and logic. The *Indian Currency and Finance* book and assiduous service as Assistant Editor and Editor of the *Economic Journal* certified to his "solidity" and scholarly craftsmanship. His early reviews, in the *Economic Journal,* of Fisher, Hobson, Mises, and of Bagehot's collected works, gave hints of the brilliance of his later literary style. The hiatus of the next few years in his scientific output is adequately explained by his service in the Treasury during the first World War.

The first extreme departure from an academic career comes, of course, with the Byronic success of the *Economic Consequences of the Peace,* which made him a world celebrity whose very visits to the Continent did not go unnoticed on the foreign exchange markets. As successful head of an insurance company and Bursar of King's College, he met the practical men of affairs on their own ground and won the reputation of being an economist who knew how to make money. All this was capped by a solid two-volume *Treatise on Money,* replete with historical accounts of the Mycenean monetary system and the rest. Being a patron of the ballet and theater, a member of the "Bloomsbury Set" of Virginia Woolf and Lytton Strachey, a Governor of the Bank of England, and peer of the realm simply put the finishing gilt on his portrait.

Why then do I say that the *General Theory* still comes as a surprise? Because in all of these there is a sequence and pattern, and no one step occasions real astonishment. The *General Theory,* however, is a mutant, notwithstanding Keynes' own expressed belief that it represents a "natural evolution" in his own line of thought. Let me turn, therefore, to his intellectual development.

As far back as his 1911 review of Irving Fisher's *Purchasing Power of Money,*[8] Keynes expressed dissatisfaction with a me-

[8] This is a characteristically "unfair" and unfavorable review, to be compared with Marshall's review of Jevons, which Keynes' biography of Mar-

chanical quantity theory of money, but we have no evidence that
he would have replaced it with anything more novel than a
Cambridge cash balance approach, amplified by a more detailed
treatment of the discount rate. All this, as he would be the first
to insist, was very much in the Marshallian oral tradition, and
represents a view not very different from that of, say, Hawtrey.

Early in life he keenly realized the obstacles to deflation in a
modern capitalistic country and the grief which this process en-
tailed. In consequence of this intuition, he came out roundly
against going back to the prewar gold parity. Others held the
same view: Rist in France, Cassel in Sweden, *et al.* He was not
alone in his insistence, from the present fashionable point of view
vastly exaggerated, that central bank discount policy might
stabilize business activity; again, compare the position of Gustav
Cassel. Despite the auspicious sentence concerning savings and
investment in its preface, the *Tract on Monetary Reform* on its
analytical side goes little beyond a quantity theory explanation
of inflation; while its policy proposals for a nationally-managed
currency and fluctuating exchange are only distinguished for their
political novelty and persuasiveness.

In all of these, there is a consistency of pattern. And in retrospect it is only fair to say that he was on the whole right. Yet this
brief account does not present the whole story. In many places,
he was wrong. Perhaps a pamphleteer should be judged shotgun
rather than rifle fashion, by his absolute hits regardless of misses;
still one must note that, even when most wrong, he is often most
confident and sure of himself.

The *Economic Consequences of the Peace* proceeds from beginning to end on a single premise which history has proved to
be false or debatable. Again, he unleashed with a flourish the
Malthusian bogey of overpopulation at a time when England
and the Western European world were undergoing a population
revolution in the opposite direction. In his controversy with Sir
William Beveridge on the terms-of-trade between industry and
agriculture, besides being wrong in principle and interpretation,
he revealed his characteristic weakness for presenting a few
hasty, but suggestive, statistics. If it can be said that he was right
in his reparations-transfer controversy with Ohlin, it is in part for
the wrong reasons—reasons which in terms of his later system are

shall tries weakly to justify. That Keynes' first publication of a few years
earlier was a criticism does not astonish us in view of his later writings.

seen to be classical as compared to the arguments of Ohlin. Again, at different times he has presented arguments to demonstrate that foreign investment is (1) deflationary, and (2) stimulating to the home economy, without appearing on either occasion to be aware of the opposing arguments.

None of these are of vital importance, but they help to give the flavor of the man. He has been at once soundboard, amplifier, and initiator of contemporary viewpoints, whose strength and weakness lie in his intuition, audaciousness, and changeability. Current quips concerning the latter trait are rather exaggerated, but they are not without provocation. It is quite in keeping with this portrait to be reminded that in the early twenties, before he had an inkling of the *General Theory*, or even the *Treatise*, he scolded Edwin Cannan in no uncertain terms for not recognizing the importance and novelty of modern beliefs as compared to old-fashioned—I might almost have said "classical"—theories.

Where a scientist is concerned, it is not inappropriate, even in a eulogy, to replace the ordinary dictum *nihil nisi bonum* by the criterion *nihil nisi verum*. In all candor, therefore, it is necessary to point out certain limitations—one might almost say weaknesses, were they not so intrinsically linked with his genius—in Keynes' thought.

Perhaps because he was exposed to economics too young, or perhaps because he arrived at maturity in the stultifying backwash of Marshall's influence upon economic theory—for whatever reason, Keynes seems never to have had any genuine interest in the theory of value and distribution. It is remarkable that so active a brain would have failed to make any contribution to economic theory; and yet except for his discussion of index numbers in Volume I of the *Treatise* and for a few remarks concerning "user cost," which are novel at best only in terminology and emphasis, he seems to have left no mark on pure theory.[9]

---

[9] Indeed, only in connection with Frank Ramsey's article on "A Mathematical Theory of Saving" (EJ, 1928) does he show interest in an esoteric theoretical problem; there he gave a rather intricate interpretation in words of a calculus-of-variations differential equation condition of equilibrium. His reasoning is all the more brilliant—and I say this seriously!—because it is mathematically unrigorous, if not wrong. The importance which Keynes attached to this article is actually exaggerated and can be accounted for only in terms of his paternal feeling toward Ramsey and his own participation in the solution of the problem. [The reader should compare Metzler's essay below on Keynes' contribution to theory—Ed.]

Just as there is internal evidence in the *Treatise on Probability* that he early tired of somewhat frustrating basic philosophic speculation, so he seems to have early tired of theory. He gladly "exchanged the tormenting exercises of the foundations of thought and of psychology, where the mind tries to catch its own tail, for the delightful paths of our own most agreeable branch of the moral sciences, in which theory and fact, intuitive imagination and practical judgment, are blended in a manner comfortable to the human intellect." (*Essays in Biography*, pp. 249–50.)

In view of his basic antipathy to economic theory, it is all the more wonder, therefore, that he was able to write a biography of Alfred Marshall which Professor Schumpeter has termed one of the best treatments of a master by a pupil.[10] Never were two temperaments more different than those of the two men, and we can be sure that the repressed Victorianism and "popish" personal mannerisms which Keynes found so worthy of reverence in a master and father would have been hardly tolerable in a contemporary.

From Marshall's early influence, no doubt, stems Keynes' antipathy toward the use of mathematical symbols, an antipathy which already appears, surprisingly considering its technical subject, in the early pages of the *Treatise on Probability*. In view of the fact that mathematical economists were later to make some of the most important contributions to Keynesian economics, his comments on them in the *General Theory* and in the Marshall and Edgeworth biographies merit rereading.[11]

Moreover, there is reason to believe that Keynes' thinking remained fuzzy on one important analytical matter throughout all his days: the relationship between "identity" and functional (or equilibrium-schedule) equality; between "virtual" and observable movements; between causality and concomitance; between tautology and hypothesis. Somewhere, I believe in his early writings, he already falls into the same analytic confusion with respect to the identity of supply and demand for foreign exchange which

[10] Keynes' discussion of Marshall's monetary theory is much better than his treatment of Marshall's contribution to theory.

[11] Keynes' critical review of Tinbergen's econometric business cycle study for the League of Nations reveals that Keynes did not really have the necessary technical knowledge to understand what he was criticizing. How else are we to interpret such remarks as his assertion that a linear system can never develop oscillations?

was later to be his stumbling-block with respect to the identity of saving and investment.

Perhaps he was always too busy with the affairs of the world to be able to devote sufficient time for repeated thinking through of certain basic problems. Certainly he was too busy to verify references ("a vain pursuit"). His famous remark that he never learned anything from reading German which he didn't already know would be greeted with incredulity in almost any other science than economics.[12] What he really meant was that his was one of those original minds which never accepts a thing as true and important unless he has already thought it through for himself. Despite his very considerable erudition in certain aspects of the history of thought, there was probably never a more ahistorical scholar than Keynes.

Finally, to fill in the last little touch in this incomplete portrait of an engaging spirit, I should like to present a characteristic quotation from Keynes:

> "In writing a book of this kind, the author must, if he is to put his point of view clearly, pretend sometimes to a little more conviction than he feels. He must give his own argument a chance, so to speak, nor be too ready to depress its vitality with a wet cloud of doubt."

Is this from the *General Theory?* No. From the *Treatise on Money* or the *Tract?* No and no. Even when writing on so technical a subject as probability, the essential make-up of the man comes through, so that no literary detective can fail to spot his spoor.

THE ROAD TO THE GENERAL THEORY

It was not unnatural for such a man as I have described to wish as he approached fifty to bring together, perhaps as a crowning life work, his intuitions concerning money. Thus the *Treatise* was born. Much of the first volume is substantial and creditable, though hardly exciting. But the fundamental equations which he

---

[12] Around 1911–1915, he was the principal reviewer of German books for EJ; also he must have read—at least he claimed to have—innumerable German works on probability. That he could not speak German with any fluency is well attested by those who heard him once open an English lecture to a German audience with a brief apology in German.

and the world considered the really novel contribution of the *Treatise* are nothing but a detour and blind alley.

The second volume is the more valuable, but it is so because of the intuitions there expressed concerning bullishness, bearishness, etc. And even these might have been prevented from coming into being by too literal an attempt to squeeze them into the mold of the fundamental equations. Fortunately, Keynes was not sufficiently systematic to carry out such a program.

Before the *Treatise* was completed, its author had already tired of it. Sir Isaac Newton is alleged to have held up publication of his theory for twenty years because of a small discrepancy in numerical calculation. Darwin hoarded his theories for decades in order to collect ever more facts. Not so with our hero: let the presses roll and throw off the grievous weight of a book unborn! Especially since a world falling to pieces is ripe to drop Pollyanna and take up with Cassandra on the rebound.

Perhaps not being systematic proved his salvation. A long line of heretics testifies that he is not the first to have tried to weld intuition into a satisfactory unified theory; not the first to have shot his bolt and failed. But few have escaped from the attempt with their intuition intact and unmarred. In an inexact subject like economics, concepts are not (psychologically) neutral. Decisions based upon ignorance or the equi-probability of the unknown are not invariant under transformation of coordinates or translation of concepts. Simply to define a concept is to reify it, to breathe life in it, to create a predisposition in favor of its constancy; viz., the falling rate of profit and the organic composition of capital, the velocity of circulation of money, the propensity to consume, and the discrepancy between saving and investment.

The danger may be illustrated by a particular instance. Shrewd Edwin Cannan, in characteristic salty prose, throughout the first World War "protested." [18] At first his insights were sharp and incisive, his judgments on the whole correct. But in the summer of 1917, to "escape from an almost unbearable personal sorrow," he undertook to set forth a *systematic* exposition of the theory of money. The transformation of Cinderella's coach at the stroke of twelve is not more sudden than the change in the quality of his thought. Here, I am not so much interested in the fact that his voice becomes shrill, his policies on the whole in retrospect bad—

[18] E. Cannan, *An Economist's Protest* (1927).

as in the fact that his intuitions were perverted and blunted by his analysis, almost in an irrecoverable way! Not so with Keynes. His constitution was able to throw off the *Treatise* and its fundamental equations.

While Keynes did much for the great depression, it is no less true that the great depression did much for him. It provided challenge, drama, experimental confirmation. He entered it the sort of man who might be expected to embrace the *General Theory* if it were explained to him. From the previous record, one cannot say more. Before it was over, he had emerged with the prize in hand, the system of thought for which he will be remembered.

Right now I do not intend to speculate in detail on the thought-process leading up to this work, but only to throw out a few hints. In the 1929 pamphlet, *Can Lloyd George do it?* written with H. D. Henderson, Keynes set up important hypotheses concerning the effects of public works and investment. It remained for R. F. Kahn, that elusive figure who hides in the prefaces of Cambridge books, to provide the substantiation in his justly famous 1931 *Economic Journal* article, "The Relation of Home Investment to Unemployment." Quite naturally the "multiplier" comes in for most attention, which is in a way too bad, since the concept often seems like nothing but a cheap-jack way of getting something for nothing and appears to carry with it a spurious numerical accuracy.

But behind lies the vitally important consumption function: giving the propensity to consume in terms of income; or looked at from the opposite side, specifying the propensity to save. With investment given, as a constant or in the schedule sense, we are in a position to set up the simplest determinate system of under-employment equilibrium—by a "Keynesian savings-investment-income cross" not formally different from the "Marshallian supply-demand-price cross."

Immediately everything falls into place: the recognition that the *attempt* to save may lower income and actually *realized* saving; the fact that a net autonomous increase in investment, foreign balance, government expenditure, consumption will result in increased income *greater* than itself, etc., etc.

Other milestones on the road to Damascus, in addition to the

Lloyd George pamphlet and the Kahn article, were Keynes' contributions to a report of the Macmillan Committee [14] and his University of Chicago Harris Foundation lectures on unemployment in the summer of 1931. In these lectures, Keynes has not quite liberated himself from the terminology of the *Treatise* (*vide* his emphasis on "profits"); but the notion of the level of income as being in equilibrium at a low level because of the necessity for savings to be equated to a depressed level of investment is worked out in detail.

From here to the *Means to Prosperity* (1933) is but a step; and from the latter to the *General Theory* but another step. From hindsight and from the standpoint of policy recommendations, each such step is small and in a sense inevitable; but from the standpoint of having stumbled upon and formulated a new system of analysis, each represents a tremendous stride.

But now I shall have to desist. My panegyric must come to an end with two conflicting quotations from the protean Lord Keynes between which the jury must decide:

> In the long run we are all dead.

> . . . The ideas of economists and political philosophers, both when they are right and when they are wrong, are more powerful than is commonly understood. Indeed, the world is ruled by little else. Practical men, who believe themselves to be quite exempt from any intellectual influences, are usually the slaves of some defunct economist. Madmen in authority, who hear voices in the air, are distilling their frenzy from some academic scribbler of a few years back. I am sure that the power of vested interests is vastly exaggerated compared with the gradual encroachment of ideas . . . Soon or late, it is ideas, not vested interests, which are dangerous for good or evil.[15]

[14] Young economists who disbelieve in the novelty of the Keynesian analysis, on the ground that no sensible person could ever have thought differently, might with profit read Hawtrey's testimony before the Macmillan Committee, contrasting it with the Kahn article and comparing it with Tooke's famous demonstration in his *History of Prices*, Volume I, that government war expenditures as such cannot possibly cause inflation—*because what the government spends would have been spent anyway, except to the extent of "new money" created.*

[15] *General Theory*, pp. 383–4.

CHAPTER XIV

The *General Theory* (4)

By GOTTFRIED HABERLER

1.

I SHALL confine myself in this essay to the purely scientific content of *The General Theory of Employment, Interest, and Money,* the most famous of Keynes' economic works, whose tenth anniversary unhappily coincided with the death of its author. In the light of ten years of intense and voluminous discussion, what remains of the Keynesian revolution, of the New Economics? What will be the verdict of a historian of economic thought one hundred years hence? There is no doubt Keynes stirred the stale economic frog pond to its depth. He has kept economists in a state of agitation for the last ten years, and probably for many years to come. The brilliance of his style, the versatility, flexibility, incredible quickness, and fecundity of his mind, the many-sidedness of his intellectual interests, the sharpness of his wit, in one word the fullness of his personality was bound to fascinate scores of people in and outside the economic profession. Only a dullard or narrow-minded fanatic could fail to be moved to admiration by Keynes' genius. But the novelty and validity of the propositions which constitute his system are a different matter altogether—quite independent of the challenging way in which he pronounced them, of the psychological stimulus afforded by his bold attack on widely accepted modes of thought, of much needed change in emphasis which we owe to his book, and of the wisdom (or unwisdom) of his policy recommendations. Apart from a few observations on alleged policy implications of the *General Theory* at the end of this paper, we shall be concerned exclusively with the logical content of the system.

2.

The tremendous appeal of the *General Theory* to theoretically-minded economists has been attributed by many to the (alleged) fact that it uses for the first time in the history of economic thought a general equilibrium approach in easily manageable, macroscopic (aggregative) terms. There is no doubt, in my opinion, that this made the theory very attractive, especially because such a system lends itself easily to refinement and dynamization. But we can safely assume that the concrete content and the policy recommendations which Keynes and others deduced from his system had even more to do with its persuasiveness (even for his theoretically-minded followers) than its theoretical beauty and simplicity.

The use of aggregative systems of general equilibrium is by no means new. All business-cycle theories run in macroscopic terms. It is true that most of the earlier business-cycle theories are incompletely stated, the number of explicitly stated relations is frequently not equal to the number of unknowns, the structure of the system is such that it is unstable (or does not oscillate, which is bad for a business-cycle theory). But even before the appearance of Keynes' *General Theory,* the work of econometricians, notably Frisch[1] and Tinbergen,[2] had done much to clarify these issues and had set higher standards of formal completeness and precision. In fact, these early models, or models of models, were superior to Keynes' system in scientific workmanship because they made a clear distinction between statics and dynamics, while Keynes' system is entirely static, as is well known (although it lends itself to dynamization).[3] Moreover, they were tentative, experimental, hypothetical, not yet frozen into a dogmatic pattern. This made them politically neutral, which, together with the fact that they were expressed in mathematical

[1] See his famous contribution to the Cassel *Festschrift,* "Propagation and Impulse Problems," 1933.

[2] For example, in "Suggestions on Quantitative Business Cycle Theory," in EC, 1935.

[3] What is strictly static in the *General Theory* is the theoretical skeleton as precisely stated in several places in the book (e.g., p. 245 *et seq.,* or p. 280 *et seq.*) and later formalized by Lange, Meade, and others. The text surrounding the theoretical statements in the *General Theory* contains, of course, many dynamic considerations. The frequent use made of the expectation concept shows the dynamic intent. But the dynamic elements are not incorporated into the theory. All the functions stated are strictly static.

terms, made them decidedly less accessible and less attractive than the Keynesian system. But there is no doubt that Keynes gave a tremendous impetus to model building, static as well as dynamic.

3.

Let us look now into the content of the system. We shall first examine the individual relationships ("functions" or "propensities") of which it is composed, and then the working of the system as a whole.

Little need be said about the marginal efficiency of capital or demand schedule for capital, because here Keynes follows conventional lines. Investment is a decreasing function of the rate of interest. In the post-Keynesian, Keynes-inspired literature, it has been more and more questioned whether the rate of interest is really such an important factor; in other words, the view has gained ground that the demand curve for capital may be fairly inelastic with respect to the rate of interest. But this is not the position of the *General Theory*, at least not of its theoretical skeleton, although Keynes in *obiter dicta* and policy recommendations frequently accepted openly or by implication the theory of lacking investment opportunities.

The liquidity preference theory of the rate of interest appeared very unorthodox and novel in 1936. The ensuing discussion has made it clear, however, that the only innovation is the assumed relationship between the rate of interest and hoarding, i.e., money held for speculative purposes (M_2) or idle deposits. (Assuming that the velocity of circulation of money, of M_1, remains the same, or if it too varies with the rate of interest, the proposition implies that the velocity of the total money stock ($M_1 + M_2$) also is positively correlated with the rate of interest.) [4] The older monetary

[4] This proposition was clearly foreshadowed in the earlier ("classical") literature. See, e.g., Lavington, *English Capital Market* (1921), p. 30. "The quantity of resources which [an individual] holds in the form of money will be such that the unit of resources which is just, and only just, worth while holding in this form yields him a return of convenience and security equal to the yield of satisfaction derived from the marginal unit spent on consumables, and equal also to the net rate of interest."

See also Pigou, "The Exchange-Value of Legal-Tender Money" in *Essays in Applied Economics* (1922), pp. 179–81. In his later, post-Keynesian writings Pigou always makes a specific assumption with respect to the policy followed by the banking system. In what he calls the "normal" case the banks act in such a way as to allow the quantity of money to rise and fall

theory assumed (more or less explicitly) that the demand for hoards is inelastic with respect to the rate of interest. Keynes assumed it to be elastic. The reasons given for this are two: (1) Hoarding is the cheaper (i.e., its opportunity cost is the lower), the lower the rate of interest; (2) the lower the rate of interest, the smaller the likelihood that it will go still lower and the greater the chance that it will rise again.[5]

The older theory was probably more realistic on this point. At any rate, cyclical and other shifts of the liquidity preference schedule are undoubtedly much more significant than its alleged negative slope. A change in the rate of interest of a few per cent, *other things being equal,* is hardly an important factor in de- termining the volume of hoards. The latter is determined pri- marily by other factors such as price expectations, general pessi- mism, temporary lack of investment opportunities, and so on.[6] It is true that some writers, e.g., Kalecki and James Tobin, have managed to compute beautiful correlations between the rate of interest, on the one hand, and the volume of idle deposits, on the other. But the reason is that both are (or until now were) the joint effect of the same cause, of the business cycle. It is quite easy, however, to imagine future ups and downs of business with-

---

with the rate of interest. (See, e.g., *Equilibrium and Employment,* p. 61.)

This latter-day Pigovian approach, institutional in nature, seems to me more realistic than the Keynesian liquidity preference theory. The latter is clearly a direct descendant of the penetratingly classical Cambridge type of quantity equation (as Hicks pointed out in his paper, "Mr. Keynes and the Classics," EC, Vol. 5, 1937), and suffers from the same weakness as its parent concept, viz., excessive utilization of a marginalistic psychology in a field where a frankly institutionalistic analysis is much more fruitful.

[5] We may, perhaps, say in Hicksian terminology: The lower the rate of interest, the smaller the elasticity of expectation of future rates.

[6] I do not deny that hoarding and changes in the velocity of circulation have been much neglected in the literature, and that it is a mistake (of omission rather than commission) to regard these phenomena as data (or as occasional disturbances) instead of explaining them systematically. The point is that the level of the rate of interest as such is a comparatively unimportant factor.

Expectations of changes in interest rates are, however, a different matter. But the state of expectation is a complicated matter, and no simple formula, such as the one suggested in the preceding footnote, can do justice to its complexity.

Professor W. Fellner in his elaborate and searching investigation of the subject reaches the conclusion "that the elasticity of liquidity provisions with respect to interest rate is not likely to be high" (*Monetary Policy and Full Employment,* Berkeley, 1946, p. 200).

out any significant changes in interest rates. I venture to predict that in such cases we shall still find idle deposits rising in the downswing and falling in the upswing, which would prove that the correlation between hoards and interest rates does not indicate a causal relationship in the sense that people hoard more when a fall in the rate of interest makes it cheaper and vice versa.

Other propositions frequently associated with Keynes' interest theory—e.g., those concerning the connection between short- and long-term rates and the alleged floor, well above zero, below which the rate of interest cannot fall—were frequently discussed in the pre-Keynesian literature.[7] But Keynes certainly improved the analysis and utilized those theorems effectively by putting them into the broader context of a general equilibrium system.

The theory of liquidity stands in great need of further elaboration. It will be necessary to distinguish a larger number of different types of assets than just money and real goods, or money, securities, and real goods. The different types of assets have to be arranged according to their liquidity, with cash on one end of the scale, certain types of finished goods on the other end, and loans, bonds, equities, raw material, etc., in between. Much work had been done along that line before the appearance of the *General Theory*[8] (and more has been done since publication of the volume), and Keynes himself contributed important elements for a comprehensive theory, especially in his *Treatise on Money*. But these refinements, indispensable though they are for a useful application of the theory to reality, were not incorporated, and were not easy to incorporate, into the body of the *General Theory* —a fact which should be kept well in mind by those who try to find empirical support for the liquidity preference theorem of the *General Theory*.[9]

[7] E.g., in I. Fisher, *The Theory of Interest* (in the third approximation of his theory), or Karin Kock, *A Study of Interest Rates* (London, 1929). See, especially, Chapter VII, "Short and Long Rates of Interest."

[8] Cf., for example, Hicks "Gleichgewicht und Konjunktur" in *Zeitschrift für Nationalökonomie*, Vol. 4, Vienna, 1933.

[9] In all attempts at verification, the liquidity preference theory is applied to the choice between (a) cash (including bank notes and deposits) and (b) the next item on the scale, viz., shortest-term securities, in other words, between (a) money and (b) near-money (i.e., money's closest substitute). For that very limited choice (i.e., the decision whether to hold one's idle funds in cash or short-term securities) the short-term rate of interest may indeed be an important factor. But that choice is an unimportant detail as far as expenditures on goods and the volume of output and employment are

We now turn to the consumption function. The idea that saving depends on the level of income—other things such as the rate of interest being equal—is an old one. Suffice to recall the fact that scores of writers made the point that inequality of the income distribution is necessary or desirable to guarantee a sufficient supply of capital, because the bulk of saving comes from the higher income brackets. Keynes' great contribution was that he strongly emphasized the income factor and used it much more systematically in the analysis of economic change than had ever been done before. It is true that the consumption function has often been overworked by Keynes and his followers; it has been too rigidly formulated and too inflexibly applied to short- as well as long-run problems without allowing for all the necessary, qualifications, such as secular shifts, cyclical fluctuations, the influence of capital gains, and other factors. But on the whole the change in emphasis toward income was needed and beneficial. The strong and exceedingly fruitful accent on income effects, which has become more and more noticeable in recent years in all branches of economics, such as price and demand analysis, international trade, etc., is largely due to Keynes. The same is true of the multiplier technique, whose usefulness should not be doubted, despite the crudity with which it is often used.

4.

Let us turn now to the interaction of the various parts and the working of the system as a whole. Even if it were true that all the materials and tools used by Keynes had been known and used before and that he did not improve them—is it not true that with their help he constructed an entirely new theoretical structure?

His demonstration that unemployment is possible in equilibrium, and his analysis of the factors determining the size and changes of employment and unemployment, are generally regarded as Keynes' most important theoretical discovery. The originality and importance of this conclusion remains unimpaired, it will be said, even if it can be demonstrated that it is derived entirely from well known premises, just as the work of a great

---

concerned. And any empirical regularities found with respect to this detail cannot be regarded as a verification of the liquidity preference theorem in a rougher model which does not distinguish a whole scale of different assets with small gradations in liquidity, but only two or three types of assets.

artist remains great even if he uses well known tools and techniques.

According to a widely held view, which can be described as a sort of simplified, popular Keynesianism,[10] the possibility of under-employment equilibrium has been denied by the "classical" school and demonstrated by Keynes. The matter, however, is not so simple as that. This becomes quite clear if we reflect upon the intricate and crucial question concerning the rôle of wage (and price) rigidity in the Keynesian system. Keynes assumes that (money) wages are rigid downward. If this assumption, which is certainly not entirely unrealistic, is rigidly adhered to, most of his conclusions follow: Under-employment equilibrium is then possible; an increase in the propensity to consume will then reduce unemployment and a decrease in the propensity to consume will produce unemployment (except if, as many classical writers assumed, the demand for idle funds, the liquidity preference proper, is wholly inelastic with respect to the rate of interest). But all this is entirely in accord with pre-Keynesian theory, although these conclusions certainly had not been generally realized and sufficiently emphasized before the appearance of the *General Theory.*

If flexible wages—"thoroughgoing competition between wage earners" (in Pigou's words)—are assumed, the situation is radically changed.[11] Obviously, under-employment equilibrium with flexible wages is impossible—wages and prices must then fall continuously, which can hardly occur without further consequences and cannot well be described as an equilibrium position.[12] This is the weak spot of the Keynesian system which is usually slurred over by the Keynesians.

[10] Unfortunately, there is much of this oversimplified version in the *General Theory* itself, especially in the three summarizing chapters in Book I. A sociology of the formation of scientific schools will attribute much importance to this fact. It helped to crystallize a compact group of followers by repelling and annoying some readers and attracting others.

[11] The crucial importance of wage rigidity in the Keynesian system has been emphasized by many critics, most systematically perhaps by Franco Modigliani in his remarkable article "Liquidity Preference and the Theory of Interest and Money," EC, January, 1944.

[12] A logical possibility would, of course, be that all money expressions (prices, wages, money values) fall continuously, while the real magnitudes including employment remain the same. That would be the implication of the assumption that the Keynesian relations remain unchanged in real terms in the face of such a situation. But this case is surely too unrealistic to be seriously contemplated.

As in many other cases, two different attempts to deal with this problem can be found in the *General Theory*. The first one, which belongs to what I called the oversimplified, popular version of Keynesianism, is stated early in the book (p. 11 *et seq.*), and has been too readily accepted by friend and foe. It simply says that when money wages fall, prices too will fall to the same extent; therefore real wages will remain unchanged, and since "an increase in employment can only occur to the accompaniment of a decline in the real rate of wages" [13] (p. 17), employment and unemployment will remain the same.

[13] Professor Hansen objects to my quoting this passage because it "fails to include the very important conditions which must be assumed to make the statement [as quoted from Keynes] true, namely, no change in 'organization, equipment and technique'; in other words, no change in productivity. Moreover, Keynes (March, 1939, EJ) explicitly repudiated the notion that employment must increase *by or through* a lowering of real wages and a movement *along* a declining so-called general demand curve for labor. In his view employment is increased by raising effective demand, thereby causing an upward *shift* in the demand curve for labor." (RES, Vol. 28, Nov., 1946, p. 185. See also Chap. XII.)

It is true Keynes did qualify his statement by the clause "with given organization, equipment, and technique" (p. 17). But in the present context the qualification is irrelevant. For in the short run (and the problem under discussion is essentially a short-run problem) Keynes always assumes "organization, equipment, and technique" constant. In EJ, March, 1939, Keynes took issue with Dunlop's and Tarshis' criticism; he there was very reluctant to give up his generalization. "I still hold," he said, "to the main structure of the argument, and believe that it needs to be amended rather than discarded" (p. 40). He tried to reconcile Dunlop's and Tarshis' findings with his theory *without* dropping the assumption of constant organization, equipment, and technique.

It is, of course, true that according to Keynes "employment is increased by raising effective demand," but he thought (with certain tentative qualifications as enumerated in the quoted article) that, by a rise in effective demand, prices are necessarily raised more and faster than money wages, and that therefore a rise in effective demand is always associated (in the short run) with a fall in real wage rates.

Keynes' reluctance to drop this hypothesis is understandable because a change of view would have required far-reaching modifications of his whole theoretical structure. He, after all, had emphasized that he was "not disputing this vital fact which the classical economists have (rightly) asserted as indefeasible" (*General Theory*, p. 17). He had argued emphatically that, if workers could effectively bargain about real wages rather than merely about money wages, unemployment could always be eliminated by wage bargains at lower wages. The disputed proposition is, thus, deeply embedded in Keynes' theory.

I personally always felt that Keynes' dogmatic insistence on the proposi-

This solution is obviously unsatisfactory and should not be regarded as Keynes' last word. This becomes clear if we consider the solution consistent with the system as a whole which can be found in Chapter 19. There it is pointed out that a reduction in money wages will usually influence employment, but in an indirect fashion, through its repercussions upon the propensity to consume, efficiency of capital, or the rate of interest. The last-mentioned route, via the interest rate, is the one most thoroughly explored by Keynes and the Keynesians. As wages and prices are allowed to fall, money is released from the transactions sphere, interest rates fall, and full employment is eventually restored by a stimulation of investment. This amounts to giving up the idea of under-employment equilibrium under a regime of flexible prices and wages except in two limiting cases: Full employment may be prevented from being reached via this route, (a) if the liquidity trap prevents a fall in the rate of interest—that is to say, if the liquidity preference schedule is infinitely elastic, i.e., if people are willing to hoard unlimited amounts of money at a positive rate of interest—or (b) if investment is quite insensitive to a fall in the interest rate. Keynes himself regarded both these situations not as actually existing but as future possibilities. But what if we do regard them as actually existing—which as a short-run proposition, allowing for dynamic disturbances through unfavorable expectations, etc., would be by no means absurd? We would still not have established a stable under-employment equilibrium, for wages and prices would still continue to fall. The truth is that what would happen in this case cannot be told within the Keynesian framework, and Keynes himself would have been the last one to stick to it through thick and thin.[14] We must assume that some of the Keynesian schedules would shift. The

tion in question was due to the excessively static nature of his theory. If Keynes had incorporated swings of optimism and pessimism in his theory, he would have had no difficulties in admitting that an expansion can raise not only money but also real wages (even in the short run, i.e., with organization, equipment, and technique unchanged). The plain fact is that Keynes' theory is not only more static but in several respects also more "classical" than, for example, Pigou's *Industrial Fluctuations,* where it had been pointed out that "the upper halves of trade cycles have, on the whole, been associated with higher rates of real wages than the lower halves." (1929 edition, p. 238.)

[14] See the following paragraph, and footnotes 16 and 17 below.

most obvious hypothesis would seem to be that the consumption function will shift upward, because of the accumulation of liquid reserves.[15] For we must assume, it seems to me, that consumption is not only a function of income but also of wealth (and liquid wealth in particular) and of other factors which we need not discuss here and which are in fact indicated in the *General Theory* (cf. Chapters 8 and 9). A similar argument would seem to hold for the investment function.

Such extensions and modifications of the Keynesian system are entirely in keeping with Keynes' own injunction against dogmatically treating any such system as rigid and sacrosanct. He warns us that the determinant relations and magnitudes of his own system (i.e., the three propensities, the quantity of money, and the wage unit) are "complex, and that each is capable of being affected by prospective changes in the other";[16] he says

[15] If wages and prices fall, the real value of the money stock will increase beyond all limits. I called attention to this fact and its probable effect on consumption in the first edition of my *Prosperity and Depression* (1937) without then using the term "propensity to consume." Pigou has since stressed it repeatedly. Kalecki in his brief note, "Professor Pigou on the Classical Stationary State—A Comment" (EJ, April, 1944, p. 131), in principle conceded the argument that a rise in the real value of the money stock will act as a stabilizer in a period of falling prices. He makes, however, the point that this argument applies only to gold and bank notes which are not issued by the banks through making loans or through purchases of private securities; for in the case of bank money issued against loans and private securities, the rise in the real value of money is canceled by the rise in the real value of the corresponding bank assets (loans and securities) which are liabilities of the public. (The net worth of the public is, therefore, not increased by the fall in the price level.)

However, as long as there is money which is not issued against private evidences of indebtedness, Kalecki's argument is invalid from the theoretical point of view, because *money* wages and prices (*note*: real wages need not fall) can always fall sufficiently to raise the real value of gold money to any level necessary, however small the (dollar) value of gold or gold certificates in circulation.

From a practical point of view, however (i.e., taking account of frictions, disturbances through expectations, etc., which are assumed away in the pure model), Kalecki's argument is important. But I need not go into that, because I believe (and I think this is also Pigou's view; cf. the Preface to his *Lapses from Full Employment*) that the model under consideration is much too simplified to be useful for practical application. (See next paragraph in the text.) It should be observed that the simplifications are essentially the Keynesian ones.

[16] *General Theory*, p. 184. What is said of *prospective* changes naturally holds also of the *actual* level and *actual* changes.

that only "sometimes" (meaning, obviously, in certain context and over limited ranges) can they be regarded as "ultimate independent variables." [17]

It should be clear, however, that even with these modifications the theory is still much too rough for direct application and must be further elaborated and supplemented before it can be used, even in a tentative fashion, for the explanation of reality. In the short run, dynamic repercussions (unfavorable expectations, disturbances caused by bankruptcies and credit crises, etc.) must be taken into consideration. Pigou was probably right when he insisted that in a cyclical depression negative wages and prices frequently would be necessary to prevent unemployment altogether or to eliminate it quickly once it appeared. [18] The situation in the long run is radically different. Unfavorable expectations and credit crises do not last forever, disturbances caused by bankruptcies disappear, and the assumption of an infinitely elastic liquidity preference and entirely inelastic marginal efficiency of capital schedule is hardly tenable as a long-run proposition. But most economists will agree that it is not only politically easier but also economically more desirable, in the long run as well as in the short, to bring about the saturation of the economy with liquid funds (if required) by increasing the quantity of money rather than by raising its value through a fall in prices. The reasons for and against that proposition (such as rigidity of long-term money contracts, avoidance of industrial disputes, and unjust and undesirable changes in the income distribution, etc.) are the same ones that were discussed extensively in the literature on money throughout the nineteenth century and later in connection with the problem of whether in a progressive economy it is better to let prices fall or to keep them stable. [19] Therefore, the

[17] *Ibid.*, pp. 246–47. Cf. also p. 297.
[18] See, e.g., his *Industrial Fluctuations*, 2nd ed. 1929, p. 225.
[19] The older literature which dealt with these questions under various guises and in outmoded terminologies is extensively reviewed in C. M. Walsh, *The Fundamental Problems of Monetary Science* (New York, 1903). In the present case the argument for increasing the quantity of money and holding the price level constant is, of course, much stronger than in the historical case mentioned, because in the present case all prices (including factor prices) would have to fall, while in the other case it was for the most part a question of keeping factor prices stable and letting product prices fall *vs.* keeping product prices stable and letting factor prices rise. But the point is that many of the arguments used there are relevant for the present case too.

question ought not to constitute an issue between Keynesians and non-Keynesians.

One last word on this important subject. There is nothing in the Keynesian theory to exclude a more direct influence of wage reductions on employment. We stated above that according to Keynes this influence works via repercussions upon the consumption function, marginal efficiency of capital, and the liquidity preference (the rate of interest). In the preceding pages, we discussed the last route. But it is clearly possible that consumption and investment might be affected more directly by a reduction in wages. A reduction in the cost of certain consumption or investment goods may well stimulate demand for them, and for consumption and investment as a whole. Is it not possible that more roads, houses, hospitals, will be built when construction cost is reduced, or that the demand for certain private consumption goods will rise when their price falls? [19a] Assume, to make it quite simple, that the elasticity of demand for some of those things, and therefore indirectly for labor, is unity.[20] Then the wage bill remains unchanged and there are no adverse effects through a fall in consumption demand of the workers. Then employment will clearly rise. In Keynesian language we shall have to say that the marginal efficiency of capital schedule or the consumption function has gone up (which one depending upon whether the newly produced goods or installations are regarded as consumption or investment goods), and that it is this shift which has brought about the increase in employment.

One may, of course, be more or less optimistic or pessimistic concerning such favorable direct influences.[21] Keynes' theory certainly does not exclude them.

[19a] It can hardly be denied that it is possible to raise construction cost of houses, etc. (to mention a much discussed case) to such an extent that the demand for houses is seriously restricted. It obviously follows from this proposition that a reduction of such cost (brought about by elimination of monopolistic and restrictive practices on the part of labor and contractors, etc.) may stimulate demand for homes (investment). It is generally assumed that cost reducing innovations (e.g., prefabrication of houses) can stimulate investment. Why should then a reduction of labor costs not be capable of bringing about the same result?

[20] If the elasticity of demand is not unity, we get a much more complicated situation, which cannot be discussed here. But much of the argument could be adapted to fit that case.

[21] It is true, Keynes calls such influences "roundabout repercussions" (p. 257) and criticizes older writers for assuming a "direct" effect of wage re-

5.

The gist of the foregoing discussion may be briefly restated from a different point of view or rather (for it amounts to nothing more) in terms of a different economic jargon. I take Paul Sweezy's brilliant obituary note on Keynes as my text.[22] Sweezy regards as the basis of the Keynesian system, and of Keynes' criticism of classical economics, the "flat rejection and denial of what has come to be known as Say's Law of Markets which, despite all assertions to the contrary by orthodox apologists, did run like a red thread through the entire body of classical and neo-classical theory. It is almost impossible to exaggerate either the hold which Say's Law exercised on professional economists or its importance as an obstacle to realistic analysis. The Keynesian attacks, though they appear to be directed against a variety of specific theories, all fall to the ground if the validity of Say's Law is assumed."[23]

What is the content of Say's Law? After the early statements of the Law by the old classical writers, the subject has become so confused by criticism and defense that neo-classical writers only rarely make use of, or allusion to, it. But I think that a careful perusal of Ricardo's formulation (which is quoted by Sweezy) should make it clear what the original meaning of Say's Law was. The passage reads as follows: "No man produces but with a view to consume or sell, and he never sells but with an intention to purchase some other commodity which may be useful to him, or which may contribute to future production. By producing then, he necessarily becomes either the consumer of his own goods, or the purchaser and consumer of the goods of some other person. . . . Productions are always bought by productions, or by services; money is only the medium by which the exchange is effected."[24]

---

ductions on employment. But, as I pointed out in my *Prosperity and Depression* (2nd or later editions, p. 241), what to call direct or indirect is a purely terminological question. The most direct effect imaginable Keynes calls "roundabout" because, by definition of the terms, it must imply a change in the propensity to consume or in the marginal efficiency of capital.

[22] *Science and Society*, Vol. X, 1946, pp. 396–406. See also Part One above.

[23] *Loc. cit.*, pp. 400–1.

[24] *Principles of Political Economy* (Gonner ed.), pp. 273 and 275. The following quotation from Say clearly conveys the same meaning: ". . . a product is no sooner created than it, from that instant, affords a market for

The meaning of this original formulation of this law seems. to me quite clear: It states that income received is always spent on consumption or investment; in other words, money is never hoarded, the money or expenditure stream, *MV* (in some sense), remains constant or, in still other terminology, money remains "neutral." (Note how clearly the last sentence in Ricardo's passage foreshadows what a hundred years later became known as "neutral money.")

If this straightforward, monetary meaning of the law is firmly kept in mind (which is not easy because of the *hocus pocus* accumulated over the years in later classical and anticlassical writings on the subject) two conclusions are obvious: First, Say's Law does not hold in reality; every depression is a proof to the contrary. Second, hardly any neo-classical economist who ever wrote on money or the business cycle thought that Say's Law did hold in reality. The major theme of their theories of money, interest, and the business cycle, is to analyze the causes and consequences of changes in the "intrinsic" or "extrinsic" value of money, of deviations of the money rate of interest from the equilibrium rate, and of other "aberrations from monetary neutrality," which are all different expressions for deviations of reality from the ideal state as postulated in Say's Law.

A few neo-classical writers, rather naively, attributed such deviations entirely to the wickedness or incompetence of those in charge of monetary policy, but many, and as time went on more and more, of them realized that these deviations are deeply rooted in the structure of the capitalist system and cannot be easily prevented or cured by slight changes in monetary policy.

---

other products to the full extent of its own value. When the producer has put the finishing hand to his product, he is most anxious to sell it immediately, lest its value should vanish in his hands. Nor is he less anxious to dispose of the money he may get for it; for the value of the money is also perishable. But the only way of getting rid of money is in the purchase of some product or other. Thus the mere circumstance of the creation of one product immediately opens a vent for other products." Jean-B. Say (*Treatise on Political Economy*, Prinsep edition, Boston, 1921.) In later editions, Say obscured and attenuated the original meaning more and more through his attempts to meet criticisms by Malthus and Sismondi. He was forced to redefine the terms until the whole proposition became an empty tautology. See, for a brief account, P. N. Rosenstein-Rodan, "A Co-ordination of the Theories of Money and Price," *Economica*, 1936, pp. 268–9; and H. Neisser, "General Overproduction: A Study of Say's Law of Markets," JPE, Vol. 42, 1934, reprinted with revisions in *Readings in Business Cycle Theory* (1944), pp. 385 *et seq.*

Some recent neo-classical writers like Hicks and Rosenstein[25] went so far as to deny the compatibility of money and static equilibrium altogether.

Our conclusion, thus, is that there is no place and no need for Say's Law in modern economic theory and that it has been completely abandoned by neo-classical economists in their actual theoretical and practical work on money and the business cycle. That should be clear to anyone who is interested in living science (theoretical as well as realistic) and knows how to distinguish it from verbal squabbles and historical reminiscences in which economists so often indulge. The question must still be asked, however, why Say's Law was more often silently dropped rather than openly repudiated. Why did some older writers (especially Say and J. S. Mill), after having been forced to emasculate the law and to make it tautological, still pay lip service to it?

Liberal prejudices, the inability to rid oneself entirely of the assumption of a pre-established harmony of interests, were undoubtedly a factor, but it would be a bit too crude and naïve to rely on this factor.[26] There is a perfectly good scientific explanation (as against a superficial explanation in terms of ideological prejudices) for the lingering doubt concerning Say's Law, the reluctance of some to repudiate it openly and the occasional attempts to uphold it in some rarefied (non-monetary) form.[26a] The reason is the difficulty, upon which I commented above, of reconciling a competitive system with the existence of unemployment. This difficulty has, as we have shown, not been solved by Keynes.

Summing up, we may say there was no need for Keynes to rid

[25] Even Hayek should be mentioned here. This becomes clear if we reflect that the extremely complicated nature of a monetary system which is neutral in his sense makes the existence of neutral money in practice utterly impossible.

[26] Very sophisticated writers whom it would be utterly absurd to accuse as capitalist or orthodox apologetics (especially inasmuch as they are often on the other side of the fence as far as their political convictions are concerned) have been attracted by the intricacies of the problem and have refrained from rejecting Say's Law out of hand. Cf., for example, the articles by Neisser and Rosenstein-Rodan mentioned above and some of the literature there quoted.

[26a] Something like the following formulation is probably in the back of the minds of many writers: Any amount of money expenditures, however small, can buy any volume of goods offered for sale, provided prices are flexible and are low enough. This is obviously an arithmetic truism which cannot be denied, but is not very useful.

neo-classical economics of Say's Law in the original, straight-forward sense, for it had been completely abandoned long ago. Keynes was unable, on the other hand, to solve the riddle of how to reconcile competition and unemployment which is at the root of some remaining qualms about the matter in the mind of some writers.

6.

We thus reach the conclusion that, as far as the logical content of Keynes' theory goes, i.e., apart from his judgment of the typical shape of the various functions and of concrete situations and apart from policy recommendations, no revolution has taken place; the *General Theory* marks a milestone, albeit a conspicuous one, but not a break or a new beginning in the development of economic theory. The impression to the contrary stems from two sources: The first is excessive and untenable claims made by Keynes and his followers (and accepted too readily at their face value by many of his critics)—claims which are based on an over-simplification of the Keynesian system itself [27] as well as misrepresentations and misinterpretations of the "classical" doctrine.[28]

The second source is differences in policy recommendations. However, if the preceding analysis is correct, differences about policy cannot logically be explained by basic theoretical disagreement but must be explained by different judgments concerning concrete situations, administrative efficiency, the possibility of rational policy making and, perhaps most important, by different attitudes concerning the broad issues of government intervention

[27] For example, the proposition that in the Keynesian system the rate of interest is independent of the marginal efficiency of capital and the propensity to save. Or the misconceptions concerning the rôle of the assumption of rigid wages.

[28] For example, the proposition, which is closely connected with the misconception of the rôle of wage rigidity in the Keynesian system, that there is no room for "involuntary" unemployment in the "classical" system. Another misconception is the view that classical economics assumed that an act of saving always brings about a corresponding act of investment, while in the Keynesian system the two types of decisions are independent of each other, although aggregate saving and investment are equalized *ex-post* by appropriate changes in income. In reality, the neo-classical literature, especially its Wicksellian branch, stressed the fact that new saving *may* fail to induce new investments, with a consequent fall in money income and usually also in real income.

and central planning versus *laissez faire*. It follows from our analysis that specific policy recommendations derivable from the Keynesian system are not at all revolutionary. They are in fact very conservative. *Laissez faire* liberals, like Michael Polanyi,[29] who wish to conserve free enterprise and freedom of consumer choice, are entirely justified in their enthusiastic acceptance of the Keynesian doctrine.[30]

A few words of justification are needed, because fairly radical proposals for equalizing income distribution, and for direct control of investment and the location of industry, have been made under the Keynesian flag, by Beveridge and his group, for example. •

In fact, as far as policy recommendations are concerned, we may distinguish two wings of the Keynesian School, a radical, interventionist or even socialistic one to which many of the younger Keynesians belong, and a liberal wing represented by John Jewkes, Polanyi, McCord Wright, and A. P. Lerner (and many others who do not count as Keynesians because, although acknowledging their debt to Keynes, they do not believe that the continuity of development of economic thought has been interrupted by the appearance of the *General Theory*). There are good reasons to believe that at the bottom of his heart Keynes himself belonged to the liberal wing of his school, especially in later years when, after what must have looked to him a victorious battle for the acceptance of his views, he regained some perspective. Even during the years immediately after the appearance of the *General Theory*, when he was carried away by his enthusiasm, he never went all the way in accepting socialism or even anything like Beveridge's radical proposal, although in the heat of the battle against hostile critics he said things that seem to give comfort to his radical followers.

But whatever his real attitude was, my point is that the radical schemes hitched to the Keynesian bandwagon have nothing to do, logically speaking, with the *General Theory*. From the point of view of the *General Theory*, what is needed to prevent mass

[29] See his *Full Employment and Free Trade* (Cambridge, 1945).

[30] As a chemist, Mr. Polanyi can be pardoned for overlooking the fact that his conclusions could have been derived from economic principles widely accepted before the appearance of the *General Theory* (which, of course, does not mean that those conclusions were *generally* accepted before Keynes).

unemployment is monetary policy and, at the most, a mild form of fiscal policy. Monetary policy would be sufficient, in most cases at least, if the monetary authorities were prepared to extend the scope of their operations, as Keynes proposed, to purchases and sales of long dated securities or possibly equities. If fiscal policy is required, it need not imply increased government expenditures and extended government activities; it could be of the milder, less interventionist form of varying revenues and thus, when necessary, creating a deficit by tax reduction instead of by public works.

I do not wish to say, nor did Keynes ever claim, that such policies would insure literally full employment all the time (much less that they would cure all economic ills and injustices). It can be argued, and I am sure Keynes would have agreed (perhaps he actually said so somewhere), that for quick results in a cyclical depression well directed increases in government expenditure (public works) would be needed in addition to tax remissions. This does not follow, however, from the *General Theory* but from supplementary assumptions about labor mobility and the distribution of productive resources among industries and localities, compared with the distribution of aggregate expenditure among types of goods and services. Let us not forget that the *General Theory* runs in broad, aggregative terms and is therefore precluded from dealing, and is not designed to deal, with sectional unemployment, which is the result of faulty allocation of resources or of shifts in demand. It is meant to deal only with general mass unemployment resulting from a deficiency in *aggregate* effective demand (deflation). Its author clearly assumed that all other problems would take care of themselves, if only aggregate effective demand was kept on an even keel or raised when necessary, for example when the wage and price level is pushed up by monopolistic and restrictive policies of aggressive trade unions or other pressure groups.

This is certainly a much too optimistic view. Keynes and most Keynesians (especially Beveridge) underestimate, it seems to me, the possible magnitude of frictional unemployment (people on the way from one job to the other) and structural unemployment (unemployed workers in special depressed areas and industries) which, unlike general (i.e., well dispersed) unemployment, cannot be cured by merely manipulating aggregate demand. They fail to realize, or at least to realize fully, the enormous difficulties, or almost impossibility in the kind of "free society" as we today know it in the western world, to restrain labor monopolies from pushing up wages and thus forcing a rise in prices whenever full employment is approached or even long before that point, in consequence of which unemployment becomes necessary to prevent inflation.[31] Socialist economists like Professors Myrdal[32] and Pigou[33] have seen this problem much more clearly than the Keynesians.

But all this is a matter of judgment about the operation of certain social forces. Although crucially important, it does not involve the principles of the *General Theory*.

7.

What has been said in these pages is not intended to detract from Keynes' claim to subjective originality or to belittle his many genuine and ingenious innovations, both in substance and emphasis, or to play down the obvious fact that the *General Theory* has exerted a tremendously stimulating influence on economic thinking. Not only did Keynes inspire a large and growing group of enthusiastic and highly competent followers, especially among the younger generation of economists, but he also spurred on to clarifying and creative work many of those who at first received the *General Theory* with suspicion and skepticism. Keynes forced them to think through things which they used to leave in an ambiguous twilight, and to draw from accepted premises conclusions of which they were unaware or which they left discreetly unexpressed. A classical treatise like Pigou's monumental work, *Equilibrium and Employment* (which is so much more general than the *General Theory* that the latter by comparison appears

[31] I do not say that historically all depressions have come about for this reason. I only say that if it were possible to stabilize aggregate demand and to prevent depressions arising from other causes, the factor mentioned in the text would make it very hard to maintain full employment for some length of time.

[32] Cf. *Monetary Equilibrium* (1939), esp. pp. 143–147 and 155–156.

[33] *Lapses from Full Employment* (1945), *passim*. See also the illuminating review of Pigou's book by Professor Hicks, EJ, Dec., 1945, pp. 398–401. Professor Hicks seems substantially to accept Pigou's conclusions, although he finds them "sour."

as a very special case),[34] would never have been written without the Keynesian challenge, although it is not in contradiction to, but rather constitutes a clarification of, Pigou's own pre-Keynesian, "classical" position.

[34] The superiority of Pigou's great work has been recognized by so Keynesian a critic as N. Kaldor (EJ, December, 1941). It is a pity that another work of outstanding originality and scholarship which was stimulated by Keynes' challenge, viz. A. W. Marget's *The Theory of General Prices* (1938–42), has not yet exerted the influence which it should have.

CHAPTER XV

The General Theory (5)

By J. M. KEYNES

1.

I AM MUCH indebted to the Editors of the *Quarterly Journal* for the four contributions relating to my *General Theory of Employment, Interest and Money* which appeared in the issue for November, 1936. They contain detailed criticisms, much of which I accept and from which I hope to benefit. There is nothing in Professor Taussig's comment with which I disagree. Mr. Leontief is right, I think, in the distinction he draws between my attitude and that of the "orthodox" theory to what he calls the "homogeneity postulate." I should have thought, however, that there was abundant evidence from experience to contradict this postulate; and that, in any case, it is for those who make a highly special assumption to justify it, rather than for one who dispenses with it to prove a general negative. I would also suggest that his idea might be applied more fruitfully and with greater theoretical precision in connection with the part played by the quantity of money in determining the rate of interest. For it is here, I think, that the homogeneity postulate primarily enters into the orthodox theoretical scheme.[1]

My differences, such as they are, from Mr. Robertson chiefly arise out of my conviction that both he and I differ more fundamentally from our predecessors than his piety will allow. With many of his points I agree, without, however, being conscious in several instances of having said (or, anyhow, meant) anything different. I am surprised he should think that those who make sport with the velocity of the circulation of money have much in

---

[1] Cf. my paper on "The Theory of the Rate of Interest," to appear in the volume of essays in honor of Irving Fisher.

common with the theory of the multiplier. I fully agree with the important point he makes (pp. 180–183) that the increased demand for money resulting from an increase in activity has a back-wash which tends to raise the rate of interest; and this is, indeed, a significant element in my theory of why booms carry within them the seeds of their own destruction. But this is, essentially, a part of the liquidity theory of the rate of interest, and not of the "orthodox" theory. Where he states (p. 183) that my theory must be regarded "not as a refutation of a common-sense account of events in terms of supply and demand for loanable funds, but as an alternative version of it," I must ask, before agreeing, for at least one reference to where this common-sense account is to be found.

There remains the most important of the four comments, namely, Professor Viner's. In regard to his criticisms of my definition and treatment of involuntary unemployment, I am ready to agree that this part of my book is particularly open to criticism. I already feel myself in a position to make improvements, and I hope that, when I do so, Professor Viner will feel more content, especially as I do not think that there is anything fundamental between us here. In the case of his second section, however, entitled "The Propensity to Hoard," I am prepared to debate his points. There are passages which suggest that Professor Viner is thinking too much in the more familiar terms of the quantity of money actually hoarded, and that he overlooks the emphasis I seek to place on the rate of interest as being the inducement *not* to hoard. It is precisely because the facilities for hoarding are strictly limited that liquidity mainly operates by increasing the rate of interest. I cannot agree that "in modern monetary theory the propensity to hoard is generally dealt with, with results which in kind are substantially identical with Keynes', as a factor operating to reduce the 'velocity' of money." On the contrary, I am convinced that the monetary theorists who try to deal with it in this way are altogether on the wrong track.[2] Again, when Professor Viner points out that most people invest their savings at the best rate of interest they can get and asks for statistics to justify the importance I attach to liquidity-preference, he is overlooking the point that it is the *marginal* potential hoarder who has to be satisfied by the rate of interest, so as to bring the desire for actual hoards within the narrow limits of the cash avail-

[2] See below.

able for hoarding. When, as happens in a crisis, liquidity-preferences are sharply raised, this shows itself not so much in increased hoards—for there is little, if any, more cash which is hoardable than there was before—as in a sharp rise in the rate of interest, i.e., securities fall in price until those, who would now like to get liquid if they could do so at the previous price, are persuaded to give up the idea as being no longer practicable on reasonable terms. A rise in the rate of interest is a means *alternative* to an increase of hoards for satisfying an increased liquidity-preference. Nor is my argument affected by the admitted fact that different types of assets satisfy the desire for liquidity in different degrees. The mischief is done when the rate of interest corresponding to the degree of liquidity of a given asset leads to a market-capitalization of that asset which is less than its cost of production.

There are other criticisms also which I should be ready to debate. But though I might be able to justify my own language, I am anxious not to be led, through doing so in too much detail, to overlook the substantial points which may, nevertheless, underlie the reactions which my treatment has produced in the minds of my critics. I am more attached to the comparatively simple fundamental ideas which underlie my theory than to the particular forms in which I have embodied them, and I have no desire that the latter should be crystallized at the present stage of the debate. If the simple basic ideas can become familiar and acceptable, time and experience and the collaboration of a number of minds will discover the best way of expressing them. I would, therefore, prefer to occupy such further space, as the Editor of this *Journal* can allow me, in trying to re-express some of these ideas, than in detailed controversy which might prove barren. And I believe that I shall effect this best, even though this may seem to some as plunging straight off into the controversial mood from which I purport to seek escape, if I put what I have to say in the shape of a discussion as to certain definite points where I seem to myself to be most clearly departing from previous theories.

2.

It is generally recognized that the Ricardian analysis was concerned with what we now call long-period equilibrium. Marshall's contribution mainly consisted in grafting on to this the marginal principle and the principle of substitution, together with some discussion of the passage from one position of long-period equilibrium to another. But he assumed, as Ricardo did, that the amounts of the factors of production in use were given and that the problem was to determine the way in which they would be used and their relative rewards. Edgeworth and Professor Pigou and other later and contemporary writers have embroidered and improved this theory by considering how different peculiarities in the shapes of the supply functions of the factors of production would affect matters, what will happen in conditions of monopoly and imperfect competition, how far social and individual advantage coincide, what are the special problems of exchange in an open system, and the like. But these more recent writers like their predecessors were still dealing with a system in which the amount of the factors employed was given and the other relevant facts were known more or less for certain. This does not mean that they were dealing with a system in which change was ruled out, or even one in which the disappointment of expectation was ruled out. But at any given time facts and expectations were assumed to be given in a definite and calculable form; and risks, of which, though admitted, not much notice was taken, were supposed to be capable of an exact actuarial computation. The calculus of probability, though mention of it was kept in the background, was supposed to be capable of reducing uncertainty to the same calculable status as that of certainty itself; just as in the Benthamite calculus of pains and pleasures or of advantage and disadvantage, by which the Benthamite philosophy assumed men to be influenced in their general ethical behavior.

Actually, however, we have, as a rule, only the vaguest idea of any but the most direct consequences of our acts. Sometimes we are not much concerned with their remoter consequences, even though time and chance may make much of them. But sometimes we are intensely concerned with them, more so, occasionally, than with the immediate consequences. Now of all human activities which are affected by this remoter preoccupation, it happens that one of the most important is economic in character, namely, wealth. The whole object of the accumulation of wealth is to produce results, or potential results, at a comparatively distant, and sometimes at an *indefinitely* distant, date. Thus the fact that our knowledge of the future is fluctuating, vague, and uncertain, renders wealth a peculiarly unsuitable subject for the methods of the classical economic theory. This theory might work very well in a world in which economic goods were necessarily consumed within a short interval of their being produced. But it requires, I suggest, considerable amendment if it is to be applied to a world in which the accumulation of wealth for an indefinitely postponed future is an important factor; and the greater the proportionate part played by such wealth-accumulation the more essential does such amendment become.

By "uncertain" knowledge, let me explain, I do not mean merely to distinguish what is known for certain from what is only probable. The game of roulette is not subject, in this sense, to uncertainty; nor is the prospect of a Victory Bond being drawn. Or, again, the expectation of life is only slightly uncertain. Even the weather is only moderately uncertain. The sense in which I am using the term is that in which the prospect of a European war is uncertain, or the price of copper and the rate of interest twenty years hence, or the obsolescence of a new invention, or the position of private wealth-owners in the social system in 1970. About these matters there is no scientific basis on which to form any capable probability whatever. We simply do not know. Nevertheless, the necessity for action and for decision compels us as practical men to do our best to overlook this awkward fact and to behave exactly as we should if we had behind us a good Benthamite calculation of a series of prospective advantages and disadvantages, each multiplied by its appropriate probability, waiting to be summed.

How do we manage in such circumstances to behave in a manner which saves our faces as rational economic men? We have devised for the purpose a variety of techniques, of which much the most important are the three following:

(1) We assume that the present is a much more serviceable guide to the future than a candid examination of past experience would show it to have been hitherto. In other words we largely ignore the prospect of future changes about the actual character of which we know nothing.

(2) We assume that the *existing* state of opinion as expressed in prices and the character of existing output is based on a *correct* summing up of future prospects, so that we can accept it as such unless and until something new and relevant comes into the picture.

(3) Knowing that our own individual judgment is worthless, we endeavor to fall back on the judgment of the rest of the world, which is perhaps better informed. That is, we endeavor to conform with the behavior of the majority or the average. The psychology of a society of individuals each of whom is endeavoring to copy the others leads to what we may strictly term a *conventional* judgment.

Now a practical theory of the future based on these three principles has certain marked characteristics. In particular, being based on so flimsy a foundation, it is subject to sudden and violent changes. The practice of calmness and immobility, of certainty and security, suddenly breaks down. New fears and hopes will, without warning, take charge of human conduct. The forces of disillusion may suddenly impose a new cónventional basis of valuation. All these pretty, polite techniques, made for a well-panelled board room and a nicely regulated market, are liable to collapse. At all times the vague panic fears and equally vague and unreasoned hopes are not really lulled and lie but a little way below the surface.

Perhaps the reader feels that this general philosophical disquisition on the behavior of mankind is somewhat remote from the economic theory under discussion. But I think not. Though this is how we behave in the market place, the theory we devise in the study of how we behave in the market place should not itself submit to market-place idols. I accuse the classical economic theory of being itself one of these pretty, polite techniques which tries to deal with the present by abstracting from the fact that we know very little about the future.

I daresay that a classical economist would readily admit this. But, even so, I think he has overlooked the precise nature of the difference which his abstraction makes between theory and practice, and the character of the fallacies into which he is likely to be led.

This is particularly the case in his treatment of money and interest. And our first step must be to elucidate more clearly the functions of money.

Money, it is well known, serves two principal purposes. By acting as a money of account, it facilitates exchanges without its being necessary that it should ever itself come into the picture as a substantive object. In this respect it is a convenience which is devoid of significance or real influence. In the second place, it is a store of wealth. So we are told, without a smile on the face. But in the world of the classical economy, what an insane use to which to put it! For it is a recognized characteristic of money as a store of wealth that it is barren; whereas practically every other form of storing wealth yields some interest or profit. Why should anyone outside a lunatic asylum wish to use money as a store of wealth?

Because, partly on reasonable and partly on instinctive grounds, our desire to hold money as a store of wealth is a barometer of the degree of our distrust of our own calculations and conventions concerning the future. Even though this feeling about money is itself conventional or instinctive, it operates, so to speak, at a deeper level of our motivation. It takes charge at the moments when the higher, more precarious conventions have weakened. The possession of actual money lulls our disquietude; and the premium which we require to make us part with money is the measure of the degree of our disquietude.

The significance of this characteristic of money has usually been overlooked; and in so far as it has been noticed, the essential nature of the phenomenon has been misdescribed. For what has attracted attention has been the *quantity* of money which has been hoarded; and importance has been attached to this because it has been supposed to have a direct proportionate effect on the price-level through affecting the velocity of circulation. But the *quantity* of hoards can only be altered either if the total quantity of money is changed or if the quantity of current money-income (I speak broadly) is changed; whereas fluctuations in the degree of confidence are capable of having quite a different effect, namely, in modifying not the amount that is actually hoarded, but the amount of the premium which has to be offered to induce people not to hoard. And changes in the propensity to hoard, or in the state of liquidity-preference as I have called it, primarily affect, not prices, but the rate of interest; any effect on prices being produced by repercussion as an ultimate consequence of a change in the rate of interest.

This, expressed in a very general way, is my theory of the rate of interest. The rate of interest obviously measures—just as the books on arithmetic say it does—the premium which has to be offered to induce people to hold their wealth in some form other than hoarded money. The quantity of money and the amount of it required in the active circulation for the transaction of current business (mainly depending on the level of money-income) determine how much is available for inactive balances, i.e., for hoards. The rate of interest is the factor which adjusts at the margin the demand for hoards to the supply of hoards.

Now let us proceed to the next stage of the argument. The owner of wealth, who has been induced not to hold his wealth in the shape of hoarded money, still has two alternatives between which to choose. He can lend his money at the current rate of money-interest or he can purchase some kind of capital-asset. Clearly in equilibrium these two alternatives must offer an equal advantage to the marginal investor in each of them. This is brought about by shifts in the money-prices of capital-assets relative to the prices of money-loans. The prices of capital-assets move until, having regard to their prospective yields and account being taken of all those elements of doubt and uncertainty, interested and disinterested advice, fashion, convention, and what else you will, which affect the mind of the investor, they offer an equal apparent advantage to the marginal investor who is wavering between one kind of investment and another.

This, then, is the first repercussion of the rate of interest, as fixed by the quantity of money and the propensity to hoard, namely, on the prices of capital-assets. This does not mean, of course, that the rate of interest is the only fluctuating influence on these prices. Opinions as to their prospective yield are themselves subject to sharp fluctuations, precisely for the reason already given, namely, the flimsiness of the basis of knowledge on which they depend. It is these opinions taken in conjunction with the rate of interest which fix their price.

Now for stage three. Capital-assets are capable, in general, of being newly produced. The scale on which they are produced depends, of course, on the relation between their costs of production and the prices which they are expected to realize in the market. Thus if the level of the rate of interest taken in conjunction with opinions about their prospective yield raise the prices of capital-assets, the volume of current investment (meaning by this the value of the output of newly produced capital-assets) will be increased; while if, on the other hand, these influences reduce the prices of capital-assets, the volume of current investment will be diminished.

It is not surprising that the volume of investment, thus determined, should fluctuate widely from time to time. For it depends on two sets of judgments about the future, neither of which rests on an adequate or secure foundation—on the propensity to hoard and on opinions of the future yield of capital-assets. Nor is there any reason to suppose that the fluctuations in one of these factors will tend to offset the fluctuations in the other. When a more pessimistic view is taken about future yields, that is no reason why there should be a diminished propensity to hoard. Indeed, the conditions which aggravate the one factor tend, as a rule, to aggravate the other. For the same circumstances which lead to pessimistic views about future yields are apt to increase the propensity to hoard. The only element of self-righting in the system arises at a much later stage and in an uncertain degree. If a decline in investment leads to a decline in output as a whole, this may result (for more reasons than one) in a reduction of the amount of money required for the active circulation, which will release a larger quantity of money for the inactive circulation, which will satisfy the propensity to hoard at a lower level of the rate of interest, which will raise the prices of capital-assets, which will increase the scale of investment, which will restore in some measure the level of output as a whole.

This completes the first chapter of the argument, namely, the liability of the scale of investment to fluctuate for reasons quite distinct (a) from those which determine the propensity of the individual to *save* out of a given income, and (b) from those physical conditions of technical capacity to aid production which have usually been supposed hitherto to be the chief influence governing the marginal efficiency of capital.

If, on the other hand, our knowledge of the future was calculable and not subject to sudden changes, it might be justifiable to assume that the liquidity-preference curve was both stable and very inelastic. In this case a small decline in money-income would lead to a large fall in the rate of interest, probably sufficient to raise output and employment to the full.[8] In these conditions we might reasonably suppose that the whole of the available resources would normally be employed; and the conditions required by the orthodox theory would be satisfied.

---

[8] When Professor Viner charges me with assigning to liquidity-preference "a grossly exaggerated importance," he must mean that I exaggerate its instability and its elasticity. But if he is right, a small decline in money-income would lead, as stated above, to a large fall in the rate of interest. I claim that experience indicates the contrary.

3.

My next difference from the traditional theory concerns its apparent conviction that there is no necessity to work out a theory of the demand and supply of output *as a whole*. Will a fluctuation in investment, arising for the reasons just described, have any effect on the demand for output as a whole, and consequently on the scale of output and employment? What answer can the traditional theory make to this question? I believe that it makes no answer at all, never having given the matter a single thought; the theory of effective demand, that is the demand for output as a whole, having been entirely neglected for more than a hundred years.

My own answer to this question involves fresh considerations. I say that effective demand is made up of two items—investment-expenditure, determined in the manner just explained, and consumption-expenditure. Now what governs the amount of consumption-expenditure? It depends mainly on the level of income. People's propensity to spend (as I call it), is influenced by many factors such as the distribution of income, their normal attitude to the future, and—though probably in a minor degree—by the rate of interest. But in the main, the prevailing psychological law seems to be that when aggregate income increases, consumption-expenditure will also increase but to a somewhat lesser extent. This is a very obvious conclusion. It simply amounts to saying that an increase in income will be divided in some proportion or another between spending and saving, and that when our income is increased it is extremely unlikely that this will have the effect of making us either spend less or save less than before. This pschological law was of the utmost importance in the development of my own thought, and it is, I think, absolutely fundamental to the theory of effective demand as set forth in my book. But few critics or commentators so far have paid particular attention to it.

There follows from this extremely obvious principle, an important, yet unfamiliar, conclusion. Incomes are created partly by entrepreneurs producing for investment and partly by their producing for consumption. The amount that is consumed depends on the amount of income thus made up. Hence the amount of consumption-goods which it will pay entrepreneurs to produce depends on the amount of investment-goods which they are producing. If, for example, the public are in the habit of spending nine-tenths of their income on consumption-goods, it follows that, if entrepreneurs were to produce consumption-goods at a cost more than nine times the cost of the investment-goods they are producing, some part of their output could not be sold at a price which would cover its cost of production. For the consumption-goods on the market would have cost more than nine-tenths of the aggregate income of the public and would therefore be in excess of the demand for consumption-goods, which by hypothesis is only the nine-tenths. Thus entrepreneurs will make a loss until they contract their output of consumption goods down to an amount at which it no longer exceeds nine times their current output of investment goods.

The formula is not, of course, quite so simple as in this illustration. The proportion of their incomes which the public will choose to consume will not be a constant one, and in the most general case other factors are also relevant. But there is always a formula, more or less of this kind, relating the output of consumption-goods which it pays to produce to the output of investment-goods; and I have given attention to it in my book under the name of the *multiplier*. The fact that an increase in consumption is apt in itself to stimulate this further investment merely fortifies the argument.

That the level of output of consumption-goods which is profitable to the entrepreneur should be related by a formula of this kind to the output of investment-goods depends on assumptions of a simple and obvious character. The conclusion appears to me to be quite beyond dispute. Yet the consequences which follow from it are at the same time unfamiliar and of the greatest possible importance.

The theory can be summed up by saying that, given the psychology of the public, the level of output and employment as a whole depends on the amount of investment. I put it in this way, not because this is the only factor on which aggregate output depends, but because it is usual in a complex system to regard as the *causa causans* that factor which is most prone to sudden and wide fluctuation. More comprehensively, aggregate output depends on the propensity to hoard, on the policy of the monetary authority as it affects the quantity of money, on the state of confidence concerning the prospective yield of capital-assets, on the propensity to spend, and on the social factors which influence the level of the money-wage. But of these several factors it is those which determine the rate of investment which are most unreliable, since it is they which are influenced by our views of the future about which we know so little.

This that I offer is, therefore, a theory of why output and employment are so liable to fluctuation. It does not offer a ready-made remedy as to how to avoid these fluctuations and to maintain output at a steady optimum level. But it is, properly speaking, a theory of employment because it explains *why*, in any given circumstances, employment is what it is. Naturally I am interested not only in the diagnosis, but also in the cure; and many pages of my book are devoted to the latter. But I consider that my suggestions for a cure, which, avowedly, are not worked out completely, are on a different plane from the diagnosis. They are not meant to be definitive; they are subject to all sorts of special assumptions and are necessarily related to the particular conditions of the time. But my main reasons for departing from the traditional theory go much deeper than this. They are of a highly general character and are meant to be definitive.

I sum up, therefore, the main grounds of my departure as follows:

(1) The orthodox theory assumes that we have a knowledge of the future of a kind quite different from that which we actually possess. This false realization follows the lines of the Benthamite calculus. The hypothesis of a calculable future leads to a wrong interpretation of the principles of behavior which the need for action compels us to adopt, and to an underestimation of the concealed factors of utter doubt, precariousness, hope, and fear. The result has been a mistaken theory of the rate of interest. It is true that the necessity of equalizing the advantages of the choice between owning loans and assets requires that the rate of interest should be *equal* to the marginal efficiency of capital. But this does not tell us at what *level* the equality will be effective. The orthodox theory regards the marginal efficiency of capital as setting the pace. But the marginal efficiency of capital depends on the price of capital-assets; and since this price determines the rate of new investment, it is consistent in equilibrium with only one given level of money-income. Thus the marginal efficiency of capital is not determined, unless the level of money-income is given. In a system in which the level of money-income is capable of fluctuating, the orthodox theory is one equation short of

what is required to give a solution. Undoubtedly the reason why the orthodox system has failed to discover this discrepancy is because it has always tacitly assumed that income *is* given, namely, at the level corresponding to the employment of all the available resources. In other words, it is tacitly assuming that the monetary policy is such as to maintain the rate of interest at that level which is compatible with full employment. It is, therefore, incapable of dealing with the general case where employment is liable to fluctuate. Thus, instead of the marginal efficiency of capital determining the rate of interest, it is true (though not a full statement of the case) to say that it is the rate of interest which determines the marginal efficiency of capital.

(2) The orthodox theory would by now have discovered the above defect, if it had not ignored the need for a theory of the supply and demand of output as a whole. I doubt if many modern economists really accept Say's Law that supply creates its own demand. But they have not been aware that they were tacitly assuming it. Thus the psychological law underlying the multiplier has escaped notice. It has not been observed that the amount of consumption-goods which it pays entrepreneurs to produce is a function of the amount of investment-goods which it pays them to produce. The explanation is to be found, I suppose, in the tacit assumption that every individual spends the whole of his income either on consumption or on buying, directly or indirectly, newly produced capital goods. But, here again, whilst the older economists expressly believed this, I doubt if many contemporary economists really do believe it. They have discarded these older ideas without becoming aware of the consequences.

PART FOUR

Special Aspects

CHAPTER XVI

Keynes on Economic Policy

By ALVIN H. HANSEN

THE INFLUENCE of Keynes' *General Theory of Employment, Interest and Money* runs in two directions. The first has to do with theoretical concepts and tools of analysis; the second has to do with practical policy.

1.

With respect to the first, an examination of recent and current literature will disclose that there has come into general use, since 1936, a considerable list of new technical terms, new concepts, and a new theoretical apparatus. With few exceptions, in the English-speaking countries at any rate, writers on monetary, business-cycle, and general theory now use as a matter of course these new concepts and tools of analysis. In this sense friend and foe alike have become Keynesians. Some have adopted the new language because they find it more convenient or more elegant than the older terminology. Many others, because they believe, in addition to these advantages, that the new technique is more useful and more powerful than the old. Thus, for example, it is difficult for me to see how anyone who examines recent business-cycle literature and compares it with the old can fail to be impressed with how powerful an instrument for theoretical analysis is the consumption function, and how much more illuminating and significant many of the older writings become when we rewrite what they were trying to say in Keynesian language. Similarly, the literature and analysis of international trade has been enriched by "income analysis" and by the introduction of the "export multiplier." And for general theory the "income effects," formerly represented by shifts in the price-demand schedules, can more neatly and effectively be analyzed by the aid of the Keynesian functions.

2.

And just as a new theoretical language has come into being, so also we have come to speak a new language in terms of practical policy. It is true that even now one encounters on occasion economists (and of course many more politicians) for whom the "new economics" is a "foreign language" which they simply do not understand. I recall, no farther back than 1941, one of my colleagues in the Federal Reserve System remarking, on the occasion of meeting with some economists representing a foreign government: "Well, we discovered that we speak the same language." He was of course not referring to the fact that we all spoke Engglish (the country by the way, was not England); he meant that we all spoke the Keynesian language both with respect to theory and policy matters.

Keynesian economics has not infrequently of late been referred to as the "new orthodoxy." One is reminded of the following laconic exposition of the evolution of new ideas:

First stage: "How absurd; can any sensible person believe such things?"

Second stage: "These ideas are dangerous; they must be suppressed."

Third stage: "Of course; everyone knows that; whoever doubted it?"

3.

Monetary thinking was greatly influenced by Keynes long before the appearance of the *General Theory*. The *Tract on Monetary Reform*, the *Treatise*, and his work on the *Macmillan Report* were important stepping stones along a difficult new path which increasingly put English informed opinion far in the forefront with respect to applied monetary economics.

Few shifts in accepted procedures and policies have occurred in monetary history so striking as those with respect to interest rate policy in the cycle. It had long been axiomatic that variation in the interest rate was appropriate cycle policy. Gradually, mainly due to Keynes' thinking, attention shifted to the importance of the maintenance of a low rate of interest. The goal of monetary policy became directed more and more away from preoccupation with the short-term or commercial loan rate to the long-term rate, in line with the emphasis placed by Keynes upon long-term investment and governmental loan financing. True, the course of events, including war financing, hastened the adoption of Keynes' ideas; but it is not altogether clear how rapidly or successfully the monetary authorities would have adapted themselves to the changing conditions, either in England and the British Dominions, or in the United States, had the ground not been prepared for them by Keynesian monetary thinking.

The role of the Central Banking System in the expansion of the flow of income is viewed very differently now than was the case back in 1933–34. Then there was very serious discussion about whether "the market could absorb" the issue of two or three billions of dollars involved in the modest deficit financing of the early Roosevelt period. At the approach of war, Keynes clearly enunciated the view that taxation and borrowing could not be adequate so long as the national income remained at low levels. The first job was to raise the level of incomes from which taxes and loans could then be extracted. War financing, he argued, should first come via monetary expansion. Once the national income had risen to near full employment levels, taxes and borrowing could then come into their own.[1] Moreover full reliance

[1] A common misconception of Keynesian theory arises from the popularized version of the "over-savings" doctrine. The mistaken view is often met that, according to Keynes, there are large current "excess savings" in the depression, and all that needs to be done is to tap these excess current savings and expend them. This is quite wrong. Current savings are a function of income; and when income is at a depression low, savings are also low, if indeed not zero or even a minus quantity. Private investment or governmental loan expenditures are in these circumstances required to lift the income, from which higher income level a larger flow of current savings will be generated. Thus the first task is to get income up; from this high level income will spring a large flow of current savings which can then be tapped through the sale of public issues.

The misconception referred to above partly stems from the frequent use (perfectly correct and legitimate) of the Robertsonian period analysis. In terms of these concepts, savings may exceed investment; such excess savings running to waste and causing a fall in the income flow. If these "excess savings" were tapped and expended on investment, income would not fall. But Robertson's "day" is very short, and the current "excess savings" will accordingly be extremely small. Moreover the *absolute* flow of current net savings (using Robertsonian language) in a deep depression may well be zero or even a minus quantity. The fact that his "day" may disclose "excess" savings only means that net investment is still smaller, both being minus quantities in periods of very serious depression, investment being the larger

should not be placed even then upon taxes. Borrowing was in considerable measure not only necessary but even desirable in order that the public (especially the mass population) should be possessed of liquid assets after the war was over. Moreover, loan financing via the banking system was a means of increasing the money supply, and this together with the sale of government securities to the public increased the liquid assets of the community. The increased monetary liquidity enabled us to fight a "2 per cent war."

The war financing was a gigantic laboratory demonstration of the monetary implications of Keynesian theory, the practical consequences of which are indeed for the most part viewed with great satisfaction even though it is often hoped that no one will discover just how it all happened. Not infrequently writers who enthuse about the great increase in the *accumulated* savings of individuals in the United States since 1940 are quite oblivious of the relation of these liquid holdings to the rise of the public debt.[2]

These developments reveal the folly of the "sound finance" timidity of the thirties. But they also place a new responsibility upon current fiscal and monetary authorities. It is easy to become facetious, especially if one reads much financial literature such as that referred to above. But the teachers and practitioners of Keynesian monetary doctrines had better watch their step lest it should turn out that a Frankenstein monster had been let loose. "A little learning is a dangerous thing." Powerful new tools require responsible handling.

---

minus quantity. Yet in these circumstances "excess savings" would actually be less than zero.

Another popular misconception relates to "idle funds." If the public holds large deposits, this is often believed to be proof of "current excess savings." But this is not the case, the current flow of net savings may well be zero, yet the holdings of money may be large. The current flow of savings is, in the Keynesian theory, a function of the level of income; while the holdings of idle money (currency and deposits) are a function of the rate of interest. Indeed the rate of interest could not be low unless large liquid assets were held by the public. "Idle funds" are often decried as an evil. In fact large public holdings of liquid assets promote expansion and a larger income flow, first in so far as a low rate of interest will stimulate investment, and second in so far as the security afforded by liquid assets induces larger spending out of current income.

[2] Such debt retirement as is necessary to offset inflationary tendencies is of course advocated by Keynesians. But this is an entirely different thing from the "sound finance" dogma of continuous debt retirement regardless of the prevailing economic conditions.

4.

Keynesian theory pushed still further off the stage the already dying "*MV*" type of monetary analysis. Followers of the *MV* analysis could never see why the "circular flow," once a certain money supply had been created, should not continue on indefinitely. So the fiction had to be invented that there was a villain in the piece. The villain was the monetary authority who maliciously at periodic intervals interfered to curtail the volume of money. Business-cycle analysis of the Spiethoff-Wicksell variety had already pointed the way to the correct answer—namely, the fall of investment. But the Keynesian theoretical apparatus not only contributed to an understanding of the drastic and sudden collapse of the marginal efficiency of capital which often occurs at the crisis point in the boom; it also revealed (through the liquidity-preference analysis) the limited scope of monetary policy as a means of raising investment. Beyond this, Keynes supplied the most powerful test of analysis yet invented—the consumption function—with which to study and measure the cumulative process. Already significant progress has been made in the use of this tool; and econometricians will continue to press on, learning from their own mistakes, despite the attacks of impatient critics. The general Keynesian theory of income determination (the beginnings of which antedate Keynes by several decades) makes the *MV* analysis look like a curious contraption from the horse and buggy stage.

5.

The Keynesian analysis has profoundly shaken the faith, stubbornly held and not yet altogether abandoned, in the efficacy of flexible wage adjustments as appropriate cycle policy. It is not without significance that Pigou declared unequivocally, in his recent volume on *Lapses from Full Employment*, that he favors attacking the problem of unemployment not by manipulating wage rates but by manipulating demand. Much printer's ink has indeed been wasted, and still is, on the question whether completely flexible wages might not cause money income to fall more rapidly than the money supply, thereby inducing a fall in the rate of interest and possibly (but this is more doubtful) a rise in the consumption function. That so clumsy a method of securing a low rate of interest and a *relative* increase in liquid assets should command the attention of able economists in a modern society equipped with a stream-lined central banking system is a mystery which I am unable to solve.

This is all the more true in view of the fact that Keynes, in Chapter 19 of the *General Theory*, mercilessly exposed the soft spots in this thesis. Moreover, the argument that the Keynesian under-employment equilibrium is only valid under the assumption that wages are not completely flexible is surely a weak reed for anti-Keynesians to lean upon. For a condition of completely flexible money wages, with wages and prices tumbling after each other in catastrophic collapse, is not tolerable or even thinkable in any modern society,[3] and indeed was never contemplated by the classical economists. The older classicists, in fact, viewed the problem (Say's Law) in non-monetary terms, and considered the exchange of goods against goods *in natura*. The later classicals, dealing with a money economy, recognized the monetary "slip between the cup and the lip"—hoarding and debt cancellation. Thereby they revealed one defect in the older statement of Say's Law.

But the neo-classicals, when they urged wage reduction as a cure for depressions, knew well that completely flexible money wages, together with the astronomical fall in prices which would accompany unremitting wage competition, would have just as chaotic consequences as astronomical inflationary developments. Such a deflationary process they saw clearly would lead to disastrously unfavorable expectations both on the part of investors and of consumers. Accordingly they favored realistically a "once and for all" cut in wages (say 20 per cent) with a secure floor underneath which would prelude expectations of a further fall. This type of wage flexibility as a cure for depression is at least arguable.[4] But the argument now travels a much rougher road than

---

[3] "The chief result of this policy would be to cause a great instability of prices, so violent perhaps as to make business calculations futile in an economic society functioning after the manner of that in which we live." (*General Theory*, p. 269.)

[4] But, as Keynes put it, a "moderate reduction in money-wages may prove inadequate, whilst an immoderate reduction might shatter confidence even if it were practicable . . . There is, therefore, no ground for the belief that a flexible wage policy is capable of maintaining a state of continuous full employment . . . The economic system cannot be made self-adjusting along these lines." (*General Theory*, p. 267.)

formerly, due to Keynesian wage theory. It encounters the analysis relating to the effect of wage rate reductions on aggregate demand; and from the standpoint of economic institutions it is confronted with the unescapable fact that such a reduction means a deflation of the entire cost structure. The collapse of an established cost structure is no light matter, involving as it does a fundamental reorganization of the entire inter-relationship of prices. A fall in prices which are unduly high by reason of temporary scarcities, for example, is to be welcomed; and so also is the continuous adjustment of price relationships springing from unequal rates of technological progress in different lines of production. But a general collapse of the cost structure (based fundamentally as it is on efficiency wages) is a serious matter. Thus it is that the Keynesian view that flexible wage adjustments are not appropriate cycle policy—that instead what is needed is to operate upon demand—has all but won the day.

6.

It has frequently of late been asserted that, toward the end of his life, the view of Keynes with respect to policy matters had substantially changed, indeed had reverted in large measure to the classical position. That Keynes' theoretical and policy conceptions would have developed along new lines, had he lived a decade or two longer, is highly probable. His was not a static mind. That his ideas would revert to the old conceptions is however more doubtful. Apart from hearsay, which is often conflicting and at best undependable, there is the interesting article, published after his death, in the June, 1946, issue of the *Economic Journal*.[4a] This article, while dealing with the balance of payments of the United States, raises some larger issues with respect to the role of automatic forces and governmental intervention.

I have studied this article carefully, but I cannot find support for the thesis that it indicates a change in his fundamental thinking, let alone a "recantation," as has on occasion been suggested. Keynes always laid stress on the important role of automatic forces in economic life. Indeed, this could not be otherwise since such state interventionism as he advocated (mainly monetary and fiscal policy) was designed to affect aggregate demand; beyond that, the automatic forces were assumed to be in control.

If we "succeed in establishing an aggregate volume of output

[4a] "The Balance of Payments of the United States," EJ, June, 1946.

corresponding to full employment as nearly as is practicable, *the classical theory comes into its own again* from this point onward" (p. 378, italics mine). Keynes was never an advocate of authoritarian government. In the *General Theory* he declared that his theory is "moderately conservative in its implications" (p. 377). No "obvious case is made out for a system of State Socialism which would embrace most of the economic life of the community" (p. 378). Again he sees "no reason to suppose that the existing system seriously misemploys the factors of production which are in use" (p. 379).[5] There "will still remain a wide field for the exercise of private initiative and responsibility. Within this field the traditional advantages of individualism will still hold good" (p. 380). These advantages he details as those of "efficiency," "decentralization" and the "play of self-interest" (p. 380). The "reaction against the play of self-interest may have gone too far" (p. 380). Individualism is the "best safeguard of personal liberty" (p. 380). It is also the "best safeguard of the variety of life," the loss of which is the "greatest of all the losses of the homogeneous or totalitarian state" (p. 380). Individualism "preserves the traditions which embody the most secure and successful choices of former generations" (p. 380). Being the "handmaid of experience as well as of tradition and of fancy, it is the most powerful incitement to better the future" (p. 380). "The authoritarian state systems of today seem to solve the problem of unemployment at the expense of efficiency and of freedom" (p. 381). But it may be possible for capitalistic individualism "to cure this disease whilst preserving efficiency and freedom" (p. 381).

It is well to remember that these phrases are not drawn from the posthumous article, but from the *General Theory* of 1936. Had they been written in 1946, many would have jumped at the conclusion that Keynes "had recanted."

In the article of 1946 he said similar things, but certainly no more in defense of individualism or the automatic forces than those I have cited above. The most telling phrases in this last publication are as follows. "In the long run more fundamental forces may be at work, if all goes well, tending toward equilibrium. . . . I find myself moved, not for the first time, to remind contemporary economists that the classical teaching embodied some permanent truths of great significance, which we are liable today to overlook because *we associate them with other doctrines*

[5] [See P. Sweezy's essay—ED.]

which we cannot now accept without much qualification. There are in these matters deep undercurrents at work, natural forces, we can call them, or even the invisible hand, which are operating toward equilibrium. If this were not so we could not have got on even as well as we have for many decades past" (p. 185, italics mine).

"I must not be misunderstood. *I do not suppose that the classical medicine will work by itself or that we can depend on it.* We need quicker and less painful aids of which exchange variation and overall import controls are the most important. The great virtue of the Bretton Woods and Washington proposals, taken in conjunction, is that *they marry the use of the necessary expedients to the wholesome long-run doctrine.* It is for this reason that, speaking in the House of Lords, I claimed that 'Here is an attempt to use *what we have learnt from modern experience and modern analysis,* not to defeat but to implement, the wisdom of Adam Smith'" (p. 186, italics mine).

There is nothing in any of these statements which even approaches a recantation of the *General Theory.* Indeed the *General Theory,* as we have seen, contains similar statements in defense of individualism and the importance of automatic forces within the framework of a full employment economy.

Since the posthumous article in particular deals with international matters and especially with the joint effort (which Keynes did so much to implement) of the United States and Great Britain to restore multilateral trade to the utmost possible extent, something needs to be said about the alleged change, in later years, in Keynes' thinking along this particular line. Discussions with Keynes about monetary and financial matters, both in Washington and in London during the year 1941, disclosed a pronounced shift in his attitude toward this problem. This shift related, however, not to any fundamental change in his economic philosophy, but rather to what appeared feasible and realistic in terms of practical policy. Toward the end of 1941, Keynes at long last became convinced that the United States could be sufficiently relied upon to play a positive role in international economic and financial matters to justify risking a program of Anglo-American collaboration designed to promote a multilateral trading world. The isolationist tariff policy of the United States during the twenties had been superseded by the Hull Trade Agreements and the lend-lease program of President Roosevelt. Keynes had previously been profoundly impressed with the danger of being tied to the American economy. Witness the speculative and feverish foreign investments of the twenties followed by a swift contraction of lending, the boom, and the bust in 1929 with its international repercussions. In this kind of world he was firmly convinced that Britain had better manage her balance of payments along "sterling area" and "payments-agreements" lines, rather than risk the play of automatic forces in a multilateral world market subjected to violent and seemingly uncontrollable fluctuations.

But by the end of 1941, he became convinced that a new foundation, with Anglo-American cooperation, could be constructed upon which to erect a new multilateral trading world—or at least the thing was worth risking. On one occasion (1941) his instant response, when the importance of multilateral trade based upon high levels of employment in the advanced industrial countries and developmental programs in the more backward areas had been urged, was: "Well, on that basis we should all favor multilateral trade."

The above cited declaration was, in no sense, a "recantation." Already in 1936 in the *General Theory* he had said: "But if nations can learn to provide themselves with full employment by their domestic policy . . . there need be no important economic forces calculated to set the interest of one country against that of its neighbors . . . International trade would cease to be what it is, namely, a desperate expedient to maintain employment at home by forcing sales on foreign markets and restricting purchases . . . but a willing and unimpeded exchange of goods and services in conditions of mutual advantage" (pp. 382–3). This point of view he again reiterated in the *Economic Journal* article of 1946. A multilateral trading world is worth striving for. It cannot work without active international collaboration on the part of the United States. But, he declares (p. 186), "One is entitled to draw some provisional comfort from the present mood of the American Administration and, as I judge it, of the American people also, as embodied in the *Proposals for Consideration of an International Conference on Trade and Employment*. We have here sincere and thoroughgoing proposals, advanced on behalf of the United States, expressly *directed towards creating a system* which allows the classical medicine to do its work" (italics mine). With respect to his attitude toward the United States in the thirties, to which I have referred above, it may be noted that he refers to "this magnificent objective approach which a few years ago we should have regarded as offering incredible promise of a better scheme of things" (p. 186). It is to be hoped that the American Congress will not shatter the faith which Keynes' ardent work in his last years inspired.

There is no evidence here of any change in his fundamental economic thinking: what had changed was his view of the rôle of the United States in international economic affairs.[6] On the basis of the official program of the American government—a multilateral trading world could, he believed, succeed. But if the program is abandoned, or if for other reasons it fails, then "we, and everyone else, will try something different."[7]

[6] An analogous case is the remark one frequently hears that "Mr. A," who is an adherent of a compensatory fiscal policy, has "changed his mind," because, forsooth, he advocated expansionist policies in the thirties, while in 1942–6 he urged restraints upon spending and a high tax policy! A man may wear an overcoat in winter and a straw hat in summer without being charged with inconsistency; but not so with respect to policy adaptations to changed economic conditions!

[7] *Op. cit.*, p. 186.

CHAPTER XVII

Public Policy—the Doctrine of

Full Employment [1]

By D. B. COPLAND

THERE ARE SO many aspects of the influence of J. M. Keynes on public policy that it is impossible to deal adequately with more than one in the space allotted to this essay. I propose to discuss the effects of his writings and public work on the doctrine of high employment. I choose this because it has had great influence in Australia, and in the past four years Australia has been the most consistent advocate of its adoption as a central feature of the post-war economic settlement among the nations. Unfortunately I write this in China away from my sources, and this may lead me to place more emphasis than is strictly correct on the Australian interpretation of the *General Theory of Employment*.

---

[1] This essay is based to some extent upon the Godkin Lectures delivered at Harvard University in January, 1945, and published in *The Road to High Employment* (Harvard University Press). The reader is referred to this book for an expansion of the thesis here advanced, and particularly for a discussion of the difficulties of administrating the policy, and of reconciling freedom with the security that the policy of high employment offers to people. Briefly this essay seeks to show that concentration on the principle of aggregate demand for resources implicit in Keynes' later writings, and emphasized during the war in all economic mobilisation plans, is the key to the approach to the problem of high employment. But its enunciation, and still more its administration, demands the application of new ideas concerning the relations between the government and private enterprise, and the respective responsibilities of the two. The self-regulating adjustment of the classical theory has to give way to a theory that recognizes the frictions and stickiness of a modern urban economy and a well regimented rural structure. Particular reference is made to the administrative problems involved, and to the changes in budget practices required. Finally, the application of the doctrine of high employment to the solution of international trade and monetary problems is briefly discussed.

AGGREGATE DEMAND FOR EMPLOYMENT

The principle of aggregate demand for resources lies at the basis of the attack upon unemployment, and this received its greatest emphasis in Keynes' writings in his *General Theory*. It is inevitably associated with the theory of economic expansion, the relation between investment and consumption and the rate of interest, which were recurring themes through all his writings, though not clarified till his last and greatest work. It was also associated with his steadily growing belief that the frictions and rigidities in the economic structure would not allow the necessary adjustments in costs and prices to take place in a changing economy, without a greater degree of control than was contemplated by his old masters. His long experimentation with a theory of money that would take due account of the frictions in the structure, and his varied experiences in business, in government, in his own college affairs, and in farming, gave him the ideal background to find a solution that would be both theoretically sound and capable of practical application, at least in a country like England that had experienced a rapidly increasing measure of government control over the economic and social system. *The End of Laissez-Faire* was a step in the path he took to reach the ultimate goal. Already in 1933 he was advising the President of the United States to live dangerously if he wanted to get the country out of the greatest depression it had ever experienced.

There, as in England in 1925, during the controversy over the parity at which the gold standard should be restored, his efforts were frustrated by undue timidity on the part of the government, and too great an adherence to the financial doctrines of the nineteenth century, during which international investment was developed on a scale never before attained and the rigidities of wages and conditions of work, and monopolistic control, had not precluded the quick adjustment of employment to changed conditions. Even so the adjustment was made only at the expense of great financial losses and human suffering. It was Keynes' special faculty to recognize the realities of the economic system to which he was applying his speculative mind, and to take account of the social effects of given lines of action.

When the war came, Keynes had established himself as the leader of an able group of young economists who had been transforming the teaching of economic theory in the British universities and following his example of critically examining the working of the economic system as they found it. When he was drawn into Whitehall to advise the Treasury in 1940 he was already heavily handicapped by ill-health. His performance at Whitehall therefore was perhaps one of the most astonishing of his remarkable career. That he had a decisive influence in making the theory of economic expansion the creed of the Treasury in its post-war plans is now well known, and it is in this aspect of his work in his last years that the doctrine of high employment was clearly enunciated. Thanks to his inspiration, there was established at Whitehall a Central Statistical Office and an Economic Section staffed by the younger generation who had come under his influence, either directly at Cambridge or through his writings. The first problem to be tackled was to prepare and publish up-to-date statistics on national income and its components, investment and savings, consumption and money incomes, to show how the budget was related to the whole national economy. It will be remembered that the Chancellor of the Exchequer commenced the practice of publishing these figures as an annex to his budget, thereby revolutionizing Treasury practice, and laying the foundations of the responsibility of the government for maintaining aggregate demand, or money income as the source of employment of resources. During the war the problem was one of making the best use of resources for given ends, rather than of ensuring that resources would be fully employed. It was vital that the information on employment and its occupational distribution, money income, savings, and related matters, should be available if the government was to marshal its resources to the best advantage in waging total war. The pioneer work done by the Central Statistical Office in Whitehall in those war years has been paralleled elsewhere—in Washington, in Ottawa, in Canberra, and later in the European countries after the liberation. All the research that had been done over so many years on problems of national income was drawn upon to produce up-to-date statistics, which gave a picture of the whole economy at any given time, and enabled the authorities to determine policy with greater certainty than before. These statistics are the tools of trade of the administrator who is concerned with applying the doctrine of high employment, as well as the basis upon which the responsible authorities must determine policy. They were useful in wartime, and they will probably be even more useful in the formulation of policy under the greater economic uncertainties of peacetime. It was Keynes' great faculty that he could inspire his associates and subordinates to follow him in his adventures in new methods and devices. Without his leadership in this matter, it is doubtful whether the use of national income as a basis for determining financial and economic policy by governments would have reached its present satisfactory state.

It is one thing to collect statistics and another to lay down a set of principles by which they can be used to construct policy. The figures were, however, collected with one predominant aim, namely, the best use of resources. They were thus ideally suited to the determination of policy on the employment of resources under given conditions. It was only necessary to lay down the guiding principles on which a policy should be decided. This was done as a consistent whole for the first time in the British White Paper on Employment Policy, published early in 1944.

COMPONENT PARTS OF AGGREGATE DEMAND

This paper sets out to show that aggregate demand is at one and the same time the source of total income and the basis on which the volume of employment is determined. If demand is not sufficient to employ all the resources, income will be lower than it need be. As demand falls, so will income. The key to the situation is thus to maintain income at the appropriate level to give high employment of resources. Since income is derived from demand, it is necessary to consider the component parts of aggregate demand. They are as follows: total consumers' demand for goods and services, the demand of the government and public bodies for goods and services, the demand of private enterprise and government and public bodies for new capital goods or private and public investment; and the net effect on domestic employment of the foreign balance. The objective of policy is, therefore, to watch the movements in the value of these component parts of demand, and to ensure, as far as possible, that the aggregate demand will remain fairly constant while money incomes remain constant. If this is done, the volume of employment can be reasonably stable. In the past the policy of the government, in its desire to balance its budget, was to cut down its own demand for goods and services at a time when private investment was reducing its commitments for new investment, and thus reducing the consumers' demand for goods and services. Such a practice inevitably made matters worse, but it was assumed that this was necessary in order that some fundamental adjustment could be made in costs and prices, so that private enterprise could rediscover its enterprise and start the process of investment again. The White Paper takes an entirely different view. To cope with the situation, the government should deliberately expand its commitments to make good the deficiency in aggregate demand caused by the lapse on the part of private enterprise. This is no new doctrine, but it is only one part of the plan embodied in the White Paper, and what distinguishes it from other discussions on public works and related matters is that the White Paper carries the authority of a government. The British Government in the White Paper pledges itself to maintain a high level of employment after the war. Many participated in the formulation of this policy, but it is not exaggerating things too much to say that it came the way it did, and the time it did, because of the inspiration of Keynes. This represents a great advance on pre-existing governmental practices and functions. It remains to be seen how far the policy will be developed in actual practice.

What are the essential features of such a policy, and what are the practical problems involved? The problem may be illustrated by reference to the place private investment plays in the economy of modern countries. Many people have thought it the key to the whole problem, but that is an exaggeration. It is the stability of private investment that matters rather than the amount, though the amount itself may have very important long-term repercussions on the problem we are discussing. Keynes showed very clearly in his famous "banana saga" the effects of declining investment on income, prices, and employment. As investment falls from a given level the effects on the total volume of employment may be disastrous. Each reduction in the amount of capital construction has repercussions, secondary and tertiary, on the demand for goods and services by the workers and industries directly affected by the reduced volume of investment. Hence the total effect on the volume of employment is much greater than the direct reduction in investment. This analysis gave rise to the idea of "the multiplier," and emphasised the cumulative effects of movements in one element of demand upon total demand. The principle, of course, works the other way. Any generating force that creates new demand for unemployed resources will have a total influence far in excess of the original force. If there are a number of com-

ponent elements in demand, it would then be less difficult to offset the influence of a change in one by changing the others. Thus,
if private investment falls off, the cumulative effects of the decline in demand may be offset by an equivalent addition to public
investment, to government demand for goods and services or to
total consumers' demand. If tackled directly and quickly at the
source, the amount of new demand that has to be created is not
of serious magnitude. On this point it has to be emphasised that
if any one of the components of total demand should commence
to fall, its fall will be lessened, or even arrested altogether, by an
increase in one or more of the other components. Moreover, if
action is not taken at least to maintain the level of the other components they will themselves fall on account of the repercussions
on total demand set up by the original fall in investment. Thus it
is necessary to contemplate some action even to protect the component parts of total demand not affected by the first influences
of contraction. The devastating effects of a decline in private investment and in aggregate demand were never more clearly
shown than in the United States in its greatest depression. In *The
Road to High Employment* (pp. 41–6), I estimated the losses
involved, and made the astonishing discovery that the cost to the
people of the United States of the entrepreneur's lack of enterprise, measured in terms of the standard of living, were greater
than the costs to the United Kingdom of waging her greatest
war in history. The standard of living in the United Kingdom fell
by 32 per cent between 1938 and 1943. This was deliberate policy
in order that the country could devote its maximum resources to
war. In the United States the standard of living fell by 36 per
cent between 1929 and 1933, in order that the country could endure the rigours of depression, which neither the government nor
private enterprise seemed able to control. Full details of the estimates on which this remarkable conclusion was reached will be
found in the above mentioned book.

THE ADMINISTRATIVE PROBLEMS

When the problem is considered in this way, it becomes clear
that no single solution is appropriate even at any one time. This
is very fully brought out in the White Paper. For a long time the
expansion of public works (public investment) has been advocated as a means of relieving the situation, but it does not necessarily promote recovery rapidly, as was only too clearly realized

by the experience of the New Deal. If the normal democratic processes are to be maintained, and enterprise is to be given some measure of freedom, no solution is available that does not rest upon the mutual respect of the government and private enterprise. In actual practice this means that solutions will differ in different countries, depending upon the extent to which private enterprise can be induced to respect the measures the government thinks it necessary to take. Moreover, there should be machinery for constant conference -between the government and private enterprise, so that the position may be kept under constant review, and private enterprise brought to realize that any decline in its enterprise must have widespread repercussions. In the days of total war there was this machinery of consultation on the economic front. Without it the great expansion of production could not have taken place, and resources could not have been organized as they were. It was easier to do it then because there was an agreed goal, and scarcely any limit to what could be produced within the ambit of that goal. It will be more difficult now to agree upon the goal, and still more difficult to agree upon the measures necessary to reach the goal once agreement has been reached. The clamor for decontrol after the war, and the unbounded confidence in the virtues of unfettered enterprise in the United States is not altogether a happy augury for the success of the new policy. But time and adversity are inexorable masters, and a free people must learn by trial and error. The very fact that these acute differences of views and emphasis exist upon the capacity of the system of private enterprise to maintain a reasonably high level of employment is itself the most compelling reason for setting up the machinery of consultation at once. It already exists in some form in all countries in *ad hoc* committees between the several government departments and the industries affected, but some form of economic General Staff is required to keep the problem under review at the highest level.

In the United Kingdom the position will be less difficult, partly because the war-time controls have not been abandoned, partly because the economic position is precarious and needs constant nurturing. It is an interesting reflection that economic adversity is the best seed bed for the doctrine of high employment, and the critics of private enterprise may well apply the aphorism that when "the devil was sick the devil a monk wou'd be." That may well be true, but it will be none the less an achievement if the

United Kingdom, or any other of the capitalistic democracies in their adversity, is able to reconcile security of employment with reasonable freedom of enterprise. It cannot be done with complete freedom of enterprise; that was clearly shown by Keynes in his writings and policy-making work over the last fifteen years of his life. Some controls are necessary; some direct government action is necessary. The objective of the British White Paper is to keep these controls and this action to the minimum required. Control of investment, banking, and the rate of interest is fundamental. All this the United Kingdom now has in sufficient measure, and for that matter most of the other democracies. Some direction of production may also be necessary through a system of priorities for materials or permits to expand industry in certain localities. It is not merely that the total volume of employment should be high but that its distribution should be conducive to the health and welfare of the people. But that opens up a question much too wide in its scope for treatment here.

THE PLACE OF PUBLIC INVESTMENT

Given the background of control, the Government has a number of weapons at its disposal with which to attack the problem of high employment. In the first place, it is itself a large spender and the most important single recipient of income. It is in a position to vary both its income and expenditure, if it has the necessary control of banking and investment and the courage to exercise that control. But it can't do this if it retains the view that its budget must be brought to balance every year, and if it regards reasonable public investment as "deficit financing." No private enterprise about to double its plant and increase its capital would think it was setting out on a course of "deficit financing." Yet in some countries budgets are so organized as to leave any excess of expenditure over revenue for whatever reason as "deficit finance." In certain circumstances it should be the policy of a government to have a deficit on current account; in all circumstances it should be the duty of a government to have a large annual capital account for investment. These two propositions are fundamental, if this problem of high employment is to be tackled successfully. As regards the first, an increase in current expenditure, or a deliberate reduction in taxes and dues may be a means of expanding consumers' expenditure at a time when one of the component elements of total demand is falling off.

This practice is contemplated in the British White Paper, and it leads inevitably to a new idea of the period for which a budget may be balanced. There is no virtue in a single year; a period sufficient to allow for the incidence of expansion and contraction in the economic system would be much better. Moreover, the attitude of business to the budget must undergo a fundamental change. Business should welcome a deficit and deplore a balanced budget in certain circumstances; in others it should be prepared to have high taxes and dues, even increases, to build up surpluses. These ideas will come slowly, and there will be much resistance to them, and perhaps too much timidity in their administration. That they are essential in any attack on the maintenance of high employment may be regarded as axiomatic.

On the other problem of capital expenditure by governments, there is still much to be done in democracies to make clear the important part that public investment plays in modern communities. There are three reasons why the amount of public investment will increase in modern communities. First, the social conscience of most modern democracies requires that the government shall own and operate what are called public utilities, and this is being done to an increasing extent. Second, there are some great projects of national importance that private enterprise cannot undertake, such as TVA in America. Third, the rising productivity of the world should bring a rising standard of living, and this expresses itself in part in improved public health, education, and social amenities provided by public authorities. For all these reasons an increase in the annual amount of public investment and of the public debt is to be welcomed. I have argued this point in *The Road to High Employment* (pp. 117-23), where it is shown that with cheap money, a high level of employment and national income, an increase in productive efficiency and a moderate increase in population, it is possible to increase the total amount of public investment substantially in normal times. This is now generally recognized, but in the United States there are still some grounds for fearing that the old idea of the burden of a public debt and the persistence in the practice of "deficit financing," will unduly restrict the development of public investment, especially at critical times. In the past too much emphasis has been placed on varying the amount of public investment, and too little on the absolute amount that is appropriate. If the amount is large, as I believe it ought to be, and if it is spread over a wide range of projects, the problem of varying it when such a course is necessary is much less difficult than is generally realized. It becomes a matter then of stepping up or down the rate of construction, rather than of developing new projects, that may take some time to initiate. If the public investment program is accompanied by a works program where the capital and equipment is small relative to the total outlay, this part of the program can be much more readily adjusted with advantage to the total volume of employment that will be demanded.

APPLICATION TO INTERNATIONAL ECONOMIC PROBLEMS

There is nothing new in this approach as far as the individual items are concerned. What is new is the recognition of the importance of continuing and positive action by the government, and the acceptance by private enterprise that its enterprise is not enough. It is not claiming too much to say that Keynes made a much greater contribution than any other economist to this reorientation of economic ideas to meet the needs of modern social structures. He was also in the vanguard of the grand adventure in administration required to put them into practice. These ideas are not less important in the international sphere than in domestic affairs. It is on this point, more than any other, that my colleagues in Australia, who have the responsibility of advising the Government and the Central Bank, have drawn most freely on the Keynesian analysis. Australia has consistently urged that the doctrine of high employment should be an integral part of the economic settlement in the post-war world. It is clear that if one country pursues a policy of high employment, and maintains relatively more of its resources in activity than others, its demand for imports will be high. Unless it has a highly favored export position its balance of payments will be disordered, and it will have to adopt one of several expedients, such as tariffs, import licences, currency depreciation, to correct the position; or it must abandon its employment policy. It is equally clear that if a number of countries maintain a high employment policy with high national incomes, their total demand for imports will be high, and the total volume of international trade will be maintained at a high level. Here again we have the doctrine of aggregate demand. It is the demand for imports that settles the volume of international trade and the objective of policy should be to maintain this at the highest possible level. This may be done in one or both of two ways. First, there is the resumption of the nineteenth century practice of international investment on the assumption that the world economy will be an expanding economy as it was then. Secondly, there are the internal measures that countries may take to maintain their respective volumes of employment at high levels with national incomes and spending power also high. If these measures are taken, the demand for imports will be high, and most countries will be able to continue their employment policies without the complications that arise through the foreign balance becoming unsatisfactory. It was the absence of international investment, and the failure to adopt employment policies in the years between the two world wars, that caused the malaise in international trade. The problem cannot be solved by agreements to reduce trade barriers of all kinds, though in more favorable circumstances the reduction of these barriers will be a contribution to a better world economy. The more fundamental solution is to tackle the problem at its source by ensuring that aggregate demand will be high. If that is done, the task of removing the barriers, and giving stability to the international monetary system, will be greatly simplified. If it is not done, there is no prospect of restoring the world economy. This explains why the Australian approach to international trade and currency problems has been through the doctrine of high employment. No country that has a high level of activity fears imported goods; it merely demands more imported goods *pari passu* with its demand for its own products. This is the atmosphere in which a constructive world policy on trade and currency can be developed.

Thus we see that the modern theory of employment is pervasive. Its adoption demands administrative skill of a high order, a willingness to accept new ideas, a courageous effort to exercise conscious control over investment, banking, and the rate of interest, which thirty years ago were regarded as self-regulating, a new attitude to the place of public investment in the economy, and a somewhat unorthodox approach to the budget problem. These conditions and the administrative problems to which they give rise would have stimulated Keynes to new adventures. Will his followers be less courageous?

CHAPTER XVIII

The Significance of Keynes' Theories
from the Econometric Point of View

By J. TINBERGEN

1.

ONE OF THE developments of economic method that recently led to new results fruitful to both practice and theory seems to be the development of econometrics. We may say that econometrics is characterised by a special language and special instruments; not that it is, in itself, replacing theories or competing with them. It was, however, and presumably will be in the future, selecting theories by rejecting some of those presented and giving numerical values to the coefficients in theories not rejected. And it also influenced the methods of theorizing, particularly as far as the combination of "elementary relations" into "derived theorems" is concerned.

It seems worth while to consider the many-sided contributions made to economic thought by John Maynard Keynes from the angle of the econometrician. I propose to do so by (i) considering some general characteristics of his work that happen to be also features of some econometric work, and (ii) considering his contributions to the successive steps of analysis usual in econometric work. It must not surprise us that there is not always agreement between Keynes' results and those of the econometricians; he worked along different lines, where his marvelous intuition often played a large rôle. This makes a comparison even more interesting, however. On the other hand, it seems to me that in many respects there is a good deal of agreement between the contributions made by Lord Keynes and those made by the econometricians, which reinforces some of the conclusions to which those contributions have led us.

2.

Among the general characteristics of Keynes' important work
is before all the use of *macro-economic concepts*. Instead of considering only prices of individual commodities, Keynes often
introduces the general price level into his reasoning; instead of
speaking of incomes of separate individuals, it is total national
income which is put into the center of interest. Not production
and consumption of commodity *i* by individual *j* is the ultimate
aim of his theories, but total production and consumption of all
commodities by the nation as a whole. Exactly the same is done
by many econometricians, particularly by those trying to explain
the mechanism of business cycles or of general development, the
two realms of practical economics on which a huge statistical
material has been collected and for which, therefore, econometric methods promise some success.

It is not by accident that this macro-economic method with
all its dangers was chosen. Indeed this method is full of dangers.
Our exact theories are made for individual prices, individual demand, and individual supply. Applying the same theories to
macro-economic concepts that have at least the name in common
with those micro-economic concepts is sometimes perfectly legitimate, sometimes only approximately correct and sometimes erroneous or useless. In any case it has to be investigated whether or
not it is correct. Quite apart, however, from the dangers and the
trouble involved, the working with macro-economic concepts is
a bare necessity for the modern theorist who wishes to contribute
to the solutions of the great economic problems of our times. The
great problems in fact are those of explaining the course of total
national employment and production, of explaining why they
could shrink as they have sometimes, and of indicating possibilities of influencing them. The great problems indeed for which
mankind wants the solution are these problems of society as a
whole; problems not solved by traditional theory, since it started
from hypotheses eliminating them beforehand. This is why a
man like Keynes tackled them; this is also why various econometrists, moved by the same desire, came to apply macro-economic concepts. They are the only way of making understandable and workable these problems of society as a whole. Our
limited mental power—and perhaps even more the limited men-

tal power of the "public"—make it a necessity to use macro-economic concepts.

By applying laws for micro-economic concepts to macro-economic problems, we shall often obtain only *approximative* laws. This is an unavoidable corollary of considering mass phenomena, to which we are now getting accustomed; in the sphere of even the most exact of natural sciences, physics, the use of statistical laws and probability notions is now daily practice. I don't say that it has always sufficiently been realized that the laws used by econometricians are often only approximative laws. I am inclined to admit that it has been overlooked several times.

What I want to emphasize is the possibility that some of the laws introduced by Keynes may, if interpreted in another way, also be considered as approximative laws and that they are, if so looked at, still of considerable importance. I am particularly thinking of the so-called *equality of savings and investments.* In Keynes' terminology this was an exact law. The terminology, however, was not accepted as appropriate by many other economists, since it did not cover the every-day meaning of the concept of savings in particular. I am inclined to admit this. But even then it might be—and I think it is—that savings in the usual meaning are approximately, for the nation as a whole, the same as savings in the Keynesian sense. And it is in itself important to say that savings are approximately equal to investments. In order to make this clear, I only want to remind the reader that in several of the older text books on business cycles it is stated that there are important differences in amplitude, during the course of the business cycle, between savings and investments. This, however, is impossible if savings and investments are approximately equal to each other.

This approximate equality is admitted indirectly, I am inclined to say, e.g., by Professor Robertson when, in order to show the difference between Keynes' and the usual concept of savings, he introduces the notion of "disposable income," showing a small lag with respect to "income earned." As soon as two variables are only different because of a small lag, they are approximately equal. Since the difference between Keynes' savings and usual savings is the same as that between income earned and disposable income, the two savings concepts are approximately equal.

3.

I am now proposing to consider some of Keynes' contributions to the ordinary *sequence of analytical steps in econometric work*. The first step in any econometric analysis consists in the *choice of the variables* included in the picture, or, as we now say, the model. These models are always merely simplified abstracts of reality. Much depends, however, on the simplifications chosen; they may be more or less appropriate to the final aim of the analysis. If, by some simplification, an essential feature of reality is eliminated, the theory will not be very trustworthy. It is one of the typical arts in scientific work to choose your simplifications well.

The outstanding feature of Keynes' models is the choice of (national) *income Y* as a central variable. This choice, to which we are now all more or less accustomed, is at variance with the "classical" set-up. As an illustration we may quote Professor Hayek's work on business cycles, where it is the composition of national product (consumers' goods and investment goods) which is considered as more important, but where, implicitly, some constancy of total production during the cycle still prevails.

Even if we do not go so far as to hold that income is the only variable determining savings and taking over the rôle of equating savings and investments, formerly ascribed to the rate of interest, as in Keynes' simplest model, I think we have to recognise the great importance of the choice of national income as the central variable for any macro-economic model.

4.

The second step in econometric analysis consists in the *choice of the relations* assumed to exist between the variables considered. Here may be found Keynes' main contribution: the formulation of the *"propensity to consume"* relation. As is generally known, it is the relation between consumption expenditure C and income Y, hence $C(Y)$, that is indicated by this term. The choice and the use of this relation have repeatedly been the subject of rather severe criticism, I think without sufficient justification. I do not deny that consumption outlay may also depend on other factors; I shall discuss this topic at some length presently. But I do think that as a first approximation the concept is very useful.

The propensity to consume is essentially a relation between

two macro-economic concepts: total consumption outlay and total national income. Now total consumption is the sum total of individual consumption outlays, and each of these will generally depend on the income of the individual concerned. In addition, there will be dependency on a number of prices and on the size of the family concerned; there may be still other factors. By adding up the analytical expressions (the formulae) for these individual consumption expenditures we get a function of:

(a) the individual incomes;
(b) a number of price variables;
(c) the size of all families involved; and, perhaps,
(d) other factors.

It is not at all certain, beforehand, that this complex function can be approximated by one depending only on total national income. As to influence (a), this is only possible if the marginal propensity to consume is a constant. Within fairly wide limits this is, in fact, a good approximation. As far as it is not accepted as an appropriate working hypothesis, one should, apart from total national income, include as a variable some measure for the distribution of incomes. Even this is not always necessary, however. The distribution of incomes may be a function of the absolute level of total income. In that case Keynes' formula would again be sufficient; but when using it one should bear in mind the functional relationship just mentioned.

The influence of the relevant prices on consumption, mentioned under (b), may, in a similar way, also be transformed into an influence on total national income. The movements of prices are, as a rule, also highly correlated with those of total national income, the primary reason being that the chief demand factor determining prices is national income. Again we must not forget, when using the formula for C, that it is partly the influence of prices that is reflected in Y. It goes without saying that it depends on the type of problem considered whether or not this price influence must be considered separately. Nevertheless, the usefulness of the concept of propensity to consume stands out.

5.

As a second example of a relation introduced by Keynes, let us consider somewhat more closely the *liquidity preference function*. By this name is indicated the functional relationship assumed to exist between either the total cash balance or a well-defined part of it, on one hand, and the rate of interest and other factors determining it, on the other. The importance of this concept lies not so much in the actual variables chosen as independent ones; the statistical evidence at hand shows that there are other factors, not always easy to determine, that are also of importance. Of more importance is the theory behind it concerning the holding of assets generally. Instead of concentrating attention on the questions: "How much of his monthly (or annual) savings will a person devote to buying shares, bonds, etc., and how much will he keep liquid?" Keynes asked: "How will that person distribute, at the end of the month, his assets over shares, bonds, etc., and money?" By so doing one gets a theory which includes, in a very simple way, at the same time a theory on the trade in "old" shares, bonds, etc. It is the well-known stock analysis, as distinct from the flow analysis. Its simplicity is evident. It is not certain beforehand, indeed, whether this stock theory in its simplest form, as given by Keynes, covers the actual behavior of investors. It could be otherwise; influences of past values of interest rates, share prices, etc. may, in principle, also play a rôle. By putting forward this type of analysis, Keynes gave an important stimulus to statistical analysis. And if it will be possible to reconcile the two competing standpoints, theory will have become considerably more determinate.

6.

As a final example, let us look into the relation determining the extent of *investment activity*. Keynes deals with this relation in different ways, according to whether he works with his simpler or with his more elaborate models. In the simpler applications of his theory, investment activity is often considered as an independent variable; in the more elaborate ones, a relation with the marginal efficiency of capital is assumed to exist. Evidently the difference in treatment must be explained by the nature of the variations in investmen activity considered. If public investments are used as a political means to influence employment, it is justified to consider investment activity as an independent variable, although it must not be forgotten that, by increasing public investment, private investment also may be influenced. It may be influenced in two directions, as the experience of the thirties has taught us: against expectations there may have been, during the New Deal, an adverse effect of public investment activity on private activity.

If private or "free" investment is made the subject of investigation, the marginal efficiency theory will be a better instrument. It may be interesting to make a comparison between that theory as formulated by Keynes and the econometric attempts I made in an investigation for the League of Nations' Secretariat to explain the fluctuations in investment activity.[1] Keynes' formulation is that investment activity is extended to the point where, in the marginal efficiency schedule, the marginal efficiency of capital equals the rate of interest. By his definition, the marginal efficiency of capital is the ratio between the accumulated discounted future yield of the last unit of capital invested and its cost of production. The marginal efficiency schedule is the curve indicating the relation between the number of capital units invested and the marginal efficiency as just defined. Indicating by v investment activity, by z the marginal efficiency and by m the rate of interest, we have, therefore, the condition:

$$z(v) = m$$

How, now, does z depend on v? According to its definition,

$z = \dfrac{y}{p}$, where y is the estimated future yield of that unit. Both

will depend on the number v of units invested. For simplicity, let us assume that both are linear functions of v; it would not be difficult to generalize the result. For these functions we write:

$$y = y_o + y_1 v \text{ and}$$
$$p = p_o + p_1 v,$$

where y_1 and p_1 are constants and y_o and p_o, respectively, are the yield at a zero level of new investment and the price at a zero level of new investment. Here y_o may be interpreted as the estimated yield of the capital already in existence; the interpretation of p_o is less easy. It is easier to keep p as one variable. Consequently we get the formula from Keynes' theory:

$$+ y_1 v = pm$$

or
$$v = f(y_o, p, m)$$

[1] *A Method and its Application to Investment Activity* (League of Nations, Geneva, 1939).

For fluctuations of small or moderate size, this function may be approximated by a linear expression if this is more convenient.

The attempts I made to explain the fluctuations in investment activity in several countries and periods were based exactly on this formula, if for y_0 we read "current actual profits." I think there is much sense in assuming that expectations for future yield are strongly correlated with current actual profits. If so, the calculations show that a large part of the observed fluctuations in investment activity may be explained by a linear combination of the three variables mentioned, provided that a lag of one-half to one year is supposed to exist. Other variables added improve the correlations only slightly. They are in particular not improved if the acceleration principle is used as a starting point, except in the case of investment in railway rolling stock.

7.

The next step in any econometric analysis—ordinarily the one given most of the efforts of econometrists—consists in the *determination of the numerical values* of the coefficients in the relations between the variables. This is the typically econometric performance. Qualitative economics as a rule was not able to indicate these numerical values, and the specific achievement of econometric work is just this very step. At the higher stages of economic analysis, by which we mean the use of combinations of elementary relations (cf. section 8), even the direction of some effect may be uncertain just because the numerical value of some elementary coefficient is unknown. If the *extent* of the reaction of quantity demanded on a given price change is unknown, then at the next higher stage of analysis it is uncertain whether total receipts will increase or decrease: here even the *qualitative* conclusion is uncertain.

Qualitative economics have sometimes been built on the assumption of high elasticities without knowing or investigating whether that assumption was justified. An important example is supplied by the theory of international trade, where the elasticities of the demand exerted by the world market for the products of a small country are usually assumed to be very high. Another example is the theory of the demand for labor, which is also, often silently, assumed to be rather elastic. Generally it may be said that there was, up to the thirties, a tendency to overestimate the elasticities, even of the nineteenth century. Much new insight has been gained, in recent decades, by studying the consequences of low elasticities. The fact of these low elasticities has several times been detected by econometrists; but equally perhaps by people with inside information or the right intuition. Lord Keynes is one of the latter group. An example of practical importance concerns the *elasticity of the demand* for German exports assumed by him in his discussion of the reparations problem.[2] Contrary to the common view, an elasticity of only 2 was supposed to exist, leading to the conclusion that an expansion in the value of exports (in world currencies) would only be possible at the cost of heavy, and in fact socially impossible, wage rate reductions. Later attempts to determine statistically the values of the relevant elasticities led me to the same value, as the median of a considerable number of observations.[3]

8.

I now propose to consider the fourth and last step in econometric analysis, consisting in the *solution of the system of equations* obtained during the foregoing stages. We may first of all state the problem somewhat more exactly. The ultimate aim of the economist's work is to find out what influence on the economic variables is exerted by a given change in the economic data of the community considered. We may illustrate this by some examples.

(i) The problem of finding out the consequences of a rise in wage rates. Ultimately a rise in wage rates is equivalent to a change in the claims of the workers, i.e., of a change in the supply function for labor, which is a datum to the economist. When speaking of "the consequences" of an increase in wage rates, we are thinking of the changes in the volume of employment, in the price level, perhaps in the national income, etc. All these concepts are economic variables.

(ii) The question of the influence of crops on the general business situation, being the topic of the "agricultural theories of the business cycle" comes to finding out what will be the effects of a change in crop yields (a datum), on the volume of exployment, on prices, etc. (economic variables).

---

[2] J. M. Keynes, "The German Transfer Problem," EJ, March, 1929.
[3] "Verdere metingen van de vervangingselasticiteit," published in English as "Some Measurements of Elasticities of Substitution," RES, Aug. 1946.

(iii) Determining the influence of a change in the volume of money on the general business situation again means determining the effect of a change in banking policy (a datum) on some economic variables.

(iv) The same applies to the problem of the effects of the execution of public works, of raising taxes, exchange rates, and so on.

In some cases, the static ones, the problem is to find one particular value of the variables; in other cases, the dynamic ones, it is to find a series of values in time, a movement of the values.

In any of these cases, the community considered—maybe a nation, or a market, or some markets—has to be described by a number of economic variables; between these variables and the data there exist certain relations given either by technical, natural, or institutional connections or by the behavior of a number of subjects; these relations we may call the elementary relations, equations, or laws. The way in which any one particular variable, say the price level, depends on some of the data, e.g., labor claims, may be an indirect one: labor claims acting directly only on wage rates, and wage rates, in their turn, on prices. Finding out such an indirect influence is a more complicated problem than stating a direct influence. It can only be done by the combination of two or more elementary relations. When combining these two relations, in the example just quoted, we eliminate the wage rate and attempt to find a relation between price level and labor claims. There are more complications to be overcome. Wage rates may and in fact do act on prices along more than one path: they are a co-determinant of costs and hence of supply, and they are a co-determinant of incomes and hence of demand for goods. This example could be multiplied. In many such cases the total effect is built up of a number of partial effects, that may be of unequal sign. We referred already above to this possibility; and we stated that the direction of the total effect depends on the relative size of the partial effects (cf. section 7). This again stresses the importance of the knowledge of the combined influence.

9.

The mental processus now under discussion is formally equivalent to what the mathematician calls an elimination process;

it is a typically mathematical operation which, however, can only be carried through if the relations are sufficiently determinate. Since the economic problem generally speaking cannot be solved without it, economists have, as far as they did not explicitly use mathematical symbols, in some way or another tried to find a substitute. In particular cases this will be possible, thanks to some peculiarity in the structure of the relations. We shall discuss some examples later.

It seems to be one of the tasks of the econometrician to elucidate, more than was hitherto done, this process of elimination. The simple execution of the mathematical calculations and the communication, to the astonished spectators, of the result, is not satisfactory. The result should be understood; the process must be "transparent." In Holland we say that we don't want to reach the end point by night train, but by day train. For this clarification it will be useful to give names not only to the elementary laws, such as the law of demand (or demand equation), but also to the whole hierarchy of derived laws or equations, obtained by combining two, three, etc., equations. A very modest beginning in the realm of one independent "small" market is the introduction of the notions of "price equation"[4] and "turnover equation." This is a possible procedure for a "small" market, i.e., a market for which the repercussions of its price on the shifts of the demand and supply curves may be neglected. For "large" markets this is no longer possible. An example is the labor market as a whole. Its price, viz., the wage rate, will influence its demand curve, since total national income will be influenced by changes in wage rates, and hence the demand for labor will be affected.

10.

We shall now discuss some of the possibilities of obtaining results without going through the mathematical process. One—very obvious, but nevertheless important—possibility is present if the economic variable we are interested in—say total employment— is the only variable in one of the equations the data of which are not varied. This is the case if a perfectly elastic labor supply is assumed to exist, as was frequently done in "classical" writings. The equation then simply expresses that total employment equals

---

[4] Cf. League of Nations, *Business Cycles in the U. S. A., 1919–1932* (Geneva, 1939), Ch. III.

the total population of working age. It is self-evident that under those conditions no change in the other data will ever lead to unemployment. Neither changes in labor productivity, nor a decrease in money in circulation, etc., can lead to unemployment. All the necessary adaptations will be in the other variables. As far as we are interested in the variable employment, the elimination process is reduced to its very simplest limit, viz., to the mere disregarding of the other equations.

An extension of this special and extremely simple case presents itself if the variable we are interested in is one of a group of variables for which the following conditions are fulfilled: (a) they occur in a group of equations whose number equals the number of variables in the group; (b) no other variables occur in these equations; and (c) none of the data to be varied occur in these equations. Evidently what was true first of the one variable considered is now true for the group of variables introduced, one of which is the variable we are interested in. Again the elimination process need not be carried through: we know beforehand that our variable will not be affected by the change in data under discussion.

11.

An example of this situation is to be found in Keynes' models. In the simplest models, the variables Y, national income, and C, consumption outlay, are connected by two relations:

$$C = C(Y)$$

and

$$C + I = Y$$

in which I, total investment, is considered as a datum. The variables p, price level, l, wage level, m, rate of interest, do not occur explicitly in this group of equations, nor are there any other data. It follows that changes in such data do not affect C or Y. Of course this is only true as long as one adheres to the simple and specific hypotheses that are basic to those equations.

Sometimes a similar situation is reached for a group of new variables, that may be introduced by a transformation of the old ones. In the well-known static systems of equations of, e.g., Walras and his school, the relative prices are determined by a set of data, among which the amount of money in circulation, considered as an institutional datum, does not occur. Any change in that circulation, therefore, owing to the same type of reasoning, will not affect relative prices, such as real wages, profit margins, etc. Of course this is true only under static conditions. The same may be held for a change, under purely static conditions, of the rate of exchange.

The contribution made by Keynes to this fourth step of econometric analysis seems to me to be only a modest beginning. What is important, however, is that his way of thinking, i.e., thinking in rather simple relations between the most important macro-economic variables, provides a way of making the elimination process understandable and transparent. We must hope that a development of methods able to handle more complicated cases will follow; we are in need now of understanding the working of more complicated structures than those presented by Keynes. It is probable that we will learn much from his work, however, when trying to develop the necessary methods.

CHAPTER XIX

Postulates: Keynes' *General Theory* and the Classicists[1]

By WASSILY LEONTIEF

"Yet after all there is no harm in being sometimes wrong—especially if one is promptly found out." (Keynes in "Alfred Marshall, 1842–1924," EJ, 1924, p. 345).

1.

IN STAGING his assault against orthodox theory, Keynes did not attack the internal consistency of its logical structure; he rather attempted to demonstrate the unreality of its fundamental empirical assumptions by showing up what he considered to be the obvious falsity of its factual conclusions. The orthodox theory proves that involuntary unemployment can not exist, but we know that it actually does exist. Since the formal logic of the orthodox proof is essentially correct, the fault must be sought in its choice of the basic empirical premises. This is the general plan of the Keynesian attack.[2] It took the overzealous enthusiasm of numerous neophytes to confuse the elegant outlines of the master's enveloping strategy by opening a non-discriminating sniping at the orthodox adversary all along the line of the argument.

Since it is the question of factual premises on which Keynes chooses to base his criticism of the traditional theory, an examination of these assumptions and of those substituted by him in

---

[1] [For comments on this essay, see Introduction to Part Eight; Cf. also the essays by Messrs. Smithies and Tobin.]

[2] Its peculiar indirect nature is clearly revealed in Keynes' willingness to accept the orthodox analysis as a valid, albeit practically unimportant, special case of his own general theory.

their place can serve as a convenient starting point for a comparative study of the two systems.

The nature of the supply of labor and that of the demand for money are the two principal points of divergence between the basic postulates of the *General Theory* and the teachings of the classical doctrine. The departure from orthodox analysis in the treatment of these two particular issues enables Keynes to lift the traditional theory off its hinges and develop his own peculiar theory of effective demand and involuntary unemployment. The problem of labor supply is technically the less intricate one of the two and we will follow Keynes' own example in taking it up first.

2.

Traditional analysis considers the aggregate quantity of labor supplied, in the case where this supply is a competitive one, to be a function of the *real* wage rates; Keynes on the contrary assumes that up to a certain point—defined by him as the point of full employment—one particular level of *money* wages exists at which the supply of labor is perfectly elastic and below which no labor can be hired at all. The deliberate exclusion of the cost of living as a determinant of labor supply makes the latter independent of the level of *real* wages.[3]

Not only are the two statements describing the nature of the labor supply incompatible, but the positions occupied by them within the theoretical structures to which they respectively belong are also different. The monetary supply curve of labor is a fundamental postulate of the *General Theory* in the true sense of the term. A starting point of a long chain of deductive reasoning, it is itself not theoretically derived within the body of the Keynesian system; if it were, if the salient properties of his labor supply function had been derived from some other, more general, propositions of the Keynesian theory, the statement of these properties itself could not have been considered to constitute a fundamental postulate. It would become one of the many deductively demonstrable theorems. A truly fundamental postulate by its very nature cannot be verified by deductive reasoning, in

[3] Keynes himself did not consider in any detail the conditions of a labor supply possibly exceeding full employment level. Most of his interpreters assume, however, that beyond that critical point the nature of the supply schedule changes and the quantity of labor offered for hire becomes a function of the real wage rate alone.

empirical science it must be accepted or rejected on the basis of direct reference to facts. In keeping with this principle, the author of the *General Theory* justifies his own assumptions concerning the nature of the labor supply curve through direct reference to immediate experience of the mechanism of actual labor markets. Taking up the criticism of the alternative, orthodox approach—which explains the magnitude of labor supply in terms of real rather than money wages—Keynes by analogy refers to it as a fundamental postulate, which it obviously is not. The extreme form of this Keynesian interpretation of the classical position is expressed in the often repeated statement that the orthodox theory assumes the existence of full employment, a statement which obviously reveals confusion between the conclusions to which an argument leads and the assumptions with which it begins.

Far from being directly assumed, the real supply curve of labor is derived by the modern non-Keynesian theory from a set of other much more general propositions. The truly fundamental postulates of the orthodox theory deal with the general nature of economic choice. Without embarking upon a technical discussion of this familiar piece of analysis, it is sufficient to make here two observations on the particular aspect of this theory which has a direct bearing upon the issue at hand: in sinking its foundations deeper in the ground of experience than does the Keynesian analysis, the traditional theory is able to use a smaller number of separate assumptions and thus to achieve a more integrated system of theoretical conclusions. Instead, for example, of making one separate assumption describing the shape of the labor supply schedule, another defining the properties of the demand schedule for consumers' goods, and yet a third stating the nature of the relationship between the income of an individual and his propensity to save, the classical economist derives all three kinds of relationship from the same set of more general assumptions. This, incidentally, enables him also to reveal the mutual interdependence of the three kinds of schedules.

In making the phenomena, which the orthodox theorist thinks himself able to explain in terms of some common principle, objects of separate fundamental postulates, Keynes imparts to his system the freedom to deal with assumed situations which from the point of view of the orthodox approach are clearly logically impossible and thus theoretically unmanageable. This characteristic double-jointedness of his analytical apparatus gives Keynes a good reason to claim that his theory is more general than that of the orthodox economists. If, on the other hand, the ability to explain a given set of phenomena on the basis of a smallest possible set of independent assumptions were used as the criterion of generality, the Keynesian approach would clearly appear less general than the classical.

3.

It is only natural that attempts have been made to place under the Keynesian postulate some kind of theoretical underpinnings which would bring the foundation of his analytical structure to the level of orthodox argument. One approach would follow very closely the line of classical procedure in deriving the monetary supply curve of labor from a general utility function. In contrast to the classical, this Keynesian utility function would include, among the ultimate constituents of an individual's preference varieties, not only the physical quantities of (future and present) commodities and services but also the money prices of at least some of them. In particular the *money* wage rate would be considered as entering directly the worker's utility function: confronted with a choice between two or more situations in both of which his real income and his real effort are the same, but in one of which both the money wage rates (and, consequently, also the prices of consumers' goods) are higher than in the other, he would show a definite preference for the former. A classical *homo economicus* would find neither of the two alternatives to be more attractive than the other.

From such a monetary utility function, a monetary supply curve of labor can be easily derived. In contrast to its classical counterpart, it will show the labor supply as dependent not only on the relative but also on the absolute prices and wage rates.[4] The same is true of all the other demand and supply curves derived from a basic monetary preference function. In particular the propensity to save—which Keynes considers as depending only on the size of the real income—will necessarily vary with even a proportional rise or fall in prices and wages.[5]

---

[4] In mathematical language, that means that all the classical supply and demand schedules are homogeneous functions (of all the present and expected future prices and wage rate) of the zero degree, while the corresponding Keynesian supply and demand curves are not.

[5] [See Tobin's essay, pp. 572–87.—Ed.]

Although neat and internally consistent, such "psychological" interpretations of the monetary element of the Keynesian theory of wages are hardly appropriate. They contradict the common sense of economic behavior. The reference to the fact that no worker has ever been seen bargaining for real wages—even if true—is obviously beside the point, since while bargaining in terms of dollars the worker, as any one else, can still be guided in his behavior by the real purchasing power of his income. Moreover, the "psychological" interpretation of the monetary element in consumers' behavior deprives Keynes' unemployment concept of its principal attribute. Why should any given rate of employment or unemployment be called "involuntary," if it is determined through conscious preference for higher money wages as against larger real income?

4.

Much more in keeping with the spirit of the *General Theory* is an interpretation which ascribes the monetary bias of the Keynes-

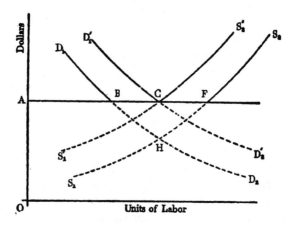

ian supply curve of labor to the influence of some outside factors, that is, factors clearly distinguishable from the preference system of the workers. A minimum wage law offers a good example of such an outside factor. Whatever the shape of the intrinsic or potential supply curve (curve S_1S_2 in the adjoining graph) no workers can be hired in this case at a wage rate which is lower than the legal minimum, *OA*. In other words, the effective supply curve would be strictly horizontal up to the point, *F*, in which the potential supply curve S_1S_2 crosses it from below. From that point on, a further addition to the labor supply can be obtained only at a price exceeding the legal minimum, and the effective supply curve thus coincides with the potential. That is precisely the type of a supply curve described by Keynes in the first chapters of the *General Theory*. If the position of the demand curve, say D_1D_2, happened to be such that it intersects the effective supply curve to the left of point F, say at B, the amount of employment, AB, is determined by the level, OA, of the minimum wage rate. The difference, BF, between this actual employment and the maximum amount, AF, which could be achieved without any change in the wage rate, provided the demand curve had shifted so as to cross the effective supply curve at F rather than at B, has been defined by Keynes as involuntary unemployment.

Although Keynes' labor market functions as if it were operating under a strictly enforced minimum wage law, the author of the *General Theory* explicitly refuses to limit the application of his theoretical scheme to obvious instances of such outside influence. The real reason for this obstinate insistence on universal validity of an apparently quite special assumption will become clearer after examination of the monetary determinants of effective demand. Keynes treats this issue as a problem of the demand for money; the orthodox economists describe it as the question of the velocity of circulation of money.

5.

The existence of a reservation price for labor would not lead to involuntary unemployment, if the relative position of the classical supply curve of labor and of the corresponding demand curve happened to be such that they intersected on or above the level of the minimum wage rate. So, for example, the supply curve $S_1'S_2'$ intersects the demand curve $D_1'D_2'$ in point C, establishing the equilibrium wage rate OA and employment AC. The corresponding Keynesian supply curve $ABCS_2'$ gives in combination with the demand curve D_1D_2 the same equilibrium position C.

Involuntary unemployment could thus always be eliminated through an upward shift of the classical monetary supply and demand curves, a shift which necessarily would follow a general rise of all prices (excluding the price of labor). Additional employment (BC) created by a reduction in the purchasing power of money which, for example, would have lifted the submerged classical equilibrium point H up to the effective minimum wage level OA, must—as can be easily noted on the diagram—be smaller than the amount of unemployment (BC) defined as being involuntary in the original situation. With a higher cost of living and a positively inclined classical supply curve of labor, the amount of labor seeking employment at the prescribed minimum wage rate will be necessarily reduced.[6]

It hardly needs to be added that any further inflation, raising the classical equilibrium point above this minimum level, can have no additional effect on the amount of employment.

6.

The theory of liquidity preference provides the Keynesian system with a deflationary mechanism which defeats, through the process of automatic hoarding, every tendency toward inflationary reduction of involuntary unemployment. The outstanding characteristic of this particular part of the *General Theory* is its exclusively dynamic character. The speculative motive—which is the very heart of this deflationary mechanism—reacts not to the absolute magnitudes of the relevant variables, which are the rate of interest and the present and expected prices, but only to the rates of change of these variables.

Keynes does not deny the possibility of maintaining a quantity of money great enough to support any given level of prices, once this quantity is already in circulation and the corresponding price level actually established. In this respect, his theory of liquidity preference does not differ in its assumptions and conclusions, although it does in formulation, from the simple quantity theory of money. In particular it can not and does not refute the classical proposition that with a given money rate of interest a proportional change in all prices will leave the *real* demand for money exactly the same as before.

It is the transition from one price level to another which according to Keynes might prove to be impossible. Without entering into the details of the argument, it is sufficient to indicate that it runs in terms of the effects of a potential change in the price level on the velocity of circulation.

Having centered his attention on the problem of change,

[8] In case of a negatively inclined supply curve of labor, additional employment achieved through a general price rise would on the contrary exceed the original amount of involuntary idleness.

Keynes does not, however, treat it in explicitly dynamic terms. True to the Cambridge tradition, he resorts to the Marshallian substitute for dynamic theory—the "short-run" analysis. The short-run analysis is related to a truly dynamic approach in the same way as the, also Marshallian, partial equilibrium theory stands in respect to the Walrasian general equilibrium analysis. In both instances the problem at hand is simplified by selective omission of some of the relevant relationships, on the one hand, and treatment as independent of some of the really dependent variables, on the other. The theory of liquidity preference considers the effects which a deviation of the interest rate from its long-run equilibrium level would have on the short-run demand for money. This relationship is analyzed on the assumption of a given price level. The conclusion that under these conditions the price level cannot be raised through an increase in the supply of money is analogous to the conclusion that one cannot walk up a flight of stairs since, if one considers the position of the left foot at the first step as given, the right foot cannot possibly reach the upper platform of the stairway. For the analytical purpose at hand, this short-run argument is hardly more adequate than a static theory satisfied with description of the two hypothetical long-run equilibria, one preceding and the other succeeding the actual ascent.

7.

Having observed the dynamic element in the Keynesian theory of money, one might turn back to his theory of wages and ask to which extent his assumption of rigid money rates possibly also represents a first awkward move in the direction of dynamic analysis. Indeed, a short-run interpretation of a time lag leads easily to treatment of the lagging variable as if it were a constant. A dynamic relationship between money wages and the cost of living, considered from the point of view of supply of labor, implies the existence of a definite lag between the former and the latter. Hence the short-run assumption that the wage rates are constant. This interpretation of the Keynesian monetary supply curve of labor seems to harmonize with the obvious reluctance of the author of the *General Theory* to commit himself to some specific institutional explanation of this particular assumption. Moreover it points the way to a further generalization of this type of reasoning which, although not advocated by the master himself, found universal acceptance among the great majority of his followers: if the stickiness assumption is a legitimate device in treatment of dynamic relationship, there is no reason why its use should be limited to the analysis of the labor market. Thus in the newer Keynesian literature not only money wage rates but also all the other prices are more often than not assumed to be fixed throughout the argument.

The limited usefulness of this simplified approach to the problem of change is unwittingly demonstrated by those authors who, on top of the typical short-run assumption of sticky money wages and fixed prices, also introduce genuine dynamic relationships into their theoretical models. The incongruity of conclusions, in which the short-run cyclical fluctuations are derived from explicitly stated dynamic relationships and long-run unemployment is explained on the basis of the short-run postulate of universal stickiness, can hardly remain unnoticed.

In the light of the foregoing observations, the principal difference between the Keynesian and the orthodox type of analysis would appear to be procedural rather than substantial. With its set of basic assumptions formulated without reference to the dynamic aspects of the problem, the classical approach suffers from what might be called theoretical farsightedness—the ability to appraise correctly the long-run trends, coupled with a singular inability to explain or even to describe the short-run changes and fluctuations. The Keynesian lenses improve somewhat but do not really correct the analytical vision so far as the short-run phenomena are concerned. However they put entirely out of focus the longer views of economic development. Only a careful reformulation of the basic postulates of the traditional theory in explicitly dynamic terms would make it applicable to the study of short-run changes without subjecting the long-run conclusion to the distorting influence of the artificial conventions of Marshallian short-run analysis.

8.

Interwoven with short-run and monetary analysis, there runs through the fabric of the *General Theory* the thread of an argument which, although at first it seems to be quite unorthodox, proves on closer inspection to be entirely in line with the basic postulates of traditional doctrine. Its subject is the relationship between the level of employment and the rate of investment, and its conclusion is the proposition that an increased rate of investment means a higher, and a reduced rate of investment a lower, rate of employment.

The orthodox demonstration of this relationship would in its simplest form run in terms of comparative utility of leisure (or disutility of labor), on the one hand, and of the products of labor —in this instance of investment goods—on the other. Increased demand for housing, machinery or any other new commodity could easily induce the society to redouble its labor efforts in the same way and for the same reason that causes the aborigines to crowd the employment offices of colonial plantation enterprises after they have been acquainted with and acquired a new "need" for imported glass beads and gaily colored cloth squares. A more artificial but not less mandatory need of paying taxes with money which cannot be secured by any other means but longer hours of work can obviously lead to the same result, as does compulsory labor service or, say, a program of planned industrialization.

The second set of examples fits the Keynesian line of thought obviously better than the first; the reason being that it inserts into the argument what might be called the distributive element. In a society as closely integrated and at the same time as greatly differentiated as ours, any particular set of new needs or, say, of new investment opportunities more often than not appears as a problem of free economic choice only to some relatively small section of the community; the rest is confronted with the indirect results of this choice in the form of "changed circumstances," favorable or otherwise. The demand for labor in particular is often expanded and contracted because of some primary change in tastes or opportunities other than those of the worker himself.

The apparent paradox of the situation lies not in the mechanics of economic interdependence—which can readily be described and explained without departure from classical postulates—but rather in its welfare implications. If all members of society were equally situated in respect to all the relevant choices and economic decisions, if each was employee and employer, saver and investor, farmer and city dweller, all at the same time, the distributive problem could not possibly arise: the fall in employment resulting from everybody's reduced demand for housing could (except in some special cases of external economies or diseconomies or of market imperfections) not be called involuntary any more than a morning headache could be called an involuntary result of a late party on the night before.

The liberal economist of the past century was prone to overlook the troublesome distributive aspects of economic change. Keynes, as Karl Marx before him, did well in pointing out this indeed most serious omission. He seemed to press, however, for reconstruction of the whole foundation in order to mend a leaky roof.

PART FIVE

International Economic Relations

CHAPTER XX

International Economics : Introduction

By SEYMOUR E. HARRIS

THE PROBLEMS AND THE CONTENTS

KEYNES PROBABLY devoted more space to problems of international economics than to any other subject. Although it is not easy to classify all passages or articles, a rough estimate yields the following: Keynes devoted about nine hundred pages in his books, and considerably more than one hundred articles, to discussions of international economics. The great interest in these matters shown by Keynes, and the important influence exercised by him in this range of subjects, justify the large amount of space given to this problem or series of problems in this volume. Besides my Introduction, this part includes (in that order) essays by Messrs. Nurkse, Bloomfield, and Hinshaw; an abbreviated version of the British Plan for a Clearing Union, to which Keynes contributed so much; his speech before the House of Lords in 1943 defending the Clearing Plan, and that in 1944 supporting the plan later to be approved at Bretton Woods; Mrs. Joan Robinson's excellent essay on the two monetary plans; and finally Keynes' first semi-public appraisal of the proposed International Bank and his speech before the House of Lords in 1945 in support of the Anglo-American Financial Agreement.[1]

Nurkse's essay deals with domestic and international equilibrium. Whereas classical economics was concerned primarily with the allocation of economic resources, Keynes was concerned pri-

---

[1] If space were available, I would have liked to include his remarks at the closing session of Bretton Woods on the influence of lawyers in Washington, and his half light and half serious speech in Savannah in 1945 at the christening of the Bank and the Fund. Both speeches are decidedly worth reproducing, though they have only a limited interest for professional economists.

marily with the level of employment. Hence Keynes' international economics, Nurkse shows, deals especially with the propagation of economic fluctuations from one country to another, and in this analysis the multiplier plays a very important part. The international aspects of effective demand and employment received little attention in the *General Theory*, which was devoted almost exclusively to domestic problems. Keynes had, however, developed a theory of international economics in his earlier writings, and it did not prove difficult for his disciples, notably Mrs. Robinson and Harrod, to apply Keynesian economics to the international field. Nurkse shows well that, under appropriate conditions, international economic policies, e.g., devaluation and tariffs, might contribute to a rise of employment and an improvement of economic conditions, and yet he shows also that Keynesian economics can offer little to the supporters of autarky, and that Keynes was above all an internationalist, a fighter for multilateralism, though he considered it essential to compensate for a reduction of demand associated with economic depression abroad; and it was also necessary to take measures to preclude an adverse balance of payments originating in full employment policies from stopping the internal expansion.

Exchange rates are the theme of Dr. Bloomfield's essay. Here the reader will find Keynes' views, at first favorable and later critical, on the theory of purchasing power parity, his attitude towards flexible exchanges, his changing views on gold. Here Dr. Bloomfield also explores the problem of finding appropriate exchange rates within the broad framework of Keynes' prescription of variable and equilibrium rates; and the reader will discover that Keynes' prescriptions were most general and give little help to the economic practitioner whose task it is to find appropriate rates. Supply and demand conditions; the volume of exports and imports; the availability of reserves; the origin of disturbances; the appropriate price and cost series to serve as guides; the nature of the economies involved; the importance of controls— all these variables are relevant. But what the relevant variables are and how much each should count are the perplexing problems towards the solution of which even Keynes, who had plowed the whole field, could offer little help. The plantings and nursing still remained to be done, as Dr. Bloomfield so well shows.

Tariffs played a significant part in Keynesian economics for but a brief period. As Dr. Hinshaw shows, Keynes only very temporarily abandoned his early devotion to free trade principles; and when more effective medicines than the tariffs as the route to international equilibrium and a source of demand became available, he said little more about tariffs. In his last years, the quest for international stabilization and financial help from the United States were intimately tied up with multilateralism.

Following the Hinshaw essay on tariffs, I have inserted literature that relates to Keynes' last important work, namely, the search for an international standard which would leave each country the maximum freedom in its domestic policies, and the Anglo-American Financial Agreement. The Clearing Union Plan and the first two speeches in the House of Lords dramatized his interest in solving British transitional problems, his desire to push a multilateral trading system, his anxiety that no country should be embarrassed in its domestic policies by pressures from abroad, and, therefore, his proposal to scrutinize capital movements and to allow a reasonable degree of exchange flexibility. In the essay by Mrs. Robinson, which is reprinted here, Keynes found support for his proposals by one of his most brilliant disciples. Mrs. Robinson stressed, as Keynes had, the responsibilities of creditor nations; but she also indicated how difficult it was for the United States to make full use of its productive capacities through producing for home use and lending abroad. Finally, the last two items (Keynes' remarks on the Bank and his speech before the House of Lords on the British Loan) reflect his abiding interest in multilateral trade and the free convertibility of all currencies inclusive of sterling. He was now looking forward to the day when blocked currencies would be freed. The reader should note in particular his ingenious defense of the Bank as a device for reducing the losses of the main creditor nation, the United States: other countries would share in the risks through a guarantee system.

Keynes' writings from 1913 to 1931 were largely concerned with money, and especially with money in its international aspects. No other subject had received as much attention in the pre-*General Theory* period, though it did receive relatively little space in the *General Theory*. And in the last few years of his life, Keynes, in quest for a monetary Utopia where the pursuit of domestic objectives might be attained without destroying the international standard, once more turned his attention to monetary problems.

MONETARY ADEQUACY AND GOLD

A fundamental tenet, in Keynes' system, was that money should serve man, rather than the other way around. It was, therefore, necessary that there should be enough money to preclude excessive rates of interest, to assure adequate demand, to prevent falling prices and increased *real* debt burdens. Perhaps in the early years and particularly in the twenties and even in 1930, the year in which the *Treatise* was published, Keynes was a little over-optimistic concerning the magic powers of money, though not unduly pessimistic on the catalytic effects of old-fashioned monetary policies in deflation periods. To Keynes, more than anyone else, goes the credit for having achieved the revolution in economics which has made money the handmaid of industry. There are few counter-revolutionists surviving who would now support restrictive monetary policies in periods of falling demand, or who would even oppose expansionist monetary policies. It has taken a generation for economists to yield to Keynes' logic, persistency, and persuasive powers. It may take another generation before the vast majority of men of affairs, less vulnerable to ideas and more hamstrung by tradition, will catch up with economists —but much progress has already been made.

In his quest for correct monetary policy Keynes rediscovered mercantilism, bitterly criticized British and French monetary policy in the twenties, and almost single-handed made an attack on the gold standard which nearly destroyed it.[2]

In discussing the mercantilist experience, Keynes emphasized (1) the gains accruing from the reduction in the rate of interest *pari passu* with the improvement in the balance of trade and the inflow of precious metals, (2) the association of a favorable balance of trade with an expansion of foreign investment, and (3) the wisdom of successive devaluations as the road to monetary adequacy.[3] Influenced by Keynes, the modern historian might

---

[2] Cf. especially *Tract*, Chaps. IV–V; *Persuasion*, Parts II and III; *Report of the Committee on Finance and Industry*, Cmd. 3897 (*Macmillan Report*), Part II and Addendum I; *Treatise*, Chaps. 21, 30, and Book VII.

[3] *General Theory*, pp. 333–349; cf. Nurkse's remarks on Mercantilism (p. 284) where he shows that Keynes' support of Mercantilism was a limited one.

well look with more sympathy than he is disposed to do upon many of the Mercantilist policies and even upon greenbackism and Bryanism of the latter part of the nineteenth century.

THE GOLD STANDARD

The gold standard was Keynes' *bête noire*. In 1923, he noted that conservatism and skepticism had joined arms in the defense of gold: the position of the supporters of gold was that gold had and would provide a reasonable standard of value, and that since managers lack wisdom, a managed currency would not be successful.[4] Early in 1925, with England's impending return to gold, he had to admit a temporary set-back. In discussing the messages of bank chairmen, he wrote:

> The first displays marriage with the gold standard as the most desired, the most urgent, the most honourable, the most virtuous, the most prosperous, the most blessed of all possible states. The other is designed to remind the intending bridegroom that matrimony means heavy burdens from which he is now free; that it is for better, for worse; that it will be for him to honour and obey; that the happy days, when he could have the prices and the bank-rate which suited the housekeeping of his bachelor establishment, will be over—though, of course, he will be asked out more when he is married; that Miss G. happens to be an American, so that in future prices of grapefruit and pop-corn are likely to be more important to him than those of eggs and bacon; and, in short, that he had better not be too precipitate.[5]

In 1930, he made his most vigorous attack on gold in a section of the *Treatise* entitled: *"Auri Sacra Fames."* Agreeing with Freud that there is subconscious support for gold, and surveying the scarcity of gold over the centuries, Keynes then continued that the supporters of gold try to envelop it with a garment of respectability as great as was ever met with in sex or religion, that its advocates support it because it is considered the "sole prophylactic against the plague of fiat moneys," and he added that gold "has become part of the apparatus of conservatism and is one of the matters which we cannot expect to see handled without prejudice."[6]

[4] *Tract*, p. 164.
[5] *Persuasion*, pp. 225–226.
[6] *Treatise*, Vol. II, pp. 289–291.

Gold was not acceptable to Keynes as a standard. He was dubious that there would be enough of it; he was impressed by its maldistribution and the failure of countries receiving it to put it to proper use; he considered the gold standard a dollar standard and, therefore, one under which British monetary policy would be subject to control from Washington and New York; he was not against the gold standard because it was a managed standard but rather because management could not be sufficiently effective under the fetters of gold.[7]

In 1913, Keynes still was relatively sympathetic with the gold standard. In his recommendations for India, he would not divorce India from gold. He was, however, even at this early date aware that some small deviations from gold were desirable: e.g., accumulations of foreign exchange and variations in gold points as means of contending with the rigidities of gold.[8] By 1923, he had become a disbeliever, a heretic. The scramble for gold and England's decision to return had greatly influenced him. Now he was clear that the British had put their economy in a strait-jacket, not only because they had returned to gold and thus had subjected the economy to the average behavior of central bankers the world over, but also because the return, consistent with gold standard theory, had been effected at too high a value for sterling.[9]

By 1930, he was prepared to yield ground. "Thus gold, originally stationed in Heaven . . . having doffed his sacred attributes and come to earth as an autocrat, may next descend to the sober status of constitutional being with a cabinet of Banks; and it may never be necessary to proclaim a republic. But this is not yet—the evolution may be quite otherwise. The friends of gold will have to be extremely wise and moderate if they are to avoid a revolution." [10]

In the thirties, Keynes once more began to express grave doubts concerning the gold standard. In 1933, he still supported a program for a qualified return to gold standard, made more

[7] Especially, *Tract*, pp. 167–76; *Persuasion*, pp. 227–236, 292–293; *Treatise*, Vol. I, pp. 329–350; Vol. II, Chaps. 35, 36; *Committee on Industry and Trade*, (*Macmillan Report*) pp. 121–29.

[8] *Indian Currency and Finance*, especially Chap. II.

[9] *Treatise*, pp. 289–301; cf. *Macmillan Report*, pp. 106–108, 124–126 (these passages were probably written by Keynes); *Persuasion*, especially Part III; *Tract*, pp. 147–154.

[10] *Treatise*, Vol. II, p. 292.

resilient by the issue of international notes; but the few passages in the *General Theory* indicate a recurrence of old doubts.[11] The international monetary plans with which Keynes' name is so prominently associated allowed gold an important place; if it was supplanted as the governing factor, it was not dethroned. It was necessary for Keynes and Mrs. Robinson (in the essay republished in this volume) to defend the stabilization of currencies in gold. Keynes could, of course, point to the liberal provisions for changes in parity, to the inconvertibility of the proposed international currency, the bancors, in relation to gold, to the interests of the Empire as a producer of gold, to the acceptance of gold as a means of settling international balances, to the general acceptance of gold as a standard of value for international purposes; and Mrs. Robinson commented on the favorable effects of gold mining upon demand under depressed conditions, though she was prepared to admit that gold mining did not provide the most productive use of resources.[12]

INDEPENDENT MONETARY POLICY

One theme was dominant in Keynes' monetary theory and policy: independence from outside influences. He would isolate the British economy from the effects of gold accumulation and sterilization by France and the United States, or from economic collapse in the latter. (How relevant Keynes' writings on this subject twenty years ago seem today!)

In 1925, Keynes wrote as follows: "A movement of gold or of short credits either way between London and New York, which is only a ripple for them, will be an Atlantic roller for us. A change of fashion by the American banks and investors towards foreign loans, of but little consequence to them, may shake us." [13]

Keynes stressed the folly of high bank rate, introduced to cope with exports of capital or gold; for the result was likely to be a discouragement of domestic investment and, in general, a rate too high to yield appropriate levels of output and employment.[14]

[11] *The Means to Prosperity*, pp. 30–33; *General Theory*, pp. 349, 382.
[12] *Proposals for an International Clearing Union*, 1943, (Cmd. 6437) p. 15 (see below, p. 327ff); *House of Lords Speech*, May 23, 1944 (Hansard Vol. 131) pp. 844–846 (see pp. 375–76); J. Robinson, "The International Currency Proposals," EJ, 1943, p. 172 (see below, p. 354).
[13] *Persuasion*, pp. 234–35; see also pp. 259–266, 292–93.
[14] *Treatise*, Vol. I, pp. 326–39.

Even an embargo on capital—as an alternative, or supplementary to high rates—was not at one time acceptable: the result would be a reduction of exports and of employment.[15] Later he was to champion control of capital movements.

In order to achieve independence, he was prepared to accept extreme measures. In the early twenties, he urged price stability as against exchange stability (in later years, price stabilization was not stressed); generous use of gold reserves; borrowing abroad; widening of the gold points; exchange depreciation or changes in gold parities; revenue tariffs and bounties on exports —all of these at one time or another and some of them concomitantly became to him the routes to domestic independence and stability.[16]

Whatever the proposal, the goal was the same: an improvement in the balance of payments, and with it an easing of bank rates, a relative increase in domestic monetary supplies, and an improvement in demand. A widening of the gold points, for example, would discourage short-term capital movements; devaluation or exchange depreciation would reduce imports and expand exports, at one and the same time raising export prices at home and depressing them abroad; a revenue tariff would directly discourage imports and yet bring about a rise of revenues, thus discouraging the Government from cutting expenditures and demand.

In the international economic relations perhaps even more than in domestic relations, Keynes was critical of the laissez-faire approach. Capital moved too easily in response to relative earnings at home and abroad; but the foreign balance—the excess of exports and other current credit items over imports and other current debit items—responded sluggishly. With elastic responses of lending to relative variations in the rate of interest, with inelastic response of costs and prices to the ensuing rise of bank rate, and of exports to the disappointing fall of prices, a serious disequilibrium develops, which is treated by penalty bank rates, monetary contraction, *et hoc genus omne*. Obviously correct policy calls for impediments to capital flows, which might embarrass the economy; and the less the countries receiving capital or any accompanying flow of gold respond through monetary

[15] *Persuasion*, pp. 254–55.
[16] *Tract*, pp. 154–8; *Persuasion*, pp. 271–287; *Treatise*, Vol. II, Chaps. 33, 36, 38.

policies, the greater will be the burden imposed on the country losing capital.[17]

Economists who are disposed to argue that Keynes' economics concentrated on purchasing power, demand, and similar over-all regulators of economic activity, and neglected the problems of structure, would do well to consider Keynes' discussion of the excessive sensitiveness of the domestic economies to influences from abroad. With Great Britain's economy tethered to more or less uniformly contracting foreign economies, or with Great Britain in a sacrificial mood, imposing contraction through a return to pre-war parity, the losses are inflicted disproportionately on export industries which are unable to cut costs and prices adequately, and on coal miners who are asked to accept a cut in wages, and who, being relatively immobile and being confronted with inadequate total demand, do not have open to them alternative occupations, as assumed in classical theory. Keynes is only too well aware that the deterioration originates not only in the inadequacy of total purchasing power and demand, but also in the failure to distribute losses evenly, in the failure to achieve the required degree of mobility, and to obtain the fluidity consistent with export prices falling, but nevertheless rising in relation to foreign prices.[18]

Keynes accused the Government of adjusting wages of doctors, charwomen, and the cost of postage to the foreign exchanges;[19] and instead of fixing wages on some fair and reasonable basis, the Government was relying on the "Juggernaut theory"—a theory of wages based on hard facts, economic pressure, equilibrium for the system as a whole, and without regard to the effects on individual groups.

We shall return to this theme. In the twenties, Keynes had made up his mind that independence in monetary policy was a *sine qua non* for sensible domestic policy; and that independence and laissez faire were not compatible.

EVOLUTION OF KEYNES' VIEWS TO 1931

In 1913, as has been noted, Keynes had scarcely begun his revolt against fixed exchanges, the international standard, and

---

[17] See especially *Treatise*, Vol. I, Chap. 21.
[18] *Persuasion*, pp. 247–253, 259–261; *Treatise*, Vol. I, pp. 326–29.
[19] *Persuasion*, pp. 249, 261–2.

subservience to foreign monetary domination. His "aberrations" were restricted largely to pointing out that all countries had not found it possible to adhere strictly to the pre-war gold standard as practised by Great Britain and had, *inter alia*, relied on foreign assets, surplus gold reserves, and some widening of the gold points—thus to some extent freeing their economies from the shackles of gold.[20]

In the twenties, Keynes' one-man revolution gained momentum. The transfer problems raised by reparations and free capital movements; the raising of the value of gold by the United States in 1920–21; Great Britain's decision to return to gold and especially at a pre-war parity; the resulting dear-money policy and unemployment over a period of ten years; the United States policy of sterilization (?) of gold in the twenties, and later her deflation and refusal to lend; the French devaluation and other continental devaluations in the twenties which put British exporters at a competitive disadvantage; French unwillingness and inability to put new gold receipts to use through adding to monetary supplies and raising prices or (and) making adequate foreign loans—all of these brought home to Keynes the dependence of the British economy on policies dictated by others, the inadequacy of classical adjustments, the urgency of independent policies for the British.

In the decade of the twenties, there was no limit to the programs proposed by Keynes for extricating the British from their subservience to international leadership. I have already noted the more important proposals. There was scarcely a reference to the excesses implicit in free exchanges—though at one point Keynes noted that prices might respond too freely to exchange movements.[21] Frustrated by the return to gold and later inhibited to some extent by having to compromise with fellow members of the Macmillan Committee, he had to renounce his major objective, a domestic standard later to be supplemented by improved international co-operation. He accepted the second best, a gold standard that should be managed in the interest of all. After noting that the return to gold had brought losses second only to the Great War, he acquiesced in the decision already made to return to gold. He was afraid now of a frontal attack on con-

[20] Cf. J. A. Schumpeter, "John Maynard Keynes, 1883–1946," AER, September 1946, p. 499, reprinted above, p. 78.
[21] *Tract*, p. 161.

servatism, "entrenched with all the advantages of possession," through the introduction of an autonomous system, for this would divide the forces of intelligence and goodwill and separate the interests of nations."[22]

In order to achieve a well managed gold standard, Keynes made some revolutionary proposals which were to have considerable influence on later policy: he opposed the immobilization of large gold resources against notes; he urged economies in gold in circulation, the use of all but a minimum amount of gold reserves by central banks, an international pricing program to lift the world out of the quagmire of deflation, the provision of an international authority which would be available to central banks and would prevent every outflow of gold from bringing contraction, the widening of the gold points as a mechanism for encouraging or discouraging gold movements and as a substitute for changes in bank rates.[23]

It has been said by Professor Schumpeter among others that Keynes, as Ricardo before him, elaborated a theory that reflected Great Britain's economic requirements.[24] Keynes' views on monetary theory and policy were undoubtedly influenced to a considerable degree by the events of the day, and in particular by economic problems confronting his country. If Great Britain had prospered under a gold standard in the twenties, undoubtedly Keynes would not have concentrated his attention on monetary matters. In fact, gold was acceptable so long as it yielded both stable prices and stable exchanges.[25] An excellent example of Keynes' nationalistic perspective is to be found in his praise of United States monetary policy in the early twenties when Keynes was stressing the need of price stabilization; but once the failure of the United States to make greater use of incoming gold seemed to react unfavorably on the British economy, Keynes' praise changed to derision. In 1923, Keynes applauded the United States for accepting gold out of convention and conservatism, but burying it out of prudence; for setting up a dollar standard on the pedestal of the golden calf![26] In 1931, he assailed both France and the United States for refusing to trade goods for gold, for taking

[22] *Treatise*, Vol. II, p. 338.
[23] *Treatise*, Vol. II, Book VII; and *The Means to Prosperity*, pp. 30–34.
[24] Schumpeter, *op. cit.*, pp. 505–6, and above, pp. 85–6.
[25] *Tract*, p. 158.
[26] *Tract*, pp. 197–199.

all the surplus gold, for their unwillingness to lend, etc.; and they were warned that they had willed the destruction of their own industries.[27]

Another example of Keynes' patriotism is his reaction when the French in 1928 finally reduced the gold franc to a value which conformed closely to his own recommendations. His approval of the action was tempered with a note of envy arising from an improvement in the competitive position of France vis-à-vis Great Britain:

> In Great Britain our authorities have never talked such rubbish as their French colleagues or offended so grossly against all sound principles of finance. But Great Britain has come out of the transitional period with the weight of her war debt aggravated, her obligations to the United States unabated, and deflationary finance still in the ascendant; with a heavy burden of taxes appropriate to the former and a million unemployed as the outcome of the latter. France, on the other hand, has written down her internal war debt by four-fifths, and has persuaded her Allies to let her off more than half of her external debt; and now she is avoiding the sacrifices of deflation. Yet she has contrived to do this without the slightest loss of reputation for conservative finance and capitalist principles. . . . Assuredly it does not pay to be good.[28]

With Great Britain's abandonment of gold in 1931, it was Keynes' turn to be exuberant. Yet his position was not consistently nationalistic. It was open to all to follow the British example and thus accept the blessings of rising prices. Those who follow would not then suffer a competitive disadvantage; but those who would not would suffer the curse of Midas. France and the United States, which had consistently refused to exchange their exports except for gold, and which refused to accept imports and yet wanted their debts to be paid—they especially were the target of Keynes' attack. And Keynes warned that the continuance of present policies would end disastrously for France and the United States and, though the depreciation would reduce the strain on the British and transfer it elsewhere, world prosperity

---

[27] *Persuasion*, pp. 292–3. I have discussed the pros and cons of United States policy in an article on dollar scarcity—this also deals with Keynes' views on dollar scarcity as revealed in his last article—"Dollar Scarcity: Some Remarks Inspired by Keynes' Last Article," EJ, June, 1947.

[28] *Persuasion*, p. 116.

could not be had without trade recovery in the United States.[29]

Although Keynes' preoccupation with money stemmed in part from his interest in the British economy, and though the gains arising from the acceptance of his views would have especially helped Great Britain, the gains for the most part were open to all who would listen. His interest in French and American monetary policies arose not only because of their direct effects on the British economy but also because of their repercussions on the world economic situation, and incidentally on the British. Adequate monetary supplies would help all countries. Flexible exchanges, a determination of money rates, monetary supplies, and investment according to domestic needs would also help all. In this sense, Keynes was an internationalist and offered his medicine to all; and to this extent, I do not agree with my colleague, Professor Schumpeter. If the Keynes theory was not for export, smuggling on a vast scale has taken place. Or if purely domestic standards were out of the question, then a gold standard managed on behalf of the interests of all was Keynes' proposal. In fact, this last proposal was presented by Keynes in his *Treatise* in 1930, and supported by him in the *Macmillan Report* issued in June, 1931. Even in the jubilant mood of September, 1931, when Great Britain went off gold, he ended his essay as follows:

> Shall we in Great Britain invite three-quarters of the world, including the whole of our Empire, to join with us in evolving a new currency system which will be stable in terms of commodities? Or would the gold standard countries be interested to learn the terms, which must needs be strict, on which we should be prepared to re-enter the system of a drastically reformed gold standard? [30]

SINCE 1936

By 1936, Keynes' interest in international economics drooped. In fact, there was far less emphasis on money, as well as on international economics, in the *General Theory* than in the *Treatise*. Since his interest in international economics was expressed largely through its effects on money and the rate of interest, a deemphasis of money was bound to be reflected in less attention to international economics. In the *Treatise*, he allowed that monetary policy through its effect on the market relative to the natural

[29] *Persuasion*, pp. 292–4.
[30] *Persuasion*, p. 294.

rate of interest and, therefore, on investment relative to savings would have a considerable effect. In the *General Theory*, however, he was "skeptical of the success of a purely monetary policy directed towards influencing the rate of interest": unfortunately the marginal efficiency of capital followed too sluggishly.[31] Relative to his early writings, Keynes devoted little space to money, and especially to international economics in his *General Theory;* and a large part of the space allocated went to a discussion not of anti-deflationary policy but rather to the anti-inflationary aspects of an expanding economy.[32] In *How to Pay for the War* (1940), Keynes continued to slight money, concentrating mainly on tax and savings policies, and secondarily on controls.

THE THEORETICAL BACKGROUND AND THE MONETARY PLANS

It was not until he began his work on international monetary co-operation in the latter part of the war that he returned once more to the monetary field and particularly to international economics. Now that the British were wedded to a policy of monetary independence, for which Keynes had fought so stubbornly, it was his task to build on the theoretical framework of his *Tract* and *Treatise;* his engineering skill proving to be as great as his theoretical aptitude. Unfortunately, however effectively his ideas had been planted in academic circles as well as on High and Downing Street, he had not had equal success on Main Street and Pennsylvania Avenue. He now fought for a strong international organization as he had in the *Treatise;* for exchange and monetary policy largely attuned to domestic needs—for liberal lending policies and responsible monetary policies by creditor nations. The United States, however, had the purse strings and was much more receptive to the gold standard than the British. Compromises had to be made.

Yet the resulting provisions in the Fund and the Bank embodied many of the principles which the world owed largely to Keynes. The gold standard, and all it stood for, now belongs to an earlier age. To appease Congress, American negotiators might argue that the gold standard had been reestablished; but the American Bankers Association knew better and it bitterly assailed the program. Keynes could inform his people and Government that he had

[31] *General Theory*, pp. 164, 316–317.
[32] *Ibid.*, Chap. 21, especially section V.

continued the fight for freedom from monetary servitude; and he had won a large victory. Having achieved this, he was now prepared to admit that some international stability was desirable, and that exchange flexibility, provision of international reserves, and international lending would help countries in a state of disequilibrium. Nations could not, however, maintain a standard of living beyond that compatible with their productive resources.

> If, indeed, a country lacks the productive capacity to maintain its standard of life, then a reduction in this standard is not avoidable. If its wage and price levels in terms of money are out of line with those elsewhere, a change in the rate of its foreign exchange is inevitable. But if, possessing the productive capacity, it lacks markets because of restrictive policies throughout the world, then the remedy lies in expanding its opportunities for export by removal of the restrictive pressure.[33]

The groundwork for this practical program, which was presented to the world in the war period, had been prepared before the *General Theory* was written. One has but to study the British Clearing Union Plan to which Keynes contributed so much, or the final plans at Bretton Woods, or his defense of the monetary plans and the Anglo-American Financial Agreement, to discover that he was now building on the foundations of 1923–1933.

Above all, he now said and reiterated that Great Britain would not subject its economy to controls from without; that a country pursuing prudent policies at home must not be embarrassed by strains originating abroad; that domestic policies of each country are the primary concern.

> More generally, we need a means of reassurance to a troubled world, by which any country whose own affairs are conducted with due prudence, is relieved of anxiety for causes which are not of its own making, concerning its ability to meet its international liabilities; and which will, therefore, make unnecessary those methods of restriction and discrimination which countries have adopted hitherto, not on their merits, but as measures of self-protection from disruptive outside forces.[34]

> For instead of maintaining the principle that the internal value of a national currency should conform to a prescribed *de jure* external value, it provides that its external value should be altered if necessary so as to conform to whatever *de facto* internal value

[33] *Clearing Union Plan,* p. 13. See below, p. 333.
[34] *Ibid.,* p. 5. See below, p. 326.

results from domestic policies, which themselves shall be immune from criticism by the Fund.[35]

In some comments on the Clearing Union plan, Keynes stressed the need of independence in wage policies.[36] Countries might get out of step in the movement of their efficiency wages, and therefore in their relative prices. In such instances, a country might run into difficulties which might be overcome by providing international currency; but in his view, countries which were out of step in their wage and price policies had a right to be out of step. The international authority might suggest to them limitations on the outflow of capital, or might make recommendations on other matters, or might, if the debtor position with the international organization became large, require deposit of reserves or, ultimately, loss of access to the organization. Its wages and price policies were its own problem, however, and this was stipulated, in no small part because of Keynes' insistence, in the final Bretton Woods plans. If efficiency wages were out of line, adjustment in exchange rates was the obvious way out.

That the monetary authorities had submitted to external dictation of the rate of interest, had particularly vexed Keynes in the twenties; and although he was less optimistic in 1936 than he had been in 1930 concerning the importance of interest rates, he remained as determined as ever in the last years of his life that each country should be free to have interest rates appropriate to its internal needs.

> . . . we intend to retain control of our domestic rate of interest, so that we can keep it as low as suits our purposes, without interference from the ebb and flow of international capital movements or flights of hot money.[37]

In discussing the need of restrictions on capital movements, he had made clear both his and the government's intentions:

> Unless the aggregate of new investments which individuals are free to make overseas is kept within the amount which our favourable trade balance is capable of looking after, we lose control over the domestic rate of interest.[37a]

[35] *House of Lords*, May 23, 1944, p. 846. See below, p. 376.
[36] J. M. Keynes, "The Objective of International Price Stability," EJ, 1943, pp. 185–187; *Clearing Union*, p. 3; see below, p. 363.
[37] *House of Lords*, May 23, 1944, p. 844; see below, p. 374.
[37a] *House of Lords*, May 18, 1943; see below, p. 364.

Behavior of creditor countries had been a particular source of annoyance to Keynes, who held them largely responsible for British difficulties in the twenties. His Clearing Union plan took cognizance of the un-cooperative behavior of creditor countries, and, in his discussions of the plans, he underlined their responsibilities. They were of course free to export as much as they wished and to import as little; but under his proposed plan, they would receive not gold, the loss of which would prove embarrassing to the debtor nations, but credits (bancors) with the Clearing Union. The creditor nations were free to stop the accumulation of bancors by introducing an inflation, raising the value of their currencies, encouraging outward capital movements, or relaxing their trade restrictions. To Keynes, the British proposals had the advantage over pre-war conditions of providing the creditor countries with a mechanism of payments which was consistent with continued excess of exports; and they had the further advantage over the American plan that no measures were to be taken to stop or reduce exports abruptly as under the "scarcity currency" provision under that plan. Here a continued drain on dollars, for example, with a resulting unavailability, would require rationing of dollars and automatic losses of export markets.[38]

Keynes used all his eloquence and persuasiveness to win the creditor nations' support for this part of his plan; but without much success.[39] United States authorities, however impressed they were by the multiplier effect of a growing excess of exports, could not take it upon themselves to persuade Congress that an unlimited credit of about $30 billion should be made available, a large part of which would be exchanged for American exports. Other countries objected to the provision that quotas should be based on trade, a provision that was favorable to British interests.

The Clearing Union Plan was clear on the issues: "No particular member States have to engage their own resources as such to the support of other particular State‚ or of any of the international projects or policies adopted. They have only to agree in general that, if they find themselves with surplus resources which

---

[38] *Clearing Union Plan*, p. 19; see below, p. 338. J. Robinson, *op. cit.*, pp. 166–67; see below, p. 348.

[39] Keynes' parallel of domestic banking and the Clearing Union plan seems to have been based on a crude fallacy of the banking process. Surely, non-withdrawal of a deposit does not allow banks to lend the deposit to others, as Keynes argued. The corresponding asset is already on the books of the bank—the failure to use the deposit simply reduces velocity.

for the time being they do not themselves wish to employ, these resources may go into the general pool and be put to work on approved purposes. This costs the surplus country nothing because it is not asked to part permanently, or even for any specified period, with such resources. . . ." [40]

Keynes said nothing of the real resources, namely exports given up in creditor countries. In his address to the House of Lords on May 18, 1943, he returned to the theme and criticized his American friends for assuming that the United States would fail to maintain satisfactory employment at home or fail to invest adequately abroad—only under these conditions would the United States accumulate large balances of bancors. He failed to note that even in prosperous times, e.g., the twenties, dollars were scarce. And his pupil, Mrs. Robinson, did not agree wholly with him in his strictures directed to creditor nations; for she stressed that in the nineteenth century the British, with their dependence on foreign food and raw materials, had much to gain from lending abroad, whereas the United States had much less to gain, and loans raise political opposition. [41] Finally in his address of May 23, 1944, in which he defended the proposed agreement, Keynes praised the American officials for having offered a plan, namely, rationing of scarce currencies, which would solve the problem of excess credits and draining of gold from debtor nations.

In his House of Lords address on the Anglo-American Financial Agreement, Keynes dwelt on the success in reconciling international with widely different domestic objectives.

> Both the currency and the commercial proposals are devised to favour the maintenance of equilibrium by expressly permitting various protective devices when they are required to maintain equilibrium and by forbidding them when they are not so required. . . . (the plans) represent the first elaborate and comprehensive attempt to combine the advantages of a freedom of commerce with safeguards against the disastrous consequences of a laissez faire system which pays no direct regard to the preservation of equilibrium and merely relies on the eventual working out of blind forces. . . . It is not easy to have patience with those who pretend that some of us, who were very early in the field to attack and denounce the false premises and false conclusions of unrestricted laissez faire and its particular manifestations

[40] *Clearing Union Plan*, p. 19.
[41] Robinson *op. cit.*, p. 169; see below, p. 351.

in the former gold standard and other currency and commercial doctrines which mistake private license for public liberty, are now spending their later years in the service of the State to walk backwards and resurrect and re-erect the idols which they had played some part in throwing out of the market place. Not so, fresh tasks now invite. . . . The work of destruction has been accomplished, and the site has been cleared for a new structure.[42]

In his last article, he wrote as follows:

I must not be misunderstood. I do not suppose that the classical medicine will work by itself or that we can depend on it. We need quicker and less painful aids, of which exchange variation and overall import control are the most important. But in the long run these expedients will work better and we shall need them less, if the classical medicine is also at work. And if we reject the medicine from our systems altogether, we may just drift on from expedient to expedient and never get really fit again. The great virtue of the Bretton Woods and Washington proposals, taken in conjunction, is that they marry the use of the necessary expedients to the wholesome long-run doctrine.[43]

Over the years, Keynes had moved from support of the old-fashioned gold standard to a domestic standard and finally back to an international standard which, though yielding a reasonable degree of stability, was at the same time consistent with domestic policies directed to sustaining demand at an adequate level. Over a period of twenty-five years, with but one brief interruption, he fought zealously and with considerable success, for free, dom from international forces which depress domestic economies.

[42] Lord Keynes in *House of Lords*, December 18, 1945; see below, p. 393.
[43] Lord Keynes, "The Balance of Payments of the United States," EJ, June, 1946, p. 186.

CHAPTER XXI

Domestic and International Equilibrium

By RAGNAR NURKSE

INTRODUCTION

THE IMPACT of Keynesian Economics on the theory of international monetary relations has been powerful. Keynes himself, though he was well aware of the international policy implications of his doctrines, did very little to apply his *General Theory* to the analysis of international equilibrium. But he provided a theoretical framework which subsequent writers had no trouble in adapting to the special case of international relations. From this work of adaptation there emerged a whole system of international economics, set up in terms of the money income and expenditure analysis.

The income approach to international trade was not by any means entirely new. For over a century, writers on international trade had referred occasionally to shifts of purchasing power or changes in relative demand.[1] The Keynesian approach, however, seemed to yield a more comprehensive and consistent account of international monetary relations than had ever been given before. It furnished at one and the same time an explanation of two related matters: (a) the adjustment process of the balance of payments and (b) the international transmission of fluctuations in economic activity and employment. The result has been a fruitful marriage of two subjects that previously led quite separate existences under the conventional names of international trade theory and business cycle theory.

---

[1] *Cf.* Jacob Viner, *Studies in the Theory of International Trade* (1937), Chapter VI.

National frontiers as such are basically irrelevant to economic analysis; it is only government policies that make them relevant. And yet a political boundary-line may be useful to the economist because it forms, as it were, a zone of light through which economic processes pass and at which at least some of them can best be observed. Customs, immigration and other officials, recording the international movement of goods, people, and money, give us information such as we do not possess for inter-regional movements within the same country. Accordingly, it is often in its international aspects that any monetary or business cycle theory is apt to meet its stiffest test in regard to verification. There have been theories that have not been successful in meeting this test of international application. For example, the traditional price-specie-flow doctrine, which represents the quantity theory of money in its international aspect, was found by one of its last distinguished proponents to be quite unrealistic.[2] Again, the "neutral money" school, when one of its leading authors attempted to apply it to international shifts, led to rather strange results.[3] By contrast, in the income-and-expenditure analysis of the Keynesian type we have a theoretical apparatus which lends itself very simply and naturally to international monetary analysis, and which yields a realistic account of both the adjustment mechanism of the balance of payments and the propagation of economic fluctuations from country to country. The "adjustment

[2] See F. W. Taussig, *International Trade* (1927): "The process which our theory contemplates . . . can hardly be expected to take place smoothly and quickly. Yet no signs of disturbance are to be observed such as the theoretic analysis previses; and some recurring phenomena are of a kind not contemplated by theory at all" (p. 239). Taussig found the facts "baffling" and "puzzling" (pp. 242, 261), and his celebrated statement that "things just happened so" was an honest admission of defeat.

[3] See F. A. von Hayek, *Monetary Nationalism and International Stability* (1937), pp. 25–34. Hayek apparently maintained that, under modern banking conditions, gold movements were bound to cause "monetary disturbances" similar to those which, in *Prices and Production*, he had described for the closed economy: deviations of the "market rate" from the "natural rate" of interest, leading to elongations and contractions in the capital structure of production. That the adjustment of the international balance of payments should necessitate such convulsions is neither plausible *a priori* nor confirmed by the facts. Taussig (*op. cit.*) found the adjustment to work more smoothly and directly than even the price-specie-flow theory had pictured it. So did many other writers, including notably C. Bresciani-Turroni (*Inductive Verification of the Theory of International Payments*, 1932) and Harry D. White (*The French International Accounts, 1880–1913*, 1933).

problem" and the "propagation problem" appear in this analysis merely as two aspects of the same dynamic process of income change. The former relates primarily to the international monetary accounts, while the latter directs attention to fluctuations in domestic income and employment. It is the "propagation" aspect that is mainly significant for the international policy implications of Keynesian economics, though the "accounting" aspect also, as we shall see, imposes itself constantly on any consideration of national policy.

Before taking up the policy implications, we must briefly indicate the nature of the income approach to the mechanics of international equilibrium. A highly simplified account is all that can be attempted in the space available.

NATIONAL INCOME AND THE FOREIGN TRADE MULTIPLIER

There is a two-way relationship between national income and foreign trade. On the one hand, changes in income generally entail changes in the same direction in the demand for imports. On the other, changes in the volume of exports tend to produce changes in domestic income.

If an expansion gets under way in one country, there will be an increase in imports into that country; which means an increase in exports for some other country. It is through this increase in exports that the expansion is transmitted to the other country. Let us see how this happens. The increase in exports will lead directly to an expansion of income and employment in the export industries. Some part of the additional income earned in the export industries may be spent immediately on imported goods, so that an equilibrating tendency toward greater imports to match the increase in exports comes into play at once. But this first increase in imports will usually be far from sufficient to restore an even balance. A part, and presumably the greater part, of the additional receipts of the export industries will be spent on home-produced goods. The increase in incomes spreads to domestic industries. At each step in the sequence of successive spending, a part of the increased money income will be diverted to swell the demand for imports.

To assume that each increment of income is entirely spent, either on imports or on home-made goods, is unrealistic; some part is likely to be saved. If there were no increased investment to absorb this saving, the rise in the total income flow would inevitably be arrested before the point at which imports become equal to the higher exports. In fact, however, the increased flow of spending on home-made goods is likely to have the "acceleration effect" of inducing a higher rate of capital expenditure, which will tend to offset the additional saving.[4]

In short, total money income in the country considered will tend to expand until the increased expenditure on imports equals the original increase in exports. In this way the increase in exports will have generated a multiple expansion in money income at home, and out of the increased income there will be an increased flow of expenditure on imports. The balance of payments comes back into equilibrium at higher levels of both national income and foreign trade.

In this successive-spending analysis, the proportion in which an increment of income is devoted to purchases of imported goods is evidently the central determinant of the process. This proportion is known as the "marginal propensity to import" or the "marginal import ratio." The higher it is, the more rapidly will imports increase after the initial rise in exports, but the smaller will be the expansion of national income associated with the restoration of external equilibrium. The smaller it is, the larger will be the ultimate increase in national income, but the longer will presumably be the time it takes for the balance between imports and exports to be restored. The increment in total income generated by the rise in exports, compared with the increment in exports itself, gives us the "export multiplier." This is simply the reciprocal of the marginal propensity to import, the reciprocal of the fraction of additional income spent on imports. If this fraction is one-third, for example, the increment in total money income will be equal to three times the increment in exports.[5]

In the event of a decline in foreign demand for the country's

---

[4] Fritz Machlup in his excellent presentation of the multiplier analysis (*International Trade and the National Income Multiplier*, 1943) excludes such induced investment by assumption. I find no need for this assumption here. The acceleration effect due to induced investment may be unpredictable; but so is the multiplier effect of the successive spending flow, since the marginal propensity to import is not likely to remain constant. In any discussion of general tendencies, both the acceleration and multiplier effects have their place.

[5] This assumes that additional saving is offset by a larger volume of investment, induced in the way just indicated. If increased domestic in-

exports, the multiplier mechanism operates in reverse. Equilibrium in the balance of payments will tend to be restored, this time at a lower level of trade, through a reduction in national income by an amount equal to the decrement in exports multiplied by the reciprocal of the marginal import ratio. Total money income will tend to fall to a level at which people's expenditure on imports will balance the diminished receipts from exports.

All these changes—upward in one case, downward in the other—which we have traced in national income, exports, and imports, are changes in terms of money value. To what extent they reflect changes in real volume will depend on the elasticity of supply. At less than full employment, supply is likely to be relatively elastic, so that movements in money value will signify real changes in the same direction. The particular supply conditions for exports and imports may show some elasticity even in a state of general full employment, so long as shifts are possible between production for the home market and for export. They may, on the other hand, be inelastic, if they depend heavily on certain specific factors of production. The extent to which money values reflect real changes need not be the same for exports, imports, and national income. For all three, however, some degree of correspondence between monetary and real changes is likely to exist below the level of general full employment.

The income approach to the study of foreign trade movements, as exemplified in the multiplier technique, is useful mainly in explaining fluctuations in the *volume* of trade. The classical doctrine of comparative costs in its various formulations was primarily concerned with the *composition* of a given volume of trade. In the international sphere, therefore, Keynesian economics has had the effect of shifting our center of attention in a manner analogous to the general shift which it promoted—from the traditional preoccupation with the optimum distribution of a given volume of employment to the analysis of the forces determining the volume of employment itself. .

It is true that the multiplier analysis, though always mechanically applicable, is most appropriate, in the sense of most likely to yield significant results in real terms, when changes in total

---

vestment does not provide the necessary offset to the additional saving, the income expansion will be arrested before imports have risen to the new level of exports, and there will remain an export surplus; which means, in effect, that the additional saving is offset by *foreign* investment.

money income come about through changes in the volume of employment rather than through changes in money wage-rates and prices.[6] It is clear that, in the adjustment process, price changes work generally in the right direction for the restoration of equilibrium. But, insofar as they occur at all, they are essentially a by-product of the changes in the volume of employment and productive activity. These latter changes are therefore to be regarded as the primary equilibrating factors.[7]

The multiplier mechanism accounts at the same time for the adjustment of the balance of payments and for the transmission of income and employment fluctuations from country to country. An increase in a country's exports leads to an expansion in the volume of domestic income, expenditure, and employment, so that external equilibrium tends to be restored through an upward shift in the country's demand for imports. We have assumed that the increase in exports is induced by a boom in a foreign country. The expansion initiated in that country is transmitted through the multiplier process, which thus tends to produce a synchronization of economic fluctuations in different countries. It is only in the rather special case of an "autonomous" increase in exports (due, say, to devaluation of the home currency, a tariff reduction abroad, or a spontaneous shift of consumer's demand as between home-made and imported goods) that the favorable effect on income and employment at home will be accompanied by an unfavorable effect abroad.

Any expansion or contraction originating in the domestic economy tends to spread abroad through its effects on the demand for imports. A domestic investment boom will "spill over" to other countries since part of the increased money income "leaks out" for the purchase of additional imports. This leakage, while it checks the growth of income at home, is what transmits the expansion process outward. The size of the leakage is determined

---

[6] Machlup's book (*op. cit.*, pp. 19 ff.) proceeds entirely on the assumption that prices remain unchanged. But even Keynes was not so Keynesian as to ignore the price effects of income and employment fluctuations. (See his admirable Chapter 21 in the *General Theory*.)

[7] "The problem may be synthesized by putting the question: Why should an inflow of gold raise industrial costs and so reduce exports? Surely only by setting up a keener competition for the means of production. . . . The mode of operation through an expansion of activity must therefore be considered the true theory and the phenomena which the classical view tends to stress a by-product." R. F. Harrod, *International Economics* (1939 edition), page 140.

by the marginal propensity to import; if it is small, the boom at home can go on for a long while before it leads to an import surplus large enough to stimulate a parallel expansion abroad; if it is large, the boom will not go so far before it "spills over" to other countries.

The special "autonomous" factors tend to produce opposite changes in income and employment in different countries, and so cancel out for the world as a whole. It is in the sphere of domestic expenditure that *general* booms and depressions originate. The propagation mechanism we have described is a passive factor from the world point of view. It is neither expansionist nor contractionist in itself, but reflects the balance of forces at play in the domestic economies, and serves to pass on from country to country the expansionist or contractionist influences originating in one place or another.

The relative strength of the expansionist or contractionist impulses which a country imparts to the outside world as a result of domestic income fluctuations is determined by its marginal propensity to import. But the relative amplitude of the fluctuations in its demand for imports may be wider or narrower than that of the corresponding domestic fluctuations. If a given percentage change in national income produces the same percentage change in imports, the "income elasticity of demand for imports" is said to be equal to unity.[8] An elasticity greater or smaller than unity means that expenditure on imports has a wider or closer percentage range of variation than the national income. A coun-

---

[8] The "marginal propensity to import" and the "income elasticity of demand for imports" are two distinct concepts, but there is a simple relation between them. The former is defined as $\dfrac{\Delta M}{\Delta Y}$ while the latter is $\dfrac{\Delta M}{M} \div \dfrac{\Delta Y}{Y}$ which can also be written as $\dfrac{\Delta M}{\Delta Y} \div \dfrac{M}{Y}$. ($Y$ stands, as usual, for income and M for imports.) Thus the income elasticity of demand is equal to the *marginal* divided by the *average* propensity to import. In the United States, $\dfrac{\Delta M}{\Delta Y}$ is relatively small, but $\dfrac{M}{Y}$ is still smaller, and the expression as a whole is therefore large. In England, on the other hand, imports are much greater in relation to income, but they consist more largely of foodstuffs, for which the demand is relatively steady; so that $\dfrac{\Delta M}{\Delta Y}$, though large, is not as large as $\dfrac{M}{Y}$ and the whole expression is smaller than unity.

try whose national income is relatively variable in itself, and whose imports, in addition, have an income elasticity of demand greater than unity, is particularly troublesome as a source of cyclical change in the world economy. The United States in recent times seems to have corresponded to this description.

The synchronization produced by the multiplier mechanism is naturally imperfect, not only because different countries have different marginal import ratios and income elasticities, but also because the successive-spending process of the multiplier analysis takes time. In consequence, fluctuations in one country will lag behind those in the other. The "lags" in the propagation aspect of the mechanism are associated, in the adjustment aspect, with "gaps" in the balance of payments.[9] Transfers of gold, exchange reserves or private short-term funds are needed to *fill* such gaps temporarily; it is the change in domestic income flows that sooner or later *closes* them. In the traditional doctrine, gold movements played a central part as a causally significant factor. In the modern view, they act rather in a passive manner as stop-gaps in the balance of payments, covering discrepancies in foreign receipts and expenditures which, in time, bring about their own adjustment through changes in domestic money incomes.

This explanation of the adjustment process applies, of course, to a system of fixed exchange rates. What it shows is essentially the working of international monetary and cyclical relations in the old days of the automatic gold standard. The gold standard was a system for maintaining equilibrium of external payments among the member countries. It paid no regard to internal equilibrium in any of the member countries, or to the equilibrium of the system as a whole. It required that countries should not seek to control their national money income deliberately by domestic means; it presupposed a laissez faire economy. These prerequisites to its smooth working came to be less and less adequately fulfilled as nations became conscious of a desire for economic stability, and as national policies were framed increasingly with a view to promoting employment and social security. The income approach to international economics would be of purely historical interest if its usefulness consisted merely in a better explanation of the international economy under Queen Victoria.

[9] See *Economic Stability in the Post-War World* (League of Nations, 1945), pp. 103 ff. and *International Currency Experience* (League of Nations, 1944), pp. 100 ff.

It is useful, more generally, in that it shows what the automatic tendencies of monetary adjustment and cyclical synchronization would be in the absence of governmental or other interferences. Above all, it is useful in any analysis of the external effects of various national policies aimed at internal equilibrium. It is a necessary foundation on which to consider the international policy problems arising from national employment policies.

If internal equilibrium is defined as a level of national income such that there is neither general unemployment nor an inflationary tendency for prices to rise, while external equilibrium is essentially a balance of payments that maintains itself without the persistent need for monetary "stop-gaps" on the one hand or, to anticipate, increased trade barriers on the other, then the central policy problem is concisely described as that of harmonizing the requirements of internal with those of external equilibrium.

Keynes gave a great deal of thought to the international policy implications of the search for internal equilibrium, but he did not explicitly set out the mechanics of external equilibrium himself. The preceding sketch does not correspond in all particulars to Keynesian doctrine.[10] The multiplier analysis admits, as Machlup has shown, of almost endless variations and refinements in detail. Yet in its essence the application of the income approach to the case of international adjustment is simple and self-evident. It is perhaps for this reason that Keynes did not undertake it himself. In his celebrated controversy with Ohlin (*Economic Journal*, 1929), he had adopted an entirely "un-Keynesian" attitude, stressing the price effects in the transfer process and largely ignoring the income effects. But Keynes never had much difficulty in repudiating his previous views, and it would be hard to believe that

---

[10] Thus, we have found no use for the "instantaneous" interpretation of the multiplier as Keynes expounds it in the *General Theory*, and have relied instead on the "serial" interpretation which expressly recognizes the time element in the successive spending process. Also, we have implicitly contradicted Keynes' statement that "the effects of loan expenditure (i.e., home investment) and of the foreign balance are in *pari materia*." (*The Means to Prosperity*, p. 36.) In our sketch, which follows Machlup's treatment in this respect, the foreign balance arising from an increase in exports leads to a flow of additional income which, so long as exports remain at the higher level, maintains itself even when the foreign balance has fallen back to zero through the induced expansion of imports. In the case of home investment, on the other hand, the net investment expenditure must go on continuously at a steady rate if income is to be maintained at the increased level.

the silence he maintained on the international aspects of the *General Theory* was due to a vested interest in his earlier position.

THE PURSUIT OF FULL EMPLOYMENT
IN AN OPEN ECONOMY

Turning to the international policy implications of Keynesian economics, the first general principle is that responsibility for the maintenance of a high and stable level of employment in any given country lies primarily in the field of domestic policy. Nothing can absolve a country from the necessity of taking measures to put its own house in order through the maintenance of a sufficient volume of effective demand at home to keep its productive resources employed at the maximum level that can be continuously sustained without an inflationary rise of prices.

The next point to recognize is that a country in pursuit of this objective—in pursuit, in short, of "full employment"—should never be deterred by difficulties, actual or anticipated, in its balance of external payments. There exist specific methods of influencing the balance of payments so that, regardless of the behavior of its neighbors, and without injuring its neighbors, a country can effectively seek to preserve external equilibrium while pursuing the full employment objective at home.

It is true that these methods can also be resorted to as instruments of a "beggar-my-neighbor" policy, aimed at improving domestic employment by creating external disequilibrium. This policy must for obvious reasons be barred. In fact, no country that knows how to keep up employment by constructive domestic measures will want to adopt it. From the point of view of a national economy, creating employment through an export surplus is just like "digging holes" at home.

The behavior of its neighbors need never deflect a country from the pursuit of full employment. The classical free trade doctrine showed that it was both beneficial and practicable for an individual country to abolish its trade barriers even in the face of a protectionist world. In the same way it is always to some extent possible for a single country to pursue a full employment policy unilaterally. The relative importance of foreign markets, the dependence on imported raw materials, and other similar conditions vary, of course, from country to country. Yet, to some extent, it is always possible for a single country to go ahead with a domestic expansion policy even in a world of depression and unemployment. The expansion will inevitably, under these conditions, produce an adverse balance of payments. So long as there are ample liquid reserves to meet the external deficit, there is no reason to worry about it. When liquid reserves have run out or are not available to start with, there is usually some change in the exchange rate that will preserve external equilibrium. Alternatively, there is the possibility of adopting import restrictions, not in order to reduce imports, but just enough to prevent them from increasing. This will prevent the expansion from "spilling over" abroad, but will not actually hurt the outside world. It is a defensive measure aimed at maintaining the equilibrium of foreign payments, and is to be sharply distinguished from the aggressive and unneighborly policy which operates through a disruption of external equilibrium.

The balance of payments is the test of whether a change in exchange rates or import restrictions is a defensive or an aggressive measure. Nothing is simpler; yet this attitude of "relativity" is repugnant to many laymen and economists alike. People often tend to regard a policy measure as either good or bad in all circumstances. In reality, "it all depends." Devaluation or import restrictions may be justifiable, as in the case of a unilaterally expanding country, when they are intended to close a deficit or preserve equilibrium in the balance of payments. They are not justifiable when their purpose is to create a surplus in the balance of payments or to enlarge a surplus already existing. The distinction was evidently quite clear in Keynes' mind when, in speaking of the Bretton Woods scheme and the U. S. Proposals for the Expansion of World Trade, he said: "Both the currency and the commercial proposals are devised to favour the maintenance of equilibrium by expressly permitting various protective devices when they are required to maintain equilibrium and by forbidding them when they are not so required."[11] The balance-of-payments test is no doubt subject to a great many qualifications in practice; but it is fairly clear in principle.[12] Surpluses and deficits in the balance of payments reflect the external employment

[11] Speech in the House of Lords, Dec. 18, 1945; see below, p. 393.
[12] The proper criterion is the balance of payments on account of all current transactions and productive capital movements, excluding for obvious reasons gold movements, short-term funds, and hot money flights. I have discussed this more fully in *Conditions of International Monetary Equilib-*

effects of economic fluctuations and policies in different countries. The balance-of-payments test may seem a superficial one, but it corresponds in every case to the deeper needs of employment policy. For instance, a country suffering a depression at home is likely to develop automatically a surplus in its balance of payments. Devaluation or import restrictions in these circumstances are the opposite of what is required for external equilibrium. Nor are they required for internal equilibrium; for it is evident that internal equilibrium, in the sense indicated earlier, can and should be attained by domestic measures of expansion; and its attainment would tend incidentally to restore the equilibrium of external payments as well.

For purposes of employment policy, import restrictions are on a par with exchange devaluation. In their effects on foreign trade, however, the two types of measures are very different. Exchange policy is far preferable to commercial policy, though the latter, being much more effective in emergencies, may have its legitimate uses for temporary purposes. Exchange adjustments and import restrictions alike may serve the ends of a defensive or an aggressive policy. The universal rise of trade barriers in the pre-war decade was due to both these policies and finds its explanation not in the theory of international trade, but in the theory of employment. But to discard permanently the gains from international trade is foolish and, besides, quite unnecessary for internal equilibrium. The case for import restrictions as a defensive measure is sometimes extended far beyond its narrow legitimate scope. It is argued that the domestic policies aimed at full employment can be more easily carried out in a closed economy than in an economy maintaining trade relations with other countries. There are two possible grounds for this proposition. The first is the fear that foreign disturbances may interfere with domestic stability and full employment, and the aim is to lessen the danger of such disturbances by reducing economic intercourse with the outside world to a minimum. This anxiety is groundless. There exists effective methods of offsetting or averting the impact of foreign disturbances by appropriate variations in domestic expenditure combined with the use of external monetary reserves, or by meas-

---

rium (Princeton University, Essays in International Finance, No. 4, 1945). Compare also *International Currency Experience* (League of Nations, 1944), Chapter IX, Section 3 ("Exchange Adjustments and Exchange Control").

ures designed to protect the equilibrium of external settlements. There is no need to sacrifice the benefits of international trade for the sake of maintaining a stable and satisfactory level of domestic activity.

The second argument for autarky amounts to saying that the employment problem is less serious in a poor community than in a rich one. There is some truth in this. The international division of labor is a labor-saving device. Destroying it, just like destroying machines, may increase the number of jobs in times of unemployment; but it will leave us permanently worse off. Balance-of-payments equilibrium which is obtained by curtailing the international division of labor cannot therefore be regarded as a true equilibrium position. Just as free trade by itself cannot ensure full employment, so the suppression of trade, though it might increase employment numerically, can never bring real prosperity. It is utterly senseless to create employment by reducing the level of economic efficiency. There are other ways of solving the employment problem.

The use of import restrictions may be inevitable when a deficit arises in the balance of payments which cannot be met from liquid reserves, and for which exchange adjustment would be too slow a remedy. Such a deficit may arise from a depression in one of a country's export markets. If the gap is closed by import restrictions, a surplus will develop in the balance of payments as soon as the foreign market recovers. The proper way then to eliminate the surplus is neither exchange appreciation, nor foreign lending, nor anything else except the removal of the import restrictions; it is the only way of restoring balance-of-payments equilibrium together with the pre-existing degree of international specialization.[13]

We have referred earlier to the case of a deficit arising in the balance of payments of a single country trying to raise its level of employment at a time of general depression. The problems of national employment policy may be considered a little more closely in the case of a country which is successfully maintaining both external and internal equilibrium at full employment, but

[13] This does not concern import barriers which a country chooses to maintain more or less permanently, for social, military, or other reasons. Starting from his *Means to Prosperity* (p. 25), Keynes repeatedly contrasted these special or structural trade barriers, which we have to take for granted, with the restrictions arising from a general search for employment or from the general state of the balance of payments.

which suddenly finds itself faced with a depression abroad. Here also, a deficit arises, but this time from a fall in exports rather than a rise in imports. The export industries will suffer a depression which, through the multiplier mechanism operating in reverse, will tend to spread to the whole domestic economy. The maintenance of internal equilibrium in these circumstances calls for offsetting the fall in foreign expenditure on the country's products by an increase in the volume of domestic expenditure. This offsetting policy, which is the opposite of what the gold standard rules would require, is subject to limitations; [14] but insofar as total employment depends on total outlay, the compensatory increase in domestic demand will tend to prevent a general depression in the given country. It does nothing, however, to correct the external disequilibrium. The gap in the balance of payments resulting from the fall in exports must be filled by drawing on the country's gold and foreign exchange reserves. How long the offsetting policy can be continued depends entirely on the size of these reserves. If they are ample, the depression abroad may right itself before they run out; it may be followed by an inflationary boom abroad, in which case the country's reserves of international liquidity will be replenished. If, however, the reserves become exhausted or unduly depleted before recovery abroad restores equilibrium in the balance of payments, then resort must be had to other measures: measures designed to correct the balance of payments.

When liquid reserves are inadequate to meet the external deficit, then and only then is the time to take measures to correct the balance of payments. Chief among these measures are exchange depreciation and import restrictions.[15] For the sake of completeness, deflation may also be mentioned here. If it were possible to carry out general wage cuts by government decree overnight, this might be an effective way of righting the foreign balance without adverse effects on domestic employment. The effect of wage reductions in a closed economy are somewhat doubtful, the Keynesian position being that they improve employment, if at all, mainly through their repercussions on the in-

---

[14] See, e.g., *Economic Stability in the Post-War World* (*op. cit.*), p. 232, or *Conditions of International Monetary Equilibrium* (*op. cit.*), pp. 11–14.

[15] This is not the place to discuss the various types of import restrictions. They include, of course, import quotas and exchange controls as well as tariffs.

terest rate. In an open economy, by contrast, the efficacy of wage reductions—though not their desirability—is undisputed. Like exchange depreciation, wage reductions act as a beggar-my-neighbor policy of stimulating home employment when their effect is to create a surplus and not, as in the present case, to close a deficit in the balance of payments. In practice, however, it is generally only through unemployment that wage reductions can be brought about. Deflation is a possible means of correcting the balance of payments, but it is destructive of internal equilibrium and therefore out of the question.

We are left with (a) changes in exchange rates and (b) measures of commercial policy. Both operate on the balance of trade either by restricting imports or promoting exports or by a combination of the two. Besides correcting the foreign balance, however, they also contribute on their own account toward offsetting the fall in expenditure and employment which tends to result from the drop in exports abroad. Those measures which operate by restricting imports serve to direct the flow of expenditure from foreign goods to the home market; those which promote exports tend to increase or rather, in the present case, to restore employment and income in the export industries. The effect on aggregate employment and expenditure in the country considered is favorable. But this favorable effect could equally well be obtained by domestic expansion. It is clear, therefore, that these measures are strictly necessary only to correct the balance of payments and are to be judged only in this capacity.

Exchange adjustments or import restrictions should come into play only when the offsetting policy which we have described cannot be continued because of a shortage of liquid reserves. Once they do come into play, however, their effects on domestic employment and expenditure make it necessary, if inflation is to be avoided, to cancel some or all of the compensatory increase in expenditure which characterized the offsetting policy. This may seem an unnecessary theoretical refinement. In practice, the effects of the successive measures can never be observed or judged so closely. Yet even for policy-making there can be no harm in clarity as to the detailed implications of full employment policy in an open economy. The general principle remains: total outlay on the country's output should be kept at a level corresponding to the maximum volume of employment attainable without inflation. The complications introduced by the existence of foreign trade relate, as we have seen, to the need to compensate for changes in foreigners' outlay on the country's products by inverse changes in domestic outlay and, similarly, to offset the incidental effect on total outlay of measures taken primarily to right the balance of payments.

So far we have discussed the problems arising from a depression in the country's export markets abroad. The opposite case, an inflationary boom abroad, has the opposite effects and calls for the opposite policy measures for the maintenance of internal equilibrium. The rise in exports, and also the fall in the marginal propensity to import due to the rise in import prices, will have to be offset by a reduction in domestic expenditure. If gold and exchange reserves become excessive, an appreciation of the currency or a lowering of import barriers is the appropriate remedy. Here again the secondary adjustments required in domestic expenditure need not be overlooked. A tariff reduction tends to direct expenditure from home-made to imported goods; its effect is deflationary; and to compensate for this, an expansion will be required in domestic expenditure so as to keep total outlay on the country's output stable.

Such, in brief, are the rules of conduct which emerge from the Keynesian system to guide an individual country in search of internal equilibrium at full employment. In the preceding pages some readers may have missed a discussion of comparative cost structures, the play of relative prices, the forces of international competition, the shifts required between production for home needs and for export, the constant adaptation of a country's export industries to changing world markets, and other similar topics. All these are valid subjects of theoretical inquiry and practical concern; they are on a different level of discourse, but they retain their validity within the Keynesian system. The classical analysis concerns itself essentially with the optimum division of labor between countries. It is under conditions of full employment that this type of analysis comes most fully into its own. The Keynesian approach demonstrates that any single country can and should do something to realize these conditions within its borders, without hurting its neighbors and without throwing away the gains from international trade. Speaking for his own country, Keynes made this resolute statement: "whilst we intend to prevent inflation at home, we will not accept deflation at the dictates of influences from outside." [16] And he welcomed the postwar trade and currency schemes as an attempt to "combine the advantages of freedom of commerce with safeguards against the disastrous consequences of a laissez faire system which pays no direct regard to the preservation of equilibrium and merely relies on the working out of blind forces." [17]

INTERNATIONAL COORDINATION OF FULL EMPLOYMENT POLICIES

As we have seen, any single country has means at its disposal for warding off or neutralizing the impact of cyclical disturbances emanating from abroad. On the other hand, each country must agree to have its freedom of action limited by the obligation to consider the effects of its policies not only on the domestic situation but also on other countries. This implies in particular an obligation to refrain from the beggar-my-neighbor policy of creating a surplus in the balance of payments and so improving the employment situation at home at the expense of other countries. Even without deliberate policy, a surplus in the balance of payments tends to result automatically when there is a depression in domestic income and employment, and will, automatically, provide some relief from that depression. But just as other countries are entitled to take steps against this disequilibrium in international settlements, so the surplus country itself should help to eliminate it, if not by domestic expansion then at any rate by such measures as foreign lending or tariff reduction. It is true that the removal of the surplus by tariff reduction would tend to have unfavorable effects on domestic employment in the surplus country; but clearly there is nothing to prevent these effects from being offset by domestic expansion.

The outlawing of beggar-my-neighbor policies means that full employment must be pursued by domestic measures alone. The international paradox of countries scrambling for export markets and shutting off imports is merely a reflection of the domestic paradox of unemployment and "poverty in the midst of plenty." A solution of the domestic problem gives a solution of the international problem as a by-product, or at any rate creates the con-

[16] Speech in the House of Lords, May 23, 1944; see below, p. 374.
[17] Speech in the House of Lords, December 18, 1945; see below, p. 393.

ditions required for the solution of the international problem. This view is expressed very strongly in the *General Theory*.[18]

In his *Means to Prosperity*, Keynes had already stated the case for international co-ordination of domestic employment policies. Writing at the bottom of the depression in March 1933, he said: "We should attach great importance to the *simultaneity* of the movement towards increased expenditure. For the pressure on its foreign balance which each country fears as the result of increasing its own loan-expenditure, will cancel out if other countries are pursuing the same policy at the same time. . . . Combined international action is of the essence of policy." [19] The same idea appears, ten years later, in the *Proposals for an International Clearing Union*, of which Keynes is believed to have been the main author: "if active employment and ample purchasing power can be sustained in the main centers of world trade, the problem of surpluses and unwanted exports will largely disappear." [20]

The doctrine of international co-ordination of national policies for the maintenance of productive activity and employment has undoubtedly a strong appeal. If it can be realized, then it is possible that a high degree of exchange stability may be secured as a result of domestic stability in the various individual countries. Few nations, if any, will nowadays endure a severe deflation or inflation just for the sake of a stable exchange parity. It is only as a result, and not at the expense, of domestic economic stability that we may hope for some stability in international currency relations as well. Under the gold standard, exchange stability was, in effect, achieved through the synchronization of business fluctuations in the various countries. Under the new system, exchange stability would be achieved not through the synchronization of business fluctuations, but through the co-ordination of national policies to keep employment and production at the maximum level attainable without a general rise in prices.[21] We may even imagine a central international authority or council directing

[18] *Op. cit.* pp. 349 and 382.
[19] *The Means to Prosperity*, p. 24.
[20] *Proposals by British Experts for an International Clearing Union* (British Information Service. New York, 1943), page 14; see below, p. 334.
[21] This maximum level may, of course, differ in the various countries, since the strength of labor unions, government controls, and other circumstances differ. In some countries the minimum degree of unemployment attainable may be 3 or 4 per cent, while in others it may be 6 or 7 per cent.

the co-ordination of national policies so as to make domestic equilibrium in the individual countries compatible with equilibrium in the international accounts.

But this idea of "combined international action," pleasing though it may be to the imagination, can be carried too far. Keynes, a master of *political* economy, seems to have viewed it with skepticism in his later years.[22] Any scheme aiming, however discreetly, at some super-national regimentation of domestic fiscal and monetary policies would be certain to encounter political and psychological obstacles in the world as we find it. Besides, it would be unnecessarily ambitious. Keynes was concerned to preserve some freedom of national action, hoping no doubt that nations would sooner or later adopt the correct internal policies spontaneously. We can hardly hope for more at the present stage. Even the gold standard system of the past was never based on any formal international convention, or possessed of any central executive machinery; it grew up freely and spontaneously through the recognition of a common primary objective (exchange stability) by a number of like-minded nations. In the same way, it is from a common recognition of the need to maintain a high and stable level of employment that a new system of stable international currency relations may spontaneously develop. Meanwhile it is right and proper that any single country pursuing this objective at home, without attempting to "export unemployment," should have access, under appropriate conditions, to exchange-rate adjustments or other "protective devices" needed to ensure equilibrium in its balance of payments.

In the world as we find it, what matters is not so much the international co-ordination of national full-employment policies as

---

[22] Here are a few quotations to illustrate his attitude: "There should be the least possible interference with internal national policies, and the plan should not wander from the international terrain." (*Proposals for an International Clearing Union*, Preface; see below, p. 324.) "The error of the gold-standard lay in submitting national wage-policies to outside dictation. It is wiser to regard stability (or otherwise) of internal prices as a matter of internal policy and politics." (EJ, 1943, p. 187.) "We must solve it (i.e., the problem of domestic stability) in our own domestic way, feeling that we are free men. The suggestion of external pressure will make the political and psychological problem of making good sense prevail more difficult." (EJ, 1944, p. 430.) In his speech of December 18, 1945, in the House of Lords, Keynes recommended the monetary and commercial policy proposals in these words: "The plans do not wander from the international terrain, and they are consistent with widely different conceptions of domestic policy."

the successful pursuit of such policies in one particular country, the United States. The effective realization, without inflationary disturbances, of stable and active employment conditions in the United States could do more than anything else to help other countries in their search for domestic as well as external equilibrium. As Joan Robinson puts it, "the problem which lies before the United States is what to do with her prodigious productive capacity—whether to use it for home consumption, to use it for the development of other countries, or to waste it in unemployment. No amount of ingenuity in devising currency schemes can influence the main issue." [23]

Apart from the variability of foreign investment, the external impact of economic fluctuations in the United States operates through the great variability of imports into the United States.[24] In contrast to British imports, where foodstuffs play the leading part, American imports consist very largely of industrial raw materials and are therefore closely geared to fluctuations in the volume of industrial production. Moreover, they consist very largely of the storable and standardized commodities in which price speculation, forward buying, and inventory fluctuations play such an important role. For this reason, as was shown by the experience of the years 1936–38, the value of imports is apt to vary even more widely than the tempo of domestic industrial activity. Buffer stocks must be mentioned here as a possible remedy for this state of affairs. Keynes was a keen advocate of this method of offsetting cyclical fluctuations in the demand for and prices of primary products.[25] It has been common in the past to speak of buffer stocks as a means of protecting primary producing countries from the effects of business cycles originating in the industrial countries. Given the circumstances just indicated, it is clear that the buffer stock idea deserves to be discussed as a means, more particularly, of mitigating the impact of American business fluctuations on the rest of the world. As far as the outside world

[23] "The International Currency Proposals," EJ, 1943, p. 169. (See below, pp. 350–1.)

[24] U. S. imports before the war constituted, on the average, only about one-tenth of total world imports. But their range of variation was such that from 1937 to 1938, for example, the reduction in U. S. imports alone accounted for about one-third of the reduction in total world imports. (See League of Nations, *Review of World Trade*, 1938, pp. 20–21.)

[25] See his article, "The Policy of Government Storage of Foodstuffs and Raw Materials," EJ, 1938.

is concerned, stabilizing the United States' demand for imports by means of buffer stocks may to some extent be an acceptable substitute for stabilizing the course of domestic business activity in the United States.

KEYNES AND ECONOMIC NATIONALISM

Keynes has been widely regarded as the high priest of economic nationalism; but even the slightest insight into the international implications of Keynesian economics must lead to a rejection of this view. In the *General Theory*, it is only incidentally that Keynes adverts to the international aspects of his doctrine. The remarks on mercantilism which he included among the "Short Notes Suggested by the General Theory" may well have misled unwary readers into believing that Keynes was advocating a reversion to mercantilism. The belief is utterly erroneous, though it is not difficult to see how it might have arisen, especially since Keynes gave us no positive and systematic account of international relationships in his system. All he was concerned to point out was that the mercantilists were essentially right in affirming, and the classical writers unrealistic in denying, that an improvement in the trade balance was likely to have stimulating effects on domestic business conditions. The multiplier analysis of foreign trade makes this proposition a self-evident one today. Keynes was quite clear as to the "beggar-my-neighbor" character of the mercantilist policies, and he was far from advocating them.[26] It was the rigid gold-standard system which, in his view, fostered a spirit of nationalism since, under conditions of laissez faire, the beggar-my-neighbor policies of mercantilism were the only means available to an individual country for the revival or maintenance of domestic employment.

The Keynesian position on international economic policy is perhaps best summarized by the following three quotations from the *General Theory*:

(1) Never in history was there a method devised of such efficacy for setting each country's advantage at variance with its neighbours' as the international gold . . . standard. For it made domestic prosperity directly dependent on a competitive pur-

[26] The plainly derogatory term "beggar-my-neighbor policies" was introduced, in print at any rate, not by Keynes himself, but by one of his earliest disciples, Joan Robinson, in *Essays in the Theory of Employment* (1937), Part III.

suit of markets and a competitive appetite for the precious metals . . .[27]

(2) But if nations can learn to provide themselves with full employment by their domestic policy . . . there need be no important economic forces calculated to set the interest of one country against that of its neighbours . . . there would no longer be a pressing motive why one country need force its wares on another or repulse the offerings of its neighbour, not because this was necessary to enable it to pay for what it wished to purchase, but with the express object of upsetting the equilibrium of payments so as to develop a balance of trade in its own favour . . .[28]

(3) And it is the simultaneous pursuit of these policies by all countries together which is capable of restoring economic health and strength internationally, whether we measure it by the level of domestic employment or by the volume of international trade.[29]

In view of this, it would not be difficult to argue that Keynes, far from being a proponent of economic nationalism, is the true internationalist among modern economists. The change which his teaching has wrought in the general approach to international economics is fundamental. International trade is not a thing apart, but is merely that section of the total volume of goods produced and exchanged which happens to cross national frontiers; and anything that lowers or raises the total volume of activity is bound to reflect itself also in the movement of foreign trade. The narrow "commercial policy" approach which has been usual in the past is quite inadequate to the task of expanding world trade.

The relationship between domestic employment and international trade is now generally recognized. Its significance has found expression in the very title of the commercial-policy proposals put forward by the United States in 1945: *Proposals for the Expansion of World Trade and Employment.* Under this scheme, the members of the proposed International Trade Organization "recognize that the attainment and maintenance of useful employment opportunities for those able, willing, and seeking to work are essential to the full realization of the purposes of the Organization. . . . Each Member shall take action designed to achieve and maintain full employment within its own jurisdiction through measures appropriate to its political and

[27] *General Theory,* p. 349.
[28] *Ibid.,* p. 382.
[29] *Ibid.,* p. 389.

economic institutions. . . . In seeking to maintain or expand employment, no Member shall adopt measures which would have the effect of creating unemployment in other countries." [30] It is clear that Keynes' general ideas have had a considerable influence on post-war plans for international trade.

INTERNATIONAL MONETARY POLICY AND MULTILATERAL TRADE

The charge of economic nationalism which has been levelled against Keynes appears even less tenable when we consider his work for the construction of a new international monetary system, to which he devoted the last years of his life. There are two reasons for dealing with this work more briefly than with the influence of his general ideas. In the first place, the specific features of Keynesian economics, concerned as they are with the creation and regulation of effective demand, do not enter into, and indeed have no place in, the international monetary arrangements for the settlement of foreign balances. The maintenance of effective demand is, in the nature of the case, primarily a matter of domestic responsibility. The balance of payments merely transmits, it cannot create effective demand.[31] Some critics, seeing the name of Keynes prominently associated with the Bretton Woods scheme, seem to have feared that adherence to the scheme would mean compulsory deficit financing in every country. They must have been reassured on reading the text of the agreement: there is nothing in it to warrant such fears. The critics may have been right in one sense: the maintenance of high and stable levels of employment in the leading member nations is, ultimately, an essential prerequisite to the smooth functioning of the international monetary system. Keynes' main concern was the more modest one of ensuring that the new international currency arrangement would at least not discourage the appropriate domestic policies. He hoped, indeed, that it would encourage them by furnishing a favorable external setting. In defending the scheme he said: "It is as providing an international framework for the policy of full employment that these proposals are to be welcomed." [32] The

[30] *Suggested Charter for an International Trade Organization of the United Nations,* U. S. Department of State (1946), p. 2.

[31] It cannot create effective demand except for one country at the expense of others, through the beggar-my-neighbor policies which we want to outlaw.

[32] Speech in the House of Lords, May 23, 1944; see below, p. 377.

Bretton Woods agreements proscribe measures "destructive of national or international prosperity." No country is to be forced into a state of deflation and unemployment as a means of adjusting its balance of payments. The agreements undoubtedly reflect a concern for economic stability and employment; yet they can scarcely be regarded as a direct offspring of Keynesian economics.

Nor can they be regarded as Keynes' personal offspring, even though his share in their formation, as well as in the formation of the Anglo-American trade and financial agreements in 1945, was very considerable. The grandiose Clearing Union proposal of 1943, which is generally attributed to him personally, foundered on the rock of creditor opposition. Even from the debtor countries' point of view, it was open to criticism since the resources which it would have made available, though ostensibly intended for international liquidity purposes, were liable to be drawn upon for post-war capital needs without, however, being distributed in anything like a fair proportion to the capital needs of different countries. John H. Williams and others suspected that the Clearing Union scheme, while cast in the form of a global plan, was essentially designed to meet Britain's balance-of-payments problem after the war. However that may be, it is interesting to note that the combined amount of the postwar loans which Keynes obtained for his country from the United States and Canada was very nearly equal to the 5.5 billion dollars which would have been the British quota in the Clearing Union. Moreover, both these loans took the form of a "line of credit," like the Clearing Union quota, to be drawn upon as and when required.

Keynes' opinions on the operation of the international monetary system under normal conditions, i.e., after the postwar transition period, may be summarized under five heads.

(1) *International Liquidity*: Keynes was well aware that the additional liquidity provided by the International Monetary Fund, just like the liquidity provided by gold and exchange reserves, is useful to any single country pursuing a full-employment policy since it affords additional protection against temporary disturbances entering from outside. On this point he expressed himself as follows: "Do the critics think it preferable, if the winds of the trade cycle blow, to diminish our demand for imports by increasing unemployment at home, rather than meet the emergency out of this Fund which will be expressly provided for such

temporary purposes? I emphasize that such is the purpose of the quotas." [33]

(2) *Exchange Rates*: Exchange stability, if it is to be achieved, must be achieved in future no longer at the expense but as the result of domestic stability of income and employment. Keynes was skeptical about the possibility of co-ordinating the internal wage-policies in different countries and consequently attached great importance to flexible ratios of exchange between the national currencies. By flexibility he did not mean continually fluctuating exchange rates, but rates subject to revision from time to time. Naturally he was in favor of the revision being performed by international agreement, under the auspices of the Fund, so as to prevent countries from taking undue advantage of exchange adjustment unilaterally. What he opposed above all, however, was any such rigidity as that imposed by the gold standard. Speaking for his own country, he declared: "We are determined that in future the external value of sterling shall conform to its internal value as set by our own domestic policies, and not the other way round." [34] In this sense, as well as in the sense that international liquidity reserves are to be used as "insulators" rather than "transmitters" of international business fluctuations, the new monetary system was described by Keynes as "the exact opposite of the gold standard." [35] There is no doubt that Keynes secured a large measure of recognition for his point of view. We need only recall that the name of the Fund, which appeared as "Stabilization Fund" in the U. S. proposal in 1943, was changed to "International Monetary Fund" in 1944.

(3) *Control of Capital Movements*: Keynes had a clear idea of the distinction between equilibrating and disequilibrating short-term capital movements. He referred to the latter in his Clearing Union plan as "movements of funds out of debtor countries which lack the means to finance them." [36] The distinction between capital movements which promote external monetary equilibrium and those which, on the contrary, create or accentuate external disequilibrium is an important one in the conduct of international monetary policy. The transfer of private funds from a country

---

[33] Speech in the House of Lords, May 23, 1944; see below, p. 372.

[34] Speech in the House of Lords, May 23, 1944; see below, p. 374.

[35] *Ibid.*

[36] *Proposals for an International Clearing Union*, paragraph 35; see below, p. 337.

with a high to one with a low interest rate, or from a country with a deficit to one with a surplus in the balance of payments, is just as contrary to the requirements of equilibrium as, for example, the export of wheat from England to Canada. There is now almost universal agreement that capital movements of the unbalancing kind—speculative transfers and capital flights—had better be subjected to control. The statutes of the International Monetary Fund not only permit, but, under certain conditions, may actually require member countries to exercise such control.

(4) *Rationing of Scarce Currencies*: Keynes welcomed the scarce-currency clause of the Fund agreement as a means of preventing the spread of depression from one country to others.[37] If a depression were to occur in a major country such as the United States, that country's imports would decline and its currency would tend to become scarce in the Fund. Under certain conditions the Fund might then proceed to ration its supplies of the scarce currency, permitting member countries to impose similar controls in their transactions in that currency. The effect would be discrimination against the exports of the depressed country, tending to eliminate the export surplus which that country automatically acquires as a result of the fall in its national income and imports. Joan Robinson was the first to point out the attractions of this rationing device for an international system concerned with full employment.[38] The application of the scarce-currency clause would evidently mean a partial suspension of multilateralism. It is presumably intended as a temporary measure, to be introduced as a last resort in an emergency. The general underlying idea is to permit discriminatory devices only when they are urgently needed for the protection of external equilibrium and to subject them to international supervision and control, rather than leave each country free, as in the past, to apply them as and when it thinks fit.

(5) *Multilateralism versus Bilateralism*: Normally, one of the supreme objectives of the new monetary and trading system is precisely to ensure full multilateralism in international settlements. On the general question of multilateral *vs.* bilateral

---

[37] Speech in the House of Lords, May 23, 1944; see below, p. 372.
[38] Joan Robinson, "The International Currency Proposals," EJ, 1943. See, however, Sir William Beveridge, *Full Employment in a Free Society*, pp. 222 ff., for a discussion of the practical difficulties in the way of carrying out this policy.

methods of settlement, Keynes' attitude, as expressed in the speeches and writings of the last three or four years of his life, was quite unequivocal. Keynes is believed to have had a mild flirtation with bilateralistic ideas at some time in the late thirties or early forties; but, if this is true, there are no traces of it in his published writings. In the Clearing Union proposal, as well as in the speech he made in defense of that proposal,[39] he appeared as a determined champion of multilateralism, and this he remained until the end. In the text of the Clearing Union proposal, the very first object of the plan was stated thus: "We need an instrument of international currency having general acceptability between nations, so that blocked balances and bilateral clearings are unnecessary."[40] In his speech of May, 1943, he said that the chief object of the scheme was "to provide that money earned by selling goods to one country can be spent on buying the products of any other country; in jargon—a system of multilateral clearing." The multilateral theme was very prominent also in his later speeches, in May, 1944, and December, 1945. No one could have put the case for multilateralism more forcefully.

This may be surprising, since one of the two principal advantages claimed for the bilateral system is the supposed convenience and security which such a system affords to a country pursuing a full employment policy at home. The proponents of bilateralism stress the fact that, under the protection of bilateral clearing agreements, a country can go ahead and expand its national income without worrying about its external accounts; for the induced increase in its imports will give rise simply to blocked balances which foreigners can use solely for increasing *their* purchases from the expanding country. In brief, it is argued that under this system a country in pursuit of full employment at home does not have to worry about its balance of payments, and is not deterred by external considerations from the pursuit of internal equilibrium. But this should always be the case, even under a multilateral system. As we have seen, there are a number of possible devices, which have all been incorporated into the international monetary and trading system which Keynes has helped to create, which enable a single country to maintain equilibrium in the over-all balance of payments while striving to achieve or to preserve internal equilibrium. These devices may

[39] Speech in the House of Lords, May 18, 1943; see below, p. 360.
[40] See below, p. 325.

be more difficult to handle than the crude and homely tool of bilateral clearing. But surely there has been some advance in economic insight among government officials in charge of international relations; and, under the guidance of new international institutions such as the Fund and the proposed I.T.O., the new devices should prove effective enough for the attainment and preservation of international equilibrium without resort to bilateralism.

The other main advantage which is claimed for the bilateral system is that it enables a country to improve its barter terms of trade by discriminatory treatment of its neighbors, by squeezing out the best possible export-import price relationships for itself, by bullying and bargaining with its weaker trading partners one by one. This policy of improving the *terms*, as distinct from the *balance*, of trade is of course a beggar-my-neighbor policy—not, indeed, as a means of creating employment through the export-multiplier mechanism, but simply as a means of extortion. Admittedly it may bring some gain, though probably only an ephemeral gain, to an individual country practising such methods. But these methods are open to all, and they inevitably lead to commercial warfare pure and simple. In defending the international currency and trade proposals, Keynes had to face constant opposition from a small but vocal group of adherents to the bilateral school of thought in his own country. What he felt about the "neo-Schachtian" school is eloquently expressed in the final paragraph of his last great speech.[41] Can any one read that paragraph and still maintain that Keynes was an economic nationalist?

What Keynes sought and, we may hope, achieved, was a multilateral solution to the postwar currency problem. His aim was a truly international monetary system. It is evident that the bilateral alternative offers, in essence, not a monetary system at all, but a -system of international barter entirely analogous to inter-personal barter in a primitive society. Just as inter-personal barter, preferable though it is to complete self-sufficiency, inhibits that division of labor which money as a medium of exchange makes possible, so the policy of bilateralism cannot but cramp and cripple the international division of labor, especially the more refined and complicated division of labor which the spread of industrial techniques all over the world tends to develop. Keynes was modern enough to see that in the modern world nothing but a multi-

[41] See p. 395.

lateral system would do. His distinctive contribution was to equip this system with the controls and safeguards required to make the pursuit of modern full-employment policies compatible with the equilibrium of international settlements. For the operation of these controls and safeguards, he left the necessary criteria—national income, employment, and the balance of payments—and, explicitly or implicitly, a set of general working principles which this essay has tried to indicate. These principles may still seem strange to some, and hard to understand; but they do possess the merit of consistency, seeking in every way to combine the advantages of international trade with the benefits of full employment.

CHAPTER XXII

Foreign Exchange Rate Theory and Policy

By ARTHUR I. BLOOMFIELD

PROMINENT among the many complex policy problems to face the International Monetary Fund will be those relating to the adjustment of exchange rates in correcting balance-of-payments disequilibria. The Fund Agreement explicitly provides for such adjustments, but lays down no clear-cut criteria for guidance. In framing their decisions on this matter, however, the managers of the Fund will be able to draw upon the varied lessons of interwar foreign exchange experience and upon a rich theoretical literature. This essay will briefly analyze the contributions of Keynes to that literature and examine some of the exchange rate policy problems of the Fund against the background of those contributions.

KEYNES ON THE FOREIGN EXCHANGES

Although Keynes was not primarily interested in the theory of foreign exchange, nor made particularly original contributions thereto, his extensive and persuasively argued writings in this field, as in many others, have exerted a great influence on thinking and policy.[1] The development of his views on the foreign exchanges (isolated here as far as possible from his views on international trade and finance generally) may be traced under the interrelated headings of (1) foreign exchange equilibrium and (2) conditions of exchange adjustment.

Foreign Exchange Equilibrium: Much of the theorizing on the

---

[1] Keynes' interest in foreign exchange problems was evident in his first book, *Indian Currency and Finance* (1913), in which he made a careful and sympathetic analysis of the operation of the gold-exchange standard in India. In that book, however, he was not interested in foreign exchange theory, nor did he lay down any major conclusions of wider application with respect to policy.

foreign exchanges since 1914, and indeed many of the practical policy problems in this field, have centered directly or indirectly about the conceptual and operational definition of an equilibrium rate of exchange.

During the period of inflation and dislocated exchanges in the early twenties, a spirited controversy was waged over the causes of the prevailing exchange fluctuations and over the determinants of the equilibrium levels towards which exchange rates allegedly tended to gravitate.[2] Some writers accounted for these fluctuations merely in terms of the over-all state of the balance of payments, but others, notably Cassel, going behind the balance of payments, argued that the dominant causal factor was relative price level movements in different countries as affected by changes in the money supply. According to Cassel's well-known purchasing-power-parity theory, the change over a period of time in the exchange ratio of two currencies will tend to be inversely proportional to the ratio of general price level changes in the two countries concerned. What he did, in effect, was to abstract from, or implicitly to assume constant, all factors other than relative price changes determining long-run movements in the balance of payments and thus exchange rates, and to assign to these changes the role of independent variable.[3]

Although in his earlier writings Keynes was sympathetic to the purchasing-power-parity theory, his analysis of its limitations and implicit assumptions in his *Monetary Reform* was among the best made up to that time.[4] He argued there [5] that: (1) if applied only to the prices of internationally-traded goods (allowance being made for tariffs and transport costs) the theory "is a truism,

[2] The literature of this controversy has been analyzed by H. S. Ellis, *German Monetary Theory, 1905–1933* (Cambridge, Mass., 1934), pp. 203–95.

[3] For a *general* equilibrium approach to exchange rate determination under a system of free exchanges, cf. J. L. Mosak, *General-Equilibrium Theory in International Trade* (Bloomington, 1944), pp. 173–74, and *passim*.

[4] But cf. also A. C. Pigou, "The Foreign Exchanges," QJE, November 1922, pp. 52–74. In this article Pigou also advances his own definition of an equilibrium rate which is much more sophisticated than Cassel's.

[5] In his earlier *A Revision of the Treaty* (New York, 1922), pp. 100–105, Keynes called attention to the influence of price movements on the fluctuations of the German mark, but laid equal emphasis on reparations payments and speculative capital movements. The term "purchasing power parity" he used only in connection with a brief reference to the French franc (*ibid.*, p. 113).

and as nearly as possible jejune"; [6] (2) if applied to domestic price levels in general, the theory requires for its validity the assumption that in the long run the prices of goods and services not entering into international trade move parallel to the prices of those that do; (3) lack of parallelism may arise from shifts in capital movements, changes in international demand and in relative efficiencies of labor, etc.; and (4) causation may run from prices to exchange rates, and vice versa. Making a statistical comparison of exchange rates and purchasing power parities for Britain, France, and Italy vis-à-vis the United States from 1919 to 1922 (with 1913 as base), Keynes found a rather good correspondence. This he attributed to the fact that relative price movements during this period were so sharp as to tend to swamp the effects of any factors at work tending to upset the correspondence between movements in international and domestic prices.

With the stabilization of European currencies in the latter half of the twenties, and with the growing *relative* importance of factors other than price changes affecting the balance of payments (notably capital movements, income changes,[7] and shifts in international demand and costs), any practical usefulness which the purchasing-power-parity theory may previously have had was greatly impaired. Although Keynes continued for a while to resort to that theory, e.g., in assessing the "appropriateness" of the exchange rates at which the pound and the franc were stabilized,[8] by 1930 his enthusiasm for it had waned. In the *Treatise* (Vol. I, pp. 69–89, 336) he argued that its basic weak-

---

[6] While it is true (when perfect markets prevail) that the prices of identical internationally-traded goods in all countries must always tend (after allowance for transport costs, tariffs, and other barriers to trade) to be equal when converted into a common currency, this relationship need not hold when applied to the prices of internationally-traded goods in the aggregate. As Viner has shown (*Studies in the Theory of International Trade* [New York, 1937], pp. 382–83), the purchasing-power-parity theory would not be a truism when applied to the prices of a variable range of internationally-traded goods, nor even to the prices of a fixed assortment of such goods if the weights used in each national index differed.

[7] The proponents of the purchasing power parity, as well as its earlier critics (including Keynes), had generally overlooked the possibility of income changes not corresponding to, nor even accompanied by, price changes, as a factor upsetting the validity of the theory, presumably in part because of the implicit assumption of full employment.

[8] Cf. *The Economic Consequences of Mr. Churchill* (London, 1925), especially p. 7, and "The Stabilization of the Franc," N&A, June 30, 1925, reprinted in *Essays in Persuasion*, pp. 113–17.

ness was the assumption that international and domestic prices tended to move together and that the statistical "verifications" of the theory (including that advanced in his *Monetary Reform*) were the result of using price indices heavily weighted with the prices of international goods. He concluded: "I used to think this theory more interesting than I think it now" (p. 74). Five years later he wrote that "no one now puts faith in the famous 'purchasing power parity' theory of the foreign exchanges based on index numbers." [9] The latter statement, however, was an exaggeration. The theory, or specific variants of it,[10] continued to be widely used during the thirties as a measure of the over- or under-valuation of exchange rates, i.e., of the degree of discrepancy of given rates from their "correct" equilibrium levels, despite the conceptual limitations of the theory, the statistical difficulties involved in its application (e.g., choice of appropriate price indices and of base dates), and its general failure to conform to the facts of actual experience.

In discarding the purchasing-power-parity theory as a reliable indicator of foreign exchange equilibrium, Keynes substituted the simpler and more direct balance-of-payments criterion. His definition of an equilibrium rate of exchange deserves to be quoted in full:

> We have to consider, on the one hand, a country's balance of payments on income account on the basis of the existing natural resources, equipment, technique and costs (especially wage costs) at home and abroad, a normal level of employment, and those tariffs, etc., which are a permanent feature of national policies; and, on the other hand, the probable readiness and ability of the country in question to borrow or lend abroad on long-term (or, perhaps, repay or accept repayment of old loans), on the average of the next few years. *A set of rates of exchange, which can be established without undue strain on either side and without large movements of gold (on a balance of transactions), will satisfy our condition of equilibrium.*[11] [Italics mine]

[9] "The Future of the Foreign Exchanges," LBMR, October, 1935, p. 528
[10] Cf. S. E. Harris, "Measures of Currency Overvaluation and Stabilization," *Explorations in Economics* (New York, 1936), pp. 35–45; H. S. Ellis, "The Equilibrium Rate of Exchange," *ibid.*, pp. 26–34; C. P. Kindleberger, *International Short-Term Capital Movements* (New York, 1937), chap. 7.
[11] See LBMR, October, 1935, p. 528.

If after "movements of gold" one added "and equilibrating short-term capital," [12] this statement would provide a very satisfactory definition of an equilibrium rate of exchange (under a system of pegged rates), and one commonly accepted today. Other writers have emphasized that there is an infinitely large number of such rates, depending upon the levels of national income prevailing at home and abroad, and that the "ideal" structure of equilibrium rates is that which maintains the balance of payments of all countries in equilibrium at full employment levels everywhere. [13]

Conditions of Exchange Adjustment: Under the pre-1914 gold standard, as is well known, monetary policy had been guided almost exclusively by the requirements of maintaining exchange rate stability, despite the deflationary (and inflationary) pressures often thereby involved. During the interwar period, however, primary emphasis tended to be placed instead on the maintenance of internal economic stability and on domestic insulation from external disturbances, especially of a deflationary character. One of the major corollaries of this attitude was a growing opposition to permanently fixed exchange rates and a corresponding receptiveness to exchange adjustments as a means of correcting balance-of-payments disequilibria. In the doctrinal shaping of these views and in the breakdown of the gold standard ideology, the writings of Keynes exerted a dominant influence.

In his *Monetary Reform* Keynes called attention to the conflict between internal price-level stability and exchange-rate stability when external price levels were fluctuating, on the grounds that balance-of-payments equilibrium would thereby be upset. [14] In-

---

[12] This omission was in keeping with Keynes' definition of balance-of-payments equilibrium as the equality of foreign lending and the foreign balance, and his lumping of *all* capital movements under the former. (Cf. *Treatise*, Vol. I, pp. 161–63). One writer has argued that in defining the standard of an equilibrium rate one should also exclude "disequilibrating" short-term capital movements from the balance of payments. Cf. R. Nurkse, "Conditions of International Monetary Equilibrium," *Essays in International Finance*, No. 4 (Princeton, 1945), pp. 4–5. But when these movements are relatively very large and are of the "capital flight" variety, I question whether the concept of an equilibrium rate itself has much meaning.

[13] Cf. J. Robinson, *Essays in the Theory of Employment* (New York, 1937), p. 208; R. F. Harrod, *International Economics* (London, 1939), pp. 117–18; and Nurkse, *op. cit.*, pp. 6–7.

[14] Implicit in this rather crude formulation of the argument is the assumption of the validity of the purchasing-power-parity theory. But a "conflict" might equally arise from differential *income* movements at home

sisting, in opposition to the traditional view, that price stability was the primary desideratum, he advocated a policy of adjustable exchange rates designed allegedly to preserve national monetary independence and especially to obviate the need for a policy of deflation in the face of persisting balance-of-payments deficits. Since he considered short-run exchange stability desirable, however, he proposed that central banks should fix buying and selling prices for gold, with a spread of about ½ of 1 per cent,[15] and that these prices should be altered only when necessary to correct a deficit threatening to upset long-run stability of internal prices. He argued that, if the leading nations were successful in maintaining internal price-level stability, exchange rate adjustments would be unnecessary. To facilitate the maintenance of short-run exchange stability, he also recommended that gold reserves be divorced from the note issue and that central banks buy and sell forward exchange at reasonable premiums or discounts (subject to change) on the spot quotations.[16]

In the *Treatise* (Vol. II, pp. 302–28) Keynes re-examined the dilemma of a gold standard, but now primarily in terms of an allegedly high degree of sensitivity of capital movements to interest rate differentials. This sensitivity, he argued, tended to force individual countries, at the risk of undergoing severe balance-of-payments disequilibria, to keep their interest rates close to the

---

and abroad, or from changes in the "substantive course of trade," even if the price-level abroad (and at home) was stable. The stress on price-level stability was in keeping with the monetary theory of the day. While Keynes (with the possible exception of Fisher) was the first modern writer to emphasize the internal-*vs.*-external stability conflict, and to recommend a flexible exchange rate policy, Viner has shown (*Studies*, pp. 209–17) that a number of writers had also done so in the early nineteenth century.

[15] The spreading of the gold points had been recommended as early as 1819 by Torrens. Cf. Viner, *Studies*, pp. 206–07. Official manipulations of the gold points had been extensively practised before 1914 as a means of controlling short-term capital and gold movements without changing the bank rate.

[16] Keynes recommended this policy as a means of improving commercial hedging facilities and of controlling short-term capital movements without altering the bank rate (and to complement his proposal for spreading the gold points). In *Monetary Reform* (and in "The Forward Market in Foreign Exchanges," MGCRE, April 20, 1922), Keynes was the first to develop a systematic theory of the forward exchanges, with the central proposition that the forward discount or premium on the exchange rate between two currencies tends to equal the difference between short-term interest rates in the two centers. Keynes' contributions in this field and their great influence on interwar thinking and policy cannot be analyzed here.

world level, and thereby to forego an autonomous interest rate policy designed to maintain internal equilibrium (now defined in terms of an equality of saving and investment). His policy proposals, designed to insulate domestic from world interest rates by controlling the flow of capital, were essentially the same, however, as in his earlier book,[17] with the additional recommendations that monetary reserves be enlarged and that direct controls be imposed over *long-term* capital exports. But accepting the gold standard as an accomplished fact, he did not suggest the possible need for moving exchange rates outside the (widened) gold points,[18] apparently considering that his proposals, especially if coupled with his plan for a Supernational Bank to maintain international stability in the value of gold, would be sufficient to preserve domestic monetary autonomy.

After the breakdown of the gold standard, Keynes again became more receptive to long-run exchange adjustments, although still insisting on the need for short-run exchange stability. Disturbed, however, by the beggar-my-neighbor depreciations of the early thirties, which he condemned as a perversion of a flexible exchange rate policy, he emphasized more strongly the need for international monetary cooperation. In *The Means to Prosperity* (1933) he outlined a scheme (foreshadowing his later Clearing Union plan) for an international currency arrangement under which, *inter alia*, currencies would be pegged *de facto* to gold (with a 5 per cent spread between the gold points), but subject to periodical adjustment, presumably under international supervision, only "to offset undesired changes in the international price level, or, occasionally, to make an adjustment, with a minimum of friction, to special national conditions, temporary or otherwise." In 1935[19] he again called for stabilization of the major currencies (the initial equilibrium parities to be arrived at by trial and error), for short-run exchange stability, and for longer run flexibility to correct deep-seated balance of payments dis-

[17] Keynes' argument and proposals were based on the assumption that capital movements were primarily of the "normal" variety. The experience of the thirties, however, demonstrated the invalidity of this assumption and the limited efficacy of Keynes' proposals to manipulate forward rates and gold points as control devices.

[18] Elsewhere in the *Treatise* (Vol. I, pp. 356–63) Keynes discussed in general terms the pros and cons of a system of freely fluctuating exchanges, but reached no clear-cut conclusions as to its net advantages or disadvantages as compared with an international standard.

[19] LBMR, October, 1935, pp. 528–34.

equilibria. He also suggested the need for a test of the severity of the strain on a country's balance of payments before its exchange rate should be adjusted, although admitting he was "a little distrustful of a cut-and-dried formula." Eight years later in his Clearing Union plan, however, he did suggest such a formula whereby a country would be entitled to depreciate once it had utilized a certain amount of its quota in the Union.

Keynes' opposition to permanently fixed exchange rates coupled with bank rate policy was reiterated in the *General Theory*. He argued there that this arrangement was the "most dangerous" imaginable, for it ruled out the objective of maintaining a domestic rate of interest consistent with full employment.[20] The *General Theory*, however, was only incidentally concerned with problems of an open economy, and it remained for other writers to demonstrate the fruitfulness of the powerful conceptual tools of that book, especially the multiplier analysis, in the development of foreign exchange theory and balance-of-payments theory generally. Emphasizing more clearly than did Keynes the *direct* disequilibrating effects on national income of balance-of-payments shifts, later writers have also stressed the need for "compensatory" internal policies to offset these effects pending a possible longer run exchange adjustment. In his formulations of the internal-versus-external-stability conflict, Keynes had generally focussed his attention only on the potentially disturbing effects of gold movements via their potential influence on interest rate policy.

Keynes' writings on the foreign exchanges inspired a voluminous and controversial literature during the interwar period centering around the meaning and validity of the conflict between internal and external stability and the merits of alternative exchange rate policies. In this great debate, systems of freely fluctuating and of permanently fixed exchanges found relatively few prominent supporters,[21] and by the end of the period the bulk of

[20] Elsewhere (p. 270) he argued that the most desirable norm of policy was a stable level of money-wages (at a full employment level), "provided that equilibrium with the rest of the world can be secured by means of fluctuating exchanges." By "fluctuating" Keynes must clearly have meant "flexible" rather than "freely fluctuating."

[21] Several of his followers, however, notably Harrod, Meade, Durbin, and Lerner, went further than Keynes by advocating, in effect, a policy of freely fluctuating exchanges (subject only to possible control in the short run to offset the influence of speculative capital movements).

informed opinion, in the light of experience [22] and under the influence of Keynesian teachings, had tended to gravitate towards an intermediate system under which exchange rates would be held stable in the short run but subject, under international supervision,[23] to periodical adjustment in the longer run when necessary to correct persisting balance-of-payments disequilibria, especially when the latter threatened to induce undesirable deflationary pressure. These attitudes were later crystallized in the various postwar international monetary plans (including the Clearing Union plan) and found formal expression in the Bretton Woods Fund Agreement.[24]

In his later writings Keynes added little to what he had already said on exchange rates. His scheme of quotas in the Clearing Union plan, by providing additional international liquidity, was designed to facilitate the maintenance of short-run exchange stability without the need for deflationary policies or additional trade restrictions, and his recommendation for direct control of disequilibrating capital movements replaced his earlier proposals of spreading the gold points and manipulating forward rates. Recognizing the desirability of longer run exchange flexibility, he laid down a formula whereby a member whose debit balance in the Union exceeded a quarter of its quota on the average of at least two years would be entitled to depreciate, but by not more than 5 per cent without the Union's consent.[25] Apart from its

---

[22] Cf. R. Nurkse, *International Currency Experience* (League of Nations, 1944), Chap. 5.

[23] The experience of the thirties clearly showed that exchange rate adjustment could not properly be left to unilateral decision. Rates tended commonly to be set either too low (as a beggar-my-neighbor device) or too high (as a means, e.g., of improving the terms of trade), and with little regard to effects elsewhere.

[24] In defending the plan for an International Monetary Fund before the House of Lords on May 23, 1944 against the charge that it was too much like the gold standard, Keynes argued that the plan incorporated three major proposals for which he had fought for 20 years: (1) henceforth the external value of a currency would be altered to conform to its internal value rather than vice versa; (2) individual countries would be enabled to retain control of their domestic rates of interest; and (3) the instruments of bank rate and credit contraction as a means of forcing a country into line with external factors were abjured. (All three proposals really amount to one.)

[25] Keynes also called attention to other possible corrective measures. He suggested, somewhat vaguely, that the Union might recommend to a member "any internal measures affecting its domestic economy which may appear to be appropriate to restore the equilibrium of its international balance" (presumably other than deflationary policies). He also suggested that coun-

somewhat arbitrary and restrictive character, however, this formula should more logically have been phrased in terms of the amount of *change* in a country's debit balance, and should have also taken account of net changes in independent reserves which a member might hold outside the Union. Keynes also argued that the only major cause of balance-of-payments disequilibrium likely to call for a longer run exchange adjustment was a differential rate of movement of prices and money-wages at home and abroad, such adjustments being needed to enable a country to pursue its own independent price and wage policy when it conflicted with that in effect elsewhere.[26]

EXCHANGE ADJUSTMENTS AND THE MONETARY FUND

Although the Fund Agreement makes provision for adjustments of exchange rates, it lays down no clear-cut prescriptions to guide the managers of the Fund in deciding upon the timing or degree of adjustment in individual cases. It specifies merely that rate changes may be sanctioned only when necessary to correct a "fundamental disequilibrium" (which is undefined).[27] The drafters of the Agreement acted wisely in leaving these matters to the discretion of the Fund, since no simple, mechanical formulae, appropriately applicable to all countries or circumstances alike, seem feasible.[28] Each case will generally have to be handled according to the conditions peculiar to it, as interpreted by the Fund.

While Keynes contributed greatly, as we have seen, to shaping the underlying philosophy of the exchange rate (and other) provisions of the Fund Agreement, he was not particularly concerned

tries with persisting surpluses should adopt such measures as domestic expansion, currency appreciation, reduction of trade barriers, or foreign investment. In his last article, "The Balance of Payments of the United States," EJ, June, 1946, p. 186, he argued that the "classical medicine" for international adjustment (to which, surprisingly, he paid homage) cannot be relied upon, and that "we need quicker and less painful aids of which exchange variation and *over-all import control* are the most important." (Italics mine.)

[26] "The Objective of International Price Stability," *ibid.*, June-September, 1943, pp. 185–87, and Speech in the House of Lords, May 18, 1943.

[27] A member has the right, however, to alter its exchange rate in the aggregate by 10 per cent without possible objection from the Fund. (I assume that this right will in most cases be used up during the transition period.)

[28] For this reason, and apart from its technical shortcomings, the formula proposed by Keynes in the Clearing Union plan cannot be accepted.

with attempting to spell out the policy details, nor do his earlier writings provide much direct help in this connection. He almost invariably assumed, moreover, that an exchange adjustment would be an adequate corrective of balance-of-payments disequilibria, without working out the conditions determining the effects of any given degree of adjustment; [29] and he touched only briefly on the relative efficacy and desirability in individual cases of rate changes as compared with alternative corrective measures (other than deflation). Nevertheless, he was the first to recognize clearly the basic problem as one of harmonizing the requirements of internal and external stability, and the relationship of exchange adjustment thereto; his writings, especially the *General Theory*, have provided the basis for a deeper understanding of balance-of-payments phenomena generally; and his definition of an equilibrium rate of exchange must, I submit, be the basic conceptual underpinning of the exchange rate policy problems of the Fund.

Equilibrium and Disequilibrium in the Foreign Exchanges: An ideal system of equilibrium rates of exchange may be defined as that which keeps the international accounts of all countries in equilibrium at full employment levels. From a policy viewpoint, however, an equilibrium rate for an individual country must be defined somewhat more modestly, along the lines of the Keynesian definition, as that which keeps the country's international accounts in equilibrium over a period of several years (on the average)[30] without having caused undue deflationary (or expansionist) pressures, or necessitated additional import restrictions, therein. To define such a rate is a relatively easy matter, but to ascertain whether or not it exists in individual cases, and especially to calculate beforehand what rate will be an equilibrium one[31] in a given instance when an existing rate is deemed

---

[29] In "The German Transfer Problem," EJ, March 1929, pp. 2 and 9, Keynes had referred briefly, however, to the theoretical possibility of a decline in the value of a country's exports following a reduction in their price, if foreign elasticity of demand was less than unity.

[30] The time period involved, however, must be flexibly interpreted, as will be noted below.

[31] The purchasing-power-parity theory cannot be relied upon, except perhaps under special conditions, as an indicator of true equilibrium rates as we have defined them. Relative price (and cost) level movements at home and abroad exert, of course, an important, often major, influence in determining the balance-of-payments pattern of a country, and thus the theoretical equilibrium level of its exchange rate, but no simple or precise relationships can safely be postulated.

out of equilibrium, will raise a variety of complex policy problems for the managers of the Fund. In any case, an approximation
to such rates must be sought for. It may be of interest to examine
some of these problems briefly from the viewpoint of the post-
transitional period,[32] and thereby to attempt to fill in some of the
policy details which Keynes had tended to neglect.

A state of "fundamental disequilibrium" must, I believe, be interpreted by the Fund in terms of the deviation of an existing
rate of exchange from its theoretical equilibrium level as defined
above. In actual practice such a deviation will tend to be reflected
most commonly in a large and persisting balance-of-payments
deficit.[33] Use of the balance-of-payments criterion would have
the practical advantage of focussing attention on what is most
relevant to the Fund, namely, the necessity of correcting persisting unbalance in international accounts threatening seriously to
distort the distribution of the Fund's holdings of individual member currencies. It would also provide a reasonably objective and
identifiable basis for policy,[34] and would preclude the possible
danger of sanctioning beggar-my-neighbor depreciations. More-

[32] The sanctioning of rate changes will raise especially difficult problems
for the Fund during the transition period in the face of direct external and
internal controls, limited export capacities and abnormal import demands.
Indeed, it may be seriously questioned whether even the concept of an
equilibrium rate will have any genuine meaning for most countries during
this period. With regard to the fixing of *initial* rates, the recent action of the
Fund in accepting in most cases the pre-existing rates appears to have been
a commonsense policy.

[33] Since exchange adjustments can, according to the Fund Agreement, be
requested only by an individual member (and apparently not by the Fund),
requests for the *appreciation* of a currency vis-à-vis all others will tend to
be exceptional, unless perhaps a balance-of-payments surplus threatens to
provoke in a country a general price inflation which cannot otherwise be
easily controlled. For this and other reasons it seems legitimate to treat a
"fundamental disequilibrium" primarily from the viewpoint of deficit countries alone.

The balance-of-payments criterion of "fundamental disequilibrium" has
been vigorously championed, to the exclusion of others, by G. Haberler,
"Currency Depreciation and the International Monetary Fund," RES, November, 1944, pp. 178–81.

[34] Theoretically, balance-of-payments equilibrium implies, in general, the
absence over a period of time of net one-sided movements of gold plus
"equilibrating" short-term capital. In actual practice, deficits will in most
cases be measurable in future with reasonable accuracy by the net decline
in a country's official holdings of gold and foreign exchange (including
private working balances), plus any net increase in its foreign short-term
liabilities and/or in the Fund's holdings of its currency.

over, by entitling countries striving to maintain high levels of income and employment in the face of depression elsewhere to depreciate their currencies if large and persisting deficits resulted thereby, this criterion would tend, along with other sanctioned protective devices and with Fund drawing-rights, to overcome any inhibitions which countries might have with regard to autonomous full employment policies. But, as will be noted below, "fundamental disequilibria" may be manifested in other forms as well.

Assuming exchange rates approximately in equilibrium to begin with, large and persisting deficits of a sort likely in future to constitute a "fundamental disequilibrium" may arise primarily from any one, or any combination, of the following: (1) differential rates of movements in different countries of national income and of prices and money costs associated with them; [35] (2) abrupt changes in the rate of flow of foreign investment; and (3) "structural" developments, including, e.g., shifts in consumer tastes, uneven rates of technological advance, and exhaustion or discovery of natural resources.[36] There is little or nothing in the Fund Agreement, *per se*, which can prevent such disequilibria from arising. The major potential cause of disequilibrium, namely (1), could be satisfactorily controlled only if all countries, or at least the leading ones, were able to maintain high and stable levels of income and employment and to keep their price-cost structures reasonably in line with each other. To the extent that success is achieved in this direction, and if coupled with appropriate operations by the International Bank,[37] the flow of foreign investment would also tend to be smoothed out. Little or nothing can be done to prevent deficits arising out of (3), but such deficits will in any case tend to develop more slowly, and generally to be on a lesser scale, than those arising from (1) and (2).

The appropriateness of the balance-of-payments criterion has

[35] Deficits of this sort would appear most clearly in the case of a country able to maintain full employment in a world of depression. Keynes focussed his attention primarily on differential rates of *price-wage* movements as a source of disequilibrium calling for exchange adjustment.

[36] These three causes of disequilibria are not, of course, mutually exclusive, and may to some degree overlap. I rule out the possibility of large and persisting deficits reflecting "hot money" movements.

[37] Cf. A. I. Bloomfield, "Postwar Control of International Capital Movements," AER, *Supplement*, May, 1946, pp. 706–09.

been questioned by Hansen and others, chiefly on the grounds that "fundamental disequilibria" of a sort calling for depreciation or other corrective measures may commonly be reflected, not in large and persisting deficits, but in price deflation and unemployment resulting from initial balance-of-payments pressure.[38] These writers argue that the criterion of "cost parity" or "price disparity" would provide a more reliable gauge of disequilibria. Now it is perfectly true that an exchange rate may not be an equilibrium one, even when no conspicuous deficit prevails, if the maintenance of that rate has involved or necessitated severe and protracted deflation; this type of situation can be gracefully subsumed under our interpretation of "fundamental disequilibrium,"[39] and would equally call for a possible depreciation. But I am inclined to believe that its importance in the future may be easily exaggerated, and that large and persisting deficits will be a more common and reliable indicator of exchange disequilibria.

Most of the leading countries may be expected to attempt, through compensatory internal policies,[40] to offset deflationary pressures caused by adverse shifts in their balances of payments, and to meet any deficits resulting therefrom by utilizing their external reserves (fortified by drawing-rights in the Fund) until the deficits cease or, if they are large and persisting, until a depreciation (or other corrective measures) are sanctioned. Now, admittedly, it is generally not possible for relatively undeveloped countries to pursue altogether effective compensatory policies, and when, e.g., exports fall off, some "primary" deflation (via the foreign-trade multiplier and the induced acceleration effect) may result in such cases. Unless accompanied, however, by a "secondary" deflation as well (via a restrictive credit policy) or by the adoption of specific corrective measures, the deficit would probably not be wiped out completely.[41] Under these cir-

---

[38] Cf. e.g., A. H. Hansen, "A Brief Note on 'Fundamental Disequilibrium,'" RES, November 1944, pp. 182–84; and M. E. Garnsey, "Postwar Exchange-Rate Parities," QJE, November, 1945, pp. 113–35.

[39] In this respect, then, both Haberler and Hansen are correct in their exchange in RES, November, 1944. I do not believe, however, that "cost parity" would be an altogether reliable gauge of the situation envisaged by Hansen, since it is subject to the conceptual and statistical limitations of purchasing power parity itself.

[40] Cf. *Economic Stability in the Postwar World* (League of Nations, 1945), chap. 17, and the British, Canadian, and Australian White Papers on Employment Policy.

cumstances the persistence of the deficit would in itself tend to justify a depreciation according to the balance-of-payments criterion.

On the other hand, if some countries work on relatively small margins of external reserves, "secondary" deflations (and the abandonment of compensatory policies if such were pursued) may indeed be necessary, unless other corrective measures are sanctioned or undertaken. In such a case a deficit resulting from some initial disturbance might be corrected in relatively short order, but only (given relative price-cost inflexibility) at the expense of considerable unemployment. This seems to be the case primarily envisaged by Hansen, and would justify a possible depreciation. But even if such a situation does arise, it would most likely have been preceded by *some* reasonably substantial and persisting deficit, which would serve as a guide to the Fund in determining whether or not to recognize a state of "fundamental disequilibrium." To declare that such a state exists merely when there is considerable unemployment not accompanied by an actual deficit (nor traceable to an immediately preceding deficit) might easily result in unintentional sanctioning by the Fund of beggar-my-neighbor depreciations. In any case, the possibility of countries being forced, even within the Fund framework, to adopt policies involving considerable unemployment because of a deficit would seem to be unlikely. For one thing, the Fund, in response to a recent request for interpretation, admitted that "steps necessary to protect a member from unemployment of a chronic or persistent character, arising from pressure on the balance of payments, are among the measures necessary to correct a fundamental disequilibrium," although the Fund reiterated its right to decide whether or not exchange depreciation was in fact necessary to correct the disequilibrium.[42] Furthermore, deficit countries would, according to the latest draft charter for an International Trade Organization (December 1946), be permitted to adopt quantitative import restrictions when, and to the extent, necessary "to stop or forestall the imminent threat of a serious decline in the level of monetary reserves."[43]

---

[41] Cf. F. Machlup, *International Trade and the National Income Multiplier* (Philadelphia, 1943), pp. 84–6 and *passim*.

[42] On the other hand, this interpretation is still sufficiently vague to leave the Fund considerable leeway.

[43] But such restrictions are to be removed when no longer required for this purpose.

It is evident from the foregoing, however, that while an actual deficit will tend to be the primary indicator of "fundamental disequilibrium," the size and duration of any particular deficit before it is to be considered to represent such a disequilibrium will have to be very flexibly interpreted by the Fund. As a general rule, the Fund will, among other things, have to recognize that a given cumulated deficit constitutes an exchange disequilibrium sooner in the case of a country with relatively small external reserves,[44] and/or perhaps which is unable to carry out effective compensatory policies, than in the case of a country for which the opposite is true. For the Fund cannot allow (nor indeed will any country be willing to undergo) severe and protracted depression caused by balance-of-payments pressure. But no hard-and-fast rules can be laid down as to precise conditions which should in any given case be considered to constitute a state of disequilibrium calling for depreciation.

Alternative Corrective Measures: It is clear, of course, that the Fund must try to avoid sanctioning depreciations over relatively short periods. For frequent depreciations and anticipations of such are disturbing to orderly trade relations and foreign investment, and are likely to have other well-known unsettling effects. No problems will arise in this connection in the case of countries with substantial monetary reserves and able through compensatory policies to maintain domestic employment in the face of deficits. But even when a member's reserves are inadequate to finance for more than a relatively short time a deficit which suddenly emerges, it might be sufficient for the Fund merely to relax its rules regarding the amount of foreign exchange it can sell to the member per unit of time, increase its aggregate drawing-rights (if possible to do so quickly), or attempt to direct short-term or even long-term loans to the member through other channels. If necessary, moreover, the Fund could attempt, through technical aid and the like, to assist the member in maintaining domestic employment in the face of the deficit. In some instances the postponement or adjustment by the International Bank of service payments on past borrowings from the Bank might serve

---

[44] In assessing the amount of external reserves available to an individual country, the Fund will have to consider the existing legal reserve requirements (if any), and the degree to which they are likely to influence the credit policy of the countries concerned. It would, of course, be most desirable, as Keynes recognized long ago, if all external reserves were freed for purposes of international settlements alone.

to tide a country over a temporary difficult period. In cases where the deficit primarily reflects an outflow of capital involving substantial drafts on the Fund's resources, the Fund can insist that the outflow be stopped at once by the imposition or tightening of restrictions.

Stop-gap measures such as these, however, may be inadequate or inapplicable. In particular, the amount of additional international liquidity that can or should be provided to a member short of reserves may, even in the short run, be insufficient if the deficit is relatively large. It might also be difficult for such a member to maintain its domestic employment. In such cases the Fund may have to sanction a depreciation at a relatively early date. If effective in correcting the deficit, depreciation would stop not only the drain of reserves, but also any "primary" deflation that was occurring and the threat of a "secondary" deflation. But depreciation may not always be an effective, or at least sufficiently speedy, corrective of deficits over short periods, particularly if the countries concerned are primary producing regions faced with relatively inelastic export demand schedules and caught in the web of a world-wide "cyclical" decline, and if the deficits are relatively large. Instead of sanctioning a depreciation, then, the Fund may instead deem it more advisable to permit temporary exchange restrictions on current account transactions.[45] Such restrictions, although clearly less desirable than depreciation in other respects, would be more predictable, and likely to be more immediate, in their ability to stop the deficit. The same may also be said for quantitative import restrictions, which, according to the draft charter for an I.T.O., can in any case be autonomously imposed by deficit countries with limited reserves. The Fund, it might be added, is enjoined (along with the I.T.O.) to consult with the countries concerned with regard to the choice of alternative corrective measures. If the underlying balance-of-payments pressure is of a "cyclical" character, or otherwise temporary, these direct controls could be / removed without the need for further corrective measures when the pressure ceased; indeed they would apparently have to be removed according to the I.T.O. draft charter.

[45] The Fund has the exclusive right to permit such restrictions. The case for direct import controls as compared with depreciation under such conditions has been argued, among others, by A. H. Hansen, *America's Rôle in the World Economy* (New York, 1945), pp. 183–87, and J. H. Williams, *Postwar Monetary Plans and Other Essays* (New York, 1945), p. xx.

Over a longer period, however, direct import controls cannot, in general, be properly countenanced, for reasons which are well known. If the underlying balance-of-payments pressure necessitating the imposition of these controls persists, a depreciation should be sanctioned, and the controls removed when (and if) the corrective effects of the depreciation work themselves out. Balance-of-payments equilibrium which can be maintained over a longer period only by means of such controls would violate our definition of an equilibrium rate of exchange, and would constitute another important case of "fundamental disequilibrium." Even if, because of substantial reserves, no direct controls were needed in the first place, a persisting deficit would in itself ultimately justify a depreciation. No clear-cut rules can be laid down, however, as to how the terms "longer period" and "persisting" should be defined.

In some cases, whether or not direct controls have been imposed, the Fund and I.T.O. may be able to alleviate or remove an underlying balance-of-payments pressure or actual deficit by *recommending* appropriate corrective measures.[46] If a deficit reflects a major "structural" development likely to endure, such as a permanent shift of foreign demand away from a country's leading exports, or the exhaustion of an important natural resource, it would be proper to recommend internal readjustments (e.g., development of new export products), and to extend loans through the Bank for this purpose. Indeed, under such conditions a mere exchange adjustment might in any case be inadequate. Corrective measures might also be recommended in many cases to individual *surplus* countries, especially if a surplus has as its counterpart substantial deficits in a large number of other countries, i.e., if a currency is threatening to become "scarce" or has formally been declared so.[47] Such recommendations might include internal expansion (although clearly not beyond a full employment level), tariff reductions, or increased foreign lending. But there is no assurance, of course, that in these cases recommended corrective measures, even if appropriate to the situa-

[46] A policy of deflation involving unemployment could not properly, of course, be one of the recommendations.

[47] Indeed, according to the I.T.O. draft charter, members agree "that in the case of a fundamental disequilibrium in their balance of payments involving other countries in persistent balance of payments difficulties which handicap them in maintaining employment, they will make their full contribution to action designed to correct the maladjustment."

tion and if acted upon, will be sufficiently effective. Here, too, a depreciation may eventually be essential.

Effectiveness of Exchange Adjustments: It has been suggested above, and it is implicitly recognized in the Fund Agreement and I.T.O. draft charter, that depreciation may always not be the most appropriate corrective of balance-of-payments disequilibria.[48] This matter may be examined briefly. The effects of a given degree of depreciation upon a country's balance of trade [49] may be divided into (a) the primary or price, and (b) the secondary or income, effects. The variables determining the primary effects, as is well known, are: (1) the price elasticity of foreign demand for a country's exports; (2) the elasticity of supply of its exports; (3) the price elasticity of demand for its imports; (4) the foreign elasticity of supply of its imports; and (5) the value of exports, and (6) value of imports, prior to depreciation.[50] A given degree of depreciation will almost invariably reduce the foreign-currency value of a country's imports,[51] to an extent depending upon (3), (4), and (6), but the foreign-currency value of its exports may rise or fall depending upon whether the foreign elasticity of demand exceeds, or is less than, unity,[52] and to an extent depending upon (1), (2) and (5). There is thus no assurance that a depreciation will necessarily improve the balance of trade, which may indeed be worsened. Even if the elasticity of foreign demand is less than unity, however, the balance of trade might still increase if the variables are of such a magnitude that

---

[48] This is also implicitly recognized in the "scarce currency clause" of the Fund Agreement, which sanctions the imposition of exchange control on current account vis-à-vis the country whose currency has been declared scarce.

[49] For convenience we focus attention upon imports and exports alone, but the effects of a depreciation upon other balance-of-payments items could also be fitted, *mutatis mutandis,* into the same framework.

[50] Cf. the brilliant essay on the foreign exchanges by Joan Robinson, *Essays in the Theory of Employment* (New York, 1937), pp. 183–209, especially the mathematical formula on p. 194. Mrs. Robinson describes her essay as an elaboration of hints thrown out by Keynes in the *Treatise.* For similar treatments, cf. A. J. Brown, "Trade Balances and Exchange Stability," *Oxford Economic Papers,* April, 1942, pp. 57–75; F. Machlup, "The Theory of Foreign Exchanges," *Economica,* November, 1939, pp. 381–88; and S. E. Harris, *Exchange Depreciation* (Cambridge, Mass., 1936), pp. 1–52.

[51] At worst, if home elasticity of demand were zero, there could be no change in the value of imports at all.

[52] If, however, home elasticity of supply were zero, there would be no change in the value of exports, regardless of the foreign elasticity of demand.

the fall in exports is exceeded by the fall in imports. The size of the demand elasticities in any given case will depend upon such factors as: the nature of the country's exports and imports, the volume of its exports and imports in relation to the world totals, the levels of national income and trade restrictions prevailing at home and abroad, the number of countries (if any) that concurrently depreciate,[53] and the length of time considered.[54] The primary effects of a depreciation on the trade balance, it might be noted, may be partly offset, or even conceivably swamped, by the secondary effects induced by income changes at home and abroad that might result from the primary shift (whether an improvement or deterioration) in the balance of trade.[55]

In recent literature it has been fashionable to assume that the relevant elasticities are so low that a depreciation may, apparently even in the long run, characteristically worsen rather than improve a country's balance of trade, or cause at best only a relatively minor improvement.[56] Now if indeed the effects were likely to be perverse [57] (and the Fund were aware of it beforehand), the appropriate solution would be to appreciate the currency concerned. But I am inclined to believe that such an effect, especially if a depreciation has had time to work itself out, will tend to be exceptional, and that the general theoretical presumption must continue to be that depreciation will improve a

[53] I.e., the more countries that depreciate, the lower the elasticity of foreign demand for the exports of any one of them. This explains, in part, why the effects on trade balances of the depreciations of the early thirties tended to be limited. One of the great advantages of the Fund is that competitive depreciations of this sort are outlawed.

[54] As intimated earlier, the corrective effects of a depreciation will generally be greater if a longer period of time is allowed, for elasticities of supply and demand tend to be higher in the long run than in the short run.

[55] The possibility of secondary effects is generally overlooked in most current discussions of depreciation. This neglect would be justified only if it is assumed that countries keep their levels of national income and output stable through compensatory policies.

[56] Cf. e.g., M. Kalecki, "Multilateralism and Full Employment," *Canadian Journal of Economics and Political Science*, August, 1946, p. 324; T. Balogh, "The International Aspects of Full Employment," *The Economics of Full Employment* (London, 1945), pp. 136–45; and especially J. Tinbergen, *International Economic Cooperation* (Amsterdam, 1946), chap. 5. The interesting arguments and assumptions of these writers cannot be treated here.

[57] The perversity referred to here is of a somewhat different sort than that possible type to which attention has been called by F. D. Graham, "Self-Limiting and Self-Inflammatory Movements in Exchange Rates," QJE, February, 1929, pp. 221–249.

country's balance of trade. Much more significant, however, is the possibility that depreciation, especially if a deficit is large in relation to the gross value of a country's foreign trade (and if the secondary effects are taken into account), may often not result in a sufficiently *large* improvement, even in the long run, to wipe out the deficit, or perhaps at best may do so only at the cost of a very severe deterioration in the depreciating country's terms of trade, or at the cost of reducing its volume of imports to a level inconsistent with domestic full employment. On this particular matter, past experience and *a priori* considerations do not cast much light, nor can too much reliance be placed as yet on the recent statistical measurements of elasticity of import and export demand coefficients.[58]

Whether or not depreciation will generally be an effective device for correcting balance-of-payments disequilibria, it is in any case clear that the Fund will face a challenging task in deciding whether and when to sanction a depreciation in any given case, and above all to what degree. The Fund can never know beforehand, except within a substantial range, what the effects of a given depreciation will be; the rates chosen may commonly be wide of the mark and so necessitate frequent unsettling readjustments. Whether or not a given rate proves to be an equilibrium one can be gauged only in the light of subsequent experience, and such a rate cannot be determined beforehand, particularly when the underlying variables affecting balance-of-payments behavior are subject to large and rapid change. The search for equilibrium rates will inevitably be one of trial and error. The possibility of considerable error in adjusting rates, as well as the possibility that depreciation may often be relatively ineffective or unsatisfactory as a corrective of disequilibria, merely strengthen the desirability of high and stable levels of income and employment in the leading countries, notably the United States, so as, among other things, to keep down the extent and duration of possible unbalance in international accounts. Indeed, if this desideratum is not realized, the multilateral world trading system currently envisaged might fail to be achieved at all, or, if achieved, might easily break down altogether. Viewed from

---

[58] For a review and analysis of some of these measurements, cf. J. Tinbergen, "Unstable Equilibria in the Balance of Payments," *Economic Research and the Development of Economic Science and Public Policy* (New York, 1946), pp. 135–142.

this angle, the greatest relevance of Keynesian economics for the exchange rate policy problems of the future may well lie in its vital contribution to our understanding of the causes and means of prevention of economic instability and under-employment.

CHAPTER XXIII

Keynesian Commercial Policy

By RANDALL HINSHAW

IN HIS ATTITUDE toward freedom of trade, Keynes was acutely conscious of the impact of changing international conditions, and thus, in this sphere, he is particularly open to the easy charge of inconsistency. Some inconsistency—that is to say, some genuine change of mind—there unquestionably was, but in the main a change in the Keynesian prescription was the result of a change in the condition of the patient; and it should be remembered that Keynes always had one patient, namely Britain, primarily in mind. Keynes was more cautious than some of his admirers in recommending the Keynesian remedies, and he reluctantly prescribed a tariff at a time when he thought a more relevant remedy— exchange depreciation—would not be acceptable. When, to his surprise, the patient accepted the more effective medicine, Keynes at once withdrew his original suggestion, and never offered it again. He did of course retain his belief in the need for import control in special circumstances, but in the final years of his life it would have been impossible to point to a more eloquent or persistent advocate of a liberal international regime. In unequivocal language, he repudiated the economic nationalists in his own country, and spent his last strength in helping to draft the blueprints for a world order designed, in his own words, "not to defeat, but to implement the wisdom of Adam Smith." [1] This apparent change in perspective was only in part because the Keynes of 1946 was different from the Keynes of 1931: the world of 1946 was a different world.

KEYNES, THE TARIFF, AND UNEMPLOYMENT

Keynes appears to have been the first economist of recognized standing to make a serious case for a tariff as a means (under

[1] "The Balance of Payments of the United States," EJ, June, 1946, p. 186.

carefully defined conditions) of increasing a nation's level of income and employment.[2] He was not always of this view. Indeed, in the early twenties, he declared that "if there is one thing that protection can *not* do, it is to cure unemployment. . . . There are some arguments for protection, based upon its securing possible but improbable advantages, to which there is no simple answer. But the claim to cure unemployment involves the protectionist fallacy in its grossest and crudest form."[3] Language could hardly be more emphatic, and it is interesting to examine the reasons which, to Keynes writing in 1923, seemed more than adequate to support a view he was later to repudiate. The reasoning is wholly classical. Keynes of course admitted (as would the most staunch classicist) that a tariff will increase employment in the protected industries, but maintained that any advantage thus gained would be offset by a corresponding contraction of employment in the export industries. Moreover, he specifically denied that a tariff can result in an increase in a country's level of income. "The protectionist," he wrote, "has to prove, not merely that he has made work, but that he has increased the national income. Imports are receipts; and exports are payments. How, as a nation, can we better ourselves by diminishing our receipts? Is there anything that a tariff could do, which an earthquake could not do better?"[4]

These are among the last published words of Keynes the classical Free Trader. Indeed it would seem that the very act of stating, thus explicitly, the classical case against protection was to result in disturbing premonitions that all was not well with the traditional view. In any case, during the next few years Keynes was to abandon the faith of his fathers that tariffs are powerless to correct unemployment. The first systematic statement of his new view is to be found in the *Treatise on Money*.[5] Here the rather tentative and hesitant case for a tariff is made in an elaborate theoretical language Keynes was later to abandon, but the argument is essentially simple and can perhaps best be presented by means of an example.

Let us consider two countries, say Britain and the United

[2] Professor Haberler's thoughtful treatment of this subject was to appear later. See the English edition of his *Theory of International Trade* (1936), pp. 259–273.

[3] "Free Trade," N&A, November 24, 1923, p. 303.

[4] "Free Trade and Unemployment," N&A, December 1, 1923, p. 336.

[5] See especially Vol. I, pp. 131–132, 326–363, and Vol. II, pp. 184–189.

States, and assume, as was the case when Keynes was writing, that both are on the gold standard. We may also assume that in the beginning both countries are enjoying prosperity and are in international equilibrium, with no net flow of gold in either direction. Let us now suppose that a severe depression occurs in the United States, and proceed to examine the various courses which are open to Britain. As a first and rather extreme case, let us assume that the British pursue a completely passive policy in this situation, allowing events to take their course without intervention of any kind. In this event, the initial result clearly will be a fall in the value of British exports, owing to the decline in American demand, and possibly also a rise in the value of British imports, owing to depressed prices in the United States.[6] Gold will flow out of Britain, and international equilibrium will be restored only when British prices and money incomes are at a lower level. In these circumstances, the fall in British prices and incomes accomplishes two purposes: the fall in prices tends to arrest, or reverse, the fall in British exports, while the fall in money incomes tends to reduce British imports. Both influences operate in the direction of equilibrium. If British money-wage rates and prices are not sufficiently flexible, international equilibrium can be regained only at a lower level of British employment; that is to say, unemployment is the only way the national income can be reduced sufficiently to achieve the necessary contraction of imports.

We have assumed, however, that nothing whatever is done by the British to protect themselves from the depression abroad. What would the classical prescription be in this situation? The traditional procedure would be to restrict an outflow of gold by means of a tight money policy. But this, according to Keynes, is simply another method of transmitting the depression from the United States to Britain. Unless British wage rates are flexible, the rise in British interest rates will result in a contraction of domestic investment and employment, and international equilibrium will be restored in as unpleasant a way as before.

In this situation, which is roughly the situation in which Britain found herself in 1930, Keynes saw three principal ways which were open to the British as means of resisting the deflationary

[6] Whether the *value* of British imports would increase in this situation will, of course, depend on the average price elasticity of the British demand for imports.

suction from abroad. These were (1) sterling depreciation, (2) "rationalization" of British industry, with the purpose of increasing productive efficiency, and (3) a moderate tariff, combined with a program of domestic expansion, possibly including some type of export subsidization. The first method Keynes regarded as politically unfeasible. The second policy he viewed as an essentially long-run solution to the British problem which offered little promise in the immediate predicament of 1930. Consequently, in the *Treatise*, Keynes hinted that he had come to look with favor on the third possibility, and early in 1931 he openly recommended a moderate tariff coupled with a program of internal expansion.[7]

According to Keynes, a tariff would assist British recovery in three ways.[8] In the first place, a tariff would protect the British balance of payments while the program of domestic expansion was being carried out. Keynes pointed out that, in the absence of effective controls, an expansionist program at home, by leading to an increase in imports, would result in an outflow of gold which would imperil the success of the program.[9] In the second place, a moderate tariff, by providing possibly substantial revenue, would aid materially in financing the program. Finally, to the extent that a tariff resulted in the substitution of domestic for foreign output, it would tend to increase domestic employment. Keynes admitted that there would be a net gain in employment only if the increased employment in the sheltered industries were not offset by a corresponding reduction of employment in the export industries, but he denied that there need be any such contraction. Exports, he pointed out, would be expected to decline (and then but gradually) only if *total* imports were to decline, and Keynes argued that his proposal did not necessarily involve a fall in the total value of imports. Indeed the *raison d'être* of the suggested tariff was to prevent the *in-*

[7] In a popular article, Keynes suggested a duty of 15 per cent on all manufactured and semi-manufactured goods and a duty of 5 per cent on foodstuffs and certain raw materials, with other raw materials (including wool and cotton) exempt. (NST&N, March 7, 1931, p. 54.)

[8] In addition to the analysis in the *Treatise*, Keynes stated his case for a tariff in a series of articles in the NST&N (March, April, 1931) and, more systematically, in Addendum I of the *Report of the Committee on Finance and Industry* (Macmillan Report, 1931).

[9] Raising the Bank rate in these circumstances would of course be ruled out as a method of preventing a gold outflow, since it would be inconsistent with a program of internal expansion.

crease in imports which would otherwise accompany an expansionist program. Certain imports, principally manufactures, would be adversely affected by the tariff, but other imports, notably food and raw materials (which either were to be admitted free or were to be subject only to a modest duty) would be favorably affected if the program of domestic expansion were successful. Thus Keynes argued that neither total imports nor total exports need fall.

It should be remembered that this proposal was made before Britain went off gold, and was offered as an alternative to sterling depreciation. Nevertheless, Keynes' fall from grace as a classical Free Trader met with a storm of denunciation from his fellow British economists.[10] Keynes, who had advanced the tariff suggestion without enthusiasm, appeared surprised at the vehemence of the criticism, and at length was disposed to write: "Whatever may be the reason, new paths of thought have no appeal to the fundamentalists of free trade. They have been forcing me to chew over again a lot of stale mutton, dragging me along a route I have known all about as long as I have known anything, which cannot, as I have discovered by many attempts, lead one to a solution of our present difficulties—a peregrination of the catacombs with a guttering candle."[11] To those who charged him with inconsistency, he remarked dryly, "I seem to see the elder parrots' sitting round and saying: 'You can *rely* upon us. Every day for thirty years, regardless of the weather, we have said "What a lovely morning!" But this is a bad bird. He says one thing one day, and something else the next.'"[12]

VIEWS ON SELF-SUFFICIENCY AND MERCANTILISM

With the British departure from gold in September, 1931, Keynes immediately withdrew his tariff proposal. However, on at least two subsequent occasions he made a qualified case for protection. In an article published in 1933, Keynes examined the arguments in favor of a greater degree of national self-sufficiency, and found some of them compelling.[13] Writing against the disturbing political background of the early thirties, Keynes

[10] See especially the correspondence in NST&N during March and April, 1931.
[11] "Economic Notes on Free Trade, III," NST&N, April 11, 1931, p. 243.
[12] "Economic Notes on Free Trade, II," NST&N, April 4, 1931, p. 211.
[13] "National Self-Sufficiency," YR, June, 1933.

was inclined to the view that extreme international specialization
and interdependence, with the accompanying rapid transmission
of economic illness from one country to another, were prejudicial
rather than favorable to world peace. At the same time, he was
of the opinion that the economic advantages of international
specialization had been somewhat exaggerated and, in any case,
were not as great as in the nineteenth century.

> A considerable degree of international specialization (Keynes
> wrote) is necessary in a rational world in all cases where it is
> dictated by wide differences of climate, natural resources, native
> aptitudes, level of culture and density of population. But . . .
> experience accumulates to prove that most modern processes of
> mass production can be performed in most countries and climates
> with almost equal efficiency. Moreover, with greater wealth, both
> primary and manufactured products play a smaller relative part
> in the national economy compared with houses, personal services,
> and local amenities . . . National self-sufficiency, in short, though
> it costs something, may be becoming a luxury which we can afford,
> if we happen to want it.[14]

Some degree of economic insularity Keynes regarded as desirable, not in itself, but as the necessary condition for certain
types of economic experimentation. For the plight of capitalist
countries, then floundering in the depths of depression, he found
little rational excuse. As then exemplified, capitalism, he wrote,
"is not a success. It is not intelligent, it is not beautiful, it is not
just, it is not virtuous—and it doesn't deliver the goods."[15]
Weighed in the balance and found wanting, the prevailing
order, Keynes felt, was doomed in the absence of heroic experimentation. Such experimentation might require (or might
involve as a by-product) a greater degree of national self-sufficiency.

Keynes' discussion of commercial policy in the *General Theory*
is well known, and adds little to the previous statements of his
position. In the "Notes on Mercantilism," Keynes made a carefully qualified case for the mercantilist system in its own historical context.[16] He made no attempt to apply this case to the international environment of 1936, and was careful to point out that

[14] *Op. cit.*, p. 760.
[15] *Ibid.*, p. 761.
[16] *The General Theory of Employment, Interest, and Money*, Chap. 23.

the advantages he saw in mercantilism were "avowedly national advantages" which were "unlikely to benefit the world as a whole." [17] Yet he was insistent that the commonly encountered efforts to explain mercantilism in terms of a naive confusion of gold with wealth were themselves naive. The mercantilist pre-occupation with the trade balance, Keynes maintained, was a rational reaction to certain influences which tend to check economic expansion. His reasoning was as follows: Economic expansion is dependent upon adequate incentives to invest, whether domestic or foreign. The level of domestic investment, Keynes held, is in the long run governed by the domestic rate of interest, while the level of foreign investment is determined by the balance of trade. But the domestic rate of interest is in part determined by the money supply, which is also affected by the trade balance. Thus, according to Keynes, mercantilist policies tended to react favorably on both domestic and foreign investment: on the former, by tending to depress the domestic rate of interest and, on the latter, by tending to create a favorable balance of trade.

LAST PHASE: KEYNES THE INTERNATIONALIST

The *General Theory* contains the last systematic statement of Keynes on the subject of commercial policy. Yet it would clearly be misleading to omit reference to the later Keynes, whose views were to wield such wide influence during the war period. If Keynes had died in 1936, he might possibly have been classified, in the sphere of commercial policy, as an apologist for economic nationalism; and doubtless there would have been those who would have maintained that he would not have been in sympathy with recent efforts toward international economic co-operation. Indeed, it is possible that some of his disciples, after consulting (with more devotion than insight) the works of their master, would have been led to take a stand against the very institutions which Keynes helped so prominently to design and to bring into being. Be this as it may, the Keynes of the war period was a consummate internationalist, and the apparent shift in his point of view appears to have been very largely the result of the change in the international environment. It should be remembered that the political and economic complexion of the thirties was not conducive to preoccupation with the long run. *Ad hoc*

[17] *Ibid.*, p. 335.

planning along national lines appeared to be the only type of planning that was politically feasible; and Keynes was never one to ignore political realities. But the drastically altered international setting of the forties offered at least the hope that long-range international planning might have some chance of success.

In his final years, Keynes clearly revealed the marks of his classical upbringing. Indeed, in a posthumously published article, he declared: "I find myself moved, not for the first time, to remind contemporary economists that the classical teaching embodied some permanent truths of great importance . . . There are in these matters deep undercurrents at work, natural forces, one can call them, or even the invisible hand, which are operating towards equilibrium."[18] Moreover, he showed scant respect for the critics (some of them "Keynesians") of the American proposals for mutilateral reduction of trade barriers. With characteristic asperity, he referred to their sentiments as "modernist stuff, gone wrong and turned sour and silly."[19] Yet it would be a mistake to assume that Keynes was simply reverting to the views he had held prior to the depression. There was no return to the ranks of the doctrinaire Free Traders. "I do not suppose," he wrote, "that the classical medicine will work by itself or that we can depend on it. We need quicker and less painful aids of which exchange variation and over-all import control are the most important. But in the long run these expedients will work better and we shall need them less, if the classical medicine is also at work."[20]

[18] "The Balance of Payments of the United States," ej, June, 1946, p. 185.
[19] *Ibid.*, p. 186.
[20] *Ibid.*, p. 186.

CHAPTER XXIV

Proposals for an International
Clearing Union

In PARLIAMENT on the 2nd February, the Chancellor of the Exchequer mentioned the need, after the war, of "an international monetary mechanism which will serve the requirements of international trade and avoid any need for unilateral action in competitive exchange depreciation . . . a system in which blocked balances and bilateral clearances would be unnecessary . . . an orderly and agreed method of determining the value of national currency units . . . We want to free the international monetary system from those arbitrary, unpredictable and undesirable influences which have operated in the past as the result of large scale speculative movements of short term capital."

On the directions of the Government this problem has been under close examination by the Treasury, in consultation with other Departments. The attached paper has been prepared and the Government has decided that it should be published as a preliminary contribution to the solution of one of the problems of international economic co-operation after the war.

[In the two following paragraphs, the provisional nature of the recommendations is emphasized.]

PROPOSALS FOR AN INTERNATIONAL CLEARING UNION

Immediately after the war all countries who have been engaged will be concerned with the pressure of relief and urgent reconstruction. The transition out of this into the normal world of the future cannot be wisely effected unless we know into what we are moving. It is therefore not too soon to consider what is to come after. In the field of national activity occupied by production, trade, and finance, both the nature of the problem and the experience of the period between the wars suggest four main lines of approach:

1. The mechanism of currency and exchange;

2. The framework of a commercial policy regulating the conditions for the exchange of goods, tariffs, preferences, subsidies, import regulations, and the like;

3. The orderly conduct of production, distribution and price of primary products so as to protect both producers and consumers from the loss and risk for which the extravagant fluctuations of market conditions have been responsible in recent times;

4. Investment aid, both medium and long term, for the countries whose economic development needs assistance from outside.

If the principles of these measures and the form of the institutions to give effect to them can be settled in advance, in order that they may be in operation when the need arises, it is possible that taken together they may help the world to control the ebb and flow of the tides of economic activity which have, in the past, destroyed security of livelihood and endangered international peace.

All these matters will need to be handled in due course. The proposal that follows relates only to the mechanism of currency and exchange in international trading. It appears on the whole convenient to give it priority, because some general conclusions have to be reached under this head before much progress can be made with the other topics.

In preparing these proposals, care has been taken to regard certain conditions, which the groundwork of an international economic system to be set up after the war should satisfy, if it is to prove durable:

(i) There should be the least possible interference with internal national policies, and the plan should not wander from the international *terrain*. Since such policies may have important repercussions on international relations, they cannot be left out of account. Nevertheless, in the realm of internal policy the authority of the Governing Board of the proposed Institution should be limited to recommendations, or at the most, to imposing conditions for the more extended enjoyment of the facilities which the Institution offers.

(ii) The technique of the plan must be capable of application, irrespective of the type and principle of government and economic policy existing in the prospective member States.

(iii) The management of the Institution must be genuinely international without preponderant power of veto or enforcement to any country or group; and the rights and privileges of the smaller countries must be safeguarded.

(iv) Some qualification of the right to act at pleasure is required by any agreement or treaty between nations. But in order that such arrangements may be fully voluntary so long as they last and terminable when they have become irksome, provision must be made for voiding the obligation at due notice. If many member States were to take advantage of this, the plan would have broken down. But if they are free to escape from its provisions if necessary, they may be the more willing to go on accepting them.

(v) The plan must operate not only to the general advantage but also to the individual advantage of each of the participants, and must not require a special economic or financial sacrifice from certain countries. No participant must be asked to do or offer anything which is not to his own true long-term interest.

It must be emphasized that it is not for the Clearing Union to assume the burden of long-term lending which is the proper task of some other institution. It is also necessary for it to have means of restraining improvident borrowers. But the Clearing Union must also seek to discourage creditor countries from leaving unused large liquid balances which ought to be devoted to some positive purpose. For excessive credit balances necessarily create excessive debit balances for some other party. In recognising that the creditor as well as the debtor may be responsible for a want of balance, the proposed institution would be breaking new ground.

I. THE OBJECTS OF THE PLAN

About the primary objects of an improved system of International Currency there is, to-day, a wide measure of agreement:

(a) We need an instrument of international currency having general acceptability between nations, so that blocked balances and bilateral clearings are unnecessary; that is to say, an instrument of currency used by each nation in its transactions with other nations, operating through whatever national organ, such as a Treasury or a Central Bank, is most appropriate, private individuals, businesses, and banks other than Central Banks, each continuing to use their own national currency as heretofore.

(*b*) We need an orderly and agreed method of determining the relative exchange values of national currency units, so that unilateral action and competitive exchange depreciations are prevented.

(*c*) We need a *quantum* of international currency, which is neither determined in an unpredictable and irrelevant manner as, for example, by the technical progress of the gold industry, nor subject to large variations depending on the gold reserve policies of individual countries; but is governed by the actual current requirements of world commerce, and is also capable of deliberate expansion and contraction to offset deflationary and inflationary tendencies in effective world demand.

(*d*) We need a system possessed of an internal stabilizing mechanism, by which pressure is exercised on any country whose balance of payments with the rest of the world is departing from equilibrium *in either direction*, so as to prevent movements which must create for its neighbours an equal but opposite want of balance.

(*e*) We need an agreed plan for starting off every country after the war with a stock of reserves appropriate to its importance in world commerce, so that without due anxiety it can set its house in order during the transitional period to full peace-time conditions.

(*f*) We need a central institution, of a purely technical and non-political character, to aid and support other international institutions concerned with the planning and regulation of the world's economic life.

(*g*) More generally, we need a means of reassurance to a troubled world, by which any country whose own affairs are conducted with due prudence is relieved of anxiety for causes which are not of its own making, concerning its ability to meet its international liabilities; and which will, therefore, make unnecessary those methods of restriction and discrimination which countries have adopted hitherto, not on their merits, but as measures of self-protection from disruptive outside forces.

[Section 2 affirms that the plan is not original. Section 3 discusses the advantage of a multilateral plan.]

4. The proposal is to establish a Currency Union, here designated an *International Clearing Union,* based on international

bank-money, called (let us say) *bancor*, fixed (but not un-alterably) in terms of gold and accepted as the equivalent of gold by the British Commonwealth and the United States and all the other members of the Union for the purpose of settling inter-national balances. The Central Banks of all member States (and also of non-members) would keep accounts with the International Clearing Union through which they would be entitled to settle their exchange balances with one another at their par value as defined in terms of bancor. Countries having a favorable balance of payments with the rest of the world as a whole would find themselves in possession of a credit account with the Clearing Union, and those having an unfavorable balance would have a debit account. Measures would be necessary (see below) to prevent the piling up of credit and debit balances without limit, and the system would have failed in the long run if it did not possess sufficient capacity for self-equilibrium to secure this.

5. The idea underlying such a Union is simple, namely, to generalize the essential principle of banking as it is exhibited within any closed system. This principle is the necessary equality of credits and debits. If no credits can be removed outside the clearing system, but only transferred within it, the Union can never be in any difficulty as regards the honoring of checks drawn upon it. It can make what advances it wishes to any of its members with the assurance that the proceeds can only be transferred to the clearing account of another member. Its sole task is to see to it that its members keep the rules and that the advances made to each of them are prudent and advisable for the Union as a whole.

II. THE PROVISIONS OF THE PLAN

[Section 6 paragraphs (1) and (2) discuss details of members and the Governing Board.]

(3) The member States will agree between themselves the initial values of their own currencies in terms of bancor. A mem-ber State may not subsequently alter the value of its currency in terms of bancor without the permission of the Governing Board except under the conditions stated below; but during the first five years after the inception of the system the Governing Board shall give special consideration to appeals for an adjustment in the ex-change value of a national currency unit on the ground of unfore-seen circumstances.

[Paragraph (4) is concerned with the relation of gold and Bancor.]

(5) Each member State shall have assigned to it a *quota,* which shall determine the measure of its responsibility in the management of the Union and of its right to enjoy the credit facilities provided by the Union. The initial quotas might be fixed by reference to the sum of each country's exports and imports on the average of (say) the three pre-war years, and might be (say) 75 per cent of this amount, a special assessment being substituted in cases (of which there might be several) where this formula would be, for any reason, inappropriate. Subsequently, after the elapse of the transitional period, the quotas should be revised annually in accordance with the running average of each country's actual volume of trade in the three preceding years, rising to a five-year average when figures for five post-war years are available. The determination of a country's quota primarily by reference to the value of its foreign trade seems to offer the criterion most relevant to a plan which is chiefly concerned with the regulation of the foreign exchanges and of a country's international trade balance. It is, however, a matter for discussion whether the formula for fixing quotas should also take account of other factors.

[Paragraphs (6) and (7) deal with obligations to accept bancors, and charges on balances, both *credit* and debit.]

[Paragraphs (8) (a) and (c) and omitted parts of (8) (b) deal with growth of debit balances and corrective measures required when these balances rise.]

(8) (b) As a condition of allowing a member State to increase its debit balance to a figure in excess of a half of its quota, the Governing Board may require all or any of the following measures:

(i) a stated reduction in the value of the member's currency, if it deems that to be the suitable remedy;

(ii) the control of outward capital transactions, if not already in force; and

(iii) the outright surrender of a suitable proportion of any separate gold or other liquid reserve in reduction of its debit balance.

Furthermore, the Governing Board may recommend to the Government of the member State any internal measures affecting its domestic economy which may appear to be appropriate to restore the equilibrium of its international balance.

[(8) (d), omitted, discusses defaults.]

(9) A member State whose credit balance has exceeded a *half* of its quota on the average of at least a year shall discuss with the Governing Board (but shall retain the ultimate decision in its own hands) what measures would be appropriate to restore the equilibrium of its international balances, including:

(*a*) Measures for the expansion of domestic credit and domestic demand.

(*b*) The appreciation of its local currency in terms of Bancor, or, alternatively, the encouragement of an increase in money rates of earnings.

(*c*) The reduction of tariffs and other discouragements against imports.

(*d*) International development loans.

(10) A member State shall be entitled to obtain a credit balance in terms of bancor by paying in gold to the Clearing Union for the credit of its clearing account. But no one is entitled to demand gold from the Union against a balance of bancor, since such balance is available only for transfer to another clearing account. The Governing Board of the Union shall, however, have the discretion to distribute any gold in the possession of the Union between the members possessing credit balances in excess of a specified proportion of their quotas, proportionately to such balances, in reduction of their amount in excess of that proportion.

(11) The monetary reserves of a member State, viz., the Central Bank or other bank, or Treasury deposits in excess of a working balance, shall not be held in another country except with the approval of the monetary authorities of that country.

[6 (12) provides for appointment of Governing Board, votes, etc.]

(13) The Governing Board shall be entitled to reduce the quotas of members, all in the same specified proportion, if it seems necessary to correct in this manner an excess of world purchasing power. In that event, the provisions of 6 (8) shall be held to apply to the quotas as so reduced, provided that no member shall be required to reduce his actual overdraft at the date of the change, or be entitled by reason of this reduction to alter the value of his currency under 6 (8) (*a*), except after the expiry of two years. If the Governing Board subsequently desires to correct a potential deficiency of world purchasing power, it shall be entitled to restore the general level of quotas toward the original level.

[6 (14) deals with statistical information, (15) to (18) with various details of administration.]

III. WHAT LIABILITIES OUGHT THE PLAN TO PLACE ON CREDITOR COUNTRIES?

7. It is not contemplated that either the debit or the credit balance of an individual country ought to exceed a certain maximum—let us say, its *quota*. In the case of debit balances this maximum has been made a rigid one, and, indeed, counter-measures are called for long before the maximum is reached. In the case of credit balances, no rigid maximum has been proposed. For the appropriate provision might be to require the eventual cancellation or compulsory investment of persistent bancor credit balances accumulating in excess of a member's quota; and, however desirable this may be in principle, it might be felt to impose on creditor countries a heavier burden than they can be asked to accept before having had experience of the benefit to them of the working of the plan as a whole. If, on the other hand, the limitation were to take the form of the creditor country not being required to accept bancor in excess of a prescribed figure, this might impair the general acceptability of bancor, whilst at the same time conferring no real benefit on the creditor country itself. For, if it chose to avail itself of the limitation, it must either restrict its exports or be driven back on some form of bilateral payment agreements outside the Clearing Union, thus substituting a less acceptable asset for bancor balances which are based on the collective credit of all the member States and are available for payments to any of them, or attempt the probably temporary expedient of refusing to trade except on a gold basis.

8. The absence of a rigid maximum to credit balances does not impose on any member State, as might be supposed at first sight, an unlimited liability outside its own control. The liability of an individual member is determined, not by the quotas of the other members, but by its own policy in controlling its favorable balance of payments. The existence of the Clearing Union does not deprive a member State of any of the facilities which it now possesses for receiving payment for its exports. In the absence of the Clearing Union, a creditor country can employ the proceeds of its exports to buy goods or to buy investments, or to make temporary advances and to hold temporary overseas balances, or to buy gold in the market. All these facilities will remain at its disposal.

The difference is that in the absence of the Clearing Union, more or less automatic factors come into play to restrict the volume of its exports after the above means of receiving payment for them have been exhausted. Certain countries become unable to buy and, in addition to this, there is an automatic tendency towards a general slump in international trade and, as a result, a reduction in the exports of the creditor country. Thus, the effect of the Clearing Union is to give the creditor country a choice between voluntarily curtailing its exports to the same extent that they would have been involuntarily curtailed in the absence of the Clearing Union, or, alternatively, of allowing its exports to continue and accumulating the excess receipts in the form of bancor balances for the time being. Unless the removal of a factor causing the involuntary reduction of exports is reckoned a disadvantage, a creditor country incurs no burden but is, on the contrary, relieved, by being offered the additional option of receiving payment for its exports through the accumulation of a bancor balance.

9. If, therefore, a member State asks what governs the maximum liability which it incurs by entering the system, the answer is that this lies entirely within its own control. No more is asked of it than that it should hold in bancor such surplus of its favorable balance of payments as it does not itself choose to employ in any other way, and only for so long as it does not so choose.

IV. SOME ADVANTAGES OF THE PLAN

10. The plan aims at the substitution of an expansionist, in place of a contractionist, pressure on world trade.

11. It effects this by allowing to each member State overdraft facilities of a defined amount. Thus each country is allowed a certain margin of resources and a certain interval of time within which to effect a balance in its economic relations with the rest of the world. These facilities are made possible by the constitution of the system itself and do not involve particular indebtedness between one member State and another. A country is in credit or debit with the Clearing Union as a whole. This means that the overdraft facilities, whilst a relief to some, are not a real burden to others. For the accumulation of a credit balance with the Clearing Union would resemble the importation of gold in signifying that the country holding it is abstaining voluntarily from the immediate use of purchasing power. But it would not involve, as would the importation of gold, the withdrawal of this

purchasing power from circulation or the exercise of a deflationary and contractionist pressure on the whole world, including in the end the creditor country itself. Under the proposed plan, therefore, no country suffers injury (but on the contrary) by the fact that the command over resources, which it does not itself choose to employ for the time being, is not withdrawn from use. The accumulation of bancor credit does not curtail in the least its capacity or inducement either to produce or to consume.

12. In short, the analogy with a national banking system is complete. No depositor in a local bank suffers because the balances, which he leaves idle, are employed to finance the business of someone else. Just as the development of national banking systems served to offset a deflationary pressure which would have prevented otherwise the development of modern industry, so by extending the same principle into the international field we may hope to offset the contractionist pressure which might otherwise overwhelm in social disorder and disappointment the good hopes of our modern world. The substitution of a credit mechanism in place of hoarding would have repeated in the international field the same miracle, already performed in the domestic field, of turning a stone into bread.

[Section 13 discusses alternative ways of achieving the objectives of the Clearing Union.]

14. It should be much easier, and surely more satisfactory for all of us, to enter into a general and collective responsibility, applying to all countries alike, that a country finding itself in a creditor position *against the rest of the world as a whole* should enter into an arrangement not to allow this credit balance to exercise a contractionist pressure against world economy and, by repercussion, against the economy of the creditor country itself. This would give everyone the great assistance of multilateral clearing, whereby (for example) Great Britain could offset favorable balances arising out of her exports to Europe against unfavorable balances due to the United States or South America or elsewhere. How, indeed, can any country hope to start up trade with Europe during the relief and reconstruction period on any other terms?

15. The facilities offered will be of particular importance in the transitional period after the war, as soon as the initial shortages of supply have been overcome. Many countries will find a difficulty in paying for their imports, and will need time and re-

sources before they can establish a readjustment. The efforts of each of these debtor countries to preserve its own equilibrium, by forcing its exports and by cutting off all imports which are not strictly necessary, will aggravate the problems of all the others. On the other hand, if each feels free from undue pressure, the volume of international exchange will be increased and everyone will find it easier to re-establish equilibrium without injury to the standard of life anywhere. The creditor countries will benefit, hardly less than the debtors, by being given an interval of *time* in which to adjust their economies, during which they can safely move at their own pace without the result of exercising deflationary pressure on the rest of the world, and, by repercussion, on themselves.

16. It must, however, be emphasized that the provision by which the members of the Clearing Union start with substantial overdraft facilities in hand will be mainly useful, just as the possession of any kind of reserve is useful, to allow time and method for necessary adjustments and a comfortable safeguard behind which the unforeseen and the unexpected can be faced with equanimity. Obviously, it does not by itself provide any long-term solution against a continuing disequilibrium, for in due course the more improvident and the more impecunious, left to themselves, would have run through their resources. But, if the purpose of the overdraft facilities is mainly to give time for adjustments, we have to make sure, so far as possible, that they *will* be made. We must have, therefore, some rules and some machinery to secure that equilibrium is restored. A tentative attempt to provide for this has been made above. Perhaps it might be strengthened and improved.

[Section 17 indicates why responsibility should be put on creditor nations.]

18. If, indeed, a country lacks the productive capacity to maintain its standard of life, then a reduction in this standard is not avoidable. If its wage and price levels in terms of money are out of line with those elsewhere, a change in the rate of its foreign exchange is inevitable. But if, possessing the productive capacity, it lacks markets because of restrictive policies throughout the world, then the remedy lies in expanding its opportunities for export by removal of the restrictive pressure. We are too ready today to assume the inevitability of unbalanced trade positions, thus making the opposite error to those who assumed the tendency

of exports and imports to equality. It used to be supposed, without sufficient reason, that effective demand is always properly adjusted throughout the world; we now tend to assume, equally without sufficient reason, that it never can be. On the contrary, there is great force in the contention that, if active employment and ample purchasing power can be sustained in the main centres of the world trade, the problem of surpluses and unwanted exports will largely disappear, even though, under the most prosperous conditions, there may remain some disturbances of trade and unforeseen situations requiring special remedies.

V. THE DAILY MANAGEMENT OF THE EXCHANGES UNDER THE PLAN

[The main subject of Sections 19–21 is the advantage of clearings over the bilateralism of the prewar period.]

22. Many Central Banks have found great advantage in centralizing with themselves or with an Exchange Control the supply and demand of all foreign exchange, thus dispensing with an outside exchange market, though continuing to accommodate individuals through the existing banks and not directly. The further extension of such arrangements would be consonant with the general purposes of the Clearing Union, inasmuch as they would promote order and discipline in international exchange transactions in detail as well as in general. The same is true of the control of capital movements, further described below, which many States are likely to wish to impose on their own nationals. But the structure of the proposed Clearing Union does not *require* such measures of centralization or of control on the part of a member State. It is, for example, consistent alike with the type of Exchange Control now established in the United Kingdom or with the system now operating in the United States. The Union does not prevent private holdings of foreign currency or private dealings in exchange or international capital movements if these have been approved or allowed by the member States concerned. Central Banks can deal directly with one another as heretofore.

[Sections 23–25 are concerned with special arrangements of particular groups of countries within the Union.]

VI. THE POSITION OF GOLD UNDER THE PLAN

26. Gold still possesses great psychological value which is not being diminished by current events; and the desire to possess a

gold reserve against unforeseen contingencies is likely to remain. Gold also has the merit of providing in point of form (whatever the underlying realities may be) an uncontroversial standard of value for international purposes, for which it would not yet be easy to find a serviceable substitute. Moreover, by supplying an automatic means for settling some part of the favorable balances of the creditor countries, the current gold production of the world and the remnant of gold reserves held outside the United States may still have a useful part to play. Nor is it reasonable to ask the United States to demonetise the stock of gold which is the basis of its impregnable liquidity. What, in the long run, the world may decide to do with gold is another matter. The purpose of the Clearing Union is to supplant gold as a governing factor, but not to dispense with it.

27. The international bank-money which we have designated *bancor* is defined in terms of a weight of gold. Since the national currencies of the member States are given a defined exchange value in terms of bancor, it follows that they would each have a defined gold content which would be their official buying price for gold, above which they must not pay. The fact that a member State is entitled to obtain a credit in terms of bancor by paying actual gold to the credit of its clearing account, secures a steady and ascertained purchaser for the output of the gold-producing countries, and for countries holding a large reserve of gold. Thus the position of producers and holders of gold is not affected adversely, and is, indeed, improved.

[Sections 28–31 discuss the place of gold reserves and the relation of bancors and gold (including convertibility and its price).]

VII. THE CONTROL OF CAPITAL MOVEMENTS

32. There is no country which can, in future, safely allow the flight of funds for political reasons or to evade domestic taxation or in anticipation of the owner turning refugee. Equally, there is no country that can safely receive fugitive funds, which constitute an unwanted import of capital, yet cannot safely be used for fixed investment.

33. For these reasons it is widely held that control of capital movements, both inward and outward, should be a permanent feature of the post-war system. It is an objection to this that control, if it is to be effective, probably requires the machinery of

exchange control for *all* transactions, even though a general permission is given to all remittances in respect of current trade. Thus those countries which have for the time being no reason to fear, and may indeed welcome, outward capital movements, may be reluctant to impose this machinery, even though a general permission for capital, as well as current transactions reduces it to being no more than a machinery of record. On the other hand, such control will be more difficult to work by unilateral action on the part of those countries which cannot afford to dispense with it, especially in the absence of a postal censorship, if movements of capital cannot be controlled *at both ends*. It would, therefore, be of great advantage if the United States, as well as other members of the Clearing Union, would adopt machinery similar to that which the British Exchange Control has now gone a long way towards perfecting. Nevertheless, the universal establishment of a control of capital movements cannot be regarded as essential to the operation of the Clearing Union; and the method and degree of such control should therefore be left to the decision of each member State. Some less drastic way might be found by which countries, not themselves controlling outward capital movements, can deter inward movements not approved by the countries from which they originate.

34. The position of abnormal balances in overseas ownership held in various countries at the end of the war presents a problem of considerable importance and special difficulty. A country in which a large volume of such balances is held could not, unless it is in a creditor position, afford the risk of having to redeem them in bancor on a substantial scale, if this would have the effect of depleting its bancor resources at the outset. At the same time, it is very desirable that the countries owning these balances should be able to regard them as liquid, at any rate over and above the amounts which they can afford to lock up under an agreed program of funding or long-term expenditure. Perhaps there should be some special over-riding provision for dealing with the transitional period, only by which, through the aid of the Clearing Union, such balances would remain liquid and convertible into bancor by the creditor country whilst there would be no corresponding strain on the bancor resources of the debtor country, or, at any rate, the resulting strain would be spread over a period.

35. The advocacy of a control of capital movements must not be taken to mean that the era of international investment should

be brought to an end. On the contrary, the system contemplated should greatly facilitate the restoration of international loans and credits for legitimate purposes. The object, and it is a vital object, is to have a means:

(*a*) of distinguishing long-term loans by creditor countries, which help to maintain equilibrium and develop the world's resources, from movements of funds out of debtor countries which lack the means to finance them; and

(*b*) of controlling short-term speculative movements or flights of currency whether out of debtor countries or from one creditor country to another.

36. It should be emphasized that the purpose of the overdrafts of bancor permitted by the Clearing Union is not to facilitate long-term or even medium-term credits to be made by debtor countries which cannot afford them, but to allow time and a breathing space for adjustments and for averaging one period with another to all member States alike, whether in the long run they are well-placed to develop a forward international loan policy or whether their prospects of profitable new development in excess of their own resources justifies them in long-term borrowing. The machinery and organization of international medium-term and long-term lending is another aspect of post-war economic policy, not less important than the purposes which the Clearing Union seeks to serve, but requiring another, complementary institution.

VIII. RELATION OF THE CLEARING UNION TO COMMERCIAL POLICY

37. The special protective expedients which were developed between the two wars were sometimes due to political, social, or industrial reasons. But frequently they were nothing more than forced and undesired dodges to protect an unbalanced position of a country's overseas payments. The new system, by helping to provide a register of the size and whereabouts of the aggregate debtor and creditor positions respectively, and an indication whether it is reasonable for a particular country to adopt special expedients as a temporary measure to assist in regaining equilibrium in its balance of payments, would make it possible to establish a general rule *not* to adopt them, subject to the indicated exceptions.

38. The existence of the Clearing Union would make it possible

for member States contracting commercial agreements to use their respective debit and credit positions with the clearing Union as a test, though this test by itself would not be complete. Thus, the contracting parties, whilst agreeing to clauses in a commercial agreement forbidding, in general, the use of certain measures or expedients in their mutual trade relations, might make this agreement subject to special relaxations if the state of their respective clearing accounts satisfied an agreed criterion. For example, an agreement might provide that, in the event of one of the contracting States having a debit balance with the Clearing Union exceeding a specified proportion of its quota on the average of a period, it should be free to resort to import regulation or to barter trade agreements or to higher import duties of a type which was restricted under the agreement in normal circumstances. Protected by the possibility of such temporary indulgences, the members of the Clearing Union should feel much more confidence in moving towards the withdrawal of other and more dislocating forms of protection and discrimination and in accepting the prohibition of the worst of them from the outset. In any case, it should be laid down that members of the Union would not allow or suffer among themselves any restrictions on the disposal of receipts arising out of current trade or "invisible" income.

IX. THE USE OF THE CLEARING UNION FOR OTHER INTERNATIONAL PURPOSES

39. The Clearing Union might become the instrument and the support of international policies in addition to those which it is its primary purpose to promote. This deserves the greatest possible emphasis. The Union might become the pivot of the future economic government of the world. Without it, other more desirable developments will find themselves impeded and unsupported. With it, they will fall into their place as parts of an ordered scheme. No one of the following suggestions is a necessary part of the plan. But they are illustrations of the additional purposes of high importance and value which the Union, once established, might be able to serve:

(1) The Union might set up a clearing account in favor of international bodies charged with post-war relief, rehabilitation and reconstruction. But it could go much further than this.

[Parts of Section 39 dealing with the financing and banking

functions of the Organization in relation to other international bodies, are omitted.]

(5) There are various methods by which the Clearing Union could use its influence and its powers to maintain stability of prices and to control the trade cycle. If an International Economic Board is established, this Board and the Clearing Union might be expected to work in close collaboration to their mutual advantage. If an International Investment or Development Corporation is also set up together with a scheme of Commodity Controls for the control of stocks of the staple primary products, we might come to possess in these three institutions a powerful means of combating the evils of the trade cycle, by exercising contractionist or expansionist influence on the system as a whole or on particular sections. This is a large and important question which cannot be discussed adequately in this paper; and need not be examined at length in this place because it does not raise any important issues affecting the fundamental constitution of the proposed Union. It is mentioned here to complete the picture of the wider purposes which the foundation of the Clearing Union might be made to serve.

40. The facility of applying the Clearing Union plan to these several purposes arises out of a fundamental characteristic which is worth pointing out, since it distinguishes the plan from those proposals which try to develop the same basic principle along bilateral lines and is one of the grounds on which the plan can claim superior merit. This might be described as its "anonymous" or "impersonal" quality. No particular member States have to engage their own resources as such to the support of other particular States or of any of the international projects or policies adopted. They have only to agree in general that, if they find themselves with surplus resources which for the time being they do not themselves wish to employ, these resources may go into the general pool and be put to work on approved purposes. This costs the surplus country nothing because it is not asked to part permanently, or even for any specified period, with such resources, which it remains free to expend and employ for its own purposes whenever it chooses; in which case the burden of finance is passed on to the next recipient, again for only so long as the recipient has no use for the money. As pointed out above, this merely amounts to extending to the international sphere the

methods of any domestic banking system, which are in the same sense "impersonal" inasmuch as there is no call on the particular depositor either to support as such the purposes for which his banker makes advances or to forgo permanently the use of his deposit. There is no countervailing objection except that which applies equally to the technique of domestic banking, namely that it is capable of the abuse of creating excessive purchasing power and hence an inflation of prices. In our efforts to avoid the opposite evil, we must not lose sight of this risk, to which there is an allusion in 39 (5) above. But it is no more reason for refusing the advantages of international banking than the similar risk in the domestic field is a reason to return to the practices of the seventeenth century goldsmiths (which are what we are still following in the international field) and to forgo the vast expansion of production which banking principles have made possible. Where financial contributions are required for some purpose of general advantage, it is a great facility not to have to ask for specific contributions from any named country, but to depend rather on the anonymous and impersonal aid of the system as a whole. We have here a genuine organ of truly international government.

X. THE TRANSITIONAL ARRANGEMENTS

41. It would be of great advantage to agree to the general principles of the Clearing Union before the end of the war, with a view to bringing it into operation at an early date after the termination of hostilities. Major plans will be more easily brought to birth in the first energy of victory and whilst the active spirit of united action still persists, than in the days of exhaustion and reaction from so much effort which may well follow a little later. Such a proposal presents, however, something of a dilemma. On the one hand, many countries will be in particular need of reserves of overseas resources in the period immediately after the war. On the other hand, goods will be in short supply and the prevention of inflationary international conditions of much more importance for the time being than the opposite. The expansionist tendency of the plan, which is a leading recommendation of it as soon as peace-time output is restored and the productive capacity of the world is in running order, might be a danger in the early days of a sellers' market and an excess of demand over supply.

42. A reconciliation of these divergent purposes is not easily found until we know more than is known at present about the means to be adopted to finance post-war relief and reconstruction. If the intention is to provide resources on liberal and comprehensive lines outside the resources made available by the Clearing Union and additional to them, it might be better for such specific aid to take the place of the proposed overdrafts during the "relief" period of (say) two years. In this case credit clearing balances would be limited to the amount of gold delivered to the Union, and the overdraft facilities created by the Union in favour of the Relief Council, the International Investment Board, or the Commodity Controls. Nevertheless, the immediate establishment of the Clearing Union would not be incompatible with provisional arrangements, which could take alternative forms according to the character of the other "relief" arrangements, qualifying and limiting the overdraft quotas. Overdraft quotas might be allowed on a reduced scale during the transitional period. Or it might be proper to provide that countries in receipt of relief or Lend-Lease assistance should not have access at the same time to overdraft facilities, and that the latter should only become available when the former had come to an end. If, on the other hand, relief from outside sources looks like being inadequate from the outset, the overdraft quotas may be even more necessary at the outset than later on.

43. We must not be over-cautious. A rapid economic restoration may lighten the tasks of the diplomatists and the politicians in the resettlement of the world and the restoration of social order. For Great Britain and other countries outside the "relief" areas the possibility of exports sufficient to sustain their standard of life is bound up with good and expanding markets. We cannot afford to wait too long for this, and we must not allow excessive caution to condemn us to perdition. Unless the Union is a going concern, the problem of proper "timing" will be nearly insoluble. It is sufficient at this stage to point out that the problem of timing must not be overlooked, but that the Union is capable of being used so as to aid rather than impede its solution.

[Sections 44–46 contain brief concluding remarks.]

CHAPTER XXV

The International Currency Proposals

By JOAN ROBINSON

THE BASIC RULE of the gold-standard game, or of any system of
multilateral international trade with stable exchange rates, is
that a country which has a favorable balance of trade on income
account must lend abroad on long term at a more or less commensurate rate; alternatively, a country whose citizens and Government are not prepared to lend abroad must not have a surplus
on income account. Any slight and temporary failure of trade
balances and rates of lending to keep in step can be provided for
by movements to and fro of gold and short-term funds, but a large
and continuous disequilibrium puts a strain upon the system
which it cannot bear.

In the text-book account of the gold standard, gold movements
of themselves set in train a mechanism to restore equilibrium.
If the surplus of exports of a country exceeds its surplus of lending, gold flows to it from the rest of the world. Consequently,
according to the text-book account, prices in that country rise,
while they fall in the rest of the world. Exports from the surplus
country to the rest of the world are therefore reduced, and its
imports from the rest of the world are increased, until its surplus
and the world's deficit are wiped out. Outside the textbooks,
matters do not go so smoothly. First, the country receiving gold
is under no necessity to check the inflow, while those who lose
gold are under an obligation, so long as they struggle to maintain the gold standard, to check the outflow, and they must set
about doing so the more quickly the smaller their reserves. Thus
the mechanism is not symmetrical, but has an inherent bias towards deflation, which is the more severe the smaller is the
amount of gold possessed by deficit countries. Secondly, a loss of
gold does not lead automatically and directly, as in the text-books,

to the fall of prices which is required to stimulate exports from a deficit country and foster its home production at the expense of imports. The process of adjustment is much more painful. To check the outflow of gold the authorities in a deficit country must restrict credit and encourage a fall in activity and incomes. This, indeed, reduces imports, but it reduces imports not only from the surplus country, but from others as well, so that countries formerly balanced are thrown into disequilibrium and have to join in the process of deflation. And it reduces not only imports, but also consumption of home-produced goods. The total loss of income is a large multiple of the reduction of imports which it is designed to bring about. If unemployment and business losses continue long enough to bring about a sufficient relative fall in money wages, relative costs are reduced, and the text-book story is completed. But meanwhile the surplus country is also suffering from unemployment through its loss of export markets. There is pressure there also to lower wages; and much else, including the gold standard itself, may give way under the strain long before equilibrium has been restored.

The aim of the two currency plans now under discussion is to provide a system of stable exchanges which is less likely to cause needless misery to the world, and is less likely to disrupt itself under the pressure of its own operations. The means proposed in both plans are, first, to provide each of the participating countries with a substitute for a gold reserve, so that the amount of disequilibrium which can occur without setting up any reaction is very much increased. This would allow a much longer breathing-space within which measures to restore equilibrium can be taken, and would provide reserves depending on some sort of rational plan, instead of on the accidental circumstances of how much gold there happens to be in any country at a particular moment. Second, to undertake measures to restore equilibrium, by consultation between the nations concerned, and to suggest measures of a less torturing kind than those imposed by the gold standard. Third, to give some degree of reality to the theoretical symmetry of the gold standard, by suggesting measures to restore equilibrium to the surplus as well as to the deficit countries.

So much is common ground. In mechanism the two plans differ considerably. For simplicity the *Proposals for an International Clearing Union*,[1] put forward by the British Chancellor of the

[1] Cmd. 6437. H. M. Stationery Office. Price 4*d*. (See above, pp. 323–41.)

Exchequer, will be referred to in what follows as the Bancor plan, and the *United States Proposal for a United and Associated Nations Stabilization Fund*,[2] as the Unitas plan. Under the Bancor plan each country is provided with overdraft facilities at the Clearing Union.[3] When any country's balance of imports exceeds its borrowing from other sources, it will make an overdraft, a corresponding credit appearing in the account of another country or countries. By this means bancor currency comes into existence. Countries can also acquire bancor credits by depositing gold with the Clearing Union, but bancor can never be withdrawn from the system. It can only be transferred from one account to another.[4] Under the Unitas scheme, each country in the first place pays, so to say, an entrance fee, by depositing a specified part of its gold reserve with the Stabilization Fund. It also puts at the disposal of the Fund a specified amount of its domestic currency, which is available to be sold to other member countries.[5] All transactions take the form of sale and purchase of currency for currency. Thus, while bancor has a real existence as an international medium of exchange, whose quantity varies as required, the Unitas plan provides no international currency. *Unitas* is simply a word, meaning gold to the value of $10 at the present price,[6] and the magnitude of the Fund is fixed at its inception. Under the Bancor plan a country's surplus on income account, not covered by lending, shows itself in the rate at which its bancor credit mounts up in the books of the Union. Under the Unitas plan it shows itself in the rate at which its initial subscription disappears from the Fund. A country's deficit shows itself, under Bancor, in its bancor debit; under Unitas, in a holding of its national currency by the Fund. The equivalent of a gold reserve is provided for each country, under Bancor, by its unused overdraft facilities. Under Unitas, gold is supplemented from the point of view of deficit countries by the amount of the currencies of surplus countries in the Fund.

Under both plans a quota is ascribed to each country, which limits its rights and obligations. The method of assessment and the function of the quotas differ considerably between the two

[2] U. S. Treasury, reprinted by H. M. Stationery Office. Price 3d.
[3] Cmd. 6437, 6 (6).
[4] *Ibid.*, 6 (10) (See above, p. 329).
[5] U. S. *Proposal*, II, 4.
[6] *Ibid.*, IV, 1.

plans. Under the Bancor plan it is suggested that the quotas should initially be three-quarters of the sum of imports and exports (presumably visible items only) on the average of the last three pre-war years, and should be continuously readjusted, when the plan is in operation, by a moving average.[7] Under the Unitas plan the quota is arrived at by an index (the details of which are not given) representing the gold holding of the country, its national income, and the fluctuations of its balance of trade.[8] It is very unfortunate that, in both plans, voting rights in the control of the schemes are based upon quotas. This naturally leads the public to suppose that the Unitas formula has been chosen so as to give the United States control of the scheme, and that the Bancor formula has been chosen to give the advantage to Great Britain. Clearly, the relative influence of various nations is a general political question very indirectly related to the technical problem of choosing the most convenient basis for fixing quotas, and the two questions should be kept distinct.

From the technical point of view, the Unitas formula seems at first sight highly irrational. What has the gold holding of a country, or the size of its national income, to do with the case? The Bancor formula certainly appears more relevant. But the function of the quotas under Unitas is different, and there would be no advantage in adopting the Bancor formula in the Unitas plan. Under Unitas, quotas determine the amount of home currency which each country places at the disposal of the Fund, and the power of the Fund to ease pressure upon debtors is limited by the amount of the currency of surplus countries which it can command. One of the contingencies which the plans are designed to meet is a repetition of the situation of the twenties when the world as a whole was running into debt to the United States, and in such a case the usefulness of the Fund would be strictly limited by its holding of dollars. Under the Unitas plan, therefore, a formula which gives a large proportionate quota to the United States might be essential to its effectiveness.

Supposing that the initial rates of exchange, when either scheme is set up, have been well chosen, and that surplus countries are regularly lending at a rate commensurate with their surpluses, the two schemes would come to much the same thing. Disequilibrium, now one way and now another, would be met by the move-

[7] Cmd. 6437, 6 (5) (See above, p. 328).
[8] *U. S. Proposal*, II, 2

ment to and fro of bancor credits in the books of the Clearing Union or by movements up and down of the holdings of various national currencies by the Stabilization Fund. Either scheme would work much as the gold standard worked in its heyday, or rather as it would work in such conditions if every country had an ample gold reserve and was never shy of losing gold.

But in such favorable conditions any scheme would work well. It is more interesting to inquire how the two schemes propose to meet situations of large-scale disequilibrium.

Consider first the position of a chronic creditor. Under the Bancor scheme no limit is set to the credit which a country can accumulate, though a mild discouragement is applied by the provision that a creditor, equally with debtors, must pay a charge of 1 per cent per annum on its average bancor balance in excess of one-quarter of its quota, and a further 1 per cent on the excess over one-half of its quota.[9] The limit to a creditor balance comes from the side of the debtors. Certain correctives (which will be discussed below) are brought into play when a debit balance exceeds one-quarter of a country's quota, and these become stringent when a debit exceeds three-quarters of a country's quota.[10] Thus in the extreme case, where there is only one surplus country, and all the rest are drawing continuously on the Clearing Union, the credit balance of the surplus country may rise to one-quarter of the sum of the quotas of all the other members, without check, and might ultimately mount up to three-quarters of the sum of these quotas.

The average of world trade (imports *plus* exports of merchandise) for the three pre-war years was $48,000 million.[11] Thus, if all the world joined the Clearing Union, the sum of quotas would be $36,000 million (if only United and Associated Nations, and their dependencies, are included the total is reduced by about $10,000 million). If all countries except one are imagined to be drawing on their quotas, it is natural to imagine that the exception is the United States. The U. S. A. quota would be $3,000 million. Thus the upper limit which the debit account of the world might reach is three-quarters of $33,000 million, that

[9] Cmd. 6437, 6 (7).
[10] Cmd. 6437, 6 (8) (a) and (c).
[11] League of Nations, *Survey of World Trade*, 1938. The figures given there in "old dollars" have been converted at the rate of 3/5.

is, about $24,000 million, though correctives would come into play before $8,000 million had been reached.

Some American critics have viewed this prospect with distaste. But, as Lord Keynes has pointed out, "there is no foundation whatever for the idea that the object of the proposals is to make the United States the milch cow of the world." [12] The scheme would not impose any compulsion upon the United States, or on any other country, and would, on the contrary, increase her freedom of action. Without the scheme, there are three alternatives before the U. S. A. First, she can raise her rate of imports to the level of her exports. This can be done in two ways; she can improve the competitive position of foreign producers by lowering her tariffs, by allowing her wage rates to rise relatively to the world level, or by appreciating her exchange, or she can bring about such an increase in employment and expenditure that the surplus is wiped out by an increase in her consumption of imported goods along with home produce. (It is worthy of note that even the moderate boom of 1935–37 gave the U. S. A. a deficit balance on income account.) The second alternative open to the United States is to lend on long-term to countries needing development at a rate equivalent to her surplus of exports. (If she chose this alternative, her surplus would doubtless grow, for the borrowers would be avid importers of American commodities. But however large the surplus of exports, there is no problem from the point of view of the exchanges so long as long-term lending keeps pace with it.) The third alternative is to accept payment for the surplus in gold, which involves pressing the rest of the world ever deeper into deflation and slump, or driving it to adopt protectionist devices, until the surplus is wiped out by means of a reduction in the demand for American exports to the level of her imports.

The Bancor scheme in no way obstructs the first two alternatives. It merely changes the character of the third, by allowing the United States to amass a bancor credit, and so to continue to run an uncovered export surplus until the debtor countries have reached the limit of their overdraft facilities. Meanwhile, when the U. S. credit balance exceeds half her quota—a point which would be reached long before the rest of the world had exhausted its borrowing rights, since the U. S. quota would not be large

[12] House of Lords, May 18, 1943 (See below, p. 365).

relatively to the sum of the quotas of the rest of the Union—the
Board of the Clearing Union would offer advice, but no more than
advice, as to what measures could be taken to restore equilibrium
by reducing the export surplus or increasing long-term lending.[13]

Thus the Bancor scheme greatly increases the possibility of
running an uncovered surplus, but by no means encourages, still
less compels, any country to do so.

The Unitas scheme is much less favorable to a creditor country. The extent of an uncovered surplus is limited by the initial
payment into the fund. The sum of quotas is given as $5,000
million [14] and it is evidently contemplated that the U. S. quota
may exceed one-quarter of this, as the maximum voting right of
any one country is limited to a quarter of the total, irrespective
of its quota.[15] One estimate puts the U. S. quota at $1,270 million.[16]
On this basis the initial subscription of U. S. A. would be $635
million. In 1938, U. S. A. had a surplus on income account of
$790 million. (Gold imports were nearly double this amount, as
it was a year of net borrowing—presumably the result of a flight
of funds from Europe.) At this rate, the dollar holdings of the
Fund would disappear in nine months. When the Fund's holdings
of a currency begin to run out, it will "inform the member countries of the probable supply of this currency and of a proposed
method for its equitable distribution, together with suggestions
for helping to equate the demand and supply for the currency.
. . . The Fund shall apportion its sales of such scarce currency.
In such apportionment, it shall be guided by the principle of
satisfying the most urgent needs from the point of view of the
general economic situation. It shall also consider the special needs
and resources of the particular countries making the request for
the scarce currency." [17] Thus, if dollars become scarce, they would
be rationed. The world would then be forced to discriminate
against American goods, for any country whose ration of dollars
was cut would be obliged to reduce its imports from the United
States correspondingly. The third alternative discussed above
would then be adopted in a modified form—equilibrium would
be restored by a decline in American exports, but the con-

[13] Cmd. 6437, 6 (9) (See above, p. 329).
[14] *U. S. Proposal*, II, 2.
[15] *Ibid.*, V, 1.
[16] *Financial News*, April 27, 1943.
[17] *U. S. Proposal*, III, 6.

traction of world demand would be concentrated on American goods, and the countries concerned would continue to consume their own and each other's products without restriction. Thus from the point of view of the deficit countries the adjustment, though troublesome, would be far less deleterious than the gold standard method of drastic deflation, while from the point of view of the creditor it would be much more severe, for the reduction in its exports, and the consequent depression, would come about immediately instead of following upon depression in the rest of the world.

Perhaps this is a misinterpretation of the Unitas scheme. Unlike the British statement, which makes the intentions of each of its proposals clear, the American document contains merely a set of rules, without explanations, and has to be read in the spirit of a detective story. The above interpretation is certainly the natural one to place upon the passage quoted, but it conflicts with other passages, which emphasize the duty to abandon exchange restrictions and discriminatory trade agreements. In particular, one of the purposes of the fund is stated to be: "To reduce the use of foreign exchange controls that interfere with world trade and the international flow of productive capital." [18] This is hard to reconcile with the proposal to ration the currency of one country, thereby imposing exchange control and discrimination upon all the others.

Perhaps the provision for rationing exchange should be taken rather as the ultimate sanction against a surplus country and the main emphasis laid upon other elements in the scheme. Unlike the Clearing Union, the Stabilization Fund has power to borrow in any member country, with the consent of its Government.[19] Under this rule, a scarce currency could be borrowed and sold without limit to all deficit countries which have not exhausted their rights to buy from the Fund. Thus, provided the Government concerned does not withhold its consent, Unitas could arrive at the same result as Bancor, loans to the Fund playing the part of a bancor credit. A loan to the Unitas Fund, however, would be a far less eligible asset than bancor. If, at any time, a creditor country wants to use its bancor balance to buy commodities or securities, it can buy from any member country it chooses; but if a lender to Unitas wants its loan to run off, it can be repaid

[18] *Ibid.*, 1, 5.
[19] *Ibid.*, III, 11 and 16 (c).

only in currencies of which the Fund happens to have a supply. It could buy only to a limited extent from a country which had been continuously in balance, and not at all from a country which had itself been consistently running a surplus. From the point of view of deficit countries, this is all to the good, as it would deflect the demand of the lending country towards their products and so help them to reduce their deficits; but, from the point of view of the lender, it means that a loan to Unitas has a much more limited purchasing power than a balance with Bancor. Thus in this respect also the Unitas plan offers less convenience to a potential creditor country than the Bancor plan.

The proposals for correcting a creditor position are similar under both schemes. The Unitas Fund has the "authority and the duty to render to the country a report embodying an analysis of the causes of the depletion of its holdings of that currency, a forecast of the prospective balance of payments in the absence of special measures, and finally, recommendations designed to increase the Fund's holdings of that currency." [20] No suggestions are made as to what type of recommendations would be offered by the Fund to the surplus country. The British White Paper is more explicit. Under Bancor, recommendations would include:

(a) Measures for the expansion of domestic credit and domestic demand.

(b) The appreciation of its local currency in terms of bancor, or, alternatively, the encouragement of an increase in money rates of earnings.

(c) The reduction of tariffs and other discouragements against imports.

(d) International development loans.[21]

All these would also be open to the Unitas Fund, and none is binding upon the Bancor Union. In this respect, therefore, the two schemes amount to the same thing.

Each, of course, is merely a scheme to regulate the exchanges, and, in the nature of the case, a currency scheme cannot solve the fundamental problems of international disequilibrium. At best it can do no more than create a setting favorable to a solution. In particular, the problem which lies before the United States is what to do with her prodigious productive capacity—

[20] *Ibid.*, III, 6.
[21] Cmd. 6437, 6 (9) (See above, p. 329).

whether to use it for home consumption, to use it for the development of other countries or to waste it in unemployment. No amount of ingenuity in devising currency schemes can influence the main issue, which cuts deeply into the internal economic position of creditor countries. English economists often point somewhat smugly to the history of the nineteenth century, and claim that when Great Britain was the leading surplus country she always played the game according to the rules and lent her surplus lavishly to the development of backward or unpeopled continents. This may be true. But it was not superior benevolence and wisdom or superior insight into economic principles, which guided her policy; it was rather the facts of geography. With population growing and industry expanding in a narrow space, Great Britain needed the development of sources of raw materials, and, even when individual rentiers lost their money, her foreign investments were an excellent speculation for the nation as a whole. For the United States, with her wide range of primary production at home, there is no unified national interest to be served, and no solution of her problem which will not cause internal conflicts. To judge by recent experience, purchasing power inside the U. S. A. cannot be maintained at a level commensurate with productive capacity except by huge Government expenditure, which raises political opposition, while lending abroad is objected to as mere charity.

Perhaps the best service which the currency plans can render is in the sphere of education. A long step forward will have been taken when the world has learned that no country can have flourishing export industries without in one way or another providing other countries with the means to buy its products. Lord Keynes attaches importance to the educative effect of Bancor: the plan "will not prevent excessive hoarding from doing harm in the long run, since this may cause other countries to suffer the anxiety of a growing debit account which would eventually reach its permitted maximum. But a country which tends to hoard bancor beyond all reason will at any rate be exhibited before the whole world as the make-mischief of the piece; and will be under every motive of reason and of benevolence and of self-interest to take corrective measures. Nor, I fancy, will the hoarding of bancor prove as attractive or as plausible as the burying of gold seems to have been, if recent experience is a guide." [22] From this

[22] House of Lords, May 18, 1943 (See below, p. 363).

point of view, the intricacies of Unitas would not bear so clear a moral. A persistent surplus would show itself, at first, by the disappearance of the currency concerned from the Fund. Then loans would be raised by the Fund. The Fund's holding of the currency would again run down, and a fresh loan would have to be raised. There would be no single sum in the books of the Fund, corresponding to a bancor balance, which would show the surplus country at any moment just how far it had gone. On the other hand, the threat to ration the currency of a persistent surplus country, and isolate it from selling in the world market, so as to prevent infection from spreading, would teach the lesson more sharply than the milder persuasion of Bancor.

We must now consider the position of deficit countries under the two plans. Under Bancor, the general principle is that any country may run an overdraft up to a quarter of its quota without any deterrent. An average overdraft between a quarter and a half of its quota must be paid for at 1 per cent per annum, and the excess over half its quota at 2 per cent. When a debit balance reaches half the country's quota, it may be asked to deposit collateral, in the form of gold or foreign or domestic currency or government bonds. To obtain permission to increase its debit above half its quota, it may be required to surrender outright a proportion of any separate gold or other liquid reserves which it possesses. Its balance may never exceed its quota, and if its balance exceeds three-quarters of its quota on the average of a year it may be declared in default and be denied further facilities.[23] These provisions are deterrent and would prevent unconscionable advantage being taken of a plan intended to ease genuine difficulties. Corrective measures designed to restore equilibrium are also provided. A country whose debit balance exceeds a quarter of its quota is permitted to depreciate its exchange on its own initiative by not more than 5 per cent, but this is once and for all, and cannot be repeated without permission from the Union. As a condition of allowing a debit balance of more than half its quota, the Union may require a depreciation to any extent it thinks fit, and, furthermore, may recommend to the government of the country any internal measures which appear appropriate to restore equilibrium.[24] The creation of slump

[23] Cmd. 6437, 6 (8).
[24] *Ibid.*, (See above, p. 328).

conditions by credit restriction would presumably not be amongst the measures recommended.

Under Unitas the rights of deficit countries are much less clear-cut, for they depend on the amount of currency subscribed to the Fund by surplus countries.[25] The upper limit is set by the provision that the Fund's holdings of the currency of any country may not exceed its quota during the first year, 150 per cent of its quota during the first two years, and 200 per cent thereafter.[26] It is not stated whether the country's original subscription to the Fund is included in this total. If so, the country may buy from the Fund at the rate of 50 per cent of its quota for each of three years (or perhaps only that part of the subscription which is in currency should be deducted; in that case the country may use 87.5 per cent of its quota in the first year).[27] But unless the world happens to be divided equally between surplus and deficit countries, or the Fund borrows from surplus countries when it is asymmetrically divided, these limits will be ineffective, since the supply of currencies to be bought will run out before rights to buy have been exhausted. A charge in gold of 1 per cent per annum is levied on the excess holding of currency over a country's quota.[28] (No similar charge is made on a surplus country. In this respect Unitas is less severe than Bancor upon surplus countries.) When a country is exhausting its rights to buy (assuming that currencies are available for it to buy) more rapidly than the Fund approves, conditions may be placed upon further sales to it.[29] There is no specific suggestion that these conditions might include depreciation, but, in other passages, alterations of exchange rates with the approval of the Fund are contemplated.[30]

Both plans encourage the control of capital movements by national governments[31] (though it is not clear how this is compatible with the Unitas prohibition of exchange control).[32] Under Bancor, a deficit country may be required by the Union to introduce control, if it has not already done so, as a condition of in-

[25] *U. S. Proposal*, III, 4.
[26] *Ibid.*, III, 3 (b).
[27] *Ibid.*, II, 4.
[28] *Ibid.*, III, 3 (e).
[29] *Ibid.*, III, 3 (b).
[30] *Ibid.*, IV, 4 and VI, 1.
[31] Cmd. 6437, 32–36 (See above, p. 335), and *U. S. Proposal*, VI, 3.
[32] *Ibid.*, VI, 2.

ı

creasing its debit balance beyond half its quota.[33] Such control would prevent the perverse movements of lending by deficit to surplus countries which bedevilled the exchanges between the wars.

Both schemes are an improvement, from the point of view of deficit countries, not only on the gold standard, but also on a regime of free exchanges. The gold standard imposes severe deflationary pressure on a deficit country and forces it to redress its balance in the most disagreeable and watchful manner. Each scheme provides alternative and less painful methods of redress. A system of free exchanges may make redress impossible. It is true that, under such a system, a deficit country can depreciate as much as it chooses on its own initiative. But all other countries are free to retaliate, and in the game of competitive depreciation there is no guarantee that the country which most needs to depreciate will in fact succeed in getting its exchange rate lowest. What is required is a system in which deficit countries can depreciate to establish equilibrium, while surplus countries are prevented from indulging in "exchange dumping" merely to increase their surpluses. A scheme of international control of exchange rates, provided that it is genuinely international and is not manipulated in favor of particular interests, promises great advantages to deficit countries, which would be well worth the sacrifice of national autonomy which it involves.

Let us now consider the use that is made of gold in the two schemes. Under Bancor, gold will be accepted by the Clearing Union at a fixed price in bancor.[34] The bancor can be used to settle accounts with any member of the Union. Thus gold-producing countries, or repentant hoarders, can make use of gold to buy what they please, or, if they do not wish to buy, to acquire an asset as good as gold. When the Union finds that it has gold on its hands, it can require surplus countries to accept it in reduction of their bancor balances.[35] Thus, in the first instance, the customary flow of gold from the bowels of the earth to the vaults of the Central Banks would be maintained. Gold mining is the archetype of "digging holes in the ground," and, as such, provides a certain corrective to world slump conditions. It has also pro-

[33] Cmd. 6437, 6, (8) (b) (ii) (See above, p. 328).
[34] *Ibid.*, 6, (10) (See above, p. 329).
[35] *Ibid.*

vided U. S. S. R. with a means of buying useful materials and equipment from the foolish capitalist world without sacrificing wheat or timber which she can consume at home. There is therefore a strong case (apart from all mysticism) for keeping gold mining alive. The Clearing Union, however, would be able to lower the price of gold in bancor, and this power could be used gradually to kill off the gold-mining industry as more useful forms of activity become available to mankind.[36]

So long as the bancor price of gold remains unchanged, each national currency has a fixed gold equivalent, and members of the Union undertake not to buy gold at any higher prices.[37] Beyond this, dealings in gold are in no way restricted. It would even be possible for a country to maintain an old-fashioned gold currency for internal circulation, if it had a mind to do so.[38] (In that case, it would have to control the export of gold; otherwise any member of the Union could buy up its gold and oblige it to accept a bancor credit in its place.) This might be a convenience for countries where Credit institutions are undeveloped or where the gold myth is still powerful.

The part played by gold in the Unitas scheme is more complicated. In the first instance, each country subscribes to the Fund a proportion of its quota in gold, the subscription being adjusted to the size of its gold holding.[39] No provision seems to be made for a country which has no gold at all, a case which will be common enough in Europe, for presumably the Nazis will have got rid of the gold which they have seized from their victims. However that may be, it seems that the gold subscribed to the Fund can be used only to buy its own currency, when this becomes scarce.[40] It is therefore merely in the nature of a token, and has no significance.

The Fund has power to buy gold,[41] but it is not obliged to buy, nor is any member country. Under this scheme, therefore, the gold-mining industry would have to depend, as heretofore, upon the willingness of national Treasuries and Central Banks to take its produce. There is one provision, however, which modifies this

[36] *Ibid.*, 31.
[37] *Ibid.*, 6 (4).
[38] *Ibid.*, 6 (30).
[39] *U. S. Proposal*, II, 4.
[40] *Ibid.*, III, 6.
[41] *Ibid.*, III, 1.

conclusion. The Fund may accept deposits in gold, and against these it will hold a 100 per cent reserve in gold.[42] Presumably this would be done by earmarking the gold wherever it happened to be, as there is no advantage in the Fund's incurring the expense of a new set of vaults. Deposits will be redeemable in gold or in any national currency. In so far as they are redeemed in gold there is no point in making them, but they would provide an owner of gold with a means of acquiring a national currency which was not directly convertible with gold, so long as the Fund was in possession of that currency. However, the currencies available to be acquired in this way would only be those of deficit countries, so that, although Unitas pays a good deal more respect to the gold myth than Bancor, it does not seem to provide the owners of gold (whether above or below ground) with equal facilities.

If it were necessary, in the interests of equilibrium, to depreciate several deficit currencies, the world price of gold would be raised, and a stimulus would be given to gold mining (as occurred on a large scale with the depreciations of the thirties). Conversely, if a surplus country consents to appreciate, gold mining is depressed. Under the Bancor scheme it would be a simple matter to counteract these effects. If it is appropriate to make some depreciations while there is no reason to desire a greater rate of gold mining, the bancor price of gold can be lowered to a sufficient extent to counterbalance the rise in value of bancor in terms of some national currencies. Similarly its price could be raised when some currencies appreciate. Under Unitas, each currency has a price fixed directly in terms of gold, and "Unitas" is a gold unit. It would therefore be impossible to keep the price of gold constant, when one currency is altered, without altering all the other currencies in the opposite sense. The same results could no doubt be attained as under Bancor, but the process would be much more complicated.

The initial choice of exchange rates will raise a formidable problem when the war is over. The Unitas plan seems to envisage fixing the rates at a single stroke, but the Bancor scheme allows for a period of experiment.[43]

A special problem will be presented at the end of the war by the balances which have arisen from payments from one United

[42] *U. S. Proposal*, IV, 3.
[43] Cmd. 6437, 6 (3) (See above, p. 327).

Nation to another for war supplies. Some of these balances are at present wholly or partially blocked, and it is out of the question that they should be freed all at once at the end of the war. The Unitas scheme provides for their liquidation.[44] Let us take, for example, sterling balances in London owned by the Government of India. The proposal is that the Fund should be free to buy a part of these balances from India, and pay for them in currencies of other countries to the extent that India needs them immediately to meet an adverse balance of payments on income account. The rest is paid in rupees out of India's initial subscription to the Fund. This automatically increases India's right to buy other currencies to the corresponding extent. If India is running a surplus on income account, the scheme does not apply. Perhaps this may be taken to imply the suggestion that a surplus country has no need or right to withdraw abnormal war balances. Repayment by Great Britain to the Fund may be postponed for three years, to allow a breathing-space. After three years, Great Britain must repurchase the sterling balances from the Fund, for gold or free currencies, at the rate of 2 per cent per annum for 20 years. India also repurchases the balances at the same rate, and the sterling thus purchased must be freed in London. From the point of view of India, this merely means exchanging one free currency for another. From the point of view of Great Britain, it means finding gold or free currency to the corresponding extent. Thus, in effect, Great Britain is required to pay off 80 per cent of the balances in free currency over 20 years. The disposal of the 20 per cent which will remain after 23 years will be the subject of consultation between Great Britain and the Fund. Great Britain and India must each pay to the Fund gold to the value of 1 per cent of the balances in the first instance, and an annual charge of 1 per cent on the outstanding balances thereafter. This charge may be regarded, from the point of view of Great Britain, as interest on debt; from the point of view of India, as payment for the convenience of having the debt redeemed in advance.

The British White Paper, naturally enough, makes no detailed proposals for the repayment of war balances, but merely suggests that the Clearing Union might make some special arrangement for converting war balances into bancor without putting an undue strain upon the debtor countries.[45]

[44] *U. S. Proposal*, III, 9.
[45] Cmd. 6437, 34 (See above, p. 336).

Either scheme is filling in only one corner of the general picture of reconstruction, and each is intended to operate alongside other institutions—in particular an investment board to foster and control long-term international lending. To quote the British White Paper: "The Clearing Union might become the instrument and support of international policies in addition to those which it is its primary purpose to promote. This deserves the greatest possible emphasis. The Union might become the pivot of the future economic government of the world. Without it, other more desirable developments will find themselves impeded and unsupported. With it, they will fall into their place as parts of an ordered scheme."[46] When all is said, the importance of a currency system lies in the kind of setting that it provides for the real economic forces which must work within it. After the experience of modern times, no one doubts that a new setting is required.

Ricardo's currency proposals were adopted in this country in 1925. Perhaps, now that history moves at such a pace, the time-lag will not be so long before some of these ideas find an expression in practice.

[46] *Ibid.*, 39 (See above, p. 338).

CHAPTER XXVI

The International Clearing Union[1]

By LORD KEYNES

My LORDS, I do not address you for the first time with any less
trepidation because the subject of our discussion this afternoon
is one with which I have become very familiar in recent months.
But I rely on your Lordships' sustaining kindness to a newcomer.
The proposals for an International Clearing Union have been
brought before Parliament at an early but not too early a stage of
their evolution. The procedure adopted is somewhat novel. I
hope your Lordships will approve it, for, if it is an innovation, it
appears to me to be a happy one. This paper has been the subject
of long preparation. To associate it too closely with particular
names is, I venture to say, to do it an injustice. It has been the
subject of intensive criticism and progressive amendment, and
the final result is the embodiment of the collective wisdom of
Whitehall and of experts and officials throughout the Commonwealth. At the same time, it has been brought to the judgment of
Parliament and of the public opinion of the world before any
final crystallization of ideas.

It seems to me to be far better that our own Treasury and the
Treasury of the United States should have decided to seek wider
counsels before concentrating on the preparation of an actual plan
—much better that they should take this course than that, without open consultation with their Legislatures or with the other
United Nations, they should have attempted to reach finality.
The economic structure of the post-war world cannot be built
in secret. Mrs. Sidney Webb, whose recent loss we so greatly
deplore, in my judgment the most remarkable woman of our
time and generation, once defined democracy to me as a form

[1] [Speech delivered before the House of Lords, London, May 18, 1943.]

of government the hall-mark of which was that it aimed to secure "the consciousness of consent." So in the new democracy of nations which after this war will come into existence, heaven helping, to conduct with amity and good sense the common concerns of mankind, the instrumentalities we set up must first win for themselves a general consciousness of consent.

The first of these instrumentalities to be considered is before your Lordships' House this afternoon—at a season in our affairs on this day of national thanksgiving when we can feel entitled, and indeed are required, to look forward to what is to come after. It is, I hope, the first of several. Indeed, it cannot stand by itself. For it attempts to deal with one aspect only of the economic problem. Your Lordships will, I take it, this afternoon be concerned chiefly with the broad purpose and method of these proposals and not with technical details. The principal object can be explained in a single sentence: to provide that money earned by selling goods to one country can be spent on purchasing the products of any other country. In jargon, a system of multilateral clearing. In English, a universal currency valid for trade transactions in all the world. Everything else in the plan is ancillary to that. Serious tariff obstacles, though we may try to abate them, are likely to persist. But we may hope to get rid of the varied and complicated devices for blocking currencies and diverting or restricting trade which before the war were forced on many countries as a superimposed obstacle to commerce and prosperity.

Now this universal currency is essential to the healthy trade of any country, and not least to our own, for it is characteristic of our trade that the best markets for our goods are often different from our best sources of supply. We cannot hope to balance our trading account if the surpluses we earn in one country cannot be applied to meet our requirements in another country. We shall have a hard enough task to develop a sufficient volume of exports, but we shall have no hope of success if we cannot freely apply what we do earn from our exports, wherever we may be selling them, to pay for whatever we buy, wherever we may buy it. This plan provides for that facility without qualification. That is the main purpose. If, however, general facilities on these lines are to survive successfully for any length of time, it will be a necessary condition that there should be a supply of the new money proportioned to the scale of the international trade which it has to carry; and, also, that every country in the world should stand possessed of a reasonable share of that currency proportioned to its needs. The British plan proposes a formula intended to give effect to both those objects. There may be a better one, and we should keep an open mind, but the aim is clear.

It is not necessary in order to attain these ends that we should dispossess gold from its traditional use. It is enough to supplement and regulate the total supply of gold and of the new money taken together. The new money must not be freely convertible into gold, for that would require that gold reserves should be held against it, and we should be back where we were, but there is no reason why the new money should not be purchasable for gold. By such means we can avoid the many obvious difficulties and disadvantages of proposing that the old money, gold, should be demonetized. The plan proposes, therefore, what is conveniently described as a one-way convertibility. What shall we call the new money? Bancor? Unitas? Both of them in my opinion are rotten, bad names, but we racked our brains without success to find a better. A lover of compromise would suggest Unitor, I suppose. Some of your Lordships are masters of language. I hope some noble Lord will have a better inspiration. What would your Lordships say to dolphin? A dolphin swims, like trade, from shore to shore. But the handsome beast also, I am afraid, goes up and down, fluctuates, and that is not at all what we require. Or bezant? The name, as the Financial Secretary to the Treasury recently recalled in another place, of the last international coin we had—the gold unit of Byzantium. In the same line of thought, Professor Brogan has recently suggested talent, named after a place which perhaps we shall soon be in a position to regard as at our service. So far every bright idea in turn has been turned down. I fancy that our Prime Minister and President Roosevelt could between them do better than most of us at this game, as in most other games, if they had the time to turn their minds to writing a new dictionary as well as a new geography.

The plan, as I have said, allots to every country an initial reserve. That is a once-for-all endowment. There is, therefore, a risk that the arrangements will break down because some improvident country runs through its stock of bancor and gold and has none left to meet its engagements. To provide against that is a very delicate matter, for it may seem to involve interference with a country's domestic policy. The plan provides in such case for consultation and advice. The country may be required to take certain specific measures. There remains in the background, if eventually unavoidable, the severe penalty of depriving the improvident country of any further facilities, which, after all, is the only effective remedy the private banker has, unless his client is actually fraudulent. It is most important to understand that the initial reserve provided by the Clearing Union is not intended as a means by which a country can regularly live beyond its income and which it can use up to import capital goods for which it cannot otherwise pay. Nor will it be advisable to exhaust this provision in meeting the relief and rehabilitation of countries devastated by war, thus diverting it from its real permanent purpose. These requirements must be met by special remedies and other instrumentalities.

The margin of resources provided by the Clearing Union must be substantial, not so much for actual use as to relieve anxiety and the deflationary pressure which results from anxiety. This margin, though substantial, must be regarded solely as a reserve with which to meet temporary emergencies and to allow a breathing space. But the world's trading difficulties in the past have not always been due to the improvidence of debtor countries. They may be caused in a most acute form if a creditor country is constantly withdrawing international money from circulation and hoarding it, instead of putting it back again into circulation, thus refusing to spend its income from abroad either on goods for home consumption or on investment overseas. We have lately come to understand more clearly than before how employment and the creation of new incomes out of new production can only be maintained through the expenditure on goods and services of the income previously earned. This is equally true of home trade and of foreign trade. A foreign country equally can be the ultimate cause of unemployment by hoarding beyond the reasonable requirements of precaution. Our plan, therefore, must address itself to this problem also—and it is an even more delicate task since a creditor country is likely to be even more unwilling than a debtor country to suffer gladly outside interference or advice. In attempting to tackle this problem, the British plan breaks new ground. Perhaps its approach may be open to criticism for being too tentative and mild; but this, I am afraid, may be inevitable until these things are better understood.

But at this point I draw your Lordships' attention to a striking feature of the proposals. Under the former gold standard, gold absorbed by a creditor country was wholly withdrawn from circulation. The present proposals avoid this by profiting from the experience of domestic banking. If an individual hoards his income, not in the shape of gold coins in his pockets or in his safe, but by keeping a bank deposit, this bank deposit is not withdrawn from circulation but provides his banker with the means of making loans to those who need them. Thus every act of hoarding, if it takes this form, itself provides the offsetting facilities for some other party, so that production and trade can continue. This technique will not prevent excessive hoarding from doing harm in the long run, since this may cause other countries to suffer the anxiety of a growing debit account which would eventually reach its permitted maximum. But a country which tends to hoard bancor beyond all reason will at any rate be exhibited before itself and before the whole world as the make-mischief of the piece; and will be under every motive of reason and of benevolence and of self-interest to take corrective measures. Nor, I fancy, will the hoarding of bancor prove as attractive or as plausible as the burying of gold seems to have been, if recent experience is a guide.

I turn now to an aspect of these proposals which has rightly caused considerable anxiety to well-judging critics. We set up a universal money; we make sure that its quantity shall be adequate; we share it out between the countries of the world in equitable amounts; we take what precaution we can against improvidence on the one hand and hoarding on the other. It is obvious that in this way we establish an immensely strong influence to expand the trade and wealth of the world, and to remove certain disastrous causes of inhibition and distress. But an obvious question arises. Are we doing this at the cost of returning, in effect, to the rigidity of the old gold standard, which fixed the external value of our national currency beyond our own control, perhaps at a figure which was out of proper relation to our wage policy and to our social policies generally?

The exchange value of sterling cannot remain constant, in terms of other currencies, unless our efficiency-wages, and those other costs of production which depend on our social policy, are keeping strictly in step with the corresponding costs in other countries.

And, obviously, to that we cannot pledge ourselves. I hope your Lordships will believe me when I say that there are few people less likely than I not to be on the lookout against this danger. The British proposals nowhere envisage exchange rigidity. They provide that changes of more than a certain amount must not be made unless the actual state of trade demonstrates that they are required, and they provide further that changes, when made, must be made by agreement. Exchange rates necessarily affect two parties equally. Changes, therefore, should not be made by unilateral action. We do indeed commit ourselves to the assumption that the Governing Board of the Union will act reasonably in the general interest, and will adopt those courses which best preserve and restore the equilibrium of each country with the rest of the world. That is the least we can do, if any form of agreed international order is to be given a chance. But if, in the event, our trust should prove to be misplaced and our hopes mistaken, we can, nevertheless, escape from all obligations and recover our full freedom with a year's notice. I do not think that we can reasonably ask any completer safeguards than that.

There is another question which can very reasonably be asked: Are we winning one freedom at the cost of another? Shall we have to submit to exchange controls on individual transactions which would be unnecessary otherwise? In this respect the plan leaves each country to act as it thinks best in its own interests, and imposes nothing. Or, rather, the only condition which is imposed is that there shall be absolute freedom of exchange remittance for current trade transactions. In the control of capital movements, which is quite another matter, each country is left to be its own judge whether it deems this necessary. In our own case, I do not see how we can hope to avoid it. It is not merely a question of curbing exchange speculations and movements of hot money, or even of avoiding flights of capital due to political motives; though all these it is necessary to control. The need, in my judgment, is more fundamental. Unless the aggregate of the new investments which individuals are free to make overseas is kept within the amount which our favorable trade balance is capable of looking after, we lose control over the domestic rate of interest.

The Chancellor of the Exchequer has made it very clear that the maintenance of a low rate of interest for gilt-edged loans is to be a vital part of our policy after the war as it has been during the war. For example, it is only if the rate of interest is kept down that the new housing we intend can be financed without excessive subsidy. But we cannot hope to control rates of interest at home, if movements of capital moneys out of the country are unrestricted. If another country takes a different view of the necessities of the situation, it is free to do otherwise. The plan leaves each country to be the judge of its own needs. Those who are experienced in these matters advise that adequate control of capital movements should be possible without a postal censorship. I mention this to believe a natural anxiety. Few of your Lordships, I expect, would stand for so gross an infringement on personal rights as a postal censorship in times of peace.

There is one important respect in which the British proposals seem to be gravely misunderstood in some quarters in the United States. There is no foundation whatever for the idea that the object of the proposals is to make the United States the milch cow of the world in general and of this country in particular. In fact, the best hope for the lasting success of the plan is the precise contrary. The plan does not require the United States, or any other country, to put up a single dollar which they themselves choose or prefer to employ in any other way whatever. The essence of it is that if a country has a balance in its favor which it does not choose to use in buying goods or services or making overseas investments, this balance shall remain available to the Union—not permanently, but only for just so long as the country owning it chooses to leave it unemployed. That is not a burden on the creditor country. It is an extra facility to it, for it allows it to carry on its trade with the rest of the world unimpeded, whenever a time lag between earning and spending happens to suit its own convenience.

I cannot emphasize this too strongly. This is not a Red Cross philanthropic relief scheme, by which the rich countries come to the rescue of the poor. It is a piece of highly necessary business mechanism, which is at least as useful to the creditor as to the debtor. A man does not refuse to keep a banking account because his deposits will be employed by the banker to make advances to another person, provided always that he knows that his deposit is liquid, and that he can spend it himself whenever he wants to do so. Nor does he regard himself as a dispenser of charity whenever, to suit his own convenience, he refrains from drawing on his own bank balance. The United States of America, in my humble judgment, will have no excessive balance with the Clearing Union unless she has failed to solve her own problems by other means, and in this event the facilities of the Clearing Union will give her time to find other means, and meanwhile to carry on her export trade unhindered.

There are really only two contingencies, in my opinion, which might lead the United States to accumulate a large balance of bancor—failure to maintain good employment at home, or a collapse of the enterprise and initiative required to invest her surplus resources abroad. Recent past history shows that in times of good employment in the United States her need for imports is so large, and her surplus of available exports so much reduced compared with other times, that a surplus in her favor does not develop; it is only if she ceases to require imports and is pressing her exports on the world that that situation arises. Why should our American friends start off by assuming so disastrous a breakdown of the economy of the United States? Moreover, if there are temporary difficulties which take time to solve, no one will gain more than a creditor if this maladjustment is prevented from starting a general slump, which eventually reaches, by repercussion, the creditor himself. I repeat that no one is asked to put up a single shilling except for so long as he has no other use for it. There is a significant difference, I suggest, between a liquid bank deposit which can be withdrawn at any time and a subscription to an institution's permanent capital.

The Motion relates to the proposals of the United States Treasury as well as to the British White Paper. Your Lordships will not expect me, nor would it be in place, to examine or criticize these proposals at any length, but there are a few remarks which I should like to make. The whole world owes to Mr. Morgenthau and his chief assistant, Dr. Harry White, a deep debt of gratitude for the initiative which they have taken. Public opinion on the other side of the Atlantic is not, I fancy, as well prepared as it is here for bold proposals of this kind, but that has not prevented the United States Treasury from putting forward proposals of great novelty and far-reaching importance. Most critics, in my judgment, have overstated the differences between the two plans, plans which are born of the same climate of opinion and which have identical purposes. It may be said with justice that the United States Treasury has tried to pour its new wine into what looks like an old bottle, whereas our bottle and its label are as contemporary as the contents; but the new wine is there all the same.

Some play, I notice, has been made with the idea that the voting power in the British proposal has been arranged in our own interest. Nothing, I can assure your Lordships, was further from our thoughts. The Chancellor of the Exchequer explained last week in the House of Commons that there is no reason to expect that the American formula, when it has been fully explained, will be unacceptable to us. Certainly to arrive at voting predominance by the use of a particular formula was neither an intention nor an essential part of our proposals. Again, the requirement in the American plan for a four-fifths majority will be found, if the paper is read carefully, to relate not to all matters by any means, but only to a few major issues. Whether on second thought any one would wish to allow a negative veto to any small group remains to be seen. For example, the American proposals might allow the gold-producing countries to prevent the United States from increasing the gold value of the dollar, even in circumstances where the deluge of gold was obviously becoming excessive; and in some ways, by reason of their greater rigidity, the American proposals would involve a somewhat greater surrender of national sovereignty than do our own.

The American plan requires the member States to provide so-called security against their overdrafts, a requirement which could certainly be met if it is thought useful; but the security in question only to a very small extent consists in an outside security in the shape of gold. It consists mainly of an I.O.U. engraved on superior notepaper, better than would be the case, perhaps, under our own scheme. I have said that, if that is thought useful and worth while, it does not involve any particular problem. The American scheme, again, sets a maximum to the liability of a creditor member to hold a credit balance, and there again that is a provision which is equally possible, if it is helpful, on either plan. But what happens when a creditor reaches his maximum is, in the American paper, somewhat obscure. I have not the slightest doubt in my mind that a synthesis of the two schemes should be possible; but it does not seem advisable to attempt it until there has been time and opportunity to discover what the expert opinion of other nations and of all the world finds difficult or unacceptable in either scheme, and what it finds sensible and good.

In the light of that opinion, the synthesis in due course should and must be attempted. I trust that your Lordships will wish the two Treasuries God-speed in their high enterprise. So ill did we fare in the years between the two wars for lack of such an instrument of international government as this that the resulting waste and dissipation of wealth was scarcely less than the economic cost of the wars themselves; whilst the frustration of men's efforts and the distortion of their life pattern have played no small part in preparing the soiled atmosphere in which the Nazis could thrive.

These papers do not present a whole story, but only the first chapter. They do, however, make a start in framing a structure without which other measures cannot be well designed or fitted in. I would also suggest, to those of your Lordships—and there are many—who have for years taken a particular interest in the evolution of international forms of government, that we here offer an essay of some importance in the new modes of international government in economic affairs, by means of which the future may be better ordered than the past. Neither plan conceals a selfish motive. The Treasuries of our two great nations have come before the world in these two papers with a common purpose and with high hopes of a common plan. Here is a field where some sound thinking may do something useful to ease the material burdens of the children of men.

CHAPTER XXVII

The International Monetary Fund[1]

By LORD KEYNES

My LORDS, it is almost exactly a year since the proposals for a Clearing Union were discussed in your Lordships' House. I hope to persuade your Lordships that the year has not been ill-spent. There were, it is true, certain features of elegance, clarity, and logic in the Clearing Union plan which have disappeared. And this, by me at least, is to be much regretted. As a result, however, there is no longer any need for a new-fangled international monetary unit. Your Lordships will remember how little any of us liked the names proposed—bancor, unitas, dolphin, bezant, daric, and heaven knows what. Some of your Lordships were good enough to join in the search for something better. I recall a story of a country parish in the last century where they were accustomed to give their children Biblical names—Amos, Ezekiel, Obadiah, and so forth. Needing a name for a dog, after a long and vain search of the Scriptures they called the dog "Moreover." We hit on no such happy solution, with the result that it has been the dog that died. The loss of the dog we need not too much regret, though I still think that it was a more thoroughbred animal than what has now come out from a mixed marriage of ideas. Yet, perhaps, as sometimes occurs, this dog of mixed origin is a sturdier and more serviceable animal and will prove not less loyal and faithful to the purposes for which it has been bred.

I commend the new plan to your Lordships as being, in some important respects (to which I will return later), a considerable improvement on either of its parents. I like this new plan and I believe that it will work to our advantage. Your Lordships will not wish me to enter into too much technical detail. I can best occupy the time available by examining the major benefits this

[1] [Speech delivered before the House of Lords, May 23, 1944.]

country may hope to gain from the plan; and whether there are adequate safeguards against possible disadvantages. We shall emerge from this war, having won a more solid victory over our enemies, a more enduring friendship from our Allies, and a deeper respect from the world at large, than perhaps at any time in our history. The victory, the friendship, and the respect will have been won, because, in spite of faint-hearted preparations, we have sacrificed every precaution for the future in the interests of immediate strength with a fanatical single-mindedness which has had few parallels. But the full price of this has still to be paid. I wish that this was more generally appreciated in the country than it is. In thus waging the war without counting the ultimate cost we—and we alone of the United Nations—have burdened ourselves with a weight of deferred indebtedness to other countries beneath which we shall stagger. We have already given to the common cause all, and more than all, that we can afford. It follows that we must examine any financial plan to make sure that it will help us to carry our burdens and not add to them. No one is more deeply convinced of this than I am. I make no complaint, therefore, that those to whom the details of the scheme are new and difficult, should scrutinize them with anxious concern.

What, then, are these major advantages that I hope from the plan to the advantage of this country? First, it is clearly recognized and agreed that, during the post-war transitional period of uncertain duration, we are entitled to retain any of those war-time restrictions, and special arrangements with the sterling area and others which are helpful to us, without being open to the charge of acting contrary to any general engagements into which we have entered. Having this assurance, we can make our plans for the most difficult days which will follow the war, knowing where we stand and without risk of giving grounds of offense. This is a great gain—and one of the respects in which the new plan is much superior to either of its predecessors, which did not clearly set forth any similar safeguards.

Second, when this period is over and we are again strong enough to live year by year on our own resources, we can look forward to trading in a world of national currencies which are inter-convertible. For a great commercial nation like ourselves, this is indispensable for full prosperity. Sterling itself, in due course, must obviously become, once again, generally convertible.

For, without this, London must necessarily lose its international position, and the arrangements in particular of the sterling area would fall to pieces. To suppose that a system of bilateral and barter agreements, with no one who owns sterling knowing just what he can do with it—to suppose that this is the best way of encouraging the Dominions to center their financial systems on London, seems to me pretty near frenzy. As a technique of little Englandism, adopted as a last resort when all else has failed us, with this small country driven to autarchy, keeping itself to itself in a harsh and unfriendly world, it might make more sense. But those who talk this way, in the expectation that the rest of the Commonwealth will throw in their lot on these lines and cut their free commercial relations with the rest of the world, can have very little idea how this Empire has grown or by what means it can be sustained.

So far from an international plan endangering the long tradition by which most Empire countries, and many other countries, too, have centred their financial systems in London, the plan is, in my judgment, an indispensable means of maintaining this tradition. With our own resources so greatly impaired and encumbered, it is only if sterling is firmly placed in an international setting that the necessary confidence in it can be sustained. Indeed, even during the transitional period, it will be our policy, I hope, steadily to develop the field within which sterling is freely available as rapidly as we can manage. Now if our own goal is, as it surely must be, the general inter-convertibility of sterling with other currencies, it must obviously be to our trading advantage that the same obtains elsewhere, so that we can sell our exports in one country and freely spend the proceeds in any other. It is a great gain to us in particular, that other countries in the world should agree to refrain from those discriminatory exchange practices which we ourselves have never adopted in times of peace but from which in the recent past our traders have suffered greatly at the hands of others. My noble friend Lord Addison has asked whether such an arrangement could be operated in such a way that certain markets might be closed to British exports. I can firmly assure him that none of the monetary proposals will do so provided that, if we find ourselves with currencies in a foreign country which we do not choose to spend in that country, we can then freely remit them somewhere else to buy goods in another country. There is no compulsion on us, and if we choose to come to a particular bargain in the country where we have resources, then that is entirely at our discretion.

Third, the wheels of trade are to be oiled by what is, in effect, a great addition to the world's stock of monetary reserves, distributed, moreover, in a reasonable way. The quotas are not so large as under the Clearing Union, and Lord Addison drew attention to that. But they are substantial and can be increased subsequently if the need is shown. The aggregate for the world is put provisionally at £2,500,000,000. Our own share of this—for ourselves and the Crown Colonies which, I may mention, are treated for all purposes as a part of the British monetary system (in itself a useful acknowledgment)—is £325,000,000, a sum which may easily double, or more than double, the reserves which we shall otherwise hold at the end of the transitional period. The separate quotas of the rest of the sterling area will make a further large addition to this. Who is so confident of the future that he will wish to throw away so comfortable a supplementary aid in time of trouble? Do the critics think it preferable, if the winds of the trade cycle blow, to diminish our demand for imports by increasing unemployment at home, rather than meet the emergency out of this Fund which will be expressly provided for such temporary purposes?

I emphasize that such is the purpose of the quotas. They are not intended as daily food for us or any other country to live upon during the reconstruction or afterwards. Provision for that belongs to another chapter of international co-operation, upon which we shall embark shortly unless you discourage us unduly about this one. The quotas for drawing on the Fund's resources are an iron ration to tide over temporary emergencies of one kind or another. Perhaps this is the best reply I can make to Lord Addison's doubts whether our quota is large enough. It is obviously not large enough for us to live upon during the reconstruction period. But this is not its purpose. Pending further experience, it is, in my judgment, large enough for the purposes for which it is intended.

There is another advantage to which I would draw your Lordships' special attention. A proper share of responsibility for maintaining equilibrium in the balance of international payments is squarely placed on the creditor countries. This is one of the major improvements in the new plan. The Americans, who are the most likely to be affected by this, have, of their own free will and honest purpose, offered us a far-reaching formula of protection against a recurrence of the main cause of deflation during the inter-war years—namely, the draining of reserves out of the rest of the world to pay a country which was obstinately lending and exporting on a scale immensely greater than it was lending and importing. Under Clause VI of the plan, a country engages itself, in effect, to prevent such a situation from arising again, by promising, should it fail, to release other countries from any obligation to take its exports, or, if taken, to pay for them. I cannot imagine that this sanction would ever be allowed to come into effect. If by no other means than by lending, the creditor country will always have to find a way to square the account on imperative grounds of its own self-interest. For it will no longer be entitled to square the account by squeezing gold out of the rest of us. Here we have a voluntary undertaking, genuinely offered in the spirit both of a good neighbor and, I should add, of enlightened self-interest, not to allow a repetition of a chain of events which between the wars did more than any other single factor to destroy the world's economic balance and to prepare a seed-bed for foul growths. This is a tremendous extension of international co-operation to good ends. I pray your Lordships to pay heed to its importance.

Fifth, the plan sets up an international institution with substantial rights and duties to preserve orderly arrangements in matters such as exchange rates which are two-ended and affect both parties alike, which can also serve as a place of regular discussion between responsible authorities to find ways to escape those many unforeseeable dangers which the future holds. The noble Lord, Lord Addison, asks how the Fund is to be managed. Admittedly this is not yet worked out in the necessary detail and it was right that he should stress the point. But three points which may help him are fairly clear. This is an organization between governments, in which Central Banks only appear as the instrument and agent of their government. The voting power of the British Commonwealth and that of the United States are expected to be approximately equal. The management will be in three tiers—a body of expert, whole-time officials who will be responsible for the routine; a small board of management which will make all decisions of policy subject to any over-riding instructions from the Assembly, an Assembly of all the member governments meeting less often and retaining a supervisory, but not an executive, control. That is perhaps even a little better than appears.

Here are five advantages of major importance. The proposals go far beyond what, even a short time ago, anyone could have conceived of as a possible basis of general international agreement. What alternative is open to us which gives comparable aid, or better, more hopeful opportunities for the future? I have considerable confidence that something very like this plan will be in fact adopted, if only on account of the plain demerits of the alternative of rejection. You can talk against this plan, so long as it is a matter of talking—saying in the same breath that it goes too far and that it does not go far enough, that it is too rigid to be safe and that it is too loose to be worth anything. But it would require great fool-hardiness to reject it, much more fool-hardiness than is to be found in this wise, intuitive country.

Therefore, for these manifold and substantial benefits I commend the monetary proposals to your Lordships. Nevertheless, before you will give them your confidence, you will wish to consider whether, in return, we are surrendering anything which is vital for the ordering of our domestic affairs in the manner we intend for the future. My Lords, the experience of the years before the war has led most of us, though some of us late in the day, to certain firm conclusions. Three, in particular, are highly relevant to this discussion. We are determined that, in future, the external value of sterling shall conform to its internal value as set by our own domestic policies, and not the other way round. Secondly, we intend to retain control of our domestic rate of interest, so that we can keep it as low as suits our own purposes, without interference from the ebb and flow of international capital movements or flights of hot money. Thirdly, whilst we intend to prevent inflation at home, we will not accept deflation at the dictate of influences from outside. In other words, we abjure the instruments of bank rate and credit contraction operating through the increase of unemployment as a means of forcing our domestic economy into line with external factors.

Have those responsible for the monetary proposals been sufficiently careful to preserve these principles from the possibility of interference? I hope your Lordships will trust me not to have turned my back on all I have fought for. To establish those three principles which I have just stated has been my main task for the last twenty years. Sometimes almost alone, in popular articles in the press, in pamphlets, in dozens of letters to *The Times*, in text books, in enormous and obscure treatises I have spent my strength to persuade my countrymen and the world at large to change their traditional doctrines and, by taking better thought, to remove the curse of unemployment. Was it not I, when many of to-day's iconoclasts were still worshippers of the Calf, who wrote that "Gold is a barbarous relic"? Am I so faithless, so forgetful, so senile that, at the very moment of the triumph of these ideas when, with gathering momentum, governments, parliaments, banks, the press, the public, and even economists, have at last accepted the new doctrines, I go off to help forge new chains to hold us fast in the old dungeon? I trust, my Lords, that you will not believe it.

Let me take first the less prominent of the two issues which arise in this connexion—namely, our power to control the domestic rate of interest so as to secure cheap money. Not merely as a feature of the transition, but as a permanent arrangement, the plan accords to every member government the explicit right to control all capital movements. What used to be a heresy is now endorsed as orthodox. In my own judgment, countries which avail themselves of this right may find it necessary to scrutinize all transactions, so as to prevent evasion of capital regulations. Provided that the innocent current transactions are let through, there is nothing in the plan to prevent this. In fact, it is encouraged. It follows that our right to control the domestic capital market is secured on firmer foundations than ever before, and is formally accepted as a proper part of agreed international arrangements.

The question, however, which has recently been given chief prominence is whether we are in any sense returning to the disabilities of the former gold standard, relief from which we have rightly learnt to prize so highly. If I have any authority to pronounce on what is and what is not the essence and meaning of a gold standard, I should say that this plan is the exact opposite of it. The plan in its relation to gold is, indeed, very close to proposals which I advocated in vain as the right alternative when I was bitterly opposing this country's return to gold. The gold standard, as I understand it, means a system under which the external value of a national currency is rigidly tied to a fixed quantity of gold which can only honorably be broken under *force majeure;* and it involves a financial policy which compels the internal value of the domestic currency to conform to this external value as fixed in terms of gold. On the other hand, the use of gold merely as a convenient common denominator by means of which the relative values of national currencies—these being free to change—are expressed from time to time, is obviously quite another matter.

My noble friend Lord Addison asks who fixes the value of gold. If he means, as I assume he does, the sterling value of gold, it is we ourselves who fix it initially in consultation with the Fund; and this value is subject to change at any time on our initiative, changes in excess of 10 per cent requiring the approval of the Fund, which must not withhold approval if our domestic equilibrium requires it. There must be *some* price for gold; and so long as gold is used as a monetary reserve it is most advisable that the current rates of exchange and the relative values of gold in different currencies should correspond. The only alternative to this would be the complete demonetization of gold. I am not aware that anyone has proposed that. For it is only common sense as things are to-day to continue to make use of gold and its prestige as a means of settling international accounts. To demonetize gold would obviously be highly objectionable to the British Commonwealth and to Russia as the main producers, and to the United States and the Western Allies as the main holders of it. Surely no one disputes that? On the other hand, in this country we have already dethroned gold as the fixed standard of value. The plan not merely confirms the dethronement but approves it by expressly providing that it is the duty of the Fund to alter the gold value of any currency if it is shown that this will be serviceable to equilibrium.

In fact, the plan introduces in this respect an epoch-making innovation in an international instrument, the object of which is to lay down sound and orthodox principles. For instead of maintaining the principle that the internal value of a national currency should conform to a prescribed *de jure* external value, it provides that its external value should be altered if necessary so as to conform to whatever *de facto* internal value results from domestic policies, which themselves shall be immune from criticism by the Fund. Indeed, it is made the duty of the Fund to approve changes which will have this effect. That is why I say that these proposals are the exact opposite of the gold standard. They lay down by international agreement the essence of the new doctrine, far removed from the old orthodoxy. If they do so in terms as inoffensive as possible to the former faith, need we complain?

No, my Lords, in recommending these proposals I do not blot a page already written. I am trying to help write a new page. Public opinion is now converted to a new model, and I believe a much improved model, of domestic policy. That battle is all but won. Yet a not less difficult task still remains—namely, to organize an international setting within which the new domestic policies can occupy a comfortable place. Therefore, it is above all as providing an international framework for the new ideas and the new techniques associated with the policy of full employment that these proposals are not least to be welcomed.

Last week my noble friend Lord Bennett asked what assumptions the experts might be making about other phases of international agreement. I do not believe that the soundness of these foundations depends very much on the details of the superstructure. If the rest of the issues to be discussed are wisely settled, the task of the Monetary Fund will be rendered easier. But if we gain less assistance from other measures than we now hope, an agreed machinery of adjustment on the monetary side will be all the more necessary. I am certain that this is not a case of putting the cart before the horse. I think it most unlikely that fuller knowledge about future commercial policy would in itself make it necessary to alter any clause whatever in the proposals now before your Lordships' House. But if the noble Viscount meant that these proposals need supplementing in other directions, no one could agree with him more than I do. In particular, it is urgent that we should seek agreement about setting up an international investment institution to provide funds for reconstruction and afterwards. It is precisely because there is so much to do in the way of international collaboration in the economic field that it would be so disastrous to discourage this first attempt, or to meet it in a carping, suspicious, or cynical mood.

The noble Lord, Lord Addison, has called the attention of your Lordships to the striking statement made by Mr. Hull in connection with the National Foreign Trade Week in the United States, and I am very glad that he did so. This statement is important as showing that the policy of the United States Administration on various issues of political and economic preparation forms a connected whole. I am certain that the people of this country are of the same mind as Mr. Hull, and I have complete confidence that he on his side will seek to implement the details with disinterestedness and generosity. If the experts of the American and British Treasuries have pursued the monetary discussions with more ardor, with a clearer purpose and, I think, with more success so far than has yet proved possible with other associated matters, need we restrain them? If, however, there is a general feeling, as I think that there is, that discussion on other matters should be expedited, so that we may have a complete picture before us, I hope that your Lordships will enforce this conclusion in no uncertain terms. I myself have never supposed that in the final outcome the monetary proposals should stand by themselves.

It is on this note of emphasizing the importance of furthering all genuine efforts directed towards international agreement in the economic field that I should wish to end my contribution to this debate. The proposals which are before your Lordships are the result of the collaboration of many minds and the fruit of the collective wisdom of the experts of many nations. I have spent many days and weeks in the past year in the company of experts of this country, of the Dominions, of our European Allies, and of the United States; and in the light of some past experience I affirm that these discussions have been without exception a model of what such gatherings should be—objective, understanding, without waste of time or expense of temper. I dare to speak for the much abused so-called experts. I even venture sometimes to prefer them, without intending any disrespect, to politicians. The common love of truth, bred of a scientific habit of mind, is the closest of bonds between the representatives of divers nations.

I wish I could draw back the veil of anonymity and give their due to the individuals of the most notable group with which I have ever been associated, covering half the nations of the world, who from prolonged and difficult consultations, each with their own interests to protect, have emerged, as we all of us know and feel in our hearts, a band of brothers. I should like to pay a particular tribute to the representatives of the United States Treasury and the State Department and the Federal Reserve Board in Washington, whose genuine and ready consideration for the difficulties of others, and whose idealistic and unflagging pursuit of a better international order, made possible so great a measure of agreement. I at any rate have come out from a year thus spent greatly encouraged, encouraged beyond all previous hope and expectation, about the possibility of just and honorable and practical economic arrangements between nations.

Do not discourage us. Perhaps we are laying the first brick, though it may be a colorless one, in a great edifice. If indeed it is our purpose to draw back from international co-operation and to pursue an altogether different order of ideas, the sooner that this is made clear the better; but that, I believe, is the policy of only a small minority, and for my part I am convinced that we cannot on those terms remain a great power and the mother of a Commonwealth. If, on the other hand, such is not our purpose, let us clear our minds of excessive doubts and suspicions and go forward cautiously, by all means, but with the intention of reaching agreement.

CHAPTER XXVIII

The Anglo-American Financial Arrangements[1]

By LORD KEYNES

MY LORDS, two days in Westminster are enough to teach one what a vast distance separates us here from the climate of Washington. Much more than the winter waste of the North Atlantic and that somewhat overrated affair, the Gulf Stream, though that is quite enough in itself to fog and dampen everything in transit from one hemisphere to the other. Yet I can well see that no one would easily accept the result of these negotiations with sympathy and understanding unless he could, to some extent at least, bring himself to appreciate the motives and purposes of the other 'side. I think it would be worth while that I should devote some part of what I have to say to that aspect. How difficult it is for nations to understand one another, even when they have the advantage of a common language. How differently things appear in Washington than in London, and how easy it is to misunderstand one another's difficulties and the real purpose which lies behind each one's way of solving them! As the Foreign Secretary has pointed out, everyone talks about international co-operation, but how little of pride, of temper, or of habit anyone is willing to contribute to it when it comes down to brass tacks.

When I last had the opportunity of discussing the Bretton Woods plan in your Lordships' House, the plan stood by itself, and its relationship to post-war policy as a whole was not clear. This was responsible for the least easily answered criticisms. All one could say in reply was that the plan was not intended to stand by itself, but one must begin somewhere. The other aspects were not yet ready for proposals, though details would be taken in hand

[1] [Speech delivered before the House of Lords, December 18, 1945.]

as soon as possible. Today the situation is different. A more or less complete outline for the reordering of commercial and currency policies in their international aspects and their reconversion to peacetime practice is now available. Each part is complementary to the rest. Whether it be well or ill-conceived, in the rounded whole which your Lordships have before you, the proposals fall into three parts: a blueprint called long-term organization of world commerce and foreign exchanges on a multilateral and non-discriminatory basis; short-term proposals for the early reconversion of the sterling area in the same direction; and an offer of financial aid from the United States to enable this country to overcome the immediate difficulties of transition which would otherwise make the short-term proposals impracticable and delay our participation and collaboration with the United States in getting the rest of the world along the lines of the long-term policy indicated.

Each of these parts has been subjected to reasonable criticism. The long-term blueprint invites us to commit ourselves against the future organization of world trade on the principle of tying the opportunity of export to import by means of bilateral and discriminatory arrangements and unstable exchanges such as are likely to involve in practice the creation of separate economic *blocs*. It is argued that this is premature and unreasonable until we have found means to overcome the temporary difficulties of transition and have more experience of the actual conditions of the post-war world, in particular of how a full employment policy works out in practice in its international aspects. The short-term proposals have been criticized on the grounds that they do not allow us enough time to liquidate the very complex wartime arrangements, or to arrange the onerous financial obligations which they heaped on us. Finally, a complaint is made of the terms of the financial aid from the United States, that the amount is insufficient and the burden of the interest too heavy.

It is not for one who has striven every day for three months to improve these proposals so as to lay them less open to these criticisms, and who perhaps knows better than most people how imperfectly he has succeeded, to take these criticisms lightly; nor on the day after my return to this country am I yet in a position to judge, with much accuracy, the mood which underlies the criticisms which are being made, and which is probably more significant than the particular complaints in which it has been finding its outlet. Nevertheless, I wonder if this first great attempt at organizing international order out of the chaos of the war, in a way which will not interfere with the diversity of national policy, yet which will minimize the causes of friction and ill will between nations, is being viewed in its right perspective. I feel sure that serious injustice is being done to the liberal purposes and intense good will towards this country of the American people as represented by their Administration and their urgent desire to see this country a strong and effective partner in guiding a distressed and confused world into the ways of peace and economic order.

Let me plunge at once into the terms of the loan and the understandings about short-term policy which are associated with it. Since our transitory financial difficulties are largely due to the rôle we played in the war and to the costs we incurred before the United States entered the war, we here in London feel—it is a feeling which I shared and still share to the full—that it might not be asking too much of our American friends that they should agree to see us through the transition by financial aid which approximated to a grant. We felt it might be proper for us to indicate the general direction of the policies which that aid would enable us to pursue and to undertake to move along those lines, particularly in terminating the discriminatory features of the exchange arrangements of the sterling area as quickly as circumstances permit, and that, subject to those general understandings, we should be left as free as possible to work things out in our own way. Released from immediate pressing anxieties on terms which would not embarrass the future, we could then proceed cautiously in the light of experience of the post-war world as it gradually disclosed its lessons.

Clearly that would have given us the best of both worlds. How reasonable such a program sounds in London and how natural the disappointment when the actual proposals fall seriously short of it. But what a gulf separates us from the climate of Washington; and what a depth of misunderstanding there will be as to what governs relations between even the friendliest and most like-minded nations if we imagine that so free and easy an arrangement could commend itself to the complex politics of Congress or to the immeasurably remote public opinion of the United

States! Nevertheless, it was on these lines that we opened our case. For three days the heads of the American delegation heard me expound the material contained in the White Paper to which the noble and learned Viscount, Lord Simon, referred. He would have done it more eloquently, but I can fairly say that I was heard not only with obvious and expressed good will and plain sympathy, but also with a keen desire on their part to understand the magnitude and the intricacies of our problem.

I must, at this point, digress for a moment to explain the American response to our claim that for good reasons arising out of the past they owe us something more than they have yet paid, something in the nature of deferred Lend-Lease for the time when we held the fort alone, for it was here that in expounding our case we had an early and severe disappointment. It would be quite wrong to suppose that such considerations have played no part in the final results. They have played a vital part; we could never have obtained what we did obtain except against this background. Nevertheless, it was not very long before the British delegation discovered that a primary emphasis on past services and past sacrifice would not be fruitful. The American Congress and the American people have never accepted any literal principle of equal sacrifice, financial or otherwise, between all the allied participants. Indeed, have we ourselves?

It is a complete illusion to suppose that in Washington you have only to mention the principle of equal sacrifice to get all you want. The Americans—and are they wrong?—find a post-mortem on relative services and sacrifices amongst the leading Allies extremely distasteful and dissatisfying. Many different countries are involved, and most of them are now in Washington to plead their urgent needs and high deserts. Some have rendered more service than others to the common cause; some have experienced more anguish of mind and destruction of organized life; some have suffered, voluntarily or involuntarily, a greater sacrifice of lives and of material wealth; and some of them have escaped from a nearer, more imminent, or deadlier peril than others. Not all of them have had out of Uncle Sam the same relative measure of assistance up to date.

How is all this to be added, subtracted, and assessed in terms of a line of credit? It is better not to try; it is better not to think that way. I give the American point of view. Is it not more practical and more realistic—to use two favorite American expressions—to think in terms of the future and to work out what credits, of what amount and upon what terms, will do most service in reconstructing the post-war world and guiding post-war economy along those lines which, in the American view, will best conduce to the general prosperity of all and to the friendship of nations? This does not mean that the past is forgotten, even though it may be beginning to fade, but in no phase of human experience does the past operate so directly and arithmetically as we were trying to contend. Men's sympathies and less calculated impulses are drawn from their memories of comradeship, but their contemporary acts are generally directed towards influencing the future and not towards pensioning the past. At any rate I can safely assure you that that is how the American Administration and the American people think. Nor, I venture to say, would it be becoming in us to respond by showing our medals, all of them, and pleading that the old veteran deserves better than that, especially if we speak in the same breath of his forthcoming retirement from open commerce and the draughts of free competition, which most probably in his present condition would give him sore throat and drive him still further indoors.

If the noble Lord, Lord Woolton, had led the Mission to Washington—as I indeed wish that he had—I would lay a hundred to one that he would not have continued in the vein in which he spoke yesterday for more than a few days. Neither pride of country nor sense of what is fitting would have allowed him, after he had sensed from every sort of information open to him how Americans responded to it, to make an open attempt to make what every American well appreciated was well enough known in men's hearts the main basis for asking for a gigantic gift. We soon discovered, therefore, that it was not our past performance, or our present weakness, but our future prospects of recovery and our intention to face the world boldly that we had to demonstrate. Our American friends were interested not in our wounds, though incurred in the common cause, but in our convalescence. They wanted to understand the size of our immediate financial difficulties, to be convinced that they were temporary and manageable, and to be told that we intended to walk without bandages as soon as possible. In every circle in which I moved during my stay in Washington, it was when I was able to enlarge on the strength of our future competitive position, if only we were allowed a breather, that I won most sympathy. What the United States needs and desires is a strong Britain, endowed with renewed strength and facing the world on the equal or more than equal terms that we were wont to do. To help that forward interests them much more than to comfort a war victim.

But there was another aspect of the American emphasis on the future benefits which were expected as a result of financial aid to Britain. Those on the American side wanted to be able to speak definitely and in plain language to their own business world about the nature of the future arrangements in regard to commerce between the United States and the sterling area. It was the importance attached on the American side to their being able to speak definitely about future arrangements that made our task so difficult in securing a reasonable time and reasonable elasticity of action. As the Chancellor of the Exchequer has explained in another place, we ran here into difficulties in the negotiations; and we accepted in the end more cut-and-dried arrangements in some respects than we ourselves believed to be wise or beneficial, as we explained in no uncertain terms and with all the force at our command. We warned them that precisely those criticisms which have been raised would be raised, and justly raised, in Parliament. They on their side, however, were not less emphatic that we should render their task impossibly difficult in commending their proposals to their own public unless we could find ways of meeting their desire for definiteness, at least to a certain extent.

Yet I must ask your Lordships to believe that the financial outcome, though it is imperfectly satisfactory to us, does represent a compromise and is very considerably removed from what the Americans began by thinking reasonable; for at the outset the peculiar complexes of our existing arrangements were not at all understood. I am hopeful that the various qualifications which have been introduced, the full significance of which cannot be obvious except to experts, may allow in practice a workable compromise between the certainty they wanted and the measure of elasticity we wanted. Negotiations of this character, in which technical requirements and political appeal must both be satisfied, are immensely difficult, and could not have been brought to any conclusion except in an atmosphere of technical collaboration between the two sides, rather than of technical controversy.

I must now turn to the financial terms of the Agreement, and first of all to its amount. In my own judgment, it is cut somewhat too fine, and does not allow a margin for unforeseen contingencies. Nevertheless the sum is substantial. No comparable credit in time of peace has ever been negotiated before. It should make a great and indispensable contribution to the strength of this country, abroad as well as at home, and to the well-being of our tired and jaded people. After making some allowance for a credit from Canada, and for some minor miscellaneous resources, it represents about as large a cumulative adverse balance as we ought to allow ourselves in the interval before we can get straight. Moreover it may not prove altogether a bad thing that there should be no sufficient margin to tempt us to relax; for if we were to relax, we should never reach equilibrium and become fully self-supporting within a reasonable period of time. As it is, the plain fact is that we cannot afford to abate the full energy of our export drive or the strictness of our economy in any activity which involves overseas expenditure. Our task remains as diffi-cult as it is stimulating, and as stimulating as it is difficult. On a balance of considerations, therefore, I think that under this heading we should rest reasonably content.

That the Americans should be anxious not to allow too hot a pace to be set in this, their first major post-war operation of this kind, is readily understandable. The total demands for overseas financial assistance crowding in on the United States Treasury from all quarters whilst I was in Washington were estimated to amount to between four and five times our own maximum pro-posals. We naturally have only our own requirements in view, but the United States Treasury cannot overlook the possible reaction of what they do for us on the expectations of others. Many members of Congress were seriously concerned about the cumulative consequences of being too easy-going towards a world unanimously clamoring for American aid, and often only with too good reason. I mention such considerations because they are a great deal more obvious when one is in Washington than when one returns here.

On the matter of interest, I shall never so long as I live cease to regret that this is not an interest-free loan. The charging of interest is out of tune with the underlying realities. It is based on a false analogy. The other conditions of the loan indicate clearly that our case has been recognized as being, with all its attendant circumstances, a special one. The Americans might have felt it an advantage, one would have thought, in relation to other transactions, to emphasize this special character still further by forgoing interest. The amount of money at stake cannot be important to the United States, and what a difference it would have made to our feelings and to our response! But there it is. On no possible ground can we claim as of right a gesture so unprecedented. A point comes when in a matter of this kind one has to take "No" for an answer. Nor, I am utterly convinced, was it any lack of generosity of mind or purpose on the part of the American negotiators which led to their final decision. And it is not for a foreigner to weigh up the cross-currents, political forces, and general sentiments which determine what is possible and what is impossible in the complex and highly charged atmosphere of that great democracy, of which the daily thoughts and urgent individual preoccupations are so far removed from ours. No one who has breathed that atmosphere for many troubled weeks will underestimate the difficulties of the American statesmen, who are striving to do their practical best for their own country and for the whole world, or the fatal consequences if the Administration were to offer us what Congress would reject.

During the whole time that I was in Washington, there was not a single Administration measure of the first importance that Congress did not either reject, remodel, or put on one side. Assuming, however, that the principle of charging interest had to be observed, then, in my judgment, almost everything possible has been done to mitigate the burden and to limit the risk of a future dangerous embarrassment. We pay no interest for six years. After that we pay no interest in any year in which our exports have not been restored to a level which may be estimated at about 60 per cent in excess of pre-war. I repeat that. We pay no interest in any year in which our exports have not been restored to a level which may be estimated at about 60 per cent in excess of what they were pre-war.

LORD BARNBY: In volume or value?

LORD KEYNES: Volume. That is very important; I should have said so. The maximum payment in any year is £35,000,000, and that does not become payable until our external income, in terms of present prices, is fifty times that amount. Again I repeat, the maximum payment in any year is £35,000,000, and that does not become payable until our external income—that is from exports and shipping and the like—is, in terms of present prices, fifty times that amount. In any year in which our income falls short of this standard, interest is fully and finally waived. Moreover, the installments of capital repayments are so arranged that we obtain the maximum benefit from this provision in the early years. For at the start the minimum payment to which we have committed ourselves is no more than £13,000,000 a year; that is to say, less than one per cent of the external income which we must attain if we are to break even, quite apart from the cost of the American loan.

It is relevant, I think, to remind your Lordships that the maximum charge to us in respect of the early years is not much more than half of what is being charged in respect of loans which the United States is making currently to her other Allies, through the Import and Export Bank or otherwise; whilst the minimum charge per cent to which we have been asked to commit ourselves in the early years is only one-fifth of the annual service charge which is being asked from the other Allies. None of those loans is subject to a five-year moratorium. All the other loans which are being made are tied loans limited to payments for specific purchases from the United States. Our loan, on the other hand, is a loan of money without strings, free to be expended in any part of the world. That is an arrangement, I may add, which is entirely consistent with the desire of the United States to enable us to return as fully as possible to the conditions of multilateral trade settlements.

Your negotiators can, therefore, in my judgment, fairly claim that the case of last time's war debts has not been repeated. Moreover, this is new money we are dealing with, to pay for post-war supplies for civilian purposes, and is not—as was mainly the case on the previous occasion—a consolidation of a war debt. On the contrary, this new loan has been associated with a complete wiping off the slate of any residual obligations from the operation of Lend-Lease. Under the original Lend-Lease agreement, the President of the United States has been free to ask for future "consideration" of an undetermined character. This uncomfortable and uncertain obligation has been finally removed from us. The satisfactory character of the Lend-Lease settlement has not, I think, received as much emphasis as it deserves. The Secretary of State for India emphasized it in his opening speech yesterday, but it was not, so far as I noticed, taken up in any of the speeches which were made by other noble Lords.

I am indeed glad that there is some part of the settlement which has commended itself to those on the Benches on this side of the House. No part of the loan which is applied to this settlement relates to the cost of Lend-Lease supplies consumed during the war, but is entirely devoted to supplies received by us through the Lend-Lease machinery, but available for our consumption or use after the end of the war. It also covers the American military surplus and is in final discharge of the variety of financial claims, both ways, arising out of the war which fell outside the field of Lend-Lease and reciprocal aid. Is it not putting our claim and legitimate expectations a little too high to regard these proposals, on top of Lend-Lease, as anything but an act of unprecedented liberality? Has any country ever treated another country like this, in time of peace, for the purpose of rebuilding the other's strength and restoring its competitive position? If the Americans have tried to meet criticism at home by making the terms look a little less liberal than they really are, so as to preserve the principle of interest, is it necessary for us to be mistaken? The balm and sweet simplicity of no per cent is not admitted, but we are not asked to pay interest except in conditions where we can reasonably well afford to do so, and the capital installments are so spread that our minimum obligation in the early years is actually less than it would be with a loan free of interest repayable by equal installments.

I began by saying that the American negotiators had laid stress on future mutual advantage rather than on past history. But let no one suppose that such a settlement could have been conceivably made except by those who had measured and valued what this country has endured and accomplished. I have heard the suggestion made that we should have recourse to a commercial loan without strings. I wonder if those who put this forward have any knowledge of the facts. The body which makes such loans on the most favorable terms is the Export-Import Bank. Most of the European Allies are in fact borrowing, or trying to borrow, from this institution. The most favorable terms sometimes allowed, as for instance in the case of France, for the purpose of clearing up what she obtained through Lend-Lease machinery, are 2⅜ per cent with repayment over thirty years, beginning next year; that is to say, an annual debt of 5⅜ per cent so that an amount equal to 34 per cent of the loan will have been paid by France during the six years before we have begun to pay anything at all. The normal commercial terms in the Export-Import Bank are, however, 3 per cent repayable over twenty years commencing at once, so that payments equal to 48 per cent of the loan would have been paid during the first six years in which we pay nothing. Moreover, the resources of this institution are limited and our reasonable share of them could not have exceeded one-quarter or one-fifth of what we are actually getting. Nor are they without strings. They are tied to specific American purchases and not, like ours, available for use in any part of the world.

What about the conditions associated with the loans? The noble and learned Viscount, Lord Simon, as have also several other critics, laid stress on our having agreed to release the current earnings of the sterling area after the spring of 1947. I wonder how much we are giving away there. It does not relate to the balances accumulated before the spring of 1947. We are left quite free to settle this to the best of our ability. What we undertake to do is not to restrict the use of balances we have not yet got and have not yet been entrusted to us. It will be very satisfactory if we can maintain the voluntary wartime system into 1947. But what hope is there of the countries concerned continuing such an arrangement much longer than that? Indeed, the danger is that these countries which have a dollar or gold surplus, such as India and South Africa, would prefer to make their own arrangements, leaving us with a dollar pool which is a deficit pool, responsible for the dollar expenditure not only of ourselves but of the other members of the area having a dollar deficit.

This arrangement is only of secondary use to us, save in the exceptional wartime conditions when those countries were, very abnormally, in a position to lend to us. We cannot force these countries to buy only from us, especially when we are physically unable to supply a large quantity of what they require. It seems to me a crazy idea that we can go on living after 1947 by borrowing on completely vague terms from India and the Crown

Colonies. They will be wanting us to repay them. Two-thirds of what we owe to the sterling area is owed to India, Palestine, Egypt, and Eire. Is it really wise to base our financial policy on the loyalty and goodwill of those countries to lend us money and leave out of our arrangements Canada and the United States? And Canada, let me add, is not less insistent than the United States—if anything she is more insistent—on our liberating the current earnings of the sterling area.

I hope I shall convince the noble and learned Viscount, for I have not yet finished. This was, anyhow, a condition very difficult to resist, for the main purpose of a loan of this magnitude was for the precise object of liberating the future earnings of the sterling area, not for repaying their past accumulations. Some have been misled by the fact that that has been expressly emphasized. Our direct adverse balance with the United States is not likely to exceed during the period more than about half the loan. The rest of our adverse balance is with the rest of the world—

VISCOUNT SIMON: The noble Lord speaks of a proposal difficult to resist. May we be informed if the experts did their best to resist it?

LORD KEYNES: They did their best to resist so early a date, but I am giving the reasons why, in being forced to surrender, the magnitude of our surrender was not so very great. I have explained so far that it would be very difficult in any circumstances to carry on the arrangements beyond that for the reasons I have explained, and I am now passing to what was, I feel, a vulnerable part of our case. That was that the precise object of having so large a loan was to make these very arrangements practicable. About half of it would be a direct adverse balance with the United States. The rest of the adverse balance is with the rest of the world, mainly the sterling area. Canada will be dealt with separately. The very object of the other half of the loan is, therefore, to provide us with dollars mainly for the sterling area. We are given not only the condition but also the means to satisfy it. I am afraid it would take more than my forensic powers to maintain that position in its most absolute form against an argument so powerful as that, if the Americans could say: "You are going to borrow all this money by impounding the earnings of the sterling area. What is the necessity for so large a loan? The calculations have been based on the contention that we have to meet the major part of your adverse balance." But that is not the end. I do not think we need repine too much.

The way to remain an international banker is to allow checks to be drawn upon you; the way to destroy the sterling area is to prey on it and try to live on it. The way to retain it is to restore its privileges and opportunities as soon as possible to what they were before the war. It would have been more comfortable to know that we could have a little more than fifteen months to handle the situation, but, nevertheless, the underlying situation is as I have described. I do not regard this particular condition as a serious blot on the loan, although I agree with the noble and learned Viscount that I would have preferred it less precise, as I would have preferred many other points to be less precise. Such a view can only be based on a complete misapprehension of the realities of the position, for, apart from the question of debt, do the critics really grasp the nature of the alternative? The alternative is to build up a separate economic *bloc* which excludes Canada and consists of countries to which we already owe more than we can pay, on the basis of their agreeing to lend us money they have not got and buy only from us and one another goods we are unable to supply. Frankly this is not such a caricature of these proposals as it may sound at first.

In conclusion, I must turn briefly to what is, in the long run, of major importance—namely, the blueprints for long-term commercial and currency policy, although I fear I must not enlarge on that. In working out the Commercial Policy Paper, to which, of course, this country is not committed, unless a considerable part of the world is prepared to come into it and not merely the United States, and in the Final Act of Bretton Woods, I believe that your representatives have been successful in maintaining the principles and objects which are best suited to the predicaments of this country. The plans do not wander from the international terrain and they are consistent with widely different conceptions of domestic policy. Proposals which the authors hope to see accepted both by the United States of America and by Soviet Russia must clearly conform to this condition. It is not true, for example, to say that State trading and bulk purchasing are interfered with. Nor is it true to say that the planning of the volume of our exports and imports, so as to preserve equilibrium in the international balance of payments, is prejudiced. Exactly the contrary is the case. Both the currency and the commercial proposals are devised to favor the maintenance of equilibrium by expressly permitting various protective devices when they are required to maintain equilibrium and by forbidding them when they are not so required. They are of the utmost importance in our relationship with the United States and, indeed, the outstanding characteristic of the plans is that they represent the first elaborate and comprehensive attempt to combine the advantages of a freedom of commerce with safeguards against the disastrous consequences of a laissez faire system which pays no direct regard to the preservation of equilibrium and merely relies on the eventual working out of blind forces.

Here is an attempt to use what we have learnt from modern experience and modern analysis, not to defeat, but to implement, the wisdom of Adam Smith. It is a unique accomplishment, I venture to say, in the field of international discussion to have proceeded so far by common agreement along a newly trod path, not yet pioneered, I agree, to a definite final destination, but a newly trod path, which points the right way. We are attempting a great step forward towards the goal of international economic order amidst national diversities of policies. It is not easy to have patience with those who pretend that some of us, who were very early in the field to attack and denounce the false premises and false conclusions of unrestricted laissez faire and its particular manifestations in the former gold standard and other currency and commercial doctrines which mistake private license for public liberty, are now spending their later years in the service of the State to walk backwards and resurrect and re-erect the idols which they had played some part in throwing out of the market place. Not so. Fresh tasks now invite. Opinions have been successfully changed. The work of destruction has been accomplished, and the site has been cleared for a new structure.

Questions have been raised—and rightly and reasonably raised —about the willingness of the United States to receive repayment hereafter. This is a large subject to which I have given a great deal of thought, but I shall not have time to develop it fully today. I am not, as a result, quite so worried as most people. Indeed, if in the next five or ten years the dollar turns out to be a scarce currency, seldom will so many people have been right.

It is a very technical matter, very emphatically within their past experience, but not so easily the subject of future prediction. I am afraid I must content myself with a few headlines. First, it is not a question of our having to pay the United States by direct exports; we could never do that. Our exports are not, and are not likely to be, as large as our direct imports from the United States. The object of the multilateral system is to enable us to pay the United States by exporting to any part of the world, and it is partly for that very reason that the Americans have felt the multilateral system was the only sound basis for any arrangement of this kind. Secondly, all the most responsible people in the United States, and particularly in the State Department and in the Treasury, have entirely departed from the high tariff, export subsidy conception of things, and will do their utmost with, they believe, the support of public opinion in the opposite direction. That is why this international trade convention presents us with such a tremendous opportunity. For the first time in modern history, the United States is going to exert its full powerful influence in the direction of reduction of tariffs, not only of itself but by all others.

Thirdly, this is a problem of which today every economist and publicist in the United States is acutely conscious. Books on economics are scarcely written about anything else. They would regard it as their fault and not ours if they fail to solve it. They would acquit us of blame—quite different from the atmosphere of ten or twenty years ago. They will consider it their business to find a way out. Fourthly, if the problem does arise, it will be a problem, for reasons I have just mentioned, of the United States vis-à-vis the rest of the world and not us in particular. It will be the problem of the United States and the whole commercial and financial arrangements of every other country. Fifthly—and perhaps this is the consideration which is least prominent in people's minds—the United States is rapidly becoming a high-living and a high-cost country. Their wages are two and a half times ours. These are the historic, classical methods by which in the long run international equilibrium will be restored.

Therefore, much of these policies seem to me to be in the prime interest of our country, little though we may like some parts of them. They are calculated to help us regain a full measure of prosperity and prestige in the world's commerce. They aim, above all, at the restoration of multilateral trade which is a system upon which British commerce essentially depends. You can draw your supplies from any source that suits you and sell your goods in any market where they can be sold to advantage. The bias of the policies before you is against bilateral barter and every kind of discriminatory practice. The separate economic *blocs* and all the friction and loss of friendship they must bring with them are expedients to which one may be driven in a hostile world, where trade has ceased over wide areas to be co-operative and peaceful and where are forgotten the healthy rules of mutual advantage and equal treatment. But it is surely crazy to prefer that. Above all, this determination to make trade truly international and to avoid the establishment of economic *blocs* which limit and restrict commercial intercourse outside them, is plainly an essential condition of the world's best hope, an Anglo-American understanding, which brings us and others together in international institutions which may be in the long run the first step towards something more comprehensive. Some of us, in the tasks of war and more lately in those of peace, have learnt by experience that our two countries can work together. Yet it would be only too easy for us to walk apart. I beg those who look askance at these plans to ponder deeply and responsibly where it is they think they want to go.

CHAPTER XXIX

The Bank for Reconstruction and Development[1]

By LORD KEYNES

It is our hope that the institution of the Bank for Reconstruction and Development, to which this Commission is to devote its work, will serve the purpose of increasing the health, prosperity, and friendship of the participating countries in two main respects.

In the first place, it will be authorized in proper cases and with due prudence to make loans to the countries of the world which have suffered from the devastation of war, to enable them to restore their shattered economies and replace the instruments of production which have been lost or destroyed. It is no part of the purpose of UNRRA to provide funds for reconstruction as distinguished from the necessary relief and rehabilitation in the days immediately following liberation. There is, therefore, at present a gap in the proposals of the United and Associated Nations which is not yet filled, and to fill which there is no proposal in view except the institution of this Bank. Yet this is a matter of the utmost urgency and importance where we should, therefore, press forward to reach agreement on methods and on details. We do not know the date of the complete liberation of the occupied countries of Europe and Asia. But we are now entitled to hope that it will be not unduly delayed. We should be bitterly failing in duty if we were not already prepared for the days of liberation. The countries chiefly concerned can scarcely begin to make their necessary plans until they know upon what resources they can rely. Any delay, any avoidable time lag, will be disastrous to the establishment of good order and good government, and may

[1] [Opening Remarks at the First Meeting of the Second Commission on the Bank, July 3, 1944.]

also postpone the date at which the victorious armies of liberation can return to their homelands.

I cannot, therefore, conceive a more urgent, necessary, and important task for the Delegates of the forty-four nations here assembled. I am confident that the members of the Commission of which I have the honor to be the Chairman will devote themselves to their work in a spirit of full responsibility, well aware how much depends on their success.

It is likely, in my judgment, that the field of reconstruction from the consequences of war will mainly occupy the proposed Bank in its early days. But as soon as possible, and with increasing emphasis as time goes on, there is a second primary duty laid upon it, namely, to develop the resources and productive capacity of the world, with special attention to the less developed countries, to raising the standard of life and the conditions of labor everywhere, to make the resources of the world more fully available to all mankind, and so to order its operations as to promote and maintain equilibrium in the international balances of payments of all member countries.

These two purposes deserve particular emphasis, but are not exclusive or comprehensive. In general, it will be the duty of the Bank, by wise and prudent lending, to promote a policy of expansion of the world's economy in the sense in which this term is the exact opposite of inflation. By *expansion* we should mean the increase of resources and production in real terms, in physical quantity, accompanied and facilitated by a corresponding increase of purchasing power. By *inflation* on the other hand, we should mean the increase of purchasing power corresponding to which there is no accompanying increase in the quantity of production. The Bank will promote expansion and avoid inflation.

Under the proposals to be brought before you, the Bank will be free to operate along three different lines.

A certain part of the Fund's subscribed capital will be called up and will be available for direct lending by the Bank for approved purposes in the currencies of the contributing members.

But the greater part of its subscribed capital will be held as a reserve fund with which to guarantee two other types of operations.

The first type of loan eligible for such guarantee will be loans for suitable purposes and on suitable terms, issued through the ordinary channels of the investment market where on account of the risks involved there would be difficulty otherwise in placing the loan on terms which the borrowing country could afford to pay.

The second type of loan secured by the assets and subscribed capital of the Bank will also be placed through the ordinary channels of the investment market but will be offered on the Bank's behalf in its own name. The proceeds of such loans will then be re-lent by the Bank to borrowing countries on terms and for purposes to be directly agreed with them.

The proceeds of both these types of loan would be freely available for the borrower to make purchases in any member country, with due regard to economy and efficiency.

Let me now explain the nature of the proposed guarantee, for this is of a novel character which may be regarded as marking in a particularly significant way the international character of the proposed institution.

It is evident that only a few of the member countries will be in possession of an investable surplus available for overseas loans on a large scale, especially in the years immediately following the war. It is in the nature of the case that the bulk of the lending can only come from a small group of the member countries, and mainly from the United States. How then can the other member countries play their proper part and make their appropriate contribution to the common purpose?

Herein lies the novelty of the proposals which will be submitted to you. Only those countries which find themselves in a specially favored position can provide the loanable funds. But this is no reason why these lending countries should also run the whole risk of the transaction. In the dangerous and precarious days which lie ahead, the risks of the lender will be inevitably large and most difficult to calculate. The risk premium reckoned on strict commercial principles may be beyond the capacity of an impoverished borrower to meet, and may itself contribute to the risks of ultimate default. Experience between the wars was not encouraging. Without some supporting guarantee, therefore, loans which are greatly in the interests of the whole world, and indeed essential for recovery, it may prove impossible to float.

Yet, as I have said, there is no reason in a case like this, where the interests of all countries alike, whether lenders or borrowers, or exporters, are favorably affected, why the unavoidable risks should fall exclusively on the lenders, for example, the investors, or the government of the United States, if it turns out that they are the chief source of available funds.

The proposal is, therefore, that all the member countries should share the risk in proportions which correspond to their capacity. The guarantees will be joint and several, up to the limit of any member's subscription, so that the failure of any member to implement his guarantee will not injuriously affect the lender, so long as the Bank has other assets and subscriptions to draw upon, resources which will, according to our proposals, be of considerable dimensions. Moreover, it is proposed that every member country should undertake to provide gold or free exchange up to the full amount of its subscription, in so far as it is called upon under its guarantee. Therefore the quality of the bonds thus guaranteed should be of the first order; at any rate, they will be a great deal better than in the case of many borrowing countries there would be any hope of offering otherwise than under the auspices of the new institution.

The bonds will be good for several different reasons. In the first place, they will have behind them the vast resources of the Bank available in gold or free exchange. In the second place, the proceeds will be expended only for proper purposes and in proper ways, after due inquiry by experts and technicians, so that there will be safeguards against squandering and waste and extravagance, which were not present with many of the ill-fated loans made between the wars. In the third place, they will carry the guarantee of the borrowing country; and this borrower will be under an overwhelming motive to do its best and play fair, for the consequences of improper action and avoidable default to so great an institution will not be lightly incurred.

But there is also a fourth safeguard, of great importance to the guaranteeing countries as well as to the lenders. There are two reasons for hoping that the guarantors will not find themselves under any insupportable or burdensome liability. In the first place, a guarantee will relate to the annual servicing of the loan for interest and amortisation. Its implementation will, therefore, be spread over a period corresponding to the term of the loan and cannot fall due suddenly as a lump sum obligation. In the second place, there is an interesting and essential feature of the proposals in the shape of a commission payable by the borrower in return for its guarantee. It is suggested that for long-term loans of the normal character this commission should be at the rate of 1 per cent per annum. This rate of commission should be the same for all members alike, for it would be a mistake, and worse than a mistake, to attempt the invidious task of discriminating between members and assessing their credit-worthiness in what is really a mutual pool of credit insurance amongst a group acting in good faith—indeed in the old language of insurers consecrated by tradition, in the spirit of *uberrima fides*, of good faith, complete, abundant, and overflowing.

This commission should not be an excessive burden on the borrower. One per cent added to the interest appropriate to a loan guaranteed by the Bank will not be onerous. On the other hand, the annual receipts from the commission will greatly augment the free reserves of the Bank available to meet its obligations before calling on the guarantors. The Bank should aim at so conducting its business that there would be a good hope of the pool of commissions being sufficient by itself to carry it most of the way.

Here are the broad outlines of the proposals which you will be asked to consider. There are other aspects and much detail for you to work out. For the Bank has not enjoyed so much discussion as has the Fund, prior to this Conference.

But I believe that we have before us a proposal the origins of which we owe primarily to the initiative and ability of the United States Treasury, conceived on sound and fruitful lines. Indeed, I fancy that the underlying conception of a joint and several guarantee of all the member countries throughout the world, in virtue of which they share the risks of projects of common interest and advantage even when they cannot themselves provide the lump sum loan originally required, thus separating the carrying of risk from the provision of funds, may be a contribution of fundamental value and importance to those difficult, those almost overwhelming, tasks which lie ahead of us, to rebuild the world when a final victory over the forces of evil opens the way to a new age of peace and progress after great afflictions.

PART SIX

*Economic Fluctuations and Trends
and Fiscal Policy*

CHAPTER XXX

Introductory : Wastage and Investment

By SEYMOUR E. HARRIS

THE PROBLEM

To KEYNES, the waste of economic resources through unemployment seemed nonsensical and suicidal. He concentrated more of his energies on the solution of this problem than of any other; and he had considerable success. The expenditure of £500 million on unemployment relief in the twenties, or the loss of £2 billion of output associated with unemployment in those years, a sum which could have financed the construction of British railroads twice over, the concomitance of two hundred and fifty thousand idle construction workers and great scarcities in housing, the large production, technical and engineering potentials alongside of unemployment—all of these vexed Keynes and made him anxious to find a solution.[1]

He was not prepared to accept the classical or the Treasury assumption that there is a fixed supply of money or capital, and, therefore, that any money or capital put at the disposal of the unemployed would be at the expense of the employed.

It has been argued that it is not possible to ensure that any particular scheme of investment will mean *additional* expenditure. It may merely cause a diversion of finance and of resources from different expenditures which would have occurred otherwise. . . . But in present circumstances, when the physical limit on further capital output is far from reached, there is no reason why the action of the banking system need stand in the way of additional investment, unless this investment was throwing too heavy a burden on the balance of trade—a contingency which we deal

[1] See, especially, *The Means to Prosperity*, pp. 5–8; *Essays in Persuasion*, especially pp. 135–156; *Macmillan Report*, Addendum I, pp. 208–209; *Treatise*, Vol. I, pp. 294–295.

with below. For the theory that there is in any sense a fixed loan fund available to finance investment which is in all circumstances fully employed, or that the amount of the savings of the public always exactly correspond to the volume of new investment, is, we think, mistaken.[2]

STAGNATION

Unemployment stems from inadequate demand; and assaults on the banking system, the rate of interest, orthodox canons of finance, institutional factors that hold consumption down and savings up—all of these should be enlisted to raise demand. This is the lesson of Keynesian economics.

Keynes was not always a stagnationist; and in fact he never developed his theory of stagnation systematically as has been done so ably by Professor Hansen. In the *Treatise*, for example, Keynes concentrated his attention upon the relative desirability of inflation and deflation. Greatly influenced by Professor D. H. Robertson's pioneer work in this field, he preferred the recurrent episodes of inflation in the nineteenth century to deflation. The latter was harmful, in his view, because with falling prices consumers gained at the expense of savings, and because large losses from unemployment followed.

Throughout the *Treatise*, Keynes was concerned with excess savings and high rates of interest. When there was unemployed capital, additional savings were bound to make matters worse. At a rate of interest in 1930, 50 per cent in excess of the pre-World War rate, and with entrepreneurs excessively gloomy concerning business prospects, there was bound to be an enormous gap between what lenders would accept and borrowers pay. Rates were abnormally high, in part because of the diversion of capital to *distress* borrowers, who had to finance losses, and to *artificial* borrowers, who were interested only in speculative gains. Recovery awaited a revision of acceptable rates by those who held billions of £ sterling in short-term money in the United Kingdom and the United States, and a reappraisal of business prospects. In the *Treatise*, he ends on a note half optimistic and half gloomy. To the historian, 1930 would appear as the death struggle "of the war rates of interest and the re-emergence of the pre-war rates."

---

[2] *Macmillan Report*, Addendum I, p. 203; also cf. p. 204. See also the excellent statement in Oxford University Institute of Statistics, *The Economics of Full Employment* (Blackwell, 1944), pp. 85–91.

Unfortunately, Keynes went on, equilibrium is finally attained only by spilling savings. How else could it be achieved, when in the financial countries savings are large enough to cause capital to increase five times faster than population! [3]

Clearly, in the *Treatise* Keynes had not presented a systematic stagnation theory, although in his emphasis on over-savings and high interest rates, and on the excess of the market rate over the natural rate, he was groping towards such a theory. As late as 1931, in fact, he assured his readers that England was suffering "from the growing pains of youth, not from the rheumatics of old age." In a rise of man-day output of 20 per cent since the pre-war and an annual increase of national income of £100 million in the years preceding the collapse of 1930, he saw evidence of growth and progress.[4]

In the *General Theory*, the reader should note three important passages dealing with the problems now under discussion. First, Keynes pointed out that the ultimate objective of economic activity is consumption. Demand might indeed be kept up temporarily by increasing capital, or might be reduced through disinvestment. In general, however, there are limits to the stimulation or discouragement of demand through a redistribution of output between consumption and capital goods. In short, capital growth can make only a limited contribution to the maintenance of demand; and gains on this score are to be written down in so far as a result of current investment, future investment will be discouraged.[5]

Second, he emphasized, as he had in the *Treatise*, the difficulty of establishing a rate of interest which both was acceptable to the wealth-owners and would allow a reasonable average of employment. *But he now expressed grave doubts concerning the possibility of attaining adequately low rates through monetary expansion.* The borrower must deduct, from the percentage of earnings which the marginal efficiency of capital allows him, the cost of bringing lenders and borrowers together, the income and surtaxes, and compensation for risk and uncertainty. The required earnings rate was too high at current interest rates. In the nineteenth century, however, the growth of population and inventions,

[3] Especially *Treatise*, Vol. II, p. 384; see also pp. 377 ff.; *Essays in Persuasion*, pp. 142–147, 151.
[4] *Essays in Persuasion*, p. 156.
[5] *General Theory*, pp. 104–6.

opening up of new lands, and the state of confidence, seem to have been adequate, at the existing propensity to consume, to establish a marginal efficiency of capital, which, at the reasonable rate of interest established by the monetary authorities, was compatible with a reasonably satisfactory level of employment. War also contributed to demand.[6]

Third, Keynes stressed the limited demand for capital: with increasing supplies, capital should, within a generation or two, lose its scarcity value, with a resulting euthanasia of the rentier class. In the long run, there is no reason for a scarcity value for capital unless the propensity to consume is so high that net saving under full employment comes to an end before the supply of capital is sufficient. Keynes would then seek to end the scarcity of capital, and he would introduce a tax system which would yield the entrepreneur adequate rewards to assure the harnessing of his labor to the service of the community. Experience would then teach how far the State should increase and supplement the inducement to invest, and how far the State should seek a rise in the average propensity to consume without abandoning the objective of depriving capital of its scarcity value.[7]

Clearly, then, by 1936, Keynes had presented more than the germs of a stagnation theory. By that time, he had emphasized over-saving, excessive rates of interest, limited demand for capital, low marginal efficiency of capital, and had noted the more favorable demand conditions in the nineteenth century: population increase, wars, new inventions, opening up of new lands, were especially important.

Keynes presented his most systematic exposition of a stagnation theory in a paper in the *Eugenics Review* for 1937—based on his Galton Lecture. Here Keynes was quite specific on the effects of a declining population, on the relation of investment and population change, on the need of combating stagnation by reducing interest rates and raising consumption through institutional measures. He was emphatic that consumption standards were unlikely to rise by more than 1 per cent per annum over the years, and that a longer production period was not probable (e.g., rise of capital per unit of output). Under conditions of full employment and a stationary population, inventions which tend to reduce labor requirements would not absorb more than one-

[6] *General Theory*, pp. 307–309. Cf. Dr. A. Sweezy's essay below.
[7] *General Theory*, pp. 375–377.

half of the annual savings, which under full-employment conditions he estimated at 8–15 per cent of national income, or 2–4
per cent of the capital stock.

His calculations for the period 1860 to 1913 are especially interesting. With 1860 as 100, he estimated real capital in 1913 at
270, population at 150, standard of life at 160, period of production at 110. His conclusion was that increasing population accounted for about one-half of the increase in capital. This source
of demand would, obviously be dried up when population became stationary. Hence the need for lower rates of interest, and
especially increased consumption standards.[8]

EXPANSION OR CONTRACTION

Before we discuss the general issues, I should remind the
reader of Keynes' position in 1925 as revealed by his evidence
before the Colwyn Committee on *National Debt and Taxation*.
He then stressed especially the danger of a rapid repayment of
the public debt, which would result in a transfer of cash from
taxpayers who might be *venturesome* to rentiers who probably
would not. At that time, Keynes was, however, not ready to consider the effects of debt repayment upon total demand: he
specifically suggested that this aspect was not very important.[8a]

Once the British had decided to return to gold, and once it
had become evident that the results were likely to be deflationary,
Keynes felt the need of an expansive policy. Yet it was not until
Great Britain had returned to gold that he began to advocate
outright an expansionary policy. His paper on the reports of the
Bank Chairmen in 1927 gives an inkling of what was to come.
From 1929 on he aggressively fought for expansion against economy; for a reduction or elimination of the Sinking Fund appro-
priations and taxes to finance unemployment; for a public investment program; against doles, against reduction of teachers'
salaries, and against wage cutting and reduction of output as the
means of cutting losses.[9] His famous banana parable eloquently
showed what was to be expected of wage-cutting as a means of

[8] J. M. Keynes, "Some Economic Consequences of a Declining Population," *Eugenics Review*, 1937, pp. 13–17.

[8a] *Committee on National Debt and Taxation* (Colwyn Report), Minutes
of Evidence, pp. 278, 283–285, 535–536.

[9] Especially *Essays in Persuasion*, pp. 161–5, 272–275; *Treatise*, Vol. 1,
pp. 160–1, 176–78; *Macmillan Report*, Addendum I, pp. 207–208; *The
Means to Prosperity*, pp. 5–16.

recouping losses. In short, there were two ways of dealing with depressed conditions: one, to maintain standards by putting to use wasted capacity, thus casting fear away; the other, to encourage a psychology of fear.

In the *Treatise*, Keynes stressed the deflationary effects imposed on the British economy by foreign economic policies and the mistaken emphasis the British put on international considerations. Interest rates were too high to assure adequate levels of employment. The way out was to reduce interest rates through monetary policy, and counter excessive demands for British capital from abroad by embargoes on British capital, control of imports, programs of domestic investment, or subsidies on domestic investment. If the rate of interest were lowered from 5 to 4 per cent and British borrowers were still unwilling to borrow at 4 per cent, then a small subsidy might make the capital available to British investors. This subsidy might well then account for an increment of wealth, and might keep capital from going abroad and keep foreign lending from rising to a dangerous level in relation to the foreign balance—in the absence of corrective measures, lending would exceed the amounts available for foreign lending.[10]

In the *General Theory*, Keynes continued to stress the need of public investment. Since he had become less optimistic concerning monetary policy in relation to its effects on the rate of interest, and since he was disturbed by the large fluctuations in, and the continuing decline of, marginal efficiency of capital, and since he was less disposed to rely on beggar-my-neighbor remedies than in his earlier writings, his attention towards public investment necessarily increased. The State could take a long view; and the State's estimate of marginal efficiency would be colored by the social advantages.[11]

With large losses associated with unemployment and wastage, a community with large accumulation of capital might not be better off than a poor community—until the latter had attained an advanced state. Failure to attain goals consistent with economic potentials might be averted by the rich nation controlling the propensity to consume and the rate of investment in the social interest. But if, even then, the rate of interest were not to fall as

[10] See, especially, *Treatise*, Vol. II, pp. 186–187, 376–377; also see *Macmillan Report*, Addendum I, pp. 201, 205; and *Essays in Persuasion*, pp. 125–128, 271–287.

[11] *General Theory*, pp. 163–164.

much as the marginal efficiency of capital, with a rate of accumulation consistent with a rate of interest equal to the marginal efficiency of capital under conditions of full employment, in that case, "even a diversion of the desire to hold wealth towards assets, which will in fact yield no economic fruits whatever, will increase well-being. In so far as millionaires find their satisfaction in building mighty mansions to contain their bodies when alive and pyramids to shelter them after death, or, repenting of their sins, erect cathedrals and endow monasteries or foreign missions, the day when abundance of capital will interfere with abundance of output may be postponed."[12]

Near the end of the book, Keynes once more dwelt on the problem of public investment. Only a somewhat comprehensive socialization of investment will secure an approximation to full employment. Manipulation of the rate of interest will not provide the optimum amount of investment; and the effects of a guided tax program on consumption, though helpful, will not of themselves yield full employment.[13]

THE CASE FOR PUBLIC INVESTMENT

Those who are inclined to belittle Keynes' contributions to economics frequently analyze his position merely as one of monetary expansion and deficit financing. Even in his discussions of public investment, however, where monetary expansion and deficit financing are indeed germane, Keynes saw much more than the merely monetary aspects of the problem. Indeed, he had anticipated many of the objections that were later to be raised against public investment.

For example, the increased demand for money following an investment program, he pointed out, would increase the rate of interest and discourage investment unless the authorities took counter measures; and with psychology confused as it was, the government's program, through its adverse effects on confidence, might well stimulate an increase of liquidity preference and diminish the marginal efficiency of capital. Thus, against any rise in public investment it was necessary to expect some decline in private investment.[14] Again, Keynes was aware that at a high

---

[12] *Ibid.*, p. 220.

[13] *Ibid.*, pp. 377–78.

[14] *General Theory*, pp. 119–120; *Macmillan Report*, p. 204; and *Essays in Persuasion*, p. 124, where Keynes seems to underestimate the inflationary potential.

level of employment, with its corresponding low marginal propensity to consume, investment measures would become less and less effective.[15] (Those who would rely exclusively on fiscal measures to eliminate all or virtually all unemployment—e.g., Beveridge's 3 per cent—should keep this point in mind.) At the actual marginal propensity to consume over the years in a modern economic society, fluctuations in employment are large, and the increment of investment which might correct the situation is so large as to preclude easy handling.[16] Keynes also pointed out that, under certain conditions, an investment program might be confronted with inadequate stocks of consumption goods, and inadequate capacity—temporarily at least there would be disinvestment in stocks, rising prices, and increased savings. Finally, the value of the multiplier, K (where the marginal propensity to consume $\frac{\Delta Cu}{\Delta Yu} = 1 - \frac{1}{K}$) would be affected by the extent to which relief was being paid out of taxes or loans, on the degree of "openness" of the economy, on the rise of savings with increasing output and profits, and generally on the changing value of $\frac{\Delta Cu}{\Delta Yu}$ as employment rose. If the system was a relatively open one (e.g., Great Britain) and the dole was being financed by loans, the multiplier might be 2–3; if the system was a closed one, and unemployment was being financed by transfers, then the net effect of a long-investment program on the nation's income would be greater, and the multiplier might be five.[17] By 1936, Keynes (and Kahn) had clearly dealt with the major problems.

It was necessary, in Keynes' view, to plan well ahead.

> The main obstacle in the way of remedying unemployment by means of organized schemes of investment is probably to be found, not so much in any of these arguments, as in the practical difficulties of initiative and organization. It is not easy to devise well-conceived plans on a large scale. It is not easy to fit them into the existing scheme of things, even when they have been conceived, without all sorts of difficulties, frictions, and delays. And, finally, the period of preliminary planning and designing, which must elapse before they will provide their full quota of employment, may be somewhat lengthy. It is difficult to *improvise* good

[15] *General Theory*, p. 127.
[16] *Ibid.*, p. 118.
[17] *Ibid.*, Chap. 10.

schemes. If they are to be thoroughly wise and economical, they may often need as much as two years' preliminary gestation.[18]

In 1931, he was prepared to make concrete proposals: "why not pull down the whole of South London from Westminster to Greenwich," thus providing housing near where the people work, more comfortable buildings, acres of parks and public spaces, "something magnificent to the eye, yet useful and convenient to human life as a monument to our age?"[19]

Though aware of the arguments that could be raised against public investment, Keynes left no doubt concerning his enthusiasm for loan expenditures. The resources out of which an investment program might yield additional employment included the savings on the dole, the putting to use of savings that otherwise would have gone to waste, and capital that would otherwise have gone abroad.[20] In 1933, Keynes showed that the burden of loan expenditures on the Exchequer was not to be taken seriously. Allowing for the saving on the dole, making a conservative estimate of the multiplier and hence of the resulting rise of income, and allowing for the rise of tax receipts with increasing incomes, Keynes found that the benefit to the Exchequer of a loan-expenditure of £3 million would be 1.5 to 2 million pounds sterling. An expenditure on housing of £100 million would yield the Exchequer at least £50 million, a sum substantially more than the subsidies required to render the housing program feasible.[21]

We should not end this section without noting the brilliant attack on existing methods of making work. For a man long out of work, the marginal disutility of labor is necessarily less than the utility of the marginal product. On this assumption, "wasteful" loan expenditure may add to the country's wealth. Keynes notes that wholly wasteful forms of loan expenditure (e.g., the dole) are preferred to partly wasteful forms (e.g., financing of improvements at below the market rate of interest). The most wasteful form of expenditure, i.e., digging gold out of the ground, adds nothing to the wealth of the community, but has the greatest appeal. Yet Keynes concludes that *so long as classical principles stand in the way of something better,* gold digging, burying and

---

[18] *Macmillan Report,* Addendum I, p. 206.
[19] *Essays in Persuasion,* pp. 153–4.
[20] *Essays in Persuasion,* pp. 123–128; cf. also p. 120.
[21] *The Means to Prosperity,* pp. 11–15.

unburying old bottles with banknotes, pyramid building, earthquakes, wars, etc., all will add to the community's wealth.

Ancient Egypt was doubly fortunate, and doubtless owed to this its fabled wealth, in that it possessed *two* activities, namely, pyramid building as well as the search for the precious metals, the fruits of which, since they could not serve the needs of man by being consumed, did not stale with abundance. The Middle Ages built cathedrals and sang dirges. Two pyramids, two masses for the dead, are twice as good as one; but not so two railways from London to York. Thus we are so sensible, have schooled ourselves to so close a semblance of prudent financiers, taking careful thought before we add to the "financial" burdens of posterity by building them houses to live in, that we have no such easy escape from the sufferings of unemployment.[22]

THE CONTENTS OF THIS PART

Above all, Keynes would rid the world of wastage of economic resources resulting from unemployment. He had, therefore, over many years, supported expansive policies. This part of the volume deals with the problems relating to economic trends and fluctuations with which Keynes was concerned. It sets out with an essay by A. G. Hart on expectations, since Keynes' theory of economic trends and stagnation is tied to his theory of the marginal efficiency of capital (roughly, anticipated net income), in turn depending largely on anticipations. Next in turn are Keynes' views on fiscal policy, that decisive corrective of deficiencies and fluctuations in his system. In his essay, Dr. Colm studies this aspect of Keynesian economics; and he well shows how difficult it is to measure the influence of Keynes' writings on public policy.[23] His great influence lay indeed in the widespread use of his approach, in the acceptance of his method of analysis with its emphasis on national income, investment, consumption, and its natural evolution from these concepts to projections, models, and the like. One might be disappointed with the progress made in fiscal flexibility,

[22] *General Theory*, p. 131.

[23] Dr. Smithies, interestingly enough, in a survey of New Deal policies, showed that fiscal gains were incidental before 1938, and that it was not until 1938 that deficit financing was invoked in order to expand demand and achieve recovery. *Cf.* A. Smithies, "The American Economy in the Thirties," *Papers and Proceedings of the American Economic Association*, 1946, pp. 16, 24–27.

in the failure to attain co-operation from state and local governments, in the antagonism aroused between Congress and the Administration associated with the greater independence of the Executive under a flexible economy, and yet be aware of large gains made—and these gains certainly are to be credited to Keynes more than to any one else.

Professor Sweezy presents an admirable survey of Keynes' views on economic maturity—a subject briefly discussed in the introduction to this part of the book. *Inter alia,* he presents the evolution of Keynes' views, the occasion for the shift of emphasis from fluctuations around the general level of activity to the general level itself, the effects on the economy once population ceases to grow and new improvements are not made.

Professor Metzler's chief concern is with Keynes' theory of the cycle. His main point is that Keynes' consumption function provides an easy answer to the problem of why both upward and downward movements are ultimately reversed. Here we have an explanation which does not rest upon limiting factors, e.g., inadequate monetary supplies.

Then, there follow two essays dealing with public investment and the multiplier. Professor Higgins lists the alternative approaches to full employment: rise in private investments or (and) export balance, increase in the propensity to consume, and public loan expenditures; and he then shows why Keynes was inclined to rely primarily on the last two as routes to improved demand. In this essay the reader will also find a discussion of the relative desirability of loan expenditures as against self-liquidating investments, and some advances made on Keynes' analysis of the multiplier.

Professor Goodwin's essay on the multiplier is on a somewhat more technical plane than the other essays in this part. Injection is spending which does not originate in current income; and it is necessary to consider this impulse and its propagation to obtain the final result. Dr. Goodwin shows the manner in which the multiplier concept, as originally applied to public investment, has become in the Keynesian system part of the general concept of income formation. Income is the sum of all past injections, each appropriately discounted. I shall not comment on the many interesting points raised by Dr. Goodwin. He stresses Keynes' failure to deal with the lag between receipt and spending of income, though he himself concludes that there may be no structural lag involved beyond the usual lag between receipt and expenditure of income. In an illuminating analysis, he shows (on various assumptions concerning the lag and the propensity to consume) how long it will require to attain a given impulse from an injection.

CHAPTER XXXI

Keynes' Analysis of Expectations and Uncertainty

By ALBERT G. HART

THE CONCERN of economics with futurity is of course implied in Jevons's famous dictum that "in economics, bygones are forever bygones": the driving force of the economy lies in the future, but in the future as visualized in the present. It is only within the last years of the inter-war period, however, that English-speaking economists have brought into the foreground the problem of anticipations—who formulates them, on the basis of what evidence, and how they are transmuted into plans for action and the plans into operations. This process of bringing anticipations out from between the lines is nowhere more dramatically illustrated than in the work of Keynes. In his *Treatise on Money*, anticipations come in only incidentally in the treatment of special topics. Six years later, in the *General Theory*, expectations are pictured as determining all business decisions and having a substantial role in consumption; while the crucial Book IV, dealing with "The Inducement to Invest," is couched in terms of anticipations throughout.

SUBSTANTIVE CONTRIBUTIONS

Of Keynes' substantive contributions to the analysis of expectations, perhaps the most serviceable is his interpretation of the "speculative motive" for holding money in terms of differences of opinion about future asset values. This line of thinking is already prominent in the *Treatise on Money*, where "bearishness" toward alternative assets is called in to motivate the holding of "savings deposits." Non-cash assets are held by those who expect their prices to rise; those who are "bearish" at existing prices part with their non-cash assets and hold cash.[1] A similar argument is applied in the *General Theory* to "liquidity-preference due to the speculative-motive."[2] The line of questions Keynes here opened up about the process by which particular households and firms select themselves to hold particular pieces of wealth is still far from being worked out.

FORWARD MARKETS

The theory of forward markets, to which Keynes devoted a good deal of work, is of course by its nature a topic in the theory of anticipations. On this topic the version of the *Treatise*[3] apparently satisfied Keynes fairly well; the only new element in the *General Theory* seems to be the rather playful discussion of "own rates of interest" on commodities,[4] which gives a first impression of great freshness and promise but on examination turns out to be a rather back-handed formulation of propositions more readily discussed in terms of "marginal efficiency."

The sheet-anchor of the theory of forward markets in the *Treatise* is a concept of "anticipated normal" price attributed to those dealing in commodities. Keynes evidently thought of this price as quite definite; at one point he states that "the estimate of the normal price . . . was about 14.5 cents per lb." for copper at the end of 1920.[5] In the terminology of Hicks,[6] this view is that price expectations are normally "inelastic" unless for very short periods ahead. From this Keynes inferred that a "crisis" naturally leads to a sharp collapse of both prices and production, after which the pressure of surplus stocks will involve a slow recovery of both prices and production.

This view is correlated with Keynes' impression[7] that in busi-

---

[1] Cash held for this purpose was described in the *Treatise* as "savings deposits"; but (cf. *Treatise*, Vol. I, pp. 250 ff., Vol. II, pp. 7 ff.) we may not infer either that all deposits Keynes would call savings deposits must be held on account of bearishness, nor that Keynes' concept of savings deposits matches the statistical classification so called.

[2] For Keynes' own view of the relations of his earlier and later opinions, see *General Theory*, pp. 169, 173–4.

[3] *Treatise on Money*, Vol. II, pp. 130–47, especially 142–44. The account of "surplus stocks" in relation of spot and future prices, carrying-costs, and productive volume, in *General Theory* (pp. 317–19), is very similar.

[4] *General Theory*, pp. 222–29.

[5] *Treatise on Money*, Vol. II, p. 139.

[6] J. R. Hicks, *Value and Capital* (1939), p. 205.

[7] *General Theory*, p. 314.

ness fluctuations "the substitution of a downward for an upward tendency often takes place suddenly and violently, whereas there is, as a rule, no such sharp turning-point when an upward is substituted for a downward tendency." Here Keynes' normally shrewd observation seems to have been at fault. In the American annals it is easy to find important instances of sharp up-turns in production as well as of smooth down-turns preceding major slumps.[8] Unless Keynes' doctrine of futures markets has much more serious defects than I can put my finger on, it seems to me we are forced to infer that antecedent normal-price standards are seriously disrupted by major slumps, and perhaps no consensus on new standards takes shape till recovery is well advanced.[9]

MARGINAL EFFICIENCY OF CAPITAL

The discussion in the *General Theory*[10] of the "marginal efficiency of capital" explicitly in terms of entrepreneurial expectations did much to emancipate the profession from unacceptable implicit assumptions on capital theory which stood in the way of a really fruitful union between monetary theory and capital theory. In his "notes on the trade cycle,"[11] Keynes explains fluctua-

---

[8] Looking quickly at a graph of the available monthly series of industrial output for the United States (the Federal Reserve series since 1919; the Ayres interpolation of the Thomas series for 1899–1915; the Macaulay "deflated clearings" for 1875–1899; Ayres "business activity" before 1875), one may form a picture of the successive troughs as forming pretty good toeholds for a climber up the icy slope of output expansion, with suitable sharp cuts on the downhill side. The decisive slumps (1873, 1893, 1907, 1920, 1929, 1938) drop away very rapidly. But closer inspection of the steps on the slope shows that the recovery in 1908 comes too quickly to give much room for the climber's toe; while he is likely to stub his toe sharply on the abrupt revivals of 1879, 1897, 1899, 1900–01, 1903–04, 1912, 1915, 1922, 1924, 1933, 1934–36, 1938–39, 1940–41. On the record, sharp down-turns may be described as normal (particularly if one uses the Keynesian doctrine of the "breathing-spell" to account for abrupt drops considerably after the down-turn in 1902 and 1907); but after major slumps, sharp upturns seem more "normal" than smooth ones.

Smooth downturns appear in 1881–82, 1887, ·1890, 1902, 1906–07, 1910, 1923.

[9] Since any *bona fide* calculation on normal prices has to rest on cost estimates, we can scarcely expect such estimates to stay put when the wage-unit is in flux. Frequent references during the 1930's to the normality of prices resembling 1913, and since the war to the abnormality of prices exceeding 1929, may be attributed to a craving to rationalize resistance to future changes.

[10] *General Theory*, pp. 135 ff.

[11] *General Theory*, pp. 313 ff.

tions—and particularly the "crisis," which draws his special attention—primarily in terms of "psychological" shifts in the marginal efficiency of capital.[12]

In this part of his work, Keynes may for once be accused of over-stressing the continuity of theoretical development in using a term with a strong affinity to traditional "marginal productivity" and thus encouraging the economist reader to slip back into regarding "marginal efficiency" as a physical rather than a psychological magnitude. My feeling is that in Keynes (and even more in the thinking of his disciples) the "objective" element in the decline of marginal-efficiency at the downturn is overstressed.[13] Admitting that in particular lines (such as housing in a specified city) an increase of capital stock tends to depress the quasi-rents of units of capital, it must be recognized that often investment opportunity in one line is created by investment in another (as road-building creates opportunities for new housing, and new housing a need for more road-building). So far as I can see, the secular decline of interest in the United States may quite as easily be due to a change in the propensity to over-value given "objective" prospects (would today's entrepreneurs build railway trunk lines to serve a wilderness?) as to any actual progress toward saturation with physical wealth.

FORMATION OF ESTIMATES AND "ANIMAL SPIRITS"

In an economics of expectations, the way in which observable events lead into entrepreneurial estimates is just as important a link in the logical chain as the way in which estimates lead into entrepreneurial decisions and resulting actions. Toward the un-

[12] ". . . . It is an essential characteristic of the boom that investments which will in fact yield, say, 2 per cent in conditions of full employment are made in the expectation of a yield of, say, 6 per cent, and are valued accordingly. When the disillusion comes, this expectation is replaced by a contrary 'error of pessimism,' with the result that the investments, which would in fact yield 2 per cent in conditions of full employment, are expected to yield less than nothing; and. the resulting collapse of new investment then leads to a state of unemployment in which the investments, which would have yielded 2 per cent in conditions of full employment, in fact yield less than nothing." (*General Theory*, pp. 321–22.)

[13] Witness Keynes' diagnosis of 1929 in the United States: "New investment during the previous five years had been, indeed, on so enormous a scale in the aggregate that the prospective yield of further additions was, coolly considered, falling rapidly. Correct foresight would have brought down the marginal efficiency of capital to an unprecedentedly low figure." (*General Theory*, p. 323.)

derstanding of the estimation process, Keynes offers a wealth of incompletely systematized ideas; direct observations of business policy-making, philosophical surmises about the theory of knowledge, and more or less impressionistic deductions from poring over economic annals, are all stirred up together into one savory stew.[14]

Perhaps most valuable of Keynes' contributions on this side is his reminder that the estimate justifying an investment may be the child of the impulse to invest rather than its parent: "Most, probably, of our decisions to do something positive, the full consequences of which will be drawn out over many days to come, can only be taken as a result of animal spirits—of a spontaneous urge to action rather than inaction, and not as the outcome of a weighted average of quantitative benefits multiplied by quantitative probabilities. Enterprise only pretends to itself to be mainly actuated by the statements in its own prospectus, however candid and sincere. . . Thus if animal spirits are dimmed and the spontaneous optimism falters, leaving us to depend on nothing but a mathematical expectation, enterprise will fade and die—though fears of loss may have a basis no more reasonable than hopes of profit had before." [15]

MAJOR DEFICIENCIES

With all his power of insight, Keynes' views of expectations had major deficiencies. Aside from the lack of a theory of estimate-forming, the most important are his failure to confront ex-ante and ex-post reasoning; his neglect of the consequences of disappointment of short-run expectations; his over-willingness to generalize about "securities" (assets in general) without regard to their heterogeneity; and his transformation of the theory of uncertainty into a search for "certainty equivalents."

EX-ANTE VERSUS EX-POST

In view of the intensive journal discussion of the relation between Keynesian and "Swedish" insights, it is needless to labor the point that while Keynes carried on both *ex-ante* and *ex-post* discussions he lost a great deal by failure to integrate them. This

[14] See in particular the Chapter on "The State of Long-Term Expectation," *General Theory*, pp. 147 ff.
[15] *General Theory*, pp. 161–62; see also pp. 150–51.

is tied in with the failure to systematize the theory of the formation of entrepreneurial estimates, which was discussed above.
The meaning of current experience for further anticipations
plainly turns largely on how current experience diverges from
earlier anticipations about it.

NEGLECT OF DISAPPOINTMENT OF SHORT-TERM EXPECTATIONS

Directly related to the failure to confront *ex-ante* and *ex-post*
reasoning is Keynes' readiness to "omit express reference to
short-term expectation, in view of the fact that in practice the
process of revision of short-term expectation is a gradual and
continuous one, carried on largely in the light of realized results;
so that expected and realized results run into and overlap one
another in their influence."[16] The grounds given would sound at
least equally reasonable as grounds for insisting on giving the
subject attention, since they imply the possibility of a cumulative
drift in one direction or another, arising from disappointment of
short-term expectation. Had a systematic inquiry been launched
into the way in which experience alters expectations, this omission
could scarcely have been tolerated.

HETEROGENEITY OF ASSETS

Taking Keynes' work as a whole, very illuminating discussions
can be found touching many sorts of assets—working capital,
surplus (or "liquid") stocks of goods, housing, industrial equipment, equity securities, debt securities, time deposits, and demand
deposits. But at crucial points—particularly in the key chapter
on "Psychological and Business Incentives to Liquidity"[17]—all
assets but debts receivable and cash drop out of sight, and it
seems to be assumed that all propositions which hold for comparisons between cash and debts will also hold for comparisons
between cash and other assets. Since of all assets debts are the
most similar to cash, letting debts represent non-cash assets is
risky; if only one type of non-cash asset is to be analyzed closely
in studying the effects of changes in cash assets, it might be more
prudent to analyze (say) houses.

The Keynesian argument that at some level of interest "liquidity

---

[16] *General Theory*, p. 50.
[17] *General Theory*, pp. 194 ff. [Cf. Lintner's essay below.]

preference becomes absolute"[18] (involving some very interesting and suggestive analyses of expectations regarding long-term interest rates)[19] seems to imply an absolute limit to the extent to which growth of the cash supply can inflate prices. Such a limit must plainly exist for prices of debts of finite maturity, on grounds which do not affect equity assets—namely, the existence of a definite upper limit to the sums of money receivable under debt contracts. But if growth of cash relative to income is capable of affecting the propensity to consume in the slightest degree, it can generate experiences which will justify raising estimates of money receipts from equity assets.

From the Keynesian standpoint, furthermore, the question deserves study whether the allowance for risk which Keynes describes as entering into investment decisions[20] should not be regarded as varying with the liquidity of the potential investor. The chief rational ground for reluctance to risk substantial losses is that an initial loss is likely to shake a firm's credit and thus pull down supplementary losses upon its head.[21] As liquidity grows, loss in one venture becomes less likely to handicap the firm in reaping the gains from its other ventures; so that the value the firm can place upon a potential asset involving chances of both gain and loss will grow if "pure interest" remains constant. Development of this line of analysis would probably narrow the gap between Keynesian and "non-Keynesian" monetary theories.[22]

CERTAINTY EQUIVALENTS

Perhaps the most crucial shortcoming of Keynes' theory of expectations is his attempt to boil down a system of contingent anticipations into what has been called a "certainty equivalent."[23]

[18] *General Theory*, p. 207. Note, however, that Keynes says "virtually absolute," and expresses doubts of the practical likelihood of finding such a point.

[19] *General Theory*, pp. 201–204.

[20] *General Theory*, pp. 144–45, 148–49, and *passim*.

[21] I have presented a moderately detailed analysis of the hazard of one loss involving another, and the effects of this hazard on rational business policy, in *Anticipations, Uncertainty, and Dynamic Planning* (Un. of Chicago Press, 1940), pp. 67 ff.

[22] Plainly the effects of growth in the stock of money will vary widely according to the nature of the chain of transactions producing the growth; but to pursue this question would carry me far outside the range of this paper.

[23] For this Keynes uses the term "expectation": "By [an entrepreneur's] expectation of proceeds I mean . . . . that expectation of proceeds which,

Despite the fact that this same attempt is made by Hicks [24] and Lange,[25] I can only characterize it as fruitless in itself and, worse, as likely to sterilize large areas of monetary theory. The certainty equivalent is a will-o'-the-wisp. Generally speaking, the business policy appropriate for a complex of uncertain anticipations is different in kind from that appropriate for any possible set of certain expectations. Trying to frame monetary theory in terms of certainty equivalents means leaving out the specific reactions to uncertainty—which happen to be of fundamental importance for monetary theory. Furthermore, it leads to absurdities if pressed very far.[26]

The key to the uncertainty problem lies in two characteristics of business planning: (a) the fact that between the present and any future calendar date (except the very nearest) additional information is to be expected, so that estimates for each date improve as the date approaches; (b) the fact that many decisions relating to the output or capital outfit of any future calendar date can be postponed (sometimes costlessly, sometimes at some cost in efficiency) until more information has come in. *Flexibility* (of which liquidity is an aspect) is worth incurring costs for, because it avoids wastage of information accruing between the date of planning and the date for which plans are made.[27] Keynes' oversights in this matter may be traced to a certain vagueness about the content of expectations. Perhaps at this point his intellectual vested interest in the view that probability is an aspect of a proposition in someone's mind, rather than an attribute of a contingent event,[28] got in the way of deeper analysis.

---

if it were held with certainty, would lead to the same behaviour as does the bundle of vague and more various possibilities which actually makes up his state of expectation when he reaches his decision." (*General Theory*, p. 24, *note* [8].) While this term has a background in the terminology of probability, its use in this sense departs both from strict probability usage (since Keynes does not identify his "expectation" with any sort of weighted mean) and also from popular usage.

[24] J. R. Hicks, *Value and Capital*, pp. 124–26.

[25] O. Lange, *Price Flexibility and Employment* (Bloomington, Indiana, 1944), pp. 31–32.

[26] Cf. the paradoxes developed by M. Friedman (in criticizing this point in Lange), AER, September 1946, pp. 627–30.

[27] Cf. my article on "Risk, Uncertainty and the Unprofitability of Compounding Probabilities," reprinted in American Economic Association, *Readings in the Theory of Income Distribution* (Philadelphia, 1946), pp. 547–57.

[28] J. M. Keynes, *Treatise on Probability* (London, 1921), pp. 3–5. It is curious that Keynes did not put more stress on the fact that the proposition

POLICY INFERENCES

On the whole, the policy inferences which Keynesian economists should properly derive from the economics of expectations seem to me to be seriously neglected. The chief exception is the universally stressed proposition that investment cannot be stimulated by depressing consumption, because the demand for investment goods is derived (via anticipations) from consumption markets; but even this is commonly stated in short-hand formulations which leave anticipations as elements between the lines.

In the United States, Keynes' wisdom on the subject of "animal spirits" and investment seems to me to have been grossly undervalued. Of course, economists cannot conscientiously advocate throwing overboard Social Security, progressive taxation, the employee's security against discharge because of political views or union membership, and everything else which offends some conservative opinions, for the sake of making entrepreneurs feel at home in the world. But economists are bound in framing policy recommendations to look out for the adverse effects on investment of uncertainty, as to the boundaries of government enterprise, for example. Our economy will be hard to keep going unless entrepreneurs can find a substantial sphere of operations where they can work with zest and a sense of social approval—other than the operation of trying to influence government agencies set up to control business.

The theoretical vice of leaving the analysis of uncertainty to chase the will-o'-the-wisp of "certainty equivalents" has its counterpart in the field of policy.[29] Reasonable adaptability of policy

---

in question generally deals with a future event, and that the accretion of evidence through time is likely to give the probability of such propositions as "On July 1, 1947, cotton will sell for between 22 and 24 cents a pound" a definite trend toward unity or zero. His chapter on "The Application of Probability to Conduct" (*ibid.*, pp. 307 ff.) is conducted on the assumption that the actor must always operate as if some one of a set of mutually exclusive probable propositions was true. The fact that decision can be postponed—involving both a change in data and a change in the character of possible positive acts—does not enter. Neither does the fact that some actions may be moderately appropriate to many of the possible contingencies, while other actions are highly appropriate to some contingencies and highly inappropriate to others.

[29] Cf. my debate on this subject with Dr. Jacob Mosak, in AER, September, 1945, pp. 531–58; March, 1946, pp. 20–43; September 1946, pp. 532–40.

within a range of reasonably likely situations is more important than perfect adaptation of policy to a "most probable" course of events (which actually is unlikely to come to pass). Economists will be able to give better counsel if they form the habit of analyzing contingencies and designing policies to hedge against uncertainties.

CHAPTER XXXII

Declining Investment Opportunity

By ALAN SWEEZY

1.

"DURING THE nineteenth century, the growth of population and of invention, the opening up of new lands, the state of confidence and the frequency of war over the average of (say) each decade seem to have been sufficient, taken in conjunction with the propensity to consume, to establish a schedule of the marginal efficiency of capital which allowed a reasonably satisfactory average level of employment to be compatible with a rate of interest high enough to be psychologically acceptable to wealth-owners. . . . Today and presumably for the future the schedule of the marginal efficiency of capital is, for a variety of reasons, much lower than it was in the nineteenth century." [1] This means that the problem of maintaining reasonably full utilization of the economic system's capacity is more difficult. We can no longer rely exclusively on the automatic forces of expansion to do the trick.

Keynes does not develop this thesis at any length; a few scattered remarks are all the reader will find. His primary concern in the *General Theory* is to explain the mechanism by which changes in investment expenditure produce changes in the volume of output and employment. For most purposes, the change in investment is given; it comes from outside the system. His analysis of the marginal efficiency of capital merely shows us where to plug in our theory of what determines investment; it does not itself provide us with a theory. For that we have only his general references to the influence of population growth, invention, territorial expansion, and war.

Although not elaborated at any length, Keynes' ideas about

[1] *General Theory*, pp. 307–8.

the long-run factors influencing investment demand, nonetheless, play an important part in shaping his treatment of the problem of income and employment. They determine to a considerable extent what is important and what is not; what is discussed and what is left out. To take one example: it is largely because he has become skeptical of the long-run adequacy of investment demand that Keynes shifts the focus of attention in the *General Theory* from the cyclical variation of the level of employment and income to the level itself. The traditional business cycle approach assumes that full employment is the norm about which activity fluctuates and to which it tends always to return. In the *General Theory*, Keynes abandons the assumption that there is any norm; the system can be in stable equilibrium at widely different levels of employment.

Acceptance of full employment as the norm of economic activity could rest either on the assumption (a) that the system contains automatic corrective forces which compensate for changes in investment, e.g., wages and interest rates; or (b) that investment tends automatically to reach whatever level is necessary for full employment. Ardent believers in laissez faire used to rely chiefly on the former; the *General Theory* so effectively destroyed the basis for their faith that they have been forced to shift to the latter.

2.

The neo-classical school, in which Keynes grew up, was the end-product of a century of almost continuous economic progress and expansion. So accustomed had people become to the appearance of ever larger investment opportunities that they forgot there could be an investment problem. "Is it that we are hearing in Bentham (though writing in March 1787 from 'Chrichoff in White Russia') the voice of nineteenth-century England speaking to the eighteenth? For nothing short of the exuberance of the greatest age of the inducement to investment could have made it possible to lose sight of the theoretical possibility of its insufficiency." [2] Keynes himself was long as much an unconscious victim of this exuberance as his contemporaries. In the *Economic Consequences of the Peace*, for example, he seems about to pose the problem of secular "over-saving." Discussing Europe before the

[2] *Ibid.*, p. 353.

war, he says: "The capitalist classes were allowed to call the best part of the cake theirs and were theoretically free to consume it, on the tacit underlying condition that they consumed very little of it in practice—so the cake increased; but to what end was not clearly contemplated. . . . Saving was for old age or for your children; but this was only in theory—the virtue of the cake was that it was never to be consumed, neither by you nor by your children after you."[3]

From this it would be a small step to ask whether the cake could keep on growing for ever and, if not, what would happen when the capitalists' ingrained habits of saving came into conflict with the diminishing possibilities for further investment. But Keynes did not take that step in the *Economic Consequences*. He was concerned about changes of an entirely different sort: "lest, population still outstripping accumulation, our self-denials promote not happiness but numbers; and lest the cake be after all consumed, prematurely, in war, the consumer of all such hopes. . . . The war has disclosed the possibility of consumption to all and the vanity of abstinence to many. Thus the bluff is discovered; the labouring classes may be no longer willing to forego so largely, and the capitalist classes, no longer confident of the future, may seek to enjoy more fully their liberties of consumption so long as they last . . ."[4] The danger is that we will have, not too much, but too little, saving. Or, if we do go on accumulating, that population will grow so rapidly as to outstrip the increase in the means of subsistence. There is not even a hint here of modern "stagnation" theory.

Much the same is true of the *Tract on Monetary Reform*. "For a hundred years the system worked, throughout Europe, with an extraordinary success and facilitated the growth of wealth on an unprecedented scale. To save and to invest became at once the duty and the delight of a large class. . . . The morals, the politics, the literature, and the religion of the age joined in a grand conspiracy for the promotion of saving. . . .

"The atmosphere thus created well harmonized the demands of expanding business and the needs of an expanding population with the growth of a comfortable non-business class."[5] To the

[3] *Economic Consequences of the Peace*, p. 20.
[4] *Ibid.*, pp. 21–22.
[5] *Monetary Reform*, pp. 9-10.

present-day reader this suggests strongly that a slowing down in the rate of population growth and of business expansion might well disrupt the harmony and lead to serious difficulties. But again Keynes had something else in mind. He was worried not about the slowing down of expansion, but rather about the adverse effect of monetary instability on the confidence of the investing classes. "As in other respects, the nineteenth century relied on the future permanence of its own happy experiences and disregarded the warning of past misfortunes. It chose to forget that there is no historical warrant for expecting money to be represented even by a constant quantity of a particular metal, far less by a constant purchasing power. . . .[6] If we are to continue to draw the voluntary savings of the community into 'investments,' we must make it a prime object of deliberate state policy that the standard of value in terms of which they are expressed, should be kept stable."[7] Keynes still thought that the encouragement of saving should be a major objective of public policy.

In the *Treatise on Money*, the reader gets a few glimpses of declining investment opportunity. At one point in the chapter on "Historical Illustrations," the problem comes briefly into full view: "Great Britain is an old country. . . . The population will soon cease to grow. Our habits and institutions keep us, in spite of all claims to the contrary, a thrifty people, saving some 10 per cent of our income. In such conditions one would anticipate with confidence that, if Great Britain were a closed system, the natural rate of interest would fall rapidly. In the rest of the world, however (though the United States may find herself in the same position as Great Britain much sooner than she expects), the fall in the rate of interest is likely to be much slower. Equilibrium under laissez faire will, therefore, require that a large and increasing proportion of our savings must find its outlet in foreign investment."[8] This is a very clear statement of the "secular stagnation" thesis. The reference to the United States is particularly striking. But it is still no more than an isolated insight, without bearing on the systematic development of the writer's thought.

Nor did the problem of investment opportunity play a significant rôle in Keynes' thinking when, in June, 1934, he wrote a letter

[6] *Ibid.*, p. 11.
[7] *Ibid.*, p. 20.
[8] *Treatise*, p. 188.

to *The New York Times* analyzing the economic situation in the United States and appraising the program of the New Deal.[9] "I see the problem of recovery in the following light: How soon will normal business enterprise come to the rescue? On what scale, by which expedients, and for how long is abnormal government expenditure advisable in the meantime?" He evidently had no doubt that private investment eventually would expand sufficiently to maintain recovery without further help from the government. The problem in 1934 was simply to overcome the obstacles which for the time being stood in the way of expansion. Chief among these obstacles was the perplexity and uneasiness of businessmen, cut loose from their moorings in a strange world of depression and reform; the fact that "many types of durable goods are already in sufficient supply, so that business will not be inclined to repair or modernize plant until a stronger demand is being experienced than can be met with existing plant"; and, finally, the "excessively high cost of building relatively to rents and incomes."

There was no chance that business left to itself would be able to initiate recovery, even if the government abandoned entirely its reform program. Only the actual experience of a larger volume of demand would put business in a position to surmount the obstacles of excess capacity and shattered confidence. Keynes thought it would be necessary for the government to raise its net outlay to $400 million a month and keep it there for at least a year to produce the expansion of demand necessary for full recovery.

Looking back now, with the advantage of our present much more elaborate statistical material, the figure of $400 million a month seems remarkably accurate. It probably would have produced reasonably full employment, though perhaps not so quickly as Keynes thought. But it is by no means so sure that private investment would then have caught on in sufficient volume to make it possible for the government to withdraw its support. Keynes was one of the first to see that the problem might go deeper. As already pointed out, he called attention to the possible long-run inadequacy of investment opportunity in the *General Theory*. The experience of the closing years of the decade made the prob-

[9] *The New York Times*, June 10, 1934. It is to be hoped that this letter will be republished, along with other of Keynes' less easily accessible writings.

lem of investment opportunity loom even larger in his mind. In an article for the *New Republic* in July, 1940, dealing with America's war potential, he said:

> At all recent times, investment expenditure has been on a scale which was hopelessly inadequate to the problem of maintaining full employment; and it is not unlikely that this would have remained true, except temporarily, even if the attendant political considerations had stimulated private-enterprise investment instead of retarding it.[10]

3.

Criticism of the declining investment opportunity, or "secular stagnation," thesis can be classified under three main headings: (1) criticism based on misinterpretation of the thesis itself; (2) disagreement as to the magnitude and timing of the important factors involved; and (3) dissatisfaction with the analysis of how these factors, particularly population growth, exercise their influence on investment.

Critics of the first group have accused Keynes, Hansen, and other "stagnationists" of holding that our economic system has become "decadent," "senile,"[11] that it is no longer capable of advancing to higher levels of output, etc. They then point to the rapid increase in man-hour productivity during the depressed thirties, or to rising output in countries with low rates of population increase by way of refutation. But the criticism misses the mark completely, since neither Keynes nor Hansen ever suggested that our economy had become technically unprogressive or "incapable" of advancing to higher levels of production and well-being. Their point is simply that private investment expenditure may not be adequate to maintain income and employment at satisfactory levels. Their whole analysis is designed to show, moreover, what sort of policies are necessary to compensate for a deficiency in investment expenditure and thus enable us to realize the full benefits of technical progress.

Critics have also represented the "stagnationists" as holding the view that there are "no" further opportunities for private investment. They then have an easy time, of course, proving that this is not so. Science and technology are still creating, and are likely to

[10] "The United States and the Keynes Plan," NR, July 29, 1940.
[11] Because it is liable to misinterpretation of this sort, the word "stagnation" is perhaps an unfortunate one.

Declining Investment Opportunity 431

fail to note is the distinction between "some" and "enough." The
"stagnationists" are worried, not that there will be "no" further
investment opportunities—that would be absurd—but that the
outlets created by technical progress will not be sufficient, in the
absence of population growth and territorial expansion, to maintain full employment of available resources.

No one can, of course, be sure what the impact of technical
change will be. This is particularly true of relatively short periods
of a decade or two. It is quite possible that the effects of a major
technical revolution might be so bunched as to give us an adequate volume of investment expenditure, even in the absence of
any other major outlets, for a considerable number of years. The
introduction of a much cheaper method of building houses or the
rapid application of atomic energy to industrial uses are possibilities that readily come to mind. But it would be foolish to rely exclusively on such developments in formulating policies for the
future. It is quite possible that radical technical changes will be
introduced gradually and that the annual investment expenditure
associated with them will be correspondingly modest.

Much the same applies to investment in economically backward parts of the world, the other great unknown in the investment outlook. No one can be absolutely sure that it will not be
possible for this country to invest five to ten billion dollars a year
in countries like China and India over the course of the next few
decades. But even less can any one confidently predict that it will
be possible. The industrialization of these countries is beset with
many difficulties; their people will also be reluctant to rely too
heavily on foreign capital. We would be rash to count on an outlet
for American capital large enough to absorb a large part of our
full employment volume of saving.

The uncertainties about future investment opportunities being
what they are, it is clearly desirable to keep our policy flexible.
Fortunately, a high degree of flexibility is possible if only we
recognize the nature of the problem and plan ahead of time to
take the appropriate measures as the need may arise. The greatest
danger comes from those who would commit us rigidly to one
single type of policy by insisting that investment will always be
adequate if only the government will leave the economic system
to run by itself.

The third type of criticism stems largely from dissatisfaction with the analysis of investment demand provided by the stagnation school. People particularly have trouble seeing how population growth affects investment. It seems paradoxical that declining population growth should cause unemployment. Fewer workers need fewer jobs and it would seem that we should have less, not more, unemployment. Moreover, how would it help to have more workers added to the labor supply in a depression when there are already plenty of unemployed available to fill any jobs that might open up? Finally, it is asked, why do we need to worry about population growth—or new industries and new methods of production, for that matter—when the existing population needs and wants more of the things we are already producing? Why is there not plenty of scope for investment in meeting more fully the wants of the people who are already here?

Unfortunately, we are still far from having completely satisfactory answers to these questions. The classical economists devoted a good deal of attention to the relation between population growth and capital accumulation, but their analysis, though extremely important for an understanding of the broad relations involved, is too general to provide answers to many of the detailed questions we encounter in connection with the theory of employment.

Keynes never went into the relation between the classical theory of capital accumulation and his own theory of employment and wages. That there is a gap to be filled can be clearly seen if one considers Mrs. Robinson's unsuccessful attempt to criticize the former from the vantage point of the latter in her otherwise excellent *Essay on Marxian Economics.* Marx—following in Ricardo's footsteps—held that "at some periods the stock of capital, which governs the amount of employment offered, catches up upon the supply of labour—real wages tend to rise and profits consequently fall." [12] She criticizes this reasoning on the ground that "an equal proportional rise in all money wages must lead to the same proportional rise in the level of prices of a given rate of output," [13] leaving profits unchanged. The difficulty here is that her criticism is based on a short-run theory of wages, which assumes that the stock of capital equipment remains unchanged, while it is directed at a long-run theory whose whole purpose is to analyze the effect of changes in the stock of capital equipment.

[12] Joan Robinson: *Essay on Marxian Economics* (London, 1942), p. 37.
[13] *Ibid.,* p. 100.

When we allow for additions to capital equipment, it appears, in fact, that the classical conclusion is quite justified.

To simplify the problem, let us suppose there are no new inventions, no shifts in demand, no new resources to exploit; in short, no outlets for, investment except in providing more equipment of existing types and more working capital for the increment of population. If, now, population ceased to grow but people continued to save and entrepreneurs continued to use the savings to acquire more capital equipment, there would soon be a shortage of labor to operate the additional equipment.[14] Entrepreneurs would bid against each other for the existing supply of labor and would thus raise wages and reduce profits. As a result of the shift in the distribution of income, there would be some increase in wage-earners' consumption, accompanied by an equal reduction in spending on non-wage earners' consumption and on capital goods. The prices of the former would rise and of the latter fall until the appropriate amount of labor had been shifted to the production of wage goods. Real wages would thus rise as soon as the necessary readjustment of production had been effected.

Wages would continue to rise and profits to fall until investors became dissatisfied with the reduced rate of return and decided either to stop saving or to hold their savings in liquid form instead of acquiring new capital goods with them. If they chose the latter alternative, they would precipitate a decline in aggregate output and employment. Thus the cessation, or slowing down, of population growth would have been responsible for the appearance of general unemployment.

This analysis shows, incidentally, why it would be impossible in the absence of population growth, new invention, etc., to "invest" in raising the standard of living of the existing population. To maintain investment under such conditions would mean

[14] Right after writing this I had a haircut. In the course of conversation, the barber told me something about his early job experience. His family had come to this country from Canada in 1900. They arrived in North Adams on a Saturday, and the following Monday morning he and his father and two of his sisters went to work in one of the mills. Shortly after that, they were approached by the agent of a Fall River mill who offered to pay their moving expenses and find them a house if they would come to Fall River to work. By way of further illustration of how things were in those days, he added: "Why, over in Adams when they finished Number 3 and Number 4 buildings of the Berkshire Mills, they couldn't find enough people to work in them, and they had to send all the way to Poland to get the people."

duplicating indefinitely textile mills, shoe factories, power plants, etc., of the types already in existence. There would soon be such a glut of capital equipment and such a shortage of labor to operate it as to make further investment unprofitable. It would be possible, of course, to maintain full employment, even in the absence of dynamic investment outlets, by shifting workers from the production of new equipment to its operation, repair, and replacement. The end result would be a one hundred per cent consumption economy; in a sense, perhaps, a "solution" for the investment problem, but scarcely one investors would be satisfied with.

In reality, of course, the process of capital formation and its relation to wages, prices, employment, etc., is far more complex than indicated in the foregoing highly simplified analysis. Many questions remain to be answered; for example, how, if at all, does population growth help to stimulate recovery from depression? [15] But it does seem clear that, given otherwise favorable conditions, population growth widens the scope of profitable investment opportunity, and that the decline in growth, which is characteristic of our present era, is likely to confront us with the long-run problem of adjusting to a lower rate of investment expenditure.

4.

In spite of the relative weakness of investment demand, it is unlikely that we will ever have another depression like 1929–32. People have learned too much about the possibilities of positive social action to sit idly by while paralysis creeps over the economic system. The question for the future is not whether we will have another great depression, but rather what means we will adopt to avoid it. We are familiar with the contrast between the Nazi way and the New Deal way of promoting recovery. Nor do these two exhaust the possibilities. In a complex international situation of the type we are likely to have in the visible future, it would be quite possible to adopt a military solution of the problem without any of the vicious social and racial trappings of the Nazi program. The danger is that, in refusing to recognize and to

[15] Keynes and Hansen have both pointed out that population growth has an effect on the composition of demand which is favorable to investment, especially through the stimulus it gives to building. This might help in initiating recovery from depression. See Keynes: *Eugenics Review*, April, 1937.

be prepared to deal with the problem of inadequate investment demand, we shall drift in that direction without being fully aware of what we are doing.

For the purpose of working out a peaceful domestic solution we are in many respects in a favorable position. We have learned a great deal about the techniques of fiscal and monetary policy. Our present budget is so large and our tax rates so high that we are faced with the pleasant task of reducing both expenditures and taxes to desirable long-run peacetime levels, instead of increasing them as in the pre-war period. Social security, health, housing, education, and public works programs, offer socially valuable spending channels adequate to compensate for any deficiency in private investment expenditure. Our most difficult problems are to achieve a reasonable measure of stability in the wage-price structure and to overcome the present dangerous disposition to abandon all efforts at intelligent planning and control in the economic sphere.

CHAPTER XXXIII

Keynes and the Theory of Business Cycles

By LLOYD A. METZLER

1.

THE PURE THEORY of business cycles was never one of Keynes' primary interests. In this field, as in other branches of economics, he found the practical problems of the day more absorbing than discussions of theory for its own sake. Economic theory was introduced and developed by him only because it seemed to be the best method, and perhaps the only method, of reaching useful conclusions with respect to current problems. On numerous occasions he emphasized that he was not attempting to make a contribution to economic theory, but simply suggesting an answer to a particular economic question. It is a tribute both to Keynes and to the usefulness of sound economic theory that, despite his practical approach and his lack of enthusiasm for pure theory, as such, he made important contributions to many different branches of economic theory. Indeed, it is obvious even at this early date that the innovations which Keynes made in economic theory will far outlive the particular problems which they were designed to solve.

This is no less true of the theory of business cycles than of other branches of economic theory. In the field of economic fluctuations, Keynes' practical outlook led him, to a considerable extent, to confine his discussion to the phase of the cycle which his country, or the world, was experiencing at the time he was writing. If high employment prevailed and prices were rising, he emphasized the factors which cause a boom to turn into a slump, and suggested measures to keep employment and output at a high level. Likewise, in periods of depression, the causes of a cumulative downward spiral, and the economic forces which govern the length of this downward movement, were his main concern. Whether there is any regularity in the sequence of events from prosperity to crisis to depression and to revival was a question of secondary interest to Keynes. He did not, however, share the view of some of his followers that the theory of cycles, in the strict sense of the expression, had been outmoded by the theory of employment. He continued to believe that fluctuations of economic activity occur with some regularity, and that this regularity can be explained on economic grounds. "We do not . . . merely mean by a *cyclical* movement," he said, "that upward and downward tendencies, once started, do not persist for ever in the same direction but are ultimately reversed. We mean also that there is some recognizable degree of regularity in the time-sequence and duration of the upward and downward movements."[1]

In attempting to explain this regularity, Keynes did not work out anything as complete as a self-contained theory of cycles. In the unsettled and disturbing state of world economic affairs during the inter-war period, practical problems were far too numerous and far too urgent to permit a man of his inclinations the luxury of anything like a complete theory of fluctuations. Moreover, the pure theory of business cycles is a subject which appeals particularly to economists with mathematical aptitude, and Keynes showed only slight inclination toward this type of rigorous analysis. It is not surprising, therefore, that his contribution to the theory of business fluctuations consisted more in the stimulus which he gave to the work of other economists than in his own direct contribution. Keynes' own contribution should not be overlooked, however, for it will be shown later that he had a considerable insight into the later developments of business cycle theory, even though he himself did not work them out fully.

I have attempted to show elsewhere that Keynes was largely responsible for at least two fundamental changes in the theory of business cycles.[2] Both changes were closely associated with the concept of a propensity to consume. The first fundamental change was in the definition of the "normal" or "equilibrium" level of economic activity, about which the economic system tends to fluctuate. The equilibrium of income was defined, in Keynes' theory of employment, as the level of income at which intended

---

[1] *General Theory*, p. 314.

[2] "Business Cycles and the Modern Theory of Employment," AER, June, 1946. Parts of the present chapter are taken from this paper.

. savings are equal to non-induced investment.[3] While this definition of equilibrium presented a number of serious statistical
problems, such as the difficulty in distinguishing between induced
and non-induced investment, it nevertheless represented an important advance in the theory of business cycles. Just how important it was can be seen by considering the concepts of equilibrium which prevailed before Keynes' theory of employment was
developed. The pre-Keynesian concepts of equilibrium were of
two sorts. First, a purely empirical concept was used, and business cycles were defined as fluctuations about some statistically-
determined smooth curve. The inadequacy of this definition of
equilibrium is apparent from the long and fruitless controversies
which appeared in the economic journals concerning the type of
trend line which should be used for this purpose. It is now apparent that no amount of statistical manipulation can succeed in
separating trend movements from business cycles unless an adequate theory of an economic norm is provided. The second concept of an economic norm to be found in traditional works on
business cycles is the concept of full employment; before publication of the *General Theory,* the usual assumption among the
more analytically-minded economists was that the economic system tends automatically toward a state of full employment, and
that any deviation from this norm represents merely a temporary
state of disequilibrium. This definition of equilibrium has frequently been in such violent contradiction with economic experience that one wonders how it survived for so long. In view of the
shortcomings of both of the traditional concepts of the normal
level of economic activity, the concept of equilibrium presented
by Keynes must be regarded as a major contribution to the theory
of business cycles.

The second important contribution of Keynes' theory of employment to business cycle analysis was in the explanation of
turning points of the cycle. Prior to the development of the concepts of propensity to consume and propensity to save, an explanation of these turning points was perhaps the most difficult
task of business cycle analysis. The traditional theory usually
assumed that the economic system was inherently unstable, in
the sense that a slight upward or downward movement of income
and employment tended to initiate a cumulative and self-reinforc-

---

[3] Although the condition of equilibrium was not stated by Keynes in precisely these terms, it was later interpreted in this manner.

ing process of expansion or contraction. In other words, it was commonly believed that an initial increase of income, employment, and prices would stimulate a further increase, and that income would continue to rise at an accelerated rate until the limits of possible expansion were reached, or until some outside force put a stop to the cumulative process.[4] The converse of this argument is, of course, that a slight downward movement is also self-aggravating, and that a depression, once started, tends to continue until some factor or factors which operate only at low levels of employment reverse the movement. Thus traditional business cycle theory conceived of the economic world as a world subject to cumulative upward and downward movements as a result of relatively small disturbances. From this conception, it followed that an explanation of the cycle was to be found in the factors which reverse the direction of the cumulative movement. Once a process of expansion or contraction was started, it was widely believed that an explanation of further movements in the same direction was relatively simple. In an expansion process, for example, the rise of income was believed to be reinforced by optimistic expectations as well as by the effect of higher demand upon the output of investment goods (the acceleration principle). And since Say's Law (supply creates its own demand) was generally accepted, it was difficult to see how producers' expectations, in the aggregate, could be disappointed. While particular industries might suffer from over-production, this would be offset by increased demand in other industries. The cumulative movement of income and prices was thus regarded as an obvious process; the real difficulty lay in the explanation of the turning points.[5]

To explain how a process of expansion is stopped and a depression initiated, economists usually introduced certain limiting factors which become operative only at high levels of economic activity. It was frequently asserted, for example, that a period of prosperity and rising income is brought to a close by the inability of the banking system to make additional loans. Faced with a declining reserve ratio as a result of previous loans and as a result

[4] The classic example of such an unstable economy is given by Wicksell, in his description of the cumulative change in prices which results from a discrepancy between the money rate of interest and the bank rate. See Knut Wicksell, *Interest and Prices* (translated from the German by R. F. Kahn, London, 1936), Chap. 9.

[5] Compare J. Tinbergen, "Econometric Business Cycle Research," RES, Volume VII, 1940.

of cash drains to support a higher volume of transactions, the banks become reluctant to make further loans. Interest rates rise, and a period of credit contraction ensues. By reducing the level of total demand for goods, this credit contraction brings all of the forces of cumulative contraction into play, and the level of output declines. Thus, according to this view, the immediate cause of the crisis was held to be the inflexibility of the banking system. Alternatively, the cause of the downturn was frequently found in a shortage of certain factors of production which made a continuation of the expansion process impossible. If the rise of output in certain segments of the economy was brought to a halt through the development of bottlenecks, it was frequently believed that this would lead to a decline in total output, through the operation of the acceleration principle.

At the other turning point, when depression ends and a revival begins, economists were much less certain about the immediate cause of revival. In some cases the upturn was attributed to a resumption of investment activity induced by an accumulated shortage of equipment. In other cases, more liberal lending policies by the banking system were believed to be the immediate cause of recovery. And in still other cases, the revival was attributed simply to a return of business confidence and to more optimistic expectations in general. But whatever the immediate cause of revival, the important fact is that in traditional business cycle theory it was thought to be necessary to introduce limiting factors which brought the period of cumulative contraction to a close.

After Keynes' *General Theory* was published, these limiting factors—bottlenecks, limits to bank expansion, etc.—lost much of their importance as explanations of the turning points of the cycle. As soon as the consumption function was introduced as a central feature of economic models, it was immediately recognized that a cumulative process of expansion may not be self-reinforcing but instead may inevitably lead to a crisis and a period of contraction even before the physical or financial limits to expansion have been reached. The crisis and subsequent depression, in the modern theory, are attributable not to the limits imposed by the banking system but to the fact that, as income is increased, the demand for consumers' goods does not increase to the same extent. Thus the explanation of the upper turning point, in modern business cycle theory, is intimately related to

Keynes' consumption function. The consumption function plays an equally important part in accounting for the lower turning point; the cumulative downward movement cannot continue indefinitely, for the simple reason that a given reduction of income is associated with a smaller reduction in the demand for consumers' goods.

In older theories of business cycles, the stabilizing influence of consumption upon the cumulative processes of expansion and contraction was not recognized, for the tacit assumption was usually made that a given change in output creates a corresponding change in the demand for this output. This acceptance of Say's Law gave an exaggerated appearance of instability to the economic system, and made it necessary to introduce limiting factors to explain the turning points of the cycle. Keynes' theory of employment changed all this by showing that the turning points of the cycles, like the periods of expansion and contraction, are inherent in the structure of production and sales. This was a considerable advance, not only in the theory of economic fluctuations but in economic policy as well, for it indicated why monetary and banking policy, by themselves, are inadequate stabilizers of the economic system. It also explained why a period of prosperity and rising economic activity frequently leads to a crisis and to depression before a condition of full employment has been attained, and before the effects of bottlenecks, shortages of credit, etc., have become apparent. Although Keynes did not participate directly in the development of business cycle theory subsequent to the *General Theory*, it will be shown later that he was fully aware of the direction this development would take, and, as in so many other fields, he anticipated, in a general way, a substantial part of the new theory.

2.

In order to illustrate Keynes' influence upon the theory of business cycles, two examples will be given of the relation between the propensity to consume and economic fluctuations. The first example is taken from the modern theory of inventory cycles, while the second deals with the acceleration principle.

The classic example of a pre-Keynesian theory of inventory cycles is that of R. G. Hawtrey.[6] Although Hawtrey attributes more significance to inventory fluctuations than most economists,

[6] R. G. Hawtrey, *Trade and Credit* (1932), Chap. 5.

his theory is typical of other theories of the pre-Keynesian era in that it describes the cycle as a sequence of unstable processes of cumulative expansion and contraction, and attributes the reversal of these processes to limiting factors which become operative only at high or low levels of output and employment. The essential feature of Hawtrey's theory, as of most other theories of the time, is an acceptance of Say's Law. Hawtrey assumed, in other words, that when output is increased or decreased, an equivalent increase or decrease occurs in the effective demand for this output.

With this conception of demand, it is easy to see how a small disturbance may start a cumulative process of expansion or contraction. Suppose, for example, that business men decide to increase their inventories. In order to do so, they must produce more than they expect to sell. But in expanding output, the business men also expand income by the same amount. Hawtrey argues that this increase of income is either spent on consumption or saved, and that most, if not all, of the added savings constitute a demand for capital goods. Considering both the demand for investment goods and the demand for consumers' goods, total demand therefore increases at an equal rate with the increase of income. As a result, producers find that their attempt to increase inventories has been frustrated by a corresponding increase in demand. Their subsequent production plans include not only a level of output sufficient to satisfy the higher demand, but also an additional output for inventories. Again, however, demand is increased by the higher level of output, and inventories remain low despite attempts to increase them. Thus a cumulative process of expansion is set in motion, and continues as long as business men attempt to increase their inventories.

A similar argument is applicable to the process of contraction. When business men attempt to *reduce* inventories by producing less than they expect to sell, they find that their total sales are correspondingly reduced, and inventories remain unchanged. "The dealers want to diminish their stocks of goods, but, when they restrict the orders they give to producers, the consumers' outlay falls off, and their sales are so reduced that their stocks are little diminished." [7]

Unqualified acceptance of Say's Law thus leads to a conception of the economy as an unstable system in which a slight contraction leads to further contraction, and a slight expansion sets off

[7] R. G. Hawtrey, *op. cit.*, p. 93.

a cumulative upward movement. In Hawtrey's opinion, these periods of expansion and contraction are brought to a close by changes in the credit policy of the banking system. During a period of rising income and prices, the banks find their cash reserves diminished both by an increase in deposits and by a drain of cash into circulation. Hawtrey argues that sooner or later the reduction of their reserves forces the banks to restrict credit. This means, among other things, that interest rates tend to rise, and with higher interest rates the carrying costs of inventories are considerably increased. Traders attempt to economize by reducing their inventories, and, as a result, the cumulative process of contraction described above is set in motion. During the period of contraction, debts are gradually liquidated, bank deposits are reduced, and cash flows back into the banks as a consequence of the decline in income and prices. Eventually the increased liquidity of the banking system leads to lower interest rates and to more liberal lending policies in general. Finding their carrying costs reduced, traders decide to hold more inventories, and a period of economic expansion ensues.

The foregoing is a brief description of the theory of inventory cycles which prevailed prior to the publication of the *General Theory*. In order to see how profoundly Keynes has influenced the theory of inventory cycles, it is only necessary to substitute his propensity to consume for Say's Law in the preceding description. It then becomes immediately apparent that, in the expansion phase of the cycle, inventories may reach a normal level, and income may therefore decline, even without the intervention of the banking system and without the appearance of any significant shortages. Likewise, when income is contracting and producers are attempting to reduce their stocks, a point will eventually be reached where stocks have reached a normal level; at this point, the depressing effects of business attempts to reduce stocks will cease, and income will begin to rise even without a change in bank policy or a change in what producers regard as normal stocks.

Consider first the expansion phase of the cycle. Suppose this phase is initiated by a decision on the part of producers to increase their inventories. As output is increased, income in the hands of consumers also rises, and a cumulative expansion is thus set in motion. The expansion cannot continue indefinitely, however, and it may be stopped far short of full employment, for the marginal propensity to consume shows that total demand increases less than the value of output. Inventories therefore gradually accumulate, although the increase in stocks, for a time at least, is less than the amounts which producers wish to add to their supplies. Eventually a point is reached at which stocks are normal, in relation to sales. At this point, producers plan no further production for stock, and total output begins to decline. Thus the upper turning point of the cycle may be explained, using Keynes' consumption function, without considering the action of the banking system.

It should be apparent, also, that the lower turning point of the cycle may be explained in a similar manner. In the early stages of the depression, output exceeds sales and inventories accumulate. Later, in attempting to get rid of these excess stocks, producers force output and employment below the level appropriate to the level of other types of investment. Since consumption normally declines less than income, however, inventories will eventually be reduced, despite the decline in demand, and will reach a level which producers regard as normal in relation to their sales. Thereafter, the fact that business men no longer find it necessary to reduce inventories will cause output to rise and the expansion phase of the cycle will begin.

The cycle just described is distinguished from the pre-Keynesian inventory cycle primarily by its self-perpetuating character. Inventory cycles, in the modern theory, are *inherent* in the structure of production and sales, whereas the traditional view envisaged the turning points as a result of credit policies and cost changes which become operative only in the extremes of prosperity and depression. In the traditional theory of inventory cycles, the length of a period of expansion was thought to be governed largely by the flexibility of the banking system and by the extent of unemployment when the expansion began; the expansion was not brought to a close until the banks were forced to restrict credit. In the modern theory, on the other hand, it is necessary to explain the length of the average cycle in terms of factors which are a part of the process of production and sales. While changes in banking policy may play some part in the turning points of the cycle, much greater emphasis is placed, in the modern theory, upon the relation of output to sales, and upon the relation of sales to production plans.

The reduced emphasis upon the influence of the banking system which is apparent in the foregoing discussion of inventory cycles is characteristic, also, of other recent developments in the theory of business cycles. An outstanding example is the theory of the relation of the acceleration principle to the cyclical process. According to this principle, the demand for certain types of producers' goods depends upon the *rate of change* of total output. For this reason, when output is rising the demand for producers' goods may nevertheless decline, simply because the rate of increase of total sales begins to fall. While this theory explains why cycles in producers' goods may precede cycles of economic activity in general, it is not, by itself, a complete theory of the cycle, for it does not explain why the rate of increase of consumers' demand begins to fall. In other words, the acceleration principle explains how the demand for producers' goods depends upon the demand for final output, but it does not go beyond this point to show how final output depends upon the level of activity in the producers' goods industries.

In attempting to develop a self-contained theory of fluctuation which included the acceleration principle as an important element, economists were frequently thwarted, in the years before the appearance of the *General Theory*, by explicit or implicit acceptance of Say's Law. As in the case of inventory cycles, the economic system built upon the acceleration principle seemed to be inherently unstable. If demand for consumers' goods were increased, for example, this led to an increased demand for producers' goods, and, if Say's Law were accepted, the rise in output of producers' goods should induce a corresponding increase in demand for consumers' goods. This, in turn, was assumed to be the cause of a further increase in demand for producers' goods, and thus the cumulative upward spiral was started. Prior to the development of Keynes' theory of employment, the acceleration principle thus seemed to account, in part, for the cumulative character of economic expansion and contraction, but failed to account for the turning points of the cycle.

Six years before the *General Theory* was published, the problem was stated by J. M. Clark as follows:

We have, then, a problem of mutually interacting forces, returning upon each other in a vicious circle of cumulative disturbance. Viewed from this angle, the challenging problem is not why there are cyclical fluctuations but why there is a limit to the fluctuations short of zero, on the one side, or the full capacity of existing productive equipment, on the other. *If there is a determinate limit short of these ultimates, it would seem that it can most easily be explained on the assumption that consumers' expenditures fluctuate less than does the income derived from productive activity.*[8]

From the italicized part of this quotation, it is evident that Clark foresaw the direction which business cycle theory was to take. It was apparent to him, even in 1932, that Say's Law was responsible for the unstable nature of economic models containing the acceleration principle. Nevertheless, it was not until Keynes had developed the notion of a consumption function that the true significance of the acceleration principle for the theory of business cycles became apparent. As soon as Say's Law was abandoned, and the consumption function was substituted in its place, it became possible to explain why the expansion process might lead to a crisis and downturn before the full limits of economic activity had been achieved. The process of expansion may come to a halt for the simple reason, which Clark stated, that the increase in consumers' expenditures is normally smaller than the increase of income.

With the aid of Keynes' consumption function, a theory of economic oscillations containing the acceleration principle as a central feature was readily developed. The new theory, or the synthesis of an old theory with Keynes' theory of employment, was first suggested by Harrod[9] and later presented in a more rigorous form by Hansen[10] and Samuelson.[11] Space does not permit a detailed discussion, here, of the relation between the propensity to consume and the acceleration principle. In any event, the important point, for present purposes, is that introduction of Keynes' consumption function into the theory of acceleration enabled economists to explain the turning points of general economic activity without resorting to limiting factors. In other words, just as in the case of inventory cycles, a genuine theory of business cycles was substituted for a theory of a cumulative

[8] J. M. Clark, "Capital Production and Consumer Taking: a Further Word," JPE, October, 1932, p. 693. Italics added.
[9] R. F. Harrod, *The Trade Cycle* (Oxford, 1939).
[10] A. H. Hansen, *Fiscal Policy and Business Cycles* (New York, 1941), Chap. 12.
[11] P. A. Samuelson, "A Synthesis of the Principle of Acceleration and the Multiplier," JPE, December, 1939.

process. And again, in making this substitution it became apparent that the inflexibility of the banking system was less important as an explanation of the turning points of the cycle than had previously been supposed.

3.

Although Keynes did not participate directly in these developments of business cycle theory, he nevertheless had a considerable insight into the direction the new theory would take, and the change in point of view which resulted from substituting his consumption function for Say's Law is clearly evident in his own writing. In his *Treatise on Money*, he attributes a major rôle to the banking system in the explanation of the upper turning point of the cycle. In the *General Theory*, on the other hand, changes in bank policy have a much less important part. The crisis and subsequent collapse, in the later work, are attributed primarily to a sudden change in expectations—a shift in the marginal efficiency of capital. ". . . we have been accustomed," he says, "in explaining the 'crisis' to lay stress on the rising tendency of the rate of interest under the influence of the increased demand for money both for trade and speculative purposes. At times this factor may certainly play an aggravating and, occasionally perhaps, an initiating part. But I suggest that a more typical, and often the predominant, explanation of the crisis is, not primarily a rise in the rate of interest, but a sudden collapse in the marginal efficiency of capital." [12] This view represents a substantial departure from the view expressed in the *Treatise on Money*, and it is a departure, as we have seen, which is justified to a considerable extent by the substitution of the consumption function for Say's Law. Thus Keynes was fully aware of the direction which his theory of employment would give to the theory of business cycles.

An even better indication of his insight into subsequent developments may be found in his discussion of the length of a depression. In the traditional theory of business cycles, the explanation of the lower turning point of the cycle always seemed more difficult than the explanation of the upper turning point. While limits to an expansion process could be explained, in part, in terms of the activities of the banking system, the effects of bottlenecks, and the influence of labor shortages upon the relation between prices and costs, none of these processes, in reverse,

[12] J. M. Keynes, *General Theory*, p. 315.

seemed adequate to explain the limits to a period of contraction. To a considerable extent, the problem of the length of a depression therefore remained an unsolved problem. In the *General Theory*, Keynes explained the length of the depression in terms of two factors, the length of life of durable assets and the time required to work off excess inventories.

> The explanation of the *time element* in the trade cycle, of the fact that an interval of time of a particular order of magnitude must usually elapse before recovery begins, is to be sought in the influences which govern the recovery of the marginal efficiency of capital. There are reasons, given firstly by the length of life of durable assets in relation to the normal rate of growth in a given epoch, and secondly by the carrying-costs of surplus stocks, why the duration of the downward movement should have an order of magnitude which is not fortuitous, which does not fluctuate between, say, one year this time and ten years next time, but which shows some regularity of habit between, let us say, three and five years.[13]

Keynes argued that the recovery could not begin until the marginal efficiency of capital had been restored, and that this could not occur until the supply of capital had been reduced through depreciation and through liquidation of excess inventories. In contrast with the view of Hawtrey, he believed that a reduction of inventories could occur without setting off an unstable, cumulative, downward movement of income. Since Keynes had rejected Say's Law, it was apparent to him that an attempted reduction of business stocks would not reduce demand by an equivalent amount, and that business men could therefore succeed eventually in disposing of excess stocks despite the decline in demand. Likewise, with respect to plant and equipment, it was evident to Keynes that an attempted disinvestment would not cause an equivalent reduction of effective demand, and that a balance between final demand and the amount of machinery and equipment required to produce this level of demand might therefore be achieved short of a complete collapse. The length of the cycle, in Keynes' later view, was therefore largely determined by technical conditions, such as the length of life of durable goods, which governs the time required to reduce the amount of capital, and the carrying costs of business inventories,

[13] *Ibid.*, p. 317.

which determine, to some extent, the willingness of business men to hold excess stocks.

These ideas, which Keynes mentioned almost incidentally, were later developed, as we have seen, into more detailed and more complete theories of economic fluctuations. In place of a single cycle, however, the later theories found at least two cycles, a short cycle dependent upon inventory fluctuations, and a longer cycle dependent upon fluctuations in the demand for plant and equipment. It would be a considerable exaggeration to say that Keynes foresaw all of these later developments, or that the *General Theory* contained anything like a complete theory of business cycles. It would also be a mistake to assert that the later cycle theories based upon Keynes' work provide an entirely satisfactory explanation of economic fluctuations. Nevertheless, it is apparent from the foregoing discussion that Keynes' consumption function filled a serious gap and corrected a serious error in the prevailing theory of business cycles, and that Keynes himself was aware of the importance which his new theory of consumption might have in later discussions of business cycles.[14]

[14] [Cf. Hart's essay above, in which he discusses the turning points and marginal efficiency of capital, and A. F. Burns, *Economic Research and the Keynesian Thinking of Our Times* (NBER, 1946), pp. 20–21.]

CHAPTER XXXIV

Fiscal Policy

By GERHARD COLM

KEYNES' INFLUENCE ON U. S. FISCAL POLICY

It is almost impossible to think of fiscal policy, as it is understood in the modern world, without thinking of John Maynard Keynes, and particularly the *General Theory*. In fact, he gave the concept of fiscal policy a new meaning and the operations of government finance a new perspective. It is perhaps not going too far to say that Keynes thought of the survival of liberal capitalism in terms of fiscal policy correctly understood and boldly carried out.

Keynes has contributed to fiscal policy in a direct and indirect manner. He has made a number of practical recommendations with respect to policies in this country as well as in his own country, but what is more important, he has greatly stimulated thinking.

Nevertheless, it is difficult to appraise at this time what direct influence Keynes, through his books, pamphlets, and talks, had on the actual policies of depression finance, war finance, and postwar policies in this country.

Of his specific recommendations the best known are the advocacy of government deficit spending during the depression of the thirties,[1] and of "deferred pay" or forced savings during the war.[2] He also proposed heavy reliance on progressive income and inheritance taxation as a long-range fiscal policy.[3] Policies resembling all these proposals have been adopted in this country.

---

[1] *The Means to Prosperity*, 1933; and "An Open Letter to President Roosevelt," December 31, 1933, NYT.

[2] *How to Pay for the War; A Radical Plan for the Chancellor of the Exchequer* (1940).

[3] *The General Theory of Employment, Interest and Money*, 1936.

The connection between them and Keynes' writings is difficult to establish, however. For example, at least until the recession of 1937–38, Government deficits were more the unintentional results of policies designed to give direct relief to farmers, home owners, business, and unemployed workers, than the conscious aim of a recovery policy through deficit spending. It is likely that, without a line written by economists on deficit spending, we would have had the same policy. Only when the recession occurred in the fall of 1937 was a comprehensive recovery program formulated and discussed by a top Government committee on monetary and fiscal policy. This program, which was, broadly speaking, in line with Keynes' recommendations for a national investment policy, never became reality because of congressional disapproval.[3a]

Keynes' "deferred pay" proposal for war finance was adopted in Great Britain to a minor extent. So far as I know, its author never publicly recommended that the same policy be applied in the United States. Nevertheless, a compulsory savings plan was proposed to President Roosevelt by members of his official family. It was suggested that compulsory saving would permit the adoption of stiffer rates than otherwise would be acceptable; thereby it would help in the curtailment of wartime purchasing power and would help in the control of wartime savings during the inflationary reconversion period. The President's Budget Message of January 6, 1943, included a reference to such a program as a possible alternative to additional taxes. However, no specific proposal was transmitted to or adopted by Congress. The compulsory savings feature of the excess profits tax might have been indirectly influenced by Keynes' proposals, although he himself did not propose such a scheme.

The debate on postwar policies, specifically on Senator Murray's original Full Employment Bill, centered to some extent around the merits of a policy of deficit spending in combatting unemployment. The bill, in its original version, provided for Government investments in case private business investments dropped below the amount necessary to sustain full employment. Opponents who feared a possible misuse of this approach proposed a provision that Government budgets must be balanced over the years as a general rule. In the final compromise both provisions were eliminated and the formulation of policy recom-

[3a] See *Message of the President to the Congress*, April 14, 1938.

mendations is left to the President, assisted by a Council of Economic Advisers, and to a joint congressional committee.

Thus it appears that Keynes' specific recommendations have not been adopted as a deliberate United States policy during the depression, during the war, or with respect to the postwar period.

Yet it would be highly superficial and misleading if these facts were accepted as the final answer to the question of Keynes' contribution to fiscal policy in the United States. While his specific proposals were not adopted, his general approach and his methods for analyzing and appraising fiscal measures had an effect on the general discussion of policies that can hardly be overestimated.

Boiled down to the simplest statement, it can be said that Keynes regarded unemployment as the result of disproportions between the desire to save and the desire to invest savings in income-creating ventures. A desire to save more than is currently being invested is, according to Keynes, likely to characterize an advanced capitalist economy, in which incomes are high on the average and capital accumulation is already large. An excess of intended savings over investment will cause a contraction of incomes and employment which may develop into a downward spiral. However, as income falls, the proportion which persons wish to save declines. When intended savings comes into balance with investment, the downward movement stops. Equilibrium may well be reached considerably below full employment of available resources, however; and from this Keynes concludes the need for compensatory Government action.

Classical theory, on the other hand, suggested that depressions are caused by "frictional" disproportions between prices and costs. Disproportions develop under conditions of relative scarcity of labor and capital during the boom and must be adjusted in and through the depression. The depression not only cushions but eliminates the causes of frictional disturbances and prepares the ground for a new upswing. This theory therefore suggests an attitude of laissez faire.

During the thirties, popular confidence in the self-healing capacity of the capitalistic system was at its lowest point. Keynes' work provided a theoretical support for popular belief which left classical theory discredited by the scholarly criticism of one of the most outstanding of the world's economists, as well as by the practical experience of the great depression. The fact that the

Employment Act of 1946 in the United States, and similar policy declarations in Great Britain, Canada, and other countries, found so little basic opposition (as distinct from the very vocal criticism of specific policy recommendations) can, I believe, be largely attributed to this theoretical as well as practical disrepute of the laissez-faire doctrine.

In order to realize the basic change in the general thinking in fiscal policy, it is useful to remember, as an example, that Congress in 1932, faced with the effect of the depression on Federal finances, increased the tax rates on individual and corporate incomes. The Ways and Means Committee voted for a manufacturers' excise tax. I do not think that in case of another severe depression now, fifteen years later, Congress would consider tax increases as the most appropriate measure. During these last fifteen years not only professional economists, but also political leaders and many laymen, have learned to consider the effects of Government finance on the economy as a whole. Fiscal policy has even become a topic for political campaign speeches. It is impossible to measure the effect of Keynes' theory in this respect. No doubt the practical experience of the depression and of war finance are mostly responsible for this change in attitude. I am inclined to believe, however, that the new developments in economic theory had a very significant though indirect effect.

KEYNES' THEORY OF ECONOMIC DYNAMICS AND
HIS FISCAL POLICY RECOMMENDATIONS

Keynes did not discuss matters of public finance *per se.* He looked at public finance as one of the instruments of a policy designed to influence employment and income. By using the term "fiscal policy" rather than the conventional "public finance," Keynes apparently intended to indicate that he was concerned only with one aspect of public finance. I do not believe that Keynes ever gave a formal definition of fiscal policy, although he certainly was one of the authors who helped to introduce, or rather reintroduce, this term into modern usage. A working definition of fiscal policy can, I believe, be derived from Keynes' writings. He used the term "fiscal policy" when referring to the influence of taxation on savings, and of Government investment expenditures financed by loans from the public. He looked at fiscal policy as one form of "State action as a balancing factor." [4]

[4] *General Theory*, p. 220.

Thus for the purpose of an interpretation of Keynes' thought, we might define fiscal policy as a policy that uses public finance as a balancing factor in the development of the economy. Then, of course, it becomes necessary to analyze why Keynes believed there was a possible lack of balance in the economy that must and can be balanced by public finance measures.

Although other chapters of this book deal intensively with Keynes' general theory, I must summarize, at least in simplified form, those essential aspects of it that have a bearing on fiscal policy. Thereby I shall focus only on the (perhaps few) dynamic elements in the theory.

Autonomous decisions to invest in privately owned capital goods or the Government plant are, according to Keynes, the main factors determining the level of income and employment. An autonomous change in investment, when there is unemployment, causes a change in income and employment which is larger than the initial movement; the relationship between cause and effect is determined by a "multiplier" which in turn is determined by the marginal "propensity to consume." Under the institutional arrangements of the capitalistic economy there is no mechanism that induces investments of just that amount necessary to maintain full employment of all available resources. Investments may be so large as to create an inflationary pressure or so low as to result in chronic unemployment. Classical economics (with few exceptions) regarded full employment as the "natural" state of affairs and had to look for specific historical causes for explaining actual under-employment. From Keynes' analysis, it follows that the economy may be in equilibrium in either a high or low level of employment, so that continuing full employment of all resources can be explained only by reference to specific historical circumstances.

As a matter of hypothesis (not as an absolute truth), Keynes stated his belief that in the modern economy equilibrium tends to be established considerably below the full-employment level unless Government intervenes as a "balancing factor," offsetting the depressive tendencies.

These assumed historical developments include, first, a declining marginal efficiency of capital. This tendency would not necessarily militate against a sufficient amount of investments, if the interest rate could decline as much as the marginal efficiency of capital. The interest rate, however, can not sink below a minimum determined by consumers' liquidity preference and by institutional factors. (No criticism of Keynes' theory of interest rate is intended here.)

The second factor is Keynes' hypothesis that "as real income increases, both the pressure of present needs diminishes and the margin over the established standard of living is increased."[5] This psychological proposition is essentially static in character, as the reference to *"established* standard of living" indicates. But it has been interpreted to imply that as income rises the ratio of consumption to savings falls. An increase in investment at a high level of income would consequently have a less stimulating effect on consumption than at a lower level. On the other hand, the declining marginal efficiency of capital at the same time limits the inducements of business to invest. The increasing desire to save and the declining incentive to invest cause the dilemma of present-day capitalism, according to Keynes' theory. Under the actual conditions of our time (except, of course, for the war period and the years immediately following the war), there is therefore the constant threat of chronic under-employment.

From this analysis follow Keynes' main recommendations for fiscal policy:

(1) Pursue a policy of low interest rates.

(2) Supplement private investments by public outlays.

(3) Devise a progressive tax system that falls more heavily on the portion of income that is saved than on the portion that is spent and thereby counteract the decline in the propensity to consume.

In appraising Keynes' theory of economic dynamics we distinguished those elements that are of a truly general nature from those of a historical nature based on a hypothesis concerning the expected actual development. From the general theory Keynes concluded that there is no effective mechanism inherent in our economic system assuring that private investments will meet exactly the requirements of a full employment level of income. Decisions to invest and propensity to save are each determined by factors independent of each other, so that they may or may not harmonize with each other. Through most of the historic periods of capitalistic development, the desire to invest pressed against the limits set by available capital supply—with a resulting vigorous expansion of the economy. The experience of that period

[5] *General Theory*, p. 251.

gave rise to the theory that it is the interest rate that balances demand for and supply of capital at full employment level. In the light of Keynes' analysis, it appears that the mechanism of interest rates could bring about that result only in a specific constellation of historical circumstances. A similar constellation of circumstances may again occur at certain periods, but may be absent at others. War destruction may have "solved" certain economic problems at least for a period of time. But we do not know for how long. In any case we must be ready for compensating action if the capitalistic system is to be preserved.

Compensating Government action can, as Keynes argued, consist either in measures affecting investment or the relation of savings to income or both. It can, of course, also consist in measures affecting the size of the labor force (hours of work, years in school, etc.).

From this analysis the following general conclusions can be drawn with respect to fiscal policy:

(1) In view of the hypothetical character of any specific prognostication, no general dogmatic rule of fiscal policy can be proposed. It must be based on a specific analysis of economic circumstances. (It will be shown in a later section that Keynes' theory has greatly stimulated the development of improved methods of statistical analysis.) Perhaps the best test of this approach is that Keynes, on the basis of his general theory, could diagnose the depression of the thirties as well as wartime inflation, and could propose fiscal policy measures for each situation.

(2) Fiscal policy is one, but not the only, device for balancing action. Keynes referred to measures influencing the size of the active labor force (hours of work, period of education, etc.) as an alternative to measures influencing investment, consumption, and saving. He said, however, that a policy designed to decrease the active labor force would be a "premature policy." [5a] It seems that Keynes regarded the formulation of a national investment program as the most important step; tax policies designed to reduce the inequalities of incomes and to reduce savings more than spending, the step next in importance.

But a policy designed to influence investments and consumption may use fiscal or nonfiscal devices. Keynes' references to a

[5a] *General Theory*, p. 326. Keynes has modified this opinion considerably according to oral statements made in recent years.

national investment program are so broad that they may include direct government expenditures as well as measures guiding and influencing private investment decisions. Still the main emphasis seems to be on direct government action. "I expect to see the State, which is in a position to calculate the marginal efficiency of capital goods on long views and on the basis of the general social advantage, taking an ever greater responsibility for directly organizing investment." [6]

(3) It is extremely doubtful if Keynes believed that price-cost adjustments could cure a depression in which the economy is in an under-employment equilibrium. At any rate, the rigidity of wages downward is an institutional fact, the persistence of which may be taken for granted. In the *General Theory*, he looked to basic disturbances and adjustments in the circular flow for the cause and cure of depressions. "Employment can only increase *pari passu* with an increase in investment; unless indeed there is a change in the propensity to consume." [7] He did not regard price-cost relations as a major factor determining either investments or consumption.

Here a critical comment may be in order. Recognition that depressions cannot be satisfactorily explained by reference to frictional maladjustments does not exclude recognition that maladjustments may exist nevertheless, and that readjustment of prices and costs may be a necessary policy in addition to fiscal policies. Using a metaphor, it is important for the motorist to know that his car runs on fuel and will stop when it runs out of fuel. It would be wrong, however, to conclude that because fuel is essential for the running of the car he need not be concerned with adjustment of the spark plugs. Price-cost disturbances may not be the basic explanation of under-employment, but they may be important factors nevertheless. It is true that unemployment resulting, for instance, from excessive monopolistic prices or from too rapid an increase in wage rates can always be overcompensated by additional employment created through government investments. But additional government investments can hardly be regarded as the most rational cure when excessive prices or costs are the cause of a disturbance. Therefore it does not follow from Keynes' theory that compensatory government policy, and par-

[6] *Ibid.*, p. 164.
[7] *Ibid.*, p. 98.

ticularly fiscal policy, are appropriate or sole cures in all kinds of depression. It seems to me that Keynes himself has not sufficiently clarified this point, and to some extent has invited the interpretation of fiscal policy as a "cure-all" in each case of under-employment. When discussing the Bretton Woods Agreement before the House of Lords, Keynes said: "Here is an attempt to use what we have learned from modern experience and modern analysis, not to defeat, but to implement the wisdom of Adam Smith."[8] In the *General Theory*, Keynes has not indicated the way in which fiscal policies may tie in with policies designed to remedy maladjustments. He has dealt with maladjustments in other publications.

(4) Inasmuch as fiscal policy is not the most appropriate measure in each situation of under-employment, it must also be emphasized that fiscal policy is not the only aspect of public finance. Keynes has used, in demonstrating the effects of Government spending, extreme examples (digging ditches or building pyramids)[9] which were interpreted as suggesting "spending for spending's sake." In this respect I believe that a didactic method of arguing is confused with policy recommendation. In a similar way, it is true that Keynes mentions taxation only in the context of a policy designed to reduce savings and to strengthen the propensity to consume, while he does not mention the possibility that taxation which is too steeply progressive may interfere with the incentives to produce or the supply of capital for business expansion. Here again the fact that Keynes did not treat taxation except in the context of his major argument does not mean that he negates other aspects of public finance. It would hardly be necessary to emphasize this, were it not for the fact that unscrupulous critics and over-enthusiastic friends have, as I believe, misinterpreted the consequences of Keynes' theory for fiscal policy in that fashion.

KEYNES' THEORY OF DYNAMICS AND DEVELOPMENT OF STATISTICAL PROJECTIONS OF THE FLOW OF INCOMES, EXPENDITURES, AND SAVINGS

The quantitative analysis of the circular flow of funds has been improved in a spectacular fashion in Great Britain, the United States, and other countries, during the last decade, and has aided in creating a factual basis for a rational fiscal policy.

[8] EJ, June, 1946, p. 186.
[9] *General Theory*, pp. 130–31.

The British White Paper on the sources of war finance [10] and the American presentation of the "Nation's Budget" [11] may be mentioned as significant examples. The latter method of presenting receipts, expenditures, and savings or absorption of funds, for each of the economic groups—consumers, business, and government—appears to be particularly suitable for a quantitative analysis of economic prospects. This method of statistical presentation is based on the truism that investment equals savings and also demonstrates that this equilibrium can be achieved on a lower or higher level of income.

While it is true that Keynes' theory of dynamics has greatly stimulated the development of statistical techniques, a particular method of statistical analysis and presentation is not necessarily related to any specific type of policy conclusion. As a matter of fact, the Nation's economic budget analysis has been used to demonstate inflationary pressures and the need for reducing Government expenditures and maintaining high taxes.[12] It has also been used to demonstrate possible alternative policies for a future postwar depression, namely, either inducement of relatively increased consumers' expenditures, or inducement of increased business outlays, or increased Government outlays.[13]

Some widely used methods of economic forecasts or projections followed the patterns of Keynesian theory pretty closely. Following Keynes they regarded changes in business investments, export surpluses, and loan-financed Government expenditures as the genuine cause, and changes in income, consumption, and employment, as the dependent variable in the economic development. Changes in consumer expenditures were estimated with the aid of an average multiplier. The multiplier was derived from past relationship between incomes and consumers' expenditures.

For a statistical analysis considerable refinement is necessary. Keynes was particularly concerned with loan-financed expenditures, since borrowed funds usually would not have been spent anyhow, and consequently the full amount of the expenditure

---

[10] *An Analysis of the Sources of War Finance and Estimates of the National Income and Expenditure in the Years 1938 to 1943* (1944); *National Income and Expenditure of the United Kingdom 1938–1945* (1946).

[11] *The Budget of the United States* (1946 and 1947).

[12] See, e.g., President Truman's Review of the 1947 Budget, August 2, 1946.

[13] *National Budgets for Full Employment*, National Planning Association (1945).

can be considered an addition to investment. Tax-financed expenditure may have a similar though weaker effect, however, since to some extent taxes fall on savings rather than funds which would have been spent for consumption. More important, there are, of course, also genuine changes in consumers' attitudes; and business investments (e.g., inventory movement and outlays for plant and equipment) are not exclusively subject to independent changes but to some extent respond to changes in consumer incomes and expenditures.

The Keynesian structure was relied on to some extent in making forecasts of the level of income and employment during the reconversion period. Business net investments and Government expenditures minus revenues were regarded as the independent or autonomous variables, while consumption was thought of as depending on the level of these components—at least for those categories of goods in which supply was equal to or in excess of demand. The multiplier relation was not accepted without modification, however, since an allowance was usually made for demand in excess of normal due to backlogs of demand for durable or semi-durable items.

This procedure of segregating categories of expenditure where supply was reasonably adequate and applying the multiplier relation to them alone has been criticized on the grounds that the multiplier must be applied to total consumption.[14] If supply is short on some items, according to this theory, demand will spill over to other categories in which goods are available.

This approach has the merit that it would have given an estimate of consumption more nearly approaching that which actually materialized in the transition period. There are no theoretical reasons for supposing the spill-over to be complete, however, so that it is probably more accurate to say that there was simply a shift in the consumption function during the postwar transition. Keynes recognized the possibility of such shifts, although emphasizing the relative stability of the function, or at least that at any time the marginal propensity to consume would be declining. In times of social upheaval or stress, the likelihood of shifts in the consumption function would, of course, be much increased.

This is not the place to discuss possible refinements in the

[14] For a discussion of this question, see L. R. Klein, "A Post-Mortem on Transition Predictions of National Product," JPE, August, 1946.

methods of forecasting. Improved methods may avoid some of the errors that have been made in the past. No method has been developed for predicting with a high degree of certainty the genuine changes in economic data. The dynamic elements in Keynes' theory have helped, however, to focus on the crucial points in the economic process where genuine changes are most likely to occur; they have also aided in the development of measuring the expected secondary effects of these primary changes. With respect to estimating prospective genuine changes the only real progress lies in the sample studies of business and consumer attitudes for which very promising starts have been made. To great extent we still rely today largely on hunches and anticipation of other people's behavior, just as the forecasters did before Keynes' writing.

Keynes' proposals for fiscal policy were predominantly designed to counteract secular depressive tendencies. In this respect they do not depend on accurate cyclical forecasts. In addition, the great uncertainty in economic prognostication suggests that fiscal planning must be of a tentative nature and must be flexible enough to take account of developments that differ from expectations. Three types of statistical analysis have been developed in recent years:

(1) Forecasts, in the literary meaning of the term, must predict both economic trends and policies which the Government is likely to adopt. They are useful—within limits—for businessmen and others who are not interested in any "iffy" statements, but want the best judgment about the outlook.

(2) More important as an aid in policy formulation are so-called "projections." They predict on the assumption that Government policies remain the same and may show the probable need for remedial policies.

(3) There are, finally, "models" which analyze the effect of alternative policies. Projections and models are most useful as a basis for policy planning.

Nobody who compares the "business barometers" of the twenties with the methods of economic forecasts, projections and models developed during the last decade can fail to observe the wholesome effect that the modern theory of dynamics, to which Keynes has made such an outstanding contribution, had on the development of our modern tools of quantitative economic analysis and of rational policy formulation. Much trial and error will still be needed before these tools can become reliable instruments of policy formulation. I believe, however, that Keynes' stimulating influence on the development of these tools will be regarded as one of his most significant contributions.

AN APPRAISAL OF KEYNES' FISCAL POLICY RECOMMENDATIONS

Keynes has not elaborated the fiscal policy recommendations that follow from his general theory. The most comprehensive and detailed discussion has been presented by Alvin Hansen [15] in this country, and by Sir William Beveridge [16] in England. A great amount of literature has been published dealing with various phases of fiscal policy, government expenditures, and other policies designed to influence investments, tax policies, and debt transactions. The discussion has proceeded from the argument of principles to an attempt to determine in quantitative terms the contribution each one of these policies can make to a policy of full employment.

With respect to the discussion in the United States, a certain cycle can be observed. During the thirties the main emphasis was on Government investments in public works as a major recovery policy. The second phase of the discussion took place during the war and explored the problem of sustaining full employment after the end of the postwar restocking period. For this period the discussion centered around the use of tax reduction as a means of supporting consumers' purchasing power and encouraging business investments. This applies particularly to the period immediately following the end of the reconversion boom. With respect to the longer range, proposals for urban redevelopment and other ambitious projects for national and international development were emphasized.

The use of public works of the conventional character as a means to combat mass unemployment has been generally recognized—within limits. The experience of the thirties in expanding public works has proved that the "multiplier" effect, that is, the effect on incomes and consumption, was approximately as expected by Keynes. It has been recognized, however, that no policy of this sort can be truly effective unless it co-ordinates Federal, State, and local action, or at least prevents State and local govern-

[15] Alvin H. Hansen, *Fiscal Policy and Business Cycles* (1941).
[16] Sir William Beveridge, *Full Employment in a Free Society* (1945).

ments from being driven into a policy contrary to the Federal policy. Keynes referred only in general terms to the tertiary effect of government investments, namely, the stimulation of business investments as income rises. In this respect much was expected by those who spoke of the "pump-priming" effect of government expenditures. The statistical record of the thirties is not quite clear, but there seems to be little evidence that there was a significant tertiary effect.[17] This fact has been explained by the following reasons: (1) that the net addition of government expenditures (i.e., after allowance for the counter-movement in State and local activities) was not very significant; (2) that business distrusted the permanence of the increase in consumers' purchasing power resulting from the recovery program; and (3) that there were other developments, particularly in the field of tax policy, labor relations, foreign economic policy, and a general anti-business attitude which may have deterred business investments. More recent proposals have been formulated on the basis of this experience.

Alvin Hansen and others have emphasized the need for the formulation of bold long-range programs as, for example, for urban redevelopment, for public health programs, and for other social programs. These programs exceed those of the depression years and are formulated on the basis of the wartime experience with respect to America's capacity to produce.

Lack of confidence by business in the stability and effectiveness of the recovery program was probably influenced to some extent by the fact that it was mainly a program of the Executive branch of the Government, only reluctantly supported by the Congress. Large parts of the program were never fully discussed or specifically acted upon by the Congress. This contributed to the charge of "boondoggling" and extravagance. This experience was one of the arguments presented by the supporters of full employment legislation.

The Employment Act of 1946 also reflects the desire to avoid the inconsistencies in the recovery policies of the thirties. Various agencies acted at cross purposes at that time, with the President the sole co-ordinating factor but practically without a co-ordinating staff. At present there are co-ordinating agencies avail-

[17] G. Colm and F. Lehmann, "Public Spending and Recovery in the United States," *Social Research*, May, 1936. Arthur Smithies, "The American Economy in the Thirties," AER, May, 1946, pp. 17–19.

able for aiding the President in that task—several, in fact, so that their exact relationship still needs to be determined. While public works planning for the future seeks to avoid some of the pitfalls that impaired its effectiveness during the thirties, there has been a growing recognition of the practical limits of a public works policy as an anti-cyclical device.

The limits of an effective fiscal policy through manipulation of expenditures were demonstrated in August, 1946, when President Truman wanted to curtail expenditures as one of the measures for combatting inflationary pressure. He cut by two billion dollars a Federal budget that exceeded forty billion dollars. The rest of the budget was regarded as largely inflexible because it is determined by legislation or allocated for Government purposes that were believed to be nondeferrable. It proved difficult to enforce even this limited curtailment program in view of resistance against the postponement of certain public works. This experience showed not only that flexibility in the Federal budget is limited, but also that our legislative and administrative machinery is not yet fully equipped to use even this limited existing flexibility.

As the limits in the variation of expenditures were discovered, more attention was paid to the possibility of using taxation as a fiscal policy device. Keynes thought of progressive taxation as a means for redistributing income and thereby affecting the propensity to consume. Studies of the American tax system during the thirties [18] showed that the rates at that time were probably progressive enough to prevent a considerable further increase in inequality, but hardly progressive enough to bring about a redistribution of incomes. It was also shown [19] that most of the regressive elements in the American tax system are in the State and local tax field rather than in the Federal field, which again raises the question of Federal-State-local co-ordination in an effective fiscal policy.

Right at the beginning of the defense and war program, recommendations were made to use tax policy as a fiscal device to stabilize the economy and to minimize the need of direct controls. Soon it became obvious that taxes sufficient to control inflation without direct controls would have to be so drastic that they

[18] G. Colm and F. Lehmann, *Economic Consequences of Recent American Tax Policy* (1938).

[19] Helen Tarasov, *Who Does Pay the Taxes?*, Supplement IV, *Social Research*, 1942.

would have impaired war production and involved avoidable as well as unavoidable curtailments in consumption. It may well be that wartime tax or savings measures should have been more drastic than they actually were, but they could not have been drastic enough to assure price stability without direct controls.

The wartime increase in tax rates created the basis for a great many proposals for postwar tax reductions. Some proposals for tax reductions are expected to support consumers' demands, others to encourage business investments. In the case of some proposals, one can hardly suppress the feeling that reduction of wartime taxes, which may well be justified on other grounds, is rationalized as part of a fiscal policy in order to give the proposal wider appeal. Perhaps it is significant that labeling a recommendation as in accord with requirements of fiscal policy is regarded, at least by some, as a means of increasing the appeal of a measure.

Wartime taxes on corporations curtailed and were intended to curtail normal incentives to invest for non-war purposes. If continued in peacetime, they would impair to some extent also the incentives to rational and economical management. The early removal of the excess profits tax was intended to restore rational business management. This measure could, however, hardly be presented on the ground of fiscal policy at a time of inflationary pressure.

The question is not whether other wartime tax rates should or should not be maintained. The question is what should be the extent and timing of a future tax reduction and the contribution of such tax reduction to a full employment policy.

With respect to the first question, most of the discussion on tax reduction was based on the illusion that postwar Federal budgets would amount to somewhere around sixteen to eighteen billion dollars, while it seems that a figure of around thirty billion dollars will be more realistic. The tax reduction that is likely to occur because of other than fiscal considerations will be of a nature that will probably strengthen individual and corporate savings more than the propensity to consume. In other words, the multiplier applicable to a reduction in income taxes which are already nearer the maximum rate of progression is relatively small. Flexibility in taxes may be politically and administratively more feasible than flexibility in expenditures, but, as a means of supporting active purchasing power, it is also much less effective.

In connection with plans for an expanded social security system, flexible employees' contributions have been considered, with the Federal budget contributing a larger share to the costs at times when economic conditions require strengthening of consumers' purchasing power. Such Federal contributions were suggested, of course, only for a time when practically universal coverage is accomplished under an expanded social security system.

During the war President Roosevelt proposed a collateral anti-inflationary policy, namely, increasing the contributions even before expanded benefit schemes became effective. Such a policy was regarded by critics as a "misuse" of the workers' Social Security funds. Similarly, the flexible contribution plan for an expanded Social Security system has been criticized with the argument that varying and large budget contributions to the Social Security system would weaken its *insurance* character. Particularly in circles of labor unions it is feared that a system that is not largely financed by contributions would not assure unaltered benefits. Here again are obstacles to the acceptance of fiscal policy which are not related to the economic merits of the proposal.

Debt transactions must be considered next to expenditure and revenue policies as a means of fiscal policy. Keynes expected that postwar redemption of forced wartime savings could be timed so that it would support active purchasing power after the end of the inflationary period. Some economists have expressed the hope that, because of the widespread holdings of war savings bonds, the propensity to consume will be very much higher than in the past and will make the task of stabilizing employment on a high level much easier.[20] This expectation implies that bonds will be redeemed by refinancing through the banking system, or that the bondholder will reduce his savings considerably. There is certainly some validity in this notion. In view of the distribution of bond holdings and the rather conservative attitude of bondholders,[21] it appears uncertain how substantial the effect on the propensity to consume will be. It is likely that the wartime accumulation of liquid assets in the form of bonds or cash may very well have some cushioning effect, once a downturn in business

[20] W. S. Woytinsky, "Postwar Economic Perspectives," Parts III and IV, *Social Security Bulletin*, Washington, D. C., February and March, 1946.
[21] See U. S. Department of Agriculture, *National Survey of Liquid Asset Holdings, Spending, and Saving*, 1946.

occurs. In 1932–33, national income sank to a rockbottom rate of forty-five to fifty billion dollars before the deflationary spiral came to an end. Under present conditions, the rockbottom equilibrium point probably lies very much higher.

In all three fields of fiscal policy—government expenditures, taxes and debt transactions—the discussion ranged between enthusiastic expectation that the device for assuring full and steady employment had been found, and disillusionment and skepticism. It seems that at the present time skepticism prevails. We may ask ourselves whether the pendulum has not swung too much to the negative side. The thinking about the possibilities of fiscal policy itself seems to be subject to cyclical swings and requires some effort toward stabilization.

A balanced appraisal would probably show that fiscal policy has been recognized as one of the devices in the arsenal of a policy designed to stabilize employment and income on a high level. The change of argumentation that has taken place in all discussions of public finance is of great significance and is bound to bear fruit. As a matter of fact, public finance measures are no longer discussed without consideration of their impact on the economy, though policy decisions are by no means made solely on that ground. It has also been recognized that the problem of economic stabilization must use other devices besides fiscal policy. It may well be that the first recession after the postwar boom may be of a nature that requires first of all measures designed to adjust costs and prices in relation to incomes, rather than fiscal policies. It may also be that fiscal policies may prove more effective as long-range rather than as short-range measures of an anti-cyclical character.

In many respects the problems of fiscal policy are not exclusively or even not predominantly problems for the economist but for the political scientist and the administrator. Our legislative and administrative arrangements are not conducive to an effective fiscal policy. The wide recognition of the economic problems and the solid theoretical foundation that these economic problems have found increase the chances that the necessary legislative and administrative arrangements for an effective fiscal policy will be made.

CHAPTER XXXV

Keynesian Economics and Public
Investment Policy

By BENJAMIN HIGGINS

AMONG THE brands of economic policy associated with Keynes is the utilization of public investment to promote full employment. This association does not arise from any priority of Keynes' as to the general idea of using public investment to alleviate unemployment. Indeed, public investment policy seems to be one of the many areas in economics where practice preceded theory. Keynes himself has suggested that Egyptian pyramids and medieval cathedrals were essentially make-work projects, which contributed directly to the prestige and indirectly to the prosperity of the societies that built them.[1] It is certain that after the English crisis of 1825, which some economic historians regard as the first "modern" cyclical downturn, the British monarch sought to reduce the unemployment of textile workers in Spitalfields by ordering Windsor castle hung with silk; and in 1919, before Keynes had published the first of his important books, the International Labour Organization in its very first session passed the following recommendation: [2]

> The Conference recommends that each Member of the International Labour Organization co-ordinate the execution of all work undertaken under public authority with a view to reserving such work as far as practicable for periods of unemployment. . . .

[1] *General Theory*, p. 131.
[2] For an account of the consistent and persistent advocacy of such policies by the I.L.O., see my report on *Public Investment & Full Employment* (Montreal [International Labour Office], 1946), Appendix A. Keynes himself pointed out "the consistent appreciation of this truth" by the I.L.O. (*General Theory*, p. 349).

Even on the analytical side, Keynes could not claim historical precedence. A very clear statement of the basic principle was presented, for example, in John M. Robertson's *Fallacy of Saving* published in 1892. After a careful demonstration that unemployment results from a tendency for savings to exceed investment in wealthy communities, he argues that: "Either (a) the principle of parsimony must be generally abandoned, and the majority must demand high-class goods or services . . . or (b) the state or the municipalities must institute important public works . . . which should extensively employ and train inexpert labour."[3]

A policy proposal may be associated with the name of a particular economist, even when the idea was not originally his, if he has done a great deal to popularize it, or if he has worked out the details of its application. Yet neither case really fits Keynes' contribution to the public investment field. True, his *Open Letter to President Roosevelt* may well have been a significant factor in Roosevelt's desertion of his proposed budget-balancing program in favor of an expansionary public works policy; but the latter policy had been initiated by Hoover, and the popularization of the somewhat more ambitious New Deal policy was left largely to American economists associated with the Administration.[4] In his own country, Keynes' ideas on public investment found their first official expression in the postwar planning of the coalition government, and have yet to be consistently applied in a period of threatened or actual unemployment.[5] Keynes' contribution to the technical literature on planning public works has been virtually nil.[6]

[3] John M. Robertson, *The Fallacy of Saving* (London 1892), pp. 121–2. Robertson anticipated "Keynesian economics" in other respects as well. For example, he opposed reduction of the National Debt on the grounds that it would reduce consumption & cause unemployment (pp. 125–6); & argued—contrary to Sidney Webb—that "it will be the principal service a pension system can render, to encourage the workers to consume and not paralyse production by restricting their demand" (p. 129).

[4] For a fairly detailed account of American public investment policy in the thirties, see my *Public Investment & Full Employment, op. cit.,* chap. IX.

[5] British public investment policy of the thirties is outlined in Chapter X of my *Public Investment and Full Employment, op. cit.* A much fuller account, together with an analysis along Keynesian lines, is presented in Bretherton, R. F., Burchardt, F. A., and Rutherford, R. S. G., *Public Investment & the Trade Cycle* (Oxford, 1941).

[6] In Addendum 1 to the *Report of the Committee on Finance & Industry* (*Macmillan Report*), 1931, which is signed by others but can safely be attributed largely to Keynes, he stressed the importance of advance planning

There is one final way in which Keynes may have justified the widespread association of his doctrines with the principle of using public investment as part of a compensatory fiscal policy. He may have provided a more complete or more satisfactory *rationale* for the policy than any one else. In search of this *rationale*, let us review briefly his major works dealing with employment policy.

WORKS PRIOR TO THE *GENERAL THEORY*

Keynes' first important work on employment policy was his *Tract on Monetary Reform* (1924). Even at this time, Keynes' attention was centered on the savings-investment relationship and the demand for cash balances. Yet the sole instrument of control recommended is monetary policy: "The governors of the system would be bank-rate and Treasury Bill policy, the objects of government would be stability of trade, prices, and employment."[7]

Six years later, in his *Treatise on Money*, Keynes confessed some doubts concerning the efficacy of monetary policy alone for maintaining investment at the full-employment level.[8] Yet the instruments on which he placed major reliance were still bank-rate and open-market policy.[9] Public investment was regarded as a remedy of last resort, to be undertaken in a special case: viz., when a country's "international disequilibrium is involving

---

of capital development schemes. "It is difficult to *improvise* good schemes," he argued, and recommended "that we should now attack the task of capital development in this country in a much more systematic and far-sighted manner than hitherto. It should not be an objection to a scheme that its execution will be spread over many years and will be somewhat prolonged." He urged particularly programs of housing and urban redevelopment, modernization of staple industries, and railway electrification (*loc. cit.*, pp. 206–208). These few remarks, however, were about the extent of Keynes' writing on techniques of planning public works.

[7] *Op. cit.*, p. 212.

[8] See especially Vol. II, pp. 351–2 and 362.

[9] For example: "Thus—in spite of qualifications which we shall have to introduce later in respect of the so-called 'open-market' operations of Central Banks—it is broadly true to say that the governor of the whole system is the rate of discount" (Vol. II, p. 211); "My remedy in the event of the obstinate persistence of a slump would consist, therefore, in the purchase of securities by the Central Bank until the long-term market-rate of interest has been brought down to the limiting point." He suggested two "specific remedies" for "the slump of 1930"; that "the Bank of England & the Federal Reserve Board . . . put pressure on their member banks . . . to reduce the rate of interest which they allow to depositors to a very low figure, say ½ per cent"; and that "these two central institutions should pursue bank-rate policy & open-market operations *à outrance*" (Vol. II, p. 386).

it in severe unemployment." [10] For in such a case, "open-market operations by the Central Bank, intended to bring down the market-rate of interest and stimulate investment, may, by misadventure, stimulate foreign lending instead and so provoke an outward flow of gold on a larger scale than it can afford. . . . Thus the desired result can only be obtained through some method by which, in effect, the Government subsidises approved types of domestic investment or itself directs domestic schemes of capital development." [11]

At about the time that the Treatise was being written, Keynes published an essay entitled "A Programme of Expansion (General Election, May, 1929)," [12] which is more modern in tone. Here he points out that the whole period of the twenties was one of unemployment in Britain, and approves Lloyd George's plan to spend £100 million per year on national development. He considered it "a very modest programme," the cost of which is negligible compared to the cost of idle resources. As he put it, "Every puff of Mr. Baldwin's pipe costs us thousands of pounds." The argument that such a program would make capital scarce and check private investment, he points out, is no more true when the program is executed by public authorities than if it is carried out by private enterprise. Such a development scheme, he further contends, would only cause inflation "after everyone is employed and our savings are being used up to the hilt."

The essays on "Saving & Spending" (January, 1931), "The Economy Bill" (September 19, 1931), and "The Economy Report" (August 15, 1931), are in the same vein.[13] In the first, Keynes asked, "why not pull down the whole of South London, from Westminster to Greenwich, and make a good job of it?" In the second, he argued that "Government borrowing of one kind or another is nature's remedy . . . for . . . a slump," and that "It is much better in every way that the borrowing should be for the purpose of financing capital works, if these works are any use at all, than for the purpose of paying doles (or veterans' bonuses)." In the third, he contended that "the Government's programme of economy is as foolish as it is wrong. Its direct effect on employment must be disastrous." [14]

[10] *Op. cit.,* Vol. II, p. 376.
[11] *Op. cit.,* Vol. II, p. 376.
[12] Reprinted in *Essays in Persuasion,* pp. 118 ff.
[13] Reprinted in Essays in *Persuasion.*
[14] *Ibid.,* pp. 148ff., 157ff., and 162ff.

These are pungent essays; but they do not provide the superior *rationale* of public investment policy that we are seeking. The analysis on which the recommendations rest is no more complete and little more sophisticated than the analysis underlying, say, the I.L.O. recommendation above. The same is true of Keynes' Halley Stewart Lecture of 1931.[15] He was by that time less sanguine than ever concerning the effectiveness of cheap money, and was fearful that, no matter how low interest rates were forced, "The lender, with his confidence shattered by his experiences, will continue to ask for new enterprise rates of interest which the borrower cannot expect to earn." [16] If so, he argued, "there will be no means of escape from prolonged and perhaps interminable depression except by direct state intervention to promote and subsidize new investment." He expressed the hope that the world would not wait for a war to undertake enough loan-financed expenditure to bring full employment, and added, "I predict with an assured confidence that the only way out is for us to discover *some* object which is admitted even by the dead-heads to be a legitimate excuse for largely increasing the expenditure of someone or something." [17]

In Addendum 1 to the *Macmillan Report,* he introduced the germ of the "multiplier" argument in support of a program of capital development: "In addition to the men occupied in making and transporting the materials required, there will be a further set of men put into work to supply the needs created by the additional purchasing and consuming power of the first set of men, and so on." [18] He also replied to some stock criticisms of public investment. It need not injure business confidence, he said, if it does not consist of "obviously wasteful, foolish, or extravagant projects." [19] If excess capacity exists, public investment need not lead to any significant increase in price. He admits that a large-scale public investment program may increase imports, but points out that this "is an objection which applies to all remedies for unemployment," and insists that "this is scarcely a reason for not providing employment." [20] Such arguments provide new sup-

[15] Salter and others, *The World's Economic Crisis* (London 1932), pp. 69–88.
[16] *Op. cit.,* p. 85.
[17] *Ibid.*
[18] *Macmillan Report,* p. 203.
[19] *Ibid.,* p. 204.
[20] *Ibid.,* p. 205.

port for, but do not essentially alter, the doctrine of public investment expressed in earlier literature.

Much the same must be said of Keynes' statements on public investment policy in *The Means to Prosperity,* published two years later.[21] In chapters 2 and 3 of this booklet, he presented what is still one of the best text book statements of the multiplier principle,[22] and applied it to public investment. He estimated that the multiplier for public works expenditures would be at least two for England, and higher for the United States. He also estimated that at least half the outlays would return to the Exchequer in increased tax receipts and reduced doles. The final conclusion was "that there is no means of raising world prices except by an increase of loan expenditure throughout the world."[23] Such essays as these were designed to diminish opposition to the use of public investment to alleviate unemployment, rather than to provide a new analytical framework to support such a policy.

In this survey of Keynes' writings prior to 1936, a fairly steady line of development of his thinking about public investment policy can be discerned. Nevertheless, it is apparent that it is in the *General Theory*, and not in earlier works, that we must seek the distinctly "Keynesian" *rationale* of public investment policy.

IMPLICATIONS OF THE *GENERAL THEORY* FOR PUBLIC INVESTMENT POLICY

When the *General Theory* was published, several countries—including the United States, the United Kingdom, Australia, New Zealand, Canada, Switzerland, and Sweden—were already embarked in some degree on programs of public works designed to alleviate unemployment.[23a] In some of these countries—especially Sweden and the United States—an analytical literature had been developed to support such a policy. Nevertheless,

[21] This pamphlet consists of articles previously published in TL and NST&N.
[22] His arithmetic is, perhaps, a little confusing to students acquainted with later versions of the principle. From a marginal propensity to consume of 0.7, he derives a multiplier of 2, by assuming that only 70% of expenditures are income-creating (*op. cit.*, p. 10).
[23] *Op. cit.*, p. 25.
[23a] These programs are all discussed in my *Public Investment & Full Employment, op. cit.*, Part IV.

Keynes' *magnum opus* opened a new era of theory and practice in the public investment field.

In the first place, the analysis of the *General Theory* conferred a new importance and a new respectability on public investment policy; it was elevated from the rank of last line of defense to major offensive strategy. The analysis led logically to isolation of four chief methods of attacking unemployment: private investment might be stimulated directly; an export surplus might be promoted; the propensity to consume might be raised; or the state might undertake investment projects itself. All methods but the last, however, have distinct and serious limitations.

Keynes' attitude towards the first method—stimulating private investment directly—underwent an almost complete reversal between the *Treatise* and the *General Theory*. "I am now somewhat skeptical," he wrote in the latter book (p. 164), "of a merely monetary policy directed towards influencing the rate of interest. I expect to see the State . . . taking an ever greater responsibility for directly organizing investment; since it seems likely that the fluctuations in the market estimation of the marginal efficiency of capital . . . will be too great to be offset by any practicable changes in the rate of interest." [24] Even if the monetary authorities had complete control over interest rates, it is questionable whether they are very powerful factors in business decisions (Chap. 17); and the pursuit of a rigorous easy money policy may have unfavorable effects on speculation in securities (pp. 319–20), and on the balance of payments (pp. 335–6). It seems better to abandon the interest rate as an instrument of control, and aim at reducing it to zero for welfare reasons (pp. 220–226, 376–7). There remains, of course, the possibility of stimulating private investment by subsidy; but this policy is limited because every increase in private investment by such artificial stimulation reduces the marginal efficiency of capital (Chaps. 11, 12, 16), and at the same time, through the accompanying rise in income, raises savings and perhaps even lowers the average propensity to consume. Thus no real hope, at least in the long run, lies in the direction of stimulating private investment. [25]

While not set forth in the *General Theory*, the limitations to

[24] The same view is expressed on pp. 319–20.
[25] [Cf. Dr. Colm's essay above.]

promotion of export-surpluses, as a device for maintaining full employment, are readily apparent. It is obviously not a remedy that all countries can adopt simultaneously, and efforts of any one country to do so in a depression period tend to prompt retaliation and to enhance international conflict. In any case, a continued export surplus is for any one country a "boondoggle" of the purest sort. Keynes' later writings and speeches concerning international trade policy indicate that he considered the proper long-run objective in this field to be trade balanced at a high level.

The importance of raising the propensity to consume—or reducing the propensity to save, which is the same thing but somehow sounds different—is perhaps the most distinctive conclusion of the *General Theory*. Measures to raise the propensity to consume share first honors among cures for unemployment with public investment: "Whilst aiming at a socially controlled rate of investment with a view to a progressive decline in the marginal efficiency of capital, I should support at the same time all sorts of policy for increasing the propensity to consume" (p. 325). Although Keynes himself provided no criterion for achieving a proper balance between these two main types of policy, the chief considerations involved are not hard to determine. One would be the relationship, stressed in the neo-classical theory of interest, of the marginal productivity of capital to the marginal rate of time preference; if additions to publicly owned capital will add more to future consumption than is necessary to offset the present consumption sacrificed, measures to increase public investment should rate higher than measures to raise current consumption. A closely related consideration would be the relative demand for goods and services that are more efficiently provided by public and by private enterprise respectively; the wider the range of goods and services that can be more efficiently produced by public than by private enterprise, the greater the scope for public investment—and vice versa. Another consideration, the weight of which should vary inversely with the expected duration of the unemployment, is its geographic and occupational distribution; depending upon the types of labor and resources that are idle, relief may be more rapidly provided by one or the other type of employment policy. Since measures to raise consumption usually involve redistribution of income in a more direct fashion than public investment, public investment will tend to be the more advantageous the more closely an optimum distribution of income has been approximated.

In any case, however, Keynesian theory surely does not suggest that policies to stimulate consumption should be carried beyond stabilization of consumer-spending at a high level, rising gradually with growth of the labor force and increases in productivity. A policy of producing countercyclical variations of consumer-spending, so that consumption would actually increase in "depression" and decrease in "prosperity," would hardly be popular, since it would require unpleasant restrictions on consumption in periods of rising private investment. Measures to raise the propensity to consume may be more important in highly developed economies for raising the *average level* of income, around which fluctuations would take place in the absence of countercyclical measures; but public investment is left virtually in sole possession of the field, when it comes to policies for offsetting fluctuations in private investment.

PRINCIPLES OF PLANNING PUBLIC INVESTMENT

There is little in the *General Theory* on principles of planning public investment. A few comments are introduced incidentally to the discussion of the multiplier, but these are not originally Keynes' but Kahn's, as Keynes readily admitted.[26] They are brief, and can be quoted in full:

(i) The method financing the policy and the increased working cash, required by the increased employment and the associated rise of prices, may have the effect of increasing the rate of interest and so retarding investment in other directions, unless the monetary authority takes steps to the contrary; whilst, at the same time, the increased cost of capital goods will reduce their marginal efficiency to the private investor, and this will require an actual *fall* in the rate of interest to offset it.

(ii) With the confused psychology which often prevails, the Government programme may, through its effect on "confidence," increase liquidity-preference or diminish the marginal efficiency

---

[26] However, as Professor Dudley Dillard has pointed out, "the basic insight and a clear explanation of practical significance" of the multiplier is expressed in a 1929 pamphlet written with H. D. Henderson, under the title *Can Lloyd George Do It? An Examination of the Liberal Pledge* ("The Pragmatic Basis of Keynes's Political Economy," *The Journal of Economic History*, Nov., 1946, p. 133).

of capital, which, again, may retard other investment unless measures are taken to offset it.

(iii) In an open system with foreign-trade relations, some part of the multiplier of the increased investment will accrue to the benefit of employment in foreign countries, since a proportion of the increased consumption will diminish our own country's favourable foreign balance; so that, if we consider only the effect on domestic employment as distinct from world employment, we must diminish the full figure of the multiplier. On the other hand, our own country may recover a portion of this leakage through favourable repercussions due to the action of the multiplier in the foreign country in increasing its economic activity.

Furthermore, if we are considering changes of a substantial amount, we have to allow for a progressive change in the marginal propensity to consume, as the position of the margin is gradually shifted; and hence in the multiplier . . . In any case, the multiplier is likely to be greater for a small net increment of investment than for a large increment; so that, where substantial changes are in view, we must be guided by the average value of the multiplier based on the average marginal propensity to consume over the range in question.[27]

The discussion arising out of the *General Theory* yielded a number of additional principles of great importance. First, the concept of "pump-priming" was largely displaced by that of "compensatory spending." The Keynesian analysis—as developed by Hansen, Samuelson, and others—made it clear that for "pump-priming" to work, *induced* private spending (*new investment* and consumption by those whose incomes are *not* directly affected by public investment, but whose anticipations are changed) would have to be positive and large. Otherwise, reduction of government loan expenditures to the initial level would tend to bring a relapse of income and employment to the starting point. In fact, however—as Keynes suggests in point (ii) above—induced private spending may be negative.

A second principle, so closely related to the first as to be hardly distinguishable from it, is that business cycle policy no longer consists of seeking "the cause" of cycles, and then eliminating "the cause," so that no further government intervention is necessary, but of stabilizing private spending as much and at as high a level as possible, and then filling the inevitable cyclical and chronic deflationary gaps by public investment. Of course,

[27] *General Theory, op. cit.,* pp. 119–121.

while irregularity of innovations and of replacement would prob-ably prevent complete stabilization of private investment, a few decades of successful full employment policy would greatly re-duce the amplitude of fluctuations in private spending, and might raise its average level as well. Nevertheless, the Keynesian anal-ysis implies a *continuity* of public investment policy that was not implicit in earlier business cycle theory.

Third, the emphasis on deficit-finance in the neo-Keynesian discussion destroyed some of the comfortable illusions about the merits of self-liquidating public works.[28] The sale of govern-ment services for a price tends to restrict consumption of goods and services produced by private firms, just as taxes do. Of course, just as increased government expenditures with a bal-anced budget, even without any redistribution of income, will raise income by the amount of the increase,[29] so public investment that is continuously self-liquidating will raise income by the amount of the investment, even if no income redistribution is affected. If income is transferred from savers to spenders in the process, the effects will be still more favorable. Also, if construc-tion is concentrated in depression periods, and liquidation is spread throughout prosperity, the net effect will be counter-cyclical. Nevertheless, it remains true that, to the extent that public investment is self-liquidating, the scale of government enterprise needed to fill a given deflationary gap must be larger.

[28] Illusions to which the writer was subject for an embarassingly long time. Cf. Higgins & Musgrave, "Deficit-Finance . . . the Case Examined," *Public Policy II.* (Cambridge, 1941) pp. 202–3.

[29] Cf. T. Haavelmo, "Multiplier Effects of a Balanced Budget," EC, Oct., 1945; and G. Haberler, R. M. Goodwin, E. E. Hagen, *Ibid.*, Apr., 1946. It is surprising that this fact, too, took so long to emerge from the discussion. Even now, it is not clearly realized that the argument applies equally well to a balanced expansion of trade, or to an increase in investment that is off-set by an equal increase in *ex-ante* savings. The essential point is that gov-ernment expenditures, private investment, or exports, are part of national in-come, while taxes, savings, or imports are not. Thus the favorable effects through the operation of the multiplier will be $(1 + C + C^2 + \ldots + C^n)$. ΔE, where E is the increased expenditures of any kind, & C is the marginal pro-pensity to consume; while the unfavorable effects are $(O + C + C^2 + \ldots + C^n)$. ΔR, where R is any "leakage." The net effect will therefore be $1 \times E$. For some reason, the initial discussion of this point, like the initial discussion of the "multiplier" itself, ran solely in terms of public investment. I am told that this type of formulation of the multiplier principle was origin-ated by W. A. Salant.

Thus restriction of public investment to self-liquidating works turns out to be a more "radical" policy than deficit-finance.

Fourth, in depression even useless works are better than none. This point has been somewhat oversold, especially in the United States, where the whole policy of public investment is associated in the minds of a large sector of the public with "boondoggling." Keynes himself never favored "make-work" projects. For example, he stated very clearly that "It would, indeed, be more sensible to build houses and the like" than to substitute for gold-mining his system of burying bank notes in disused coal mines and digging them up again, stating merely that "If there are political and practical difficulties in the way of (sensible projects)," then "the above would be better than nothing" (p. 129). Indeed, the logical conclusion to be derived from the Keynesian system is that if the recipients of the initial outlay on useful and on waste-projects have the same marginal propensity to consume, the useful projects will have greater multiplier effects just by the value of the direct services they yield. If the useful projects are worth what they cost, their multiplier effects on gross national product or income will be:

$$(1 + C + C^2 + \ldots + C^n).\ \Delta E,$$

where C is the marginal propensity to consume, and E the amount of public investment. If "wasteful" projects are completely worthless, their contribution to income (ignoring "relation" and other leverage effects) will be:

$$(O + C + C^2 + \ldots + C^n).\ \Delta E$$

The difference in the rise of gross national product or income in the two cases is therefore ΔE. By the same token, public investment will, other things being equal, have greater multiplier effects than social security expenditures, or any other transfer payment, since the latter are not part of gross national product, create no direct demand for a production of goods and services, and are therefore "wasteful" expenditures in the above sense.

Multiplier effects are not, of course, the sum total of "leverage" effects of public expenditures on national income. The direct "relation" effects of social security expenditures are, of course, zero; no goods and services are demanded directly. There is therefore a presumption that the relation effects of public in-

vestment expenditures will exceed those of social security outlays; the "relation" effects of the increased consumption resulting
from, say, family allowances would have to be very great indeed
to outweigh the "relation" effects of both primary and secondary
increases in demand for goods and services resulting from public
investment. Much will depend, of course, upon the size of the
stock piles of raw materials and equipment utilized in public
investment projects, and the extent of excess capacity for producing such raw materials and equipment, when the program
is initiated. On the other hand, it is possible that "induced
private investment" will be less in the case of public investment
than in the case of transfer payments, if the program is permitted
to lend to a rise interest rates or in the prices of labor, materials,
and equipment utilized by private enterprise, or if business men
simply dislike government investment more than government
doles.[30]

KEYNES AND PUBLIC INVESTMENT PRACTICE

Keynesian public investment economics has had enormous
practical success. During the downswing of 1929–32, almost no
government advocated increased public investment. Now many
governments give lip-service to the principles outlined above.
At a session of the International Development Works Committee
of the I.L.O., meeting in Montreal in January, 1946, the representatives of ten governments, together with representatives of
labor and management, had no difficulty in reaching an agreement on ten points of public investment policy formulated in
Keynesian terms.[31] The English, Canadian, and Australian "White
Papers" on employment policy, and the original United States
Full Employment Bill of 1945, are all essentially Keynesian
documents. Moreover, several governments have passed legislation to put such principles into effect, and a few have even set
about resolutely to prepare in advance programs of public in-

[30] There is some evidence that the businessmen of this continent do prefer
outlays on social security benefits to public works. If we can judge from some
remarks of Dr. Kalecki, the reverse is true of England. He states that
"subsidizing mass consumption is much more violently opposed by these
(business) 'experts' than public investment. For here a 'moral' principle of
the highest importance is at stake. The fundamentals of capitalist ethics require that 'You shall earn your bread in sweat'—unless you happen to have
private means." (M. Kalecki, "Political Aspects of Full Employment," PQ,
October-December, 1943, p. 326.)

[31] [Cf. the essay of Dr. Colm above.]

vestment to meet the postwar recession if, as, and when it develops.[32] Much remains to be done before all governments will be adequately prepared to meet a recession with a well-planned public investment program; but Keynes and his followers have provided a *rationale* for a full-employment public investment policy so simple, so clear, and so convincing, that few democratic governments will be able to forgo its adoption when all is no longer quiet on the employment front.

[32] Public investment planning of various countries up to the end of the first postwar year is outlined in Part V of my *Public Investment & Full Employment, op. cit.*

CHAPTER XXXVI

The Multiplier

By RICHARD M. GOODWIN

LORD KEYNES did not discover the multiplier; that honor belongs to Mr. R. F. Kahn.[1] But he gave it the rôle it plays today, by transforming it from an instrument for the analysis of road building into one for the analysis of income building. From his own and subsequent work we now have a theory, or at least its sound beginnings, of income generation and propagation, which has magnificent sweep and simplicity. It set a fresh wind blowing through the structure of economic thought.

THE ELEMENTS OF THE THEORY

At any one moment we may divide all income-generating expenditure into two classes: there is that which is determined by the level of income; and there is the remainder consisting in any spending not out of income. The latter we may call *injections.* All the expenditure, including the injections, becomes income, so that its future career will be entirely accounted for as spending out of income. If, then, we are careful to include current spending not out of income, all possible sources of income are reckoned with. In such a fashion we describe the injection of income and its transmission through economy, or, alternatively, the impulse and its propagation. Expenditure out of income constitutes the bulk of the whole, comprising ordinary consumer expenditures on perishable goods and services. Government and private investment are the most important injections, but some part of war or relief expenditures, as well as consumer spending for durable goods, must be included.

[1] Cf. his famous article, "The Relation of Home Investment to Unemployment," EJ, June, 1931.

To make the reason for the distinction clear, we may consider a typical injection, an act of investment by a firm. The spending is undertaken not because of current but rather expected output, and ordinarily it cannot be financed out of current receipts. The amount of the investment will accrue, directly and indirectly, as income, and from then on it is a question of the propagation of the impulse through the economy. After varying lengths of time, the income receivers will spend a certain portion of the added income. This will subsequently lead to still more income and so on indefinitely—indefinitely, but not without limit, for the fact that any but an abnormal society will have a marginal propensity to consume between zero and one, means that it is a dwindling series of successive additions to income. If all injections are taken into account, and likewise all spending out of income, since the former leads to the latter, nothing relevant is omitted. To determine in practice what an injection is requires much ingenuity, even though the principle is clear and fairly simple.

When once understood, the distinction disposes of the spurious objection that what is done with savings has been ignored. If they lead to injections then it is obviously not so, and if they do not, then they ought properly to be left out of account so far as income is concerned. It should be noted that there is no implication of any inherent tendency to die down. If the injections equal the savings out of income, then income will remain constant; if they exceed savings, it will increase.

To bring out clearly the nature and problems of multiplier analysis, we must make rather narrow and somewhat unrealistic assumptions. I shall not attempt to discuss the more difficult task of when and how to relax them. Except when specified to the contrary, I shall assume throughout a closed economy, constant prices, and some sort of unchanged distribution of income. With a fixed distribution, we may take an average of the various individual marginal propensities to consume, and reason as if all individuals had the same marginal propensity: α. It may not be too far wrong further to assume that, for a limited variation in income, α is constant. In these circumstances each dollar injected will give rise, at succeeding intervals, to incomes of .

$$1, \alpha, \alpha^2, \alpha^3, \alpha^4, \ldots \ldots \ldots$$

These may be "added" to find the total result of the injection in all subsequent time. It is

$$\frac{1}{1-a}$$

and is called the multiplier, since it tells us by how much the original injection is multiplied to obtain the final result. This set of numbers gives the typical life history of any dollar spent. Should one dollar be injected at regular intervals for some time, all stages in the progress of an expenditure from birth to death will come to be represented simultaneously. The group will exemplify the life history of the individual. Today's spending is in full force, yesterday's in the first stage of dissolution, day-before-yesterday's in the second, and so on. Therefore, if the injections have been continuing, substantially all the stages will be represented, so that a steady injection will, after a time, raise income to the multiplier value, and keep it there.[2]

The multiplier, which began as an analysis of the effects of public spending, has thus broadened into a general concept of income formation. The income received at any time may be regarded as the result of all past injections in various stages of dissolution, a kind of backward-looking multiplier effect. There is, of course, no simple, observable multiplier, either forward or backward, where the rate of injections is changing. Income at any time is equal to current injections plus a fraction of the previous period's income, which was in turn the sum of the previous injection and income, and, thus regressing backward in time, we may explain present income as the sum of all past injections, each appropriately discounted. If we call $y(t)$ income at time t, and $i(t)$ the injections, then we have

$$
\begin{aligned}
y(t) &= i(t) + ay(t-1) \\
&= i(t) + ai(t-1) + a^2 y(t-2) \\
&= i(t) + ai(t-1) + a^2 i(t-2) + a^3 i(t-3) + \ldots\ldots
\end{aligned}
$$

$$(1) \qquad = \sum_{n=0}^{\infty} a^n i(t-n).$$

[2] For a formal proof, cf. P. A. Samuelson, "A Fundamental Multiplier Identity," EC, July-October, 1943.

The terms in the series rapidly become negligible. In this manner the propagation mechanism is completely stated.[3] Any time shape of injections can be easily handled, so that the problem becomes one of stating what determines the level of injections, or of finding out what they have been, are, or will be.

The multiplier is essentially and necessarily dynamic since the various quantities involved must be dated, else it loses all realistic content. Although only noted in passing, this point is made clearly in Kahn's original paper.

I am here considering the position in the final position of equilibrium when everything has settled down. But some time will, of course, elapse between the point when the primary employment begins, and the point when the secondary employment reaches its full dimensions, because wages and profits are not spent quite as soon as they are earned. I do not enter into the question of this time-lag.[4]

For some reason or other Keynes chose to ignore this dynamical aspect in his presentation of the multiplier in the *General Theory*. He stated it as a combination of a consumption function:

(2) $c = ay$,

and an income equation:

(3) $y = i + c$,

where c is consumption and i investment.
By substitution one gets:

(4) $y = \dfrac{1}{1-a} i$,

which apparently is instantaneously true at all points of time. Actually there is a time lag between the receipt of income and its spending in equation (2), and between its spending and subsequent re-emergence as income, as implied in equation (3). Therefore, the solution (4) only tells us the position which will

---

[3] Strictly speaking this only explains the movements around some level. The level is determined by a minimum consumption, i.e., that consumption which people would make if they had no income. If this be regarded as a constant new injection (since it is not determined by income), then the theory becomes complete.

[4] EJ, June, 1931, p. 183 n.

be approximated after a lapse of time, *if the rate of injection, i, remains constant.* Should it change, equation (4) will never, except by chance, give us the correct answer. In some passages Keynes admitted this, but defended his interpretation by saying that it would hold where there was perfect foresight.[5] This was true but useless, since entrepreneurs would have to foresee not only the consumption, but their own, and others', reactions to it, and the reactions to the reactions, etc., *ad infinitum.*

The difficulty is seen most forcibly if we imagine the marginal propensity to consume to be unity. Then the injection of one dollar would result *immediately* in an infinite income. If, on the other hand, we insert a lag, a dollar is added to income each period without end until something else changes; this is, in fact, merely what the quantity theory of money would predict where the injections are financed out of new money. One may imagine, however unlikely, an *α* greater than one, with the absurd result that an injection would lower income. A dynamic analysis shows that income would simply rise faster and faster with a constant rate of injection. The difficulty with using equation (4) here is that one is attempting to add something that has no sum.

The multiplier is thus seen to fulfill the most fundamental criterion of any theory—simplicity. We merely divide all expenditures, omitting inter-firm transactions and the like, into two classes, those springing from previously received income and all others. These injections of purchasing power then become income, so that if we have a quantitative theory of how income leads to further income, then we have a complete account of the genesis of all income. If it is permissible to assume that each unit of income in turn leads to a constant fraction (less than one) of itself in further income, the theory takes on an extremely simple form. Proceeding in this manner, we may regard national income at any point of time as the result of all past injections, reduced in accordance with how long ago they occurred. Or we may project into the future, by taking account of present income, present and forthcoming injections.

The actual process of "multiplying" income necessarily takes time, though Keynes chose to ignore this fact. While his manner of presenting it avoids complications, it hinders the student in grasping the essential nature of the mechanism. If the rate of injection is changing, for example, income will not be a multiple

[5] *General Theory*, p. 122.

of the concurrent rate of injection. However, the longer the period considered, the more nearly will it be so. In order to get some concrete idea of how long the process does require, it is desirable to look a little closer at the actual sequence of events.

THE NATURE OF THE LAG

Perhaps as a result of Keynes' static formulation, there has been surprisingly little discussion of the actual process by which income is multiplied. In dealing concretely with the lag, the problem cannot be avoided. The lag has usually been associated with the Robertsonian income expenditure period, taken over from monetary theory. Two points should be made about such a view. If one examines the matter closely, it is by no means certain, granted an average lapse of time between receipt of money and its spending, that there is any necessary structural lag between the level of income received and the rate of spending out of it. Secondly, if the lag does exist, it is very short for most incomes.

On the other hand, a much more important lag has been generally overlooked. It has been assumed implicitly in the literature that the spending of money for goods is *ipso facto* the generation of another income. In a certain logical sense this might be held to be true, since production is not validated as income until it is sold to the final user. But actually, by virtue of capitalistic production, all the incomes incident to the creation of goods (except the final profit or loss) have long since been paid out. The actual sale represents the unfreezing of capital. In the case of excessive inventories, for example, an injection may be stopped dead in the second round, merely liquidating capital which may then be held idle or used to repay bank loans. The vital question is: how does a change in sales affect the current rate of income payments by firms? Stated in this way, much of the simplicity of the analysis appears to be lost, since entrepreneurial reactions are undoubtedly complicated. We may, in part, save the simple multiplier theory by defining a passive action of firms as that which equates current production starting to current sales which means that current receipts will always exactly be disbursed. Any deviation from passivity involves an injection, positive or negative. In a sense this method solves nothing, since it transfers all the difficulties to another department, the theory of investment.

The fact that, even when the volume of sales is a direct guide to production, a significant lag will exist was first pointed out by Professor Frisch.[6] If an increase in sales is immediately matched by production started, there will be, nonetheless, a lag in the rate of earning of income behind the sales. Under ordinary circumstances, the lag will be to a good approximation one-half the fabrication time, and is therefore by no means negligible. That it is a lag of considerable magnitude is shown dramatically in a change-over to war or to peace production. It exists apart from such things as lethargy, reaction times, perverse anticipations, time to transmit orders, etc.

There can be no serious doubt that there is a lapse of time between the receipt of income and the receipt of another income caused by the spending of the first. It does not matter too much whether the explanation is Robertson's, or Frisch's or a combination of the two. But even if one accepts the existence of a lag, one may doubt that its magnitude is significant, and this was undoubtedly Keynes' belief. Probably the best evidence on the size of the lag comes from the statistics of income velocity. It is obvious, from the way the problem is stated, that the time from income creation to income creation implied in the velocity concept is the same as the over-all lag in the multiplier. On this point, and on this point alone, the two concepts coalesce, and the multiplier analysis can make important use of the rich empirical evidence from monetary studies. One should say, rather, that the two concepts agree if we mean the income velocity of active money. Keynes always accepted the hypothesis that the velocity of active money is substantially constant.[7] The evidence for such a constancy is considerable. The average value of income velocity in the United States for 1909–18 was 3.11, and for 1919–28 it was 3.08, according to Professor Angell.[8]

This constancy was maintained in spite of large variations in both money and income. By taking note only of long periods, we have some hope of eliminating most of the effects of idle money. In any case the lag cannot be longer than ⅓ year and might be ¼ or ⅕ year, since the velocity of active money was not less than 3 per year. It is worth pointing out explicitly that this does not utilize the hypothesis of the constancy of the velocity of

[6] Cf. his paper in *Essays in Honor of Gustav Cassel*. The concept was developed and applied more generally by Tinbergen, Kalecki, and others.
[7] *General Theory*, p. 201.
[8] *The Behavior of Money* (1936), Appendix.

money as an essential, explanatory device. The multiplier and the quantity hypothesis are contradictory. One may describe the multiplier process in velocity terms, but it may, and ordinarily will, require a variable velocity of all money. Consequently velocity has no explanatory value, since it is to multiplier, not velocity, theory that one has to turn for the explanation of the variations.

FURTHER DISCUSSION OF THE MECHANISM

The commonest assumption is the attribution of the whole lag to the delay between the receipt and the spending of income. I shall assume that all injections are in the form of investment, though with slight alterations the cases of, say, relief or bonus payments can be handled. Also, to avoid difficulties of analysis, I shall make the assumption, not in serious conflict with the empirical evidence, of a constant marginal propensity to consume.

For the consumption function we have:

$$(5) \quad c(t) = ay(t - \theta) + K.$$

The consumption is c, the marginal propensity to consume α, the average lag θ, and the amount of consumption with no income, a constant, K. If we call i investment, income received will be:

$$(6) \quad y(t) = ay(t - \theta) + K + i(t).$$

The complete solution will be the sum of two parts. The first, obtained by setting K and i equal to zero, is the propagation mechanism and is given by:

$$(7) \quad y(t) = Ya^{t/\theta}, \qquad t = \theta, 2\theta, 3\theta, \ldots .$$

where Y is a constant to be determined by whatever the value of $y(t)$ is at time zero. The second part is obtained by getting the particular results of the impulses, or injections, i and K. Should i be a constant, I, we get:

$$(8) \quad y(t) = \frac{K + I}{1 - a}.$$

The complete solution will consist in the sum of (7) and (8).

It may seem pointless to consider so often the improbable case of a constant level of investment. Actually, it is only a pedagogical device which is convenient for delineating the nature of the mechanism, but it may be justified in the following way. Wherever the marginal propensity to consume is constant, we may utilize the superposition theorem, which states that the propagation of any one impulse through the system is independent of all others, so that the net result of many impulses can be found by simple addition of the solutions for each one separately. Any increment or decrement to investment may be treated as an isolated impulse, which is propagated through society quite independently

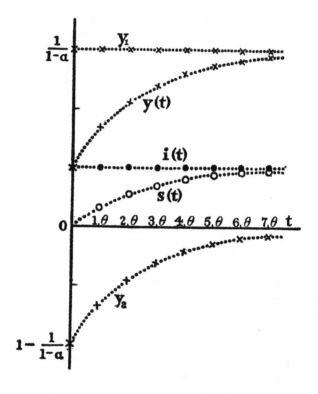

of any other impulses past or present. When investment increases, we can calculate the behavior of income as if the addition would last forever, and add the results to the previously determined income. Then, if investment decreases, we can treat the reduction as a negative investment which lasts forever, the permanent increase and decrease combining to make one which lasts for the actual duration. By adding the effects of constant positive and negative shifts, we get the correct result of the actual ever-varying investment.

In Figure 1, an analysis is given of the results of the imposition of a constant rate of investment of one dollar per period. If I dollars are invested, by addition we get simply I times the solution for one dollar. Since the impulse may be studied by itself, we may ignore what income would have been otherwise and simply call it zero. The arbitrary constant Y in (7) must be determined so that y equals one when t equals zero. The solution for any one dollar invested is, then:

$$y(t) = \left(1 - \frac{1}{1 - a}\right)a^{t/\theta} + \frac{1}{1 - a}.$$

As is evident in the diagram, the solution is the sum of two parts, y_1 and y_2, a constant level and a dwindling series.

We may define a time constant, τ, as that time in which the direct results of an impulse are nine-tenths achieved, i.e.:

$$a^{\tau/\theta} = .1.$$

This requires that:

$$(9) \quad \tau = \theta \frac{\log .1}{\log a}.$$

Evidently the longer the lag and the smaller the marginal propensity to consume, the longer the time required to attain, substantially, the multiplier effect. If τ is small, then Keynes was perhaps justified in ignoring the dynamical problem. Taking θ as ¼ year, we find τ to be 5.6 years for $\alpha = .9$, 1.6 years for .7, and .8 year for $\alpha = .5$. None of these can be called small with respect to any but quite long-run problems.

This model gives a convenient vantage point from which to view the Keynes-Robertson controversy about the equality, or lack of it, between savings and investment.[9] It was a disagreement about definitions, and about definitions there can be no question of truth; the only criterion is usefulness. On this score there can be, I think, little doubt that the Robertsonian definitions are preferable. This is, of course, only so if there is a significant lag. The existence of the lag is not at all a matter of definition, but an hypothesis about reality which is either true or false.

If we define savings, $s(t)$, as the same thing as investment, then, naturally, they remain equal throughout any change. In

[9] An excellent treatment of it will be found in G. Haberler, *Prosperity and Depression* (1941), pp. 170–195.

Figure 1, $s(t)$ would be identical with $i(t)$ and hence would certainly not have any explanatory value. If, following Professor Robertson, we call the flow of savings:

(10) $s(t) = y(t - \theta) - ay(t - \theta) - K$,

then $s(t)$ is in general not equal to $i(t)$, which is given by (6). Subtracting (10) from (6) we have:

(11) $i(t) - s(t) = y(t) - y(t - \theta)$.

Savings and investment will only be equal for a constant level of income, i.e., $y(t) = y(t - \theta)$, as is suggested by Figure 1. When investment exceeds saving, income must be increasing. When saving exceeds investment, income must be decreasing. It is precisely these differences which cause income to increase or decrease, and it is the gradual equating of the two that determines the level that income gradually approaches. This way of regarding the matter surely makes Keynes' point, but does it with greater clarity and persuasiveness. In passing, we may note how strikingly similar is this statement of the problem to the formulation in the *Treatise*. The similarity is, in part, illusory because the definitions and reasoning are different.

The Robertsonian definitions are best thought of in terms of the supply of savings (out of yesterday's income) and the demand for funds for today's investments. If a gap occurs between the two, it must be made up by a change in the amount of active money, either by the creation or destruction of money, or by changes in hoards, or both. At this point occurs the connection with monetary analysis. If the regular injection of one dollar is commenced, the new funds needed but not available out of current savings will be successively:

$$1, a, a^2, a^3, \ldots \ldots \ldots \ldots \ldots$$

This is the multiplier series for a single impulse, so that we find, as it should be, that the additional money required is just equal to the increased level of income. Income is reckoned per period, which means that income velocity for active money is *one*. Were we to use the year as time unit, we would multiply income, but not the stock of money, by the number of periods per year to get annual velocity. If all the new active money is newly created money, and if there was no idle money before, the velocity will remain constant, otherwise not.

It is worth noting that the expansion of active money falls off rapidly even though the injections continue. In general, so long as a spending program does not tend to grow indefinitely, it will become self-financing in the sense of inducing the necessary savings out of income: this is simply another way of stating the tendency of income to rise sufficiently for savings to become equal to investment. The inverse proposition is that a depression brings its own monetary solution by drying up savings and ending hoarding.

It is not difficult to see that most of the forgoing conclusions apply equally if the essential lag is in the productive rather than in the consumptive process. In this case we have:

$$(12) \quad c(t) = ay(t) + K,$$

and:

$$(13) \quad y(t + \epsilon) = ay(t) + K + i(t).$$

From (12) and (13) it follows that:

$$(14) \quad i(t) - s(t) = y(t + \epsilon) - y(t),$$

which has the same consequences as (11). Income increases, decreases, or remains stationary, depending on the difference between saving and investment. All the events are the same for the two different hypotheses; only the timing is somewhat different. When investment is undertaken, income does not rise until the following period. The complete solution in this case for a constant $i(t)$ is simpler:

$$(15) \quad y(t) = \frac{I}{1 - a}(1 - a^t).$$

If we calculate the new active money required, we find:

$$(16) \quad m_1 = \sum_{t = 1}^{\infty} \left\{ y(t + 1) - y(t) \right\} = \frac{I}{1 - a} \sum_{t = 1}^{\infty} \left\{ a^t(1 - a) \right\}$$

$$= \frac{I}{1 - a}.$$

Again there is complete agreement with monetary analysis.

Formally it will obviously not make much difference which lag we utilize. Aside from some difference in the rate, both systems proceed to the same limit in obedience to the same kinds of rules. The chief distinction is in the nature of the lag. The effective production lag in many industries may easily be six months or more, so that an average lag of three months is quite possible. It is difficult to see how the average income-expenditure lag could be so great, since the bulk of all payments are on a weekly basis. If both lags are significant, then we may construct easily a combined system, the qualitative results of which are the same as the other two.

Great importance attaches to the question of just what is the magnitude of the multiplier. There are unfortunately some obstacles in the way of statistical estimates. The theory is simple, but its simplicity is partly achieved by leaving out complications. Even on the safe ground of pure theory there is no such thing as an observable multiplier, because of the necessity of postulating some kind of lag. From equation (1), we can see that current income is not a constant multiple of current injections, but is rather a mélange of the effect of many past ones. Therefore the multiplier cannot be estimated directly from national income data. A somewhat more satisfactory procedure is to attempt from time series to estimate the consumption function, from which we can then infer the multiplier. As an alternative, one may use budget studies of savings. While this method is in theory preferable, in practice it is not easy. It may not take adequate account of business savings, which are very important. Also it requires explicit handling of the question of the distribution of incomes, whereas the more slipshod time series procedure may make a rough allowance by lumping any systematic shifts in distribution with the true consumption function.

Another difficulty, which we have assumed away, is presented by foreign trade. This represents one of the special aspects of the multiplier which cannot be treated here because of limitations of space. Suffice it to say that an import (or import service) is a source and an export (or export service) a sink of spending much like savings and investment. The way in which these payments are introduced makes a considerable difference in countries with large foreign payments.

In his original paper, Kahn estimated the British employment multiplier at between one and a half and two. This figure is low because no account was taken of exports. Later, Mr. Colin Clark, by a somewhat dubious procedure, attempted to take account of both imports and exports, with the resulting values of 2.1 and 3.2 for two periods.[10] Keynes put the value of the multiplier for the United States at around 2.5.[11] Utilizing later and more complete data, Professor Samuelson obtained the value of 2.2.[12] Needless to say, all estimates refer to the static or limiting value of the multiplier. What is surprising, indeed impressive, is the degree of agreement, not the discrepancies.

THE MULTIPLIER WITH FULL EMPLOYMENT

Throughout, we have assumed that variations in money income were variations in real income, i.e., that prices were constant. If prices change, complications arise, because, while consumers may be taken, as a first approximation, to consider only real income, it is money income that flows through the economy. To facilitate discussion, it is convenient to assume that there is a perfectly elastic supply of everything up to full employment, then perfectly inelastic beyond.

"When full employment is reached, any attempt to increase investment still further will set up a tendency in money-prices to rise without limit, irrespective of the marginal propensity to consume; i.e., we shall have reached a state of true inflation." [13] That it is so may be seen by considering the fact that a stationary state can only be reached when income receivers are saving just as much as investors want. If investors succeed in increasing the rate of *real* investment, prices must rise at a certain rate, since only the impossible, a rise in real income, would bring greater savings out of a steady level of income.

Perhaps of greater importance is the analysis of the results of a monetary injection, either a single pulse or a constant level. From Figure 2 we can easily see what happens. The consumption function is *eb* up to full employment income, *f*, after which proportions are kept constant, so that we follow along a straight line through the origin, *bh*, leaving real consumption and real savings constant with higher prices and higher money incomes. The line *bh* will be straight even if *eb* is not. The marginal propensity to consume, the slope of *bh*, will be higher but necessarily less than

---

[10] "The Determination of the Multiplier from National Income Statistics," EJ, Sept., 1938.

[11] *General Theory*, p. 128.

[12] Appendix to Chap. XI, in Hansen, *Fiscal Policy and Business Cycles* (1941).

[13] *General Theory*, p. 118.

one: therefore any expansion will terminate. If the constant rate of investment, *bd*, is raised by *dj*, then income and prices must rise until the real value of the larger money investment is reduced to its previous level, at which point the public's flow of money savings will be equal to the larger rate of money investment. This point may be found graphically by drawing a line through *j* parallel to *bh*. Where it intersects *od* at *k*, income will come to rest. It does not follow that there is no addition to the rate of real investment: there will be a passing rise, which is gradually wiped

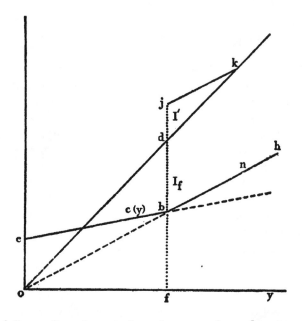

out. It follows that there is forced saving through price rises, so that we have the Keynesian analogue to the Wicksellian theory. A single injection gives the same result, except that the series of decreasing increments, in the one case, are the set of declining total effects in the other. In either case, the multiplier for money income is larger in the region of full employment, since the marginal propensity to consume is greater. It also follows, though not obviously, that the process of reaching the multiplier value takes longer.

To discuss the problem, I propose to assume a production rather than a consumption income lag, which may be set equal to one time unit. The results will differ depending on the relative behavior of production and consumption goods. I shall make the simplest, though scarcely the most realistic, assumption, namely, that they move together, so that one price level, p, is applicable to everything. If the subscripts r and m are used to denote real and monetary, then we have for the consumption function:

(17) $c_r(t) = ay_r(t) + K$,

and for the income equation:

(18) $y_m(t) = c_m(t - 1) + i_m(t - 1)$.

The price level is given by:

(19) $p(t) = 1/Y_f \; y_m(t + 1)$,

where Y_f is the constant level of full employment, real income. The solution, in monetary terms, for the propagation mechanism is:

(20) $y(t) = Y \left(\dfrac{a}{1 - K/Y_f} \right)^t$.

If a one dollar per period investment is commenced and maintained from $t = O$, the complete solution is:

(21) $y(t) = \dfrac{1}{1 - (a + K/Y_f)} \left\{ 1 - \left(\dfrac{a}{1 - K/Y_f} \right)^t \right\}$.

The full employment multiplier is, therefore:

(22) $\dfrac{1}{1 - (a + K/Y_f)}$,

which is larger than the under-employment multiplier but necessarily finite. The quantity $a + K/Y_f$ is the slope of bh in Figure 2, and hence one sees easily that the closer is the "break-even point," $c = y$, to full employment, the larger the multiplier becomes. Although income rises faster above full employment, it has further to go to reach the multiplier value. The time taken by the process is longer, the time constant being:

(23) $\tau = \dfrac{log \ .1}{log \left(\dfrac{a}{1 - K/Y_f} \right)}$,

which is larger than in the ordinary case (9).

If at full employment a constant level of money investment, I', is undertaken, we may calculate the total forced saving, or capital added, as a result. The added real investment at any time will be:

$$i'_r(t) = \frac{I_f + I'}{p(t)} \doteq I_f.$$

Total forced saving will be the sum of these for all subsequent time, and can be shown to be:

$$(24) \quad \sum_{t=0}^{\infty} i'_r(t) = \frac{I_f \, I'}{I_f + I'} \sum_{t=1}^{\infty} \frac{h^t}{1 - \frac{I'}{I_f + I'} h^t},$$

where:

$$h = \frac{a}{1 - K/Y_f}.$$

Although convergent, the limit of the sum of the series is not easily found. If, however, the increment of investment, I', is a small portion of the total, forced saving will be approximately:

$$\frac{I_f}{I_f + I'} \, I' \left\{ \frac{1}{1 - h} - 1 \right\}.$$

Wicksell pointed out that the rise in prices would in turn push up the marginal efficiency of capital, so that even with no other change, the money rate of investment would be likely to increase, counteracting the attenuation in the real rate of investment due to rising prices. It was for this reason that he called it a cumulative process: it does not stop until some outside factor breaks the spiral. The simplest case corresponding to these conditions would be a rate of added monetary investment varying so as to keep the real rate constant. This will be so if:

$$(25) \quad i_m(t) = p(t) \, (I'_r + I_f)$$

where I'_r is the constant added rate of real investment. Inserting (25) into (17), (18), and (19), we get:

$$(26) \quad \left(1 - \frac{K + I'_r + I_f}{Y_f} \right) y(t) - a y(t-1) = 0.$$

The complete solution will be:

$$(27) \quad y(t) = Y \lambda^t,$$

where:

$$\lambda = \frac{a}{1 - \dfrac{K + I'_r + I_f}{Y_f}} = \frac{Y_f - K - I_f}{Y_f - K - I_f - I'_r}.$$

Since $\lambda > 1$, the system is dynamically unstable: income will grow exponentially.

The great value of Keynes' work lies, and was meant to lie, in the realm of under-employment equilibria. In view of this, it is extraordinarily impressive to see with what ease and elegance the Keynesian apparatus deals with the "classical" question of the dynamics of inflation with full employment.

THE MULTIPLIER WITH IMPERFECTLY ELASTIC AGGREGATE SUPPLY

Before, perhaps well before, full employment is reached aggregate supply will in fact cease to be perfectly elastic. If the price rise is general, we may treat the problem by a judicious combination of the results from the two extremes of perfect elasticity and perfect inelasticity. Precise and complete analysis is difficult, because the equations cease to be linear.

It is clear that the result is not independent of whether, or by how much, prices rise. We cannot calculate the money multiplier as usual and deflate by prices to find the real income multiplier. The multiplier for money incomes is necessarily increased by price rises, with the consequence that the weakening effect of increasing prices on real income is mitigated. Real income will, however, not rise so much with increasing prices as without. To see this, one has only to reflect that as prices rise the real value of a constant money investment will decrease, so that it will come into equality with real savings at a lower real income than it would with constant prices. These conclusions do not apply to a constant level of real investment, since this will multiply real income by the usual value in any case. By how much more money income must increase will simply depend on how prices go up with the higher real output. In all cases the process takes longer than with constant prices.

PART SEVEN

Money and Prices

CHAPTER XXXVII

The Theory of Money and Prices

By JOHN LINTNER

No VOLUME dealing with the development and significance of Keynes' writings on economic subjects could be complete without a consideration of the relations between money supplies and general price levels. Not only did these issues concern Keynes through much of his active life, but his major writings made substantial contributions to the analysis of these problems.

It is particularly appropriate to review and analyze Keynes' work on money and prices at this time, because the significance of his work in this area has been somewhat overshadowed in the last ten years by the more immediately challenging problems of primary factors determining the levels of income and employment analyzed in the *General Theory*. With the recovery of high levels of employment accompanied by marked inflationary pressures during the years of the war effort and early postwar transition, and with public policy turning more strongly toward maintenance of high levels of activity throughout the system, problems of monetary policy and price levels come once more back toward the fore. In such times it is especially important to recognize that all of Keynes' valuable work was not encompassed by the "economics of depression" presented in the *General Theory;* that the latter work was indeed a *General* Theory of Employment, Interest *and* Money, making substantial contributions to our understanding of the behavior of the economic system at high levels of employment as well as low, and that the *General Theory* itself emphasized the importance of monetary influences on price movements as factors positively affecting changes in the level of income and employment.

A comparison of the contemporary analyses of inflationary pressures in the United States in World Wars I and II will provide a convenient framework for our consideration of Keynes' work on money and prices. Inflationary pressures in the first war were explained largely in terms of the quantity theory of money (which Keynes at that time accepted), whereas the analysis of inflation in the second war was conducted, by "Keynesians" and "non-Keynesians" alike, largely in terms of projected balance sheets of national income and the application of analytical concepts and relationships integrated for the first time in Keynes' *General Theory*. The first section of this essay consequently will review the analysis of inflationary pressures in this country during the first World War. The second section will briefly consider the importance of national income statistics, as developed between the wars, in measuring inflationary pressures. The third section will then review critically the progressive development of Keynes' theoretical analyses of money and prices as he moved from the simple quantity theories of the first war gradually on to the more sophisticated and more realistic income analysis of the *General Theory*. This section will attempt to identify the important contributions to the problem made in each of his major works, and it will emphasize the essential continuity in the development of his thinking. It will give particular attention to the *qualitative* character of the changes introduced at each new formulation, because these will provide clues to modifications in the generally accepted body of "Keynesian" analysis which may be required in the development of a still more adequate theory. The final section will review briefly the application of this analysis to the problem of inflation in the second World War.

1.

During the first World War, inflationary pressures due to war financing were discussed largely in terms of a simple quantity theory relating the supply of money and the supply of goods. Most discussions at the time were little more sophisticated than the statement that a larger percentage increase in money supplies than in the output of goods will "naturally" lead to an increase in general prices. Since total output was fixed within reasonably narrow limits by the quantity of basic productive resources available, inflationary price increases were charged primarily to increased money supplies due to war borrowing. While most writers were too cautious to expect that the rise in prices would be exactly equal to the percentage excess of the increase in circulating media over available supplies of goods, surprisingly little attention was given to the underlying factors which would alter the velocity of monetary circulation in wartime. Moreover, the whole analysis largely confined itself to a comparison of aggregate money supplies and *total* output (or transactions); it did not clearly distinguish between war output and production available for civilian purchase, and it did not allow for factors other than total money balances which will influence civilian demands for goods.

The report on "Fiscal Aspects of Bank Credit and Currency" of the *Committee on War Finance of the American Economic Association*, presented in March, 1919, is typical of contemporary analyses of the problem.[1] After reviewing the financial operations of the Treasury during the war, in which particular emphasis is given to the large increases in direct bank holdings of governments and in collateral loans against governments in connection with "borrow and buy" campaigns, the report comments that "the manifestation of the effects of war financing, aside from taxation, . . . is twofold: (1) changes in the volume of the currency and banking credit of the country and (2) changes in the price level."[2] Most of the report is taken up with statistics to indicate changes in physical volume of business, money in circulation, deposit currency, general prices, and wages. Recommendations are designed simply to "restore normal currency and banking conditions" through various measures to limit and/or reduce the current expansion of bank credit. Even though brief recognition is given in the Summary[3] to the fact that "some changes in prices and wages" are inevitable in wartime because of "the increasing demand for many types of commodities for war purposes, and the decrease, or rising cost, in the supply due to the diminution of the labor force," principal emphasis is given throughout to the side of currency and bank credit, following at least implicitly a simple quantity theory of money.

[1] The representative character of the report may be indicated by the distinguished membership of the Committee: Ernest L. Bogart, Charles J. Bullock, Fred R. Fairchild, Henry B. Gardner, Robert M. Haig, Jacob H. Hollander, Edwin W. Kemmerer, Alexander D. Noyes, Carl C. Plehn, William A. Scott, H. Parker Willis, and Edwin R. A. Seligman, Chairman.

[2] *Ibid.*, p. 93. It might be noted that in spite of this statement, which seems so clearly to imply a rather simple quantity theory, we find on p. 108 that "the committee expresses no opinion as to the general theory of what is called inflation or as to the comparative influences of the different forces at work, but leaves the facts to speak for themselves"!

[3] *Ibid.*, p. 125.

Kemmerer, who had been a member of the Committee on War Finance and Chairman of its subcommittee on Fiscal Aspects of Bank Credit and Currency, amplified the prevailing view in a paper on "The Causes and Progress of Inflation" before the Academy of Political Science in 1920. Distinguishing between causes connected with the war and those not directly related, he found the principal non-war causes to be the large gold production up to 1916 which increased available reserves, and three features of the Federal Reserve Act which economized on the use of these reserves—the reduced reserve requirements for member banks, the new Federal Reserve note, and the Federal Reserve clearing and collection system. He continues:

> The chief war causes of inflation were the heavy net importations of gold into this country resulting from Europe's unprecedented demands upon us for war supplies, the gold embargo, the great wartime reductions made in legal reserve requirements of our national banks and of many other member banks, the extensive resort by the government to loans for financing the war, particularly loans at artificially low rates of interest that were floated largely by the aid of very low discount rates at the federal reserve banks for war paper, and by the aid of undue encouragement of the public to borrow and buy. . . . The slackening of the usual rate of increase of physical production because of wartime readjustments and because of the depletion of our labor force, the more direct routing from producer to consumer of the goods produced, the wholesale destruction of the products of industry, and the speeding-up of the rates of monetary and deposit currency turnover, all contributed their part to the wartime inflation.

While most economists at the time generally accepted this analysis of the inflationary problem, some insisted on more or less important qualifications. One group, led by H. Parker Willis[4] and B. M. Anderson, Jr.,[5] inclined to put great emphasis on the "inferior quality" as well on the increased quantity of credit. Moulton[6] urged that the quantity theory was primarily adapted to explaining price levels in the exchange of goods already produced. Since the volume of output itself depends on the volume of busi-

[4] "The Federal Reserve System and Inflation," *Proceedings of the Academy of Political Science*, Vol. IX, pp. 42–55.
[5] *Ibid.*, pp. 63–66.
[6] "Banking Policy and the Price Situation," AER, *Supplement*, March, 1920, pp. 156–175; and "War Finance and the Price Level," JPE, October, 1919, pp. 694–715.

ness borrowing, a restriction of credit will not necessarily reduce prices, the price level of newly produced goods being determined primarily by costs of production. Others, led by Wesley Mitchell,[7] and R. C. Leffingwell,[8] Assistant Secretary of the Treasury, preferred to explain the rise in prices primarily in terms of a tremendous increase in demands for goods, due to the government's war needs, which could not be matched by increases in output. For them, credit expansion was more of a passive factor, sustaining and diffusing the increase in prices, than it was for the quantity theorists, but even this group considered factors increasing the quantity of outstanding credit to be of substantial importance in increasing demands and in causing further increases in prices.

Even though this last approach seems in many respects to be much the most realistic of those current during the earlier conflict, it remained essentially an explanation of prices at a given time in terms of the then existing supply and demand relationships. Reasonably cogent analysis was made of the *supplies* of different types of goods which could be offered in the market in wartime but there was little explanation (apart from quantity theories) of what determined the level of demands outside the war-goods sector dominated by the government, nor was the *process* of successive inflationary increases in these demands adequately explained. While proponents of the prevailing monetary analysis professed to explain both the level of demands at given times and the process of inflation, it is now clear that by concentrating on the volume of outstanding circulating media they were both oversimplifying and distorting the problem. They were oversimplifying it because they did not clearly distinguish demands for different important groups of products, and, indeed, could not estimate them separately in terms of the simple quantity theory they were using. They were distorting the problem because they assigned primary causal importance to one factor, the volume of money in circulation, which was, in fact, much more a reflection of *past* decisions with respect to the volume of expenditures and the form in which savings would be held, than a primary determinant of future demands for goods. By attaching primary significance to this secondary factor, they turned at-

---

[7] "Prices and Reconstruction," AER, *Supplement*, March, 1920, pp. 129–155.

[8] "Treasury Methods of Financing the War in Relation to Inflation," *Proceedings of the Academy of Political Science*, Vol. IX, pp. 16–41.

tention away from other elements of much greater importance in determining prospective demands for goods.

2.

Very great progress has been made in the analysis of inflationary pressures since the first World War. The improvement in realism and usefulness of the analysis is indeed so great that it constitutes an enduring tribute to the efforts of economists over the last quarter-century, and a promise of what may yet be accomplished in the development of a still more realistic and useful body of economic analysis of the problems of peace as well as those of war. This remains true even when full allowance is made for the uncertainties, confusion, and error, that marked some of the policy reports during the recent war.

This great advance between the wars in understanding of inflationary pressures is the result of two related lines of research. The first involved the development of a much more detailed and integrated statistical picture of the country's various economic activities than had been available during the earlier conflict. Largely after the first war, a whole system of accounting for the national economy was evolved in the form of national income and product statistics. These "balance sheets of the economy" in their various breakdowns meaningfully related the different elements of the increasingly rich body of data available covering current production and the allocations of output and resources between different principal uses, and the flows of income in the aggregate and for different major groupings of recipients, and the disposition of these incomes in the purchase of different types of goods and in different types of savings. These various balance sheets of national product and income data, when supplemented with information on employment and the available labor force, provided an important basis for estimating output potentials and the diversions of resources and production which would be required to meet military needs. When supplemented by data on consumption patterns, tax structures, and the allocations of savings, as well as base period and current holdings of assets by major groups in the economy, they provided an even more valuable benchmark for estimating probable demands in different important groups of markets.

This framework provided economists in the second World War with a realistic basis for appraising *simultaneously* both the supplies of various types of goods which would probably be forth-coming in the next quarter or year, and the pressures of demands which could be expected in corresponding groups of markets. By comparing the probable aggregate dollar demands for each class of goods with the supplies expected to be made available (both valued at prices prevailing at the start of the period), esti-mates of the upward pressure on prices for different broad cate-gories of goods—popularly known as "inflationary gaps"—could be obtained. Even though at various times there was considerable confusion between different "gaps," and inadequate or inappro-priate allowances made in the "benchmark estimates" for changes in patterns of consumer expenditure and business inventory be-havior which would be induced by the war and alternative public policies, nevertheless such simultaneous estimates of inflationary pressure in different parts of the economy provided a valuable guide to policy. This guide had been almost entirely lacking in the first conflict, because both the statistical basis and logical framework for such estimates were not then available.

Perhaps the greatest virtue of the methods used in the second war arose from the fact that the national income and product statements in their various breakdowns indicated for any period necessary *relationships between the totals* of various items of data on production, income flows, and allocations of income to expenditures and savings of different types. The different "sources and uses of income" statements for the economy as a whole must balance at the end of any period just as surely as the balance sheets or "source and application of funds" statements for an individual business. National income statements consequently provided not only a basis for estimating different important *ex-ante* "inflationary gaps," but also the framework within which they would necessarily have to work themselves out by the end of the period, when all books must balance and all gaps for the period just concluded must have become zero. There are, of course, a multitude of ways in which inflationary gaps may be resolved *ex-post*—price increases, "unexpected" [9] increases in out-put or unexpected drafts on inventories, unexpected or induced increases in savings, etc. Moreover, all of these may again be in-fluenced by policy decisions with respect to taxation, bond sales, priorities, allocations, and rationing, as well as price, inventory,

[9] "Unexpected" in this context implies developments not anticipated or adequately provided for in the construction of the estimates.

and other controls. But even though the basis for estimating the extent of each of these developments *individually,* and for estimating the specific *individual* effects which would be induced by different contemplated modifications of policy, were rough and often relatively insecure, the national income balance sheets nevertheless provided a framework of necessary relations which was a valuable check upon the *consistency* of these individual estimates. This was indeed a great step forward, for while it is quite possible to hold a consistent set of expectations each of which is individually in error (and this in fact occurred frequently), this framework at least made it possible to eliminate the still cruder errors of inconsistent sets of expectations.

The totals at which the national income statements would balance were, of course, not precisely known in advance, and were subject to estimate just like all the individual components in the statement. This led to the final two advantages of using this framework of analysis. First, the fact that almost all estimates to be used as a basis for policy had to be expressed in terms of *ranges* of probable values rather than as precise figures, helped encourage planners of the war program to adopt flexible plans, and also, because of the national income framework and the known relations between its various elements, to allow for the effects which the realization of the extreme value for one factor would have on the other elements of the statement and on the income totals themselves. Secondly, economists could allow in their estimates for the effects which price changes and other developments in particular groups of markets would have on income totals, accumulated balances, etc., and so be in a position to estimate probable inflationary pressures in various markets for an ensuing period. By tracing through these various alternative adjustments, the *process* of inflationary price movements could be studied realistically in terms of the summary balance sheets for the whole economy.

3.

The second line of research, which led to better understanding of inflationary pressures in the second World War, developed in the field of monetary theory. As shown in Section 1., most leading economists during the first World War blamed inflationary pressures primarily on the large volume of money in circulation, because apparent changes in over-all velocity was relatively small and because total output was fixed within relatively narrow limits by the available supplies of productive resources. Not only did the analysis run almost entirely in terms of the M, V, and T of the Fisher quantity equation, but it used a simple form of the quantity theory in which money supplies, adjusted for velocity, were held to be the primary causal factor determining the level of demands for output.

Now it must be admitted at once that the quantity equations, and even most of the quantity theories, however inadequate and misleading they may have been when improperly applied, represent major forward steps in the historic development of monetary theory. The quantity equation is, of course, simply an identity, but it did serve to focus attention on certain important over-all aggregates reflecting the activity of the economy, and it served as a convenient classificatory device for the discussion of the other features of the economy which determine why M, V, and T behave as they do. Just as the proposition that in free markets "price is determined by supply and demand," represented a major advance in the early development of economics, so did the quantity equations.

It is worth recalling, however, that the most fruitful developments in price theory have come only as a result of the *subsequent* efforts of economists to get back behind supply and demand in order (a) to identify more clearly and completely the individual, more basic, factors which are significant in determining "supply" and "demand" themselves, (b) to establish the way(s) in which changes in each of these underlying factors will affect "supply" and/or "demand," and (c) to determine the way(s) in which changes in each one of the basic factors will react upon all the others and, through them, on "supply" and "demand." *The process, in short, has been one of (1) continually drawing distinctions which can be shown to make a difference in results, and (2) determining at each stage the ways in which the more complete set of "building blocks," so identified, are related to each other and to demands and supplies offered in different market situations.* On the one hand, these developments have grown out of continuously more rigorous and general theoretical analysis, designed to develop the full implications of the conditions assumed in different theories, and, conversely, to determine the conditions and relationships which are both necessary and sufficient to validate the conclusions of various theoretical models previously enunciated. On the other hand, these developments have grown out of empirical work designed to test the realism and relevance of the conditions and relationships that had to be postulated in different theories, with the result that previous assumptions were modified and new elements and relationships were introduced into the theoretical analyses.

The development of monetary theory has, of course, followed along exactly the same lines. Investigations, during the last quarter-century, of the more basic factors which determine or influence the summary items M, V, P, and T of the equation of exchange, and particularly the investigations of the ways in which these underlying factors react on each other, have led to such substantial improvements in the whole theoretical analysis that scarcely more than the relationship of ancestry remains discernible when the recent writings, even of those such as Viner, Holm, Angell, or Fellner, who still use the framework of the old quantity equations, are compared with the work of, say, Kemmerer or Fisher at the time of the first war.

Unfortunately, it will be impossible to trace through all these developments in this paper. It will be possible, however, to trace this same kind of development in Keynes' writings on money and prices by reviewing briefly his analysis of these problems in the *Tract on Monetary Reform*, the *Treatise*, the *General Theory*, and his last volume, *How to Pay for the War*. This seems appropriate in view of his major contributions to monetary theory, the tremendous influence currently of his more recent writings, and the character of the present volume. Such a review will serve further to emphasize the essential continuity of the development of Keynes' theoretical writing, which has been unduly discounted recently, particularly among his more devoted followers. By confining attention to Keynes' contributions, however, the author does not wish to discount the value and significance of the contributions to the analysis made by other writers.

Keynes, until several years after the first World War, analyzed the factors determining the price level almost entirely in terms of the quantity theory of money, and accepted the validity of the theory without serious question. In reviewing Fisher's *Purchasing Power of Money* in 1911,[10] Keynes approved of Fisher's analysis and wanted merely to supplement it with Marshall's evidence before the Gold and Silver Commission and the Indian Currency Committee, in order to fill out the account of the way in which,

[10] EJ, September, 1911, pp. 393–8.

via strengthened bank reserves and an easier lending policy, an increase in gold stocks will have its *initial* effect in raising prices. In his *Indian Currency and Finance* in 1913, he used the quantity theory in a straightforward way to relate the sharp fluctuations in Indian prices to gold flows from other countries. He argued that these violent fluctuations in the internal price level had serious undesirable effects on both production and employment within the country, and proposed that the gold reserves should be centralized so that extraordinary drains could be met without serious disruption of the Indian economy. But while the proposal of a "managed" gold standard was unorthodox, the entire argument was conducted in terms of the orthodox quantity theory. The *Economic Consequences of the Peace* was equally orthodox in its treatment of money supplies and price movements.

Keynes' *Tract on Monetary Reform*, in 1923, likewise held the quantity theory to be "fundamental. Its correspondence with fact is not open to question." [11] He used the Cambridge "cash-balance" quantity equation throughout, interpreted so that the cost of living price level, p, depended passively on (a) the public's demand for cash balances, k and k' (measured in "consumption" units),[12] (b) the volume of cash and bank deposits, n, made available by the banking systems, and (c) the banks' reserve ratio, r. Keynes' objective in the *Tract* was to stabilize the price level in order "to avoid cyclical fluctuations" of boom and depressions.[13] Since business cycles were characterized in the past by fluctuations in the price level, due to the "tendency of k and k' to diminish during the boom and increase during the depression" uncompensated by changes in n and r, Keynes argued that there should be a strong Central Bank which should (1) exercise a stabilizing influence over k and k' by varying the bank rate, and, in so far as this failed or was impracticable, (2) deliberately vary n and r so as to counterbalance the movements in k and k'.[14] As

[11] Macmillan and Co., London, 1923 edition, p. 74. All other references will be to this edition.

[12] *Ibid.*, p. 78. This demand for real balances was held to reflect the wealth of the community and the habits of the public. These "habits are fixed by its estimation of the extra convenience of having more cash in hand as compared with the advantages to be got from spending the cash or investing it. The point of equilibrium is reached where the estimated advantages of keeping more cash in hand compared with those of spending or investing it."

[13] *Ibid.*, pp. 85, 82–3.

[14] *Ibid.*, p. 85. It should be noted that Keynes held that lowering the bank rate could somewhat counteract a tendency of k' to increase, because "easy

in the *Indian Currency,* Keynes' recommendations were unorthodox in favoring a strong Central Bank policy and a managed currency, but once his dubious assumption that stabilization of the internal price level will eliminate the business cycle is admitted, the rest of the argument depends on an orthodox, if somewhat improved, version of the quantity theory.

In spite of improvements over earlier quantity theories,[15] important confusions and unwarranted assumptions marred the analysis presented in the *Tract.* Before turning to the *Treatise,* it will be well to consider a few of the most important of these deficiencies, since Keynes' subsequent recognition of these defects and his efforts to allow for them realistically played such an important part in determining the development of his later theoretical analysis. First, even though Keynes at this time explicitly recognized that changes in price levels will induce corresponding changes in levels of output and employment—this was indeed one of his major reasons for wanting to stabilize the price level—he nevertheless failed to see that his analysis of the relation of money supplies and price could be valid only if output were in fact (relatively) constant. Other quantity theories which had total output as an explicit variable in their equations were in a somewhat better position than Keynes in this regard, but, like

---

lending diminished the advantage of keeping a margin for contingencies in cash," and conversely. Even though the k's were determined by relative advantages at the margin of holding cash as against spending *or investing* it, Keynes did not allow for a direct effect of changes in bank rate on the relative advantage of investing funds.

[15] The Cambridge "cash-balance" quantity theory, used and developed by Keynes in the *Tract,* represented a substantial advance over the Fisher type, prevailing in America, in at least two respects. First, it dealt with the cost-of-living price index which is a less ambiguous and more significant measure than the rather nebulous and conglomerate average price level of *all* transactions used in the Fisher equation. Secondly, it had the advantage that in working with the "real balances" the public would desire to hold, determined by comparisons at the margin of the relative advantages of holding money as against spending or investing, the analysis focused attention on subjective valuations of individuals and business firms much more directly than did most current discussions of "velocities." (V/T and k are of course reciprocals, reflecting identical underlying causal factors, when the universe of trade against which they are held and ultimately spent is properly defined.) This shift in viewpoint led later to the recognition and removal of important confusions still latent in the analysis and to the identification of *qualitatively distinct* motives of holding funds, as well as to the later synthesizing of the previously separate "monetary" and "price" theory.

Keynes, they had no adequate theory of the determination of the level of output as a whole or of the interaction between output and money supplies, price levels, velocities, real or money balances, etc. This most important defect of the Tract, as of other quantity theories, was not to be overcome until the appearance of the *General Theory* a decade later—and, as will be indicated below, much work yet remains to be done. Second, and next most important, the *Tract*, in keeping with other quantity theories, treated money solely as a (current) medium of exchange.[16] Precautionary motives were treated vaguely and incidentally; motives related to money as a store of value involving speculative decisions were never mentioned. Third, there were serious confusions because the balances of all the public were lumped together. Actually, of course, as was later recognized, the liquid balances of different important groups of holders behave very differently because they reflect the influence of substantially different sets of underlying determinants; moreover, shifts in balances between different types of holders may be of substantial importance, quite apart from changes in the totals of all balances held.[17]

The second and third of these major deficiencies of the *Tract* were largely, if not entirely, eliminated in the *Treatise,* published seven years later, and some definite, but confused, effort was made to meet the first. Much of the analysis of the *Treatise* was, of course, loose and incomplete, and at times it was confused and even contradictory (especially where the level of output was involved as a significant variable). Nevertheless, this effort "to find a method which is useful in describing, not merely the characteristics of static equilibrium, but also those of disequilibrium, and

[16] *Ibid.,* p. 75. "The theory flows from the fact that money as such has no utility except what is derived from its exchange value, that is to say, from the utility of the things which it can buy . . . What the public wants is not so many ounces, or even so many £ sterling of currency notes, but a quantity sufficient to cover a week's wages, or to pay their bills, or to meet their probable outgoings on a journey or a day's shopping. When people find themselves with more cash than they require for such purposes, they get rid of the surplus."

[17] As an example of this confusion, the *Tract* related the balances of individuals and business firms (which together made up Keynes' "public") directly to the price of the "consumption unit" or the cost-of-living index, even though the bill of goods against which business firms hold balances differs significantly from the consumers' basket.

to discover the dynamical laws governing the passage of a monetary system from one position of equilibrium to another," [18] represented a necessary intermediate stage in the development of Keynes' analysis between the *Tract* and the *General Theory*. Even though it clearly shows the growing pains of Keynes' struggle to get his theoretical analysis on a sound and realistic footing, its important contributions to the development of monetary theory must not be discounted on this account.

The most important contribution of the *Treatise* to monetary theory lay in the improved analysis of the motives for holding money and the factors which will determine the amount of different types of balances the public will desire to hold. Earlier writers had, of course, recognized that money served as a store of value as well as a medium of current exchange, and cash hoards were frequently mentioned in the literature, but the *Treatise* for the first time explained these motives for holding money as an integral part of a theory of the relations of money supplies and price levels. The importance of this innovation in monetary theory can scarcely be overemphasized—only the integration of the theory of money with a theory of output as a whole can take precedence. Theory no longer *assumed* that the public held balances only to spend them and that a change in its balances necessarily led to a corresponding change in current spending. Income receivers no longer were permitted in the theoretical models to choose *only* between currently spending or saving their incomes. Theory at last allowed for the decision whether to spend or save, *and* for the further decision whether the current money savings (and the accumulated savings from the past) would be held as money balances *or* invested, and for the important underlying factors determining that decision.

This great advance involved an important *qualitative* distinction between balances held for spending on the one hand and money balances held as savings deposits on the other. The volume of the first type of balances which individuals and business firms would want to hold, called "income deposits" in the *Treatise*, was related to the level of total incomes by way of the velocity of circulation of income deposits.[19] But the formal similarity of this

---

[18] *A Treatise on Money*, Preface, p. v, also cf. Vol. I, p. 133.

[19] This velocity was determined in turn by the intervals between receipts of income, the regularity of its disbursement, and the proportion of income carried over for spending from one income date to the next.

treatment to the earlier quantity theories must not be allowed to obscure its essential differences: (1) only income deposits, not total deposits, were directly related to incomes by velocity of circulation; and (2) since other types of balances were being held simultaneously, the restrictive and unrealistic assumption of earlier theories that money balances determined spending (income) could be relaxed, and necessary allowances made in the theory for the fact that the size of income balances the public desired was as much or more a *result* of the level of income (or, with output constant as Keynes still frequently assumed, a result of the level of *prices* of goods and services) as it was a determinant of them. An increase in money supplies, even with output and income velocities constant, would not necessarily increase prices proportionately, because the new balances might be held as savings deposits rather than as income deposits. The importance of this theoretical advance in interpreting inflationary pressures arising from increased money supplies, both in times of depression, such as the thirties, or in times of war, should be obvious.

The volume of savings deposits, in contrast to income deposits, the public would desire to hold was related not to the price level of goods and services or current incomes, but to the attractiveness of current investments which could be made with the funds.[20] The relative desirability of savings deposits and other investments will depend on the rate of interest that can be obtained on the former and, *ceteris paribus,* on the price level of the latter. Consequently, said Keynes, at any given rate of interest on savings deposits, together with a given set of anticipations of the public regarding (a) the income streams expected to be realized from the ownership of different investments *and* (b) the expected future changes in the price of investments (its "degree of bearishness"), there will be a functional relationship between the amount of savings deposits the public will desire to hold and the price level of investments. Since the volume of savings deposits actually available for the public to hold is determined by the banking system, the price level of investments will settle at the level indicated by the bearishness function at which the public

---

[20] "It is the criterion of a savings deposit that it is not required for the purpose of current payments and could, without inconvenience, be dispensed with if, for any reason, some other form of investment were to seem to be preferable." *Treatise,* Vol. 1, p. 36.

will *want* to hold neither more nor less than the amount of savings deposits available. Moreover, "the amount by which the creation of a given quantity of deposits will raise the price of (investments) above what their price would otherwise have been depends on the shape of the public's demand curve for savings deposits at different price levels of (investments)." [21]

This "bearishness function" of the *Treatise* is indeed the true parent of the "liquidity preference" so much emphasized in the *General Theory*.[22] The idea had been conceived, the relationship had been formulated, only clarification and refinement remained to be done to get this important "building block" of the *General Theory*. Keynes in the *Treatise* consistently considered "savings deposits" or "financial circulation" to include all balances not required for income purposes (the "transactions motive" of the *Theory*) or to provide against contingencies (the "precautionary motive" of the *Theory*), and if "investments" are limited to fixed coupon securities the bearishness function of the *Treatise* is in fact the liquidity preference of the *General Theory*, since, for such securities, "price" varies inversely with the interest rate.

Keynes in the *Treatise*, of course, still lumped debts with equity securities and non-liquid assets generally, and he used the relation to determine the general average price of this polyglot "investment" rather than the rate of interest. Moreover, while uncertainties and bearishness as to expected movements of the future price levels of investments were explicitly recognized and emphasized as determinants of the *position* of the bearishness function, he had not yet pushed his analysis to the point where he saw that these uncertainties and risks would determine the general *shape* of the function as well.

But it should be recognized that even though distinctions between assets had yet to be drawn, and relations of anticipated yields, risks, prices, and interest rates, still had to be clarified and refined, in some respects the analysis of savings deposits and bearishness in the *Treatise* is superior to that of liquidity prefer-

[21] *Treatise*, Vol. I, p. 143.

[22] Professor Schumpeter (AER, September, 1946, p. 506) finds "liquidity preference in embryonic form" in the variability of k in the *Tract*, but Keynes there allows only for the fact that "easy lending diminishes the advantage of keeping a margin for contingencies in cash" and does not otherwise relate k to the interest rate (*Tract*, p. 85). If this be embryonic liquidity preference (and it is so only in a "fin and gill" stage, if at all), then credit must go back at least to Fisher's *Purchasing Power of Money*.

ence in the *General Theory*. In the first place, Keynes in the *Treatise* emphasizes that the public's relative preferences for savings deposits and other assets depend on "expectations of the future return to be obtained from savings deposits and from other (assets) respectively, which is obviously affected by the price of the latter—*and also by the rate of interest allowed on the former.*"[23] In the *General Theory*, and in ensuing discussions, liquidity preference has been analyzed too much in terms of a comparison of net expected return from bonds and a zero rate on "speculative balances." The importance of recognizing interest return on these balances is indicated by the fact that on July 1, 1946, the public had roughly $50 billion in deposits drawing interest of from 1 to 3½ per cent, while adjusted demand deposits and circulating currency (a very large part of both being held for transactions and precautionary purposes) amounted to a fraction over $106 billion.[24] While the institutions holding these interest-bearing deposits were comparing adjusted bond yields with zero rates, the public holders obviously were not.

Moreover, the importance of autonomous shifts of the bearishness functions is emphasized as much, or more, in the *Treatise* ·as in the *General Theory*—a consideration of increasing importance as economic theory turns more and more to an analysis of the dynamics of transition periods, and as the public holds even larger volumes of easily shiftable assets, including government and other bonds, stocks, deposits, currency, etc. Finally, it should be noted that, even though the analysis of the prices of non-fixed coupon assets in the *Treatise* was inadequate, the *Treatise* did recognize and allow for the fact that the public's demand for "financial balances" depends as much or more on the prices, anticipated yields, and expected price movements of these other assets, such as equities, real estate, capital plant and equipment, etc., as it does on bonds and debts. In contrast, the *General Theory*, rather than clarifying and refining these important relationships, interpreted the public's demand for speculative balances in terms of net anticipated yields on bonds and debts

[23] *Treatise*, Vol. I, pp. 141–2.
[24] FRB, November, 1946. The first figure includes time deposits of commercial banks, mutual savings banks, postal savings, as well as $7.4 billion in accounts in savings and loan associations (*Federal Home Loan Bank Review*, November, 1946, p. 42), giving a total of $59.2 billion, which must be reduced somewhat to allow for the fact that some commercial banks were not paying interest in their (usually small) savings departments.

alone.[25] The importance of this lapse may be judged from the fact that the total funded debt of all American corporations in 1941 was only $36 billion as compared with book equities of $128 billion.[26] Not only must an adequate theory allow for the direct relation of these "other assets" to interest rates, but qualitative distinctions between these assets must be incorporated into the analysis. This lapse has been made good on an abstract theoretical level by Hicks, Marschak, and Timlin, who determine the rate of interest as a marginal rate of substitution between all assets— but even this formulation leaves out of account very significant institutional factors.

Before proceeding to other matters, it should also be noted that Keynes' discussion in the *Treatise* of the relations between anticipations, uncertainties, and the price level of assets, led him to formulate what he later termed the "marginal efficiency of capital." For he argued in the *Treatise* that the price level of new investment goods "depends on the anticipated price level of the utilities which these investments will yield up . . . and on the rate of interest at which these are discounted," [27] and the volume of new investment which will be undertaken will depend on the relation of this value of new investment goods to their costs. Moreover, these latter two factors (excluding cost of borrowing) were used to determine a "prospective net yield of new capital," [28] which falls short of the marginal efficiency of capital of the *General Theory* by only minor refinements.

The second important line of theoretical development in the *Treatise* lay in its separate treatment of the different types of balances held by business firms and by individuals. Keynes not only distinguished between different *qualitative types* of balances, with the important results discussed above, but he recognized in the body of his theory that both transactions and speculative balances held by business firms will behave differently from those held by individuals, because business firms and indi-

[25] *General Theory*, p. 197.
[26] U. S. Treasury Department, *Statistics of Income*, Part 2, 1941, p. 102. Funded debt was taken to be "bonds, notes, and mortgages, payable with maturities of one year or more." "Book equity" includes $74 billion as the book value of preferred and common stock outstanding and $54 billion of book surplus attributable to equity securities.
[27] *Treatise*, Vol. I, p. 180.
[28] See, e.g., *Treatise*, Vol. I, 204.

viduals are in essentially different positions in the economy and will be responding to distinct, though related, sets of underlying economic data. Unfortunately, much of this valuable analysis of the *Treatise* was not retained in the models of the *General Theory* —to the detriment of the latter with respect to its treatment of money, prices, and interest rates, if not of employment levels as well. The models of the *General Theory* need to be broadened, to allow separately not only for different liquidity preference schedules of individuals and business firms, but also at least for commercial banks and other financial institutions. The schedules for each of these types of institutions will have a different position and shape, and show distinctive characteristic movements over the business cycle, and indicate important differences in response to different hypothesized changes in underlying parameters such as an increase in money supply. This will be true because of the known differences in terms (both quantitative and qualitative) on which they obtain their funds; their different functions, responsibilities, and objectives; and the important differences in patterns of decision-making behavior as determined by historical precedents and legal restrictions, as well as their different position in current operations. These distinctions are nonetheless important for not having been included in the *"General" Theory.*[29]

[29] A related omission of substantial importance in the *General Theory* arises from the fact that it considers only the total volume of realized savings and does not allow for the different *forms* in which these savings accrue. For instance, the choice between institutions to hold the saved funds has important repercussions, since the lending (investment) policies of different institutions are so substantially different in types of borrowers served and in terms and maturities offered. Productive new investments will be undertaken only if the necessary funds are available (a) to the specific units desiring to make them, (b) at the time and in the amount required, and (c) on terms, financial and otherwise, which make them acceptable to the units contemplating the investments. Capital markets do not form one homogeneous unit. If the channeling of savings to different institutions does not make those savings effectively available to units needing funds for new investments, the *level of income may fall even though the volume of intended investment* (which could be effected if capital markets were in fact homogeneous) *exceeds* ex-ante *savings.* If it is to be adequate for use in connection with national policy, the Keynesian theoretical structure must be broadened to allow realistically for these important institutional features of the economy. Cf. J. Keith Butters and John Lintner, *Effect of Federal Taxes on Growing Enterprises,* Chaps. VII, VIII, and IX, esp. pp. 131–133; also Charles C. Abbott, *Financing Business during the Transition* (1944), Chap. VII, esp. pp. 98–101.

For one thing they play a most important part in explaining both the term structure of interest rates on a given type of security, such as government bonds, and the relative rates on different types of securities and lending. Even though the importance of both these latter factors has been recognized, the distinctions and relationships necessary to handle them adequately have not been incorporated into the theoretical models.

The final important development in Keynes' theoretical analysis shown by the *Treatise* lay in his treatment of the factors determining the levels of savings and investment, and his deliberate, though still very confused and faulty, efforts to relate fluctuations in savings and investment to changes in price levels, income, and output as a whole. In this regard, the *Treatise* begins by drawing a sharp distinction [30] between decisions concerning savings and investment, holding that "the decisions which determine savings and investment, respectively, are taken by two different sets of people, influenced by different sets of motives, each not paying very much attention to the other . . . Not only are the decisions made by different sets of persons; they must also in many cases be made at different times." [31] This distinction in the *Treatise* is fully as sharp as that embodied in the *General Theory*.[32] It is explained in another passage as follows:

> Saving is the act of the individual consumer and consists in the negative act of refraining from spending the whole of his current income on consumption. Investment, on the other hand, is the act

[29] In the Preface to the *Tract*, Keynes had foreshadowed this later distinction by noting that "We leave saving to the private investor, and we encourage him to place his savings mainly in titles to money (whereas) we leave responsibility for setting production in motion to the businessman, who is mainly influenced by the profits which he expects," but this distinction was used in the *Tract* only to distinguish between the effects of fluctuating prices upon "investors" and "businessmen." (*Tract*, p. v, Chap. I, pp. 1–27.) Savings were not directly related to the increment of real investment, nor was the interaction of changes in these magnitudes related to fluctuations in output, incomes, and price levels.

[31] *Treatise*, Vol. I, p. 279.

[32] Indeed, the distinction is drawn *too* sharply in both the *Treatise* and *General Theory* to square with known facts of the situation, since it fails to allow for the fact that some (perhaps substantial) volume of investment will be undertaken only if the particular units contemplating the investment can save the required funds. Cf. Butters and Lintner, *op. cit.*, and Henry C. Wallich, "The Effect of Taxation on Investment," *Harvard Business Review*, Summer, 1945, pp. 442–451.

of entrepreneur whose function it is to make the decisions which determine the amount of the nonavailable output.[33]

This, indeed, reads like a quotation from the *General Theory,* except for the fact that Keynes in the *Treatise* was excluding windfall profits by definition from income and hence from savings. Savings and investment would be equal, *by definition,* only in equilibrium, and were free to vary independently. While this definition of income and savings is nonoperational and artificial, and got him into trouble in his final theoretical structure, nevertheless it may be significant that by defining saving and investment so that they would be unequal, except in "equilibrium," he was led to examine more carefully into the factors determining them, with important results for the development of his analysis.

This examination, in fact, led him to conclude that "a disequilibrium between savings and investment . . . is much more often due to fluctuations in the rate of investment than to sudden changes in the rate of savings."[34] Thus, in the *Treatise,* as later in the *General Theory,* irregularities in the rate of investment are the primary dynamic initiating cause of change.[35] Professor Schumpeter's emphasis on *innovations*—involving practical application of new discoveries and inventions, development of *new* forms of organization, introduction of *new* products, conquest of *new* markets, shifting trade channels, etc.—as the primary explanation for these major fluctuations in investment is "unreservedly accepted."[36]

In contrast to this primary emphasis on the basic importance of fluctuations in autonomous investment, Keynes considered that "the business of saving is essentially a steady process. If there are disturbances in the economic world, these *by affecting prosperity* may react on the rate of savings. *But a disturbance will seldom or never be initiated by a sudden change in the proportion of current income which is being saved.*"[37] Similarly, though Keynes in the *Treatise* expected an increase in interest rates to increase

[33] *Treatise,* Vol. I, p. 172.
[34] *Ibid.,* Vol. II, p. 95.
[35] *Treatise,* Vol. I, p. 280.
[36] *Treatise,* Vol. II, pp. 95–6. The list within the dashes paraphrases Mitchell's summary (*Business Cycles,* p. 21) which Keynes quotes directly. Others, including Robertson and Spiethoff, are also cited with approval. *Ibid.,* pp. 100–101.
[37] *Treatise,* Vol. I, p. 280. Italics added.

savings, he allowed that "the amount of the effect may often be quantitatively small in practice, especially over the short period." [38]

He was, however, more optimistic about the possibilities of influencing, if not controlling, the volume of investment by varying interest rates. Since the attractiveness of new investments depends on their prospective returns *relative* to the interest cost of financing their production, [39] Keynes argued that the banking system through changes in its own terms of lending, and through its control over the supply of money and savings deposits (which via the "bearishness function" determine the price level of investments and interest rates), could strongly influence the volume of investment undertaken. Indeed, he goes so far as to argue at several points that, even though "the *net* result depends on the policy of the banking system as a free agent acting with design, it can, by coming in as a balancing factor, control the final outcome." [40]

The rest of the *Treatise* may be treated very briefly. It is significant that Keynes moved quite close to a "cost of production" theory of the price levels of goods and services, relating them directly to the normal earnings that would have to be offered different productive factors to secure their services in production. But the so-called fundamental equations, intended to reveal the dynamic causes and processes of income and price movements, were unessential, confusing, and erroneous. [41] Because of the artificial definition of income, a difference between savings and investment could only *reflect* a change in prices and could not exert a causal influence on prices. [42] Moreover, the whole work displayed a confused vacillation between arguments implicitly assuming output to be constant, [43] and those involving its fluctuation as a significant factor determining price movements. [44] But most fundamentally, the structure fell down because it lacked a

[38] *Ibid.*, p. 201.

[39] *Ibid.*, p. 154.

[40] The quotation is from *Treatise*, Vol. I, p. 183. It might be noted that Keynes is somewhat more doubtful as to the "influence of the interest rate on the volume of investment" in the *General Theory*.

[41] Cf. Alvin H. Hansen, "A Fundamental Error in Keynes' *Treatise on Money*," AER, September, 1932; and Keynes' reply, *Ibid.*, December, 1932. Also, Hansen, *Full Recovery or Stagnation?* (1938), Appendix I.

[42] Cf. Hawtrey, *The Art of Central Banking* (1932), esp. p. 349.

[43] See, for instance, *Treatise*, Vol. I, p. 173.

[44] As, for instance, *Ibid.*, p. 181.

coherent theory of the determination of income and output as a whole, and of the interrelationships between these variables and the other primary elements of the economy, including price levels. This was the great task remaining for the *General Theory*.

It certainly is true of the *Treatise*, as Keynes recognized in the Preface, that "its parts are not all entirely harmonious with one another . . . it represents a collection of material rather than a finished work." [45] The book had taken several years, during which his theories had been developing and changing, with the result that:

> There is a good deal in this book which represents the process of getting rid of the ideas which I used to have and of finding my way to those which I now have. There are many skins which I have sloughed still littering these pages . . . I feel like someone who has been forcing his way through a confused jungle. [46]

There were still more skins to slough, more jungle to cut through, more significant distinctions to be drawn, and more important operational relationships between variables to develop. But it is important to emphasize that at the time of the publication of the *Treatise*, Keynes was much farther along the road to the *General Theory* than has been generally recognized or admitted. Indeed, however badly their significance was obscured by confusing, faulty, or irrelevant observation and argument, almost all the important elements of the *General Theory* were already present in the *Treatise*—the major emphasis on fluctuations in autonomous investment, the primary dependence of consumption and saving on the level of income and only secondarily on interest, the basic dependence of transactions balances on income levels instead of the reverse, the bearishness function which was but a short step removed from liquidity preference and the investment-interest relation which was to become marginal efficiency of capital. Several of these elements had still to be refined and made more precise; one most important relationship (the consumption function) which was only implicit in the *Treatise* had to be made explicit and its implications developed; and all these elements had yet to be integrated into a coherent theory. But this involved no more than continuing the arduous, self-critical, and struggling process of developing his theories that Keynes had already been following for years. There was indeed

[45] *Ibid.*, pp. v and vi.
[46] *Ibid.*

no "break with his past" in the *General Theory*, but only the attainment of a new plateau in a progressive development that runs continuously from the *Tract* onward.

The development of Keynes' theoretical analysis in the *General Theory* may be reviewed rather briefly, in spite of its great importance, both because it is much better known and because several of its building blocks have already been introduced. Moreover, this discussion is concerned primarily with the *structure of the theory* rather than with recommendations with respect to depression policy.

The transition from the *Treatise* to the *General Theory* essentially involved two steps. First of all, the rather artificial, and certainly non-operational, definition of income in the earlier work had to be abandoned in favor of the more straight-forward definition of income developed by students of national income analysis. This had the advantage that it placed the rich empirical resources of national income statistics, and the conceptional framework of national income accounting, at the disposal of the rest of economic theory. Income, savings, consumption, and investment, *as defined in the theory*, all became measurable, observable entities, which led to the formulation of refutable hypotheses regarding their relationships. Indeed, one of the greatest virtues of the *General Theory* is that more of its elements are defined in an "operational,"[47] measurable manner, and more of its assumed relationships between variables are in the form of refutable hypotheses, than was generally the case in earlier theories. Adopting the definition of income used in studies of national income was the most important step in this direction taken in the *General Theory*. Unfortunately, however, the fact that, under these definitions, observed savings and investment will always be equal obscured the much more important fact that savings and investment enter the theory as *schedule relations* against income, being numerically equal only at the point of intersection.[48]

[47] Cf. Percy W. Bridgman, *Logic of Modern Physics* (1927).

[48] Rereading the *General Theory* is enough to confirm one's suspicion that Keynes himself contributed to the later embarrassing confusions in the literature by his dual and obscure discussions of the identity and diverse (virtual) changes in savings and investment. As Samuelson has well said (EC, July, 1946, p. 197) he never became clear on "the relationship between 'identity' and functional (or equilibrium-schedule) equality; between 'virtual' and observable movements; between causality and concomitance; between tautology and hypothesis"—even though these distinctions formed the neces-

The second step involved the formulation of the consumption function and the development of its implications. Keynes in the *Treatise* had observed that expenditure on consumption out of a given level of income will be relatively stable and little affected by interest rates, but he had not perceived a *schedule relation* between levels of consumption (or saving) and income. Once this relation was formulated, tentatively tested, *and assumed fixed*, then there must be a related stable relationship between fluctuations in investment and changes in the level of income—the famous "multiplier" relationship first enunciated by Kahn[49] and adopted by Keynes in his little pamphlet, *The Means to Prosperity*, in 1933. In the *General Theory*, Keynes used the consumption function to relate the *equilibrium levels* of investment and income, as well as their fluctuations. Indeed, this formed his basic theory of income determination: since the consumption function shows savings in a fixed schedule relation to income, and since the volume of investment which will be undertaken at a given time is autonomously given (or, *ceteris paribus*, related in a schedule sense to income levels), income will settle at the level indicated by the intersection of the two schedules, just as price in the Marshallian market diagram settles at the intersection of the demand-price and supply-price schedules (curves).

The great significance of this simple theory of the determination of income has been fully expounded by others, and no further encomiums need be offered here. But a few features of this theory of income and effective demand may be noted. First, it depends on the autonomous character of investment, either in absolute volume or in a schedule sense. This had been clearly foreshadowed in the *Treatise*. Secondly, it integrates into a coherent theory the vague premonitions of the *Tract* and the strong and at times rather fully developed arguments of the *Treatise* that all attempts to increase saving do not necessarily or automatically increase new investment expenditures.[50] It was this divorcement

sary analytical basis for the most significant contributions of the *General Theory!* His intuitions were later clarified by the work of the mathematical economists.

[49] R. F. Kahn, "The Relation of Home Investment to Unemployment," EJ, June, 1931.

[50] Some parts of the *Treatise*, e.g., the parable of the banana plantation, had even ascribed this to induced reductions in income levels, but the theory had not been made coherent, nor consistent with the balance of the theoretical structure of the work.

of acts of savings and of investment (cross-petitions for which had been filed by Keynes several years earlier) which led to the possibility of this "simple" theory of under-employment equilibrium and the overthrow of Say's Law. Thirdly, the formal similarity of Keynes' "savings-investment-income" cross, with the Marshallian "demand-supply-price" cross is significantly suggestive. Everyone by now is well aware of the tremendous weight on *ceteris paribus* in the Marshallian cross, but the fact that the theory of income embodied in the Keynesian cross correspondingly depends on assumptions of *ceteris paribus* has been obscured, perhaps by its aggregative character.[51] The frequent failure of some of the more ardent "Keynesians" to allow for these impounded factors, even when they rather obviously affect the argument, has brought much needless discredit upon the entire body of analysis.[52]

But Keynes' *General Theory* integrated this simple theory of income into a somewhat more general theoretical structure in which income, output, employment, consumption, investment, savings, money supplies, interest rates, and price levels enter as true variables in an interdependent system of schedule relationships. Several important factors left out of account in the simple truncated Keynesian income theory are consequently included as significant variable factors in this more general model, so that the burden of assumed *ceteris paribus* on this model is somewhat less severe than on the simple theory. A few comments on the need for further development and modification of this more general

---

[51] It should be noted that logical validation of this Keynesian theory depends not only upon impounding other aggregative elements in *ceteris paribus*, but also granting the rather dubious assumption of appropriate equilibrium adjustments in the entire structure of relations between individual units underlying the aggregates. Both these factors can be of the greatest practical significance when the theory is used for policy purposes.

[52] Errors in policy recommendations have also arisen because of (a) unquestioning use of such unrealistic Keynesian assumptions as that changes in wages and prices will be proportional, (b) unwarranted assumptions of constancy in value or position of basic variables and schedules of the Keynesian system, leading to unjustified extrapolations of past relationships, and (c) concentration on comparative statics and use of these models for policy purposes in a way that involves an implicit assumption of instantaneous adjustment of the system to "equilibrium" values, overlooking the important fact that in the realistic *process* of adjustment the other data of the system and the position of the schedules will be modified so that the final adjustment will not be that indicated by the original values of the other parameters of the system.

theoretical structure are offered at various points in this paper. At this point it only needs to be noted that the "general" theory included the simple theory as a special case, and that the additional relations (with one exception—the rather realistic assumption that wage rates are relatively sticky in the downward direction) were taken from the *Treatise* and from orthodox classical analysis. The schedules of "speculative liquidity preference" and "marginal efficiency of capital," as well as the analysis of the demand for transactions and precautionary balances, come directly from the *Treatise*, with only a rather straightforward development.[53] The employment-real-income and the wage-marginal-cost-price relations were taken over unchanged from classical models.

Special emphasis needs to be given to the fact that this more general structure of the *General Theory* made substantial contributions to the theory of money and prices and points the way to still other important developments. The importance of its work on the theory of money and prices has not been adequately recognized—probably because that section of the book was incompletely developed and because its theory of income determination was a more important, timely, and striking contribution. But there is no good reason for continuing myopia, and it is well to recall that the broader theoretical structure of the *General Theory* itself emphasized the importance of wages, price levels, and price movements, in determining fluctuations in income, output, and employment.

It is this more general theoretical structure of the *General Theory* which provided its most significant contributions to the theory of money and prices. The character and importance of these contributions may be seen by briefly considering the structure of the analysis currently accepted prior to the *General Theory*. While differences in detail and emphasis were great, almost all of the earlier theories of money and prices could be fitted

[53] That there would be at any time a minimum below which the rate of interest would not fall followed quite naturally when the uncertainties and risks of movement in security prices (analyzed in the *Treatise* to determine the *position* of the speculative balances function) were related to security price levels and unadjusted yields and seen to determine the general *shape* of the function as well. This development from the *Treatise* was very straightforward after allowance was made for risks related to the expected period of investment (Cf. Hicks' brilliant article, based on the *Treatise*, in *Economica*, February, 1935) and the cost of security transactions.

into the following pattern rather closely: 1. An increase in money supplies will increase the flow of money expenditures or effective demand (a) by increasing cash balances, (b) by easing banks' lending policies, and/or (c) by reducing market rates of interest relative to the "equilibrium" or "natural" rate; (2) this increase in money demand will increase prices; (3) this increase in prices will directly increase incomes and, together with the reduction in market rates of interest, will increase output because of increased profits. This linear sequence of causation involved an assumption, whether implicit or explicit, that the adjustment of price levels and interest rates following an increase in money supplies would occur with output completely (or at least relatively) constant, and that it would be only after prices and interest rates had been affected that changes in income or output would be induced. Since the *General Theory* included income and output as genuine variables in an interdependent system of schedule relationships, it could dispense with these unrealistically restrictive assumptions (which at best could be approximated only under conditions approaching universal perfect competition) and allow for the direct effects which fluctuations in the flow of money may have on output, even if price levels are unchanged. This served to make the analysis of money and prices much more realistic than it had been, and considerably modified the character of many important conclusions, particularly when the analysis was applied to depression conditions in an economy having substantial sectors operating under quasi-monopolistic market conditions.

Moreover, most earlier monetary theory had been centered on definitional equations involving an identity based either on the total money value of all transactions or total income payments during a given period of time. Examination of underlying factors determining the elements explicitly included in these equations led to important advances in monetary theory, and, since the identities must always be satisfied *ex-post*, they imposed important standards of consistency on the separate consideration of probable variations in the different elements in the equation.[54] Furthermore, analysis centering on definitional identities is always incomplete because the equations merely state necessary

[54] Unfortunately, this latter feature was frequently vitiated by careless, unrealistic, or inconsistent use of implicit assumptions, particularly with respect to variations in output.

relations between realized numerical values of the explicit variables;[55] a change in one variable may be counteracted by changes in two or more variables, so that conclusions regarding the induced changes in any one factor, such as prices, will depend either upon unrealistically restrictive assumptions of constancy of other factors, such as output or velocity, or else they will depend on a theoretical analysis lying "behind" the equation but not introduced explicitly into the formal analytical structure. In this regard, the *General Theory* represents a substantial advance, because at least a considerable part of this "background" analysis enters explicitly into an integrated theoretical structure comprising *an interrelated system of schedule relationships*, some of which are in the form of refutable hypotheses. Unfortunately, the importance of this qualitative advance over previous theories has been largely overlooked because its full implications were not developed.

The consideration given specifically to the theory of prices is, indeed, sketchy and incomplete. Turning first to the special case where productive units are homogeneous and interchangeable and are supplied at fixed unit costs, Keynes argues that output and employment will increase up to a point of "full employment" in proportion to the increase in effective demand brought about by enlarging the money supply; but that, beyond this limit of output, further increase in effective money demands will proportionately increase prices and factor costs. But the effect of an increase in money supply on the level of effective demand depends on whether (a) the new money initially accrues as someone's income or (b) represents merely an enlargement of bank credit due to a non-income transaction.[56] In the first case, typified by private or public bank borrowing to meet current productive expenditure, income and effective demand will initially increase by the amount of additional money supplies. Since, however, after the first round of expenditure, income will not continue sufficiently high for transactions balances to absorb the entire increase in money supply, there will be an increase in speculative balances similar to those arising in case (b), typified by bank

[55] Cf. Jacob Marschak, "Identity and Stability in Economics: a Survey," EC, 1942, pp. 61–74.
[56] This important distinction is introduced in Chap. 15, pp. 200–209, but is unfortunately not considered in Chap. 21 on the theory of prices.

purchases of outstanding securities from non-bank holders. The increase in effective demand due to added speculative balances will, in turn, depend upon (1) the liquidity preference schedule, (2) the schedule of marginal efficiency of capital, and (3) the investment multiplier determined by the schedule of (marginal) propensities to consume. The greatly increased power and realism of this analysis using three distinct schedule relationships rather than the one "blanket" factor V should be obvious. Moreover, Keynes warns strenuously that these schedules are not independent, and that *movements along one may induce shifts in the position of others* [57]—and that other factors still to be considered may affect each of these three schedules.

Keynes goes on to allow for the fact that prices may be expected to rise with increasing output even before the point of full employment for four reasons. First, since productive resources are not homogeneous, an increase in output will generally involve diminishing returns and increasing supply prices, even though the unit-costs of all factors remain unchanged. Secondly, wage rates will almost certainly increase as output is increased, though not continuously. Thirdly, the prices of other factors entering into marginal costs will also rise in varying proportions. Finally, prices will also rise before full employment is reached because the short-period supply schedules in different markets will show varying degrees of elasticity, with the result that supplies in some markets will become completely inelastic while others are still quite elastic. For this reason, as output increases, a succession of "bottlenecks" will be reached, where supplies in particular markets cannot be increased in the short run, and their

[57] Unfortunately, this most important matter was allowed to remain in a strong general statement and was not implemented or made specific in the rest of the analysis. One illustration of the resulting deficiency in the analysis may be considered at this point. Keynes expects an increase in idle balances to influence effective demands primarily by way of a change in the rate of interest. In so far as the liquidity preference schedule is highly elastic at low rates of interest, however, the effect of increased idle balances (when these balances are already large) on the *position* of the consumption function may well have a more important and more direct effect on effective demand than does the small or negligible change in interest rate. This, indeed, may have been the case in America in 1946. The classics certainly overemphasized the direct effects of cash balances on effective demand, but they were not entirely wrong in holding them to be one considerable factor, particularly when large. This factor can easily be introduced explicitly in the Keynesian models. (See A. Smithies, "The Quantity of Money and the Rate of Interest," RES, February, 1943, pp. 69–76.)

prices have to rise to whatever level is necessary to divert demand to other markets. These bottleneck levels of employment were of crucial importance in planning the war effort in all countries.[58]

Even though many, if not most, of the elements of Keynes' analysis had been foreshadowed in the earlier works of other writers, and particularly in his own *Treatise*, the *integration* of these elements into a unified and interdependent theoretical structure, which included an operational theory of the determination of income and output, stands as a major achievement in the history of monetary theory. It is indeed unfortunate that the implications of this theoretical structure for the analysis of price levels and price movements were not more fully developed.[59] But even as it stood, (1) the careful distinction between the influence on effective demands of increases in money supplies which enter directly into income payments from those which do not, (2) his development of the importance of successive "bottleneck" levels of output, (3) his (partial) integration of global price and output theory with cost and production functions within the firm and industry, and (4) his analysis of the effects of increases in investment expenditures and/or cash balances on prospective demand for goods by way of (a) the liquidity preference schedule, (b) the investment-interest-income function, and (c) the consumption function which implicitly determined the investment multiplier—all these made important contributions to monetary analysis in general, and contributed significantly to our understanding of inflationary pressures during the recent war.

In the *General Theory*, however, Keynes did not go on to consider the process and timing of inflationary movements. All the essential tools were ready at hand, but his task was left for his small tract on *How to Pay for the War*, published three years later. In the *General Theory*, Keynes had held that after "full employment" was reached, prices and wages would both rise in pro-

---

[58] Keynes also developed some necessary relationships, based on identities, between elasticities involving prices, money supplies, output, employment, and wage rates. These were in the nature of a supplement to the broader analysis, and did not, as Marget has claimed (*Theory of Prices*, II, [1942] p. 741) amount to a reversion to "the type of framework.for the study of the Theory of Money and Prices which is represented by these familiar Quantity Equations" since Keynes' analysis of money and prices was set throughout in the broader framework of his general theoretical structure made up of an interrelated system of schedule relationships.

[59] See, for example, Donald M. Fort, "A Theory of General Short-Run Equilibrium," EC, October, 1945, pp. 293–310.

portion to further increases in effective demand.[60] He needed to broaden his theory to allow for the empirical fact that, in the past at least, increases in wages have not been proportional to rises in prices and have lagged behind them. This involved reformulating his statical models in dynamic terms. By taking "investment expenditure" in wartime to be equal to government war expenditure plus government-sanctioned private capital outlays, Keynes was able to develop a rather realistic sequence analysis of the process and timing of inflation by using his consumption function and introducing appropriate wage-price lags.[61]

4.

This theoretical structure was combined with national income statistics to analyze inflationary pressures during the last war in the following manner: [62] Expenditures on goods and services by government and on capital formation by business plus consumers' expenditures will determine (gross) national income. War expenditures are autonomous in the sense that they are determined by war needs rather than by income or interest rates, and non-war outlays of government and private capital formation are rigorously controlled, but the volume of intended or desired consumer expenditures depends primarily on disposable income payments to individuals. Since, moreover, consumers' disposable income is functionally related in turn to gross income, the volume of consumer demand for goods can be estimated more or less closely when the volume of prospective war outlay is known. The excess of total effective demands over available supplies of *all* goods at base prices yields a "total income gap," and the corresponding excess of intended consumer outlay over supplies of such goods available gives the "consumer expenditure gap." Using similar relationships, a variety of other "gaps" could be estimated, and, by introducing appropriate calculated relationships of tax

[60] *General Theory*, pp. 295, 303.

[61] Keynes left the analysis in numerical form, but it was quickly generalized by Koopmans (RES, May, 1942) and Smithies (QJE, Nov., 1942).

[62] For fuller treatments see: W. A. Salant, "The Inflationary Gap: Meaning and Significance for Policy Making," AER, June, 1942, pp. 308–314; Milton Friedman, "Discussion of the Inflationary Gap," AER, June, 1942, pp. 314–320; R. V. Gilbert and V. Perlo, "The Investment Factor Method of Forecasting Business Activity," EC, June-October, 1942; S. E. Harris, *Inflation and the American Economy* (1945), esp. Chap. XI and other references there cited.

yields to income bases, the indicated increases in different taxes necessary to close other gaps could be inferred.

It is clear that this more realistic and powerful analytical structure used in the second war in every major Allied country stems from both (a) the development of national income analysis and (b) Keynes' analysis of the interaction of the volume of independently-determined war outlay on demands and income by way of the consumption function. While it is possible that, given the development of national income statistics, and given the theoretical advances made by other writers between the wars, the understanding of inflationary pressures might have been nearly as good, and the techniques nearly the same, as they were even if the *General Theory* had not been written—the *General Theory* remains of basic importance because it provided the theoretical structure actually used, and because it did integrate the consumption function into a theory of income and output in usable form for the first time. Moreover, the importance of the *General Theory* cannot be minimized by suggesting that, given the development of adequate breakdowns of national income for a series of years, eager statisticians engaged in their much-beloved "fishing expeditions" might have discovered the consumption function independently, for once more it was the *integration* of this relationship into a structural theory of income and output which was the important development. Great importance must also be attached to Keynes' work in the *Treatise*, which broke down the earlier assumption that effective demands depend primarily upon money balances and substituted the more realistic analysis of transactions balances whose size *depends upon* income, and other balances which *may* be accumulated in very large volume before there is any effect upon current effective demands in the market.

There can be no doubt that the analysis of inflationary pressures during the recent war represents a great improvement over that current during the earlier conflict, nor can Keynes' contribution to that development be seriously questioned. But in spite of the great advances which have been made, and the admitted usefulness of the analysis as a general guide to policy, it remains true that the *application* of this analysis during the war remained very inaccurate and often quite confused.[63] Apart from sheer confusions, these imperfections were due to inadequate statistical

[63] Cf. Professor Harris' summary of this experience, *op. cit.*

methods and data, as well as to remaining deficiencies of substantial consequences in the theoretical analysis. Professor Friedman has well summarized the situation in these terms: [64]

> The present state of gap analysis is unsatisfactory, not only because it does not go far enough, but also because the estimates that are made are subject to such wide margins of error . . . One of the main by-products of attempting (to estimate the gap) is a keener realization of how little we know about the quantitative interrelationships of the economic system, and how much there is to know. To estimate the gap, and the consequences that will flow from it, requires precise and quantitative knowledge of economic change—of how impulses are transmitted throughout the economic system, of lags in adjustment, technical possibilities, and human reactions.

This characterization is perhaps even more true of the theory of money and prices in general and the theory of income and output determination in peacetime, as it was of "gap" analysis during the war. In particular, the *General Theory* has made great contributions to our knowledge in both these important and closely related areas, but it remains an oversimplified and imperfect analytical structure which needs substantial modification, generalization, and development. Latent assumptions need to be brought out into the open and subjected to empirical test; "blanket concepts," covering up distinctions which can be shown to make a difference in results,[65] need to be broken down and their significant elements incorporated into a still broader theoretical structure; unrealistic assumptions of economic behavior [66] and relations between variables need to be modified and brought into closer conformance with observable individual and institutional behavior. Preoccupation with equilibrium values [67] must give way to a truly dynamic analysis of the process of economic

[64] Friedman, *op. cit.*, p. 319.

[65] See, for example, above, pp. 519–21, 528, 532.

[66] Cf., for instance, James Tobin, "Money Wage Rates and Employment," below; Franco Modigliani "Liquidity Preference and the Theory of Interest and Money," EC, January, 1944, and Fort, *op. cit.*

[67] Jacob Marschak, "A Cross Section of Business Cycle Discussion," AER, June, 1945, pp. 368–381; esp. p. 371, where the following comment is made: "It is the equilibrium values, and not the process of reaching them, nor the question of whether they are reached at all, that has interested most economists (since) Keynes' book of 1936 was read and digested."

change, with hypotheses formulated in refutable form and subjected to extensive statistical tests.[68]

These efforts will be but a continuation of Keynes' own work over his more productive working life. Qualitatively, as this paper has shown, these were the steps by which the *General Theory* itself was developed in a natural evolution from his earlier theoretical structures. Keynes, far more than most economists, was always re-examining the postulates and structures of his theories, abandoning old ideas and incorporating new elements and relationships in the gradual evolution of a more realistic and fruitful analysis. It is a challenge to modern economists to be equally critical in re-examining the basis of existing theory and equally zealous in their theoretical speculations and their empirical observation and testing as they continue their efforts to build analytical structures that are more realistic and useful in interpreting and guiding economic developments.

[68] Cf. Marschak, *op. cit.*, and the exemplary emphasis on empirical work in Arthur F. Burns, "Economic Research and the Keynesian Thinking of Our Times," in the *Twenty-Sixth Annual Report* of NBER.

PART EIGHT

Effective Demand and Wages

CHAPTER XXXVIII

Introduction : Keynes' Attack on Laissez Faire and Classical Economics and Wage Theory

By SEYMOUR E. HARRIS

THE CONTENTS

THE ESSAYS in this part of the book are concerned especially with the postulates of classical and Keynesian economics, and with the main areas of disagreement—wages and money—resulting from different postulates. In this introduction, I shall deal primarily with the attitude of Keynes towards laissez faire and classical economics as revealed in the pre-*General Theory* period. Since Messrs. Leontief, Smithies, and Tobin deal fully with the postulates of both classical and Keynesian economics, and since they also elaborate Keynesian economics, once certain unrealistic assumptions are removed, I shall only present here the *elements* of wage theory as a preliminary to the discussion in the body of this section.[1]

As Dr. Smithies observes, supporters and detractors of Keynesian economics in the popular press will find little support for high wage theories in the *General Theory*. In fact the thesis of Keynes' book, subject to reservations, is that a change in money wages will not influence real wage rates, employment, or output. Association of Keynes' name with high wage theories rests on his earlier writings and particularly on his antagonism to wage cutting in the inter-war period.

---

[1] Since Prof. Leontief's essay deals both with postulates and wages, it appears above.

LAISSEZ FAIRE

In his biography of Marshall, Keynes noted both that the former was aware of the conflict between the social and private interest, and that Professor Pigou had elaborated on this theme.[2] The lesson was not lost on Keynes, who also emphasized this conflict, and, following Bentham, he would distinguish (but anew) the *agenda of government* from the *non-agenda*, and he would be sympathetic with a political system within a democratic framework which would be capable of accomplishing the agenda—and a broader one than that supported by Bentham.[3]

In many fields of economic activity, laissez faire had broken down.

First, there is the area of money, which is discussed fully elsewhere. In that area, Keynes' main complaint was that the monetary system tended to operate in a manner which yielded a smaller income than intelligence, industry, and resources made possible.[4] The difficulty was in part the fear of management of interference, which stemmed from the laissez faire philosophy, and in part from the fear of poor management.[5] In his early writings, Keynes had stressed the need of monetary stability, lamenting with equal eloquence those inflationary episodes which destroyed savings—at that time considered a desideratum—and those deflationary episodes which tended to increase risks and reduce business enterprise.[6] Yet even in 1923 he saw in the depreciation of money a "weighty counterpoise against the cumulative results of compound interest and the inheritance of fortunes," as well as a loosening influence "against the rigid distribution of old-won wealth and the separation of ownership from activity." [7] His general position, and especially in the last 20 years, was that monetary authorities were not disposed to interfere aggressively, and thus to shackle the forces tending to deflate the economy. It was the right of the State to control vested interests and revise contracts that had become intolerable. The task of the monetary authority was to free a country from outside forces that tended to raise interest rates and restrict monetary supplies and, if neces-

---

[2] *Essays in Biography,* p. 227.
[3] *Essays in Persuasion,* pp. 312–313.
[4] *General Theory,* pp. 217–220, 339.
[5] Cf. *Tract,* pp. 164–67.
[6] *Tract,* pp. 34–37; *Essays in Persuasion,* pp. 90–92.
[7] *Ibid.,* p. 87.

sary, to introduce controls (e.g., ban on capital exports) which would preclude the export of money from having unsettling effects on the international position. Above all, correct monetary policy stipulated a monetary system sufficiently elastic to keep the rate of interest low enough to assure investment at an adequate level—even in the *General Theory*, when he had lost some of his early enthusiasm for monetary policy, he still supported expansionist monetary policies.[8]

Second, laissez faire policies were bound to result in deficient demand, unemployment, wasted resources, etc. Keynes' analysis of the classical system, which was the foundation of his own, led him to reject the laissez faire philosophy. Although he was prepared to admit that the modern classicist did not embrace Say's Law in its crude form, he nevertheless insisted that classical economics was primarily interested in the distribution of the product, and not in the employment of resources, and that in general it was assumed that all income earned in producing output would also be used to purchase it. At any rate, no adequate attempt had been made to study effective demand and its relation to the supply function.[9]

In quarters where Say's Law was accepted, there would be no obstacle to full employment. Keynes, however, found in the failure to spend current income on consumption and investment goods the cause of unemployment. It was, therefore, necessary to control consumption, savings, and investment. Most of the proposals to flout the laws of the market place originated in the quest for adequacy of demand. It was necessary to control and reduce savings, and to raise consumption in conditions of less than full employment—through taxation and deficit spending *inter alia*—to increase investment through reductions in the rate of interest, stimulation of consumption, and public programs of investment. Keynes was even prepared to give serious consideration to usury laws, which were directed to discouraging use of capital to finance transfers, and to stamped money, as a means of forcing money into productive channels.[10]

Third, Keynes considered the application of laissez faire principles to some sectors of the economy (e.g., exchange markets)

---

[8] *Treatise*, Vol. II, pp. 188–189; *Tract*, p. 67; *General Theory*, pp. 235–6, 339.
[9] *General Theory*, especially, pp. 18–22, 26.
[10] *General Theory*, pp. 351–58 and Chap. 24.

may be especially injurious when other parts (e.g., the labor markets) are inflexible. Wages might move upwards too rapidly and thus interfere with the growth of an economy—he contended that in Spain, for example, the planned expansion following the gold discoveries of the sixteenth century was nipped by wage inflation. Falling wages in response to declining prices and rising exchange rates might not yield an equilibrium position short of complete economic exhaustion; and besides, modern trade-unionism precludes the required downward adjustment of wages. At any rate, Keynes was not inclined to allow the threat of the economic Juggernaut—that wages should be determined by economic pressures and the economic machine should crash along, irrespective of what was done to individual groups.[11]

CAPITALISM OR SOCIALISM

Although Keynes was critical of the excesses of the capitalist system, he was far from friendly to Marxism or to any form of socialism. He could not accept a doctrine based entirely on an economic textbook which he knew "to be not only scientifically erroneous but without interest or application in the modern world." Nevertheless, he had much in common with Marx. They both were aware of exploitation by capitalists, of deficient demand and over-savings, of declining marginal efficiency of capital, and the unwisdom of capital exportation. Marx, of course, considered the last an attempt of capitalist nations to find an outlet for their surplus commodities, whereas Keynes was critical, not because exploitation of borrowing nations was involved, but rather because the uncontrolled flow of capital abroad reduced the gains of capitalism for Great Britian vis-à-vis the debtor nations and imposed upon the British economy monetary contraction and unemployment.[12]

Keynes would indeed try to preserve capitalism by ridding it of its parasitic elements. Excess savings; high rates of interest; the hereditary principle and its debilitating effect on capitalism; the preference of the future over the present—these were the special targets of his criticism.[13]

[11] *Essays in Persuasion*, pp. 261–2; *Treatise*, Vol. I, pp. 176–178, 273; Vol. II, pp. 155–56. Keynes' attacks on the classical postulate that the marginal disutility of labor = the real wage will be discussed later.
[12] *Essays in Persuasion*, p. 300; *Treatise*, Vol. I, chap. 21; Vol. II, pp. 184–196, 312–13; cf. the essay by P. Sweezy, above.
[13] *Treatise*, Vol. II, p. 313; and *General Theory*, pp. 220–21 and chap. 24.

Money-making and the quest for profits were indeed acceptable pursuits in Keynes' views: it was better to tyrannize over pocketbooks than over lives. In fact a large part of the *Treatise* is devoted to a defense of money-making and enterprise against thrift. It was the quest for profits and its ensuing profit inflation which, in the years 1500–1700, produced modern capitalism. Keynes, however, envisaged the day when, with continued accumulation of capital and improvements in technology, the pursuit of monetary gains would become a much less important feature of everyday life, the problem then becoming one of effectively using leisure time. And one of the few features of the Russian experiment that appealed to Keynes was its attempt to reduce the importance of money-making.[14]

In 1926, he concluded that capitalism could still "be made more efficient for attaining economic ends than any alternative system yet in sight," but it was nevertheless in many ways extremely objectionable. At this time, he was not yet prepared to give the State as much authority or right to intervene as he was ten years later. The State should concern itself with the amount of savings, the population problem, central banking policy, and provide information for business decisions—thus making capitalism more efficient.[15] In later years, the breakdown of capitalism undoubtedly contributed to a revision of his views concerning the province of the State. In particular, its responsibility for underwriting demand became a central part of his program.

Yet it is far from the truth to classify Keynes as a socialist or even as a destroyer of capitalism. In his attacks on the Labor Party, on the tyranny of trade unionism, on socialism and communism, in his unwillingness even in wartimes to deprive consumers of their rights to choose among alternative commodities, Keynes showed that to the very end he remained a defender of capitalism, of a system of private enterprise, but that this was to be adapted to modern institutional requirements. Keynes' faith in capitalism is well revealed in his brilliant essay on "Economic Possibilities for our Grandchildren" (1930). Here Keynes contrasted the pessimists of the left who would save us by revolution and the pessimists of the right who considered "the balance of our economic and social life so precarious that we must risk no

[14] *General Theory*, p. 374; *Treatise*, chap. 30; *Essays in Persuasion*, pp. 302–303, 366–373.
[15] *Essays in Persuasion*, pp. 312–322.

experiments." It was the forces of compound interest, the accumulation of gold and profits, which had yielded the modern economic society. A further annual rise of capital by 2 per cent per year would increase capital equipment by 7½ times in one hundred years. He concluded that, if the problems of war and population could be solved, then the *economic problem* might be solved within one hundred years. Man's problem, then, would be to learn how to use his freedom from material cares and how to enjoy and profit from his leisure.[16]

To many, the *General Theory* may seem to be a frontal attack on capitalism. Yet what are Keynes' final words on the issue of statism *vs.* liberalism?

> Our criticism of the accepted classical theory of economics has consisted not so much in finding logical flaws in its analysis as in pointing out that its tacit assumptions are seldom or never satisfied, with the result that it cannot solve the economic problems of the actual world. But if our central controls succeed in establishing an aggregate volume of output corresponding to full employment as nearly as is practicable, the classical theory comes into its own again from this point onwards. If we suppose the volume of output to be given, i.e., to be determined by forces outside the classical scheme of thought, then there is no objection to be raised against the classical analysis of the manner in which private self-interest will determine what in particular is produced, in what proportions the factors of production will be combined to produce it, and how the value of the final product will be distributed between them. . . . Thus, apart from the necessity of central controls to bring about an adjustment between the propensity to consume and the inducement to invest, there is no more reason to socialize economic life than there was before.[17]

Keynes then goes on to argue that the present system has broken down, not in the *direction* of its employment, but rather in the actual *amounts* of employment made available.[18] In his view, the advantages of the system are the efficiency of decentralization, the play of self-interest. Individualism, if it can be purged of its excesses and defects, will greatly widen the field for the exercise of formal choice; and the proposed controls are

[16] Keynes' views on issues raised in this paragraph may be found, for example, in *Persuasion*, pp. 312–322, 358–369; *How to Pay for the War*, pp. 7, 52, 55; *Treatise*, Vol. II, p. 163.

[17] *General Theory*, pp. 378–79.

[18] Cf. P. Sweezy above.

the only manner of salvaging private enterprise and assuring the exercise of individual initiative.[19]

VARIANTS OF KEYNESIANISM

Keynes was particularly critical of socialist economics. It is difficult to understand his rather extreme and unfair attack on both Marxian and Russian economics. In his view, there was nothing to be learned from Russian economics.[20] Perhaps Keynes would not take this extreme position today, in view of the remarkable accomplishments of the Soviet, and particularly since 1928. Over a period of twelve years (1928–1940), individual output rose by 650 per cent and real per capita income by 350 per cent; and there were significant rises in productivity. (Russian figures indeed are not thoroughly reliable, and corrections for price changes offer many difficulties; but all competent observers agree that there has been no significant attempt to manipulate the figures.) The gains indeed were absorbed primarily in the production of capital goods and war goods and did not contribute adequately to an improved standard of living. Capitalist nations may not approve of Russian methods, nor did Keynes: control of the allocation of economic resources, serious infringements on private liberty, etc. But the Russians nevertheless have shown that if a country is prepared to pay the price in curtailment of personal liberty, then rapid rates of industrialization, very rapid advance from a low level of output, and full employment without the large inflationary pressures that seem to accompany full employment in democratic countries, and particularly the United States—all of these can be achieved. The Soviet has shown the capitalist world that through co-ordinated rationing, allocation, taxing, pricing, and saving policies, the State can achieve a balanced growth of the economy, and can largely determine the distribution of goods.[21]

This brings me to the variations of the Keynesian theme that now prevail. All groups involved accept one fundamental feature of Keynesian economics: the imperative necessity of underwrit-

[19] *General Theory*, pp. 379–380.
[20] *Essays in Persuasion*, pp. 297–311, especially, p. 306.
[21] See especially A. Baykov, *The Development of the Soviet Economic System*, pp. 290, 384; A. Yugow, *Russia's Economic Front in Peace and War* (1942), p. 199; L. H. Bean, "International Industrialization and Per Capita Income" in NBER, Conference on Research in National Income and Wealth, *Studies in Income and Wealth*, Vol. VIII (1946), p. 732.

ing, subsidizing, socializing, or guaranteeing, demand, that is, the responsibility of the Government to assure an adequacy of demand.

At one extreme is the Beveridge group.[22] Beveridge and his followers would not only socialize demand; they would also control the distribution of labor and capital, take strong measures to curb inflation, even to the extent of restricting activities of trade unionism, discouraging make-work practices, etc.; and they might even impose upon the public, through control of allocation of economic resources, proper consumption standards. In the international field, they are prepared, if necessary, to have recourse to bilateralism, minute control of foreign trade, bulk commodity agreements, etc. The most extreme position is taken by Dr. Balogh in the Oxford volume noted.

At the other extreme, Polanyi would rely exclusively on monetary manipulation—his work is based more on the *Treatise* than on the *General Theory*. According to Polanyi, the Government should manufacture enough money to assure a demand adequate to exclude spilled savings, that is, the gap between savings and investment must be filled. At some point in this expansionary process, the public will begin to disgorge its hoards. Once the monetary supplies become excessive (i.e., the gap becomes negative), the government can reverse its policies by withdrawing cash through a proper tax policy. Above all, it is not the job of the government to waste resources on public works or to interfere in any manner with the allocation of economic resources. Polanyi undoubtedly overestimates the effectiveness of purely monetary measures and underestimates the institutional difficulties of reversing inflationary or deflationary policies.[23] Lerner, in his functional finance theories, approaches the Polanyi position, but in other respects comes closer to the Beveridge position.

In the middle we shall find the doctrines of Keynes and perhaps of a majority of his followers. They are content to rely primarily on monetary expansion and socialization of demand. They are aware of structural maladjustment, but are impressed by the practical difficulties, within the time available, to treat these sore

[22] Sir W. Beveridge, *Full Employment in a Free Society* (1944), especially Parts I, IV, V, VI; and *The Economics of Full Employment*, Studies Prepared by the Oxford University Institute of Statistics (1944), especially Chaps. III and IV.

[23] M. Polanyi, *Full Employment and Free Trade* (1945), Chap. 1, especially pp. 64–66.

spots effectively—though, of course, they would make earnest efforts to do so. In the London *Times*, Keynes emphasized, for example, the difficulties involved in dealing with distressed areas through specific measures.[24]

WAGES AND DEMAND

Few economists and few businessmen are now unaware of the relation of wages and demand. That this relationship is a matter of common knowledge, and general acceptance, is a reflection of Keynes' influence on both economic theory and practice. As has been noted, this popular association of wage rates and demand originates in his earlier writings. Long before the days of the *General Theory*, Marx had put forth a theory of exploitation, inadequate wages, and deficiency of demand. But theories associated with Socialism were not palatable in a free enterprise system. It remained for a bourgeois economist, whose views would command some respect among economic practitioners in a capitalist society, whose presentation could more readily be understood than Marx's, and whose views might more easily percolate, to convince the economist first, and the lay public second, of the dependence of demand on wages.

Keynes' views on wages evolved gradually. In his *Tract*, he had little to say about wages: his main point was that real wages had risen both during the war and the early post-war period.[25] In the second half of the twenties, he began to pay more attention to the wage problem. The decision to return to gold at pre-war parity had made necessary a deflationary policy which encountered its greatest difficulties, particularly of an institutional kind, in the assault on wage rates, and particularly in export industries. At first, indeed, Keynes was inclined to emphasize justice against the laws of supply and demand, the former suggesting maintenance of wages against the pressure of a rising £ sterling.[26] But it was not long before he had contrasted the cost *vs.* demand aspects of wage-cutting. A reduction of money wages brings a corresponding decline of demand; the analogy of favorable effects of general wage reductions with those of wage cutting by one employer does not hold; reduction of wages in export industries might increase export trade, but it might be countered by

[24] LT, January 12, 1937.
[25] *Tract*, pp. 27–30.
[26] *Essays in Persuasion*, pp. 257–262.

similar reductions elsewhere; a better attack in the international field would be a re-allocation of economic resources and an international program for increasing prices; and finally, Keynes contended in 1930–31 that money wages in Great Britain were not too high, given the British output potential and allowing for the severe cyclical decline, which would presently run out.[27]

WAGES IN THE *GENERAL THEORY*

In general, Keynes' discussion of wages revolved around the effects of a reduction of wages upon demand and output. There is relatively little said about rises in wage rates. In the *Treatise*, indeed, Keynes had been careful to point out that wage inflation had brought an early end to a profit inflation in Spain stimulated by the inflow of gold.[28] In the *General Theory* he urged that, in periods of technical progress, rising wages and stable prices, as against the alternative of stable wages and falling prices, would bring the gains of progress largely to the active members of society, and proper incentives would be assured to stimulate the transfers of workers from less to more productive occupations.[29] These discussions of rising wages were rare, however; and they related to the long run.

What was Keynes' theory of wages? Since the determinants of effective demand, employment, and output, were the marginal efficiency of capital, the rate of interest, and the propensity to consume, changes in wage rates could not influence output unless they affected one or more of these variables.[30] The general presumption is against a change in money wage rates influencing output; or at least that the net effect was not easy to predict.

Keynes could envisage conditions under which a reduction of money wages might have favorable effects; but this was not the likely outcome. First, there was the adverse effect of the transfer of income from workers to capitalists, the former having a higher marginal propensity to consume. Keynes was particularly critical of the classical economists, who were too quick to assume that demand would rise with a reduction of wages and prices and with the ensuing increased purchases by non-wage-earners. They

[27] *Treatise*, Vol. I, pp. 176–178 and chap. 21; *Macmillan Report*, Addendum I, pp. 193–199.
[28] *Treatise*, Vol. II, chap. 30, pp. 155–56.
[29] *General Theory*, pp. 269–271.
[30] *General Theory*, pp. 260–1.

were disposed to leave out of account the effect on output of the decline in wages, without which consideration the assumption of expanded demand by non-wage-earners was not very meaningful. The crucial point in this discussion of demand is that, even if entrepreneurs should mistakenly expand their output in response to a decline in the wage rates, their expectations would be disappointed—unless the marginal propensity to consume were unity [31] or unless the difference between the actual propensity and unity were made up by a rise in investment. This would only happen if the marginal efficiency of capital should rise relatively to the rate of interest. No reason is adduced for this to happen.

Second, would the marginal efficiency of capital react favorably to a reduction in the wage rate? Entrepreneurs might indeed expand output on the assumption that wage-cutting would help them; but their expectations, as was just pointed out, are bound to be disappointed. Keynes also points out that one decisive wage cut, on the understanding that this would be the one and only cut, might stimulate investment. A reduction of these proportions is not, however, practical; and a series of downward revisions would be the signal for entrepreneurs to wait until wages had reached rock bottom. Marginal efficiency of capital is then not likely to rise.

Third, what of effects via the rate of interest? Here Keynes is hopeful, because, with wage and price reductions, the demand for cash might well be reduced. (Labor, dissatisfied and fearful of the consequences of wage-cutting might, however, increase its hoards.) If the favorable effects are to be had through what amounts to an expansion in monetary supplies, then Keynes, spurning wage-cutting and its unfortunate social and economic consequences, would directly expand monetary supplies, though at the same time warning the reader of the limitations of monetary expansion as a weapon for expanding output and employment.[32]

THE ATTACK ON THE CLASSICAL THEORY OF WAGES AND EMPLOYMENT

Classical economics, in Keynes' view, assumes that the marginal disutility of labor is equal to the real wage. Against this postulate,

---

[31] If the marginal propensity were less than unity, then the reduction of demand by workers would not be offset by a corresponding rise of demand by other groups.

[32] Cf. *General Theory*, especially pp. 257–260, 265–271.

Keynes contends that involuntary unemployment generally prevails, a condition associated with an excess of the real wage over the marginal disutility of labor. Involuntary unemployment prevails when demand is deficient. Unemployed workers are prepared to work at current real wage rates or at reduced real wage rates (i.e., at higher than current money wage rates but not rising as much as the cost of living); but they are unable to bring about the required reduction in real wage rates. In short, though a large proportion of the unemployed are prepared to work at lower real wages, they are unable to depress the real wage rate; and hence they remain involuntarily unemployed. As Mr. Tobin puts it, labor is beset by a money illusion and hence will work at a lower real wage rate, and yet labor is powerless to take advantage of the potential demand for its services at lower real wage rates, because a reduction in the money wage rate will not bring about a decline in the real wage rate.

Messrs. Leontief, Smithies, and Tobin all discuss the classical and Keynesian postulates. In Professor Leontief's view,[33] for example, the classicist, in starting with the general nature of consumers' choice, relied much more on experience than did Keynes, who built on three postulates, (1) the demand schedule for consumers' goods, (2) the slope of the labor supply schedule, and (3) the relation of income and savings. According to Professor Leontief, the postulate that labor supply was a function of the real wage rate was not the fundamental one of classical economics. Dr. Smithies points out that in the Keynesian system *real income is determined independently of changes in money and income;* that the main factors determining the distribution of income are independent of wages and prices; that real output and employment are not dependent on conditions of labor supply; and that real wages are independent of the money bargain—they depend on the relative equilibrium value of prices and wages. Mr. Tobin shows clearly the relation of Keynes' consumption function—that *real* consumption expenditure is a unique function of *real* income with a positive value of less than unity—to changes in wage rates. So far as consumption expenditure is concerned, a change in money wage rates could not affect the volume of employment and output.

None of these authors is prepared to accept Keynes' discussion

[33] See his essay above.

as the final word on the relation of wage rates and employment, though they all agree that Keynes made important contributions. Even Professor Leontief, who is the most critical of the three towards Keynes, sees in Keynes' treatment an improvement over classical short-run theory; and he finds that Keynes, like Marx before him and unlike the classicists whom Keynes criticized, made important contributions to the distributive aspects of economics. (In contrast, Keynes was inclined to criticize the classicists for their concentration on distribution and their failure to deal with the level of employment. Keynes and Leontief are not necessarily in disagreement here, for to some extent the level of employment and output is a problem of distribution.)

In the three essays under consideration, the authors attempt to reconcile Keynes' economics with classical economics. Professor Leontief, for example, critical of the universality given to involuntary unemployment by Keynes, suggests the manner in which classical economics might deal with the problem. It would only be necessary to obtain an upward shift in the classical monetary supply and demand curve—prices would rise and real wages decline. Unfortunately, Keynes' liquidity preference stops the proposed expansion of money from bringing about the required rise of prices and the elimination of involuntary unemployment.

Keynes built his system on over-simplified assumptions; and therefore it is necessary to relax some of the unrealistic assumptions. Both Smithies and Tobin deal with this problem in some detail. Smithies, for example, relaxes the assumptions of constancy of techniques and equipment; of perfect competition; of noninterference by Government; of a closed system; of irrelevance of relative wages and prices; of static analysis. Even in short periods, he holds, techniques change, and, therefore, average productivity may continue to rise and marginal productivity of labor to decline (and therefore labor's share to fall). The removal of the assumption of perfect competition suggests the possibility of expanding employment, rising real wage rates (as Tobin says in criticism of Keynes, real wages are not a declining function of output) and a reduction of supply price. Government fiscal policy in an inflationary period would bring a greater rise of receipts than expenditures, and, therefore, employment and output would not be determined independently of wage and price levels. Again, the reintroduction of international trade under a system where trade

is important, exchanges fixed, domestic and foreign trade industries closely related, would bring about a situation in which wage
rates would seriously influence employment and output.

Tobin also suggests the limitations of Keynes' assumptions. He
deals with monopoly and considers the effects of monopoly on
distribution and demand. He does not see (nor does Leontief)
why the effects of the money illusion should be restricted to a discussion of the effects on the supply schedule of labor. The money
illusion may also influence the consumption function. Keynes'
failure to consider factors of production other than labor is also a
subject for criticism. In attacking the problem in this manner,
Keynes fails to take into account the possibility of changes in
wage rates resulting in substitution for labor of other factors, or
vice versa. And why should not the money illusion relate to the
prices acceptable by owners of non-labor factors?

WAGE THEORY AND WAGE POLICY

In a simplified discussion, Keynes showed that the presumption
was against wage-cutting, and primarily because favorable effects
upon employment via the propensity to consume and the marginal efficiency of capital were not anticipated, and any favorable effects through a reduction in the rate of interest could more
easily be achieved through monetary expansion. In developing a
theory of wages which was integrated especially with demand as
against the classical concentration on costs, Keynes made a notable advance. Even though he did not consider all relevant
variables, and even though, as the contributors to this volume
show, this involved making heroic assumptions, the theory was
much more nearly adequate than earlier classical theories with
their emphasis on costs, their neglect of demand, their assumptions of a fixed supply of money, their assumptions (or, as Leontief
says, their goal) of full employment, and hence their concern
with the availability of wage-goods, and in general with their
failure to deal with important variables.[34]

Other virtues can be found in Keynes' wage theory, not the
least of which is that it fitted in well with institutional requirements. That Keynes' wage theory was the outgrowth of the economic history of the inter-war period is not in my opinion a black
mark against it. The case against wage-flexibility or wage-cutting

[34] Cf. *General Theory*, pp. 272–279; and S. E. Harris, "Professor Pigou's
Theory of Unemployment," QJE, Feb. 1935, pp. 286–324.

stemmed from, *inter alia*, the difficulties of cutting wages, and from the injustices that resulted. Once the authorities became aware of wage rigidities, moreover, they would be less disposed to impose exchange rates, which in turn might require downward wage adjustments. Above all, Keynes, in contrast to Professor Pigou, would not attempt to stabilize wage rates in terms of wage goods; for every small fluctuation in the propensity to consume or inducement to invest would cause prices to rush violently between zero (should output rise) and infinity (should output fall).[35]

Keynes was not by any means unaware of the imperfections of markets and the need for taking measures to attain the optimum allocation of economic resources. His theory that marginal disutility of labor was not equal to the real wage originated in his concern with market imperfections and irrational behavior. He defended his long-run policy of stable prices and rising wage rates on the grounds, *inter alia*, that the wage incentive would then attract workers into the more productive occupations. And he devoted a whole chapter to the employment function, concerning himself especially with the problem of the varying effects upon employment of a given rise in effective demand.[36] The last is some evidence that his discussions were not limited to over-all demand.

Keynes' main concern over the years was with the relation of wage changes and demand; and he gave much more attention to downward than to upward revision of money wages. His attitude towards our *current* wage problems would indeed be an interesting matter for speculation. In *How to Pay for the War*, he made clear his opposition to wages rising with the cost of living in a war period when taxes, employment, and output were rising.[37] With the Government requiring a large part of current output, he proposed forced loans and relative wage stability as programs for *excluding* inflation. His views since the days of the *Treatise* had changed: at that time he urged an *inflationary* program as the only way to assure the State adequate resources in war—prices and wages both rising but the latter with a lag.[38]

Undoubtedly Keynes in 1946–47 would object to wage increases

---

[35] *General Theory*, pp. 238–39.
[36] Chap. 20; cf. Smithies' essay below.
[37] *How to Pay for the War*, pp. 72–74.
[38] *Treatise*, Vol. II, pp. 173–174.

which were not related to rising productivity, although he looked with favor upon a rise of money wages in the United States which would tend to bring the supply and demand for dollars once more in equilibrium.[39] It would be interesting to conjecture how he would deal with the problem of sterilization of purchasing power. Workers now are not only interested in the relation of money wages and the cost of living index—a concern with real wages which, as Leontief suggests, Keynes was inclined to under-estimate—but their decisions concerning offer of work are related to the extent to which their dollar claims on goods can be vali-dated. Finally, would Keynes continue to stump for a policy of advancing wages and stable prices in a world where the *organized* workers arrogate to themselves the main gains of progress, and one-half or three-quarters of the population are squeezed? The latter may not only not share in the gains but may actually lose, whilst organized workers, farmers, and businessmen gain.

CONCLUSIONS ON WAGES

In the pre-*General Theory* era, Keynes stressed the relation of wage rates, demand, and output. His discussion of inter-war British economic policy might well be interpreted as one sup-porting high wages, or at least against falling wage rates. From these early discussions, the modern supporter of Keynesian eco-nomics in the public arena undoubtedly finds support for high wage theories. Yet Keynes had little to say in favor of rising wage rates; and, as has been noted, he was critical of wage inflations which brought an end to expansion in the years 1500–1700. That the proponents of high wage theories still find support in the *General Theory* for their theories can be explained by their failure to understand the *General Theory*, by *their* improvement on the *General Theory* through the introduction of more realistic as-sumptions which to some extent point to favorable effects of rising wages, and perhaps by their confusion of Keynes' general em-phasis on the marginal propensity to consume and the desirability of raising it with the relation of rising wage rates and the pro-pensity to consume.[40] Perhaps their support is also found in his

[39] Lord Keynes, "The Balance of Payments of the United States," EJ, June, 1946, p. 185.

[40] Cf. S. H. Slichter, "Wage-Price Policy and Employment," and com-ments by A. P. Lerner, *Papers and Proceedings of American Economic As-sociation*, May, 1946, pp. 304–318, 330–335. Here Lerner, adhering closely to the *General Theory* version of wage theory, contends against Slichter

effective attack, in the *General Theory*, on the classical theory that unemployment is associated with excessive wage rates. It was a great contribution of Keynes to show that employment depends on effective demand, and that rises in effective demand come via changes in consumption, the marginal efficiency of capital, and the rate of interest—even if the shift of emphasis from wage rates to effective demand was carried too far.

that a rise of wage rates leads to a reduction of employment in Slichter's formulation only because the latter fails to take into account the rise of prices following the rise in wage rates.

CHAPTER XXXIX

Effective Demand and Employment[1]

By ARTHUR SMITHIES

MY PURPOSE in this essay is to inquire what levels of employment and what rates of real wages are associated with given levels of effective demand. I shall consider the question first within the framework of the Keynesian equilibrium system, and then consider the extent to which removal of the special assumptions of that system affects the conclusions of Keynes' theory of employment.

THE ASSUMPTIONS OF THE KEYNESIAN SYSTEM

Before embarking on our discussion of the theory of employment, it will be convenient to set out the main assumptions of the *General Theory* as a whole. Since this subject has been treated in detail elsewhere in this volume, I shall confine the present discussion to a brief summary.

(1) Keynes assumes that techniques of production and the amount of fixed capital used in production are unchanged throughout the periods with which he is dealing. Thus the analysis is limited to periods sufficiently short for the new investment that takes place during them to have no effect on techniques.

(2) However, the analysis usually assumes that the equilibrium positions achieved after the longest periods compatible with the assumption of constant techniques has been reached. While there are many illuminating remarks on the process of moving from one equilibrium position to another, no complete explanation is attempted.

(3) Perfect competition is assumed throughout. Thus questions of changing degree of monopoly, or what we call "wage-

[1] This paper has benefited greatly from the criticisms of Professor J. Marschak and Professor J. R. Hicks.

price policy," are largely ignored. Furthermore, in the *General Theory* this, in conjunction with the assumption of unchanging techniques, has led to the assumption of diminishing returns and increasing cost. But Keynes has subsequently conceded that this assumption may be invalid.[2]

(4) The rôle of Government, either as a taxer or a spender, is not explicitly recognized in the formal part of the *General Theory*.

(5) The formal part of the analysis is carried out in terms of a closed economy.

(6) The *General Theory* deals in aggregates and ignores questions of changes in relative prices and wages.

(7) The *General Theory* is static and consequently does not take into account the fact that economic events at one point of time are not independent of what went before and will not fail to influence what will occur subsequently.

Of course the *General Theory* abounds with *obiter dicta* that violate these assumptions. Its true greatness could never have been achieved had its author been fully dependent on the analytic tools he forged.

THE THEORY OF EMPLOYMENT

The Keynesian theory of employment can be summarized in the following propositions.

(a) Aggregate real demand for goods and services (consumption plus investment) depends on real income and the rate of interest. The aggregate real supply "price" is identical with real income. Thus the equilibrium value of real income (output) is determined where aggregate real demand is equal to real income, or, what comes to the same thing, where the equilibrium values of saving and investment are equal.[3]

---

[2] See "Relative Movements of Real Wages and Output," EJ, March, 1939. I am inclined to believe that the evidence on which Keynes was persuaded may have been inconsistent with the unchanging techniques assumption.

[3] In this statement I have taken some formal liberties with the *General Theory* but none of substance. In Chap. 3, Keynes states that aggregate demand and aggregate supply in terms of money wage units depend on employment. He later agrees that employment is a function of real output, so there is no difficulty about making the latter the independent variable in the demand and supply functions. I have preferred to express demand and supply in real terms rather than in terms of money wage units, because Keynes' demand and supply functions in Chap. 3 involve the question of the relation of prices to wages, which can be more conveniently introduced at a later stage.

(b) The rate of interest depends on the quantity of money in the sense that the money supply can be adjusted so as to establish the rate of interest at any desired level above a certain lower limit. For purposes of the present argument, I shall assume that the rate of interest is held constant. In modern conditions in the United States, this assumption seems to be the most realistic one to make.

(c) The effect of (a) and (b) is that real income is determined independently of changes in money wages and prices. This result is supported by the assumptions of perfect competition and constant techniques. They imply that the main factors affecting the distribution of income and, hence, the propensity to consume, are independent of wages and prices. If this is so, and the rate of interest is also constant, the inducement to invest in equilibrium may also be assumed to be independent of money wages and prices. Keynes recognizes that changes in wages and prices would bring about a redistribution as between rentiers and entrepreneurs, but considers it to be of minor importance. As we shall see, money wage and price changes turn out to be more important when we venture outside the walls of the Keynesian garden.

(d) Employment is determined by the technical relation of employment to output.

This proposition depends on the assumption of unchanging techniques of production, but it requires the additional assumption that the distribution of any given aggregate demand among industries is not subject to changes that would affect the total stability of employment in relation to output. Keynes recognizes this point (pp. 286–288), but confines his discussion of it to a brief discussion of short period problems (i.e., short from his point of view). Further discussion might prove necessary if changes in relative prices were under consideration.

(e) Money wages are adjusted in such a way as to evoke the supply of labor required to produce the equilibrium real income.

That the supply of labor does not depend uniquely on the real wage is, of course, central to the *General Theory* (e.g., p. 13), but Keynes nowhere flatly asserts that it depends uniquely on the money wage. He is caught between his intuition and his logic, and as usual his logic has to give way. For his logical system permits only the conclusion that the labor supply depends on the money wage, since real output and employment do not depend on the conditions of labor supply. Dependence of the labor supply on the real wage would be inconsistent with propositions (a), (b), and (c). For the time being, therefore, we must accept proposition (e).

The question of the money wage-rate adjustments necessary to produce the equilibrium supply of labor does not occupy much of the *General Theory*. In 1936, the possibility of shortages of labor seemed very remote, and Keynes was content to assume that in general the supply of labor was perfectly elastic with respect to the money wage. He does recognize (e.g., p. 296) that money wages will rise as full employment is approached, but assumes implicitly that the adjustment would be readily made. These assumptions would possibly be valid if everyone were convinced that the economy was on the road to stable equilibrium. It is far less valid if it is widely thought that we are on our way to the peak of an inflationary boom.

(f) Prices are adjusted so that the money wage is equated to the value of the marginal product of labor.

This proposition follows from the assumptions of perfect competition and a closed economy. It is in line with the argument of Chapter 19 and is necessary to validate the proposition that real income is independently determined. For if prices did not behave in this way, income would be redistributed, and consequently effective demand and real income would change.

(g) Real wages are thus independent of money wage bargains, but depend on the relative equilibrium values of prices and wages. How many of those who praise or vilify Keynes in the popular press realize that this is one of the central theses of the *General Theory?* It means that, in a closed economy, concerted action by the whole labor movement to increase money wages will leave real wages unchanged. Real wage gains by a single union are won at the expense of real wages elsewhere. Furthermore, even if the trade unions could ordain the general level of money wages, the most they could aspire to would be to perform the functions of a central bank (p. 267), and, even then, real wages would be increased by pulling money wages down rather than putting them up—for this would tend to lower interest rates.

According to the *General Theory*, an increase in employment is necessarily associated with diminishing real wage rates. This follows from the assumption of perfect competitive equilibrium and, its necessary condition, diminishing returns. An increase in employment is associated with a decrease in output per head, and a smaller proportion of that output going to wages. The classical economists said real wage rates could be increased by increasing the wages-fund; Keynes would say by increasing the rate of investment—but actually the *General Theory* does not deal with that question. Yet in this country, the *General Theory* almost qualifies for the *index expurgatorius* of conservatism and "Keynesian" is synonymous with radical.[4]

THE "CLASSICAL" THEORY

We need not debate Keynes' use of the term "classical" here. Suffice it to say that what Keynes describes as classical is the theory that was generally taught and held in pre-Keynesian economics. Given the general assumptions of the Keynesian theory set out in Section I, the classical theory of employment set out in chapter 2 of the *General Theory* can be summarized as follows.

(α) The aggregate demand and the aggregate supply functions for real output are identical. Under this assumption, propositions (a), (b), and (c) of the Keynesian theory thus yield an indeterminate result for real income and employment.

(β) From the employment function which relates employment to real income, there can be derived a real marginal product function for labor.

(γ) The real supply function of labor determines the quantity of labor that will be available at given rates of real wages. It will in general be positively inclined, and at every point on it the marginal disutility of labor will be equal to the marginal utility of the real wage.

Real output and employment are then determined by the intersection of the marginal product function and the supply function.

Keynes holds that, in general, the limitations on effective demand determine output and employment at levels where the marginal product of labor is greater than its supply price according to the classical theory, so that "involuntary unemployment" exists. If effective demand is sufficient, however, output and employment will reach the classical equilibrium position, and, by definition, full employment will be achieved.

If effective demand is just sufficient to raise employment to the full employment position, there is some possibility of harmony

[4] These propositions of the Keynesian theory and those of the classical theory which follows are set out formally in an appendix.

between the Keynesian and the classical influences; but if effective demand is excessive there will be discord.

Suppose, to be concrete, the Government decides to finance a given "real" program by spending enough money to bid away goods from private purchasers. The excessive demand will raise prices so that real wages will fall. In line with the classical theory, the supply of labor will fall off until new money wage demands which seek to restore the old real wage are met. The Government will increase money expenditures and raise prices further. This inflationary spiral will continue unless the process of inflation itself reduces real effective demand. If the Government and labor both remained intransigent in their policies, the chief way in which this could come about would be through the increased yield of a progressive tax system.

Further, as Keynes stresses, (e.g., p. 301) at full employment there is likely to be a general tendency for money wages to increase autonomously. In terms of the classical theory, labor will revise its notions of what its supply schedule ought to be. Attempts to increase real wages will be met by higher prices, and so on. Under our assumptions, the process would only stop if real effective demand were reduced, e.g., by fiscal policy; but then full employment would no longer be maintained. It may turn out that reasonable stability of prices and full employment can only be compatible if there is general recognition that the wage bargain should determine the real wage. Such an outcome, incidentally, is not consistent with the assumption of perfect competition.

Keynes recognizes (p. 301) that the tendency for money wages to rise may occur before full employment. He does not recognize, however, that with a non-homogeneous labor force the classical theory may hold in certain sectors of the economy, and that this may influence the level of output as a whole. A complete short-run theory of employment probably requires a more intimate association of the Keynesian and the classical theories than is found in the *General Theory*.

TOWARD A MORE GENERAL THEORY

I must repeat that any attempt to formalize the *General Theory* inevitably does it less than justice. One is constantly "discovering" qualifications to the main thread of its argument, only to end up by finding at least recognition of the point lurking somewhere in its pages. Yet a clear understanding of Keynes' system cannot be obtained without formalization. Let us now relax the assumptions summarized in Section I and consider what this does to the theory of employment. To complete this program would require a treatise rather than an essay. My chief aim will be to point to problems rather than to solve them.

(1) *Constant equipment and techniques.* It is this assumption that accounts for much of the difference between Keynes and the classics (by classics I now mean the English Classical School and not all orthodox pre-Keynesians). The Classical School was concerned with methods of increasing the demand for labor at given rates of real wages. Their answer was by the accumulation of capital and improved industrial techniques. If full employment can be assumed, it is accumulation and not consumption that increases the demand for labor—or, to use the classical slogan, "the demand for commodities is not the demand for labor."

The trouble with any slogan is that one is apt to forget the assumptions behind it, and the classical slogan led to a general approbation of thrift as the way to progress. The *General Theory* refutes not the classical theory but this unwarranted extension of it. Keynes demonstrates that excessive thrift may lead to chronic unemployment, and a thrifty nation may save and accumulate less than one whose propensity to consume is high enough to maintain full employment.

But, in correcting the classical error, Keynes has not answered the classical question. Discussion of full employment policies under his inspiration has paid little attention to determination of the optimum rate of accumulation.

The assumption of constant techniques ignores the question of substitution. Is it not possible that the technology of the future may raise the average productivity of labor, but lower its marginal productivity? This could mean that, despite an increase in effective demand, real wage rates could fall and the total share of labor in the national product be reduced. The economic and political effects could be profound, and drastic changes in the whole process of wage determination might be required.

I have the impression that Keynes considers the constant technique assumption valid for longer periods than is permissible in the United States. For instance, on page 270 he states: "I am now of the opinion that the maintenance of a stable general level of money wages is, on the balance of considerations, the most advisable in a closed system. . . . This policy will result in a fair degree of stability in the price level. . . ." It is only in "the long period" (p. 271) that a rising money wage level is held necessary for price stability. The rate of increase of productivity in the United States is sufficiently rapid to render conclusions on wage policy based on the assumption of constant techniques and constant productivity of very limited usefulness. In advancing industries, productivity changes become significant over a period of months rather than years and must be taken into account in dealing with both short and long-run questions. The *General Theory* thus omits, for the most part, one of the most critical factors that should be taken into account in money wage determination; and, in determining the amount of employment that results from a given level of effective demand, it is dangerous ever to ignore the possibility of changes in productivity.

(2) *Adjustment problems.* Both Chapter 3, where the general theory is introduced, and Chapter 18, where it is summarized, attest to the fact that the main concern of the book is with stable equilibrium positions; and it is only for the case of stable equilibrium, as Keynes defines it, that the Keynesian system is fully determined. But it is also fully recognized (e.g., pp. 286–298) that the relation of effective demand to employment will differ during the period of adjustment from its eventual equilibrium value. Keynes argues (p. 288) that the elasticity of employment in relation to effective demand will increase as time elapses and will reach its greatest value at the equilibrium position. This conclusion derives from the assumption of unchanging techniques. Under the impetus of new demand, productivity may increase rapidly, and it is quite possible that employment will be less in the equilibrium position than at some stage in the adjustment process. In the same passage (p. 287), he remarks that an increase in effective demand will increase employment less rapidly if directed to consumers' goods than if to investment—because consumers' goods represent the "last stage" of production. I draw attention to this obviously fallacious argument merely because it touches on a matter of practical importance. Space does not permit more than these illustrative comments of Keynes' treatment of the adjustment process. Whatever the details, everything comes out right in the end, and the economy arrives happily at a state of stable equilibrium.

(3) *Perfect competition.* When the assumption of perfect com-

petition is abandoned, several major amendments to the *General Theory* become necessary.

In the first place, it is no longer necessary to assume, in addition, diminishing returns and therefore increasing marginal costs. If monopoly or imperfect competition is the rule, it is possible to have in the short run an increase of employment and an increase of real wages at the same time. This modification of his original position received a tentative assent from Keynes in 1939.[5]

In the second place, the effects of changes in the degree of monopoly deserve an important place in the theory of employment. A reduction in the degree of monopoly will reduce the supply price of real output in terms of wage units. It will also affect both consumption and investment demand, but that is beyond the scope of this paper. Suffice it to say here, for a given level of money demand, output and employment will increase and real wage rates will increase.

Finally, if wage rates are determined by bargains between monopolistic labor and monopolistic business, the wage-price relation will become indeterminate. In such a situation, some of the dilemmas of full employment that we discussed above may be resolved. Business and labor at any rate have the freedom to negotiate a compromise as to the relation that should obtain between real wages and profits.

(4) *Rôle of Government.* When the fiscal operations of the Government are considered, it becomes difficult to accept the Keynesian thesis that real income and employment are determined independently of wage and price adjustments. In the United States at the present time, the progressiveness of the income tax means that revenues of the Federal Government increase more than proportionately to the general price level. Expenditures, on the other hand, tend to increase less than proportionately, since a substantial part of the Government's commitments, such as interest on the national debt, are fixed in terms of money. Hence the automatic operation of the budget tends to reduce total effective demand and employment as money wages and prices rise.

(5) *International Trade.* Consider the case of a "dependent" economy, the prices of whose exports and imports are determined externally and whose domestic trade is fully competitive with its foreign trade in the sense that there is full mobility of resources.

[5] See EJ, 1939.

Assume further that it pursues a policy of fixed exchange rates. In such a country, the money wage rate would determine real wages, production, and employment. The propensities to consume and to invest at home would determine the rate of domestic capital formation and foreign investment. Relative costs of production would govern the distribution of imports between consumers' goods and capital equipment. On the other hand, the Government could conceivably pursue a policy of flexible exchange rates, supplemented if necessary by direct controls, which would validate the Keynesian analysis.

In the United States, of course, the Keynesian theory of employment has much more validity, even if fixed exchange rates are maintained. World prices are not independent of prices here, and foreign trade accounts for only a small part of the national product. But even here, I doubt whether the assumption of a closed economy provides an adequate approximation.

It has been thought that the closed economy assumption, plus the "Notes on Mercantilism," imply that Keynes supports a policy of curing unemployment through "exporting" it by means of foreign investment. Nothing can be further from the truth. Let him speak for himself: "If nations can learn to provide themselves with full employment by their domestic policy . . . there need be no important economic forces calculated to set the interest of one country against that of its neighbours. There would still be room for international division of labour and international lending in appropriate conditions. . . . International trade would cease to be what it is, namely, a desperate expedient to maintain employment at home . . . , but a willing and unimpeded exchange of goods and services in conditions of mutual advantage" (p. 382). It was the Keynes of the *General Theory* who became the great British architect of Bretton Woods and the international trade proposals. Would that all Keynesians agreed with him! [6]

(6) *Relative Wages and Prices.* It is implicit in the *General Theory* that a change in relative wages might affect the distribution of incomes and in that way the propensity to consume, effective demand, and employment. But this possibility is evidently not considered sufficiently important to be recognized explicitly.

Changes in relative wages may have other effects on the relation of effective demand to employment that cannot be ignored

[6] [Cf. Dr. Nurkse's essay above.]

even in a first approximation. An increase in wages in the investment industries in relation to those in consumer goods industries will tend to lower the rate of investment and hence effective demand; while relative increase of wages in the consumer goods industries may spur the introduction of labor saving methods. Questions such as these were commonplace in neoclassical economics. Although they lead to no easy generalizations, they deserve their place in aggregative theory.

(7) *Static Analysis.* I have characterized the *General Theory* as static, because its main preoccupation is with equilibrium positions or with the process of change from one equilibrium position to another. These changes come about through the influence of factors exogenous to the Keynesian system. There is no question of the interrelations of the endogenous variables giving rise to cyclical fluctuations. A dynamic analysis may lead to somewhat different conclusions.

The statistical evidence can be interpreted to indicate that in 1937 and 1946 money wage increases increased labor's share of the national income. For a given effective demand, the real wage at which a given amount of labor found employment increased. I also believe that the wage increases in 1937 contributed to the subsequent depression. Why did not prices adjust themselves fully to the new wage level so that everything would go on as merrily as before?

In the first place prices probably adjust themselves only with a lag. But, during that lag, lower profit rates may become reflected in investment plans and a lower rate of investment in the future.

Secondly, business may fear that if they make the full price adjustment they will "price themselves out of the market." What this means in analytic terms is that consumers believe that prices will be lower in the future and consequently lower their propensity to consume while they consider prices to be too high. In static analysis, the Keynesian assumption that consumers' expenditure is a function of income alone may be valid. In a dynamic situation this may not be true—we may find that consumer demand has a price elasticity of more than unity.

These are examples of the need to regard the Keynesian analysis as a special case of a general dynamic theory. But I do not want to overemphasize the point. Equilibrium analysis does provide the norm about which fluctuations take place, so that for many of the major problems of practical importance the Keynesian static [7] analysis is sufficient.

CONCLUSION

I have stressed the limitations of Keynes' theory of employment and the need for a more general theory. Great though it is, the *General Theory* is not the last word in economics. But, in the present stage of capitalism, it should be the first word. It has brought to modern economics a Ricardian illumination. The parallel between Keynes and Ricardo is striking.[8] Both constructed simple analytic models with the aid of highly restrictive assumptions. It may turn out that each will have exercised his greatest influence in fields to which his formal analysis did not apply. The *General Theory* is a most constructive tool for those who are aware of its limitations, but a dangerous one for those who ignore them.

APPENDIX

Let Y denote money income; W, the money wage rate; P, the price level; N, employment; r, the rate of interest; and M, the quantity of money. Let D and Z represent respectively the aggregate money demand for and the aggregate money supply price of real output. The Keynesian system described above can then be expressed as follows:

$$(1) \quad \frac{D}{P} = f\left(\frac{Y}{P}, r\right) \qquad \text{(Aggregate demand function for consumption } plus \text{ investment)}$$

$$(2) \quad \frac{Z}{P} = \frac{Y}{P} \qquad \text{(Aggregate supply function)}$$

[7] It is thought by some writers that the concept of the multiplier makes the Keynesian analysis dynamic. In a sense it does, since the multiplier process represents the path from one equilibrium position to another under highly simplified conditions. But the temporary changes in the marginal propensity to consume, which that process represents, are relatively unimportant from the point of view of a complete dynamic analysis. There have been numerous formulations of the relation of the Keynesian theory to dynamic analysis. I take the liberty of referring to my own. See "Process Analysis and Equilibrium Analysis," EC, January, 1942.

[8] I find that Professor Schumpeter has also been struck with the similarity. I hesitate to repeat what he has said so brilliantly, but the point should be made more than once. See J. A. Schumpeter, "John Maynard Keynes, 1883–1946" AER, September 1946. (See above p. 94.)

(3) $D = Z$

(4) $M = L_1(Y) + L_2(r)$ (Liquidity preference relation)

(5) $N = \psi\left(\dfrac{Y}{P}\right)$ (Production equation)

(6) $W = \chi(N)$ (Wage determination function)

(7) $P = W\psi'\left(\dfrac{Y}{P}\right)$ (Price determination function)

If $M - L_1$ (Y), and consequently r, are held constant, real income $\dfrac{Y}{P}$, is determined by (1), (2), (3), and (4); then N, W, and P are successively determined by (5), (6), and (7).

In the classical theory of employment (6) is replaced by the supply function of labor,

$$(6')N = \theta\left(\frac{W}{P}\right)$$

Relations (5), (6), and (7) would then determine $\dfrac{Y}{P}, \dfrac{W}{P}$, and N, and their values would not necessarily be equal to those determined by (1), (2), (3), and (4) in the Keynesian system. The substitution of $(6')$ for (6), together with our monetary system, would make the Keynesian system homogeneous of order zero in W and P, and, so, overdetermined.

In Chapter 3, Keynes expresses aggregate demand and supply in terms of money wage units as functions of employment. This is entirely consistent with the scheme set out above. If we multiply both sides of (1) by $\dfrac{P}{W}$ we have:

$$\frac{D}{W} = \frac{P}{W}f\left(\frac{Y}{P}, r\right)$$

and, by using (7):

$$\frac{D}{W} = \psi'\left(\frac{Y}{P}\right)f\left(\frac{Y}{P}, r\right)$$

Keynes ignores r in Chapter 3, and since $\dfrac{Y}{P}$ is a function of N by (5), we can write:

$$\frac{D}{W} = F(N)$$

Similarly, from (2):

$$\frac{Z}{W} = \frac{Y}{P} \cdot \frac{P}{W}$$

or:

$$= \frac{Y}{P} \psi' \left(\frac{Y}{P}\right)$$

$$\frac{Z}{W} = \Phi(N)$$

CHAPTER XL

Money Wage Rates and Employment

By JAMES TOBIN

WHAT IS THE effect of a general change in money wage rates on aggregate employment and output?[1] To this question, crucial both for theory and for policy, the answers of economists are as unsatisfactory as they are divergent. A decade of Keynesian economics has not solved the problem, but it has made clearer the assumptions concerning economic behavior on which the answer depends. In this field, perhaps even more than in other aspects of the *General Theory*, Keynes' contribution lies in clarifying the theoretical issues at stake rather than in providing an ultimate solution.

PRE-KEYNESIAN SOLUTIONS TO THE MONEY WAGE PROBLEM

How considerable this contribution is can be appreciated from a brief review of pre-Keynesian attempts to solve the problem.[2] These solutions rested on one of the following assumptions: (a) that the price level is unchanged,[3] (b) that aggregate money demand (MV) is unchanged,[4] or (c) that some component of

[1] This question concerns the effects of a general change in money wage rates which is expected to be permanent. A fall in money wage rates which is expected to be followed by further reductions will discourage output and employment, and a rise which is expected to continue will stimulate output and employment. On these propositions there is no disagreement.

[2] It should be noted that R. F. Harrod ("Review of Professor Pigou's *Theory of Unemployment*," EJ, XLIV, March, 1934, p. 19) anticipated the Keynesian solution.

[3] J. R. Hicks, *The Theory of Wages* (London, Macmillan, 1936), pp. 211-2.

[4] Cf. Hicks, "Mr. Keynes and the Classics: A Suggested Interpretation," EC, V, April, 1937, p. 147.

aggregate money demand, e.g., non-wage-earners' expenditure, is unchanged.[5] Naturally, if money demand is assumed to be maintained in any of these ways, the conclusion follows easily that a money wage cut will increase, and a money wage rise diminish, total employment and output. These assumptions, or any variant of them, beg the central question raised by the fact that money wage-rate changes are double-edged. They change money costs, but they change at the same time money incomes and hence money expenditures. Even the money expenditures of non-wage-earners cannot be assumed unchanged, for their incomes depend in part on the expenditures of wage-earners.

THE RÔLE OF THE CONSUMPTION FUNCTION IN KEYNES' SOLUTION

Keynes replaced these assumptions with a proposition which, whatever its shortcomings, is certainly a more plausible description of actual economic behavior. This proposition is his consumption function: that *real* consumption expenditure is a unique function of *real* income, with the marginal propensity to consume positive but less than unity. So far as consumption expenditure alone is concerned, therefore, Keynes concluded that a change in money wage rates could not affect the volume of employment and output. Because the marginal propensity to consume is less than unity, any increase in output and real income would fail to generate enough of an increase in real consumption expenditure to purchase the additional output. Any decrease in output and real income would cause, for the same reason, an excess of aggregate real demand over supply. The result of a change in money wage rates would be, still considering only reactions via

[5] A. Smithies, "Wage Policy in the Depression," *Economic Record*, December, 1935, p. 249.

A. C. Pigou, *Theory of Unemployment* (London, Macmillan, 1933), pp. 100–106.

In "Real and Money Wage Rates in Relation to Unemployment" (EJ, XLVII, September, 1937, p. 405), Pigou relaxed this assumption to provide in effect that non-wage-earners' money expenditure, although not constant, is uniquely determined by the volume of employment. This variant has the same significance as the three assumptions discussed in the text. Later, under the prodding of Nicholas Kaldor ("Professor Pigou on Money Wages in Relation to Unemployment," EJ, XLVII, December, 1937, p. 745), Pigou in "Money Wages and Unemployment" (EJ, XLVIII, March, 1938, p. 134), accepted in essence the Keynesian position.

consumption expenditure, a proportionate change in prices and money incomes and no change in employment, output, real incomes, or real wage rates.

These are the implications of Keynes' systematic theory. In the course of remarks which are, from the standpoint of his systematic theory, *obiter dicta*, Keynes considered two possible effects of a money wage cut on the propensity to consume: "redistribution of real income (a) from wage-earners to other factors entering into marginal prime cost whose remuneration has not been reduced, and (b) from entrepreneurs to rentiers to whom a certain income fixed in terms of money has been guaranteed."[6] The effects on consumption of the second type of transfer, (b), Keynes thought doubtful and apparently unimportant. The first type of transfer, (a), from wage-earners to other prime factors, would, if it occurred, be likely to diminish the propensity to consume; it would, therefore, be unfavorable to employment. However, Keynes over-estimated the likelihood of such a redistribution of income. Maintenance of the prices of other variable factors in the face of a wage cut would encourage substitution of labor for these factors; such substitution would not only be directly favorable to employment of labor but would also diminish or reverse the transfer of income from labor to non-wage-earners. On the other hand, if the owners of other variable factors sought to avoid such substitution, they would, as Lerner has shown, reduce their prices in the same proportion as the wage rate and consequently would not gain income at the expense of labor.[7]

EFFECTS OF MONEY WAGE RATE CHANGES ON INVESTMENT

The possibility remains that a change in money wage rates may induce a change in the other component of Keynes' effective demand, real investment. So far as real investment is itself dependent on the level of real income or the volume of real consumption expenditure, there is clearly no reason for such a change. Likewise, the marginal efficiency of capital, so far as it is objectively determined by the amount of additional output which can result from an increment of capital, is not altered by a change

[6] *General Theory*, p. 262.
[7] Problems raised by the existence of variable factors other than labor are discussed below, pp. 578, 582–3.

in money wage rates. Three types of reactions on the rate of real investment are left:

(a) Conceivably, a change in money wage rates may affect that delicate phenomenon, the state of business confidence. However, the direction of this influence cannot be predicted in a general theory.[8] Individual business men making investment decisions may be impressed chiefly by the fact that a money wage cut reduces their costs. On the other hand, a fall in wages and prices embarrasses entrepreneurs by increasing the real burden of their debt. Without underrating the importance of these types of reactions, therefore, Keynes had to exclude them from his theoretical structure.[9]

(b) In an open economy, a change in the general wage rate and price level will affect the balance of trade. A reduction of money wage rates and prices will stimulate demand for exports and shift domestic demand to home goods in preference to imports. Such a change in the balance of trade is equivalent to an increase in real investment and has a multiplied effect on home real income and employment. This effect may be strengthened by a worsening of the terms of trade, which increases the employment necessary to obtain the equilibrium level of real income and real saving. A rise in money wage rates would have the opposite effects. On this score there is little dispute. These effects may be nullified, however, by similar wage adjustments in other countries or by changes in exchange rates.

(c) A change in the level of money wage rates, prices, and money incomes alters in the same direction the demand for cash balances for transactions purposes. With an unchanged quantity of money, a reduction of money wage rates leaves a larger supply of money to satisfy the demand for cash balances from precautionary and speculative motives. The result is a reduction in the rate of interest, which should lead to an increase in the rate of real investment. Similarly a rise in money wage rates increases the interest rate and restricts real investment. It was only by this circuitous route that Keynes found any generally valid theoretical reason for expecting in a closed economy a relationship between money wage rates and employment.

---

[8] Except in the case discussed in footnote [1] above, or in the opposite case when wage expectations are inelastic.

[9] He considered the various possibilities in detail. *General Theory*, Chap. 19, especially pp. 262–4.

THE CENTRAL THESIS OF THE *GENERAL THEORY*

Such is the Keynesian solution to the money wage problem. It is important to view it in the broad setting of the *General Theory*. Keynes set himself the goal of establishing, first, that there may be involuntary unemployment of labor and, second, that there may be no method open to labor to remove such unemployment by making new money wage bargains. There may be involuntary unemployment because additional labor would be offered at the going money wage rate at the same or lower real wage rates.[10] Labor, beset by a "money illusion," will permit its real wage to be reduced by price rises without leaving the market, even when it will not accede to the same reduction in its real wage by a money wage cut. At the same time, labor is powerless to take advantage of the potential demand for its services at lower real wage rates, because a reduction in the money wage may not lead to a reduction in the real wage.

The linkage between money wage rates and employment via the rate of interest appears to destroy the second half of this central thesis. For, if money wage rates were flexible, they could presumably fall enough to lower the rate of interest to a level which would induce the volume of investment necessary to maintain full employment. This linkage is, however, extremely tenuous. It can be broken at either of the following points: (a) The interest elasticity of the demand for cash balances may be infinite; (b) the interest elasticity of the demand for investment may be zero.[11] Condition (a) is likely to be approximated at low interest rates, and condition (b) is supported by the evidence that interest calculations play an insignificant part in business investment decisions. The Keynesian thesis that labor cannot erase unemployment by revising its money wage bargains is, therefore, not seriously damaged by admitting the effect of money wage rates on the demand for cash balances.

---

[10] *General Theory*, chap. 2. See footnote [18] below.

[11] F. Modigliani ("Liquidity Preference and the Theory of Interest and Money," EC, XII, January, 1944, pp. 45–89) emphasizes that except when condition (a), which he calls the "Keynesian case," is satisfied, unemployment is attributable to an improper relationship between the quantity of money and the money wage rate, i.e., to rigid wages. He does not mention that condition (b) would constitute another and very important exception to the wage rigidity explanation of unemployment.

ASSUMPTIONS OF KEYNESIAN MONEY WAGE THEORY

It is damaged, however, by removal of certain of the restrictive assumptions of the Keynesian model; and their removal is logically necessary because they clash with other basic assumptions. To demonstrate this, the main assumptions of Keynesian money wage theory will be examined. They are: (1) that real wages are a decreasing function of the volume of employment, (2) that labor is the only variable factor of production, (3) that pure competition exists throughout the economy or that the degree of monopoly is constant, (4) that "money illusion" affects the supply function for labor, and (5) that "money illusion" does not occur in other supply and demand functions.

(1) *Diminishing Marginal Productivity*

Adopting the traditional postulate of diminishing marginal productivity, Keynes assumed that real wage rates and employment are inversely related. Consequently, an increase in employment at the same money wage can occur only if there is a rise in prices sufficient to compensate business firms for the increase in marginal costs associated with an expansion of output. For this reason, the question whether labor will accept increased employment at a reduced real wage brought about by such a price rise becomes Keynes' criterion for the existence of involuntary unemployment. Keynes ventured the guess that real wages and money wages would usually be found to move in opposite directions, since money wages usually rise in periods of increasing employment and fall when employment is decreasing.[12] This conjecture provoked several statistical investigations designed to check the traditional postulate.[13] Statistically these investigations were inconclusive;[14] in any case the issue, though of great interest in

[12] *General Theory*, pp. 9–10.

[13] J. T. Dunlop ("The Movement of Real and Money Wages," EJ, XLVIII, September, 1938, p. 413) and L. Tarshis ("Changes in Real and Money Wages," EJ, XLIX, March, 1939, p. 150) concluded, from English and U. S. experience respectively, that Keynes was wrong in his conjecture and that real and money wage rates generally moved in the same direction. J. H. Richardson ("Real Wage Movements," EJ, XLIX, September, 1939, p. 425) supported the traditional, here also the Keynesian, position. M. Kalecki (*Essays in the Theory of Economic Fluctuations,* London, Allen & Unwin, 1939) held that approximately constant marginal costs prevail.

[14] Cf. R. Ruggles, "Relative Movements of Real and Money Wage Rates," QJE, LIV, November, 1940, pp. 130–149.

itself, is not crucial for Keynes' central thesis. Equilibrium with decreasing marginal costs throughout most of the economy is
∨ conceivable in a world of monopolies. In such an economy, the involuntary nature of unemployment at a given money wage would be even clearer than on Keynes' definition. Increased employment would not be purchased at the expense of a higher cost of living but would yield higher real wages. The question raised by the second proposition of Keynes' central thesis—can unemployment be removed by a money wage cut?—remains the same whether increasing or decreasing marginal productivity prevails.

(2) No Variable Factors Other than Labor

The assumption that labor is the only variable factor is more serious. By this simplification, Keynes rules out the possibility of substitution as a result of money wage rate changes. If the possibility of substitution between labor and other factors is admitted, the Keynesian solution of the money wage problem can be saved only by introducing another assumption. Paradoxically, this postulate is that all factors other than labor are fully employed and that their prices are completely flexible. Then their prices will always change in the same direction and proportion as the money wage rate.[15] If the money wage rate increases, business firms will attempt to economize on labor by substituting other factors. But since these other factors are already fully employed, attempted substitution can only result in bidding their prices up until the incentive to substitute vanishes. Likewise, if there is a cut in the money wage rate, business firms will attempt to substitute labor and reduce the employment of other factors. But since the prices of these factors are perfectly flexible, this substitution will be prevented by a lowering of the prices of these factors to keep them fully employed. If the price of any other factor were rigid, a change in the money wage rate would cause substitution between labor and that factor. A money wage cut would increase the employment of labor and a money wage rise reduce it.

(3) Pure Competition or Constant Degree of Monopoly

Under conditions of pure competition, prices would be free to

[15] Cf. A. P. Lerner, "Mr. Keynes' *General Theory of Employment, Interest, and Money*," ILR, XXXIV, October, 1936, p. 435; "The Relation of Wage Policies and Price Policies," AER, *Supplement*, March, 1939, p. 158; *The Economics of Control*, New York, Macmillan, 1946, Chap. 23, especially pp. 287–8.

move up or down in the same ratio as the money wage rate, as Keynesian theory requires. Under monopolistic conditions, these proportionate price movements oan occur only if the degree of monopoly—the ratio of the difference between price and marginal cost to price—remains the same. Monopolistic conditions lead to price rigidity and stickiness. Consequently a cut in the money wage rate will increase the degree of monopoly. Disregarding other results of the money wage cut, the increase in the degree of monopoly will increase the relative share of the national income going to non-wage-earners. Since non-wage-earners may be assumed to have a lower marginal propensity to consume than wage-earners, this redistribution of income reduces the real demand for consumption goods. In this respect, a money wage cut is detrimental to employment and output. A money wage rise has the opposite effect. This is presumably the *rationale* of the arguments of proponents of raising wages as an anti-depression policy.[16]

Rigidities in the prices of other factors of production, including unfinished goods and services, also lead to the substitution effects discussed in the previous section. The substitution effects of a money wage cut not only tend to increase employment directly, but also limit or prevent entirely the adverse effects on consumption expenditure from redistribution of income. Even though the degree of monopoly is increased, the increase in employment due to substitution tends to maintain labor's relative share. Monopolists in the finished and near-finished goods markets gain, possibly at the expense of labor but certainly at the expense of the sellers of factors with rigid prices, including the monopolists of unfinished products. Between the marginal propensities to consume of these two groups of non-wage-earners—monopolists in the final stages of production and monopolists in the early stages plus landlords and other property-owners—there is little to choose. Taking substitution effects into account weakens the argument that because of price rigidities a money wage cut redistributes income adversely to consumption expenditure. Indeed, if the elasticity of substitution is high enough, the redistribution of income may be favorable to consumption.

(4) *"Money Illusion" in the Supply of Labor*

Economic theory is usually predicated on the premise that,

[16] Kalecki *op. cit.* Chap. 3, especially pp. 80–86.

given their schedules of preferences for goods and services and leisure, individuals behave consistently and "rationally." A consumer is not supposed to alter his expenditure pattern when his income doubles, if the prices of the things he buys all double at the same time. Nor is a business firm expected to change its output, if the price of its product and the prices of all factors it employs change in the same proportion. Generalized, this premise is what Leontief calls the "homogeneity postulate," namely, that all supply and demand functions, with prices taken as independent variables, are homogeneous functions of the zero degree.[17] Applied to the supply of labor, this postulate means that a proportionate change in the money wage and in all current prices will leave the supply of labor unchanged. Considering the real wage rate as the ratio between the money wage rate and the current price level of goods consumed by wage-earners, the postulate means that a given real wage rate will bring forth the same amount of labor whatever the level of the money wage rate—that labor will react in the same way towards a 10 per cent cut in its real wage whether this cut is accomplished by a reduction of its money wage rate or by a rise in current prices. Any other behavior seems inconsistent and "non-rational," based on a "money illusion" attributing importance to dollars *per se* rather than on an understanding of their real value.

Clearly one of Keynes' basic assumptions—Leontief calls it *the* fundamental assumption—is that "money illusion" occurs in the labor supply function.[18] Labor does attach importance to the money wage rate *per se,* and more labor will be supplied at the same real wage the higher the money wage. This assertion concerning the behavior of wage-earners is indispensable to Keynes in establishing the existence of involuntary unemployment.

[17] W. Leontief, "The Fundamental Assumption of Mr. Keynes' Monetary Theory of Unemployment," QJE, LI, November, 1936, p. 192.

[18] Leontief, (*op. cit.*) pointed out also that the wording of Keynes' definition of involuntary unemployment does not necessarily repudiate the "homogeneity postulate" ("Men are involuntarily unemployed if, in the event of a small rise in the price of wage-goods relatively to the money wage, both the aggregate supply of labor willing to work for the current money wage and the aggregate demand for it at that wage would be greater than the existing volume of employment." *General Theory,* p. 15.) It could be interpreted to mean merely that the supply schedule for labor with respect to its real wage is negatively inclined. To Keynes' definition should be added the condition that the amount of labor demanded at the lower real wage must be greater than or equal to the amount supplied.

What are the reasons for such "non-rational" behavior on the part of labor? First, high money wage rates are a concrete and immediate accomplishment of the leadership of individual unions. The object of individual labor groups in wage bargaining is to protect and if possible to advance their wages relative to other groups. Each union will resist a cut in money wages in order to avoid a relative reduction in real wages. The cost of living is a remote phenomenon, apparently beyond the control of organized labor, certainly beyond the control of any single bargaining unit. Money wage bargains must be made for periods during which the cost of living may frequently change. Second, wage-earners have obligations fixed in terms of money: debts, taxes, contractual payments such as insurance premiums. These obligations are a greater burden when money wage rates are cut, even though all current prices may fall proportionately. Third, labor may have inelastic price expectations; a certain "normal" price level, or range of price levels, may be expected to prevail in the future, regardless of the level of current prices.[19] With such price expectations, it is clearly to the advantage of wage-earners to have, with the same current real income, the highest possible current money income. For the higher their money incomes the greater will be their money savings and, therefore, their expected command over future goods. Wage-earners with inelastic price expectations will resist money wage cuts even when prices are falling, not only because they fear that wages will not rise again when prices rise but also because the expected price rise would reduce the real value of their current saving. Fourth, labor may be genuinely ignorant of the course of prices or naïvely deceived by the "money illusion." Judged by labor's consciousness of the cost of living in the United States in 1946, this explanation, if it ever was important, is not now significant. Altogether, the support for Keynes' assumption in regard to the supply of labor is convincing; his denial of the "homogeneity postulate" for the labor supply function constitutes a belated theoretical recognition of the facts of economic life.

(5) *Absence of "Money Illusion" Elsewhere in the Economy*

Wage-earners are the only inhabitants of the Keynesian economy who are so foolish or so smart, as the case may be, as to act under the spell of the "money illusion." They are under its spell

[19] Hicks, *Value and Capital* (Oxford, 1939), pp. 269–272.

only in their capacity as suppliers of labor. The "homogeneity postulate" is denied for the labor supply function; for all other demand and supply functions it is retained. Without the retention of the "homogeneity postulate" for all supply and demand functions except the labor supply function, the Keynesian money wage doctrine cannot be maintained. The dependence of the doctrine on this procedure and the justification for the procedure will be considered for (a) the supply functions of other factors, and (b) the consumption function.

(a) Supply of Other Factors

When the existence of variable factors other than labor is admitted, Keynesian theory requires that these factors be fully employed and that their prices be perfectly flexible.[20] This is where the "homogeneity postulate"—the assumption of "rational" behavior—enters with respect to the supply functions of these factors. If the sellers of these factors were, like the sellers of labor, influenced by the "money illusion," their prices would be rigid like wages and there could be unemployment of these factors. A change in the money wage rate could then alter the employment of labor by causing substitution between labor and other factors.

Keynes, since he assumes away the existence of other factors, presents no reasons for this distinction between labor and other factors. Lerner, however, asserts that it is "plausible and in conformity with the assumption of rationality of entrepreneurs and capital-owners, who would rather get something for the use of their property than let it be idle, while labor has non-rational money-wage demands."[21] It is important to note what is included in "other factors:" not only the services of land, other natural agents, and existing items of capital equipment, but also services and unfinished goods which are the products of some firms but serve as inputs for other firms. The sellers of these factors have much the same reasons as wage-earners for having "non-rational" money-price demands. Perhaps to a greater extent than labor, they have obligations fixed in terms of money. If their price expectations are inelastic, they have the same interest in high money rates of remuneration, whatever their current real returns, to

[20] P. 578 above.

[21] "Relation of Wage Policies and Price Policies," AER, *Supplement*, March, 1939, p. 163.

protect their current savings against future price rises. They too must make money bargains for the sale of their services, contracts which will last over a period of many possible price level changes. Business firms which control the supply of intermediate goods and services often attempt to stabilize money-prices, letting their output and sales fluctuate widely. Such price rigidities are money-price demands on the part of entrepreneurs analogous in effect to the "non-rational" money-wage demands of labor.

The "money illusion" will frequently influence the suppliers of other factors. Consequently there can be price rigidities in all markets and fluctuations in the use of all factors of production. In such an economy the money wage rate is an independent determinant of the volume of employment.

(b) Consumption Decisions

The Keynesian consumption function, which is crucial to the Keynesian solution to the money wage problem,[22] is framed in real terms: real consumption expenditure is uniquely determined by real income.[23] It is not affected, for example, by a doubling of money income and of all prices. This is the application of the "homogeneity postulate" to the consumption function. If "money illusion" occurred in consumption and saving decisions, real consumption expenditure would depend on the level of money income as well as on the level of real income, just as the supply of labor depends on the money wage rate as well as on the real wage. A change in the money wage rate, changing the level of money incomes and prices, would alter the real demand for consumption goods and therefore affect the volume of both output and employment. Here again, therefore, retention of the "homogeneity postulate" is an essential assumption for Keynesian money wage doctrine.

But if wage-earners are victims of a "money illusion" when they act as sellers of labor, why should they be expected to become "rational" when they come in to the market as consumers? Most of the reasons which compel them to behave "non-rationally" in making money wage bargains would logically compel them to act "non-rationally" as consumers. And if, as argued above, labor has no corner on such non-rationality, the whole body of consumers would be influenced by the "money illusion."

[22] P. 573 above.
[23] This is the significance of Keynes' use of wage-units.

In which direction would the "money illusion" be expected to operate on the consumption function? With real income given, will an increase in money income cause an increase or a decrease in real consumption expenditure? The logic of the other assumptions of Keynesian theory leads to an inverse relationship between money income and real consumption expenditure, with real income constant. For wage-earners are assumed to feel worse off when their money wages are cut; and when consumers feel worse off, they are supposed to devote a greater part of their real incomes to consumption and less to saving.

Consistency with other Keynesian assumptions is not, however, the most weighty argument in favor of such a relationship. One reason for non-homogeneous behavior in the supply of labor, we have seen, is the holding of inelastic price expectations. Such price expectations will also influence current consumption expenditure. If current prices are below the "normal" level expected to prevail in the future, consumers will substitute present purchases for future purchases, save less now and plan to save more in the future. If current prices are above expected future prices, consumers will reduce present consumption expenditure in favor of future expenditure, increase current saving at the expense of future saving. From the same real income, real consumption expenditure will be less the higher the current level of money incomes and prices. Inelasticity of price expectations is, therefore, one source of an inverse relationship between money income and real consumption expenditure out of a given real income.

If price expectations are not inelastic, a different but equally effective reason for the same relationship comes into operation. It is now widely recognized that the volume of accumulated savings held by consumers affects their propensity to consume.[24] The greater the volume of such holdings, the more consumers have already satisfied their desire to save, the greater the part of a given current income which will be spent for consumption. These assets are, except for equities, fixed or very nearly fixed in money value. Now if current price changes are expected to persist, a general decline in money prices and incomes will increase the real value of accumulated savings, and a general rise in money prices and incomes will reduce their real value. An increase in the real value of these assets should increase the propensity to consume,

[24] Cf., for example, A. P. Lerner, "Functional Finance and the Public Debt," *Social Research*, X, February, 1943, p. 49.

and a decrease in their value reduce it.[25] Such behavior on the part of consumers is quite consistent and rational; it appears to be the consequence of a "money illusion" only when current prices and incomes are taken as the sole variables relevant to consumption decisions.

Assuming that real consumption expenditure is, for these ✓ reasons, an inverse function of the level of money income, as well as a direct function of real income *à la* Keynes, a decrease in money wage rates must lead to an expansion of output and employment, and an increase in money wage rates to a curtailment of output and employment. A money wage cut, for example, will cause a general decline in prices and money incomes. This decline will stimulate an increase in the real demand for consumption goods and thereby cause a general expansion of output, real income, and employment. In the new equilibrium, prices will be lower: they will fall less than the money wage if increasing marginal costs prevail, and more than the money wage if decreasing marginal costs predominate. In the latter case, the expansion of output and employment will be greater either because more substitution of present for future consumption is induced or because the increase in real value of accumulated savings is larger. A rise in the money wage rate, of course, has the opposite effects.

These effects of changes in the money wage rate are superimposed on the substitution effects already discussed and act on the employment of labor in the same direction.

CONCLUSION

The central thesis of the *General Theory* contains two complementary propositions: first, that because labor has "non-rational"

[25] Since the assets held by consumers are the debts of other economic units, price changes affecting the real value of consumers' assets will also affect the real burden of debt. Changes in the real burden of debt may influence business investment decisions. The resulting changes in investment will act in the opposite direction from the changes in consumption described in the text. (Keynes [*General Theory*, p. 264] and Hicks [*Value and Capital*, p. 264] both considered the possible depressing influence of price and wage reductions in increasing the burden of debt without mentioning the favorable effects of the increased real wealth of creditors.) But only part of consumers' assets are, directly or indirectly, business debts; the assets of ˂ private economic units exceed private debt by the total of public debt, the monetary gold reserve, and the supply of government-issued currency. Hence, a given price change will cause a greater change in the real value of consumers' assets than in the burden of business debt.

money wage demands, involuntary unemployment of labor is possible; second, that labor is in any case powerless to remedy this unemployment by altering its money wage bargains. (The second proposition Keynes qualifies by admitting the possibilities of reactions on employment via the rate of interest, but this qualification, for reasons given above, is of limited practical importance.) The second proposition of the central thesis rests on assumptions logically inconsistent with the assumption contained in the first; and the premises of the second proposition are as unrealistic as the assumption underlying Keynes' labor supply function is realistic. If Keynes' denial of the "homogeneity postulate" is extended to supply and demand functions other than the labor supply function—if, in other words, "money illusion" operates elsewhere than on the sellers' side of the labor market—then employment is inversely affected by money wage rate changes. Labor is not powerless to reduce unemployment by reducing its money wage demands. Changes in employment follow from changes in the money wage because of substitution between labor and other factors and because of the effects of "money illusion" on real consumption expenditure. The substitution effect can be avoided only by assuming, as in the *General Theory*, that labor is the only variable factor or, if other factors are considered, by assuming that the suppliers of these factors, unlike labor, have no "non-rational" money-price demands. The consumption effect can be avoided only by assuming that wage-earners—and the suppliers of other factors if they are admitted to behave like wage-earners—act "rationally" as buyers even though they are "non-rational" as sellers, and by neglecting the effect of inelastic price expectations or accumulated savings on the propensity to consume. These two effects, or either one of them alone, make the money wage rate a determinant of the volume of employment. The consumption effect makes it also a determinant of the level of output and real income.

To summarize, a change in the money wage rate may alter the level of employment in the following ways:

1. By its effect on business confidence, which is not theoretically predictable, a change in the money wage rate may alter the volume of real investment.

2. In an open economy, a wage cut will have an effect equivalent to an expansion of investment by increasing the balance of

trade. A wage rise will have the opposite results and affect employment adversely.

3. By reducing the demand for cash balances, a wage cut *may* reduce the rate of interest; reduction of the interest rate *may* stimulate investment and employment. A wage rise may have the opposite effects.

4. A wage cut may induce substitution of labor for other factors, and a wage rise may diminish employment by causing substitution of other factors for labor.

5. A wage cut may cause an increase in the real demand for consumption goods and therefore in both output and employment. Increased consumption demand would result either from substitution of present consumption for future consumption, when price expectations are inelastic, or from the increased real value of accumulated savings. A wage rise would have the contrary effect.

6. An effect contrary in direction to the four preceding possibilities is that a money wage cut will, because of price rigidities, redistribute income adversely to labor and thereby reduce the propensity to consume. For similar reasons, a money wage rise would be favorable to employment. This effect will be the stronger the weaker is the substitution effect; if substitution is considerable, it may be entirely absent.

Solution of the money wage problem was greatly advanced by replacing arbitrary assumptions concerning the price level or the level of money expenditure with Keynes' analysis of effective demand. Further progress towards a solution, and ultimately towards a quantitative solution, depends on refinement and extension, both theoretical and statistical, of the basic Keynesian system. What are the variables other than real rates of remuneration affecting the supply of labor and of other factors of production, and what effects do these variables have? What variables other than real income determine real consumption expenditure, and how? What variables lie behind the marginal efficiency of capital, and how do they enter business investment calculations? Only when economists have more satisfactory answers to these broader questions will they be able to give an acceptable solution to the money wage problem.

PART NINE

Some Earlier Discussions

CHAPTER XLI

Keynes and Traditional Theory

By R. F. HARROD

IN THIS PAPER I do not propose to ask or answer the question, Has Keynes succeeded in establishing the propositions which he claims to have established? nor again, What kind of evidence is required to establish or to refute those propositions? I shall confine myself to a narrower question, namely, what are the propositions which Mr. Keynes claims to have established? And in order to restrict my subject matter still further, I propose to confine myself to those propositions, which he claims to have established, that are in conflict with the theory of value in the form in which it has hitherto been commonly accepted by most economists. In other words, my question is: What modifications in the generally recognized theory of value would acceptance of the propositions that Keynes claims to have established entail?

In order to clarify the issues involved, it may be well to divide commonly accepted theory into the general theory and its specialized branches. The general theory consists primarily of a number of functional equations expressing individual preference schedules and a number of identities, such as that supply must be equal to demand, and the elucidation of such questions as whether there are as many equations as there are unknowns and whether the solutions are single or multiple. The result of these enquiries should make it clear whether the equilibrium of the system as a whole is stable or unstable or undetermined, whether there are alternative positions of equilibrium, etc. There may be some clues as to the general form of some of the functional equations, provided by such principles as the law of diminishing utility, to use old-fashioned terminology, which may make it possible to predict the direction of changes in the values of the various unknowns due to a given change in one of them. More precise prediction can only be achieved if or when it becomes possible, as a result of the labors of such investigators as Dr. Schultz, to write down the actual terms of the functional equations. Within the corpus of this general theory may be included the formulation of the market conditions that are required for the realization of some kind of maximum. Thus if one individual A is indifferent whether he produces commodity X or commodity Y for a certain consideration, and another individual B *prefers* X to Y, the maximum is not realised if the market so operates that A normally produces Y and not X for B. On this condition the maxim of free trade is fairly securely founded, the more general maxim of laissez faire much less securely so.

In contrast with the theory of value in this very general form, may be set the special theories formulated to deal with specific problems such as interest, profit, joint production, discriminating monopoly, etc. The normal method used in dealing with these departmental studies is to assume that certain terms, which appear as variables in the general system of equations, may be treated as constants for the special purpose in hand. For instance in studying the behavior of duopolistic producers of a given commodity, it may be assumed that the duopolists can obtain the services of factors of production at rates the determination of which in the market will not be appreciably affected by the duopolists' behavior. Such methods constitute short cuts to the unravelling of particular problems and they are often perfectly legitimate. In the minds of most economists, other than those who stand, so to speak, at the philosophical end of the economic array, the conclusions reached by these short-cut methods constitute the main findings of economic theory.

I may say at once that in my opinion Keynes' conclusions need not be deemed to make a vast difference to the general theory, but that they do make a vast difference to a number of short-cut conclusions of leading importance. Thus to those whom I may perhaps call without offence the ordinary working economists they ought, if accepted, to appear to constitute quite a revolution. Whether they entail a substantial modification of the more general theory depends on how that is stated. I need hardly observe that there is no authorized version. Those whose main interest is in the general theory, may, if they have laid their foundations well and carefully, be able to look down with a smile of indifference on the fulminations of Keynes. Pavilioned upon their Olympian fastness, they are not likely to show much irritation.

It is convenient to take Keynes' theory of interest as the starting point of this exposition. In the commonly accepted short-cut theory there are two unknowns and two equations. The two unknowns are the volume of saving (= the volume of investment) and the rate of interest. Of the new-fangled view, sponsored by some out-of-the-way definitions in Keynes' *Treatise on Money*, that the volume of saving may be unequal to the volume of investment, it is not necessary to say anything, since it has played no part in the standard short-cut formulations of interest theory (although it has figured in recent writings concerned with practical monetary problems). The commonly accepted interest theory, from the time of the early classical writers onward, entails that saving is always and necessarily equal to investment.

The two equations in the traditional theory of interest correspond to the demand and supply schedules relating to a particular commodity. First there is the demand equation:

$$y = f(x),$$

y, the marginal productivity of capital, depending on x, the amount of capital invested per unit of time. So much capital will be invested that its marginal productivity is equal to the rate of interest; that is,

$$y = y',$$

where y' is the rate of interest. Since both the traditional theory and Keynes hold that investment is undertaken up to the point at which the marginal productivity of capital is equal to the rate of interest, y' may be suppressed, and y made to stand for the rate of interest which is equal to the marginal productivity of capital.

Then there is the supply equation:

$$x = \phi(y);$$

x, the amount which individuals choose to save, which is equal to the amount of investment, depends on the rate of interest. Thus there are two unknowns, the rate of interest and the volume of saving, and sufficient equations to determine them. It is not necessary for the present purpose to consider controversies concerning the forms of these equations, such as whether a rise in the rate of interest tends to cause people to save more or less.

This treatment of interest and saving is analogous to that of the price of a particular article and the amount of it produced. The treatment depends on the short-cut assumption of *ceteris paribus*. This is often legitimate in the case of particular commodities, although it is recognised that in certain cases it is idle not to bring in certain other variables, for instance the prices of close substitutes. Among the "other things" which are supposed to be "equal" is the level of income in the community under discussion. In many cases it may be true that, when we are trying to determine how much of a particular commodity a producer is likely to produce, his decision to produce a little more or a little less will not have a sufficiently large effect on the total income of the community to react on the market for his goods in such a way as to make an appreciable difference to him. This particular short-cut is in that case justified. I suggest that the most important single point in Keynes' analysis is the view that it is illegitimate to assume that the level of income in the community is independent of the amount of investment decided upon. No results achieved by the short-cut of such an assumption can be of any value.

How does Keynes' analysis proceed? His first equation is substantially the same as that of the traditional analysis

$$y = f(x).$$

The marginal productivity of capital is a function of the amount of investment undertaken. The marginal productivity of capital appears in Keynes' book under the title of marginal efficiency. It does not appear that there is a difference of principle here. It is true that Keynes makes an exhaustive and interesting analysis of this marginal efficiency and demonstrates that its value depends on entrepreneurial expectations. The stress which he lays on expectations is sound and constitutes a great improvement in the definition of marginal productivity. This improvement, however, might be incorporated in traditional theory without entailing important modifications in its other parts.

When we come to the second equation, the level of income must be introduced as an unknown term, giving

$$x = \phi(y, i),$$

where i is the level of income. The amount of saving depends not only on the rate of interest, but on the level of income in the community.

It might be thought that to introduce the level of income as an unknown at this point is tantamount to abandoning all attempt to have a departmental theory of the volume of saving, since the level of total income appears in all the equations of the general theory and it is impossible to determine its value without taking all factors into account. This would mean that we should have to leave the ordinary working economist without any departmental theory of saving and interest which he could grasp, and to let him flounder in the maze of $n \times r \times s$, etc., equations governing the whole system. Keynes has, however, come to the rescue and carved out a new short-cut of his own. In his view the value of the unknown level of income can be determined in a legitimate and satisfactory manner by the departmental equations relating to saving and interest only. To the legitimacy of this assumption it will be necessary to return presently.

Meanwhile, since there are three unknowns and but two equations in the savings/interest complex, another equation is needed. Before proceeding to that, it may be well to recur to the second equation,

$$x = \phi(y, i).$$

This may be transposed into the form

$$i = \psi(x, y).$$

The level of income depends on the amount of investment (= that of saving) and the rate of interest. In this form the second equation shows itself as the doctrine of the multiplier. The multiplier is the reciprocal of the fraction expressing the proportion of any given income which, at a given rate of interest, people consume. If the value of the multiplier is known for any given rate of interest and level of income, the actual level of income can be deduced directly from the volume of investment. Those to whom the doctrine of multiplier seems an alien morsel in the corpus of economic doctrine should remember that it is merely a disguised form of the ordinary supply schedule of free capital, but with the level of income treated as a variable.

In discussing this doctrine, for the sake of a still shorter cut, Keynes is inclined to let the rate of interest drop out of sight. Thus the equation becomes

$$i = \psi(x);$$

the level of income depends on the volume of investment. The justification for this procedure is that whereas the relation of the level of income to the amount of investment is in the broadest sense known—it may be assumed that people save a larger absolute amount from a larger income—the relation of the amount which people choose to save to the rate of interest is a matter of controversy. Moreover in Keynes' view the level of income has a more important effect on the amount which people choose to save than the rate of interest. However, there is no need to pick a quarrel here. The rate of interest may be brought back into this part of the picture without affecting the main argument. The propensity to consume may be regarded as depending on the rate of interest, although for the sake of brevity and clarity mention of this need not be insisted on at every point in an exposition of the doctrine of the multiplier.

What of the third equation? We have

$$y = \chi(m),$$

where m is the quantity of money, a known term, depending on banking policy. This is the liquidity preference schedule. Probably i, the level of income, ought to be inserted in this equation, thus:

$$y = \chi(m, i),$$

since the amount of money required for active circulation by consumers and traders depends on the level of income. Ought not the price level to come in also? That may be taken to be subsumed under i, the level of income, in a manner that I shall presently explain. The residue of money, not required for active circulation, is available for ordinary people who are discouraged by their brokers from immediate investment, and, more important, for firms who may want cash for capital extensions or similar purposes within six months or a year or two and are unwilling to hold their reserves in the form of securities to which some risk of depreciation within the prescribed period is attached. Since the amount of money available for liquid reserves is strictly limited and cannot be increased by the mere desire on the part of firms to hold more money than that, the prospective yield of less liquid reserves must be sufficient to confine those who insist on a money reserve to the amount of money available for that purpose. The less the amount of money available the higher the rate of interest will have to be, both because the high rate is a *quid pro quo* against the risk of depreciation of the capital and also because the higher the present rate the less probability is there of depreciation within the prescribed period.

It is not necessary to give a final pronouncement on the significance of the liquidity preference equation. It appears that, even if some modification is required in this third equation, which determines the rate of interest, a type of analysis similar in its general structure to that of Keynes may be maintained.

We now have three equations to determine the value of the three unknowns, level of income, volume of saving (= volume of investment), and rate of interest (= marginal productivity of capital).

For the working economist these results may be set out in still briefer shorthand as follows. The amount of investment (= amount of saving) depends on the marginal productivity of capital and the rate of interest; the level of income is connected with the amount of investment by the multiplier, i.e., by the propensity to consume; and the rate of interest depends on the desire for liquid reserves and the amount of spare cash in the community available to satisfy that desire. The amount of this spare cash depends on the policy of the banks in determining the quantity of their I.O.U.'s that are outstanding and on the level of income (the higher this, the more money will be taken away into active circulation).

Thus, if the schedules expressing the marginal productivity of capital, the propensity to consume, and the liquidity preference are known and the total quantity of money in the system is known also, the amount of investment, the level of income, and the rate of interest may readily be determined.

The next topic for consideration is the legitimacy of the assumption that the level of income may be regarded as determined by the complex of considerations expressed in the savings/interest equations, rather than by the whole system of equations. In general, the level of activity is traditionally conceived as depending on the preference schedules of the various factors expressing their willingness to do various amounts of work in return for income, and on the schedules expressing the relation between the amount of work done and the income accruing from it (laws of returns). In considering the former schedules we have to take into account all the factors of production. Now in Keynes' system, the supply of capital has already been dealt with by the savings/interest equations. For the supply of risk-bearing, we may provisionally content ourselves with the elegant device which he provides in his footnote to page 24. He writes, "by his (the entrepreneur's) expectation of proceeds I mean, therefore, that expectation of proceeds, which, if it were held with certainty, would lead to the same behaviour as does the bundle of vague and more various possibilities which actually makes up his state of expectation when he reaches his decision." Thus considerations affecting the supply of risk-bearing are subsumed in the equations which determine the volume of investment.

There remain the factors other than those covered by the category of investment. Of these we are only concerned with those the supply of which can be varied. Thus we are left with those which may roughly be designated prime factors. What is the nature of their supply-schedule? What is the form of their preference for income in relation to the work required to obtain it?

In this field Keynes' argument is vitally dependent on his observation of real conditions. The work/income preference schedule exerts its power upon the economic system through the terms on which the prime factors are willing to sell their services. The contracts or bargains of the entrepreneurs with prime factors are normally fixed in money, with no proviso regarding the general level of prices. In the exceptional cases in which there is such a proviso, it is none the less usually the case that a rise in prices involves *some* fall in real rewards to prime factors and conversely. It is true that in a time of rising prices the factors may press for a rise in rewards, but, even if they achieve this, there is still no proviso to safeguard them against a further rise of prices, and prices may, for all the new bargains laid down, and indeed are very often in fact observed to, run on ahead of rewards. Conversely in a time of falling prices. This gives the supply schedules of the prime factors a very special kind of indeterminacy which undermines their power to determine the general level of activity. Keynes discusses this matter in Book I, and its importance in his logical edifice justifies him in giving it pride of place.

Consider next the second set of schedules determining the general level of activity, namely those expressing the relations between the amount of work done and the income accruing from it (laws of returns). Since the bargains with prime factors are expressed in money, the returns due to their employment should be expressed in money also. But the money value of these returns depends on the level of prices. The general price level might be regarded as determined by the quantity theory of money; Keynes does not so regard it for reasons which will be explained below. On the contrary he regards the general price level as completely malleable and determined by the equations in the general field without reference to the quantity of money.

The consequence of the conclusions yielded by the interest/savings equations, if these are accepted, is that the level of income and activity is determined. Now suppose the entrepreneurs decide to produce more than the amount so determined. Owing to a deficit propensity to consume, they will find deficient purchasing power, and either accumulate stocks or sell at a loss. If they do the former, the accumulation of stocks will constitute an additional (involuntary) investment on the part of the community, which, when added to the intended investment, makes the total investment of the community such as to be consistent, in accordance with the interest/savings equations, with the higher level of activity which entrepreneurs are choosing to indulge in. But such a position is unstable. So long as stocks are accumulating, they will reduce activity and continue to do so, until it reaches the point indicated by the interest/savings equations. If on the other hand they sell at a loss, they will be dissaving; the propensity to consume will be temporarily raised, so that the higher level of activity which they are choosing to indulge in becomes consistent with that required by the interest/savings equations. But again the position is unstable. The marginal propensity to consume will not be permanently sustained at an abnormally high figure by these means. To avoid losses, entrepreneurs will restrict and continue to do so, until activity and income are reduced to a level, which satisfies the interest/savings equations, with the marginal propensity to consume normal for that level of income. Converse arguments would apply in the case of entrepreneurs deciding to produce too little.

Now if the level of activity so determined is indeed the equilibrium level of activity, the price level must be appropriate to it. Let us suppose that the price of each commodity is determined by the marginal money cost of production, in the crude way that a tyro might describe erroneously supposing himself to be explaining the true classical theory of cost of production. If the law of diminishing returns prevailed on balance, as Keynes supposes that it does anyhow in the short period, the general price level would be expected to rise with increases of output and to fall with decreases. To make the matter still more crude and common, suppose prices to vary not merely in proportion to changes in the number of units of factors required per unit of output, as output varies, but also in proportion to changes in rates of reward to the factors. In this case we should find, as output rose and diminishing returns came into play, that the rise of prices would just sufficiently exceed the rise of wages, etc., if any, to cover the increased real marginal cost of production per unit. Factors might press for a rise of rewards, but though they might gain on balance in *some* trades, they would always be beaten by the price level in the system as a whole.

Now this is precisely what Keynes supposes actually to happen. It is, however, "subject to the qualification that the equality (between marginal cost and price) may be disturbed, in accordance with certain principles, if competition and markets are imperfect" (page 5). The objections to this view which upholders of the quantity theory of money might raise must be considered. But first observe its relation to the determination of the level of activity.

Take a period within which prime factor bargains do not change. The supply of each of these in money terms may then be represented by a horizontal straight line. But if prices vary in proportion to costs (cost variations including allowance for overtime rates, the employment of less efficient labor, etc.), then the money value of the marginal net product of each factor must be represented by a co-incident horizontal straight line. Therefore on these conditions the two sets of schedules leave the level of output entirely indeterminate. If the matter is expressed in real terms, both sets of schedules are downward sloping to the right; they are still co-incident. If money rewards to factors are raised or lowered in response to changes in the level of employment, *and* prices are adjusted accordingly, the same result ensues. Thus this complex of equations does *not* determine the level of activity; therefore it leaves that level free to be determined by the savings/interest complex. Q.E.D.

Thus the crux of the matter seems to have shifted to the quantity theory of money. The essence of the difference between the traditional theory and Keynes' theory can be put thus: In the traditional theory the supply and demand schedules of all the factors stand on the same footing; the level of activity is an unknown, but the price level is determined by the monetary equation. This determination of the price level enables the level of activity to be determined by the factors' money supply schedules, and by their marginal productivity schedules. In Keynes' theory, the level of activity is determined by the equations governing the savings/interest complex. In the general field, in which we are now only concerned with the demand and supply of prime factors, the level of activity is conceived as determined *ab extra*. It is a known quantity. But the price level is conceived to be completely malleable. If it were not, the system in the general field would be over-determined. Thus the monetary equation is shorn of its former powers. The level of activity being a known quantity the price level is determined by the money cost of production, with suitable modifications for imperfect competition.

What right has Keynes to gut the monetary equation in this way? Has, then, the banking policy no power to influence the situation? Yes, certainly it has. The fact is that the power residing in the monetary equation has already been used up in Keynes' system in the liquidity preference equation and it cannot therefore exert any direct influence in the general field. To make it do so would be to use its determining influence twice over. In fact in Keynes' system all the old pieces reappear, but they appear in different places.

Explanation is necessary. It will be remembered that, according to the liquidity preference equation, the rate of interest is determined by the desire of people for liquid reserves and the quantity of money available for that purpose. The quantity of money available for that purpose is equal to the total quantity of money in existence less that required for active trade.[1] Now if the quantity required for active trade were perfectly indeterminate, as it must be by the quantity theory—for according to that the price level depends on the quantity of money available for active trade, and therefore it is unknown what quantity of money any given amount of active trade will absorb—the residue would be indeterminate also. But if the m in

$$y = \chi(m)$$

is indeterminate, there are too many unknowns in the interest/savings set of equations. Thus it is necessary to the validity of Mr. Keynes' solution of the problem of investment and interest that the amount of money available for liquid reserves should be determinate, and that involves that the price level should be de-

---

[1] In his liquidity preference equation, Keynes includes the demand for money for whatever purpose, and the quantity of money that appears in it is the total quantity of money in the community. It has appeared simpler in this part of the exposition to divide this total into two parts, the amount required for active circulation and the residue, to define the quantity of money which appears in the liquidity preference equation as that residue, and the demand which the equation expresses as the demand for purposes other than those of active circulation. This re-definition of terms is merely an expository device and does not imply any departure from Keynes' essential doctrines.

termined otherwise than by the monetary equation. And so, in Keynes' system, it is.

The matter may be put thus: The savings/interest equations suffice to determine the level of activity, subject to the proviso that the quantity of money which appears in the liquidity preference equation is a known quantity; and this will be known if the price level, and therefore the amount absorbed in active trade, is known. The equations in the general field suffice to determine the price level, subject to the proviso that the level of activity is known. Thus there is after all mutual dependency. The level of activity will be such that so much money is absorbed in active trade that the amount left over enables interest to stand at a rate consistent with that level of activity.

The mutual interdependency of the whole system remains, but the short-cuts indispensable to thinking about particular problems, as Keynes has carved them out, remain also.

The amount of investment depends on the marginal productivity of capital and the rate of interest. The level of income and activity is related to the amount of investment by the multiplier, that is by the marginal propensity to consume; the price level is related to the level of activity by the marginal money cost of production (which depends on the amount of activity undertaken); the amount of money absorbed in active trade depends on the volume of trade; and the price level, the amount of money available for liquid reserves, is equal to the total amount of money in the system less that required for active trade; and the rate of interest depends on the amount of money available for liquid reserves and the liquidity preference schedule.

It may be well to do some exercises. Suppose the banks to increase the total amount of money available by open market operations. The increment may eventually be divided between active circulation and liquid reserves. An increase of money available for liquid reserves will tend to reduce the rate of interest, and so to increase investment. This will increase the level of income through the multiplier, in accordance with the marginal propensity to consume. If the fall in the rate of interest increases the marginal propensity to consume, the increase of income will be *pro tanto* greater, but it is not certain that it does so. The increase of income involves an increase of turnover, and of prices in accordance with the law of diminishing returns. This involves an increased use of money in active circulation. Thus the fall in the rate of interest will not be so great as it would be if all the new money went into liquid reserves. The money will be divided between the two uses, but there is no reason whatever to suppose that the increments in each use will be in proportion to the amounts of money previously employed there, as is assumed in a quantity theory using a compendious index number. The comparative size of the increments will depend on the current elasticity of the liquidity preference schedule and the current elasticity of the marginal productivity of capital schedule (which involves expectations).

Suppose a fall in rewards to prime factors. The price level will drop. Money will be released from active circulation for liquid reserves. This will tend to make the rate of interest fall and to react on the level of investment and activity accordingly. Thus the stimulus to activity is very indirect, and its effectiveness depends on the same factors as that provided by an increase in the quantity of money. This is very different from the view that a reduction of rewards will stimulate activity because costs fall while prices are sustained by the quantity of money remaining the same.

It appears to me that the achievement of Keynes has been to consider certain features of traditional theory which were unsatisfactory, because the problems involved tended to be slurred over, and to reconstruct that theory in a way which resolves the problems. The principal features so considered are (1) the assumption that the level of income could be taken as fixed in the departmental theory of interest and saving, (2) the peculiar nature of the supply schedules of the prime factors which arises from their bargains being fixed in money without proviso as to the price level, and (3) the failure of monetary theory to explain how the total stock of money is divided between liquid reserves and active circulation; or, in other words, the unsatisfactory character of the theory of velocity of circulation.

I stated above that the old pieces in the traditional theory reappear, but sometimes in new places. It might at first be thought that the liquidity preference schedule is a new piece, and that therefore either the new system is over-determined or the traditional writers must have been wrong in supposing that their system was determined. But it is not really a new piece. The old theory presupposed that income velocity of circulation was somehow determined. But precisely how was something of a mystery.

Thus the old theory assumed that there was a piece there but did not state exactly what it was. Keynes' innovation may thus be regarded as a precise definition of the old piece.

By placing it where he does, he overcomes a difficulty which has been assuming an alarming prominence in recent economic work. In monetary literature, the rate of interest has been treated, and increasingly so, as an influence of vital importance in the monetary situation. But in traditional theory, neither in the general system of equations nor in the departmental theory of interest does it appear that the rate of interest is more intimately connected with the *numéraire* than the price of any other factor of production. This is a striking discrepancy. Keynes introduces the liquidity preference schedule at a point which makes it a vital link between the general system of equations and monetary theory. His treatment is in harmony with recent literature, in that he justifies the special connection of the price of this particular factor with monetary problems. It is an immense advance on recent literature, because it removes the discrepancy between the treatment of interest in the two branches of study.

In my judgment Mr. Keynes has not affected a revolution in fundamental economic theory but a readjustment and a shift of emphasis. Yet to affect a readjustment in a system, which in its broad outlines, despite differences of terminology, has received the approval of many powerful minds—Marshall, Edgeworth, and Pigou, the Austrian School, the School of Lausanne, Wicksell, Pantaleoni, Taussig, and Clark, to mention but a few—is itself a notable and distinguished achievement. And in the sphere of departmental economics and shortcuts, which are of greatest concern for the ordinary working economist, Keynes' views constitute a genuine revolution in many fields. .

The foregoing account has attempted to expound, not to appraise. The only criticism of Keynes which I venture to offer is that his system is still static. Note has been taken of the fact that at certain important points, e.g., in his definition of the marginal efficiency of capital, Keynes lays great stress on the importance of anticipations in determining the present equilibrium.

But reference to anticipation is not enough to make a theory dynamic. For it is still a static equilibrium which the anticipations along with other circumstances serve to determine; we are still seeking to ascertain what amounts of the various commodities and factors of production will be exchanged or used and what prices will obtain, so long as the conditions, including anticipations, remain the same. But in the dynamic theory, as I envisage it, one of the determinants will be the rate of growth of these amounts. Our question will then be: What rate of growth can continue to obtain, so long as the various surrounding circumstances, including the propensity to save, remain the same?

Saving essentially entails growth, at least in some of the magnitudes under consideration. No theory regarding the equilibrium amount of saving can be valid, which assumes that, within the period in which equilibrium is established, other things, such as the level of income, do not grow but remain constant.

I envisage in the future two departments of economic principles. The first, the static theory, will be elaborated on the assumption that there is no growth and no saving. The assumption that people spend the whole of their income will be rigidly maintained. On this basis it will be possible to evaluate the equilibrium set of prices and quantities of the various commodities and factors, excluding saving. In the second department, dynamic theory, growth and saving will be taken into account. Equilibrium theory will be concerned not merely with what size, but also with what rate of growth of certain magnitudes, is consistent with the surrounding circumstances. There appears to be no reason why the dynamic principles should not come to be as precisely defined and as rigidly demonstrable as the static principles. The distinguishing feature of the dynamic theory will not be that it takes anticipations into account, for those may affect the static equilibrium also, but that it will embody new terms in its fundamental equations, rate of growth, acceleration, deceleration, etc. If development proceeds on these lines, there will be a close parallel between the statics and dynamics of economics and mechanics.

But to develop this theme further would take me too far from my subject.

CHAPTER XLII

A Simplified Model of Keynes' System

By J. E. MEADE

THE OBJECT of this article is to construct a simple model of the economic system discussed in Keynes' *The General Theory of Employment, Interest and Money,* in order to illustrate:

First: the conditions necessary for equilibrium;

Second: the conditions necessary for stability of equilibrium; and

Third: the effect on employment of changes in certain variables.

To simplify the exposition, the following assumptions are made:

(1) There is a closed economy.

(2) There is perfect competition, so that every price is equal to the marginal cost of production.

(3) Two industries are examined—one producing goods for consumption and the other producing durable capital goods.

(4) The short-period elasticity of supply of capital goods is the same as that of consumption goods.

(5) In each of these industries the wage of labor is the only prime cost.

(6) Fixed capital equipment, which is assumed to last for ever, is the only other factor of production. In consequence, the total expenditure of money on consumption goods *plus* total expenditure on newly constructed capital goods is equal to the national income, which is distributed between wage-earners and the owners of fixed capital equipment.

(7) We shall deal only with short-period equilibrium. The short period is defined as the period of time in which the ratio between the output of new capital goods and the existing stock of capital goods is small, so that we can neglect changes in the stock of capital goods. It is, however, assumed that, within this short

period, (a) producers have time to adjust their output until the marginal prime cost is equal to the price of the product, and to adjust the rate at which they expand their capital equipment until the rate of interest is equal to the marginal efficiency of capital, and (b) all individuals have time to adjust appropriately their expenditure and their savings in consequence of any change in their incomes.[1]

THE CONDITIONS FOR EQUILIBRIUM

Our first task is to examine the conditions in which the system will be in equilibrium. The following eight conditions determine the position of short-period equilibrium:

(1) The price of a unit of capital goods equals its marginal prime cost.

(2) Similarly, the price of a unit of consumption goods equals its marginal prime cost.

(3) Total income equals the amount received for the sale of newly produced capital goods *plus* the amount received for the sale of consumption goods.

(4) Total income equals total profits *plus* the amount paid out in wages.

(5) The total volume of employment equals employment in producing capital goods *plus* employment in producing consumption goods.

(6) The amount spent on consumption goods is determined by the size of the national income. We shall suppose that, with a given propensity to consume, people always spend a constant proportion of their income on consumption. This satisfies Keynes' psychological law that out of an increase in real income people

---

[1] Without any fundamental change in the method of analysis, we could make allowances for foreign trade, imperfect competition, raw material and depreciation costs, etc. But to modify assumption (7) might involve far-reaching changes in method. If, for example, the time-lag between a change in income and the consequent change in demand for consumption goods were longer than the period in which changes in the size of the capital stock are negligible, we should be obliged to relate expenditure in any one short period to conditions existing in a previous short period. We should be obliged to relate certain terms by means of time-lags to other terms at an earlier time, and to write the stock of capital at any one point of time as the sum of outputs of capital goods over previous periods of time. But if we assume that these time-lags are short, we can postulate a given stock of capital, and suppose that the system finds an equilibrium before this stock can alter significantly.

spend part on consumption and save part, although it is a simple and special case of that law.

(7) The rate of interest equals the marginal efficiency of capital. We shall suppose that the same yield is expected in each future year on a unit of capital installed now, and that this expected yield depends solely upon the profits being made at present in industry—a rise in present profits causing some rise in the yield expected in future years. The expected annual yield divided by the current cost price of a unit of capital goods is the rate at which we must discount the future annual yields to make the present value of a unit of capital equal to its present supply price; and in equilibrium this must equal the current rate of interest.

(8) The supply of money equals the demand for money, which is determined (a) by the volume of monetary transactions to be financed, and (b) by the rate of interest ruling in the market. We suppose that the total amount of money can be divided into two parts: (a) the amount of money held to finance business transactions, which bears a constant ratio to the money income of the community, and (b) an amount of "idle" money held to satisfy the precautionary and speculative motives for liquidity. A rise in the rate of interest causes people to shift from "idle" money to non-liquid assets; and to simplify our model we shall suppose that the ratio between the value of non-liquid assets held and the amount of "idle" money held is a function of the rate of interest.

By means of these eight relationships we can show [2] that the volume of employment is determined for every given supply of money, for every given money wage-rate, and for every given proportion of income saved.[3]

THE CONDITIONS FOR STABILITY OF EQUILIBRIUM

The system is in short-period equilibrium when these eight relationships are satisfied. But is this equilibrium stable? Suppose

[2] See Appendix, §§ 1 and 2.

[3] If we suppose that the money wage-rate would fall so long as any labor were unemployed, the system cannot be in equilibrium without full employment. In this case, the money wage-rate is no longer given, but the equilibrium volume of employment is now a given quantity—namely, the given volume of labor seeking employment. In this case, the eight relationships would determine the money wage-rate in terms of the supply of money, the volume of labor to be employed, and the proportion of income saved.

that the money wage-rate and the proportion of income saved remain constant, but that there is an accidental increase in total expenditure on commodities, accompanied by the appropriate increases in output of capital and consumption goods. This will have two effects: (a) It will increase incomes and so the amount which people desire to save. (b) It will also cause profits to rise and thus cause the expectation of profit to increase, and this will increase the incentive to borrow money for investment. If a chance rise in incomes increases the incentive to save more than the incentive to invest, then the system is in stable equilibrium; for if incomes rose, people would wish to save a larger increment of income than they wished to invest, so that incomes would fall again to their previous equilibrium level. If a chance rise in incomes increased the incentive to invest more than the incentive to save, incomes would continue to grow, until some entirely new position of short-period equilibrium were reached. In this case equilibrium is unstable.

In order to test the conditions in which equilibrium is stable, we must distinguish between two possible banking policies. The banks may (i) keep the rate of interest constant, or (ii) keep the amount of money constant.

(i) If the former policy is adopted, the amount of money must be increased as the volume of business activity increases, so as to maintain a constant ratio between the value of non-liquid assets and the amount of "idle money," so that with a given liquidity preference function the rate of interest will be unchanged. Equilibrium will be stable on this assumption if the eight relationships show that, with a constant money wage-rate and a constant proportion of income saved, a fall in the rate of interest is necessary to preserve equilibrium when employment increases. For this means that, unless the rate of interest falls, any chance increase in incomes, profits, and employment would stimulate investment less than savings, so that any such expansion is impossible to maintain. But if the eight relationships show that a rise in the rate of interest is necessary to preserve equilibrium as employment increases, this means that a chance increase in incomes, profits, and employment would stimulate investment more than savings, so that some discouragement of investment by a rise in the rate of interest would be necessary to preserve equilibrium. Or, in other words, with a constant rate of interest equilibrium would be unstable.

It will be shown [4] that, on the assumption that the banks keep the rate of interest constant, equilibrium is stable or unstable according as $\pi \gtrless 1 - l$, when $(1 - l)$ measures the proportion of the national income which goes to profits and π measures the elasticity of expected future yields to changes in the present profitability of industry.[5] Since less than the whole national income must go to profits, we can conclude that equilibrium cannot be stable if a 1 per cent rise in present profits causes a 1 per cent or greater rise in the expectation of profits; and we may add that equilibrium is the more likely to be stable (a) the less sensitive are expected profits to changes in present profits, and (b) the larger the proportion of the national income which goes to profits.

(ii) If the banks keep the amount of money constant, the condition for stability of equilibrium is less severe. As before, any chance increase in incomes and expenditure, in addition to causing an increase in savings, will also stimulate investment by raising the present profitability of industry and so the yields expected in the future. But in this case the increased volume of business activity will leave less of the given stock of money to be held in excess of the requirements to finance current transactions. The ratio between the value of non-liquid property and the amount of "idle money" will increase, which will cause the rate of interest to rise. This in itself will diminish the incentive to invest, so that there is less probability that the incentive to invest will increase more than the incentive to save in consequence of any chance increase in total incomes.

When the banks keep the amount of money constant, equilibrium is stable, if the eight equilibrium relationships discussed above show that, with a constant money wage-rate and a constant proportion of income saved, the supply of money must increase in order to preserve equilibrium as employment increases. This means that conditions are such that, unless the rate of interest is kept down by an increased supply of money, the incentive to save would grow more rapidly than the incentive to invest, so that an expansion would be impossible. If, however, the eight equilibrium relationships show that the supply of money must be diminished in order to preserve equilibrium as employment rises, then

[4] See Appendix, § 4.

[5] If, for example, a 1 per cent rise in present profits causes a 2 per cent rise in expected profits, then $\pi = 2$.

equilibrium is unstable with a constant supply of money. For in this case a chance expansion of employment and incomes would increase the incentive to invest so much more than the incentive to save that an actual diminution in the supply of money would be required to raise interest rates sufficiently to maintain equilibrium.

It will be shown [6] that equilibrium in this case is stable or unstable according as

$$\pi \underset{>}{\overset{<}{=}} (1 - l)\left(1 + \frac{1 + \eta[1 - m]}{m\lambda}\right)$$

where η is the short-period elasticity of supply of goods in general, m is the proportion of the total stock of money which is held idle to satisfy the speculative motives for liquidity, and λ is the elasticity of the liquidity preference schedule, i.e., the percentage increase in the ratio between the value of non-liquid assets and the value of "idle" money divided by the percentage rise in the rate of interest necessary to cause this shift to non-liquid assets. With the assumption that the banks kept the rate of interest constant, we found that equilibrium would be stable if $\pi < 1 - l$. It follows that if equilibrium would be stable with a constant rate of interest, it will certainly be stable with a constant supply of money; whereas equilibrium may be stable with a constant supply of money in conditions in which it would not be stable with a constant rate of interest. We conclude that equilibrium is the more likely to be stable (i) the smaller are π, l, m, and λ, and (ii) the greater is η.

It is of course possible that in the real world the system is unstable. But in what follows we shall assume that equilibrium is stable, since it is not possible to discuss the effect of given changes on the volume of employment, if any small jerk to the system may start it off in one direction or the other in search of a completely new equilibrium.

THE EFFECT OF CHANGES IN CERTAIN VARIABLES ON THE SHORT-PERIOD DEMAND FOR LABOR

We can now examine the effect on employment of (1) a reduction in interest rates, (2) an increase in the total supply of money, (3) a reduction in money rate-wages, and (4) a reduction in the proportion of income saved.

[6] See Appendix, § 5.

(1) We suppose that the money wage-rate and the proportion of income saved are constant, and that the banks reduce the rate of interest by a certain proportion and then keep it constant at this new level. We wish to evaluate ϵ_i, the elasticity demand for labor in terms of the rate of interest. It can be shown [7] that:

$$\epsilon_i = -\eta \cdot \frac{1-l}{l} \cdot \frac{1}{1-l-\pi}$$

If equilibrium is to be stable when the banks first lower and then stabilize the rate of interest, ϵ_i must be < 0; for we have already argued that, for equilibrium to be stable with a constant rate of interest, conditions must be such that an increase in employment cannot take place without a fall in the rate of interest. If equilibrium is stable, a reduction in interest rates will therefore increase employment, and will be more effective in doing so (i) the greater is η, and (ii) the greater is π. If the short-period elasticity of supply of goods is large, a given rise in expenditure will cause a large increase in output and employment. If the sensitiveness of expected profits to changes in present profits is large, a given rise in profits will cause a large rise in expected yields, which will help to stimulate investment, and so expenditure, still further.

(2) We now suppose that the money wage-rate and the proportion of income saved are constant, but that the banks increase the total supply of money by a certain proportion and then keep it constant at this new figure. We wish to evaluate ϵ_M, the elasticity of demand for labor in terms of the supply of money. It can be shown that: [8]

$$\epsilon_M = \eta \frac{1-l}{l} \cdot \frac{1}{(1-l)(1+\eta[1-m]+m\lambda) - m\lambda\pi}$$

For equilibrium to be stable when the banks first increase and then stabilize the supply of money, ϵ_M must be > 0; for we have already argued that, for equilibrium to be stable with a constant supply of money, conditions must be such that an increase in employment must be accompanied by an increase in the supply of money. We conclude, therefore, that, if equilibrium is stable, an increase in the supply of money will increase employment, and that it will be more effective in doing so (i) the greater is η, (ii) the greater is π, (iii) the smaller is λ, and (iv) the smaller is m.

[7] *Ibid.*, § 4.
[8] *Ibid.*, § 5.

If the short-period elasticity of supply of goods is large, a given increase in expenditure will cause a large increase in employment; if the sensitiveness of expected profits to changes in present profits is large, a given increase in present profits will cause a large increase in investment expenditure; if people's willingness to shift from non-liquid assets to "idle" money is only slightly increased by a fall in the rate of interest, a given proportionate increase in the supply of "idle" money must be accompanied by a large fall in interest rates, and will therefore greatly stimulate investment; if the amount of money held "idle" is a small proportion of the total holding of money, a given increase in the total supply of money will represent a large proportionate increase in the supply of "idle" money, and so, with a given liquidity preference elasticity, will cause a large fall in interest rates.

(3) Our next object is to examine the effect on employment of a given reduction in money wage-rates, on the assumption that the proportion of income saved and the total supply of money are constant. For this purpose we wish to evaluate ε_w, the elasticity of demand for labor in terms of money wage-rate. It will be shown [9] that $\varepsilon_w = -\varepsilon_N(1-m\lambda[\pi-1])$ where ε_N has the value given above.

It is to be observed that if $\pi = 1$, $\varepsilon_w = -\varepsilon_N$. This is what we should expect. Suppose that there were a 10 per cent reduction in all money wage-rates combined with a 10 per cent reduction in the supply of money. Then, *if* output and employment remained unchanged, the marginal prime cost and so the price of all commodities would fall by 10 per cent in view of the 10 per cent fall in the money wage-rate; and in consequence all money incomes would fall by 10 per cent. Ten per cent less money would be required to finance current transactions, and, as the total supply of money is also reduced by 10 per cent, the supply of "idle" money would also have fallen by 10 per cent. But since the price of capital goods would have fallen by 10 per cent, the ratio between the value of non-liquid assets and the amount of "idle" money would be unchanged, so that with a given liquidity preference schedule the rate of interest would be unchanged. Money savings would have fallen by 10 per cent because of the 10 per cent fall in money incomes. Money investment would also have fallen by 10 per cent, if expected profits had fallen by 10 per cent; for, the rate of interest being unchanged, and the supply price of

. [9] *Ibid.*, § 6.

capital goods and the expected money yield on them having fallen by 10 per cent, there would be no incentive to change the value of *real* investment, so that the money value of investment would have fallen in the same ratio as the price of capital goods. If $\pi = 1$, expected profits would in fact have fallen by 10 per cent; for the output of goods being constant and the price of goods and of the factor labor having fallen by 10 per cent, present money profits would have fallen by 10 per cent; and, if $\pi = 1$, this would have caused expected yields to be 10 per cent lower. In other words, the system would be in equilibrium with the same volume of output and employment, if $\pi = 1$ and there were a 10 per cent reduction in both the money wage-rate and the total supply of money. A 10 per cent reduction in the money wage-rate without any reduction in the supply of money may therefore be expected to have the same effect as a 10 per cent increase in the supply of money without any change in the money wage-rate. We should therefore expect that, if $\pi = 1$, a given reduction in money wage-rates will have the same effect in increasing employment as an equal proportionate increase in the supply of money.

If, however, π is < 1, a 10 per cent fall in the present profitability of industry causes expected future yields to fall by less than 10 per cent. In this case a 10 per cent reduction in money wage-rates, as it tends to reduce both the present money supply price of capital goods and the present money yields on capital, tends to increase the ratio between expected profits and the supply price of capital goods, and so to encourage real investment. In this case, therefore, a given reduction in money wage-rates is more effective in increasing employment than an equal proportionate increase in the supply of money. Conversely, if π is > 1, the fall in expected money yields is more than in proportion to the present fall in money profits and money costs; and a reduction in the money wage-rate tends, therefore, to lower the marginal efficiency of capital.

(4) Finally, we can examine the effect on employment of a change in the proportion of income saved, on the assumption that the money wage-rate and the supply of money are constant. We wish to evaluate ϵ_s, the elasticity of demand for labor in terms of the proportion of income saved. It can be shown [10] that:

$$\epsilon_s = -\frac{(1 + \lambda)m}{1 + \eta} \cdot \epsilon_M,$$

[10] *Ibid.*, § 7.

where ε_M has the value given above (page 612). As we have already argued, if equilibrium is to be stable in this case in which the supply of money is constant, ε_M must be > 0; ε_s is therefore < 0, so that a decrease in the proportion of income saved will cause an increase in employment.

This is what we should expect. A fall in the proportion of income saved will increase expenditure on consumption; and there will therefore be an increase in total expenditure and in employment, unless investment falls by as much as consumption increases. But investment will fall only if there is a rise in the rate of interest, and the rate of interest will rise only if there is a decrease in the supply of "idle" money. But, with a given total supply of money, the supply of "idle" money will decrease only if there is an increase in total expenditure, causing an increased demand for money to finance current transactions. The rate of interest cannot, therefore, rise sufficiently to diminish investment by as much as expenditure on consumption has increased.

MATHEMATICAL APPENDIX

§ 1. On the seven assumptions stated on page 606 we can construct eight equations corresponding to the eight relationships discussed on pp. 607–8.

The price of a unit of capital goods equals its marginal prime cost, or

$$p_x = w\frac{dN_x}{dx} \tag{1}$$

where p_x equals the price of a unit of capital goods, w equals the money wage-rate and N_x equals the volume of employment in capital goods industries. Since labor is the only prime factor of production, $\frac{dN_x}{dx}$ equals the marginal labor cost and $w\frac{dN_x}{dx}$ equals the marginal prime cost.

Similarly, for consumption goods

$$p_y = w\frac{dN_y}{dy} \tag{2}$$

where p_y equals the price of a unit of consumption goods and N_y equals the volume of employment in consumption goods industries.

Total income equals the amount spent on newly produced capital goods plus the amount spent on consumption goods, or

$$I = xp_x + yp_y \tag{3}$$

where I equals income, x equals output of capital goods, and y equals output of consumption goods.

Total income equals profits plus wages, or

$$I = P + wN \tag{4}$$

where P equals profits received and N equals total employment.

Total employment equals employment in capital goods plus employment in consumption goods industries, or

$$N + N_x + N_y \tag{5}$$

Amount spent on consumption equals a constant proportion of income, or $yp_y = (1 - s)I$, where s is the proportion of income saved. From (3) it follows that

$$xp_x = sI \tag{6}$$

The rate of interest equals the marginal efficiency of capital, or

$$i = \frac{E(P)}{p_x} \tag{7}$$

where i equals the rate of interest and $E(P)$ equals the yield expected in each future year on a unit of capital goods installed now at a price p_x.

The ratio between the value of non-liquid assets and the amount of "idle" money is a function of the rate of interest, or

$$\frac{p_x K}{M - kI} = L(i) \tag{8}$$

where K equals the constant stock of capital goods in existence, so that $p_x K$ equals the value of existing non-liquid assets. If M equals the total supply of money and k equals the proportion of income which people wish to hold in money at any moment of time to finance current transactions, kI equals the amount of money held for business purposes and $M - kI$ equals the amount of "idle" money available to satisfy the speculative and precautionary motives for liquidity.

§ 2. In these eight equations we have eight unknowns: [11]

$$x, y, p_x, p_y, I, P, i, \text{ and } N,$$

two constants:

$$k \text{ and } K,$$

and three independent variables:

$$M, w, \text{ and } s,$$

so that the volume of employment, N, is determined in terms of the supply of money, the money wage-rate, and the proportion of income saved.

§ 3. If we differentiate each of the equations (1) to (8), allowing the eight unknowns and the three independent variables to vary, we obtain the following equations:

From (1) $\dfrac{dp_x}{p_x} = \dfrac{dw}{w} + \dfrac{d_x}{x} \cdot \dfrac{1}{\eta}$ (1a)

where $\eta =$ the short-period elasticity of supply of capital goods = the proportionate increase in output divided by the proportionate rise in marginal labor cost

---

[11] If we count N_x and N_y, as well as x and y, among the unknowns, we have two additional equations, $N_x = \phi(x)$ and $N_y = \psi(y)$, since N_x depends solely on x and N_y solely on y.

$$= \frac{dx}{x} \div \frac{d\left(\frac{dN_x}{dx}\right)}{\frac{dN_x}{dx}}$$

From (2) $\dfrac{dp_y}{p_y} = \dfrac{dw}{w} + \dfrac{dy}{y} \cdot \dfrac{1}{\eta}$ \hfill (2a)

where η = the short-period elasticity of supply of consumption goods, which we assume (*vide* assumption 4) to be the same as the short-period elasticity of supply of capital goods.

From (3) $\dfrac{dI}{I} = s\left(\dfrac{dp_x}{p_x} + \dfrac{dx}{x}\right) + (1 - s)\left(\dfrac{dp_y}{p_y} + \dfrac{dy}{y}\right)$ \hfill (3a)

where s = the proportion of income saved = $\dfrac{xp_x}{I}$

From (4) $\dfrac{dI}{I} = (1 - l)\dfrac{dP}{P} + l\left(\dfrac{dw}{w} + \dfrac{dN}{N}\right)$ \hfill (4a)

where l = the proportion of total income which goes to wages = $\dfrac{wN}{I}$

From (5) $\dfrac{dN}{N} = \dfrac{s}{l}\dfrac{dx}{x} + \dfrac{l - s}{l} \cdot \dfrac{dy}{y}$ \hfill (5a)

For $\qquad \dfrac{s}{l} \cdot \dfrac{dx}{x} = \dfrac{xp_x}{wN} \cdot \dfrac{dx}{x} = \dfrac{xw\frac{dN_x}{dx}}{wN} \cdot \dfrac{dx}{x} = \cdot \dfrac{dN_x}{N}$, and similarly

$$\dfrac{1 - s}{l} \cdot \dfrac{dy}{y} = \dfrac{dN_y}{N}$$

From (6) $\dfrac{ds}{s} + \dfrac{dI}{I} = \dfrac{dp_x}{p_x} + \dfrac{dx}{x}$ \hfill (6a)

From (7) $\dfrac{di}{i} + \dfrac{dp_x}{p_x} = \pi\dfrac{dP}{P}$ \hfill (7a)

where $\pi = \dfrac{P}{E(P)} \cdot \dfrac{dE(P)}{dP}$ = the percentage rise in expected profits divided by the percentage rise in present profits which causes the rise in expected profits.

From (8) $m\lambda\dfrac{di}{i} = m\dfrac{dp_x}{p_x} - \dfrac{dM}{M} + (1 - m)\dfrac{dI}{I}$ \hfill (8a)

where $m = \dfrac{M - kI}{M}$ = the ratio of "idle" money to the total supply of

money and $\lambda = \dfrac{i}{L(i)} \cdot \dfrac{dL(i)}{di}$

= the percentage rise in the ratio between the value of non-liquid assets and the amount of "idle" money divided by the percentage rise in the rate of interest which causes this shift from "idle" money to non-liquid assets.

§ 4. If w and s are constant, we can eliminate $\dfrac{dx}{x}, \dfrac{dy}{y}, \dfrac{dp_x}{p_x}, \dfrac{dp_y}{p_y}, \dfrac{dI}{I}$ and $\dfrac{dP}{P}$

from equations (1a) to (7a), and we obtain

$$\epsilon_i = -\eta \cdot \frac{1-l}{l} \cdot \frac{1}{1-l-\pi} \tag{9}$$

where $\epsilon_i = \frac{i}{N} \cdot \frac{dN}{di}$. This expresses the elasticity of demand for labor in terms of the rate of interest. We have argued in the text (pp. 608–9) that equilibrium will be stable or unstable when the banks stabilize the rate of interest, according as $\frac{di}{dN} \lessgtr 0$. It follows from (9) that equilibrium will be

stable or unstable in these conditions according as $\pi \lessgtr 1 - l$.

§ 5. Assuming again that w and s are constant, we can eliminate $\frac{dx}{x}, \frac{dy}{y}, \frac{dp_x}{p_x}, \frac{dp_y}{p_y}, \frac{dI}{I}, \frac{dP}{P}$, and $\frac{di}{i}$ from equations (1a) to (8a) and we obtain

$$\epsilon_M = \eta \cdot \frac{1-l}{l} \cdot \frac{1}{(1-l)(1+\eta[1-m]+m\lambda) - m\lambda\pi} \tag{10}$$

where $\epsilon_M = \frac{M}{N} \cdot \frac{dN}{dM}$, which expresses the elasticity of demand for labor in terms of the supply of money. We have argued in the text (page 610) that, when with a constant wage-rate and a constant proportion of income saved the banks stabilize the supply of money, equilibrium will be stable or unstable according as

$\frac{dM}{dN} \gtrless 0$, i.e., from (10) according as

$$\pi \lessgtr (1-l)\left(1 + \frac{1+\eta[1-m]}{m\lambda}\right)$$

§ 6. Assuming next that s and M are constant, we can eliminate $\frac{dx}{x}, \frac{dy}{y}, \frac{dp_x}{p_x}, \frac{dp_y}{p_y}, \frac{dI}{I}, \frac{dP}{P}$, and $\frac{di}{i}$ from equations (1a) to (8a), and we obtain

$$\epsilon_w = -\epsilon_M(1 - m\lambda[\pi - 1]) \tag{11}$$

where ϵ_M has the value given in (10), and $\epsilon_w = \frac{w}{N} \cdot \frac{dN}{dw}$ = the elasticity of demand for labor in terms of the money wage-rate.

§ 7. Assuming now that w and M are constant, but that there is some change in the proportion of income which people decide to save, we can eliminate $\frac{dx}{x}, \frac{dy}{y}, \frac{dp_x}{p_x}, \frac{dp_y}{p_y}, \frac{dI}{I}, \frac{dP}{P}$, and $\frac{di}{i}$ from equations (1a) to (8a), and we obtain

$$\epsilon_s = -\frac{(1+\lambda)m}{1+\eta} \cdot \epsilon_M \tag{12}$$

where ϵ_M has the value given in (10) and $\epsilon_s = \frac{s}{N} \cdot \frac{dN}{ds}$ = the elasticity of demand for labor in terms of the proportion of income saved.

CHAPTER XLIII

Saving Equals Investment

By ABBA P. LERNER

KEYNES AND I and most people would say that a man saves something in a given period, if he spends on consumption (consumes) in that period less than his income in the period. The only unambiguous measure of the amount of his saving is obtained by subtracting his (expenditure on) consumption in the period from his income in the period: y (income) $- c$ (consumption) $= s$ (saving) by definition. If he consumes more than his income, he is doing the opposite of saving, dissaving, and we similarly measure the amount of his dissaving by subtracting his income from his consumption. $c - y = -s$ is the same equation (with the signs changed) in which $-s$ can be called dissaving.

Investment is the expenditure of money on things other than consumption. There is no reason why, for any individual, there should be any particular relationship between his investment, i, and the items y, c, and s mentioned above. But when we consider a whole (closed) economy, we see that there emerges a relationship between these items that does not appear to exist for the individual.

The equation $y - c = s$, since it is true for every individual in the economy, is also true for any two

$$y_1 - c_1 = s_1$$
$$y_2 - c_2 = s_2$$
$$(y_1 + y_2) - (c_1 + c_2) = (s_1 + s_2)$$

or any other number of individuals in the economy. If we take *all* the individuals together and add up their incomes and consumptions and savings (using capital letters to represent these sums for the whole economy), we get $Y - C = S$. In this respect, then, the whole economy is like any individual.

But for the whole economy there is another relationship. The sum of the incomes of all the individuals in the economy, Y, is equal to the sum of the expenditures of all kinds by the individuals of the economy, since these expenditures *are* nothing but the payments, the receipt of which constitutes all the incomes. The sum of all the payments must be equal to the sum of all the receipts in the same period, since these are the same thing, only looked at from different angles. The sum of expenditures of all kinds, which is equal to Y, must consist of C, the sum of expenditures on consumption, *plus I*, the sum of expenditures on things other than consumption, since these two make up all possible expenditures. This gives us the equation $Y = C + I$ or $Y - C = I$. We know that $Y - C$ is also equal to S, and, since quantities that are equal to the same quantity are equal to one another, we get the result that $S = I$. The sum of the savings of all individuals is equal to the sum of their investments in the same period.

The resistance that this piece of very simple arithmetic arouses in many people can usually be traced back to one or more of the following five causes:

(1) A failure to recognize that all the items considered are *payments* (or differences between payments) over a *period*, and never *amounts* existing at some *point* of time (such as the beginning or the end or some intermediate point within the period to which our proposition relates). They are all of the nature of *flows* which can be measured either as *so much in a given period* (as in the simplest case examined above) or as *so much per unit of time* (if we suppose the flows to continue at an unchanged rate over several units of time). They can never be measured as *so much* existing at any moment of time. That can only be done of *stocks*, not of flows, and our proposition deals only with flows.

This failure to keep clear of irrelevant considerations of stocks (of money) may take the form of:

(a) An insistence on the discussion of the velocity of circulation of money. The velocity of circulation is nothing but the ratio between some total of money payments in a period (which, being a flow, may be relevant to our proposition) and some *stock* of money existing at some point of time (which, since it is a stock, is on a different plane and can have no relevance to our proposition).

(b) An insistence on the discussion of "hoarding" (and "dishoarding"). Sometimes "hoarding" means a reduction in the velocity of circulation, the irrelevance of which has been shown. Sometimes it means simply holding stocks of money. Sometimes it means increasing one's stock of money. And most frequently it mysteriously means all three of these simultaneously, as well as a lengthening of the period an individual holds particular coins or notes. The concept of *stocks* inherent in all of these usages renders irrelevant any validity that the particular meaning of "hoarding" may retain.

Lack of clarity as to whether stocks or flows are being discussed has played a great part in feeding useless discussions in economics in the past. The Wages Fund is a conspicuous example of an ambiguous word used to cover such a confusion, and in modern theory of capital the same confusion is a great stumbling block. The proposition that $I = S$ is a proposition about flows and has nothing to do with stocks.

(2) A failure to understand the paradox that, while each individual separately is free to save either more or less than he invests, all the individuals together are not so free, since the sum of the investments, I, is always equal to the sum of their savings, S. How does this compulsion work? If it does not affect any individual, how can it affect the whole economy, which is simply the sum of the individuals?

To understand paradoxes of this nature is the special province of the economist, and many other similar paradoxes have by their familiarity ceased to terrify and become part of the stock in trade of all economists. Any country is free to import more goods than it exports or vice versa, but world imports always equal world exports (plus freight charges, etc.). Any individual can take his money out of the bank tomorrow morning, but all individuals together cannot. And we have the converse paradox. One bank or one country cannot expand its credit indefinitely; all the banks, or all the countries, keeping in step, can do so. To insist that what is true of each individual must be true of all individuals together is the simple fallacy of composition.

But how does the compulsion work, if it does not affect individuals? This question leaves many students uneasy. The answer is that the individual is by no means as free to decide how much he is going to save as has been suggested. There are very few individuals who would not like to have larger incomes than they actually have and to save more out of these larger incomes. Each individual is constrained to save the amount that he does by the size of his income; and the size of his income is determined by other people's expenditures on the goods that he produces. Each individual considers his own income as given and independent of his own expenditure (since in a large community the repercussions on his own income of any variations in an individual's expenditure are in general likely to be small enough to be legitimately neglected); and, not being interested in the effect of his expenditures in creating income for somebody else, he sees no connection between income and expenditure. This does not mean that the connection does not exist for the individual. It merely means that he is not interested in it, in so far as his own expenditure affects other people's incomes (though he may have a lively interest in the effect of other people's expenditure on his own income). The economist has a wider outlook, must concern himself equally with the incomes of all the individuals, and so must recognize that for the whole community the excess of total incomes over that part of incomes that is created by expenditure or consumption must have been created by investment (or expenditure on other things), so that $I = S$.

The failure to face up to the paradox of social necessity with apparent individual freedom sometimes takes the form of trying to extract from the total of an individual's actual saving (i.e., the excess of his income in a period over his consumption in the period) some part of it that really is "free" or "voluntary" or "*ex ante*" and declaring that the rest of his saving is "forced" or "involuntary" or "really saved by somebody else" (i.e., the investor who produced something that cannot be consumed) so that it should not be counted. All such attempts necessarily fall to the ground for the lack of any situation, to serve as a basis for comparison, in which the individual can with any plausibility be said to be unconstrained in his saving or even less constrained than in the period discussed. It is much more satisfactory to recognize that in a determinate universe all saving, like everything else, is "forced" and that free will is nothing but a pleasant illusion.

Related to this difficulty is the unconscious assumption—taken from the point of view of the individual and illegitimately transferred to society—that while expenditure is varied, income remains the same. From this it would follow that an increase in saving always means a reduction in consumption (and never an increase in income, consumption remaining constant). The assumption of constant income is then dropped, and the fall in consumption is allowed to diminish income, so that any increase in saving appears necessarily to involve a diminution of income. From this type of argument any number of surprising results naturally follow, such as that, although there is an increase of saving (to which the fall in expenditure is due), there is no change in saving (since income has fallen as much as consumption).

(3) A tendency to regard expenditure, not as a flow during a period coincident with the flow of income during the same period, but as something coming "out of" the income received in the period. "Saving" is on this view the income received in a period *minus* the expenditure made "out of" that income.

One possible meaning of this is simply that only that expenditure is to be counted which takes place *after* some or all of the income is received. If the ambiguities in this are overcome—as they can be—by some arbitrary ruling as to when we are to begin counting the expenditure, we will, of course, find that S so defined is greater than I by all the expenditure that took place too early in the period to be considered to be "out of" the income received in the period, so that we did not count it. If this procedure were carried to its logical conclusion, this expenditure, not being "out of income," would have to be considered as dissaving and subtracted from S and so reduce it to exactly the same value as I. It is, however, not usually carried to its logical conclusion, and is considered to be a demonstration of the falsity of our proposition that I = S.

Another meaning of the insistence on counting C, I and S only in so far as they come "out of" the income received during the period is that we must count only the expenditure (or laying up) of the particular notes or coins received as income during the period. Thus if something is bought with money received before the period began, it is not expenditure "out of" income. On this line of analysis, Peter, who took his wages-bag to the grocer, has spent all his income and saved nothing, while Paul, who put his wages-bag into his safe and took last week's bag to the grocer, has saved all his income. At this stage of the argument, it is again not necessary for I to equal S. Of course, if this method of counting were carried to its logical conclusion and the expenditure of coins other than those received as income in the period were regarded as dissaving, we would find ourselves back at our arithmetical result that I = S; but to do that would be to destroy the whole purpose of this new method of counting.

Correlative with the objection to counting *spending* that is not "out of income" is an objection to counting as *saving* the unspent income with which a man is caught at the end of a period, even though he may not have the slightest intention of saving it.[1] This looks like a serious divergence from the ordinary man's idea of what is meant by saving, and has inspired Mr. Robertson to another of his delightful quotations from *"Alice."* [2] This would be justified if by saving were meant particular coins or notes received as income and not spent. But we are not interested in particular notes or coins, and what is included in the saving of an individual, apart from the saving that he has used to buy assets other than money, is the *excess* of the money he holds at the end of a period over the money he had at the beginning. If a man started a period with £20 and finds himself at the end of the period with £25, it does not conflict with common sense to say that he has saved £5 in that period, even if it is his intention to spend the whole £25 (or more) in succeeding periods. Of course if we take highly artificial periods—say, of ten minutes each—our definitions acquire an artificial flavor too. We would then have to say that in the ten-minute period in which a man receives his weekly wage he saves (nearly) all of it, and that in all the other ten-minute periods in which he makes any expenditures he dissaves. But if we take reasonable periods, this artificiality disappears.

There is, of course, a sound idea underlying the notion of considering only such expenditure as comes after or "out of" income. It is that an individual's expenditure is determined more by income in the past, which is known and has been received, than by income in the present, which is uncertain. This may be true to a certain extent, although the effect of expected income on a man's expenditure must not be left out altogether. It is important for the real economic problems of forecasting expenditure and income, and has its place in economic theory, much more important than our piece of simple arithmetic; but it cannot be used to show that two and two are five.

(4) The failure to realize that the proposition $S = I$ is only an analytical proposition, and not about the real world at all. What is taken to be a statement about the real world excogitated from

---

[1] I am grateful to Dr. H. W. Singer for drawing my attention to this form of my third type of difficulty—an important form which I had overlooked.
[2] EJ, September, 1937.

an armchair is naturally looked upon with suspicion. Our proposition is not based upon observation of the real world. It therefore cannot tell us anything we did not know; neither can it turn out to be mistaken. It follows from and is implicit in our definitions of income, consumption, savings and investment, and the postulate that in any period moneys paid out are equal to moneys received. It is a proposition of the same order as the proposition that the area of the square of the hypotenuse of a right-angled triangle is equal to the sum of the areas of the squares on the other two sides. It has been called a truism, often in tones of contempt, telling us nothing but that something is equal to itself. In a sense this accusation is justified. All the propositions of mathematics are similarly truisms, since they tell us nothing that is not implied in the basic definitions and postulates. To one who sees these implications in the postulates themselves, the enunciation of the propositions of mathematics are nothing but an array of truisms and a waste of time, and I understand that there are born mathematicians for whom propositions like Pythagoras' and the multiplication table are unnecessary encumbrances. The usefulness of propositions of this mathematical nature is an inverse function of their obviousness. The abundant discussion that has grown up around the proposition, made famous by Keynes, that $S = I$, is abundant proof that its truth is not instantaneously obvious to all men; and if without adducing any new information it leads them to see some implications previously overlooked, it carries out the purpose for which it was designed.

(5) A belief that the short period equilibrium which is discussed in the analysis that makes use of our proposition is a necessary condition for the realization of the equality. This would indeed be suspicious, since the proof of the equality—e.g., as given in the first pages of this article—does not mention equilibrium. This seems to go with a belief that it is the ultimate goal of Keynes and his followers to show that $I = S$ and then to retire from the field of economics. The equality of I to S has nothing whatever to do with any kind of equilibrium. Equilibrium is discussed as a condition for some kind of stability of Y and C (and consequently also of I and S). The equation of I to S is always true and serves as a check, since any result that makes them unequal must involve a mistake either in logic or in counting.

CHAPTER XLIV

Saving and Investment : Definitions, Assumptions, Objectives

By ABBA P. LERNER

DEFINITIONS

IT IS POSSIBLE to define saving (S) and investment (I) in many different ways. Five of the best known sets of definitions are given below. The relationship between S and I will naturally depend on which set of definitions is used.

(1) If, as in Keynes' *General Theory of Employment, Interest, and Money,* S is defined as the income earned in a period *minus* the consumption in the same period, and I is defined as the expenditure in this same period on investment (and therefore also the income in that period earned other than in the production of consumption goods), then I is always equal to S. Any talk of the difference between saving and investment must be based either upon other definitions or upon confusion.

(2) If, as in Mr. Keynes' *Treatise on Money,* S_t is defined as "normal" (instead of actual) income *minus* consumption, and is therefore less than the S of the *General Theory* by as much as "normal" income is less than actual income; while I_t is defined just like I in the *General Theory*, then $I_t - S_t$ (which is the same as $S - S_t$) will represent the excess of actual over "normal" income—"abnormal profits."

(3) If, as in Mr. Robertson's writings, S_r is defined as income earned yesterday (instead of today—and therefore "disposable" today) *minus* today's consumption, and is therefore less than S by as much as income earned yesterday is less than income earned today; while I_r is defined in the same way as I, then $I_r - S_r$ (which

is the same as $S - S_r$) will represent the excess of income earned today over income earned yesterday.

(4) If, as in the work of the Swedish writers—Ohlin, Lundberg, and especially Myrdal—S_e is defined as *expected* or *ex-ante* saving and I_e is defined as *expected* or *ex-ante* investment, it is possible to give an almost unambiguous meaning to these concepts by so interpreting them that they fall into the Robertsonian scheme of discrete and extremely short "days." S_e is equal to income *minus* consumption as expected at the beginning of the "day" by the recipients of the income and the spenders on consumption. The "day" is so short that the plans for consumption are always carried out, expected consumption is always equal to actual consumption, and expected saving, S_e, is less than S by the extent to which expected income is less than actual income. The difference $(S - S_e)$ may be called "unexpected income."[1] I_e, investment as expected at the beginning of the day by the investors, is greater than I to the extent that there is an unexpected depletion of stocks arising from a discrepancy between what sellers expect to sell and what buyers expect to, and actually do, buy. $I_e - S_e$ therefore represents unexpected depletion of stocks *plus* "unexpected income."

(5) If, as in Mr. Hawtrey's *Capital and Employment*, I_a is defined as "active" or intended investment and S_a is defined as "active" or intended saving,[2] so as to leave out "passive" or unintended investment, which arises when an unexpectedly large demand leads to a depletion of stocks, and "passive" or unintended saving, which is the result of an unexpectedly large income earned in the period, the procedure is identical with the above described interpretation of *ex-ante*. $I_a - S_a$, like $I_e - S_e$, represents unexpected depletion of stocks *plus* "unexpected income."

ASSUMPTIONS

The first of these five sets of definitions seemed to me the simplest and the most convenient. Dr. F. A. Lutz, who prefers the third or Robertsonian set of definitions, declares[3] that: "In con-

---

[1] Dr. Lutz fails to distinguish between the excess of actual over expected income and the excess of actual over "normal" income, calling them both "profits." (Cf., "The Outcome of the Saving-Investment Discussion," QJE, Aug., 1938.)

[2] Mr. Hawtrey does not apply this distinction to saving.

[3] *Op. cit.*

tradiction to Mr. Lerner's view, it is the contention of this article that the assumption of a time lag between receipts and expenditure in Robertson's sense is closer to reality than the assumption of simultaneity between them and is necessary for the analysis of economic events over time."

Simultaneity between receipts and expenditures is implicit in the proposition that $I = S$ only in the sense that there is no interval between the moment that A receives a payment from B and the moment when B makes this same payment to A. Between this receipt and expenditure there can be no time lag, because they are merely different names for the same event. This simultaneity is hardly open to dispute. Mr. Robertson's time lag is, however, something quite different. It is the time elapsing between the moment that A receives his income from B and the moment when he spends this income (appropriately defined) on (consumption) goods purchased from C. Simultaneity between such receipt and expenditure would be not merely unrealistic, as Dr. Lutz suggests, but impossible, as I have pointed out in the very article referred to.[4] However, this kind of simultaneity is nowhere assumed by Keynes or by myself, so that criticisms of the Keynesian definitions and approach on this score[5] must be based on a confusion between the two meanings of a time lag between receipts and expenditures. The difference between the two approaches is in definition and in method, not in any conflicting assumptions about the real world. (Even the special assumptions that the Robertson method has to make about the nature of the time lags, so as to be able to fit them into "days," are not contradicted by the absence of any such special assumptions on the other approach as to the nature of the time lag between an individual's receipts and his subsequent expenditures.) We may, therefore, in judging between the usefulness of different sets of *definitions* of I and S, dismiss as irrelevant any alleged differences in assumptions, since any set of assumptions may go with any set of definitions, and to consider the realism of assumptions at the same time as the usefulness of definitions can hardly have any other effect than to confuse the issues.

[4] "Saving Equals Investment," QJE, February, 1938, pp. 306–307.
[5] As, e.g., by Dr. Haberler in "Mr. Keynes' Theory of the Multiplier" (*Zeitschrift für Nationalökonomie*, 1936), where he declares that the multiplier doctrine implies an infinite velocity of circulation.

OBJECTIVES

The main reasons given by Dr. Lutz for rejecting the Keynesian in favor of the Robertson-*ex ante* definitions are based upon an examination of the suitability of the different definitions for three different purposes: (a) to provide some indication either of the level of economic activity or of any tendency for it to expand or contract; (b) to provide a guide for credit policy; and (c) to develop a dynamic or causal process analysis of economic activity through time. It is granted that the Keynesian definitions have the advantages of simplicity and of freedom from the difficulties associated with the concept of a period which is supposed to be simultaneously identical with time lags of different length. Against this is set the disadvantage of the absence of any difference $I - S$ which might act as a guide for the purposes enumerated above. What is surprising is that the disadvantage is rated higher than the advantages, after a demonstration that the difference $I - S$ cannot be used for any of these purposes.

Whatever the manner in which Dr. Lutz would like to have the different procedures (1) to (5) compounded to form his interpretation of the Robertson-*ex ante* definition, $I - S$ will consist of some or all of the four elements: abnormal profits, excess of income earned today over income earned yesterday, unexpected income, and unexpected depletions in stocks. Dr. Lutz has shown that none of these can tell us unambiguously what the level of economic activity is or whether economic activity is going up or down in the near future, that they cannot provide anything that can seriously be considered as a guide for credit policy, and that their usefulness for dynamic analysis is vitiated by the impossibility of fitting all the relevant time lags into the Robertsonian "day." Furthermore, in so far as any of these concepts are of some use, it would appear to be more reasonable to call them by recognizable names—such as those used in this paragraph—rather than to speak of $I - S$, which might stand for any or all of them. In this way it would be possible to utilize such of these concepts as may be useful, without confusing them with each other and without giving up any of the advantages of the Keynesian terminology.

Dr. Lutz gives two subsidiary reasons for his conclusions and one final argument that belongs to quite another universe of discourse. He declares that: "Keynes himself has confused his definitions in two ways: first, by associating the doctrine of the saving-investment relation with the multiplier; secondly, by asserting that his terminology marks a return to the classical doctrine of the relation between saving and investment." [6]

The second point can be dismissed as a misunderstanding for which Mr. Keynes' mischievous style might perhaps be blamed. Mr. Keynes and his followers will completely agree about the differences that Dr. Lutz points out between the classical and the Keynesian theories of the rate of interest. The first of these two points is, however, based on a complete misunderstanding of the concept of the multiplier which is so common that Keynes' presentation cannot escape the suspicion of lack of clarity.

Since S is equal to I by definition, it is as impossible for the multiplier to "bring them into equality" as it is for the rate of interest (which is supposed to do this on the classical theory). The phrase is unfortunate but almost unavoidable in attempts to describe the mechanism by which a change in the level of investment brings about a change in the level of income or employment that is indicated by the multiplier. Neither Keynes nor any of his followers would deny that "the saving-investment relation (in the sense of their equality) is independent of the multiplier." [7] More significant is the suggestion [8] that the multiplier (and therefore also its inverse, the marginal propensity to save) are *ex-post* concepts and so cannot be identified with any previously known *ex-ante* psychological propensities, which alone could provide any independent, non-tautological, information as to the effect of an increase in the rate of investment on the level of income or employment.

It is true that Keynes claims that the multiplier holds good for any period of time we may choose, and that, if he is taken up on this and very short or otherwise non-typical periods are considered, some very strange results appear. By appropriately choosing a very short period, the marginal propensity to consume, and consequently the multiplier, too, can be "discovered" to have almost any desired value. At one extreme will be the period in which there is an increase in income (compared with some corresponding previous period) but no increment in (expenditure on) consumption (because the shops are shut or because such expendi-

[6] *Ibid.*, p. 608.
[7] *Ibid.*, p. 609.
[8] Also put forward by Dr. Haberler, *op. cit.*

tures as are made in this period are rigid). This would give a marginal propensity to consume of zero and a multiplier of unity. If a period is chosen in which the increment in consumption is equal to the increment in income, the marginal propensity to consume will be unity and the multiplier equal to infinity. At the further extreme would be the case where the period taken was a Saturday evening, when there is no increment of income from investment but an increase in expenditure on consumption as compared with a previous Saturday evening following a week in which earnings were less. In this case the marginal propensity to consume is infinite and the multiplier might be anything.

I think Keynes can legitimately be criticized for making it appear plausible that he would consider such "propensities to save" to represent a useful form of psychological generalization about human behavior. But surely this is merely a matter of presentation. Consumption and saving can be considered to be stable functions of income only if periods are considered that are long enough for the elimination of the discontinuities that give such strange results. In other words, unless some special period is indicated, *the* marginal propensity to consume which gives *the* multiplier, and which is based upon "psychological law," must be understood to refer to *short period equilibrium,* where the abnormalities due to discontinuities and to failure of adjustment of the output of consumption goods to the new level of investment will have been overcome. Thus "except in conditions where the consumption industries are already working almost at capacity, so that an expansion of output requires an extension of plant, there is no reason to suppose that more than a brief interval of time need elapse before employment in the consumption industries is advanced *pari passu* with employment in the capital-goods industries, with the multiplier operating near its normal figure." [9] If we consider periods long enough for short period equilibrium to be reached, the propensity to save will correspond closely enough to the habits of the people to enable us to say how much the level of employment will have moved up as a result of a given increase in the level of investment and saving. Saving will be greater by the increase in investment, not because people have received income and are waiting for the shops to open so they can spend it, but because the greater rate of saving is in correspondence with the greater level of employment and income.

[9] *General Theory,* pp. 124–5.

This brings us to a legitimate criticism, or rather limitation, of Keynes' approach which would seem to underlie much of the criticism that it has received. It is not as dynamic as some would wish. It is concerned most of the time with short period equilibrium and with the movement of such an equilibrium through time. In assuming such equilibrium to be continuously maintained, it gives up, for the sake of simplicity, the process analysis that the Robertson approach attempts. If successfully carried out, the latter would be more complete and more realistic than Keynes' equilibrium analysis, but it seems at the moment to be stalemated by the complexity of the problem and the multiplicity of the time lags which have to be considered. Keynes' greatest fault is perhaps his failure to point out with sufficient emphasis that he is in the main concerned with equilibrium analysis. This has led to much wasted argument. But there is no reason whatever for supposing an indissoluble bond to exist between the static or equilibrium approach that characterizes the greater part of Keynes' *General Theory* and the Keynesian definitions of saving and investment.

Those who are optimistic as to the possibilities of dynamic or process analysis have not only the right but the duty to carry on with their work, and there can be no quarrel between workers on the different approaches who will continue to be of service to each other. It would be well, however, if the difference between equilibrium and process analysis approaches were not hampered by traditional loyalties to particular terminologies. The high respect that all economists have for Mr. Robertson's work has made his definitions, or some definitions that can be made to look something like his, almost imperative for workers on process analysis. I would like to submit, with all the diffidence of one who has been working almost entirely on the other line, that the greater clarity of the Keynesian definitions and the necessity, if these are used, for finding specific names for the various things that might be hidden under $I - S$ would prove advantageous even in process analysis. Dr. Kalecki's work [10] would seem to substantiate this view.

The final argument raised by Dr. Lutz against the Keynesian definitions is that "they do not allow us to distinguish investment which is financed out of inflationary credit, or dishoarding, from

[10] "A Theory of the Trade Cycle," *Review of Economic Studies*, February, 1937.

investment that is financed out of the current supply of voluntary savings. There is no doubt, however, that it makes a lot of difference whether investment is financed from the one source or the other; and a terminology that conceals this difference hardly seems commendable." [11] If this means that the use of the Keynesian terminology prevents us from discussing the effects of increases in the amount of money or of diminutions in liquidity preference or increases in the marginal efficiency schedule of investment, it clearly is incorrect. It would seem rather that these matters can be discussed so clearly in the Keynesian terminology that the bogey of "forced saving" loses the portentousness lent to it by a dimmer light. Dr. Lutz appears to lament the theoretical capital lost in the "forced saving" venture, but until a clear and significant meaning is discovered for "voluntary" saving it would be best to call it a bygone and to leave open the question whether or not the undefined distinction makes "a lot of difference."

[11] *Op. cit.*, p. 612.

CHAPTER XLV

Alternative Formulations of the
Theory of Interest

By ABBA P. LERNER

THE FIRST PART of this article develops a technique for analyzing the more recent developments of interest theory. This is used in the second part to show that several apparently different theories of the rate of interest really say the same thing. In the third part, the different formulations of interest theory are examined for hidden implications concerning the relative importance of elements they all recognize.

1.

From the "classical"[1] view that the rate of interest is the price that equates saving to investment, to the "modern" view that it is the price that equates the demand for holding cash to the sup-

[1] I have put the word "classical" in quotation marks throughout this article because I believe that the theory of the rate of interest referred to by that label here and in Keynes' writings was not clearly held by many economists who have right to that title. In the writing, if not in the mind, of the classical economists the total stock of capital played a more important rôle than the rate of investment, and some long-period time preference was more significant than the actual rate of current saving. It is only when applying some unclarified notions as to what the rate of interest would be in a stationary state with full employment (where, of course, there can be no saving or investment) and trying, in an elementary text-book, to present these as a theory of the current rate of interest, that some orthodox economists have been forced, in attempting to avoid some much cruder confusions, to present something like the "classical" theory of the rate of interest. Some economists who have been maneuvered into defending such lightly proposed formulations have discovered a strong attachment, born of chivalry, for their newly adopted charges. A study of the development of classical theories of interest, as a result of such a situation, would, however, form the subject of another article.

ply of cash,[2] there are two steps. The first step—a fairly easy one—is to recognize that "hoarding," "dishoarding," and changes in the amount of money also have something to do with the supply of "credit" and the rate of interest—in the short period, at any rate. The second step—one that for most trained economists is a terrifying and long-postponed departure into uncharted waters— is to recognize that, by simple arithmetic, saving and investment are always equal to each other (for the whole economy) whatever the level of the rate of interest or anything else.

When these two steps have been taken, the rest is merely a matter of re-establishing one's equilibrium in the new position and of taking one's bearings. There remains only some arbitrariness in the language in which the new position is described.

An obvious way of bringing in the complications connected with "hoarding," "dishoarding," and changes in the quantity of money (i.e., of taking the first step from the "classical" to the "modern" position) is simply to add these elements to (or subtract them from) the "classical" supply and demand curves for saving. The rate of interest is the price paid for loans or "credit." If the only suppliers of loans on the loan market in any period were people who saved some of their income in the period and every one of these supplied exactly the amount he had saved, then the supply of loans would be equal to the amount of saving. Similarly on the other side of the market; if the only people to demand loans were investors and no investor borrowed either more or less than he invested, then the demand for loans would be equal to the amount of investment. The rate of interest, then, in equating the supply and demand for loans (or "credit") would thereby equate saving to investment.

To some extent these conditions may be relaxed without impairing the purely "classical" argument that the rate of interest equates saving to investment. If some savers "hoard" or lend less than they save, but this is exactly compensated by others who "dishoard" or lend more than they save, the total amount saved is still equal to the amount loaned on the market. Similarly, if some investors "hoard" or borrow more than they invest, but this is exactly offset by other borrowers who "dishoard" or invest more than they borrow, then the total amount invested is still equal to

---

[2] This is, of course, one particular formulation of the "modern" theory of interest (namely the "Keynesian"). That other "modern" formulations come to practically the same thing is the thesis of Part 2 of this article.

the total amount borrowed. Or again, if there is a balance of net "hoarding" (or "dishoarding") by savers, but there is an equal balance of "dishoarding" (or "hoarding") by investors, the pure "classical" theorem would still hold. Saving would no longer be equal to lending or the supply of "credit," nor would investment be equal to borrowing, or the demand for "credit," but saving would be greater (or less) than lending by the same amount as investment is greater (or less) than borrowing, so that the rate of interest that made lending equal to borrowing would also equate saving and investment. In general, any one of the conditions given above may be relaxed if there is another compensating deviation in the opposite direction from the same or any other condition.

If there is no such exact equality between "hoarding" by some and "dishoarding" by others, and there is a balance of net "hoarding" in the whole economy (net "hoarding" will be a negative quantity if there is a net balance of "dishoarding"), then net "hoarding" is the measure of that amount of saving that does not get invested but is "hoarded" either by the savers themselves or by people who borrow from them. The rate of interest which must always equate lending to borrowing then fails to equate saving to investment but makes saving equal to investment *plus* net "hoarding." To get the equilibrium, net "hoarding" must be added to the investment curve to give the net demand for "credit."

An increase in the amount of money has an effect opposite to that of net "hoarding," and therefore identical with that of net "dishoarding." The borrowers of the new money may invest it, in which case the creation of the new money, like "dishoarding," has permitted an increase of investment *not* balanced by any increase in saving. The borrowers of the new money may spend it on consumption goods, and in this case, again like "dishoarding," it has permitted a diminution of saving (or an increase in dissaving) not balanced by any decline in investment. Or, finally, the borrowers of the new money may neither invest it nor spend it, but just "hoard" it, and in this case the creation of the new money, once more just like an act of "dishoarding," has permitted an equal and opposite volume of "hoarding" to take place and to cancel the effect that the increase in the amount of money might have had on the relationship between saving and investment. In the absence of any net "hoarding," the rate of interest that equates lending to borrowing does not equate saving to investment because some of the lending is provided not by savers, but by the monetary authorities who loan out the new money. What the rate of interest does is to equate investment, which is equal to the demand for "credit," to the supply of "credit," which is equal to the saving *plus* the increase in the amount of money. Of course the opposite is true for a decrease in the amount of money.

Taking into account the effect both of *net* "hoarding" and of net changes in the amount of money, we can restate the position as it appears after the "first step" has been taken. The formula would now run: The rate of interest is the price that equates the

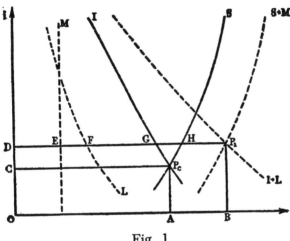

Fig. 1

supply of "credit," or saving *plus* the net increase in the amount of money in a period, to the demand for "credit," or investment *plus* net "hoarding" in the period. Our argument up to this point is illustrated by Figure 1.

S is the supply schedule of saving, showing how much would be saved (measured horizontally) at each rate of interest (measured vertically). I is the schedule of investment, showing how much would be invested (measured horizontally) at each rate of interest. These two schedules intersect at P_c, the "classical" point of equilibrium, which shows the rate of interest being determined at that level (AP_c) at which saving equals investment, both being equal to OA. L is the schedule showing the amount of net "hoarding" that would take place at each rate of interest. In the figure this is shown as a *positive* amount (i.e., at all the rates of interest considered there would be a net balance of "hoarding" and not a net balance of "dishoarding") which is greater for lower rates of interest. There is no reason for expecting "hoarding" always to outbalance "dishoarding" in the economy, and this is taken to be so in the figure merely for the purpose of simplifying the diagram. "Hoarding" could be taken as a negative quantity at some or at all rates of interest (and shown by the *L* curve falling to the left of the vertical axis) without affecting the argument in any way. There is, however, a good reason for net "hoarding" to be greater (or net "dishoarding" to be less) the lower the rate of interest, so that the *L* curve slopes down to the right. This is because the higher the rate of interest the greater the benefit lost by "hoarding" money instead of lending it out at interest, and the greater the temptation to "dishoard" and benefit by the receipt of interest.

The *M* curve shows the increase in the amount of money in the period, and is here shown as a positive amount and independent of the rate of interest. Both of these conditions are postulated merely for the purpose of simplifying the diagram. A *decrease* in the amount of money could be shown by drawing the *M* curve to the *left* of the vertical axis, signifying a *negative increase* in the amount of money. It might be the policy of the monetary authorities to take the rate of interest into account when deciding by how much to increase (or decrease) the amount of money. Thus if they increase the amount of money more (or diminish it by less), the higher is the rate of interest, then the M curve will slope *upward* to the right. But all such differences in assumptions would merely complicate the diagram without affecting our argument in any way.

The *M* curve is now added horizontally to the *S* curve, giving the total net supply schedule of loans (or "credit") marked *S* + *M*. The *L* curve is added to the *I* curve, giving the total net demand schedule for loans (or "credit") marked *I* + *L*. The two new curves intersect at *P₁*, giving an equilibrium into which the complications due to "hoarding" and to changes in the amount of money appear to have been incorporated. This is the position as it appears when the "first step" has been taken.

It is at once apparent that Figure 1 contains a good deal of muddle, and in this it reflects the state of mind of voyagers in the middle of our two-stage trip. In the apparent equilibrium indicated by *P₁*, saving is not necessarily equal to investment (in the figure it is greater by *GH*), while the amount of money hoarded is not necessarily equal to the increase in the amount of money (in the figure it is greater by *EF*, which is equal to *GH*). This exactly portrays the disturbed state of mind of people who declare that saving can be greater than investment if the difference is hoarded.

The second step clears up the muddle. As soon as it is recognized that saving must always equal investment,[3] we get Figure 2, where the *S* and *I* curves coincide, giving the new curve *SI*. For each scale of investment there is a corresponding level of

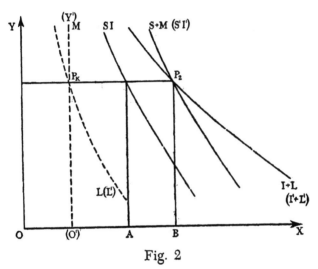

Fig. 2

income. This is determined by the propensity to consume. For each level of income, there is a corresponding supply schedule of saving (with respect to the rate of interest) just like the *S* curve in Figure 1. Thus for any particular rate of interest there is a particular scale of investment, measured by the abscissa of the point corresponding to that rate of interest on the investment curve, and a particular supply schedule of saving showing how much would be saved at different rates of interest if income were at the level corresponding to the particular rate of interest, so that the two curves will have this point in common. All other

[3] Any reader who still feels uneasy on this point might read one of my articles—"Mr. Keynes' General Theory of Employment" ILR, October, 1936, or "Saving Equals Investment" QJE, February, 1938 [Cf. pp. 619–25, above.]

points on the particular supply schedule of saving are illegitimate, and may be left out of the picture, because they contradict themselves in assuming a rate of interest other than that which forms the postulate on which the whole curve is constructed. Such a point would indicate how much would be saved at a rate of interest of 5 per cent, if the level of income were such as could exist only if the rate of interest were 4 per cent. The only legitimate point on the supply curve of saving is the one which falls on the investment curve and shows that at that particular rate of interest the amount saved will be equal to the amount invested. The locus of such legitimate points for different rates of interest must coincide with the I curve, making it an SI curve.

The SI curve is added to the M and L curves, as in Figure 1, to give the supply of "credit" $(S + M)$ and the demand for "credit" $(I + L)$. Equilibrium is reached at P_1, where the supply of "credit" is equal to the demand for it. There can now be no divergence between saving and investment such as was possible in the equilibrium visualized after the first step had been taken (GH in Figure 1), nor can there now arise a difference between the increase in the supply of money in the period and the amount "hoarded" (EF in Figure 1). P_1 must always be of the same height as P_2 (the intersection of M and L which shows "hoarding" equal to the increase in the supply of money).

We must now examine a little more closely the nature of the items we have been handling: S (saving), I (investment), L ("hoarding"), and M (changes in the amount of money). S and I are essentially and naturally of the nature of *flows*. They must be measured as "so much per unit of time" or as "so much in a given period." In the absence of any change in the running of the whole economy, it is reasonable to suppose that their values will be proportional to the period taken. At the same rate of interest, if we consider a period twice as long, we would expect to find that twice as much is invested and saved. It is not so clear in the case of L and M.

Let us first consider L or "hoarding." "Hoarding" by any individual was used to indicate an excess of S over l (lending) or an excess of b (borrowing) over I. $S = Y$ (income) $- C$ (expenditure on consumption). "Hoarding," therefore, $= (Y - C - l) + (b - I) = (Y + b) - (C + I + l)$. Now, $(Y + b)$ is equal to total money receipts, and $(C + I + l)$ is equal to the total money outlays. The excess of the former over the latter, which is what we have called "hoarding," is *the increase in the amount of money held*. This item can indeed be measured as "so much in a given period," but there is no reason for supposing that at each rate of interest, everything else remaining unchanged, an individual will continue to "hoard" (or "dishoard") the same amount in successive periods in the way in which he may be expected to continue to save at the same rate. If the rate of interest has been the same for some time, an individual will neither "hoard" nor "dishoard." Only when there is a *change* in the rate of interest (and for a short period after the change) will "hoarding" or "dishoarding" take place.

The reason for this difference between the ways in which S and I respond to the rate of interest and the way in which L ("hoarding") responds to the rate of interest is as follows. Saving, investing, and "hoarding" all take place only when there is some kind of maladjustment. Saving takes place when the capital value of an individual's assets (representing future yields) is considered by the individual to be too small as compared with his current income, so that he uses some of his income to increase the stock (and value) of his assets. The rate at which he saves is equal to that rate of saving which equates the marginal utility of income forgone to the utility of the marginal increment of assets acquired (or that of the future consumption that it may represent). Investment takes place whenever the capital stock of society is too small as compared with the rate of interest, in the sense that, if the capital stock were just maintained, the marginal rate of return on the activity of maintaining it would be greater than the rate of interest. In such circumstances the capital stock is augmented. The rate of investment that takes place is the rate that makes the marginal rate of return on investment equal to the rate of interest.

In both of these cases, the acts of saving and of investment have some tendency to wipe out the maladjustment that calls them forth, in so far as saving tends to increase the value of assets held by an individual, thus rendering further saving less urgent, while investment tends to increase the stock of capital, and thus to lower the marginal rate of return on maintaining it. Both of these tendencies, however, are very weak in the short run, because the amount that can be saved or invested in a short period, limited in the way indicated above, is small compared with the total value of assets or the total stock of capital, so that many periods must elapse before there is any noticeable effect on these and on the rate of saving or investment that corresponds to a given rate of interest.

The maladjustment which calls forth "hoarding" is an inequality between the marginal utility of the stock of money held initially by any individual and the rate of interest which is the price that has to be paid (or the reward that has to be forgone) for the sake of enjoying this marginal utility. It does *not* take a long time to eliminate such a maladjustment which arises when there is a change in the rate of interest, since there is no increasing cost of "hoarding," as there is of saving (because of the diminished marginal utility of income) or of investment (because of the diminished marginal efficiency of investment). It is possible for an individual to borrow or lend (or withdraw or repay loans) and thereby very quickly to adjust the marginal utility of his stock of money to the rate of interest. As soon as these transactions are completed, no more "hoarding" or "dishoarding" takes place until the rate of interest (or something else) changes again.

What all this means is that while I and S, the *levels* of investment and saving, depend on the *level* of the rate of interest, "hoarding" depends on a *change* in the rate of interest. In this it is more like a *change* in I or S, which would also depend upon a change in the rate of interest. This is quite natural, for "hoarding," as we have seen, is nothing but a *change* in the amount of money held. From this it follows that the true parallel to I and S would be not "hoarding" or the *change* in the amount of money held, but the total *amount* of money people wish to hold, for that, just like I and S, could be expected to stay put as long as the rate of interest (and other influences) remained unchanged.

If the period under consideration is taken to be long enough for the amount of money held to be completely adjusted to the change in the rate of interest, it is a simple matter to adjust our argument and reinterpret our diagram in accordance with this consideration. "Hoarding," or the *increase* in the amount of money held in the period at each rate of interest (L in Figure 2), is the excess of the amount of money people wish to hold at each rate of interest over the amount of money they held at the beginning of the period. We can therefore obtain the curve showing the *total amount* of money people wish to hold, by simply *adding* this initial amount of money held to the L curve—i.e., by moving the whole curve to the right, by a distance representing the amount of money held at the beginning of the period. We can suppose the L curve in Figure 2 to have been treated in this way, so that it now represents the total amount of money people will wish to hold at each rate of interest. This curve is now recognizable as the demand curve for money to hold. It will naturally have a positive value for all rates of interest as it is shown to have in the figure.

An analogous treatment can be applied to the M curve which represented the *increase* in the supply of money. This can be turned into a curve showing the total amount of money available in the new position (at the new interest rate) by adding to the *increase* in the supply of money the initial supply of money or the amount of money available at the beginning of the period. On the new interpretation, the M curve will be the supply curve of money.[4]

Now, the total *supply* of money, or the total amount in existence or available at the beginning of the period, must necessarily be equal to the total amount of money *held* at the beginning of the period, because all money in existence must be held by somebody, and all money held by anybody must be in existence. This means that the M curve and the L curve will both have been shifted to the right by *exactly the same amount*. It follows that the relationship between the two curves and the ordinate or height of their point of intersection P_k will not have been affected by this change. The ordinate of P_s will also be unaffected, since the $S + M$ and the $I + L$ curves will also have been shifted to the right by exactly equal distances.

We must now observe that in substituting the supply of money for the change in the amount of money, and substituting the demand for money to hold or liquidity preference for "hoarding," we would appear to have involved ourselves in a greater difficulty than the one from which we wished to escape by this measure. We now find that to get the $S + M$ and the $I + L$ curves we have to add the M and L curves, which now measure *definite* amounts of money, independent of the length of any period, to the SI curve, which measures an amount of saving and investment

[4] For some suggestions which I have found useful in the preceding paragraphs I am indebted to Dr. L. M. Lachman, at the London School of Economics, who must not, however, be held responsible for anything I say in this article.

which is *indefinite* unless some arbitrary length of period is postulated.[5]

This difficulty disappears as soon as it is observed that the arbitrariness of the *SI* curve does not matter at all. We get exactly the same result whatever the length of the period considered. If the period is longer, we add equally larger amounts to both M and L (the supply and demand curves for money), and so the height $BP_{\bullet}$ (which gives us the rate of interest) is unaffected; and however small the period, the height of $BP_{\bullet}$ is unaffected. When we see this, we also see that the whole business of adding the *SI* curve to the M and L curves is quite unnecessary. We can get the answer to our question more directly by just looking at the M and L curves (the amount of money and the liquidity preference schedule) and their intersection P_k. This is nothing but the diagrammatical representation of the formulation of the modern interest theory favored by Keynes.

When one has reached the new position and adjusted oneself to its implications, a backward glance at the two steps that led from the "classical" to the "modern" theory of interest (at any rate in its "Keynesian" formulation) shows them to be as Machiavellian as they seem terrifying to a "classical" economist who is making up his mind to venture on them. For the first, easy step is the insinuation of liquidity preference as a junior partner in the old-established one-man firm in the business of interest-determination, and the second, much more nasty, step is to put saving-investment, the senior partner, to sleep, as a preliminary to kicking him out.

While the tougher economists, like Keynes, are not impressed by the wickedness of such a procedure, and the slightly less tough salve their consciences with a shrug of the shoulder and a murmured plea that in science the end justifies the means, other economists who have ceased to be "classical," but are still somewhat "romantic,"[6] will be very loth to dispose of the "Old Man"

---

[5] The addition appears even more strange, indeed quite impossible, if we consider the S and I curves to represent not *amounts* saved or invested in some arbitrarily chosen *period*, but as *rates* (or *intensities*) of saving and investment. However, it is always possible to consider some finite *period* in which saving and investment are *amounts*, instead of concentrating on the limiting *ratio* between saving (or investment) and the period of time which constitutes the *flow*, so that our difficulty is seen to consist only in the arbitrariness of the period chosen.

[6] See D. H. Robertson, EJ, September, 1937, p. 436, n. 2.

so summarily, and will prefer to keep him on in the firm as a sleeping-partner with suitable honors and harmless occupations. In this way we find other formulations of the modern theory of interest, differing from Keynes' in the letter rather than in the spirit. The analysis of these formulations by means of the apparatus used above will enable us first to see the differences, if any, in this logical form, and then to examine the pros and cons of the differences in their emphasis on, or implications concerning, the various objective factors involved.

2.

The clearest of such modern formulations of interest theory seems to be that of Professor Bertil Ohlin.[7] According to Professor Ohlin, the rate of interest is the price that equates the supply and demand for "credit" which may be measured *gross* or *net*. The *net* supply of credit (or the supply of *new* credit) is the amount saved *plus* any net dishoarding (or *minus* any net hoarding) by lenders, since it is this sum that they lend on the credit market. The net demand for credit (or the demand for *new* credit) is the amount invested *plus* any net hoarding (or *minus* any net dishoarding) by borrowers, that being the sum borrowed on the credit market. These supplies and demands are both considered not as simple quantities, but as schedules relating the various quantities of new credit that would be supplied or demanded at the different rates of interest. Since Professor Ohlin—as this account of his theory shows—has not only taken the first step from the "classical" towards the "modern" theory of interest, but has emphatically stated that saving must always be equal to investment, thereby making the second step, it is possible to explain and illuminate his theory by means of our Figure 2. We will consider first his *net* formulation in terms of the supply and demand for *new* credit. There are two different ways of doing this.

The simple way is to interpret the *M* curve as showing dishoarding by lenders and the *L* curve as showing hoarding by borrowers, both being schedules showing the different amounts that would be hoarded or dishoarded at different rates of interest. The *SI* curve shows investment (and therefore also saving) as a function of the rate of interest just as before. The addition of this

[7] "Some Notes on the Stockholm Theory of Saving and Investment," II, EJ, June, 1937, and his rejoinder to Keynes in "Alternative Theories of the Rate of Interest," EJ, September, 1937.

curve to the M curve gives us the total supply schedule of new credit $S + M$. Its addition to the L curve gives us the total demand schedule for new credit $I + L$. The intersection of these supply and demand schedules for new credit at P_i gives us the rate of interest BP_i. Again we see that we could have saved ourselves the trouble of adding the SI curve and gone direct to P_i as the equilibrium point showing the rate of interest $O'P_i$.

This interpretation of Figure 2 has the disadvantages: (a) that it suggests that the lenders will always dishoard a fixed amount, irrespective of the rate of interest (unless we re-draw the M curve, making it slope upward to the right to show that they would be induced to dishoard more at higher rates of interest), and (b) that it implies that at all rates of interest it is the lenders on the whole who dishoard and the borrowers who hoard. There is no reason for supposing this to be the case, since it is possible for lenders to hoard by lending something less than their total saving, and for borrowers to dishoard by investing (or spending on consumption) more than they borrow. These are not fundamental objections, since they boil down to nothing more than the unavoidable arbitrariness of a base line for our measurements. It is nevertheless worth while, for the sake of dispelling any uneasiness that may remain, to go on to the slightly more complicated second interpretation (or rather adaptation) of our Figure 2 as an illustration of Professor Ohlin's argument.

Since hoarding is not peculiar to borrowers and dishoarding is not restricted to lenders, and since it is only the net balance of hoarding and dishoarding that matters to us, we can use one curve to measure the *net* hoarding or dishoarding by the whole economy, in a schedule showing this as a function of the rate of interest. This is the new meaning of the L curve. The M curve then becomes a new Y axis (which we mark $O'Y'$), since at the rate of interest OP_i hoarding equals dishoarding, so that net hoarding equals zero. At higher rates of interest net hoarding is negative (dishoarding is greater than hoarding or net dishoarding is positive), and at lower rates of interest net hoarding is positive. We therefore rename our L curve L', to remind us that it is now considered with respect to the vertical axis $O'Y'$, which it cuts at P_i. With the shifting of our vertical axis a distance OO' to the right, the saving-investment curve must also be shifted the same distance to the right to show the same schedule of saving-investmens. This merely means re-naming, as $S'I'$, the previous $S + M$

curve. This curve (in its investment aspect, I') is then added to the L' curve of *net* hoarding (positive for rates of interest less than $O'P_k$ and negative for higher rates of interest) to give $I' + L'$, which is the same as the previous curve, $I + L$. The intersection of these two curves at P_s gives us the rate of interest at which the supply of credit (which consists of saving plus net dishoarding by savers) is equal to the demand for credit (which consists of amounts borrowed and used for investment plus net hoarding by people other than savers), the various items being rearranged somewhat so that all uncancelled (or *net*) hoarding or dishoarding is included in the second curve.

Once more we get the same answer, and we see again that the incorporation of saving and investment is completely unnecessary for the purpose of getting the answer to our question. P_s gives the point where saving is equal to investment *plus* net hoarding. Since we know that saving is always equal to investment, we can remove these from both sides of our equation without losing anything, and we see that P_s gives us the rate of interest at which net hoarding equals zero. By going directly for this, we, and Professor Ohlin, would have saved ourselves a lot of trouble. Our only comfort is that all this empty ceremony about saving and investment may have done something to preserve the dignity of our ancient monarch, deprived of all influence in the real affairs of state. The effects of such ceremonial activities will be dealt with in the third section of this article, when we consider the importance of differing formulation with the same logical content.

We can now consider Professor Ohlin's *gross* formulation. Keynes says that the rate of interest is the price that equates the supply and demand for *cash*. Professor Ohlin says that it is the price that equates the supply and demand for *credit*. The identity of meaning of these two propositions is shown in Figure 3.

Along the vertical axis is measured the rate of interest. The M curve shows the amount of money available in an economy. If the amount of money is fixed independently of the rate of interest, this curve will be perpendicular, as it is drawn in our diagram. If the supply of money is governed by the rate of interest (as it may be if the monetary authorities are influenced by the rate of interest in determining the amount of money), the M curve will have a corresponding shape. The horizontal distance between the M curve and the A curve shows the value, at each rate of interest, of all the other assets in the economy. The lower the rate of interest the greater the value of these assets, because then the expected future incomes which these assets represent will lose less in being discounted to give the present value of the assets.

At each rate of interest—and the corresponding value of the assets—people will wish to distribute their wealth in a certain proportion between cash and other assets. At a higher rate of interest, people will wish to hold less cash, partly because of the higher reward for holding other assets, partly because the value of other assets shrinks relatively to the value of a given amount of money, and partly because at the higher rate of interest invest-

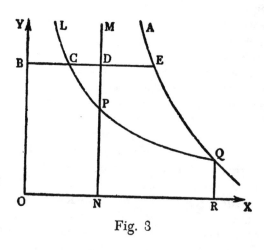

Fig. 3

ment and incomes will be less. The *L* curve shows the way in which at each rate of interest people desire to distribute their wealth between cash and other assets. Thus if the rate of interest is *OB*, the amount of cash (here shown fixed independently of the rate of interest) being *BD*, the value of other assets is *DE*, so that the total value of assets including cash is *BE*. At this rate of interest (and the corresponding value of other assets) the owners of wealth wish to hold in cash not *BD*, the amount of cash actually available for them to hold, but *BC* (i.e., *BD minus CD*); and they wish to hold in the form of other assets not *DE*, the value of the existing other assets, but *CE* (i.e., *DE plus CD*).

At the rate of interest *OB*, then, all property-owners together will try to exchange *CD* of cash for the same cash value of other assets by exchanging with each other. Of course they cannot succeed in doing this, because, whatever the extent to which cash and other assets change hands, the total of cash remains at BD, which is CD too much—and the total of other assets remains at DE, which is CD too little. But the attempt to get rid of cash and to acquire other assets has the effect of raising the price of these assets, and thus of lowering the rate of interest.

This process continues, the line BE moving down, DE, the value of other assets, increasing, and CD, the excess of cash or the deficit of other assets, diminishing until it disappears, C and D meeting in P. P is the point of equilibrium, there being no further incentive for the value of assets and the rate of interest to change. NP is the equilibrium rate of interest.

Keynes calls the L curve the demand for money and the M curve the supply of money, measuring both of these in the familiar way from the Y axis towards the right. The rate of interest is determined by the equilibrium shown at P, where the demand for BC is equal to the supply BD. Professor Ohlin looks at the picture from the other side, measures his quantities from the A curve towards the left. The M curve then measures the supply of assets which is the demand for credit, and the L curve measures the demand for assets which is the supply of credit.[8] The equilibrium giving us the rate of interest is shown at P, where the supply of credit, ED, is equal to the demand for credit, EC; and it is thus that the rate of interest is determined. Our figure shows very simply that the equation of BC to BD is the same thing as the equation of EC to ED.

[8] We may assume that when Prof. Ohlin says that the supply and demand for assets "govern" the demand and supply of credit, he means that the former are the schedules which determine both the *quantity* of credit *supplied* (and demanded) on the market and the *price* or rate of interest in which alone we are here interested. Such an interpretation is supported by a passage in Prof. Ohlin's article in EJ, September, 1937, p. 423, where he says: "When it is said in pure theory that the price of a commodity is governed by supply and demand, the meaning is that it is determined by the demand and supply *curves*, which express the planned sales and purchases at different possible prices during a certain future period." It must be presumed that by the quantity of credit supplied (and demanded, since supply must equal demand) Prof. Ohlin means not the amount of credit that actually changes hands on the market, for that belongs to the *net* rather than to the *gross* analysis, but the total value of assets in existence (which is the actual demand for credit or capital-disposal) and the value of assets people wish to hold (which is the actual supply of credit or capital-disposal). Prof. Ohlin's somewhat obscure expression for this familiar form of showing an equilibrium by the intersection of supply and demand schedules is related to his use of the *ex-ante* concept.

As Figure 3 is drawn, one might get the impression that the Keynesian argument is more reasonable because it is represented by the more normal procedure of measuring supply and demand from the Y axis towards the right, while Professor Ohlin's argument is very peculiar because it entails measurement from some strange-looking curve and towards the left. This, however, is entirely arbitrary, since the figure could quite easily be re-drawn the other way round and show the supply and demand for assets (the demand and supply of credit) measured from the Y axis towards the right, and the supply and demand for cash measured towards the left, and from a curve of exactly the same shape as the A curve in our figure. Any reason for preferring one of these formulations to the other must be based on quite different grounds.

In concluding this analysis of the logical content of Professor Ohlin's *net* and *gross* formulations of the theory of interest, I would like to mention two points.

First, in the *gross* formulation, even as given by Professor Ohlin himself, there is no mention whatever of saving or of investment. Poor senior partner has been completely forgotten. Secondly, although Professor Ohlin insists that the distinction between *ex-ante* and *ex-post* analysis is essential for dealing with these problems, I have been able, I think, to present the whole of his interest theory without making any use of that mechanism.

The differences between Professor Ohlin's formulation of the theory of interest and that of other "modern" but not quite Keynesian" economists, like Dr. Hicks and Mr. Robertson, are very slight and need not occupy much space. Dr. Hicks speaks of the rate of interest being determined by the supply and demand for *loans* in place of Ohlin's *credit*, but any difference between these can only be in the nature of some arbitrary variation of the base line for measurements which affect supply and demand equally and give the same rate of interest as the answer. Dr. Hicks' supply and demand for loans can be illustrated in our Figure 2 in exactly the same way as Professor Ohlin's supply and demand for credit. Dr. Hicks emphasizes the arbitrary nature of the choice between speaking in terms of *loans* or of *cash*, declaring that, if we equate the supply and demand for money, the equation of the supply and demand for loans follows automatically, and, if we equate the latter, the former equation is otiose. This is shown very clearly in our Figure 3.

The kernel of Mr. Robertson's theory of interest is also the same, although it is not so easy to disentangle it, on the one hand from his peculiar terminology and on the other hand from the numerous side issues that he delights to bring in. In his last rejoinder to Keynes,[9] however, he consents, under protest, to use Keynes' terminology for a while, so that saving is always equal to investment, and this enables the reader to see that his "loanable funds," the supply and demand for which determine the rate of interest, is parallel with Professor Ohlin's "credit" and Dr. Hicks' "loans," so that Mr. Robertson is right when he says that his apparatus and Keynes' are "but alternative pieces of machinery," from which it follows that the vigorous attacks made so frequently by Mr. Robertson on Keynes' formulation must rest either on minor terminological quibbles, which we cannot discuss here, or on differences in implicit assumption about the data which determine the relative convenience of the different formulations. These we can discuss in the next section.

3.

Just as in the examination of the different formulations of interest theory we found it convenient to use Professor Ohlin's largely as representative of the others, so we shall find it convenient here to compare his formulae with that of Keynes, now looking not for similarities in their analytical content, but for differences in their empirical implications and suggestions. On this we may come to a judgment as to these relative merits as tools for economic investigation.

Professor Ohlin's *gross* formulation has the advantage (as compared with Keynes') of making it harder for the student to forget that there is a different rate of interest for every different kind of "credit" determined by the supply and demand for that kind of "credit" (or the demand and supply of the corresponding assets). The emphasis in the *asset* side also diminishes the danger, which is quite considerable if, like Keynes, we look only on the money side, of overlooking the effect on the rate of interest of changes in the total value of other assets. There is then a shift of the L curve to the right, but there is no change in purely psychological propensities to draw our attention to this shift.

Professor Ohlin's *gross* formulation, or a simple variant of it, is also a more useful method for the discussion of the intricate

[9] EJ, September, 1937, p. 428.

complementarities that arise when there are several different kinds of assets. It enables us, for example, to deal more easily with the question: How will an increase in the desire to hold equities, due to an expectation of increased yields, affect the (bond) rate of interest? The answer is that, if equities are complementary with bonds against money, the rate of interest will fall, while if equities are complementary with money against bonds, the rate of interest will rise. Or the same results can be put, not quite so simply, in terms of the different elasticities of substitution between bonds, equities, and money. In any case this analysis [10] presupposes an awareness of the problem in terms of the demand for holding different values of various assets. The same treatment is suitable for all questions, like those concerning the relationship between long- and short-period interest rates, which concern the demand for different kinds of assets. (In this case, bonds and bills.)

Against these advantages must be set the danger in Professor Ohlin's formulae of forgetting that the ceremonies performed in honor of saving and investment are quite empty. Although it is clear that they play no real part in either of his formulations, Professor Ohlin is extraordinarily and suspiciously emphatic in declaring that they really do affect the result. Thus: "Does this mean that [the height of the] rate of interest has no connection with the disposition of individuals and firms to save . . . ? Of course not. But it has such connections only indirectly." [11] And even more emphatically at the end of his last article: "The quantity of claims . . . *provides a direct link with saving, investment, and the whole economic process.*" [12] Our analysis has shown that the real connections between saving and investment and the rate of interest (for, of course, everything in an economy is connected with everything else) are of a far more indirect nature than would be suggested by their simple and purposeless addition to both the supply and demand schedules for cash or credit.

This leads to another disadvantage, from which Professor Ohlin's *net* formulation suffers more than his *gross* formulation, namely, that readers may easily take the attentions paid to savings and investments too seriously and suppose it to be very little

---

[10] Based on the general lines laid down by Hicks and Allen in "A Reconsideration of the Theory of Value" (*Economica*, 1934).

[11] EJ, June, 1937, p. 221.

[12] *Ibid.*, September, 1937, p. 427 (his italics).

removed from the "classical" theory of the supply and demand for savings. Keynes himself has fallen into this trap.[13]

Dr. Hicks seems to have been successful in keeping all of these in what seems to me to be a right perspective. Essentially he has put in a more mathematical manner what I have endeavored to show in my curves.

Mr. Robertson, on the other hand, seems to be more to blame than Professor Ohlin, and gives one the impression that his very deep pseudo-classical formulations really contain more than empty ceremony. His concession, in this last article,[14] in employing the Keynesian language shows him quite definitely to have taken the two steps from the "classical" to the modern view, and his ancient trappings are justified, when challenged, by quite new and very ingenious arguments in terms of the modern theory. Yet one still feels that there is behind all this a harking back to the old system that provides the energy for his cunning. I wish to consider here only one of his points—namely, that the marginal efficiency of capital "can exercise a direct influence on the rate of interest." A closer examination of this shows that Mr. Robertson is assuming that if there is an increase in investment, there is an increase in the demand for cash to hold to finance the investment, or else a tendency for the increase in income, formed by the increase in investment, to be hoarded.[15] This may be so to some extent if we consider a very short period, but it cannot be generalized, so that it is better to consider such effects as changes in the demand for money rather than as "direct" effects of the increase in investment to be measured by the schedule of the marginal efficiency of capital.

Certainly there is no very simple relationship between such increases in the demand for holding cash, which are most directly related to the *rate of increase* of the rate of investment (or the level of incomes), and the *level* of the rate of investment on which the unsophisticated "classical" argument is based.

This effect, which fits without any difficulty into the simplest Keynesian formula of the supply and demand for money, should be distinguished from another which does not fit so easily into that scheme. An increase in the marginal efficiency of capital may

[13] "Alternative Theories of the Rate of Interest," EJ, June, 1937, p. 245. (See above p. 647.)

[14] *Op. cit.*, p. 428.

[15] I am indebted on this point to a discussion with Dr. M. Kalecki.

be accompanied by an increase in share values, and this may affect the rate of substitution between bonds and cash,[16] and in this way the rate of interest. To consider this as an effect (direct or indirect) of an increase in the marginal efficiency of capital on the rate of interest is not correct, for it is not the change in the marginal efficiency of capital that has the effect, but the change in the total value of shares. An increase in the marginal efficiency of capital, while increasing the profitability of *new* investments, can lower as well as raise the value of *existing* investments, and may leave it unchanged. There is, of course, the consideration that the new investment, by adding to the total of assets, may tend to increase their value, and thus to have some effect, of the nature here discussed, on the rate of interest, but this effect is certainly negligible in the short-period determination of the rate of interest to which all this argument refers.

We see, then, that against the very simplified form of the Keynesian system, which speaks as if there were only one kind of asset and only one rate of interest, the other formulations have an advantage against which several disadvantages have to be put. We are saved from the task of weighing these advantages and disadvantages by the consideration that a more sympathetic interpretation of both systems, bringing in both cash and assets as in our Figure 3, gives us the advantages of both.

[16] See p. 652.

CHAPTER XLVI

Interest Theory—Supply and Demand for Loans, or Supply and Demand for Cash?

By ABBA P. LERNER

WHEN I say, as a Keynesian, that the rate of interest is determined by the supply and demand for cash, i.e., the *stock* of cash and the quantity of cash that the public wishes to *hold* at various rates of interest, I do not, of course, mean to deny that in the economic universe everything is to a greater or less degree dependent on everything else. The whole system of Walrasian equations is necessary to describe the determination of the equilibrium of the economic system as a whole. Nevertheless, it seems to me that there is more meaning in my statement than is admitted by critics like Dr. Fellner and Dr. Somers,[1] who prefer to say that the rate of interest is determined by the supply and demand for loans, and who declare that my statement is correct only on the assumption that all the other prices and quantities in the Walrasian scheme are given. This means that "The rate of interest equates the demand and supply of cash only in the sense in which the shoe price can also be said to perform this function if all other prices are given."[2]

It cannot be denied that the rate of interest, being the price paid for a loan, must be at the level where the demand for loans is equal to the supply of loans. But to say that the rate of interest is determined by the supply and demand for loans is unsatisfactory. because such a formulation, unlike most partial analyses of this kind, does not even give the first approximation provided by

[1] "Alternative Monetary Approaches to Interest Theory," RES, xxiii, 1941, pp. 43–48.
[2] *Ibid.*, p. 48.

a statement like "The price of shoes is determined by the supply and demand for shoes." [3]

In the case of shoes, such a simplification from the Walrasian formulation of general equilibrium is permissible because an increase in the demand for shoes (say, because a shortage of rubber makes people walk more) does not as a rule have a very important effect on the supply of shoes. In the case of *loans*, this relative independence does not hold. When there is an increase in the demand for loans, say because businessmen want to borrow more money in order to spend it, there is likely to result from this an increase in the supply of loans. The increased spending on the construction of new factories or in the purchase of additional consumption goods will increase incomes, and part of these incomes will be saved and offered on the loan market. The part of these incomes that is not saved but spent will increase incomes still further and part of these further additions to income will be saved and offered on the loan market. Such induced increases in the supply of loans may partly or wholly offset the effect of the increase in the demand for loans. (Similarly, if there is a decrease in the supply of loans because some lenders decide to spend their money instead of lending it, this will increase the amount of money in the hands of those from whom the purchases are made, and these may directly or indirectly increase the supply of loans; or the money spent by the erstwhile lenders may flow into the hands of erstwhile borrowers who will now decrease their demand for loans.)

There may be delays in the working out of these effects. Some may argue that any increase in demand for loans can increase the supply only in a degree smaller than the increase in demand. Others may argue that the supply would increase in an equal degree and in some circumstances in a greater degree. These complications, important as they are for other purposes, are not significant for the present issue. As long as the change in demand for loans *may* have an important effect on the supply of loans (or a change in the supply of loans may have an important effect on the demand for loans, or a change in demand or supply by some

---

[3] The proposition that the rate of interest is determined by the supply and demand for loans is often called the "loanable funds" theory of interest. This phrase seems to be ideally suited to cloud the distinction between the supply and demand for *loans* and the supply and demand for the *cash* (funds) in which the loans are made.

can have an important effect on the demand or supply by others),
we cannot use this partial analysis. We are then faced with the
question of whether we can find some way of correcting this fault
in the partial analysis or must give it up and go back to the correct but not very illuminating statement of general analysis that
the rate of interest, like any other price, depends on everything
in the entire economy.

One solution is to construct simplified Walrasian or general-
equilibrium schemes in which there are a small number of variables representing composite quantities, such as output of consumption goods in general or output of investment goods in general. Perhaps the most enlightening of these schemes, and the
easiest for the non-mathematical economist to understand, is that
constructed by Professor Oscar Lange.[4] Such schemes, although
they raise difficulties of their own in the unavoidable implications
of some sort of homogeneity in the really non-homogeneous entities to which they refer (like the output of consumption goods
or the output of investment goods or even the output of goods in
general), are of great value in elucidating some of the more complex interrelationships between the different variables. But they
are much more difficult to understand than the simple supply
and demand partial analyses to which all of us are accustomed.

Many economists and all non-economists still do not feel quite
satisfied when they are shown that there are n equations to determine n unknowns, and are not much happier when they are
shown a simplified account which they do not fully understand
and which they suspect of all kinds of skulduggery, even though
there are only six unknowns and six equations. Is it not possible to
apply something like the familiar supply and demand analysis
and yet give not too inaccurate an account of the determination
of the rate of interest?

The partial supply and demand analysis can be salvaged. The
clue to this lies in noticing that the disturbing effects of a change
in demand on the supply (and vice versa) arise only in those
cases where the increase in demand for loans is not for the purpose of holding the extra cash but for the purpose of spending it.
To the extent that the borrower increases his own holding of cash,
his borrowing cannot indirectly increase the supply of loans. And
even when he does spend the money he borrows, there can be

---

[4] "The Rate of Interest and the Optimum Propensity to Consume" (*Economica*, v [N. S., 1938], pp. 12–32).

no increase in the supply of loans if the person who receives the money from him keeps it and adds it to *his* previous stock of cash. In fact, if we consider all such increases of cash in the hands of all the members of society who receive any of this money in the course of its wanderings through the economy, we can say that the money which people in general wish to add to their stores of cash cannot come on to the loan market again as an additional supply of loans resulting from the original increase in demand for loans, but that the money which nobody wishes to add to his store of cash keeps on moving until it is offered again on the market for loans.[5]

Thus by bringing in the demand for cash to hold (and in parallel fashion the supply of cash), we can eliminate the effects of demand on supply (and of supply on demand) which threatened to frustrate the attempt at partial analysis. In the demand for loans we must count only that part of the demand which the borrowers, or the other people who indirectly receive the borrowed money, wish to add to their stock of cash. Similarly, in the supply of loans we must count only those loans which come from new issues of money or which the lenders are able to supply because they wish to decrease their holdings of cash. Any other loans indicate a withdrawal of cash by the lenders from other parts of the economy (where the lenders would have spent it if they had not loaned it out), and the withdrawals have the effect of increasing the demand for loans or decreasing the supply of loans in these other parts of the economy. When this is done, the corrected demand for loans consists of the demand for additional cash to be held by the borrower or by those who directly or indirectly receive the money from the borrowers when they spend their borrowings. The corrected supply of loans consists of newly created cash *plus* the cash set free by the lenders (who may be lending only indirectly, spending the spare cash which eventually finds its way into the hands of the actual lenders). The demand for loans is nothing but the demand for additional cash, and the

---

[5] It is not necessary for this to attempt to follow the adventures of the identical dollars that start the train of additional spendings and receipts. This is impossible anyway, even theoretically, unless all the money in the economy is hard cash and there is no credit whatever. We merely mean the increases in anybody's payments (and therefore, in every case, in somebody's receipts) which are induced directly or indirectly by the initial increase in spending by the borrowers of the new loans or by the erstwhile lenders who spend the money instead of lending it.

supply of loans is nothing but the supply of additional or spare cash. If we add the stock of cash actually in existence to both sides of this supply and demand, and subtract the decrease in demand for cash from both sides (i.e., the cash set free and loaned out, directly or indirectly), we have the demand for loans translated into the demand for cash and the supply of loans translated into the supply of cash.

We are then tempted to deny that we have a supply-and-demand-for-loans theory of interest and to say that the rate of interest is determined by the supply and demand for the stock of cash, since it is this supply and demand for cash which determines the equilibrium of the supply and demand for loans. It is only when the supply or stock of cash is equal to the demand for it that the supply of loans is equal to the demand for them.

It cannot be overemphasized that the supply and demand for cash refers to the *stock* of cash, while the supply and demand for loans refers to the *flow* of lending and borrowing which is measured as so much *per period of time*. If the stock of cash in existence is in accord with the stock that people wish to hold, there will be no attempt by individuals to increase their holdings of cash by increasing the rate of borrowing (or reducing the rate of lending), and there will be no attempt by individuals to decrease their holdings of cash by increasing the rate of lending (or decreasing the rate of borrowing). The equilibrium of the supply and demand for the stock of cash is therefore a necessary and sufficient condition for the equilibrium of the supply and demand for the flow of loans. The actual rate of borrowing must be equal to the actual rate of lending (since these are merely different aspects of the same phenomenon), and there is no desire on the part of borrowers or lenders to vary these rates of borrowing or lending.

In saying that the "cash" theory of interest is preferable to the "loans" theory, I do not deny that the actual rate of interest is in fact agreed upon by the suppliers and demanders for loans. I only mean to assert that in estimating the effect of any event on the rate of interest we are likely to be misled unless we take into account the effects of the event on the supply and demand for the stock of cash. For example, the simple "loans" theory might lead to the conclusion that an increase in the profitability of investment in new capital goods, by increasing the demand for loans, must raise the rate of interest. But if the investors and

others are led by the same increase in the profitability of investment to reduce their own holdings of money by investing or
spending out of their previous stocks of cash, the supply of loans
will increase more than the demand for loans and the rate of interest will fall. This is liable to be overlooked if we concentrate
on the effect on the demand for loans, but is seen at once if attention is directed to the effects of the initial event on the supply
and demand for the stock of cash.

It might be argued that the "loans" analysis is adequate if we
consider a short period in which there is no time for the increased
spending by the borrowers to bring about the increase in lending
by those whose income will be increased.[6] It is true that in this
case an increase in the demand for loans will have the effect of
raising the rate of interest, but even then we cannot say that the
rate of interest is a function of the supply and demand for loans.
Rather it is a function of the *rate of change* in the supply (or demand) for loans. If there is a once for all increase in the demand
for loans of this nature, there will at first be an increase in the demand for loans without any increase in the supply. After some
delay, the increased spending by the lenders will increase incomes and savings. The part of the increased income which is not
saved will be spent and will increase other incomes. In this way,
saving *immediately* increases by the amount of increase in investment (since that is the amount by which income increases in
relation to consumption), and the supply of loans *gradually* ex-
pands (as the increased rate of investment raises income to the
corresponding higher level) until it has increased as much as the
demand for loans. After this, both the supply and the demand for
loans will be greater than before in the same degree, and there is
no reason why the rate of interest will be maintained at the
higher level unless the *rate at which the demand for loans increases* continues at the higher level. The rate of interest in this

---

[6] For this it is necessary to assume that the increase in the profitability
of investment or in the attractiveness of consumption which brings about
the increase in the demand for loans (or the decrease in the supply of loans)
does not induce the borrowers (or the erstwhile lenders) to increase their
expenditure out of their previous holdings of cash in anticipation of the
forthcoming borrowings (or reduced lendings out of their income). If
there should be such an anticipatory increase in spending, the increased
lending to which it gives rise may come about even before the increased
demand for loans, leading to a (temporary) *fall* in the rate of interest.

case is raised not by the greater *demand* for loans but by the greater rate of increase in the demand for loans.[7]

Of course, a higher level of economic activity will probably bring with it a need for more cash to be held in connection with the greater volume of transactions, and the increase in the demand for cash will tend to raise the rate of interest. This looks something like the proposition criticized in the preceding paragraph, but there is no reason for believing that the greater need for cash that accompanies the greater volume of transactions is the same as the cash temporarily absorbed by the borrowing (which may initiate an increased volume of transactions) in the interval between the initial borrowing and the time when it results in increased income saving and lending. The increased *transactions* demand for cash may be greater or less than this transitional increase in the demand for cash, and in any case it fits perfectly into the formula that the rate of interest is determined by the supply and demand for cash.

Methodologically, Lord Keynes' contribution was to point out that partial analysis can be made a little more complicated, bringing in three or four variables instead of the Marshallian two, and yet remain manageable. For some economists who are accustomed either to the black and white of the very simplest kind of partial analysis, with only two variables, or else to the complete Walrasian general equilibrium with everything depending on everything else, this point of Lord Keynes seems difficult to grasp. The liquidity preference theory of interest is an example of this kind of more complicated partial analysis, bringing in the supply and demand for cash to support the supply and demand for loans. Perhaps some difficulty has been caused by the shorthand method of expressing it which may seem to imply that borrowing and lending have nothing to do with the rate of interest.

[7] If the demand had previously been constant, the rate of increase in the demand for loans was zero, and now during the change it is positive. When the demand for loans is stabilized at the higher level, the rate of increase in the demand for loans is again zero and the rate of interest falls to the previous level.

PART TEN

Bibliography of Keynes' Writings

Bibliography of Keynes' Writings[1]

By SEYMOUR E. HARRIS and MARGARITA WILLFORT

(1) BOOKS AND PAMPHLETS BY J. M. KEYNES

Indian Currency and Finance, 1913.

The Economic Consequences of the Peace, 1919 (German transl. by M. J. Bonn and C. Brinkmann, 1920; French transl. by P. Franck, 1920; also *Der Friedensvertrag von Versailles* (Europäische Bücherei), 1921).

Mr. Lloyd George's General Election, 1920 (Extract from *The Economic Consequences of the Peace*).

A Treatise on Probability, 1921 (German transl. by F. M. Urban, 1926).

A Revision of the Treaty, 1922 (German transl. by F. Ransohoff, 1922; French transl. by P. Franck, *Nouvelles considérations sur la révision de la paix*).

A Tract on Monetary Reform, 1923 (German transl. by E. Kocherthaler, 1924; French transl. by P. Franck, 1924; Italian transl. by P. Sraffa, 1925).

The Economic Consequences of Sterling Parity, 1925 (In Great Britain: *The Economic Consequences of Mr. Churchill;* reprinted, in part, in *Essays in Persuasion*).

A Short View of Russia, 1925 (Reprinted in *Essays in Persuasion*).

The End of Laissez-Faire, 1926 (Reprinted, in part, in *Essays in Persuasion;* German transl. by K. Hilferding, 1926).

Laissez-Faire and Communism, 1926.

Réflexions sur le franc, 1928 (Transl. by R. Lelis; reprinted in part in *Essays in Persuasion*).

A Treatise on Money, 2 Vols., 1930 (German transl. by C. Krämer, *Vom Gelde,* with new introduction by Keynes, 1932; Italian transl.).

---

[1] Please consult Chap. VII.

Essays in Persuasion, 1931.
Essays in Biography, 1933.
The Means to Prosperity, 1933.
The General Theory of Employment, Interest, and Money, 1936
 (German transl. by F. Waeger, 1936; French transl. by J. de
 Largentaye, 1942; Spanish transl. by E. Hornedo, 1943).
How to Pay for the War, 1940.

(2) BOOKS AND PAMPHLETS BY KEYNES WITH OTHERS

Keynes, J. M., and D. H. Henderson: *Can Lloyd George Do It?*
 1929 (Reprint from N&A, May 11, 1929).
 How to Conquer Unemployment, 1929.
Keynes, J. M., Sir A. Salter, Sir J. Stamp, Sir B. Blackett, H. Clay,
 Sir W. H. Beveridge: *The World's Economic Crisis and the
 Way of Escape*, 1932.

(3) CONTRIBUTIONS BY J. M. KEYNES TO OFFICIAL REPORTS

Annex to the *Report of the Royal Commission on Indian Cur-
 rency*, 1914.
Testimony before the Colwyn Committee; see *Final Report of the
 Committee on National Debt and Taxation*, 1927, *Minutes of
 Evidence*, pp. 277–287, and 534–540.
Speeches before the House of Lords, on:
 Clearing Union (May 18, 1943, Hansard Lords, Vol. 127).
 Bretton Woods Agreement (May 23, 1944, Hansard Lords,
 Vol. 131, pp. 838–849).
Anglo-American Financial Arrangement (Dec. 18, 1945, Hansard
 Lords, Vol. 138, pp. 777–794).
Britain's Industrial Future (1928). (Liberal Party Program—
 Keynes was a member of the board and greatly influenced
 the report.)
Report on British Finance and Industry (*Macmillan Report*),
 1931; Cmd. 3897. (Keynes was a member of the committee
 and signatory of Report and Addendum I without reserva-
 tions.)
Final Report of the Committee on Industry and Trade (*Balfour
 Report*), 1929; Cmd. 3282. (Keynes was a witness in an indi-
 vidual capacity between 1924 and 1927.)

Plan for an International Clearing Union, 1943 (Keynes greatly influenced this plan).

(4) REVIEWS BY J. M. KEYNES OF OFFICIAL REPORTS, ETC.

(arranged chronologically)

Review of *Report of the National Monetary Commission of the United States, 1912*, EJ, Mar., 1912, pp. 150–151.

"*Report on Indian Paper Currency*," EJ, Mar., 1912, pp. 145–7.

Review of *Report Upon the Operations of the Paper Currency Department of the Government of India, 1910–1911*, EJ, Mar., 1912, pp. 145–149.

"*Reports on Irish Finance*," EJ, Sept., 1912 (a review of three official reports).

Review of *Report of the Commission on the Cost of Living in New Zealand*, EJ, Sept., 1912, pp. 595–9.

"*Tables Showing for 1910–11 the Estimated Value of Imports and Exports of the United Kingdom at Prices of 1900*," EJ, Dec., 1912, pp. 630–631.

Keynes on the Departmental Committee on Matters Affecting Currency of the British West African Colonies and Protectorates, and Minutes of Evidence, EJ, Mar. 1913, pp. 146–7.

Review of Departmental Committee. . . . : *The Currency of British West Africa*, EJ, Sept., 1913.

"*The Forty-Third Annual Report of the Deputy Master of the Mint, 1912*," EJ, Mar., 1914.

"*Currency in 1914*," EJ, Mar., 1914, pp. 152–157. (Review of *Forty-Third Annual Report of the Deputy Master of the Mint*.)

"*The Trade of India, 1913–14*," EJ, Dec., 1914, pp. 639–642. (Review of two official reports.)

"*The Report of the Committee on the Currency and Bank of England Note Issues, 1925*," EJ, June, 1925, pp. 299–304.

"*The United States and Gold*," in *European Currency and Finance* (Commission of Gold and Silver Inquiry, U. S. Senate), EJ, 1925.

"*The Committee on the Currency: Comment on Report*," EJ, June, 1925.

"*The Colwyn Report on National Debt and Taxation*," EJ, June, 1927, pp. 198–212.

"The Report of the Bank for International Settlements, 1933–34," EJ, Sept., 1934, pp. 514–518.
"The Supply of Gold," EJ, Sept., 1936, pp. 412–418.

(5) BOOKS REVIEWED BY J. M. KEYNES

(arranged alphabetically by name of author)

Walter Bagehot: The Works and Life of Bagehot, EJ, Sept., 1915, pp. 369–375.

Sir D. Barbour: The Standard of Value, EJ, June, 1913, pp. 390–393.

Chen Huang-Chang: The Economic Principles of Confucius and His School, EJ, Sept., 1912, pp. 584–588.

C. R. Fay: English Economic History, EJ, June, 1940, pp. 259–261.

M. M. Fishel: Le Thaler de Marie-Thérèse, EJ, 1914, pp. 257–260.

I. Fisher: The Purchasing Power of Money, EJ, June, 1911, pp. 393–398.

I. Fisher and H. G. Brown: The Purchasing Power of Money, EJ, Sept., 1911, pp. 393–398.

H. G. Funkhouser: Historical Development of the Graphical Representation of Statistical Data, EJ, June, 1938, pp. 281–282.

W. I. J. Gun: Studies in Hereditary Ability, N&A, Mar. 27, 1926.

R. G. Hawtrey: Currency and Credit, EJ, June, 1920, pp. 362–365.

Sir Alfred Hoare: Unemployment and Inflation, EJ, 1933, pp. 474–475.

J. A. Hobson: Gold, Prices, and Wages, EJ, June, 1913, pp. 393–398.

A. M. Innes: What Is Money? EJ, Sept., 1914, pp. 419–421.

T. S. Jevons: Theory of Political Economy, EJ, Mar., 1912, pp. 78–80.

T. S. Jevons: The Future of Exchanges and the Indian Currency, EJ, Mar., 1923, pp. 60–65.

J. W. McIbraith: The Course of Prices in New Zealand, EJ, Sept., 1912, pp. 595–598.

J. E. Meade: Consumers' Credits and Unemployment, EJ, Mar., 1938, pp. 67–71.

F. C. Mills: The Behaviour of Prices (NBER), EJ, Dec., 1928, pp. 606–608.

L. V. Mises: Theorie des Geldes, EJ; Sept., 1914, pp. 417–419, and
   F. Bendixen: Geld und Kapital, ibid.
T. Morison: The Economic Transition in India, EJ, Sept., 1911,
   pp. 426–431.
J. F. Shirras: Indian Finance and Banking, EJ, June, 1920, pp.
   396–397.
Warren-Pearson: Interrelationships of Supply and Prices, EJ,
   Mar., 1929, pp. 92–95.
M. de P. Webb: The Rupee Problem, EJ, Sept., 1910, pp. 438–440.

(5a) MISCELLANEOUS REVIEWS, INCLUSIVE OF SEMI-OFFICIAL ITEMS

Review of *The Works of Walter Bagehot,* EJ, Sept., 1915, pp.
   369–375.
"An American Study of Shares *vs.* Bonds as Permanent Invest-
   ments," N&A, May 2, 1925. (Review of *E. L. Smith: Common
   Stocks as Long-Term Investments.*)
"Trotsky on England," N&A, Mar. 27, 1926. (Review of *Where Is
   Britain Going?*)
"Mr. Churchill on the War," N&A, Mar. 5, 1927. (Review of *The
   World Crisis, 1916–1918.*)
"Russia and Britain: A Contrast" (About Loveday's *Britain and
   World Trade*) N&A, Nov. 8, 1930.
"Is There Enough Gold? The League of Nations Inquiry," N&A,
   Jan. 19, 1929.
"Mr. Churchill on the Peace," N&A, Mar. 9, 1929 (Review of *The
   World Crisis: The Aftermath*).
"*The Bank for International Settlements: Fourth Annual Report,
   1933–34,*" EJ, Sept., 1934.
"*The Report of the Union Corporation for 1935,*" and other pub-
   lications. EJ, Sept., 1936, p. 412 (see "The Supply of Gold").
"*Professor Tinbergen's Method,*" (Review of *Tinbergen: Statisti-
   cal Testing of Business Cycles,* I), EJ, Sept., 1939, pp. 558–
   578.
   Tinbergen's "Reply," *ibid.,* Mar., 1940, pp. 141 et seq., and
   Keynes' "Comment," *ibid.,* Mar., 1940, pp. 154–156.
"*The Process of Capital Formation,*" EJ, Sept., 1939, pp. 569–74.
   (Review of *League of Nations: Statistics Relating to Capital
   Formation,* 1938.)
[See also, below, Section 6 (p).]

(6) ARTICLÆS BY KEYNES [2]

*(Items italicized are from scientific journals; arrangement for each
group is chronological).*

(a) EMPLOYMENT, UNEMPLOYMENT, ETC.

KEYNES, J. M. "Currency Policy and Unemployment," N&A, Aug.
11, 1923.

"What Can Great Britain Do?" NR, Aug. 15, 1923.

ANON. "Unemployment, Protection, and Stable Money," N&A, Nov.
10, 1923.

KEYNES, J. M. "Does Unemployment Need a Drastic Remedy?"
N&A, May 24, 1924.

ANON. "The Government and Unemployment," N&A, May 31,
1924.

KEYNES, J. M. "A Drastic Remedy for Unemployment: Reply to
Critics," N&A, June 7, 1924.

ANON. "Unemployment: The Blind Spot," N&A, Jy. 4, 1925.

"Trifling with Unemployment," N&A, Nov. 26, 1927.

"Unemployment and Industrial Progress," N&A, Mar. 17,
1928.

"The Problem of the Distressed Areas," N&A, Apr. 7, 1928.

"Unemployment and Treasury Policy," N&A, Aug. 4, 1928.

"The Need for Economic Preparedness," N&A, Sept. 8, 1928.

"Unemployment and the Housing Subsidy," N&A, Nov. 17,
1928.

"The Objections to Capital Expenditure," N&A, Feb. 23, 1929.

"The Slum, the Taxpayer, and the Unemployed," N&A,
Mar. 2, 1929.

"Mr. Lloyd George and his Pledge," N&A, Mar. 9, 1929.

"Unemployment Fallacies in the Open," N&A, Mar. 23, 1929.

"Ninepence for Nothing," N&A, Apr. 6, 1929.

"Mr. Churchill's Secret," N&A, Apr. 13, 1929.

"The School Age and Unemployment," N&A, Jy. 13, 1929.

"The Issue," N&A, Mar. 16, 1929.

"Is There Any Unemployment?" N&A, May 4, 1929.

"Can Mr. Thomas Conquer Unemployment?" N&A, Jy. 27,
1929.

[2] Anonymous articles which appeared in N&A during Keynes' chairmanship may have been written by him, or at least may have been discussed with
him before publication. When they seem to have been written by him or
greatly influenced by him, they are included here. (Mr. H. D. Henderson
undoubtedly was responsible for many of the anonymous articles.)

"Unemployment, Mr. Thomas, and the Bank," N&A, Oct. 12, 1929.

"Unemployment and the Budget," N&A, Mar. 15, 1930.

KEYNES, J. M. "The Industrial Crisis," N&A, May 10, 1930.

Letter to the Editor on "Mr. Baldwin and Unemployment," N&A, Aug. 2, 1930.

ANON. "The Menace of the Dole," N&A, Aug. 16, 1930.

"The Challenge of Unemployment," N&A, Aug. 30, 1930.

KEYNES, J. M. "The Great Slump of 1930," N&A, Dec. 20 and 27, 1930.

"The Causes of World Depression," *Forum*, Jy. 1931.

ANON. "Dole Gatherers," N&A, Feb. 7, 1931.

KEYNES, J. M. "An Economic Analysis of Unemployment," in *Unemployment as a World Problem* (ED. Q. Wright), 1931, pp. 3–42.

"The Problem of Unemployment," *The Listener*, Jan. 14, 1931.

"The World's Economic Outlook," *Atlantic Monthly*, May, 1932.

"A Programme for Unemployment," NST&N, Feb. 4, 1933.

"Der Stand und die nächste Zukunft der Konjunkturforschung," in *Festschrift für Arthur Spiethoff*, 1933, pp. 123–125.

"Letter to President Roosevelt," NYT, Dec. 31, 1933 (reprinted in NICB: *American Affairs*, Apr., 1946).

"Mr. Roosevelt's Experiments," TL, Jan. 2, 1934 (see editorial comment, *ibid.*, Jan. 2, 1934, and other comments, *ibid.*, Jan. 8, 1934).

"The Progress of the United States in the Direction of Recovery," LA, Aug., 1934.

"The General Theory of Employment," QJE, 1936–7, pp. 209–223.

"How to Avoid a Slump," LA, Mar., 1937.

KEYNES, J. M., and N. KALDOR, *"Professor Pigou on Money Wages in Relation to Unemployment,"* EJ, Dec., 1937, pp. 743–745.

(b) WAGES AND PRICES

KEYNES, J. M. in discussion of R. H. Hooker, *"The Course of Prices at Home and Abroad, 1890–1911,"* JRSS, 1911, pp. 45–47.

KEYNES, J. M. "The Measure of Deflation—An Inquiry into Index Numbers," N&A, Oct. 27, 1923.

ANON. "The Inflation Bogey and the Moral," N&A, Oct. 27, 1923.

KEYNES, J. M. "Sheltered and Unsheltered Price Levels," N&A, Feb. 26, 1927.

ANON. "The Background of Trade and Prices," N&A, June 29, 1929.

KEYNES, J. M. "The Question of High Wages," PQ, Jan., 1930, pp. 110–124.

"Professor Pigou on Money Wages in Relation to Unemployment," EJ, Dec. 1937, pp. 743–745.

"Relative Movements of Real Wages and Output," EJ, Mar., 1939, pp. 34–51.

"The Objective of International Price Stability," EJ, June-Sept., 1943, pp. 185–187.

(*See also* Hayek and Graham, *ibid.*, Dec., 1944, pp. 422–429.)

KEYNES, J. M. "Note," EJ, Dec., 1944, pp. 429–30.

(c) CONSUMPTION, SAVINGS, AND INVESTMENT

KEYNES, J. M. *"Mr. Robertson on Saving and Hoarding,"* EJ, Dec., 1933, pp. 699–701. (*See* Robertson, *ibid.*, Sept., 1933, pp. 399–413; and Hawtrey and Robertson, *ibid.*, Dec., 1933.)

"Fluctuations in Net Investment in the United States," EJ, Sept., 1936, pp. 540–547.

"Mr. Keynes's Consumption Function: Reply," QJE, Aug., 1938, pp. 708–709 (a reply to Holden, *ibid.*, Feb., 1938; *see also* Keynes, *ibid.*, Nov., 1938, p. 160; and Holden's *"Rejoinder," ibid.*)

"Mr. Keynes on the Distribution of Income and the Propensity to Consume: A Reply," RES, Aug., 1939, p. 129. (*See* Staehle, *ibid.*, Aug., 1938, pp. 128–141; and Aug., 1939, pp. 129–130.)

(d) PUBLIC SPENDING AND TAXATION

KEYNES, J. M. "The Inflation of Currency as a Method of Taxation," MGCRE, July 27, 1922.

ANON. "The Cant of Economy," N&A, Apr. 23, 1927.

KEYNES, J. M. "A Note on Economy," N&A, Apr. 30, 1927, and May 21, 1927.

ANON. "Economy or Development," N&A, July 30, 1927.

"The Labour Party's Surtax," N&A, Sept. 24, 1927.

"The Truth About Economy," N&A, Oct. 29, 1927.

"The Sinking Fund Wangle," N&A, Apr. 28, 1928.

"The League, Economy, and Humbug," N&A, July 7, 1928.

"The Issues of the Derating Scheme," N&A, Nov. 24, 1928.

"The Conversion to National Development," N&A, Jan. 26, 1929.

"The Objections to Capital Expenditure," N&A, Feb. 23, 1929.

"The Slum, the Taxpayer, and the Unemployed," N&A, Mar. 2, 1929. (*See also* under Section 6 (a) above.)

"The Government's Decision," N&A, Apr. 20, 1929.

KEYNES, J. M. "Mr. Snowden and the Balfour Note," N&A, Apr. 20, 1929.

ANON. "How Much Taxation?" N&A, July 20, 1929.

KEYNES, J. M., AND H. D. HENDERSON, "The Cost of the Liberal Scheme," N&A, May 11, 1929 (reprinted in *Can Lloyd George Do It?*)

ANON. "The Coming Deficit," N&A, Nov. 23, 1929.

"The Limits of Insular Socialism," Nov. 30, 1929.

KEYNES, J. M. "The Treasury Contribution to the White Paper," N&A, May 18, 1929.

ANON. "A New Sort of White Paper," N&A, May 18, 1929.

"The Problems of the New Government," N&A, June 8, 1929.

"The Revolt of the Commons," N&A, Dec. 14, 1929.

"The Labour Party and Expenditure," N&A, Jan. 11, 1930.

"Mr. Snowden's Problem," N&A, Apr. 5, 1930.

"In Private Life We Cut Our Coat According to Our Cloth; as a Nation We Reverse the Process," N&A, May 3, 1930.

"Taxing the Rich," N&A, May 3, 1930.

KEYNES, J. M. "Spending and Saving," *The Listener*, Jan. 21, 1931 (reprinted in *Essays in Persuasion*).

ANON. "Economy," N&A, Feb. 14, 1931.

KEYNES, J. M. "Some Consequences of the Economy Report," NST&N, Aug. 15, 1931 (reprinted in *Essays in Persuasion*).

"The Budget," NST&N, Sept. 19, 1931 (reprinted in *Essays in Persuasion*).

"The Means to Prosperity," TL, Mar. 13–16, 1933. (reprinted in an enlarged version as a pamphlet; *see also* letters and comments, *ibid.*, in the weeks following, interrogation of

Keynes in the House of Commons, Mar., 1933, as well as Keynes "Reply").

KEYNES, J. M. "The Multiplier," NST&N, Apr. 1, 1933.

(e) WAR ECONOMICS

KEYNES, J. M. "*War and the Financial System, Aug., 1914,*" EJ, Sept., 1914, pp. 460–486.

"*The City of London and the Bank of England,*" QJE, Nov., 1914, pp. 48–71.

"*The Economics of War in Germany,*" EJ, Sept., 1915, pp. 443–452.

"Compulsory Saving," TL, Nov. 14, Nov. 15, and Nov. 29, 1939 (reprinted in *How to Pay for the War*).

"*The Income and Fiscal Potential of Great Britain,*" EJ, Dec., 1939, pp. 626–635 (with two appendices by E. Rothbarth); see also, *ibid.*, June, 1940.

"*The Concept of National Income: A Supplementary Note,*" EJ, Mar., 1940, pp. 60–65.

"*The Concept of National Income,*" EJ, Sept., 1940, pp. 340–342; Mar., 1940, pp. 61–65; and June-September, p. 341; Keynes, *ibid.*, Dec., 1939; and see A. L. Bowley, *ibid.*, pp. 340–1 and p. 342; also Bowley in *Manchester Statistical Society,* Nov. 8, 1939, "The Measurement of Real Income").

"British Finances after a Year of War," *London Calling,* Oct., 1940.

(f) REPARATIONS, INTERALLIED DEBTS, ETC.

KEYNES, J. M. "Europe After the Treaty," NR, Jan. 14, 1920.

"How to Mend the Treaty," NR, Jan. 21, 1920.

"The Peace of Versailles," *Everybody's Magazine,* Sept., 1920. (See Tardieux, *ibid.*, Nov., 1920, and Keynes, *ibid.*, Jan., 1921.)

"German Reparations Again," LA, Mar. 12, 1921.

"America and the Peace Conference," LA, Aug. 1, 1921.

"La reconstruction de l'Europe," MGCRE, 1922–1923.

"The Reconstruction of Europe: A General Introduction," MGCRE, May 18, 1922.

"The Genoa Conference," MGCRE, June 15, 1922.

"Is a Settlement of the Reparation Question Possible Now?" MGCRE, Sept. 23, 1922.

"Speculation in the Mark and Germany's Balances Abroad," MGCRE, Sept. 23, 1922.

"The State of Opinion in Europe—The Underlying Principles," MGCRE, Jan. 4, 1923.

"The German Offer and the French Reply," N&A, May 12, 1923.

"The International Loan," N&A, May 26, 1923.

"The Situation in Germany," N&A, June 9, 1923.

"The German Loan Delusion," NR, June 13, 1923.

"The Austrian Loan and Reparations in South-Eastern Europe," N&A, June 16, 1923.

"The Diplomacy of Reparations," NR, June 27, 1923.

"Mr. Baldwin's Prelude," N&A, July 21, 1923.

"Is a Settlement of Reparations Possible?" N&A, July 28, 1923.

"The Legality of the Ruhr Occupation," N&A, Aug. 18 and Aug. 25, 1923; NR, Aug. 29, 1923.

"The American Debt," N&A, Aug. 4 and Aug. 18, 1923.

"The Reparations Plan," NR, Aug. 8, 1923.

"How Much Has Germany Paid?" N&A, Oct. 27, 1923; NR, Nov. 7, 1923.

ANON. "Reparations: The Next Phase," N&A, Mar. 29, 1924.

KEYNES, J. M. "The Experts' Reports," N&A, Apr. 12 and Apr. 19, 1924.

"How Can the Dawes Plan Work?" NR, Apr. 23, 1924.

KEYNES, J. M. "The London Conference and Territorial Sanctions," N&A, July 26, 1924.

"The American Debt," N&A, Aug. 4, 1924.

"The Reparation Recovery Act," N&A, Sept. 20, 1924.

"The Dawes Scheme and the German Loan," N&A, Oct. 4, 1924.

"What the Dawes Plan Will Do," NR, Oct. 22, 1924.

"The Inter-Allied Debts," N&A, Jan. 10, 1925; NR, Jan. 21, 1925.

"The Balfour Note and the Inter-Allied Debts," N&A, Jan. 24, 1925 (reprinted in *Essays in Persuasion*).

"Germany's Coming Problem," N&A, Feb. 6, 1926; NR, Feb. 17, 1926.

"The Need of Peace by Negotiation," NR, May 19, 1926.

"The Progress of the Dawes Scheme," N&A, Sept. 11, 1926; NR, Sept. 29, 1926.

"The Progress of Reparations," N&A, July 16, 1927.

"The Coming Crisis in Reparations," NR, Aug. 3, 1927.

"The Financial Reconstruction of Germany," N&A, Jan. 7,

1928; NR, Jan. 25, 1928. (A review of C. *Bergmann: The History of Reparations,* and H. *Schacht: The Stabilisation of the Mark.*)

"The Financial Path to Peace," NR, Jan. 18, 1928.

"The War Debts," N&A, May 5, 1928 (reprinted in *Essays in Persuasion*).

"The London View of the War Debts," NR, May 23 and July 4, 1928.

ANON. "Back to Reparations," N&A, Nov. 3, 1928.

KEYNES, J. M. "A Rejoinder" to *The Reparation Problem* by Ohlin, EJ, Mar., 1929, pp. 179–182. (*See also* Ohlin, *ibid.;* Rueff, *ibid;* and Keynes, *ibid.,* pp. 1–7.)

"A Reply to 'A Criticism of Mr. Keynes' View on the Transfer Problem,' by A. Rueff," EJ, Sept., 1929, pp. 404–408. (*See also* Rueff in *Revue d'Economie Politique,* 1929, pp. 1067–1081.)

ANON. "Great Britain and Reparations," N&A, May 11, 1929.

KEYNES, J. M. "Mr. Snowden and the Balfour Note," N&A, Apr. 20, 1929. "The Reparations Crisis," NR, May 1, 1929.

ANON. "Mr. Snowden's Diplomacy," N&A, Aug. 17, 1929.

KEYNES, J. M. "The Report on the Young Committee," N&A, June 15, 1929.

ANON. "Mr. Snowden's Victory—and After," N&A, Aug. 31, 1929. "The Hague Balance Sheet," N&A, Sept. 14, 1929.

KEYNES, J. M. "The Draft Convention for Financial Assistance by the League of Nations," N&A, Mar. 8 and Mar. 15, 1930.

Letter to the Editor on "The Draft Convention for Financial Assistance by the League of Nations," N&A, Apr. 5, 1930.

ANON. "Germany and Geneva," N&A, Sept. 20, 1930.

KEYNES, J. M. "Reaping the Whirlwind of the Peace Treaty," *Golden Book Magazine,* Jan., 1932.

"An End of Reparations?" NST&N, Jan. 16, 1932.

"Britain for Cancellation," NR, Jan. 27, 1932.

"A Policy for Lausanne," TL, June 15, 1932.

"The World Economic Conference, 1933," NST&N, Dec. 24, 1932.

(g) EXCHANGES AND GOLD

KEYNES, J. M. "The Forward Market in Foreign Exchange," MGCRE, Apr. 20, 1922.

"The Stabilisation of the European Exchanges," MGCRE, Apr. 20, and Dec. 7, 1922.

"The Theory of Exchanges and 'Purchasing Power Parity'," MGCRE, Apr. 20, 1922.

"The Foreign Exchanges and the Seasons," N&A, May 19, 1923.

"Gold in 1923," N&A, Feb. 2, 1924; NR, Feb. 27, 1924.

"The Prospects of Gold," N&A, Feb. 16, 1924; NR, Mar. 12, 1924.

"The Franc," N&A, Mar. 15, 1924; NR, Mar. 26, 1924 (reprinted in *Réflexions sur le franc*).

ANON. "Professor Cassel's Advice," N&A, June 21, 1924.

KEYNES, J. M. "The Return Towards Gold," N&A, Feb. 21, 1925; NR, Mar. 18, 1925.

"The Problem of the Gold Standard," N&A, Mar. 21, 1925.

"Is Sterling Overvalued?" N&A, Apr. 4 and 18, 1925.

"Is The Pound Overvalued?" NR, May 6, 1925.

"The Gold Standard," N&A, May 2, 1925.

"The Gold Standard—A Correction," N&A, May 9, 1925.

"England's Gold Standard," NR, May 20, 1925.

ANON. "Gold and the Trade Outlook," N&A, May 30, 1925.

KEYNES, J. M. *"The Gold Standard Act,"* EJ, June, 1925, pp. 312–313.

"The Arithmetic of the Sterling Exchange," N&A, June 13, 1925.

"Great Britain's Cross of Gold," NR, Sept. 16, 1925.

"The French Franc," N&A, Jan. 9, 1926 (reprinted in *Réflexions sur le franc*); also NR, Jan. 27, 1926.

"The French Franc—A Reply," N&A, Jan. 16, 1926 (reprinted in *Réflexions*).

"Last Reflections About the Franc," N&A, Jan. 30, 1926 (reprinted in *Réflexions*).

"The First-Fruits of the British Gold Standard," NR, June 2, 1926.

"The First Fruits of the Gold Standard," N&A, June 26, 1926.

"The Franc Once More," N&A, July 17, 1926 (reprinted in *Réflexions*).

"The Future of the Franc," NR, July 17, 1926.

"The Autumn Prospects for Sterling," N&A, Oct. 23, 1926.

"The Stabilisation of the Franc," N&A, June 30, 1928; NR,

July 18, 1928 (reprinted in *Essays in Persuasion*).

"The French Stabilisation Law," EJ, Sept., 1928, pp. 490–494.

"Is There Enough Gold?" N&A, Jan. 19, 1929.

ANON. "The Rock of Gold," N&A, Oct. 4, 1930.

"Notes on the Situation," NST&N, Aug. 20, 1931.

KEYNES, J. M. "On the Eve of Gold Suspension," *The Evening Standard*, Sept. 10, 1931 (reprinted in *Essays in Persuasion*).

"A Gold Conference," NST&N, Sept. 12, 1931.

"The End of the Gold Standard," *The Sunday Express*, Sept. 27, 1931 (reprinted in *Essays in Persuasion*).

"After the Suspension of Gold," TL, Sept. 28, 1931 (reprinted in *Essays in Persuasion*).

"The Prospects of the Sterling Exchange," YR, Mar., 1932.

"Reflections on the Sterling Exchange," LBMR, Apr., 1932.

"The World Economic Conference," NST&N, Dec. 24, 1932.

"President Roosevelt's Gold Policy," NST&N, Jan. 20, 1934.

"The Future of the Foreign Exchange," LBMR, Oct., 1935.

"The Supply of Gold," EJ, Sept., 1936, pp. 412–418.

Letter in: W. Lück, *Monetäre Unabhängigkeit*, 1939.

(h) OTHER ASPECTS OF INTERNATIONAL ECONOMIC RELATIONS

KEYNES, J. M. "*The Foreign Trade of the United Kingdom at Prices of 1900*," EJ, Dec. 1912.

ANON. "Mr. Baldwin on Protection," N&A, Nov. 3, 1923.

"Free Trade," N&A, Nov. 24, and Dec. 1, 1923.

ANON. "The Fear of Peace," N&A, Dec. 8, 1923.

"Free Trade for England," NR, Dec. 19, 1923.

"Economic Notes on Free Trade," NST&N, Mar. 28, and Apr. 11, 1931.

"Foreign Investment and National Advantage," N&A, Aug. 9, 1924.

"Some Tests for Loans to Foreign and Colonial Governments," N&A, Jan. 17, 1925.

"The Problem of the Export Trades," N&A, Aug. 22, 1925.

KEYNES, J. M. "Will England Restrict Foreign Investments?" NR, Dec. 1, 1926.

"*A Model Form for Statements of International Balances*," EJ, Sept., 1927, pp. 472–476.

ANON. "The Balance of Trade," N&A, Oct. 1, 1927.

KEYNES, J. M. "*The British Balance of Trade, 1925–27*," EJ, Dec., 1927, pp. 551–565.

"*Note on the British Balance of Trade,*" EJ, Mar., 1928, pp. 146–47.

ANON. "The Trade Setback," N&A, June 2, 1928.

"The Tariff Trend," N&A, June 23, 1928.

"The Cabinet and Protection," N&A, Aug. 11, 1928.

"How Does Free Trade Stand?" N&A, Aug. 25, 1928.

KEYNES, J. M. "*The United States' Balance of Trade in 1927,*" EJ, Sept., 1928, pp. 487–489.

ANON. "The Labour Party and Free Trade," N&A, Dec. 22, 1928.

"The McKenna Duties," N&A, Jan. 14, 1930.

"Our Heresy," N&A, Jan. 18, 1930.

"Empire Free Trade," N&A, Feb. 8, 1930.

"Mr. Baldwin's Surrender," N&A, Mar. 8, 1930, pp. 755–6 (about protection).

"The Bankers' Resolution," N&A, July 12, 1930.

"Mr. Baldwin's Ideal," N&A, July 26, 1930.

"The Empire at the Crossroads," N&A, Sept. 27, 1930.

"Imperial Preference," N&A, Oct. 18, 1930.

KEYNES, J. M. "Proposals for a Revenue Tariff," NST&N, Mar. 7, and Mar. 21, 1931 (the first section reprinted in *Essays in Persuasion*).

"Economic Notes on Free Trade," NST&N, Mar. 28, Apr. 4, and Apr. 11, 1931.

"National Self-Sufficiency," NST&N, July 8 and 15, 1933; YR, Summer, 1933. (German transl., *Schmollers Jahrbuch,* Aug., 1933.)

"Economic Sanctions," NST&N, Sept. 28, 1935.

"*The Balance of Payments of the United States,*" EJ, June 1946, pp. 172–187.

(i) MONEY

KEYNES, J. M. "*The Recent Economic Events in India,*" EJ, Mar., 1909.

"*The Prospects of Money, Nov. 1914,*" EJ, Dec., 1914, pp. 610–34.

"The Influence on Society of Changes in the Value of Money," MGCRE, July 27, 1922.

"Professor Jevons on the Indian Exchange," EJ, Mar., 1923, pp. 60–65.

"The Speeches of the Bank Chairman," N&A, Feb. 23, 1924 (reprinted in *Essays in Persuasion*).

KEYNES, with Cannan, Sir Ch. Addis, and Lord Milner: "Monetary Reform," EJ, 1924.

KEYNES, J. M. "*A Comment on Professor Cannan's Article 'Limitation of Currency or Limitation of Credit?'*" EJ, Mar., 1924, pp. 65–68. (*See* Cannan, *ibid.*)

"The Policy of the Bank of England," N&A, July 19, 1924.

In a discussion about A. Hoare, "*The Bearing of Labour Unrest upon . . . Sound Currency*," JRSS, 1925, pp. 395–7.

KEYNES, J. M. "Speeches of the Bank Chairmen," N&A, Feb. 21, 1925 (reprinted in *Essays in Persuasion*).

"Mr. McKenna on Monetary Policy," N&A, Feb. 12, 1927 (reprinted in *Essays in Persuasion*).

"Conditions of Amalgamation," TL, May 12, 1928.

"*The Amalgamation of the British Note Issues*," EJ, June, 1928, pp. 321–328.

In a discussion about R. G. Hawtrey, "*Money and Index Numbers*," JRSS, 1930, pp. 86–88.

"A Rejoinder" to D. H. Robertson, EJ, Sept., 1931, pp. 412–423. (*See* Robertson, "Mr. Keynes' Theory of Money," *ibid.*)

"Member Bank Reserves in the United States," EJ, Mar., 1932, pp. 27–31.

"Banks and the Collapse of Money Values," *Vanity Fair*, Jan., 1932.

"The Monetary Policy of the Labour Party," NST&N, Sept. 17 and 24, 1932.

(j) INTEREST RATES

KEYNES, J. M. "The Rise in Gilt-Edged Securities," N&A, May 5, 1923.

"Further Reflections on Gilt-Edged Securities," N&A, May 12, 1923.

"Is Credit Abundant?—The Grand Trunk Railway," N&A, July 7, 1923.

"Bank Rate at Four Per Cent," N&A, July 14, 1923.

"Bank Rate and Stability of Prices—A Reply to Critics," N&A, July 21, 1923.

"The Bank Rate," N&A, Mar. 7, 1925.

"The Bank Rate: Five-and-a-half Per Cent," N&A, Feb. 16, 1929.

"The Future of the Rate of Interest," *Index* (Sweden), 1930.

"*Saving and Usury,*" EJ, Mar., 1932, pp. 135–137. (*See also* Somerville, *ibid.*, Dec., 1931; and Cannan, Adarkar, and Sandwell, *ibid.*, Mar., 1932, in "Saving and Usury—A Symposium"; and L. Dennis and H. Someroide, "Usury and the Canonists," *ibid.*, June, 1932, pp. 312–323).

"*A Note on the Long-Term Rate of Interest in Relation to the Conversion Scheme,*" EJ, Sept., 1932, pp. 415–423.

"The Theory of the Rate of Interest," in *The Lessons of Monetary Experience* (in honor of I. Fisher), 1937, pp. 145–152.

"The Rate of Interest," *Round Table*, Mar., 1937.

"*Alternative Theories of the Rate of Interest,*" EJ, June, 1937, pp. 241–252. (*See* Ohlin, Robertson, and Hawtrey, *ibid.*, Sept., 1937).

"*The 'Ex-Ante: Theory of the Rate of Interest,*'" EJ, Dec., 1937, pp. 663–669. (*See* Pigou, Ohlin, Robertson, and Hawtrey, *ibid.*, Sept., 1937).

(k) SPECIAL PROBLEMS OF INDUSTRY, TRADE, AND FINANCE

KEYNES, J. M. "Some Aspects of Commodity Markets," MGCRE, Mar. 29, 1923.

"The Slump in Industrials," N&A, May 26, 1923.

"Trustee Investments—Home, Colonial, and Indian," N&A, June 2, 1923.

KEYNES (with R. B. Lewis, J. W. F. Rowe, and G. L. Schwartz): *Stocks of Staple Commodities* (London and Cambridge Economic Service), 1923–1930.

KEYNES, J. M. "Investment Policy for Insurance Companies," N&A, May 17, 1924.

"Coal: A Suggestion," N&A, Apr. 24, 1926.

"Back to the Coal Problem," N&A, May 15, 1926.

ANON. "Coal: The Way Out," N&A, May 29, 1926.

"The Coal Dispute: Hours or Wages?" N&A, June 5, 1926.

KEYNES, J. M. "The Control of Raw Materials by Governments," N&A, June 12, 1926.

"The Position of the Lancashire Cotton Trade," N&A, Nov. 13, 1926.

"The Prospects of the Lancashire Cotton Trade," N&A, Nov. 27, 1926.

"The Cotton Yarn Association," N&A, Dec. 24, 1926.

"The Progress of the Cotton Yarn Association," N&A, Aug. 27, 1927.

ANON. "Coal and Cotton," N&A, Nov. 12, 1927.

KEYNES, J. M. "The Retreat of the Cotton Yarn Association," N&A, Nov. 19, 1927.

ANON. "What is Rationalization?" N&A, Dec. 10, 1927.

"The Master Cotton Spinners Go Silly," N&A, Jan. 7, 1928.

"Industry and the Banks," N&A, Jan. 28, 1928.

"Attend to Coal and Cotton," N&A, Feb. 18, 1928.

ANON. "Transference and Capital Development," N&A, July 28, 1928.

"The Plight of the Coalfields," N&A, Dec. 8, 1928.

KEYNES, J. M. In a discussion about G. W. Daniels and J. Jewkes, *"The Post-War Depression in the Lancashire Cotton Industry,"* JRSS, 1928, pp. 198–200.

"The Lancashire Cotton Corporation," N&A, Feb. 2, 1929.

ANON. "The Government and the Coal Mines," N&A, June 22, 1929.

"The Cotton Dispute," N&A, Aug. 3, 1929, pp. 586–7.

"Coal: The Latest Phase," N&A, Oct. 26, 1929.

"The Wall Street Collapse," N&A, Nov. 2, 1929, pp. 162–3.

"From India to Coal," N&A, Nov. 9, 1929, pp. 194–5.

"The Coal Mines Bill," N&A, Dec. 21, 1929, pp. 422–3.

"The Coal Problem Now," N&A, Dec. 28, 1929, pp. 450–1.

KEYNES, J. M. "The Industrial Crisis," N&A, May 10, 1930.

ANON. "The Lords and the Coal Bill," N&A, July 13, 1930.

KEYNES, J. M. "Address" (as Chairman) before *Annual Meeting of the National Mutual Life Assurance Company*, Feb., 1936 (reprinted in part in NST&N, Feb. 22, 1936).

"Storage and Security," NST&N, Sept. 10, 1938.

"The Policy of Government Storage of Foodstuffs and Raw Materials," EJ, Sept., 1938, pp. 449–460.

"Comments on Robertson's 'Mr. Keynes and Finance,' " EJ, June 1938, pp. 318–322.

(1) HISTORY OF ECONOMIC THOUGHT

KEYNES, J. M. *"Alfred Marshall, 1842–1924,"* EJ, Sept., 1924, pp. 311–372 (reprinted in *Memorials of Alfred Marshall*, 1925).

"Edwin Montagu," N&A, Nov. 29, 1924. (See also *Essays in Biography*.)

"Bibliographical List of the Writings of Alfred Marshall,"

EJ, Dec. 1924, pp. 627–637 (reprinted in *Memorials of Alfred Marshall,* 1925).

Memorials of Alfred Marshall, 1925. (See also *Essays in Biography.*)

"Walter Bagehot," *The Banker,* Mar., 1926. (See also EJ, Sept., 1915.)

"A Personal Note on Lord Oxford," N&A, Feb. 25, 1928.

Essays in Biography, 1933. (A note at the end mentions that the following essays had been published previously):

Politicians:

1. "The Council of Four, Paris, 1919," in *The Economic Consequences of the Peace,* 1919;
2. "Mr. Bonar Law," in N&A, May 26, 1923;
3. "Lord Oxford," in N&A, Feb. 25, 1928;
4. "Edwin Montagu," in N&A, Nov. 29, 1924;
5. "Winston Churchill," in N&A, Mar. 5 and 9, 1929;
6. "The Great Villiers Connection," in N&A, Apr. 28, 1928;
7. "Trotsky on England," in N&A, May 27, 1926.

Economists:

1. *"Alfred Marshall,"* in EJ, Sept., 1924;
2. *"F. Y. Edgeworth,"* in EJ, Mar., 1926;
3. *"F. P. Ramsey,"* in EJ, Mar., 1930, and another part in NST&N, Oct. 3, 1931.

"Francis Ysidro Edgeworth," in EJ, Mar., 1926, pp. 140–153. (See also *Essays in Biography.*)

Obituary notices on:

The Earl of Balfour, EJ, June, 1930, pp. 336–8.

F. P. Ramsey, EJ, Mar., 1930, pp. 153–4..

C. P. Sanger, EJ, Mar., 1930, pp. 154–5.

A. A. Tschuprow, EJ, Sept., 1926, pp. 517–8.

KEYNES, J. M. *"Commemoration of T. R. Malthus,"* EJ, June, 1935, pp. 222–234.

"Sir Henry Cunynghame," EJ, June., 1935, pp. 398–406.

"William Stanley Jevons," JRSS, No. 3, 1936, pp. 516–48, 554–5.

"Herbert Somerton Foxwell," EJ, Dec., 1936, pp. 589–611; "Bibliography," pp. 611–614.

H. S. Foxwell, 1849–1936 (*British Academy Proceedings,* Vol. XXIII), 1937.

KEYNES AND P. SRAFFA: "Introduction" to *David Hume: An Abstract of a Treatise of Human Nature,* 1938.

KEYNES, J. M. "*Adam Smith as Student and Professor*," *Economic History* (EJ, *Supp.*), Feb., 1938, pp. 33–46.

KEYNES and CLARA COLLET: "*Obituary: Henry Higgs*," EJ, Dec., 1940, pp. 546–558.

KEYNES, J. M. "*Mary Paley Marshall*," EJ, June-Sept., 1944, pp. 268–284.

(m) ECONOMIC INSTITUTIONS

KEYNES, J. M. "Am I a Liberal?" N&A, Aug. 8 and 15, 1925 (reprinted in *Essays in Persuasion*).

"Soviet Russia," N&A, Oct. 10, 17 and 24, 1925; NR, Oct. 28, and Nov. 11, 1925.

"Liberalism and Labour," N&A, Feb. 20, 1926; NR, Mar. 3, 1926 (reprinted in *Essays in Persuasion*).

ANON. "*The Psychology of Labour*," N&A, Aug. 14, 1926.

KEYNES, J. M. "The End of Laissez Faire," NR, Aug. 25, and Sept. 1, 1926.

ANON. "Liberalism and Labour," N&A, Feb. 2, 1929.

"Trade Unions and the Law," N&A, Jan. 3, 1931.

KEYNES, J. M. "The Dilemma of Modern Socialism," PQ, Apr.-June 1932, pp. 155–161; NR, Apr. 13, 1932. (*See* "Reply" by A. L. Rowse, PQ, July-Sept. 1932, pp. 409–415.)

"Professor Laski and the Issue of Freedom," NST&N, July 21, 1934.

"A Self-Adjusting Economic System?" NR, Feb. 20, 1935.

KEYNES and K. MARTIN: "Democracy and Efficiency," NST&N, Jan. 28, 1939.

(n) POLITICAL PROBLEMS

KEYNES, J. M. "When the Big Four Met," NR, Dec. 24, 1919 (reprinted in *Essays in Biography*).

"Russia," MGCRE, July 6, 1922.

"The British Policy in Europe," NR, Mar. 23, 1923; N&A, Mar. 5, 1923.

"Mr. Baldwin's Prelude," N&A, July 21, 1923.

"Mr. Baldwin's Task," NR, Aug. 1, 1923.

"The Aims of Mr. Poincaré," N&A, Oct. 13, 1923.

"Lord Grey's Letter to *The Times*," N&A, Oct. 13, 1923.

ANON. "The Liberal Party," N&A, Nov. 17, 1923.

KEYNES, J. M. "Public and Private Enterprise," N&A, June 21, 1924.

"The Balance of Political Power at the Elections," N&A, Nov. 8, 1924.

"The Balance of Political Power in Great Britain," NR, Nov. 26, 1924.

"Lord Oxford and Mr. Lloyd George," N&A, June 19, 1926.

ANON. "An Industrial Policy," N&A, Feb. 4, 1928.

"The Reception of the Industrial Report," N&A, Feb. 11, 1928.

"The Liberal Industrial Conference, N&A, Mar. 24, 1928.

KEYNES, J. M. "Mr. Churchill on Rates and the Liberal Industrial Inquiry," N&A, Apr. 28, 1928.

ANON. "Mr. Churchill Breaks Out," N&A, June 16, 1928.

"Aunt Tabitha and Mr. Churchill," N&A, June 23, 1928.

"Some Election Issues," N&A, Oct. 13, 1928.

"An Economic Council," N&A, Feb. 1, 1930, pp. 598–99 (about creation by the government of an economic advisory council).

KEYNES, J. M. "The League and the Underdog," *Sat. Rev. Lit.*, Mar. 8, 1930.

ANON. "Mr. Lloyd George and the Government," N&A, Oct. 25, 1930, pp. 126–7 (about liberal politics and national development).

"The Call for a National Government," N&A, Dec. 6, 1930.

KEYNES, J. M. "Sir Oswald Mosley's Manifesto," N&A, Dec. 13, 1930.

"The Monetary Policy of the Labour Party," NST&N, Sept. 17, 1932.

Letter on "Use of a Secret Document" to TL, Nov. 28, 1933.

"Economic Sanctions," NST&N, Sept. 28, 1935.

"British Foreign Policy," NST&N, July 18, Aug. 8, 15, 29, Sept. 12, 1936; July 10, 1937.

"A Positive Peace Programme," NST&N, Mar. 26, and Apr. 9, 1938.

"The British Peace Program," NR, Apr. 13, 1938.

"Mr. Chamberlain's Foreign Policy," NST&N, Oct. 8, 1938.

"Un-Commonsense About the War," NST&N, Oct. 14, 1939.

(o) POPULATION

KEYNES, J. M. Letters on "Influence of Parental Alcoholism," JRSS, 1911, pp. 114–7, 339–45.

"An Economist's View of Population," MGCRE, Aug. 17, 1922.

"A Reply to Sir William Beveridge's 'Population and Unemployment,'" EJ, Sept., 1923, pp. 476–486. (*See also* Sir W. Beveridge, *ibid.*, pp. 447–475.)

"Population and Unemployment," N&A, Oct. 6, 1923.
"Is Britain Overpopulated?" NR, Oct. 31, 1923.
"*Population and Unemployment*," EJ, Dec. 1923.
ANON. "Population and Birth Control," N&A, Mar. 29, 1930, pp. 882–3.
KEYNES, J. M. "Population and Prosperity," *Spectator*, Feb. 19, 1937.
"Some Economic Consequences of a Declining Population," *Eugenics Review*, Apr., 1937.

(p) MISCELLANEOUS

KEYNES, J. M. "*Principal Averages, and Laws of Error Which Lead to Them*," JRSS, 1911, pp. 322–31.
"Are Books Too Dear?" N&A, Mar. 12, May 26, 1927.
"Letter to the Editor of N&A about *Essays on Wordsworth*," N&A, June 25, 1927.
"Lord Oxford," NR, Mar. 14, 1928 (reprinted in *Réflexions sur le franc*).
"He's a Relation of Mine," N&A, Apr. 28, 1928; NR, May 16, 1928 (review of W. T. J. Gun: *Studies in Hereditary Ability*).
"Shaw on Wells on Stalin," NST&N, Nov. 10, 1934.
"The National Theatre," NST&N, Aug. 13 and 27, 1938.
"Enjoying Russia" (review of Low's drawings), NST&N, Dec. 12, 1932.
"Clissold," (Review of Wells' *World* . . .), N&A, Jan. 22, 1927 (reprinted in *Essays in Persuasion* and *Réflexions sur le franc*).
"One of Mr. Wells' Worlds," NR, Feb. 2, 1927.
"The Camargo Ballet," NST&N, July 8, 1933.
"A. F. R. Wollaston," N&A, June 14, 1930.
ANON. "Mr. Simon's 'Indiscretion,'" N&A, Aug. 9, 1930.
KEYNES, J. M. "Economic Possibilities for Our Grandchildren," N&A, Oct. 11 and 18, 1930; *Sat. Eve. Post*, Oct. 11, 1930 (reprinted in *Essays in Persuasion*).

NOTE: Mention should perhaps also be made of the essay on *The Method of Index Numbers* which won for Keynes the Adam Smith Prize in 1909; the important speeches of Keynes at the annual meetings of the National Mutual Life Assurance Company, 1921–1937 inclusive (reprinted in some instances in TL and N&A); and the translations of numerous articles in the *Wirtschaftsdienst* (e.g., 1936). Correspondents kindly suggested these items after this book went to press. S.E.H.

[i]

Index